332.6
OSH

332.6   O'Shaughnessy, James
OSH   P.

             What works on Wall
             Street.

$34.95

DATE		
ILL 10/1/05		
OCT 2 7 2005		
ILL 12/18/06		
9/6/07 ILL		
2/22/12 ILL		
5/3/15 ILL		

BAKER & TAYLOR

WHAT WORKS ON WALL STREET

OTHER BOOKS BY JAMES P. O'SHAUGHNESSY

Invest Like the Best: Using Your Computer to Unlock the Secrets of the Top Money Managers

How to Retire Rich: Time-Tested Strategies to Beat the Market and Retire in Style

WHAT WORKS ON WALL STREET

A Guide to the Best-Performing Investment Strategies of All Time

JAMES P. O'SHAUGHNESSY

Third Edition

McGraw-Hill
New York Chicago San Francisco Lisbon London Madrid
Mexico City Milan New Delhi San Juan Seoul
Singapore Sydney Toronto

1 2 3 4 5 6 7 8 9 0   DOC/DOC   0 9 8 7 6 5

ISBN 0-07-145225-7

McGraw-Hill books are available at special discounts to use as premiums and sales promotions, or for use in corporate training programs. For more information, please write to the Director of Special Sales, Professional Publishing, McGraw-Hill, Two Penn Plaza, New York, NY 10121-2298. Or contact your local bookstore.

Library of Congress Cataloging-in-Publication Data

O'Shaughnessy, James P.
  What works on Wall Street : a guide to the best-performing investment strategies of all time / by James P. O'Shaughnessy.
      p. cm.
  Includes bibliographical references and index.
  ISBN 0-07-145225-7 (hardcover : alk. paper)
  1. Investments—United States.   2. Investment analysis—United States.   I. Title.
  HG4910.O828   2005
  332.6—dc22
                                                                              2005006812

To Lael, Kathryn, Patrick, and Melissa

ABOUT THE AUTHOR

James P. O'Shaughnessy is the Director of Systematic Equity for Bear Stearns Asset Management and a Senior Managing Director of the firm. O'Shaughnessy's investment strategies have been featured in *The Wall Street Journal*, *Barron's*, *The New York Times*, *The Washington Post*, *Investor's Business Daily*, *The Financial Times*, London's *Daily Mail*, Japan's *Nikkei Shimbun Daily*, and many other publications worldwide, as well as on NBC's "Today Show," ABC's "The Oprah Winfrey Show," CNBC, and CNN.

Wait for the wisest of all counselors, time.
—Pericles

CONTENTS

Preface   xviii
Acknowledgments   xx

Chapter 1

Stock Investment Strategies: Different Methods, Similar Goals   1

Traditional Active Management Doesn't Work   2

What's the Problem?   3

Studying the Wrong Things   5

Why Indexing Works   5

Pinpointing Performance   7

Discipline Is the Key   7

Consistency Wins   8

A Structured Portfolio in Action   8

Overwhelmed by Our Nature   9

Case Study: The Dogs of the Dow   9

Chapter 2

**The Unreliable Experts: Getting in the
Way of Outstanding Performance   13**

Human Judgment Is Limited   14

What's the Problem?   15

Why Models Beat Humans   15

Base Rates Are Boring   17

The Individual versus the Group   18

Personal Experience Preferred   19

Simple versus Complex   20

A Simple Solution   21

Additional Reading   23

Case Study: Using Long-Term Data to Make
Predictions about the Future   24

Chapter 3

Rules of the Game   31
Short Periods Are Valueless   32
Anecdotal Evidence Is Not Enough   34
Potential Pitfalls   35
Rules of the Game   38

Chapter 4

Ranking Stocks by Market Capitalization: Size Matters   49
Best of Times, Worst of Times   51
How Much Better Are Small-Cap Stocks?   55
Reviewing Stocks by Size   57
Small Stocks and Market Leaders   59
Small Stocks Are the Winners, But Not by Much   60
Market Leaders and Small Stocks: A Better Way to Create an Index   60
Implications for Investors   69
Our Two Benchmarks   70

Chapter 5

Price-to-Earnings Ratios: Separating the Winners and Losers   71
The Results   72
Large Stocks Are Different   76
High PE Ratios Are Dangerous   77
Large Stocks Fare No Better   83
Best- and Worst-Case Returns   84
Deciles   84
Implications   84
Following This Advice in Real Time   88

Chapter 6

Price-to-Book Ratios: A Better Gauge of Value   91
The Results   92
Large Stocks Are Less Volatile   93
Large Stocks Base Rates Are More Consistent   95

High Price-to-Book Stocks—A Wild Ride to Nowhere 96
Large Stocks Are No Different 101
Best- and Worst-Case Returns 102
Deciles 103
Implications 104

Chapter 7

Price-to-Cashflow Ratios: Using Cash to Determine Value 109
The Results 110
Large Stocks Are Less Volatile 112
Worst-Case Scenarios and Best and Worst Returns 113
High Price-to-Cashflow Ratios Are Dangerous 116
Large Stocks Hit Too 120
Worst-Case Scenario and Best and Worst Returns 122
Deciles 123
Implications 126

Chapter 8

Price-to-Sales Ratios: The King of the Value Factors 127
The Results 128
Large Stocks with Low Price-to-Sales Ratios Do Well 131
Best- and Worst-Case Scenarios 132
High PSR Stocks Are Toxic 134
Large Stocks Do a Little Better 135
Deciles 139
Implications 142

Chapter 9

Dividend Yields: Buying an Income 143
The Results 144
Large Stocks Entirely Different 148
Worst-Case Scenarios 150
Deciles 151
Implications 153

Chapter 10

The Value of Value Factors   155
Risk Doesn't Always Equal Reward   156
Is It Worth the Risk?   157
Embrace Consistency   159
Large Stocks Are More Consistent   160
Implications   163
Learning to Focus on the Long Term   165

Chapter 11

Do High Earnings Gains Mean High Performance?   167
Examining Annual Earnings Changes   168
Large Stocks Do Worse   170
Best- and Worst-Case Returns   171
Buying Stocks with the Worst Earnings Changes   173
Large Stocks Do Better   174
Best- and Worst-Case Scenarios   178
Deciles   180
Implications   180
Case Study: Do Sales Increases Work Better Than Earnings Gains?   183

Chapter 12

Five-Year Earnings-per-Share Percentage Changes   185
The Results   185
Large Stocks Slightly Outperform Universe   189
Best- and Worst-Case Returns   191
Deciles   192
Implications   194

Chapter 13

Profit Margins: Do Investors Profit from Corporate Profits?   197
The Results   197
Large Stocks Do Better   199
Best and Worst Case Returns   203

Deciles 205
Implications 205

Chapter 14

Return on Equity 209
The Results 209
Large Stocks Are the Same 213
Worst-Case Scenarios and Best and Worst Returns 215
Decile 216
Implications 218

Chapter 15

Relative Price Strength: Winners Continue to Win 221
The Results 222
Large Stocks Do Better 227
Why Price Performance Works While Other Measures Do Not 229
Worst-Case Scenarios and Best and Worst Returns 230
Buying the Worst Performing Stocks 230
Large Stocks Also Hit 232
Best- and Worst-Case Returns 234
Deciles 235
Implications 238
Case Study: How Well Does Longer-Term Relative Strength Work? 238

Chapter 16

Using Multifactor Models to Improve Performance 243
Adding Value Factors 243
Base Rates Improve 245
What about Other Value Factors? 245
Price-to-Sales Has Similar Returns 247
Combining the Three Strategies 248
Test for Deviation from Benchmark 249
Additional Factors Add Less to Large Stocks 250
Price-to-Sales Ratios Do Well, Too 252
What about Growth Factors? 253

Two Growth Models   253

Return on Equity Does Better   255

Large Stocks Less Dramatic   256

Implications   257

Chapter 17

**Dissecting the Market Leaders Universe:
Ratios That Add the Most Value   259**

New Period Examined   261

Summary Results for Various Market Leaders Strategies   262

Multifactor Strategies Also Do Well   264

Base Rates   264

Worst-Case Scenarios   265

Implications   265

Best of Market Leaders Found in Chapter 19   267

Chapter 18

**Dissecting the Small Stocks Universe:
Ratios That Add the Most Value   269**

Monthly Data Reviewed, Summary Data Accessed   270

Base Rates   273

Worst-Case Scenarios   274

Implications   275

Case Study: A Note on Small-Cap Concentrated Investing   277

Chapter 19

Searching for the Ideal Value Stock Investment Strategy   281

Focusing on Downside Risk and Return   282

A Superior All-Stocks Value Strategy   282

Market Leaders by Dividend and Shareholder Value   284

Improving on the Best   286

Digging Deeper   288

Real-Time Performance   289

Investing in a More Concentrated Portfolio   289

Implications   291

Chapter 20

Searching for the Ideal Growth Strategy   295
Original Cornerstone Growth Strategy Revisited   295
Traditional Growth Factors Work, But Provide Lower Overall Return   298
Large Stocks Cornerstone Growth Strategy Works Well, Too   299
Improving the Original Strategy   301
Base Rates Also Improve   303
Implications   303
Case Study: Using More Concentrated Versions of the Growth Strategy   307

Chapter 21

Uniting Strategies for the Best Risk-Adjusted Performance   309
The Results   310
50-Stock Version Works Well, Too   311
A Broader Approach   313
Implications   316

Chapter 22

New Research Initiatives   319
Limited Statistics   320
Seasonal Analysis   321
Testing Holding Periods   324
Randomization of In-Sample Data and Testing
Strategies on Other Databases   325
Sector-Specific Analysis   326
Summation Models   327
Correlation Matrix Analysis   327
Regression to Long-Term Mean within Strategies   331
Future Projects   332

Chapter 23

Ranking the Strategies   335
The Results   336
Absolute Returns   337
The Downside   346

Risk-Adjusted Returns   347
Ranking by Sharpe Ratio   356
The Worst Risk-Adjusted Returns   357
Downside Risk   357
The Downside   365
Maximum Decline   366
The Downside   367
Blended Strategies   367
Implications   376

Chapter 24

Getting the Most Out of Your Equity Investments   377
Always Use Strategies   378
Ignore the Short-Term   379
Use Only Strategies Proven over the Long-Term   380
Dig Deep   381
Invest Consistently   381
Always Bet with the Base Rate   382
Never Use the Riskiest Strategies   382
Always Use More Than One Strategy   382
Use Multifactor Models   383
Insist on Consistency   383
The Stock Market Is Not Random   383

Appendix   385
Bibliography   393
Index   403

PREFACE

The more original a discovery, the more obvious it seems afterward.
—Arthur Koestler

Patrick Henry was right when he proclaimed that the only way to judge the future was by the past. To make the best investment plans for the future, investors need access to unbiased, long-term performance results. It doesn't matter if they are aggressive investors seeking fast growth or conservative investors seeking low-risk, high-yielding stocks for their retirement account. Knowing how a particular investment strategy performed historically gives you vital information about its risk, variability, and persistence of returns. Access to long-term performance results lets you make informed choices, based on facts—not hype.

This third edition of *What Works on Wall Street* continues to offer readers access to long-term studies of Wall Street's most popular investment strategies. Prior to its initial publication, no widely available, comprehensive guides were available to which strategies are long-term winners and which are not. Here, I show how a careful reader of earlier editions could have avoided much of the carnage the bear market of 2000 through 2002 inflicted—simply by *avoiding* the types of stocks that, while popular during the stock market bubble of the late 1990s, had historically shown themselves to be horrible long-term performers. All these recommendations were in place *prior* to the stock market bubble and ensuing bear market. Most of the advice derived from this long-term analysis is the same today as it was nine years ago. Of great interest is to see how well these strategies have performed in real time, thus helping us take the guidance history offers us to heart.

All the tests in this book continue to use Standard & Poor's Compustat database, the largest, most comprehensive database of U.S. stock market information available. In this edition of this book, I use FactSet's Alpha Tester and Backtester to run the tests.

ORIGINS

It took the combination of fast computers and huge databases like Compustat to prove that a portfolio's returns are essentially determined by the factors that define the portfolio. Before computers, it was almost impossible to determine what strategy guided any given portfolio. The number of underlying factors (characteristics that define a portfolio like price-to-earnings [PE] ratio, dividend yield, etc.) an investor could consider seemed endless. The best you could do was look at portfolios in the most general ways. Sometimes even a professional manager didn't know which particular factors best characterized the stocks in his or her portfolio, relying more often on general descriptions and other qualitative measures.

Computers changed this. We now can analyze a portfolio and see which factors, if any, separate the best-performing strategies from the mediocre. With computers, we also can test combinations of factors over long periods, showing us what to expect in the future from any given investment strategy.

MOST STRATEGIES ARE MEDIOCRE

What Works on Wall Street shows that most investment strategies are mediocre, and the majority, *particularly those most appealing to investors over the short-term*, fail to beat the simple strategy of indexing to the S&P 500. This book also provides evidence that conflicts with the academic theory that stock prices follow a *random walk* scenario.

Rather than moving about without rhyme or reason, the stock market methodically rewards certain investment strategies while punishing others. *What Works on Wall Street*'s 52 years of returns show there's nothing random about long-term stock market returns. Investors can do *much better* than the market if they consistently use time-tested strategies that are based on sensible, rational methods for selecting stocks.

DISCIPLINE IS KEY

What Works on Wall Street shows that the only way to beat the market over the long-term is to consistently use sensible investment strategies. Eighty percent of the mutual funds covered by Morningstar fail to beat the S&P 500 because their managers lack the discipline to stick with one strategy through thick and thin. This lack of discipline devastates long-term performance.

HIGHLIGHTS

After reading *What Works on Wall Street*, investors will know that:

- Most small-capitalization strategies owe their superior returns to micro-cap stocks having market capitalizations below $25 million. These stocks are too small for virtually any investor to buy.
- Buying low PE ratio stocks is most profitable when you stick to larger, better-known issues.
- The price-to-sales ratio is the most consistent value ratio to use for buying market-beating stocks.
- Last year's biggest losers are among the worst stocks you can buy.
- Last year's earnings gains alone are *worthless* when determining if a stock is a good investment.
- Using several factors dramatically improves long-term performance.
- You can do ten times as well as the S&P 500 by concentrating on large, well-known stocks with high shareholder yield.
- Relative strength is the only growth variable that consistently beats the market, but it must *always* be matched with other factors to mitigate its high levels of risk.
- Buying Wall Street's current darlings having the highest PE ratios is one of the *worst* things you can do.
- A strategy's risk is one of the most important elements to consider.
- Uniting growth and value strategies is the best way to improve your investment performance.

ACKNOWLEDGMENTS

This book would not have been possible without the help of many people. When I started this project several years ago, Jim Branscome, then head of S&P Compustat, was a champion of the project at every turn. His successor, Paul Cleckner, was also extraordinarily supportive and is an outstanding example of a businessman who understands that the best way to help the bottom line of your business is to help the bottom line of thousands of ordinary investors. Mitch Abeyta, the current head of Compustat, has also been wonderful to work with on the ongoing effort to improve the strategies and data covered in the book.

I owe a special thanks to my colleague, Whit Penski. A virtual wizard at setting up backtests within the FactSet environment, Whit spent several years teaching other professionals how to get the most out of the database, and he now assists me on all portfolio testing and implementation. Whit spent many late nights helping me update the new and continued tests for this edition. I am extremely grateful to him for his important contributions. Thanks also to my assistant portfolio manager, Luis Ferreira, who meticulously proofread the entire text. Like Whit, Luis has graciously given many hours of his personal time in diligently auditing all the tables and graphs in this edition of the book, and I deeply appreciate his efforts. Also helpful was Chris Meredith, a summer intern and soon to be employee who also gave his personal time to constructing tables and graphs for this edition.

But this book would not have been finished without the continual help, support, and encouragement of my wife Melissa. I am extremely indebted to her for editing every line in this book. Without her expert hand, this book might never have been finished. In addition to loving her dearly, I owe any success I have as an author to her.

Thanks also to my entire team at Bear Stearns for their support on this project.

1
C H A P T E R

STOCK INVESTMENT STRATEGIES: DIFFERENT METHODS, SIMILAR GOALS

Good intelligence is nine-tenths of any battle.
—Napoleon

There are two main approaches to equity investing: active and passive. The active approach is most common. Here, managers attempt to maximize their returns at various levels of risk by buying stocks they believe are superior to others. Usually, the managers follow similar routes to investigating a stock. They analyze the company, interview management, talk to customers and competitors, review historical trends and current forecasts, and then decide if the stock is worth buying.

Active investors are guided by styles, broadly called *growth* and *value*. What type of stock they buy depends largely on their underlying philosophy. Growth investors buy stocks that have higher-than-average growth in sales and earnings, with expectations for more of the same. Growth investors believe in a company's potential and think a stock's price will follow its earnings higher.

Value investors seek stocks with current market values substantially below true or liquidating value. They use factors like price-to-earnings (PE) ratios and price-to-sales ratios to identify when a stock is selling below its intrinsic value. They bargain hunt, looking for stocks in which they can buy a dollar's worth of assets for less than a dollar. Value investors believe in a company's balance sheet, thinking a stock's price will eventually rise to meet its intrinsic value.

Actively managed funds often use a hodgepodge of techniques from both schools of investing, but the most successful have strongly articulated strategies. The majority of mutual funds, professionally managed pension funds, and separately managed individual accounts are managed with an active approach.

TRADITIONAL ACTIVE MANAGEMENT DOESN'T WORK

This makes perfect sense until you review the record of traditional, actively managed funds. The majority do not beat the S&P 500. This is true over both short and long periods. Figure 1-1 shows the percentage of those actively managed mutual funds in Morningstar's database that beat the S&P 500. The *best* 10 years, ending December 31, 1994, saw only 26 percent of the traditionally managed active mutual funds beating the index. When you dig deeper and look at the percentage by which they beat the index, the news gets worse. Of the 362 funds beating the Vanguard Index (an index fund that replicates the S&P 500) for the 10 years ending May 31, 2004, only 152 of the winning funds managed to beat the index by more than 2 percent a year on a compound basis. What's more, this record *overstates* traditionally managed active funds' performance, because it doesn't include all the funds that failed to survive over the 10-year period.

Passive indexing has exploded in the past decade as a result. Here, investors buy an index that they think broadly represents the market, such as the S&P 500, and let it go at that. Their objective is to match the market, not outperform it. They are willing to give up their shot at outperforming the market for the security of not underperforming it. Since the publication of the first edition of this book in 1996, index managers have continued to see their assets under management soar: According to the September 15, 2003 issue of *Pensions & Investments*, "worldwide indexed assets under management climbed to $2.8 trillion as of June 30... (and) U.S. equity indexed assets made up $1.5 trillion, or 54% of all worldwide indexed assets." The institutional pension plans have led the way, but retail investors are right on their heels. As of December 31, 2003, over 300 Index Funds were listed in Morningstar's Principia database, and Vanguard's 500 Index fund is now the largest equity mutual fund in the United States, with over $96 billion in assets under management. What's more, since 1996, the popularity of Exchange Traded Funds (ETFs)—index funds that are listed and traded on exchanges like stocks—has exploded, furthering what amounts to a revolution in investment management characterized by investors continuing to flock to more structured, disciplined investment strategies.

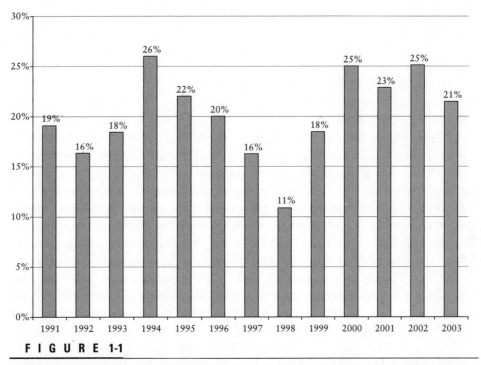

FIGURE 1-1

Percent of all equity funds with 10-year track records beating Standard & Poor's 500 for the 10 years ending December 31 in each year.
Source: Morningstar, Inc.

WHAT'S THE PROBLEM?

Conventional academics aren't surprised that traditionally managed funds fail to beat the market. Most have long held that markets are efficient and that current security prices reflect all available information. They argue that prices follow a *random walk* and move without rhyme or reason. According to their theories, you might as well have a monkey throw darts at a stock page as attempt analysis, because stock prices are random and cannot be predicted.

The long-term evidence in this book contradicts the random walk theory. Far from following a random walk, the evidence continues to reveal a purposeful stride. The 52 years of data found in this book proves strong return predictability. What's more, this return predictability continues to persist even *after* the first edition of this book was published in 1996. The market clearly and consistently rewards certain attributes (e.g., stocks with low price-to-sales ratios) and clearly and consistently punishes others (e.g., stocks with high price-to-sales ratios) over long periods. Yet the paradox remains: If our historical tests, as well as the real-time results we have generated with the strategies since the initial publication of this book, show such high return predictability, why do 80 percent of traditionally managed mutual funds continually fail to beat the S&P 500?

Finding exploitable investment opportunities does not mean it's easy to make money, however. To do so requires the ability to consistently, patiently, and slavishly stick with a strategy, even when it's performing poorly relative to other methods. One of the central themes of this book is that all strategies have performance cycles in which they over- and underperform their relevant benchmarks. The key to outstanding long-term performance is to find a strategy that has the highest base rate, or batting average, (more on that later) and then *stick with that strategy*, even when it is underperforming other strategies and benchmarks. Few are capable of such action. Successful investors do not comply with nature, they defy it. Most investors react very emotionally to the short-term gyrations of the market, and I've seen many who follow my strategies and portfolios in real time say: "Well, these strategies used to work, but they don't anymore" after just a few months of underperformance. In the next chapter, I argue that the reason traditional management doesn't work well is because human decision-making is *systematically flawed and unreliable*. This provides an opportunity to those who use a rational, disciplined method to buy and sell stocks using time-tested methods, essentially allowing the disciplined investor to arbitrage human nature.

Since the first edition of this book was published in 1996, a school of academic thought called *Behavioral Economics* has emerged to explain why these performance anomalies continue to exist even after being written about extensively. This work has received a great deal of public attention and centers around a new paradigm for evaluating how people *actually* make investment choices. In his book *Behavioral Finance: Insights into Irrational Minds and Markets*, James Montier writes:

> This is the world of behavioral finance, a world in which human emotions rule, logic has its place, but markets are moved as much by psychological factors as by information from corporate balance sheets...[T]he models of classical finance are fatally flawed. They fail to produce predictions that are even vaguely close to the outcomes we observe in real financial markets...Of course, now we need some understanding of what causes markets to deviate from their fundamental value. The answer quite simply is human behavior.

While I will examine some of the tenants of behavioral finance in Chapter 2, one of the principal reasons classically trained economists were getting the wrong answers was because they were asking the wrong questions.

STUDYING THE WRONG THINGS

It's no surprise that academics find traditionally managed stock portfolios following a random walk. Most traditional managers' past records cannot predict future returns, because their behavior is inconsistent. You cannot make forecasts based on inconsistent behavior, because when you behave inconsistently, you are unpredictable. Even if a manager is a perfectly consistent investor—a hallmark of the best money managers—if *that* manager leaves the fund, all predictive ability from past performance is lost. Moreover, if a manager changes his or her style, all predictive ability from past performance is also lost. Traditional academics, therefore, have been measuring the *wrong* things. They assume perfect, rational behavior in a capricious environment ruled by greed, hope, and fear. They have been contrasting the returns of a passively held portfolio—the S&P 500—with the returns of portfolios managed in an inconsistent, shoot-from-the-hip style. Track records are worthless unless you know what strategy the manager uses and if it is still being used. When you study a traditionally managed fund, you're really looking at two things: first, the strategy used and second, the ability of the manager to implement it successfully. It makes much more sense to contrast the one-factor (in this case, market capitalization) S&P 500 portfolio with other one or multifactor portfolios.

WHY INDEXING WORKS

Indexing to the S&P 500 works because it sidesteps flawed decision-making and automates the simple strategy of buying the big stocks that make up the S&P 500. The mighty S&P 500 consistently beats 80 percent of traditionally managed funds over the long-term by doing nothing more than making a disciplined bet on large capitalization stocks. Figure 1-2 compares the returns on the S&P 500 with those for our Large Stocks universe, which consists of all the stocks in the Compustat database having market capitalizations greater than the database mean in any given year. This effectively limits us to the top 15 percent of the Compustat database by market capitalization. Stocks are then bought in equal dollar amounts. *The returns are virtually identical.* $10,000 invested in the S&P 500 on December 31, 1951, was worth $2,896,700 on December 31, 2003, a compound return of 11.52 percent. The same $10,000 invested in our Large Stock universe was worth $3,173,724, a compound return of 11.71 percent. (Both include the reinvestment of all dividends.) And it's not just the absolute returns that are so similar—risk, as measured by the standard deviation of return, is also virtually

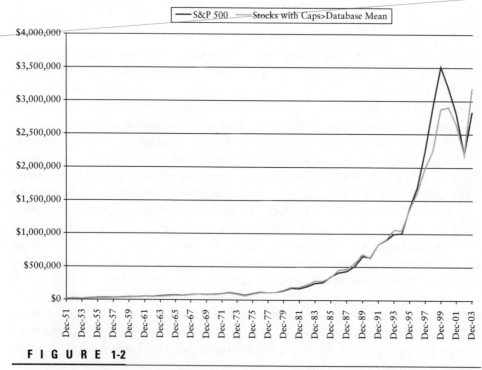

FIGURE 1-2

Comparative Returns, December 31, 1951–December 31, 2003.

identical for the two strategies. The S&P 500 had an annual standard deviation of return of 17.61 percent, whereas the Large Stocks universe's was 16.84 percent.

Thus, far from being "the market," the S&P 500 is the result of a simple strategy that says: "Buy big cap stocks." The reason this works so well is that the S&P 500 never varies from this strategy. It doesn't wake up in the morning and say "You know, small cap stocks have been doing well recently, I think I will change and become a small cap index," nor does it watch Alan Greenspan give testimony to Congress and say "Yikes! Today I'm going to become the S&P cash and bond index!" It just continues to passively implement the strategy of buying big stocks, and that's why it is so effective.

Yet, indexing to the S&P 500 is just one form of passive implementation of a strategy, in this case consistently buying big stocks. Buying the 10 highest-yielding stocks in the Dow Jones Industrial Average each year is another strategy that works consistently. From 1928—when the Dow was expanded to 30 stocks—through 2003, the strategy consistently beat the S&P 500. Indeed, it beat the S&P 500 in almost all rolling 10-year periods, with only two 10-year rolling periods during which it failed to do better than the S&P

500. (See the case study of the Dogs of the Dow.) You'll find a number of other winning strategies in this book.

PINPOINTING PERFORMANCE

It took the combination of fast computers and huge databases like Compustat to prove that a portfolio's returns are essentially determined by the factors that define the portfolio. Before computers, it was virtually impossible to determine what strategy guided the development of a portfolio. The number of underlying factors (characteristics that define a portfolio like PE ratio, dividend yield, etc.) an investor could consider seemed endless. The best you could do was look at portfolios in the most general ways. Sometimes even a professional manager didn't know what particular factors best characterized the stocks in her portfolio, relying more often on general descriptions and other qualitative measures.

The computer changed this. We now can analyze quickly the factors that define any portfolio and see which, if any, separate the best-performing funds and strategies from the mediocre. With computers, we also can test combinations of factors over long periods, thus showing us what to expect in the future from any given investment strategy. This area of research has blossomed in the years since the original edition of this book was published, with many managers running a long-term test of their investment strategies in a manner similar to the tests in this book. One potential problem with the proliferation of this kind of research—which I will expand upon later—is the potential for *data mining*. When you test an infinite number of strategies, statistically you are bound to find several that have vastly outperformed the market, however odd they may appear. That's why we insist on using great restraint when testing a strategy. Generally, the strategy must make intuitive sense, generate similar findings when using similar variables (i.e., low price-to-sales and low price-to-cashflow should demonstrate similar findings), and perform well in all holdout periods. I will cover this in greater depth in Chapter 3.

DISCIPLINE IS THE KEY

If you use a one-factor model based on market capitalization—as in the examples above—you get the same results. If, however, you change a portfolio's underlying factors so that they deviate significantly from the S&P 500, say by keeping price-to-sales ratios below one or dividend yields above a certain number, you can expect that portfolio to perform differently from the market. S&P 500 index funds are nothing more than *structured portfolios* that make disciplined bets on a large capitalization factor. *Many other factors perform much better.* Systematic, structured investing is a hybrid of active and passive management that automates buy and sell decisions. If a stock meets the criteria, it's bought. If not, not. No personal, emotional judgments enter the process. Essentially, you are indexing a portfolio to a specific investment strategy and, by doing so, unite the best of active and passive investing. The disciplined implementation of active strategies is the key to performance. Traditional managers usually follow a hit-and-miss approach to investing. Their lack of discipline accounts for their inability to beat simple approaches that *never vary* from underlying strategy.

Imagine what the Dow would look like today if, in the 1950s, the editors at Dow Jones & Company decided to revamp the Dow Jones Industrial Average, basing it on reasonably priced value stocks instead of big industrial companies. If they expanded the list to 50 names and each year simply bought the 50 large stocks with the lowest price-to-sales ratio, the "market" today would be five times higher than it is!

CONSISTENCY WINS

In a study for my book *Invest Like the Best*, I found that the *one* thing uniting the best managers is consistency. I am not alone. In the 1970s, AT&T did a study of its pension fund managers and found that successful investing required, at a minimum, a structured decision-making process that can be easily defined and a stated investment philosophy that is consistently applied. John Neff, of the Windsor fund, and Peter Lynch, of Magellan, became legends because their success was the result of slavish devotion to their investment strategies.

A STRUCTURED PORTFOLIO IN ACTION

Very few funds or managers stick with their strategies for long periods. The ING Corporate Leaders Trust (ticker symbol LEXCX) is one that did, and it is most unusual because it is a structured portfolio in action. Formed in 1935, the trust was designed to hold 30 stocks that were leaders in their industries. The fund's portfolio is *share-weighted*, holding the same number of shares in each company regardless of price. Since 1935, seven companies have been eliminated, and two spin-offs added, so that the fund currently holds 25 stocks. Yet this single-factor portfolio is a market-slayer—between January 1, 1976 and December 31, 2003, $10,000 invested in the fund grew to $315,567, a compound return of 13.12 percent a year. That beat the S&P 500's return of 13.08 percent and the majority of traditionally managed funds. The strategy lagged the S&P 500 in the bubble years of 1997 through 1999, but came roaring back in the bear market years of 2000 through 2002. Indeed, if you look at its most recent performance, for the three years ending July 31, 2004, its return of 3.95 percent per year was some 5.54 percent better than the S&P 500 and better than 91 percent of its peer funds in the Morningstar Universe. What's more, its charter prevents rebalancing the portfolio, which would allow it to reflect changes in corporate leaders. Imagine how it would have performed if it bought today's leaders like Microsoft and Intel! Indeed, a structured strategy like the high-yielding Dow approach mentioned earlier, where you are allowed to refresh the stocks every year, posted *much better* returns. There, $10,000 invested on January 1, 1976 was worth $558,616 as of December 31, 2003, a compound return of 15.45 percent, considerably more than both the S&P 500 and the ING Corporate Leaders Fund.

OVERWHELMED BY OUR NATURE

Knowing and doing are two very different things. As Goethe said, "In the realm of ideas, everything depends on enthusiasm, in the real world, all rests on perseverance." While we may *intellectually understand* what we should do, we usually are overwhelmed by our nature, allowing the intensely emotional present to overpower our better judgment. When someone questioned the General Secretary of the former Soviet Union, Mikhail Gorbachev, about actions he had taken against his better judgment, he replied, "Your question is academic because it is abstract. People don't have the luxury of living in the abstract. They live in the real, emotional, full-blooded world of reality."

It is in the full-blooded world of reality that our problems begin, for both investors and other professions. Let's see why this is so.

CASE STUDY: THE DOGS OF THE DOW

The Dogs of the Dow is one of the best known—and simplest—investment strategies around: Start with the 30 internationally famous Blue Chip stocks that make up the Dow Jones Industrial Average, and then sort them by dividend yield, from high to low. Once a year, buy the 10 that have the highest dividend yield. Hold them one year, and repeat the process, replacing any that have fallen off the list with the then 10 highest yielding Dow stocks. That's it. What could be simpler? Yet this simple strategy has been a market slayer since 1929, consistently beating the S&P 500 over all but two rolling 10-year periods (Table 1-1).

T A B L E 1-1

Average Annual Compound Rates of Return by Decad

Universe	1930s	1940s	1950s	1960s	1970s	1980s	1990s	2000s*
S&P 500	–0.05%	9.17%	19.35%	7.81%	5.86%	17.55%	18.20%	–5.34%
Dogs of the Dow	2.76%	10.91%	20.17%	8.86%	12.75%	20.64%	17.24%	4.36%

*Returns for 2000–2003

Since 1928, an investor who annually invested in the 10 highest yielding Dow stocks would have seen $10,000 grow to over $57,662,527 at the end of 2003 (excluding taxes and commission costs). That's a compound return of 12.24 percent per year since 1928 (Table 1-2). If the same investor had invested in the S&P 500, his $10,000 would have been worth just $10,366,726 at the end of 2003, a compound return of 9.70 percent per year!

And it's not just in the long-term that the strategy has shined. For the 10 years ending December 31, 2003, the Dogs of the Dow gained 11.88 percent per year, well ahead of the 9.08 percent return earned by all U.S. stock funds and much better than just a handful of large-cap funds covered by Morningstar. It's also better than the S&P 500's return of 11.06 percent over the same period. Keep in mind that, for a large portion of this 10-year period, large-cap growth stocks were powering most of the S&P 500's return.

All told, the Dogs of the Dow have had just *two* rolling 10-year periods since 1929 during which they failed to beat the S&P 500: the 10 years ending December 31, 1972, and the 10 years ending December 31, 1999. What's interesting is that, in both instances, its underperformance preceded the two most devastating bear markets of the last 60 years: the bear market of 1973–1974, during which the S&P 500 lost over 42 percent, and the more recent 2000–2002 bear market, during which the S&P 500 lost more than 45 percent.

With such overwhelming evidence in favor of the Dogs of the Dow strategy, and with so much public awareness, you would expect that many people would not only be using the strategy through thick and thin but that they would also understand that it doesn't beat the market every year. Indeed, in the early to mid 1990s, when the Dogs *were* doing well, the media heaped praise on them, and investors flocked to the strategy. A *Barron's* headline read: "Faithful Friends: Dogs of the Dow climb 4% in '94, beating 90% of stock mutual funds," and most media outlets and individual investors were singing

T A B L E 1-2

Summary Return and Risk Results for Annual Data, Standard & Poor's 500 and Dogs of the Dow, December 31, 1928–December 31, 2003

	S&P 500	Dogs of the Dow
Arithmetic Average	11.67%	14.31%
Geometric Average	9.70%	12.24%
Median Return	14.31%	13.77%
Standard Deviation of Return	20.31%	21.21%
Downside Risk—lower is better	9.12%	8.37%
Correlation with S&P 500	1.00	0.90
T-Statistic[1]	4.98	5.84
Sharpe Ratio	0.38	0.49
Number of Positive Periods	52	57
Number of Negative Periods	23	18
Maximum Peak-to-Trough Decline	−64.22%	−68.18%
Beta	1.00	0.94
$10,0000 becomes:	$10,366,726.00	$57,662,527.00
Minimum Annual Return	−43.34%	−48.88%
Maximum Annual Return	53.99%	66.73%
Minimum *Expected* Return*	−28.95%	−28.11%
Maximum *Expected* Return**	52.29%	56.73%

[1] T-Statistic measures the likelihood that results are due to chance. Observations of ±1.95 indicate results are not random at the 95 percent level of confidence.

*Minimum Expected Return is Arithmetic Return minus 2 times the standard deviation.
**Maximum Expected Return is Arithmetic Return plus 2 times the standard deviation.

their praise. But did investors pay attention to the long-term data and stick with the Dogs when things got rough? Nope. We now can examine first hand the recent reaction investors and the media had when the Dogs of the Dow were not doing well. The last time the Dogs seriously underperformed the S&P 500 for a sustained number of years was in the 10 years leading up to the market collapse of the 1970s. Because few people were aware of the strategy then, we can't look at the reactions of investors of that era. We can, however, look at the media's reaction to the more recent underperformance of the Dogs, in the 1997 to 1999 period. I collected all the articles in real time because they show us that despite all the long-term knowledge, people almost always judge investment strategies based on their short-term performance.

Time Magazine got the ball rolling with an article entitled "The Dow's Dogs Won't Hunt," pronouncing the strategy dead. (Given *Time*'s predictive track record, that was great news for Dogs fans. Remember their confident prediction that the movie *Titanic* would be a flop?) Many other newspapers and magazines joined the fracas, lamenting and explaining that the strategy

T A B L E 1-3

Worst Case Scenarios for Dogs of the Dow: All Declines Exceeding 10 Percent from December 31, 1928 through December 31, 2003 (Drawdown Analysis Using Annual Data)

Peak Date	Peak Index Value	Trough Date	Trough Index Value	Recovery Date	Decline (%)	Decline Duration	Recovery Duration
Dec–28	1	Dec–31	0.318239176	Dec–36	–68.18	3	5
Dec–36	1.036389842	Dec–37	0.707128789	Dec–38	–31.77	1	1
Dec–39	1.105859826	Dec–41	0.894617929	Dec–42	–19.1	2	1
Dec–65	44.0499425	Dec–66	37.15172151	Dec–67	–15.66	1	1
Dec–68	52.40459631	Dec–69	45.70728891	Dec–72	–12.78	1	3
Dec–00	5171.496432	Dec–02	4480.38282	Dec–03	–13.36	2	1

used to work, but doesn't anymore. After all, the naysayers said, look at 1997. And 1998. And 1999. The Dogs failed miserably! The *Philadelphia Enquirer* chimed in with "'DOGS' VS DOW: No Clear Victor" and a host of other media outlets piled on, with the inevitable words: "It used to work, but it doesn't anymore."

Investors followed suit and left the strategy in droves, presumably piling into the then hot large cap growth category. What happened next is what seems to *always* happen next: The Dogs resurged phoenix-like, while large cap growth sank like a stone. This story neatly demonstrates why investors tend to do so poorly over time—they are forever focusing just on what is working *now*, without any thought to how it has stood the test of time. Everyone wants to believe that "it's different this time" and extrapolate current trends in the market *ad infinitum*. But the facts are irrefutable—strategies that demonstrate a consistent ability to outperform over the long-term tend to return to doing so just as everyone has lost faith in them. Take this message to heart if a long-term strategy you are using has a few bad years. Chances are, it is getting set to rebound.

2 CHAPTER

THE UNRELIABLE EXPERTS: GETTING IN THE WAY OF OUTSTANDING PERFORMANCE

What ails the truth is that it is mainly uncomfortable, and often dull.
The human mind seeks something more amusing, and more caressing.
—H. L. Mencken

Everyone is guilty of faulty decision making, not just the scions of Wall Street. An accountant must offer an opinion on the creditworthiness of a firm. A college administrator must decide which students to accept into a graduate program. A psychologist must decide if a patient's ills are neurosis or psychosis. A doctor must decide if it's liver cancer or not. More prosaically, a bookie tries to handicap the next horse race.

All these are activities in which an expert predicts an outcome. They occur every day and make up the fabric of our lives. Generally, predictions are made in two ways. Most common is for a person to run through a variety of possible outcomes in his head, essentially relying on personal knowledge, experience, and common sense to reach a decision. This is known as a *clinical* or *intuitive* approach, and is how most traditional active money managers make choices. The stock analyst may pore over a company's financial statements, interview management, talk to customers and competitors, and finally try to make an overall forecast. The graduate school administrator might use a host of data, from college grade point average to interviews with applicants, to determine if students should be accepted. This type of judgment relies on the perceptiveness of the forecaster.

13

Psychologists have shown in numerous studies that when people are confronted with vast amounts of data, their brains create mental shortcuts to make decisions. These shortcuts, called *heuristics*, are the rules of thumb on which most intuitive forecasters rely when making any number of complex decisions or forecasts in their field.

The other way to reach a decision is the *actuarial*, or *quantitative*, approach. Here, the forecaster makes no subjective judgments, nor does she rely on a rule-of-thumb heuristic. Rather, only empirical relationships between the data and the desired outcome are used to reach conclusions. This method relies solely on proven relationships using large samples of data, in which the data are systematically weighted and integrated. It's similar to the structured portfolio selection process I described in Chapter 1. The graduate school administrator might use a model that finds college grade point average highly correlated to graduate school success and admit only those who have made a certain grade. A money manager might rely on a stock selection technique that employs long-term, empirical tests (like those in this book) that proves the strategy's efficacy over the span of 50 or more years. In almost every instance, from stock analysts to doctors, we naturally prefer qualitative, intuitive methods. In most instances, we're wrong.

HUMAN JUDGMENT IS LIMITED

David Faust writes in his revolutionary book, *The Limits of Scientific Reasoning*, that: "Human judgment is far more limited than we think. We have a surprisingly restricted capacity to manage or interpret complex information." Studying a wide range of professionals, from medical doctors making diagnoses to experts making predictions of job success in academic or military training, Faust found that *human judges were consistently outperformed by simple actuarial models*. Like traditional money managers, most professionals cannot beat the passive implementation of time-tested formulas.

Another researcher, Paul Meehl, offered the first comprehensive review of statistical prediction (similar to an empirical, systematic approach) and clinical prediction (similar to an intuitive, traditional heuristic approach) in his 1954 study, *Clinical versus Statistical Prediction: A Theoretical Analysis and Review of the Literature*. He reviewed 20 studies that compared clinical and statistical predictions for three things: academic success, response to electroshock therapy, and criminal recidivism. In almost every instance, Meehl found that simple actuarial models outperformed the human judges. In predicting academic success in college, for example, a model using just high school grade point average and the level attained on an aptitude test outperformed the judgments of admissions officers at several colleges.

Robyn Dawes, in his book *House of Cards: Psychology and Psychotherapy Built on Myth*, tells us more. He refers to Jack Sawyer, a researcher who published a review of 45 studies comparing the two forecasting techniques: In *none* was the clinical, intuitive method—the one favored by most people—found to be superior. What's more, Sawyer included instances in which the human judges had more information than the model *and* were given the results of the quantitative models before being asked for a prediction. *The actuarial models still beat the human judges!*

Psychology researcher L. R. Goldberg went further: He devised a simple model based on the results of the Minnesota Multiphasic Personality Inventory (MMPI), a personality test commonly used to distinguish between neurosis and psychosis, to determine into which category a patient falls. His test achieved a success rate of 70 percent. He found that no human experts could match his model's results. The best judge achieved an overall success ratio of 67 percent. Reasoning that his human judges might do better with practice, he gave training packets consisting of 300 additional MMPI profiles to his judges, along with immediate feedback on their accuracy. Even after the practice sessions, none of the human judges matched the model's success ratio of 70 percent.

WHAT'S THE PROBLEM?

The problem doesn't seem to be lack of insight on the part of human judges. One study of pathologists predicting survival time following the initial diagnosis of Hodgkin's disease, a form of cancer, found that the human judges were vastly outperformed by a simple actuarial formula. Oddly, the model used exactly the same criteria that the judges themselves said they used. *The judges were largely unable to use their own ideas properly.* They used perceptive, intelligent criteria, but were unable to take advantage of its predictive ability. The judges themselves, not the value of their insights, were responsible for their own dismal predictive performance.

WHY MODELS BEAT HUMANS

In a famous cartoon, Pogo says: "We've met the enemy, and he is us." This illustrates our dilemma. Models beat human forecasters because they reliably and consistently apply the same criteria time after time. In almost every instance, *it is the total reliability of application of the model that accounts for its superior performance.* Models never vary. They are always consistent.

They are never moody, never fight with their spouse, are never hung over from a night on the town, and never get bored. They don't favor vivid, interesting stories over reams of statistical data. They never take anything personally. They don't have egos. They're not out to prove anything. If they were people, they'd be the death of any party.

People, on the other hand, are far more interesting. It's more natural to react emotionally or personalize a problem than it is to dispassionately review broad statistical occurrences—and so much more fun! It's much more natural for us to look at the limited set of our personal experiences and then generalize from this small sample to create a rule-of-thumb heuristic. We are a bundle of inconsistencies, and although making us interesting, it plays havoc with our ability to successfully invest our money. In most instances, money managers, like the college administrators, doctors, and accountants mentioned above, favor the intuitive method of forecasting. They all follow the same path: analyze the company, interview the management, talk to customers and competitors, etc. *All* money managers think they have the superior insights and intelligence to help them to pick winning stocks, yet 80 percent of them are routinely outperformed by the S&P 500. They are victims of their own overconfidence in their ability to outsmart and outguess everyone else on Wall Street. Even though virtually every study conducted since the early 1950s finds that simple, actuarially based models created with a large data sample will outperform traditional active managers, they refuse to admit this simple fact, clinging to the belief that, while that may be true for other investors, it is not the case with *them*.

Each of us, it seems, believes that we are above average. Sadly, this cannot be true statistically. Yet, in tests of people's belief in their own ability—typically people are asked to rank their ability as a driver—virtually everyone puts their own ability in the upper 10 to 20 percent! In his 1997 paper *The Psychology of the Non-Professional Investor*, Nobel laureate Daniel Kahneman says: "The biases of judgment and decision making have sometimes been called cognitive illusions. Like visual illusions, the mistakes of intuitive reasoning are not easily eliminated…Merely learning about illusions does not eliminate them." Kahneman goes on to say that, like our investors above, the majority of investors are dramatically overconfident and optimistic, prone to an illusion of control where none exists. Kahneman also points out that the reason it is so difficult for investors to correct these false beliefs is because they also suffer from *hindsight bias*, a condition that he describes thus: "psychological evidence indicates people can rarely reconstruct, after the fact, what they thought about the probability of an event before it occurred. Most are honestly deceived when they exaggerate their earlier estimate of the probability that the event would occur…Because of another hindsight bias, events that the best-informed experts did not anticipate often appear almost inevitable after they occur."

If Kahneman's insight is hard to believe, go back and see how many of the "experts" were calling for a NASDAQ crash in the early part of the year 2000 and contrast that with the number of people who now say it was inevitable. What's more, even investors who are guided by a quantitative stock selection system can let their human inconsistencies hog-tie them. A September 16, 2004 issue of the *Wall Street Journal* includes an article entitled *A Winning Stock Picker's Losing Fund*, showing how this is possible. The story centers on the Value Line Investment Survey, which is one of the top independent stock-research services and has a remarkable long-term record of identifying winners. According to the *Wall Street Journal*, "But the company also runs a mutual fund, and in one of Wall Street's odder paradoxes, it has performed terribly. Investors following the Value Line approach to buying and selling stocks would have racked up cumulative gains of nearly 76 percent over the five years ended in December, according to the investment-research firm. That period includes the worst bear market in a generation. By contrast, the mutual fund—one of the nations oldest, having started in 1950—lost a cumulative 19 percent over the same period. The discrepancy has a lot to do with the fact that the Value Line fund, despite its name, hasn't rigorously followed the weekly investment advice printed by its parent Value Line Publishing." In other words, the managers of the fund ignore their own data, thinking they can improve on the quantitative selection process! The article goes on to point out that another closed-end fund, called the First Trust Value Line Fund, does adhere to the *Value Line Survey* advice, and has performed much better and more consistently with the underlying research.

BASE RATES ARE BORING

The majority of investors, as well as anyone else using traditional, intuitive forecasting methods, are overwhelmed by their human nature. They use information unreliably, one time including a stock in a portfolio and another time excluding it, even though in each instance the information is the same. Our decision-making is systematically flawed because we prefer gut reactions and individual, colorful stories to boring base rates. Base rates are among the most illuminating statistics that exist. They're just like batting averages. For example, if a town of 100,000 people had 70,000 lawyers and 30,000 librarians, the base rate for lawyers in that town is 70 percent. When used in the stock market, base rates tell you what to expect from a certain *class* of stocks (e.g., all stocks with high dividend yields) and what that variable *generally* predicts for the future. But base rates tell you nothing about how each individual member of that class will behave.

Most statistical prediction techniques use base rates. Seventy-five percent of university students with grade point averages above 3.5 go on to do well in graduate school. Smokers are twice as likely to get cancer. Stocks with low PE ratios outperform the market 65 percent of the time. The best way to predict the future is to bet with the base rate that is derived from a large sample. Yet, numerous studies have found that people make full use of base rate information only when there is a lack of descriptive data. In one example, people are told that out of a sample of 100 people, 70 are lawyers and 30 are engineers. When provided with no additional information and asked to guess the occupation of a randomly selected 10, people use the base rate information, saying all 10 are lawyers, since by doing so they assure themselves of getting the most right.

However, when worthless yet descriptive data are added, such as "Dick is a highly motivated 30-year-old married man who is well liked by his colleagues," people largely ignore the base rate information in favor of their "feel" for the person. They are certain that their unique insights will help them make a better forecast, even when the additional information is meaningless. We prefer descriptive data to impersonal statistics because it better represents our individual experience. When stereotypical information is added, such as "Dick is 30 years old, married, shows no interest in politics or social issues, and likes to spend free time on his many hobbies, which include carpentry and mathematical puzzles," people totally ignore the base rate and bet Dick is an engineer, despite the 70 percent chance that he is a lawyer.

It's difficult to blame people. Base rates are boring; experience is vivid and fun. The only way anyone will pay 100 times a company's earnings for a stock is if it has got a tremendous story. Never mind that stocks with high PE ratios beat the market just 35 percent of the time over the last 52 years—the story is so compelling, you're happy to throw the base rates out the window.

THE INDIVIDUAL VERSUS THE GROUP

Human nature makes it virtually impossible to forgo the specific information of an individual case in favor of the results of a great number of cases. We're interested in *this stock* and *this company*, not with this *class* of stocks or this *class* of companies. Large numbers mean nothing to us. As Stalin chillingly said: "One death is a tragedy, a million, a statistic." When making an investment, we almost always do so stock-by-stock, rarely thinking about an overall strategy. If a story about *one* stock is compelling enough, we're willing to ignore what the base rate tells us about an entire *class* of stocks.

Imagine if the life insurance industry made decisions on a case-by-case basis. An agent visits you at home, interviews you, checks out your spouse and children, and finally makes a judgment based on his gut feelings. How many people who *should* get coverage would be denied, and how many millions of dollars in premiums would be lost? The reverse is also true. Someone who should be denied might be extended coverage because the agent's gut feeling was *this* individual is different, despite what actuarial tests say. The company would lose millions in additional payouts.

The same thing happens when we think in terms of individual stocks, rather than strategies. A case-by-case approach wreaks havoc with returns, because it virtually guarantees that we will base many of our choices on emotions. This is a highly unreliable, unsystematic way to buy stocks, yet it's the most natural and the most common. In the seven years since the initial publication of this book, I have given hundreds of presentations about its findings. I always note people nodding their heads when I tell them that low price-to-sales stocks do vastly better than stocks with high price-to-sales. They agree because this is a simple fact that makes intuitive sense to them. But when I give them some of the actual names of the stocks that fit this profile, their demeanor visibly changes. Hands will go up with statements like: "what a dog" or "I hate that industry," simply because we have now provided them with specific individual stocks about which they have many ingrained prejudices. Combating these personal feelings, even when we are aware of the bias, is a very difficult task indeed.

PERSONAL EXPERIENCE PREFERRED

We always place more reliance on personal experience than impersonal base rates. An excellent example is the 1972 presidential campaign. The reporters on the campaign trail with George McGovern unanimously agreed that he could not lose by more than 10 percent, even though they knew he lagged 20 percent in the polls and that no major poll had been wrong by more than 3 percent in 24 years. These tough, intelligent people bet against the base rate because the concrete evidence of their personal experience overwhelmed them. They saw huge crowds of supporters, felt their enthusiasm, and trusted their feelings. In much the same way, a market analyst who has visited a company and knows the president may ignore the statistical information that tells him a company is a poor investment. In social science terms, he's overweighting the vivid story and underweighting the pallid statistics.

In regards to the market, many have hypothesized that analysts get much more confident about their predictions after they have met the management of the company and formed personal opinions about their talent—or lack thereof. And they often can be seen clinging to these opinions even after factual events have proved them wrong. Think of all the investors who, at the end of the 1990s, based their investment decisions just on their most recent personal experience in the market. For this intuitive investor, the only game in town was in technology shares and other large-cap growth fare. Every bit of evidence that they had personally experienced suggested that it was different this time, that a new era had dawned, and that only those who implicitly rejected history would do well going forward. And the majority of them held on through the crash, so certain were they that a rebound was right around the corner. Only after two and a half years of "new personal experience" did the hapless intuitive investor learn that alas, it wasn't different this time. And even with the personal experience of losing a fortune in the bear market, many investors were *still* unable to make use of these new facts because of the inherent bias towards overconfidence. In their article, *The Courage of Misguided Convictions*, which appeared in the November/December 1999 issue of the *Financial Analysts Journal*, Brad M. Barber and Terrance Odean report:

> Moreover, people have unrealistically positive self-evaluations. Most individuals see themselves as better than the average person and better than others see them. They rate their abilities and their prospects as higher than their peers…In addition, people overestimate their contributions to past positive outcomes; they recall information related to their successes more easily than information related to their failures. Fischhoff wrote that they even misremember their own predictions so as to exaggerate in hindsight what they knew in foresight.

SIMPLE VERSUS COMPLEX

We also prefer the complex and artificial to the simple and unadorned. We are certain that investment success requires an incredibly complex ability to judge a host of variables correctly and then act upon that knowledge.

Professor Alex Bavelas designed a fascinating experiment in which two subjects, Smith and Jones, face individual projection screens. They cannot see or communicate with each other. They're told that the purpose of the experiment is to learn to recognize the difference between healthy and sick cells. They must learn to distinguish between the two using trial and error. In front of each are two buttons marked Healthy and Sick, along with two signal lights marked Right and Wrong. Every time a slide is projected, they guess if it's healthy or sick by pressing the button so marked. After they guess, their signal light will flash Right or Wrong, informing them if they have guessed correctly.

Here's the hitch. Smith gets true feedback. If he's correct, his light flashes Right, if he's wrong, it flashes Wrong. Because he's getting true feedback,

Smith soon gets around 80 percent correct, because it's a matter of simple discrimination.

Jones' situation is entirely different. He doesn't get true feedback based on his guesses. Rather, the feedback he gets is based on Smith's guesses! It doesn't matter if he's right or wrong about a particular slide; he's told he's right if Smith guessed right and wrong if Smith guessed wrong. Of course, Jones doesn't know this. He's been told that a true order exists that he can discover from the feedback. He ends up searching for order when there is no way to find it.

The moderator then asks Smith and Jones to discuss the rules they use for judging healthy and sick cells. Smith, who got true feedback, offers rules that are simple, concrete, and to the point. Jones, on the other hand, uses rules that are, out of necessity, subtle, complex, and highly adorned. After all, he had to base his opinions on contradictory guesses and hunches.

The amazing thing is that Smith doesn't think Jones' explanations are absurd, crazy, or unnecessarily complicated. He's impressed by the "brilliance" of Jones' method and feels inferior and vulnerable because of the pedestrian simplicity of his own rules. The more complicated and ornate Jones' explanations, *the more likely they are to convince Smith*.

Before the next test with new slides, the two are asked to guess who will do better than the first time around. All Joneses and most Smiths say that Jones will. In fact, Jones shows no improvement at all. Smith, on the other hand, does significantly worse than he did the first time around, because he's now making guesses based on some of the complicated rules he learned from Jones.

A SIMPLE SOLUTION

William of Ockham, a fourteenth-century Franciscan monk from the village of Ockham, in Surrey, England, developed the *principle of parsimony*, now called *Occam's Razor*. For centuries it has been a guiding principle of modern science. Its axioms—such as "what can be done with fewer assumptions is done in vain with more," and "entities are not to be multiplied without necessity"—boil down to this: Keep it simple, sweetheart. Occam's Razor shows that most often, the simplest theory is the best.

This is also the key to successful investing. Successful investing, however, runs contrary to human nature. We make the simple complex, follow the crowd, fall in love with the story about some stock, let our emotions dictate decisions, buy and sell on tips and hunches, and approach each investment decision on a case-by-case basis, with no underlying consistency or strategy. We are optimistically overconfident in our own abilities, prone to hindsight bias, and quite willing to ignore over half century of facts that show this to be so. When making decisions, we view everything in the present tense. And, because we time-weight information, we give the most recent events the greatest import. We then extrapolate anything that has been working well recently very far out into time, assuming it will always be so. How else could the majority of investors have concentrated their portfolios in large-cap growth stocks and technology shares right before the technology bubble burst and the biggest bear market since the 1970s ensued?

It's extremely difficult not to make decisions this way. Think about the last time you really goofed. Time passes and you see: *What was I thinking! It's so obvious that I was wrong, why didn't I see it?* The mistake becomes obvious when you see the situation historically, drained of emotion and feeling. When the mistake was made, you had to contend with emotion. Emotion often wins, since, as John Junor says, "An ounce of emotion is equal to a ton of facts."

This isn't a phenomenon reserved for the unsophisticated. Pension sponsors have access to the best research and talent that money can buy, yet are notorious for investing heavily in stocks just as bear markets begin and for firing managers at the absolute bottom of their cycle. Institutional investors *say* they make decisions objectively and unemotionally, but they don't. The authors of the book *Fortune & Folly* found that, although institutional investors' desks are cluttered with in-depth, analytical reports, the majority of pension executives select outside managers using gut feelings. They also keep managers with consistently poor performance simply because they have good personal relationships with them.

The path to achieving investment success is to study long-term results and find a strategy or group of strategies that make sense. Remember to consider risk (the standard deviation of return) and choose a level that is acceptable. *Then stay on the path.*

To succeed, let history guide you. Successful investors look at history. They understand and react to the present in terms of the past. Yesterday and tomorrow, as well as today, make up their *now*. Something as simple as looking at a strategy's best and worst years is a good example. Knowing the potential parameters of a strategy gives investors a tremendous advantage over the uninformed. If the maximum expected loss is 35 percent, and the strategy is down 15 percent, instead of panicking, an informed investor can feel happy that things aren't as bad as they could be. This knowledge tempers expectations and emotions, giving informed investors a perspective that acts as an emotional pressure valve. Thinking historically, they let what they *know* transcend how they *feel*. This is the only way to perform well.

The data in this book give perspective. It helps you understand that hills and valleys are part of every investment scheme and are to be expected, not feared. It tells you what to expect from various classes of stocks. Don't second guess. Don't change your mind. Don't reject an individual stock—if it meets the criteria of your strategy—because you think it will do poorly. Don't try to outsmart. Looking over 52 years, you see that many strategies had periods during which they didn't do as well as the S&P 500, but also had many that did much better. Understand, see the long-term, and let it work. If you do, your chance of succeeding is very high. If you don't, no amount of knowledge will save you, and you'll find yourself with the 80 percent of underperformers thinking: "What went wrong?"

Let's now look at a case study focusing on how I actually used these data to make predictions about the market's direction, in which virtually all the predictions were based on the idea that everything ultimately reverts to its long-term mean.

ADDITIONAL READING

A whole crop of books have been published on Behavioral Finance over the last seven years. For those readers interested in a more in-depth understanding of the field, here's a recommended reading list of newer titles, along with a few classics:

Why Smart People Make Big Money Mistakes and How to Correct Them: Lessons From the New Science of Behavioral Economics by Gary Belsky and Thomas Gilovich

Outsmarting the Smart Money: Understand How Markets Really Work and Win the Wealth Game by Lawrence A. Cunningham

Rational Choice in an Uncertain World: The Psychology of Judgment and Decision Making by Reid Hastie and Robyn M. Dawes

Behavioural Finance: Insights into Irrational Minds and Markets by James Montier

Investment Madness: How Psychology Affects Your Investing...and What to Do About It by John R. Nofsinger

Inefficient Markets: An Introduction to Behavioral Finance by Andrei Schleifer

Beyond Greed and Fear: Understanding Behavioral Finance and the Psychology of Investing by Hersh Shefrin

Beyond the Random Walk: A Guide to Stock Market Anomalies and Low Risk Investing by Vijay Singal

The Winner's Curse: Paradoxes and Anomalies of Economic Life by Richard H. Thaler

CASE STUDY: USING LONG-TERM DATA TO MAKE PREDICTIONS ABOUT THE FUTURE

In this chapter, I focused on the various mistakes intuitive investors make by filtering the short-term data through their emotions and assuming that current events will continue indefinitely. This type of decision-making led investors, in the late 1990s, to believe that they were participating in a "new era" for investors, one in which the business cycle was repealed and people who followed the old valuation methods were doomed. But what about the predictive ability of long-term data? Is there any way to forecast the future by looking to the past? Instead of making intuitive, gut-level forecasts based on recent history, what happens if you simply assume that events will revert to the long-term base rate?

That is precisely what I did at my former firm, O'Shaughnessy Capital Management, when I wrote commentaries about what to expect in the stock market. I wrote many commentaries for our website, and the single most important thing I let guide my forecasts was the assumption that the markets would revert to their long-term historical averages. This simple notion made for some fairly accurate predictions. What follows is a sampling of several commentaries written in the late 1990s. (All the commentaries are available in their entirety at www.whatworksonwallstreet.com.)

ON THE DOGS OF THE DOW

On May 21, 1998, I posted a commentary entitled *In Defense of Man's Best Friend*, supporting the Dogs theory. Here is an excerpt:

> I'm greatly amused by the negative opinion the Dogs of the Dow strategy has aroused recently in the financial press. The strategy—which is a component of our *Dogs of the Market Fund*—is very simple: you buy the 10 highest-yielding stocks from the Dow Jones Industrial Average, and hold them one year. Every year you rebalance the portfolio so you always buy the 10 highest yielders.
>
> I've studied this strategy all the way back to 1928, when the modern 30-stock Dow Jones Industrial Average was born. As you can see from the table below, it's been a great way to buy blue-chip stocks. Starting in 1928, one dollar invested in the S&P 500 would be worth $830 by the end of 1997 (excluding taxes or trading costs). The same dollar invested in the Dogs of the Dow strategy would be worth $4,133! So, even though 69 years of data show that the strategy beats the S&P 500 in almost every 10-year period back to 1928,

the headlines are announcing that it's not going to work anymore because it had *one bad year*... Sadly, these people are ignoring history. Look at the table again and you'll see that the Dogs failed to beat the market in 25 of the last 69 years. What's more, the Dogs have had several periods where they trailed the S&P 500 for two or three years in a row. In 1992, I wrote an article for *Barron's* about the Dogs strategy's performance since 1928. But if I'd written that article in 1972, a shortsighted reader might have said—'Well, the strategy used to work, but it doesn't anymore. Look at the last three years—it's lagged the market since 1968! I'm not putting my money there!'

What I said six years ago in that article is equally valid today: 'Had you been making decisions like the average pension fund manager does in the United States, you'd have fired a manager using [the Dogs of the Dow] strategy at the end of 1972, because it had done worse than the S&P 500 over the preceding five-year stretch. Most likely you'd have given your money to a manager who'd turned in great gains over the previous five years. Back in 1972, this would have been a manager from the go-go growth crowd, willing to pay any price for the "nifty fifty" growth stocks. In the ensuing bear market, this manager's portfolio—and your investment—would have been crushed.' Strategic investors let time give them a perspective that those who follow the "hottest story" will never have...In the coming months, I'll be showing you the results of other value measures on the Dow, such as price-to-sales ratios and price-to-cashflow ratios. In the meantime, stick with the Dogs—even if you have to spend some time in the doghouse.

As already noted, the Dogs *did* underperform the S&P 500 for the 10 years ending December 31, 1999, but then went on to be a fairly good place to hide in the ensuing bear market years of 2000–2002, just like they were in the bear market years of 1973–1974. *(Note: Between December 31, 1997 and December 31, 2003, the Dogs of the Dow compounded at 5.33% versus 3.78% for the S&P 500.)*

ON USING THE PAST TO DETERMINE THE FUTURE

On October 5, 1998, during the worst part of the market turmoil brought on by the collapse of Long-Term Capital Management and the Asian crisis, I published a commentary entitled *To Divine the Future, Study the Past*, to bring a logical point of view to the crisis. Here's an excerpt:

Well, here we have it—a selling panic in the stock market. Sadly, in times like these, most investors forget that selling panics have happened many times before. And they will happen many times again.

According to the *Wall Street Journal*, 'The three months ending September 30th saw the biggest decline in the average U.S. stock fund since the third quarter of 1990, when the average fund posted a 16.07 percent negative return.' In the face of this decline, investors are selling, of course. Mutual funds saw net outflows in August 1998 for the first time since—you guessed it—1990. The philosopher George Santayana's observation that 'Those who fail to remember the past are condemned to repeat it,' is chillingly appropriate in these panicked—but not uncommon—times.

The only way for long-term investors to really suffer during these times is to turn a temporary loss into a permanent one by reacting emotionally and selling. I believe an emotional response to selling panics robs most of us of the perspective that is required for successful investing.

This said, I also believe that many people right now are *trying* to be good investors, attempting to ignore the market's gyrations and stay focused on why they're investing in the market in the first place—usually to ensure that when they retire they'll have enough money to support themselves. In my opinion, the majority of stock market investors should have very long time horizons. After all, the average baby boomer isn't going to retire for another 20 years.

In my previous commentary, I tried adding some fuel to the fire of longer-term perspective by examining the last two times we saw sharp declines in the market, in 1990 and 1987. I found that someone who invested in the Cornerstone Growth Strategy *right before* those declines would still have earned returns close to the average return for the Strategy since 1952, but only *if they stayed invested*.

But that got me thinking—was that true for the Cornerstone Growth and Cornerstone Value Strategies in all downturns? Do wonderful springs and lush summers always follow bleak winters?

First I looked at the Strategies' five worst months, going back to 1974 for the Cornerstone Growth Strategy and 1980 for the Cornerstone Value Strategy. Here's what I found:

Cornerstone Growth Strategy

Five Worst Months Since 1974	Return	Return in the Subsequent 12 Months
October 1978	−24.13%	Return from Oct. 31, 1978 to Oct. 31, 1979 **+41.26%**
March 1980	−17.34%	Return from Mar. 31, 1980 to Mar. 31, 1981 **+88.86%**
October 1987	−28.02%	Return from Oct. 31, 1987 to Oct. 31, 1988 **+21.05%**
August 1990	−14.98%	Return from Aug. 31, 1990 to Aug. 31, 1991 **+33.62%**
August 1998	−26.60%	Return from Aug. 31, 1998 to Aug. 31, 1999 **???%**

While past performance does not guarantee future results, the jolt that Cornerstone Growth experienced this past August could well indicate an exceptional buying opportunity for the Strategy... So, do these data argue for market timing? Of course not. No one can predict these losses ahead of time. Rather than letting market declines fill you with despair, you should take solace from what history shows us comes afterwards. If we use history as our guide, we see that events that generally lead people to sell in terror should lead them to buy aggressively, or, at the very least, stay the course with their investment. But this means you must overcome your emotions. But this isn't easy to do, because *today's* headlines scare many of us silly. They sound so all knowing and sure of themselves—*how can they be wrong?*

The best way for you to short-circuit the panic that you will inevitably feel over the course of your investment program is *to focus on all the other panics and what happened afterwards.* Remember that not even the Great Crash and Depression of the 1930s would have destroyed a long-term investor who *stuck with a superior investment strategy.* And remind yourself that even if you *did* know what was going to happen, you'd probably let that information lead you to the wrong conclusions...I know that bear markets are part of the deal we make as equity investors. But it is our ability to look beyond short-term losses that will help us succeed in the future and enjoy the long-term fruits of stock market investing.

(Note: The return for the fund for the period August 31, 1998 through August 31, 1999 was +38.30%.)

ON THE ATTRACTIVENESS OF SMALL-CAP STOCKS

The bubble years of the late 1990s were not kind to small-cap stocks, which languished as large-cap growth stocks soared. On January 1, 1999, I published a commentary on the attractiveness of small-cap stocks entitled *Looking Back to the Future: History Says Buy Small-Cap Stocks Now*. Here's an excerpt from the article:

Since 1994, the stock market has been extraordinarily biased toward big-cap growth stocks. Virtually all of the returns generated by the S&P 500 this year are due to the stunning performance of just a handful of big growth stocks—the top 10 performers in the index accounted for 56% of the S&P 500's returns through the end of November. If your large-cap stock wasn't a Microsoft, Pfizer, or Lucent, chances are it was flat for the year.

As for stocks outside the big-cap growth arena, this year's market has been a virtual wasteland. Value and small-cap stocks have suffered terribly. According to the December 27, 1998 *New York Times*, "If it seems that your value stocks are spinning their wheels, it probably isn't a reflection of your stock-picking prowess. Last month, the difference in 12-month performance between the S&P/Barra Value and S&P/Barra Growth Indexes was the largest in 11 years." In other words, value stocks really stunk in 1998.

And if you want to see *really bad*, all you have to do is take a look at small-cap stocks. Those laggard big-cap value strategies look positively wonderful when compared to the plight of small-cap stocks. The small-cap Russell is down more than 7% as of December 24, 1998. And even that figure masks the true shellacking the average small stock has endured—25% of the stocks in the Russell are down more than 50% from their highs this year! And if you look at our O'Shaughnessy Small-Cap Universe (7,964 stocks with market-caps below $1 billion), you'll see a median loss of 15.07% between January 1, 1998 and November 30, 1998...It's been a long and lonely draught for small stocks. Even though history shows that small capitalization stocks outperform large stocks over almost all long periods of time (someone investing $10,000 at the start of 1929 would have $18.5 million more if he simply held small stocks rather than the S&P 500) there are some long periods where the patience of Job is required. Luckily, I believe we're near the end of big-cap growth's out-sized performance and a renaissance for value and small-cap strategies. Why? Look at history.

I believe this week marks an historical opportunity for small stock investors. For the first time since the mid-1960s, *large stocks will outperform small stocks over the 20-year period ending December 31, 1998.* So, rather than being distraught about the market, I find myself delighted! For if history is a good guide, we can expect small-cap stocks to embark on a multi-year rally that will send them soaring above their bigger, better known brethren that currently dominate the S&P 500...I find the current valuations of small stocks extremely compelling. But no one rings a bell and announces it's time for us to move from big-cap growth stocks to small-cap stocks. It takes foresight and courage to buck the big-cap growth trend, yet that is what history is telling us to do. So, as if on cue for our investment philosophy, Winston Churchill said: 'The further backward you can look, the farther forward you are likely to see.'

(Note: From January 1, 1999 [when this was written] through December 31, 2003, the small-cap Russell 2000 index is up 41.64% compared to a loss of –2.67% for the S&P 500.)

ON THE INSANITY OF INTERNET VALUATIONS

On April 22, 1999, I published a commentary called *The Internet Contrarian*, which looked at the valuation of Internet stocks through the long-term data valuation matrix by which we judged all stocks. Here's an excerpt from the commentary:

Monday, April 19, 1999 was not a banner day for Internet stocks. They took their biggest one-day hit ever, with the Dow Jones Internet Index plunging nearly 19%. Over the next several days, most of them bounced back almost to the levels from which they fell, leading many to believe that Monday was just a one-day event. If you are a big investor in Internet issues, use April 19th as your wake up call and run, don't walk, to the exit. For while the Internet stocks may make a short-term come back, current Internet stock prices make absolutely no sense. No other market mania has ever produced such outlandish valuations, and I believe that when the inevitable fall comes, it will be harder and faster than anything we've ever witnessed.

Don't get me wrong. I'm wildly bullish about how good the Internet will be for consumers. But I'm incredibly bearish about the prospects about the ongoing profitability of most of the current high-flying web businesses. It seems to me that the only successful business model found to date is to create a web company, do an IPO, and get rich quick selling your shares to gullible investors.

We are currently witnessing the biggest bubble the stock market has ever created. When the Internet insanity ends, truckloads of books will be turned out; endless comparisons to Dutch Tulip bulbs and Ponzi schemes will be made; and a whole generation of ex–day-traders will rue the day they were seduced by the siren song of the Internet. This mania is a creation of fantasy and ludicrous expectations and of the childlike notion that hope can prevail over experience. Legions of inexperienced people—many of whom can't even begin to understand a balance sheet—believe that all they need to do to secure their fortune is to plunk down their money on Anything.com and watch the profits roll in.

For the patient, educated, long-term investor who knows that over time the market is bound by the rules of economics, the last year and a half has been pretty sickening.

Near the top of any mania, you'll often see outright stupidity rewarded. The current myopia cannot and will not last. After *every other market mania*—from tulip bulbs in 17th century Holland, to radio stocks in the 1920s, to aluminum stocks in the 50s, to computer stocks in the mid 1980s, and the biotech craze of the early 1990s—those boring laws of economics *always* rear their very sane heads. Ultimately, a stock's price must be tied to the future cash payments a company will make to you as an owner. History shows us that the more you pay for each dollar of a company's revenue, the lower your total return. It does this because *it has to*—that's why economics is called "the dismal science."

Because the numbers ultimately have to make sense, the majority of all currently public Internet companies are predestined to the ash heap of history. And even if we could see the future and identify the ultimate winner in e-commerce, at today's valuations it is probably *already* over-priced. When people realize that the mania has dried up, and that "the greater fool" isn't there anymore, they'll all rush for the exits at the same time. And the same thing that drove Internet prices up—lack of liquidity married to irrational investors—will drive them down, only *more* quickly.

(Note: Since the publication of this commentary through December 31, 2003, the Dow Jones Internet Index is down –75.33%, despite a gain of over 88% in 2003.)

Since I joined Bear Stearns, I've used historical data to put the bear market of 2000–2002 in perspective, and I have called for a return to equity investing. Yet the point of these commentary excerpts is not self aggrandizement. *Any* investor with access to long-term data who also understands that markets are ultimately rational will be able to make similar forecasts. The key, as always, it holding fast to the efficacy of the long-term data and to the belief that regression to the mean is bound to occur.

3 CHAPTER

RULES OF THE GAME

It is amazing to reflect how little systematic knowledge Wall Street has to draw upon as regards the historical behavior of securities with defined characteristics. We do, of course, have charts showing the long-term price movements of stock groups and individual stocks. But there is no real classification here, except by type of business. Where is the continuous, ever growing body of knowledge and technique handed down by the analysts of the past to those of the present and future? When we contrast the annals of medicine with those of finance, the paucity of our recorded and digested experience becomes a reproach. We lack the codified experience which will tell us whether codified experience is valuable or valueless. In the years to come we analysts must go to school to learn the older established disciplines. We must study their ways of amassing and scrutinizing facts and from this study develop methods of research suited to the peculiarities of our own field of work.
—Ben Graham, the father of securities analysis, in 1946

In the early 1990s, when I began the research for what became *What Works on Wall Street*, little had been done to address Graham's challenge. Now, however, real strides are being made. The first version of *What Works on Wall Street*, published in 1996, covered many of the variables that Graham was looking for 50 years earlier. Over the past several years, many academ-

31

ics have also gone over decades of stock market data and offered their findings to the general public. Of particular note is the brilliant *Triumph of the Optimists: 101 Years of Global Investment Returns,* by Elroy Dimson, Paul Marsh, and Mike Staunton, which catalogs returns over the last 101 years in 16 different countries. The book also looks at the results by country for various investment strategies, such as growth and value.

Other academics, such as Eugene Fama and Ken French, have built growth and value indices for small- and large-cap stocks going back to 1927. Fama and French use the price-to-book ratio of a company to assign the stock to the value or growth camp, with stocks with low price-to-book ratios falling into the value index and stocks with high price-to-book ratios going into growth. Their data give us the longest return history on the two main styles of investing available today.

Many academics took their own research to heart and started money management firms to take advantage of the results of their research. After publishing their seminal paper, *Contrarian Investment, Extrapolation and Risk,* professors Josef Lakonishok, Andrei Shleifer, and Robert W. Vishny formed asset manager LSV, which currently uses strategies perfected through long-term research to manage over $25 billion. And, as their website claims, they stick very close to their tested strategies: "The quantitative investment strategies offered by LSV Asset Management are the result of over 20 years of academic research, rigorous testing of techniques, and strict application of risk controls. Our ongoing research and product refinement are conducted by Josef Lakonishok, Robert Vishny, and Menno Vermeulen." You can read all their research papers directly online at www.lsvasset.com. Their research indicates that not only decades of U.S. data show that certain factors are consistently associated with superior returns, but that the same is true in Europe and Japan as well.

Yet, all this research is valuable precisely because it covers returns over decades—not days. Many investors believe a five-year track record is sufficient to judge a manager's abilities. But, like Alexander Pope's maxim that a little learning is a dangerous thing, too little time gives investors extremely misleading information. Richard Brealey, a respected data analysis researcher, estimated that to make reasonable assumptions about a strategy's validity (i.e., to assume it was 95 percent likely to be statistically relevant), you would need more than 25 years of data.

SHORT PERIODS ARE VALUELESS

Consider the "Soaring Sixties." The go-go growth managers of the era switched stocks so fast they were called gunslingers. Performance was the name of the game, and buying stocks with outstanding earnings growth was the way to get it.

In hindsight, look at how misleading a five-year period can be. Between December 31, 1963 and December 31, 1968, $10,000 invested in a portfolio that annually bought the 50 stocks in the Compustat database with the best one-year earnings-per-share percentage gains soared to almost $35,000 in value, a compound return of more than 28 percent per year. That more than doubled the S&P 500's 10.16 percent annual return, which saw $10,000 grow to just over $16,000. Unfortunately, the strategy didn't fare so well over the next five years. It went on to *lose* over half its value between 1968 and 1973, compared to a gain of 2 percent for the S&P 500.

More recently, the mania of the late 1990s provided yet another example of people extrapolating shorter term results well into the future. Here, it wasn't "gunslingers" pouring money into just the stocks with the highest gain in earnings, but rather new-era disciples pouring money into Internet companies that in many instances had little more than a PowerPoint presentation and a naïve belief that they were going to revolutionize the economy. In both cases, things ended very badly.

IT'S DIFFERENT THIS TIME

People want to believe the present is different than the past. Markets are now computerized, block traders dominate, the individual investor is gone, and in his place sit huge mutual funds to which he has given his money. Some people think these masters of money make decisions differently, and believe that looking at how a strategy performed in the 1950s or 1960s offers little insight into how it will perform in the future.

But not much has really changed since Isaac Newton—a brilliant man indeed—lost a fortune in the South Sea Trading Company bubble of 1720. Newton lamented that he could "calculate the motions of heavenly bodies but not the madness of men." Herein lay the key to why basing investment decisions on long-term results is vital: The price of a stock is still determined by *people*. And as long as people let fear, greed, hope, and ignorance cloud their judgment, they will continue to misprice stocks and provide opportunities to those who rigorously use simple, time-tested strategies to pick stocks. Newton lost his money because he let himself get caught up in the hoopla of the moment; he invested in a colorful story rather than the dull facts. Names change. Industries change. Styles come in and out of fashion, but the underlying characteristics that identify a good or bad investment remain the same.

Each era has its own group of stocks that people flock to, usually those stocks with the most intoxicating story. Investors of the Twenties sent the Dow Jones Industrial Average up 497 percent between 1921 and 1929, buying into the "new era" industries such as radio and movie companies. In 1928 alone, gullible investors sent Radio Corporation from $85 to $420, all based on the hope that this new marvel would revolutionize the world. In that same year, speculators sent Warner Brothers Corporation up 962 percent—from $13 to $138—based on their excitement about "talking pictures" and a new Al Jolson contract. The 1950s saw a similar fascination in new technologies, with Texas Instruments soaring from $16 to $194 between 1957 and 1959, and other companies like Haloid-Xerox, Fairchild Camera, Polaroid, and IBM taking part in the speculative fever as well.

The point is simple. Far from being an anomaly, the euphoria of the late 1990s was a predictable end to a long bull market, where the silliest investment strategies do extraordinarily well, only to go on to crash and burn. A long view of returns is essential, because only the fullness of time uncovers basic relationships that short-term gyrations conceal. It also lets us analyze how the market responds to a large number of events, such as inflation, stock market crashes, stagflation, recessions, wars, and new discoveries. From the past, the future flows. History never repeats exactly, but the same types of events continue to occur. Investors who had taken to heart this essential message in the last speculative bubble were those least hurt in the aftermath.

ANECDOTAL EVIDENCE IS NOT ENOUGH

Investment advice bombards us from many directions, with little to support it but anecdote. Many times, a manager will give a handful of stocks as examples, demonstrating how well they went on to perform. Unfortunately, these managers conveniently ignore the many other stocks that also possessed the preferred characteristics but *failed*. A common error identified in behavioral research on the stock market is this tendency to generalize from the particular, with evidence showing that people often "delete" from their memory instances in which they did poorly. This leaves them with the strongest memories centered on the few stocks that performed very well for them, and the faintest memory for those that performed poorly. They also have demonstrated a consistent tendency to equate a good company with a good stock, assuming that because the company is highly thought of, it also will turn out to be an excellent investment.

We, therefore, must look at how well overall *strategies*, not individual stocks, perform. There's often a chasm of difference between what we *think* might work and what *really* works. This book's goal is to bring a more methodical, scientific method to stock market decisions and portfolio construction. To do this, I have tried to stay true to those scientific rules that distinguish a method from a less rigorous model. Among these rules:

- **An Explicit Method.** All models must use explicitly stated rules. There must be no ambiguity in the statement of the rule to be tested. No allowance is made for a private or unique interpretation of the rule.
- **A Public Rule.** The rule must be stated explicitly and publicly so that anyone with the time, money, data, equipment, and inclination can reproduce the results. The rule must make sense and must not be derived from the data.
- **A Reliable Method.** Someone using the same rules and the same database must get the same results. Also, the results must be consistent over time. Long-term results cannot owe all their benefit to a few years.
- **An Objective Rule.** I have attempted to use only rules that are intuitive, logical, and appeal to sensibility, but in all cases the rules are objective. They are independent of the social position, financial status, and cultural background of the investigator, and they do not require superior insight, information, or interpretation.
- **A Reliable Database.** Many problems exist with backtesting, and the quality of data is the top concern. *All* large collections of historical data contain many errors. A review of Standard & Poor's Compustat Active and Research database reveals that the data are remarkably clean. Nevertheless, problems remain. Undoubtedly, the database contains stocks where a split was unaccounted for, where a bad book value persisted for several years, where earnings were misstated and went uncorrected, where a price was inverted from 31 to 13, etc. These problems will be present for any test of stock market methods and must not be discounted, especially when a method shows just a slight advantage over the market in general. For this version of the book, we continue to use the Compustat Active and Research database. But for the period of 1994 through 2003, we are using a new backtesting engine to generate results. For 1994 forward, we use the FactSet Alpha testing engine to determine results. FactSet's Alpha tester is the new gold standard for generating backtests, because it allows much more flexibility in the backtest environment. We have also maintained real-time portfolios since 1994, and the FactSet engine closely duplicates them over the same period.

POTENTIAL PITFALLS

Many studies of Wall Street's favorite investment methods have been seriously flawed. Among their problems:

- **Data-Mining.** It takes approximately 42 minutes for an express train to go from Greenwich, Connecticut to Grand Central Station in Manhattan. In that time, you could look around your car and find all sorts of statistically relevant characteristics about your fellow passengers. Perhaps a huge number of blondes are present, or 75 percent have blue eyes, or the majority were born in May. These relationships, however, are most likely the result of chance occurrences and probably wouldn't be true for the car in front of or behind you. When you went looking for these relationships, you went data-mining. You've found a statistical relationship that fits *one set of data very well, but will not translate to another*. If you torture the data long enough, they will confess to anything. If no sound theoretical, economic, or intuitive common sense reason exists for the relationship, it's most likely a chance occurrence. Thus, if you see strategies that require you buy stocks only on a Wednesday and hold them for 16 1/2 months, you're looking at the results of data-mining. The best way to confirm that the excess returns are genuine is to test them on different periods or subperiods or in different markets, such as those of European countries. Preliminary research we have conducted in EAFE (Europe, Australasia, and the Far East) countries show the strategies performing with a similar level of excess returns as those in the United States. Another frequently used technique is to separate the database by random number, ticker symbol, or subperiods to make certain that all follow the same return pattern.

- **A Limited Time Period.** *Anything* can look good for five or even 10 years. Innumerable strategies look great during some periods but perform horribly over the long-term. Even zany strategies can work in any given year. For example, a portfolio of stocks with ticker symbols that are vowels, A, E, I, O, U, and Y, beat the S&P 500 by more than 11 percent in 1996, but that doesn't make it a good strategy! It simply means that in 1996, chance led it to outperform the S&P 500. This is referred to in the literature as the *small sample bias*, whereby people look at a recent five-year return and expect it to hold true for *all* five-year periods. The *more* time studied, the greater the chance a strategy will continue to work in the future. Statistically, you will always have greater confidence in results derived from large samples than in those derived from small ones.

- **Micro-Capitalization Stocks Allowed.** Many studies are deeply flawed because they include tiny stocks that are impossible to buy. Take stocks with a market capitalization below $25 million. During the 52 years of our study, $10,000 invested in all the stocks in the Compustat database with a market capitalization below $25 million would have grown to over $3.9 *billion* dollars! That's a compound return of over 28 percent a year over the last 52 years! Unfortunately, no one can realistically buy these stocks at the reported prices. They possess virtually no trading liquidity, and a large order would send their prices skyrocketing. For the second edition of this book, my former firm, O'Shaughnessy Capital Management, commissioned Lehman Brothers to do a liquidity study of all the stocks in the Compustat with market capitalizations below $25 million in the first quarter of 1997. They found that the majority of the issues had virtually no trading volume and that the difference between the bid and the asked price was many times more than 100 percent! More, the trading costs incurred, even if the stocks could be bought, would be enormous. More recently, a liquidity study conducted by my Systematic Equity Group at Bear Stearns Asset Management continues to find liquidity constraints similar to those found in 1997, with the smallest issues being virtually impossible to buy or sell without huge impact on the underlying prices.

Most academic studies define small capitalization stocks as those making up the fifth (smallest) market capitalization quintile of the New York Stock Exchange. Yet many of these stocks are impossible to trade. Indeed, on December 15, 2003, the median market cap of the fifth (smallest) market capitalization quintile of the New York Stock Exchange was $266.4 million, and the largest company in the quintile had a market cap of $509.8 million. In contrast, the geometric average market cap of the 1,215 mutual funds in Morningstar's all equity, small-cap category was $967 million. Of these, only 35 had average market caps at or below the smallest quintile median of $266.4 million. Thus, although many small cap funds use academic studies to support their methods, no fund can actually buy the stocks that fuel their superior performance. *On paper*, these returns look phenomenal, but no way exists to capture them in the real world. This is vital to keep in mind when you are looking at results that show astonishing returns.

Look at how a strategy's performance is affected by different levels of market capitalization: Consider 1967, a time of go-go growth stock investing. Had you bought the 50 stocks with the best one-year earnings-per-share gains for the previous year, the returns by market capitalization would be as follows:

- Capitalization greater than $1 million (almost all stocks in the database): +121.3 percent
- Capitalization greater than database median (the upper half of stocks in the database): +83.9 percent
- Capitalization greater than database average (largest 15 percent): +29.6 percent

- **Survivorship Bias, or Then It Was There, Now It's Thin Air.** Many studies don't include stocks that fail, thus producing an upward bias to their results. Numerous companies disappear from the database because of bankruptcy, or more brightly, takeover. Although most new studies include a research file made up of delisted stocks, many early ones did not.
- **Look-Ahead Bias, or Hindsight Better than 20/20.** Many studies assumed that fundamental information was available when it was not. For example, researchers often assumed you had annual earnings data in January; in reality, it might not be available until March. This upwardly biases results.

RULES OF THE GAME

I have attempted to correct these problems by using the following methodology:

- **Universe.** Our universe is the Standard & Poor's Compustat Active and Research Database from 1951 through 2003. These 52 years of data are, to my knowledge, the longest period ever used to study a variety of popular investment strategies. Although the Fama and French data series on growth and value investing go back to the 1920s, they only use a single variable—price-to-book ratio—to segregate stocks into the growth and value categories. I cannot overstate the importance of testing strategies over long periods. Any study from the early 1970s to the early 1980s will find strong results for value investing, just as any study from the 1960s and 1990s will favor growth stocks. Styles come in and out of fashion on Wall Street, so the longer the period studied, the more illuminating the results. From a statistical viewpoint, the strangest results come from the smallest samples. Large samples always provide better conclusions than small ones. Some pension consultants use a branch of statistics called *reliability mathematics* that use past returns to predict future performance. They've found that you need a minimum of 14 periods to even begin to make accurate predictions about the future.

    Compustat's research file includes stocks originally listed in the database but removed due to merger, bankruptcy, or other reason. This avoids *survivorship bias*. I developed most of the models tested herein between 1994 and 1995. Thus, the period 1950–1993 serves as the time when no modifications were made on any of the strategies. Other studies call this the *out-of-sample* holdout period. For this edition of the book, all the Compustat data from 1994 to 2003 is being accessed through FactSet through their Alpha Testing module.

- **Market Capitalization.** Except for specific small capitalization tests, I review stocks from two distinct groups. The first includes only stocks with market capitalizations in excess of $185 million (adjusted for inflation), called "All Stocks" throughout the book. Table 3-1 shows how I created the deflated minimums. The second group includes larger, better-known stocks with market capitalizations greater than the database average (usually the top 15 percent of the database by market capitalization). These larger stocks are called "Large Stocks" throughout the book. Table 3-2 shows the number of stocks having market capitalizations above the database mean. In all cases, I remove the smallest stocks in the database from consideration. For example, at the end of 2003, more than 4,867 stocks were jettisoned because their market capitalization fell below an inflation-adjusted minimum of $185 million. In the same year, only 1,025 stocks had market capitalizations exceeding the database average.

T A B L E 3-1

Inflation-Adjusted Value of $150 Million in Each Year with the Five-Year Averages Used as Minimums

Year Ending:	Inflation	Inflation-Adjustment Factor	Value of $150 Million	Five-Year Average
31-Dec-52	1%	5.51	$27,242,396.24	
31-Dec-53	1%	5.46	$27,482,129.33	
31-Dec-54	−1%	5.42	$27,652,518.53	
31-Dec-55	0%	5.45	$27,514,255.94	
31-Dec-56	3%	5.43	$27,616,058.68	$27,501,472
31-Dec-57	3%	5.28	$28,405,877.96	
31-Dec-58	2%	5.13	$29,263,735.48	
31-Dec-59	2%	5.04	$29,778,777.22	
31-Dec-60	1%	4.96	$30,225,458.88	
31-Dec-61	1%	4.89	$30,672,795.67	$29,669,329
31-Dec-62	1%	4.86	$30,878,303.40	
31-Dec-63	2%	4.80	$31,255,018.70	
31-Dec-64	1%	4.72	$31,770,726.51	
31-Dec-65	2%	4.67	$32,148,798.16	
31-Dec-66	3%	4.58	$32,766,055.08	$31,763,780
31-Dec-67	3%	4.43	$33,863,717.93	
31-Dec-68	5%	4.30	$34,893,174.95	
31-Dec-69	6%	4.11	$36,540,132.81	
31-Dec-70	5%	3.87	$38,772,734.92	
31-Dec-71	3%	3.67	$40,901,358.07	$36,994,224
31-Dec-72	3%	3.55	$42,275,643.70	

(continued on next page)

T A B L E 3-1

Inflation-Adjusted Value of $150 Million in Each Year with the Five-Year Averages Used as Minimums *(Continued)*

Year Ending:	Inflation	Inflation-Adjustment Factor	Value of $150 Million	Five-Year Average
31-Dec-73	9%	3.43	$43,717,243.15	
31-Dec-74	12%	3.15	$47,564,360.55	
31-Dec-75	7%	2.81	$53,367,212.54	
31-Dec-76	5%	2.63	$57,108,254.14	$48,806,543
31-Dec-77	7%	2.51	$59,855,161.16	
31-Dec-78	9%	2.35	$63,907,355.57	
31-Dec-79	13%	2.15	$69,678,189.78	
31-Dec-80	12%	1.90	$78,952,356.84	
31-Dec-81	9%	1.69	$88,742,449.08	$72,227,102
31-Dec-82	4%	1.55	$96,676,024.03	
31-Dec-83	4%	1.49	$100,417,386.16	
31-Dec-84	4%	1.44	$104,233,246.84	
31-Dec-85	4%	1.38	$108,350,460.09	
31-Dec-86	1%	1.33	$112,435,272.43	$104,422,478
31-Dec-87	4%	1.32	$113,705,791.01	
31-Dec-88	4%	1.26	$118,720,216.39	
31-Dec-89	5%	1.21	$123,967,649.96	
31-Dec-90	6%	1.16	$129,732,145.68	
31-Dec-91	3%	1.09	$137,658,779.78	$124,756,917
31-Dec-92	3%	1.06	$141,871,138.44	
31-Dec-93	3%	1.03	$145,985,401.46	
31-Dec-94	3%	1.00	$150,000,000.00	
31-Dec-95	3%	0.97	$153,909,296.12	
31-Dec-96	3%	0.94	$159,194,555.36	$150,192,078
31-Dec-97	2%	0.93	$161,947,665.68	
31-Dec-98	2%	0.91	$164,597,688.46	
31-Dec-99	3%	0.89	$169,130,382.72	
31-Dec-00	3%	0.86	$175,065,089.24	
31-Dec-01	2%	0.84	$177,821,319.70	$169,712,429
31-Dec-02	2%	0.82	$182,156,647.92	
31-Dec-03	2%	0.81	$185,646,807.91	

T A B L E 3-2

Large Stocks as Percentage of Compustat, 1952–2003

Year Ending:	Number of Stocks with a Market Capitalization above the Database Mean	Number of Stocks in the Database	Percent
31-Dec-52	110	560	20%
31-Dec-53	137	581	24%
31-Dec-54	153	629	24%

(continued on next page)

T A B L E 3-2

Large Stocks as Percentage of Compustat, 1952–2003 *(Continued)*

Year Ending:	Number of Stocks with a Market Capitalization above the Database Mean	Number of Stocks in the Database	Percent
31-Dec-55	147	657	22%
31-Dec-56	136	682	20%
31-Dec-57	141	692	20%
31-Dec-58	148	797	19%
31-Dec-59	160	860	19%
31-Dec-60	177	1447	12%
31-Dec-61	220	1622	14%
31-Dec-62	300	1792	17%
31-Dec-63	272	1986	14%
31-Dec-64	342	2136	16%
31-Dec-65	377	2351	16%
31-Dec-66	402	2487	16%
31-Dec-67	430	2698	16%
31-Dec-68	479	2969	16%
31-Dec-69	525	3132	17%
31-Dec-70	539	3155	17%
31-Dec-71	541	3414	16%
31-Dec-72	580	3684	16%
31-Dec-73	589	3639	16%
31-Dec-74	584	3644	16%
31-Dec-75	544	3695	15%
31-Dec-76	599	3832	16%
31-Dec-77	635	3852	16%
31-Dec-78	667	3980	17%
31-Dec-79	670	4262	16%
31-Dec-80	739	4478	17%
31-Dec-81	712	4917	14%
31-Dec-82	814	5030	16%
31-Dec-83	830	5531	15%
31-Dec-84	868	5476	16%
31-Dec-85	833	5537	15%
31-Dec-86	860	5992	14%
31-Dec-87	842	6130	14%
31-Dec-88	830	6009	14%
31-Dec-89	842	5877	14%
31-Dec-90	833	5457	15%
31-Dec-91	806	5891	14%
31-Dec-92	845	6554	13%
31-Dec-93	947	7312	13%
31-Dec-94	1008	7919	13%
31-Dec-95	1158	8718	13%
31-Dec-96	1214	9326	13%
31-Dec-97	1250	9852	13%

(continued on next page)

T A B L E 3-2

Large Stocks as Percentage of Compustat, 1952–2003 *(Continued)*

Year Ending:	Number of Stocks with a Market Capitalization above the Database Mean	Number of Stocks in the Database	Percent
31-Dec-98	1108	9861	11%
31-Dec-99	1079	10078	11%
31-Dec-00	1020	9569	11%
31-Dec-01	1069	9207	12%
31-Dec-02	1045	8832	12%
31-Dec-03	1025	8178	13%
Average	638	4557	15%

I originally chose the $150 million value in 1995 (now an inflation-adjusted $185 million) after consulting traders at several large Wall Street brokerages. They felt it was the minimum necessary if they were investing $100 million in 50 stocks in 1995. Due to inflation, the number now stands at $185 million. I use this figure to avoid micro-cap stocks and focus only on those stocks that a professional investor could buy without running into liquidity problems. Inflation has taken its toll: A stock with a market capitalization of $27 million in 1950 is the equivalent of $185 million stock at the end of 2003.

- **Avoiding Look-Ahead Bias.** I use only publicly available, annual and monthly information. For the period 1951–1994, I also time lag the data by a minimum of 11 months for the annual data and 45 days for the monthly data, so only data available at the time the portfolio was constructed are used. Although 11 months may seem excessive on the annual data, it conforms to what you would find using the current database on an annual basis. For the new data from 1994 to 2003, we are using the FactSet Alpha Tester, suitably time-lagged, to generate returns.

One potential problem with the earlier data is the changing nature of the Compustat database. As Figure 3-1 shows, Standard & Poor's has continually expanded the database. Many smaller stocks have been added, including up to five years of retroactive data. And because these firms were usually added because they were successful, the likelihood of a look-ahead bias becomes a real concern. Though *What Works on Wall Street* may suffer from this bias, I think because I eliminate the smallest stocks from consideration, the problem is greatly diminished.

- **Annual Rebalance with Risk-Adjusted Figures.** I construct and rebalance portfolios annually. We have information on many strategies in which we rebalance more frequently, but for the majority of strategies tested,

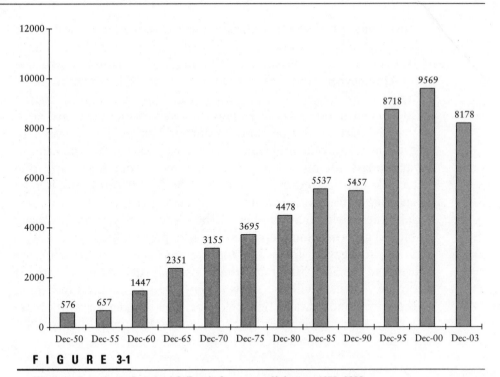

F I G U R E 3-1

Number of stocks in Standard & Poor's Compustat Universe, 1950–2003.

the annual rebalance proved optimal. The annual rebalance also allows us to use the data from 1951 through 1963, where all we have available is annual data. Stocks are equally weighted with no adjustments for beta, industry, or other variable. Foreign stocks (in the form of American Depository Receipts, or ADRs) included in the Compustat Universe are allowed. Due to data limitations, for the period 1951–1994, I was forced to add dividend returns to capital appreciation to arrive at a total return for the year. This results in a slight understatement of the compounding effect of dividend reinvestment. From 1994 on, the results reflect total returns, with full dividend reinvestment.

In this edition of the book, I am also including risk statistics obtained through the monthly data, thus allowing me to focus on things like: How often did the strategy do well? What was the worst-case scenario? How long did it take the strategy to recover?

I assume no trades are made throughout the year. This may bias my results slightly, because it rewards trade-averse strategies, but I believe many excellent strategies that require numerous trades turn mediocre once trading costs are included. I also examined annual returns and removed stocks with extreme returns or data that were inconsistent with outside information.

I also compare absolute and risk-adjusted returns and look at the beta generated by each strategy. Risk-adjusted returns take the volatility of a portfolio—as measured by the standard deviation of return—into account when considering absolute returns. Generally, investors prefer a portfolio earning 15 percent a year, with a standard deviation of 20 percent, to one earning 16 percent a year, with a standard deviation of 30 percent. A 1 percent absolute advantage doesn't compensate for the terror of a wild ride. I use the well-known *Sharpe ratio* of reward-to-risk for my calculations, with higher numbers indicating better risk-adjusted returns. To arrive at the Sharpe ratio, simply take the average return from a strategy, subtract the risk-free rate of interest, and then divide that number by the standard deviation of return. (Table 3-3 gives an example.) The ratio is important because it reflects risk. The strategy in Table 3-3, for example, had a higher *absolute* return than the S&P 500, but a *lower* risk-adjusted return because it was more volatile. I will also show *downside risk*—which is measured by the semi-standard deviation below zero—allowing me to measure how risky a strategy is when stock prices are declining. I believe that this is a more exact measurement with which to measure risk.

T A B L E 3-3

Determining a Strategy's Risk-Adjusted Return

Year Ending:	S&P 500	Strategy	T-bills	S&P 500-T-bills	Strategy-T-bills
31-Dec-93	9.99%	7.00%	3.00%	6.99%	4.00%
31-Dec-94	1.31%	5.00%	4.25%	−2.94%	0.75%
31-Dec-95	37.43%	42.00%	5.49%	31.94%	36.51%
31-Dec-96	23.07%	18.00%	5.21%	17.86%	12.79%
31-Dec-97	33.36%	24.00%	5.26%	28.10%	18.74%
31-Dec-98	28.58%	16.80%	4.86%	23.72%	11.94%
31-Dec-99	21.04%	23.57%	4.68%	16.36%	18.89%
31-Dec-00	−9.11%	−5.00%	5.89%	−15.00%	−10.89%
31-Dec-01	−11.88%	−5.18%	3.83%	−15.71%	−9.01%
31-Dec-02	−22.10%	−28.00%	1.65%	−23.75%	−29.65%
31-Dec-03	28.70%	48.00%	1.02%	27.68%	46.98%
Average	12.76%	13.29%	4.10%	8.66%	9.19%
Standard Deviation	19.43%	20.83%	1.52%		

Risk-adjusted ratio for the S&P 500 equals 8.66% divided by 19.43%, or 44.57.
Risk-adjusted ratio for the strategy equals 9.19% divided by 20.83%, or 44.11.

- **Minimum and Maximum Expected Returns.** Also, in all summary information about a strategy, I provide the maximum and minimum projected returns, as well as the actual maximum and minimum over the past 52 years. This is extremely useful information, because investors can glance at the worst loss and decide if they can stomach the volatility of any particular strategy.

- **Summary Statistics.** For each strategy, I now include a number of measurements not available in earlier editions of this book. I generate all the summary statistical information using the Ibbotson EnCorr Analyzer program. In addition to the concepts already covered, each summary result report includes the following:
  - **Arithmetic Average:** The average return over the period
  - **Geometric Average:** The average annual compound return over the period
  - **Median Return:** The return that has 50 percent of all returns above it and below it
  - **Standard Deviation of Return:** The extent to which observations in a data series differ from the average return for the entire series. The larger the standard deviation, the "riskier" the strategy. But since approximately 70 percent of all observations are positive, I think that using this to measure overall risk in a portfolio can be misleading. After all, when stocks are going your way, you want as much "risk" as possible. Therefore, I prefer to look at:
    - **Semi-Standard Deviation of Return below Zero (Downside Risk):** I believe that this is a much better measurement of the risk of a strategy, because it focuses on the portion of risk that is to the left of all observations below zero return. It essentially focuses on downside risk, and the lower this number is, the lower the risk of the strategy when stock prices are falling;
    - **T-Statistic:** Measures how likely it is that results are due to chance. Typically, a T-statistic of ±1.96 (where there are at least 20 observations) indicates a statistically significant selection return at the 95 percent level of confidence. Thus, a T-statistic exceeding ±1.96 suggests that you can be 95 percent certain that the results were not due to chance. You can test this by generating a series of random numbers over the period being analyzed. For example, a randomly generated list of numbers over the period 1951–2003 generated a T-statistic of –1.18.
  - **Correlation with the S&P 500:** The correlation range is between –1 and +1, with –1 indicating a strategy that is perfectly negatively correlated with the S&P; 0 indicating a strategy with no correlation with the S&P 500, and +1 indicating a strategy with perfect correlation with the S&P 500.
- **25-to-50 Stock Portfolios.** Except for Chapter 4, which reviews returns by market capitalization, all portfolios contain 25 to 50 stocks. In the original edition of the book, we used only 50 stock

portfolios, but we learned in real time that many of our investors preferred more concentrated portfolios to enhance overall returns. Thus, for several of the strategies featured in this edition, we also report on the results of a more concentrated 25-stock portfolio. A cursory review of private and institutional money managers reveals that 50 stocks are a common portfolio minimum. Many of the popular averages, such as the S&P 500, use more, yet many, such as the Dow Jones Industrial 30 Stock Average and *Barron's* 50 stock average, use the same or fewer. Next, I considered the benefits of diversification. Researchers Gerald Newbould and Percy Poon are professors of Finance at the University of Nevada. They studied the effect that the number of stocks held in a portfolio has on overall volatility and total return. They found that holding between 8 and 20 stocks—a common recommendation—wasn't nearly enough to adequately diversify a portfolio. Rather, they found that to be within 20 percent of the commonly quoted risk and reward figures, an investor has to expand the number of stocks she owns to at least 25. And, if your portfolio contains smaller capitalization stocks, you should hold 50 or more.

We'll also include information on the returns to various ratios and market capitalization categories by decile.

- **Discipline.** I test investment disciplines, not trading strategies. My results show that United States equity markets are not perfectly efficient. Investors *can* outperform the market by sticking with superior strategies over long periods. Simple, disciplined strategies—such as buying the top 10-yielding stocks in the Dow Jones Industrial Average, for example—have worked over the last 75 years because they are immune to the emotions of the market and force investors to buy industrial stocks when they are under distress. No one wants to buy Union Carbide after the Bhopal explosion or Exxon after the Valdez oil spill, yet it is precisely these times that offer the best buys.

- **Costs.** Transaction costs are not included. Each reader faces different transaction costs. Institutional investors making million dollar trades face costs substantially different from an individual, odd-lot trader. Thus, each will be able to review raw data and remove whatever costs fit their situation. Since the first edition of this book was published in 1996, however, online brokers have seriously reduced the transaction costs that individual investors pay for trading stocks. In many instances, an individual can now trade any number of shares for a flat $9.99 commission. This makes buying a large number of stocks a far more realistic idea for the individual, because he now faces costs similar to those of large institutional investors. Some innovative new brokers also allow clients to trade groups of stocks in baskets, thus you can now implement many of the strategies featured in this book in an economical fashion.

Now, let's look at the tests. We'll start with a review of return by market capitalization and then look at returns by single- and multifactor combinations.

4
C H A P T E R

RANKING STOCKS BY MARKET CAPITALIZATION: SIZE MATTERS

*Order and simplification are the first steps toward the mastery of
a subject.*

—Thomas Mann

First, I look at the returns for the two universes I use as benchmarks against which I measure all other strategies. These benchmarks are based on market capitalization and are called All Stocks and Large Stocks. All Stocks are those having market capitalizations in excess of a deflated $185 million. Large Stocks are those with a market capitalization greater than the Compustat database average (usually the top 15 percent of the database by market capitalization). I also look at a universe of small capitalization stocks that have liquidity adequate to allow large-scale trading, and I look at a universe of large capitalization stocks comprised of market-leading companies. In addition to these investable groups, I also focus on shares by various levels of market capitalization.

In all cases, I start with a $10,000 investment on December 31, 1951 and rebalance the portfolio annually. As with all my tests, the stocks are equally weighted, all dividends are reinvested, and all variables such as common shares outstanding are time-lagged to avoid look-ahead bias. I will also use the monthly data from January 1963 forward to establish *worst-case scenarios* that look at how badly all the various strategies did over the last 40 years.

Figure 4-1 shows the results for All Stocks, Large Stocks, and the S&P 500. As mentioned in Chapter 1, virtually no difference exists in performance between stocks with market capitalizations above the Compustat mean (Large Stocks) and the S&P 500. $10,000 invested in the S&P 500 on December 31, 1951 was worth $2,896,700 on December 31, 2003 and $3,173,724 if invested in the Large Stocks Universe. This is not surprising, because investing in the S&P 500 is nothing more than a bet on big, well-known stocks. Table 4-1 summarizes the results for each universe. You can find the annual returns for all universes at www.whatworksonwallstreet.com.

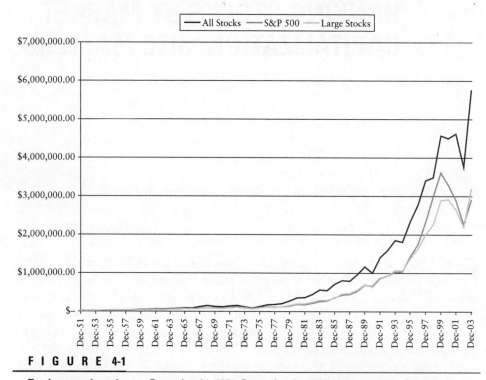

F I G U R E 4-1

Total returns by universe, December 31, 1951–December 31, 2003. Year-end 1951=$10,000.

The All Stocks group did considerably better than the S&P 500 and Large Stocks Universe: $10,000 grew to $5,743,706. The performance was not without bumps, however. The All Stocks portfolio had a higher standard deviation of return, as well as a higher downside risk, than the Large Stocks portfolio. Also, if you look at the year-by-year results at www.whatworksonwallstreet.com, you will see that during several periods, All Stocks significantly outperformed Large Stocks and, other times, the reverse was true. Large Stocks did quite a bit worse than All Stocks between December 31, 1975 and December 31, 1983, only to turn around and do

T A B L E 4-1

Summary Return and Risk Results for Annual Data, Large Stocks, All Stocks, and Standard & Poor's 500, December 31, 1951–December 31, 2003

	S&P 500	Large Stocks	All Stocks
Arithmetic Average	12.92%	12.99%	14.79%
Geometric Average	11.52%	11.71%	13.00%
Median Return	15.40%	15.75%	16.80%
Standard Deviation of Return	17.61%	16.84%	20.11%
Downside Risk—lower is better	6.33%	5.86%	7.17%
Correlation with S&P 500	1.00	0.95	0.87
T-Statistic	5.29	5.56	5.30
Sharpe Ratio	0.43	0.45	0.46
Number of Positive Periods	39	39	39
Number of Negative Periods	13	13	13
Maximum Peak-to-Trough Decline (using monthly data series)	−44.73%	−46.59%	−50.12%
Beta	1.00	0.89	0.99
$10,000 becomes:	$2,896,700.00	$3,173,724.00	$5,743,706.00
Minimum Annual Return	−26.47%	−26.70%	−27.90%
Maximum Annual Return	52.62%	45.07%	55.90%
Minimum *Expected* Return*	−22.30%	−20.69%	−25.43%
Maximum *Expected* Return**	48.14%	46.67%	55.01%

*Minimum Expected Return is Arithmetic Return minus 2 times the standard deviation.
**Maximum Expected Return is Arithmetic Return plus 2 times the standard deviation.

better between December 31, 1984 and December 31, 1990. The All Stocks Universe also had a larger worst-case scenario than Large Stocks: Between January 1963 and December 2003, All Stocks had 11 peak-to-trough declines exceeding 10 percent, with the largest occurring between November 1972 and September 1974, when the group lost 50.12 percent. The most recent decline occurred between February 2000 and September 2002, with All Stocks losing 30.04 percent. Table 4-1 summarizes the results for each group for the period 1951-2003 and Table 4-2 shows the returns by decade.

BEST OF TIMES, WORST OF TIMES

For this edition of the book, I'll list the best and worst returns for the strategies for each one-, three-, five-, and 10-year period. We'll also look at the worst-case scenario for each group and list any time they declined by more

T A B L E 4-2

Average Annual Compound Rates of Return by Decade

Universe	1950s*	1960s	1970s	1980s	1990s	2000s**
S&P 500	17.33%	7.81%	5.86%	17.55%	18.20%	−5.34%
Large Stocks	15.33%	8.99%	6.99%	16.89%	15.34%	2.40%
All Stocks	19.22%	11.09%	8.53%	15.85%	14.75%	5.91%

*Returns for 1952–1959.
**Returns for 2000–2003.

than 10 percent; how long the decline lasted, and how long it took them to get back to solid ground.

The information in Table 4-3 shows the best and worst returns using the annual data, whereas Table 4-4 uses the monthly data. The difference between the two is that most of the time, bear or bull markets don't start on December 31. The monthly data capture all interyear movements in the various strategies. These data should serve as a framework for investors trying to determine what the worst and best case might be over the periods indicated. For example, an investor with a five-year time horizon who wanted to invest in the All Stocks Universe might see that in all monthly periods over the last 40 years, the *worst* five years saw a loss of 8.94 percent per year for the All Stocks universe whereas the *best* five years saw a gain of 27.02 percent. Translating this into dollars, if the investor put $10,000 in the All Stocks universe and got a return over the next five years that matched the worst ever recorded over the last 40 years, his portfolio would be worth $6,260, an overall loss of 37.4 percent or a decline of 8.94 percent per year. Alternatively, if he received a return matching the *best* recorded over the last 40 years, his $10,000 would grow to $33,064, an overall gain of 231 percent, or an increase of 27.02 percent per year. Investors should search for strategies that have the best upside with the lowest downside, so we feature these data for all of our main strategies.

T A B L E 4-3

Best and Worst Average Annual Compound Returns over Period for Annual Data 1951–2003

For Any	1-Year Period	3-Year Period	5-Year Period	10-Year Period
S&P 500 Minimum Compound Return	−26.47%	−14.55%	−2.36%	1.24%
S&P 500 Maximum Compound Return	52.62%	31.15%	28.55%	19.19%
Large Stocks Minimum Compound Return	−26.70%	−11.93%	−4.37%	1.21%
Large Stocks Maximum Compound Return	45.07%	24.39%	22.40%	17.01%
All Stocks Minimum Compound Return	−27.90%	−16.48%	−7.81%	1.26%
All Stocks Maximum Compound Return	55.90%	31.23%	27.77%	21.31%

T A B L E 4-4

Best and Worst Average Annual Compound Returns over Period for Monthly Data 1963-2003

For Any	1-Year Period	3-Year Period	5-Year Period	10-Year Period
S&P 500 Minimum Compound Return	−38.93%	−16.10%	−4.15%	0.49%
S&P 500 Maximum Compound Return	61.01%	33.40%	29.72%	19.48%
Large Stocks Minimum Compound Return	−42.05%	−13.80%	−6.05%	−0.20%
Large Stocks Maximum Compound Return	68.49%	32.79%	28.65%	19.57%
All Stocks Minimum Compound Return	−41.65%	−16.82%	−8.94%	0.68%
All Stocks Maximum Compound Return	81.51%	29.46%	27.02%	21.46%

In this case, we see that the three major indexes featured here occasionally get out of sync with each other. For example, the worst three-year decline the S&P 500 ever suffered over the last 50 years was for the three years ending March 2003, when the index lost 16.10 percent per year, whereas the largest three-year decline for the All Stocks and Large Stocks Universes were the three years ending on December 31, 1974. This tells us that the most recent bear market affected the S&P 500 much more than the average stock traded in the United States. The data allow you to see just how far out of whack the S&P 500 got during the bubble years of 1997–2000. During those years, the S&P 500—really a handful of large growth names in the index—drove all performance and created a huge difference between it and almost every other stock in the market. Keep that in mind when you equate investing in the market with buying an S&P 500 Index fund.

Tables 4-5, 4-6, and 4-7 show various worst-case scenarios. Scanning the data for the S&P 500 shows that in the last 40 years, there were four times when the S&P 500 lost more than 29 percent from high to low and two times when it fell by more than 40 percent. The average decline for all losing periods was a loss of nearly 25 percent, and it took 13 months on average to post the decline. This information is extremely useful to review whenever we next find ourselves in a bear market, for it also shows that stocks always go on to recover from even the nastiest of declines.

T A B L E 4-5

Worse-Case Scenarios: All 10 Percent or Greater Declines for Standard & Poor's 500, December 31, 1962–December 31, 2003

Peak Date	Peak Index Value	Trough Date	Trough Index Value	Recovery Date	Decline (%)	Decline Duration	Recovery Duration
Jan-66	1.62	Sep-66	1.37	Mar-67	−15.64	8	6
Nov-68	2.08	Jun-70	1.47	Mar-71	−29.25	19	9
Dec-72	2.58	Sep-74	1.48	Jun-76	−42.63	21	21

(continued on next page)

T A B L E 4-5

Worse-Case Scenarios: All 10 Percent or Greater Declines for Standard & Poor's 500, December 31, 1962–December 31, 2003 *(Continued)*

Peak Date	Peak Index Value	Trough Date	Trough Index Value	Recovery Date	Decline (%)	Decline Duration	Recovery Duration
Dec-76	2.75	Feb-78	2.36	Jul-78	−14.13	14	5
Nov-80	4.40	Jul-82	3.66	Oct-82	−16.91	20	3
Aug-87	13.95	Nov-87	9.83	May-89	−29.53	3	18
May-90	16.84	Oct-90	14.36	Feb-91	−14.7	5	4
Jun-98	65.31	Aug-98	55.27	Nov-98	−15.37	2	3
Aug-00	89.90	Sep-02	49.68		−44.73	25	NA
Average					—24.77	13.00	8.63

T A B L E 4-6

Worse-Case Scenarios: All 10 Percent or Greater Declines for Large Stocks, December 31, 1962–December 31, 2003

Peak Date	Peak Index Value	Trough Date	Trough Index Value	Recovery Date	Decline (%)	Decline Duration	Recovery Duration
Jan-66	1.62	Sep-66	1.36	Mar-67	−15.8	8	6
Nov-68	2.16	Jun-70	1.43	Dec-71	−33.73	19	18
Nov-72	2.50	Sep-74	1.33	Sep-76	−46.59	22	24
Aug-78	3.07	Oct-78	2.70	Mar-79	−11.81	2	5
Jan-80	3.77	Mar-80	3.25	Jun-80	−13.65	2	3
May-81	5.07	Jul-82	4.22	Oct-82	−16.79	14	3
Jun-83	7.26	Jul-84	6.35	Dec-84	−12.55	13	5
Aug-87	15.31	Nov-87	10.83	Apr-89	−29.27	3	17
Aug-89	18.01	Oct-90	14.66	Feb-91	−18.62	14	4
Apr-98	59.43	Aug-98	46.81	Jan-99	−21.25	4	5
Aug-00	82.34	Sep-02	53.54	Dec-03	−34.98	25	15
Average					−23.19	11.45	9.55

T A B L E 4-7

Worse-Case Scenarios: All 10 Percent or Greater Declines for All Stocks, December 31, 1962–December 31, 2003

Peak Date	Peak Index Value	Trough Date	Trough Index Value	Recovery Date	Decline (%)	Decline Duration	Recovery Duration
Apr-66	1.77	Sep-66	1.49	Jan-67	−15.99	5	4
Nov-68	2.89	Jun-70	1.66	Mar-72	−42.67	19	21
Nov-72	2.93	Sep-74	1.46	Dec-76	−50.12	22	27
Aug-78	4.12	Oct-78	3.42	Apr-79	−17.04	2	6
Jan-80	5.21	Mar-80	4.33	Jul-80	−16.82	2	4

(continued on next page)

T A B L E 4-7

Worse-Case Scenarios: All 10 Percent or Greater Declines for All Stocks, December 31, 1962–December 31, 2003 *(Continued)*

Peak Date	Peak Index Value	Trough Date	Trough Index Value	Recovery Date	Decline (%)	Decline Duration	Recovery Duration
May-81	7.20	Jul-82	5.88	Oct-82	−18.34	14	3
Jun-83	10.85	Jul-84	9.16	Jan-85	−15.56	13	6
Aug-87	20.01	Nov-87	13.67	Apr-89	−31.66	3	17
Aug-89	22.68	Oct-90	17.10	Mar-91	−24.58	14	5
Apr-98	74.33	Aug-98	54.06	Jun-99	−27.28	4	10
Feb-00	97.15	Sep-02	67.97	Oct-03	−30.04	31	13
Average					−26.37	11.73	10.55

Finally, I will always look at base rates for how well each of the strategies does against our two main benchmarks, All Stocks and Large Stocks. Table 4-8 shows the base rate for All Stocks versus Large Stocks. Looking at returns for rolling five- and 10-year periods to establish a base rate, we see that All Stocks outperformed Large Stocks in 33 of the 48 rolling five-year periods, or 69 percent of the time. All Stocks also outperformed Large Stocks in 30 of the 43 rolling 10-year periods, or 70 percent of the time. The returns show that, for most strategies, you're better off fishing in the larger pond of All Stocks—which include many smaller cap stocks—than exclusively buying large, well-known stocks.

T A B L E 4-8

Base Rates for All Stocks Universe and Large Stocks Universe, 1951–2003

Item	"All Stocks" Beat "Large Stocks"	Percent
Single-Year Return	30 out of 52	58%
Rolling Five-Year Compound Return	33 out of 48	69%
Rolling 10-Year Compound Return	30 out of 43	70%

HOW MUCH BETTER ARE SMALL-CAP STOCKS?

Most academic studies of market capitalization sort stocks by deciles (10 percent) and review how an investment in each fares over time. The studies are nearly unanimous in their findings that small stocks (those in the lowest four deciles) do significantly better than large ones. We too have found tremendous returns from tiny stocks.

The glaring problem with this method, when used with the Compustat database, is that it's virtually impossible to *buy* the stocks that account for the performance advantage of small capitalization strategies. Table 4-9 illustrates the problem. On December 31, 2003, approximately 8,178 stocks in the active Compustat database had both year-end prices and a number for common shares outstanding. If we sorted the database by decile, each decile would be made up of 818 stocks. As Table 4-9 shows, market capitalization doesn't get past $150 million until you get to decile 6. The top market capitalization in the fourth decile is $61 million, a number far too small to allow widespread buying of those stocks.

TABLE 4-9

Compustat Database Sorted by Market Capitalization Decile on December 31, 2003

Decile	Largest Market Capitalization of Top Stock
1	$2 million
2	$9 million
3	$26 million
4	$61 million
5	$128 million
6	$261 million
7	$551 million
8	$1.2 billion
9	$3.7 billion
10	$311 billion

This presents an interesting paradox: Small-cap mutual funds justify their investments using academic research that shows small stocks outperforming large ones, yet the funds themselves *cannot buy the stocks that provide the lion's share of performance because of a lack of trading liquidity.*

A review of the Morningstar Mutual Fund database proves this. On December 31, 2003, the median market capitalization of the 1,215 mutual funds in Morningstar's all equity, small-cap category was $967 million. That's right between decile 7 and 8 from the Compustat universe—hardly small.

When you look at the returns to the All Stocks Universe by market capitalization decile, a fairly different picture emerges. Looking at Figure 4-2, we see that within the universe of investable stocks, there *is* an advantage to smaller cap stocks, but it's not of the magnitude of other studies that allow noninvestable micro-caps. Here, the smallest two deciles by market capitalization had the highest compound return between December 31, 1951 and December 31, 2003, and the largest two deciles had the lowest compound returns, but the amounts are not huge: The ninth decile had the highest return

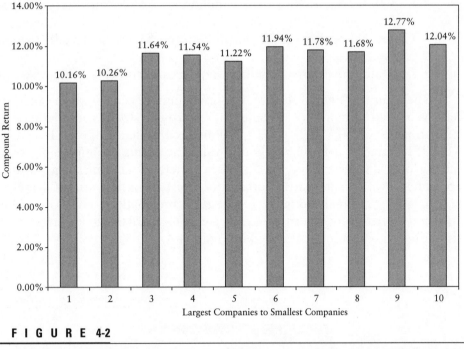

FIGURE 4-2

Average annual compound return by decile, All Stocks universe. December 31, 1951–December 31, 2003.

at 12.77 percent per year, whereas the first decile (largest stocks) had the lowest return at 10.16 percent, with the deciles in between showing no real discernable pattern to their returns.

REVIEWING STOCKS BY SIZE

In addition to reviewing the All Stocks universe by decile, it's illuminating to review performance by grouping stocks in absolute size categories. This conforms to how active managers look at stocks. They don't think about a stock being in the sixth decile, they think of it as a mid-cap stock.

Thus, I split up the universe by absolute market cap, adjusted for inflation:

- Capitalization less than $25 million (noninvestable micro-cap stocks)
- Capitalization between $25 million and $100 million (micro-cap stocks individuals might be able to invest in)
- Capitalization between $100 million and $250 million (micro-cap stocks that institutional investors can invest in)

- Capitalization between $250 million and $500 million (small-cap stocks)
- Capitalization between $500 million and $1 billion (small- to mid-cap stocks)
- Capitalization above $1 billion (liquid, larger stocks)

The returns, shown in Figure 4-3, are stunning. Almost all the superior returns offered by small stocks come from micro-cap stocks with market capitalizations below $25 million. $10,000 invested in that group on December 31, 1951 soared to over $3.9 billion in value, achieving a compound growth rate of over 28 percent for the 52 years reviewed. The micro-cap returns absolutely dwarf their nearest competitor, the $25 million to $100 million group. They even manage to overcome their breathtaking risk—an annual standard deviation of return of 47.51 percent—and land at the top of the risk-adjusted return index featured in Figure 4-4.

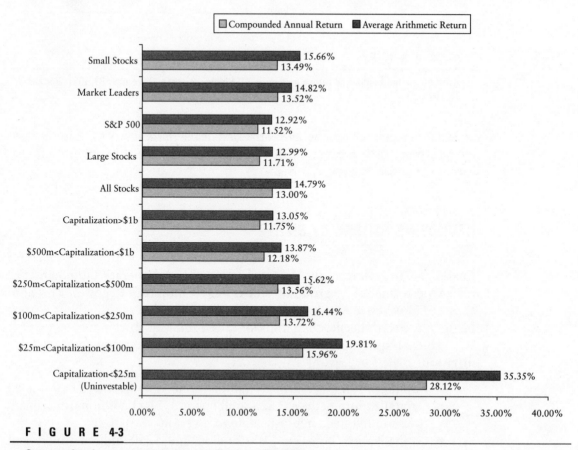

FIGURE 4-3

Compound and average returns by capitalization, 1951–2003.

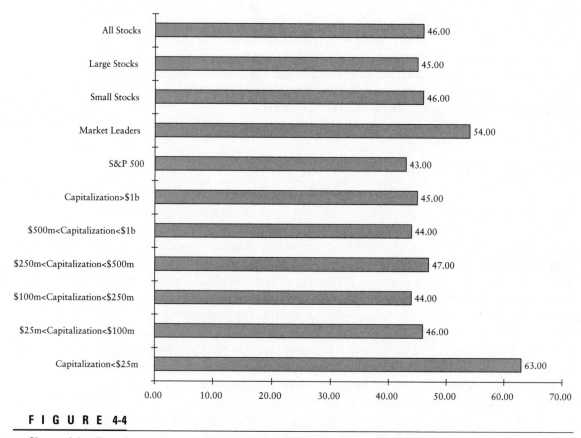

F I G U R E 4-4

Sharpe risk-adjusted return by market capitalization, 1951–2003 (higher is better).

As I mentioned in the previous chapter, these micro-cap stock returns are an illusion. The only way to achieve these stellar returns is to invest only a few million dollars in over 2,000 stocks. Precious few investors can do that. The stocks are far too small for a mutual fund to buy and far too numerous for an individual to tackle. So there they sit, tantalizingly out of reach of nearly everyone. What's more, even if you could spread $2,000,000 over 2,000 names, the bid–ask spread would eat you alive.

SMALL STOCKS AND MARKET LEADERS

I also look at two additional distinct groups of stocks—Small Stocks, or stocks that have market capitalizations greater than a deflated $185 million but less than the database average, and Market Leaders. Market Leaders are like Large Stocks on steroids. They come from the Large Stocks universe but also possess characteristics beyond mere size. To be a market leading company, you must be a nonutility stock with a market capitalization greater than the average, shares outstanding greater than the average, cashflow greater than the average, and finally, sales 50 percent greater than the average stock. Applying these factors to the overall Compustat database leaves just 6 percent of the database qualifying as Market Leaders.

SMALL STOCKS ARE THE WINNERS, BUT NOT BY MUCH

If we ignore the micro-cap stocks in Figure 4-3 as unobtainable, the results show that investors who pay no heed to risk or other factors are best off concentrating on smaller stocks from the Compustat database. As we'll see later, this is appropriate only for investors who want to make market capitalization the sole criterion for stock selection. These results confirm the academic studies showing smaller stocks beating large stocks, but once micro-caps are removed, by not nearly the large margins that many studies have found. What's really fascinating is the performance of the stocks with capitalizations between $500 million and $1 billion. They perform *nearly the same* as Large Stocks and considerably worse than All Stocks, Small Stocks, and Market Leaders. This contradicts the belief that, simply because a stock is in the smaller category, it offers the greatest potential to investors.

Ironically, we have found that when you use strategies like those featured in this book that are looking for maximum return, they *inevitably* lead you to stocks in the small- and mid-cap category. I believe this is not because of market capitalization alone, but rather because the stocks in this category are the least efficiently priced. Currently, around 400 stocks account for approximately 75 percent of the U.S. stock market capitalization, whereas literally thousands of stocks make up the remaining 25 percent. The sheer number of names in the small- and mid-cap category makes them far more difficult for analysts to adequately cover, providing great opportunities to investors willing to use a systematic, disciplined approach to finding those names that possess the factors that have a long association with higher returns. Tables 4-10 and 4-11 summarize the findings for these stocks.

MARKET LEADERS AND SMALL STOCKS: A BETTER WAY TO CREATE AN INDEX

Two additional universes bear special note. As mentioned, Market Leaders are large, market-leading companies with annual sales 50 percent greater

T A B L E 4-10

Summary Return and Risk Results for Annual Data, Micro-Cap Stocks (Less than $25 Million), $25M < Market Caps < $100 Million Stocks, and $100M < Market Cap < $250M, December 31, 1952–December 31, 2003

	Micro-Cap <$25 Million	$25 Million<Market Cap<$100 Million	$100 Million<Market Cap<$250 Million
Arithmetic Average	35.35%	19.81%	16.44%
Geometric Average	28.12%	15.96%	13.72%
Median Return	21.43%	21.43%	14.40%
Standard Deviation of Return	47.51%	30.75%	24.85%
Downside Risk—lower is better	8.78%	10.03%	9.18%
Correlation with S&P 500	0.54	0.66	0.87
T-Statistic	5.37	4.65	5.30
Sharpe Ratio	0.63	0.46	0.46
Number of Positive Periods	40	38	39
Number of Negative Periods	12	14	13
Maximum Peak-to-Trough Decline (using monthly data series)	−59.90%	−62.30%	−62.44%
Beta	1.45	1.16	1.08
$10,000 becomes:	$3.9 Billion	$22,123,631.29	$8,020,770.56
Minimum Annual Return	−33.22%	−37.00%	−35.80%
Maximum Annual Return	190.94%	113.42%	71.22%
Minimum *Expected* Return*	−59.67%	−41.69%	−33.26%
Maximum *Expected* Return**	130.37%	81.31%	66.14%

*Minimum Expected Return is Arithmetic Return minus 2 times the standard deviation.
**Maximum Expected Return is Arithmetic Return plus 2 times the standard deviation.

than average, and Small Stocks are all stocks in the Compustat database with market capitalizations greater than a deflated $185 million but less than the database average. These universes offer a good approximation for the *category* of blue chip and small stocks. Table 4-12 shows the returns of each against our All Stocks and Large Stocks universes, and Tables 4-13 through 4-18 feature worst-case scenarios; best and worst returns by holding periods; returns by decades; and base rates for Market Leaders versus Large Stocks and Small Stocks versus All Stocks. Returning to the example of what $10,000 would be worth over any five-year period given earlier for All Stocks, if you look at the best- and worst-case for Market Leaders, you would find your $10,000 declining to $8,709 over five years, if you received a return equal to the *worst* seen over the last 40 years, and appreciating to $39,542 if you got a return equal to the *best* seen in any five-year period. That compares favorably with the minimum and maximum generated by the All Stocks universe.

T A B L E 4-11

Summary Return and Risk Results for Annual Data, $2250M < Market Caps < $500 Million, $500M < Market Cap < $1 Bil and Market Cap < $1 Bil, December 31, 1952–December 31, 2003

	$250 Million<Market Cap<$500 Million	$500 Million<Market Cap<$1 Billion	Market Cap> $1 Billion
Arithmetic Average	15.62%	13.87%	13.05%
Geometric Average	13.56%	12.18%	11.75%
Median Return	17.11%	15.70%	15.52%
Standard Deviation of Return	21.46%	19.34%	16.98%
Downside Risk—lower is better	7.96%	7.19%	5.94%
Correlation with S&P 500	0.82	0.84	0.95
T-Statistic	5.25	5.17	5.54
Sharpe Ratio	0.47	0.44	0.45
Number of Positive Periods	40	38	38
Number of Negative Periods	12	14	14
Maximum Peak-to-Trough Decline (using monthly data series)	−59.14%	−56.41%	−49.40%
Beta	1.00	0.93	0.91
$10,000 becomes:	$7,443,644.15	$3,939,023.97	$3,227,329.01
Minimum Annual Return	−31.99%	−29.75%	−26.46%
Maximum Annual Return	56.53%	52.48%	47.91%
Minimum *Expected* Return*	−27.30%	−24.81%	−20.91%
Maximum *Expected* Return**	58.54%	52.55%	47.01%

*Minimum Expected Return is Arithmetic Return minus 2 times the standard deviation.
**Maximum Expected Return is Arithmetic Return plus 2 times the standard deviation.

T A B L E 4-12

Summary Return and Risk Results for Annual Data, Large Stocks, All Stocks, Market Leaders, and Small Stocks, December 31, 1952–December 31, 2003

	Market Leaders	Large Stocks	All Stocks	Small Stocks
Arithmetic Average	14.82%	12.99%	14.79%	15.66%
Geometric Average	13.52%	11.71%	13.00%	13.49%
Median Return	18.35%	15.75%	16.80%	17.75%
Standard Deviation of Return	17.37%	16.84%	20.11%	22.16%
Downside Risk—lower is better	4.94%	5.86%	7.17%	8.00%
Correlation with S&P 500	0.94	0.95	0.87	0.82
T-Statistic	6.16	5.56	5.30	5.02
Sharpe Ratio	0.54	0.45	0.46	0.46
Number of Positive Periods	41	39	39	38
Number of Negative Periods	11	13	13	14
Maximum Peak-to-Trough Decline (using monthly data series)	−38.98%	−46.59%	−50.12%	−53.82%
Beta	0.92	0.89	0.99	1.03

(continued on next page)

T A B L E 4-12

Summary Return and Risk Results for Annual Data, Large Stocks, All Stocks, Market Leaders, and Small Stocks, December 31, 1952–December 31, 2003 *(Continued)*

	Market Leaders	Large Stocks	All Stocks	Small Stocks
$10,000 becomes:	$7,316,665.00	$3,173,724.00	$5,743,706.00	$7,202,765.00
Minimum Annual Return	−21.40%	−26.70%	−27.90%	−31.20%
Maximum Annual Return	66.00%	45.07%	55.90%	66.00%
Minimum *Expected* Return*	−19.92%	−20.69%	−25.43%	−28.66%
Maximum *Expected* Return**	49.56%	46.67%	55.01%	59.98%

*Minimum Expected Return is Arithmetic Return minus 2 times the standard deviation.
**Maximum Expected Return is Arithmetic Return plus 2 times the standard deviation.

T A B L E 4-13

Worst-Case Scenarios: All 10 Percent or Greater Declines for Market Leaders, December 31, 1952–December 31, 2003

Peak Date	Peak Index Value	Trough Date	Trough Index Value	Recovery Date	Decline (%)	Decline Duration	Recovery Duration
Jan-66	1.74	Sep-66	1.48	Feb-67	−14.89	8	5
Nov-68	2.38	Jun-70	1.66	Mar-71	−30.25	19	9
Dec-72	2.94	Sep-74	1.79	Jan-76	−38.98	21	16
Dec-76	3.62	Feb-78	3.22	Apr-78	−11.01	14	2
Aug-78	4.07	Oct-78	3.64	Mar-79	−10.48	2	5
Jan-80	4.93	Mar-80	4.37	Jun-80	−11.45	2	3
May-81	6.59	Jul-82	5.72	Oct-82	−13.13	14	3
Aug-87	23.28	Nov-87	16.75	Apr-89	−28.06	3	17
May-90	28.36	Oct-90	23.32	Feb-91	−17.77	5	4
Apr-98	102.33	Aug-98	84.04	Dec-98	−17.88	4	4
Jan-01	148.35	Sep-02	107.56	Oct-03	−27.85	20	13
Average					−20.16	10.18	7.36

T A B L E 4-14

Worst-Case Scenarios: All 10 Percent or Greater Declines for Small Stocks, December 31, 1962–December 31, 2003

Peak Date	Peak Index Value	Trough Date	Trough Index Value	Recovery Date	Decline (%)	Decline Duration	Recovery Duration
Apr-66	1.93	Sep-66	1.60	Jan-67	−16.98	5	4
Nov-68	3.46	Sep-74	1.60	Apr-77	−53.82	70	31
Aug-78	5.22	Oct-78	4.17	Apr-79	−20.06	2	6
Aug-79	6.12	Oct-79	5.51	Dec-79	−10	2	2
Jan-80	6.74	Mar-80	5.45	Jul-80	−19.21	2	4

(continued on next page)

T A B L E 4-14

Worst-Case Scenarios: All 10 Percent or Greater Declines for Small Stocks, December 31, 1962–December 31, 2003 *(Continued)*

Peak Date	Peak Index Value	Trough Date	Trough Index Value	Recovery Date	Decline (%)	Decline Duration	Recovery Duration
May-81	9.51	Jul-82	7.71	Oct-82	−18.92	14	3
Jun-83	14.95	Jul-84	12.37	Jan-85	−17.25	13	6
Jun-86	21.31	Sep-86	18.89	Jan-87	−11.37	3	4
Aug-87	24.94	Nov-87	16.55	Apr-89	−33.67	3	17
Sep-89	27.43	Oct-90	19.39	May-91	−29.33	13	7
Jan-94	44.48	Jun-94	39.79	Apr-95	−10.53	5	10
May-96	63.23	Jul-96	55.97	Dec-96	−11.48	2	5
Apr-98	88.67	Aug-98	62.24	Nov-99	−29.81	4	15
Feb-00	114.84	Sep-02	80.83	Aug-03	−29.62	31	11
Average					−22.29	12.07	8.93

T A B L E 4-15

Best and Worst Average Annual Compound Returns for Annual Data 1951–2003

For Any	1-Year Period	3-Year Period	5-Year Period	10-Year Period
S&P 500 Minimum Compound Return	−26.47%	−14.55%	−2.36%	1.24%
S&P 500 Maximum Compound Return	52.62%	31.15%	28.55%	19.19%
Large Stocks Minimum Compound Return	−26.70%	−11.93%	−4.37%	1.21%
Large Stocks Maximum Compound Return	45.07%	24.39%	22.40%	17.01%
Market Leaders Minimum Compound Return	−21.40%	−6.33%	−0.19%	4.39%
Market Leaders Maximum Compound Return	66.00%	29.82%	24.27%	19.72%
All Stocks Minimum Compound Return	−27.90%	−16.48%	−7.81%	1.26%
All Stocks Maximum Compound Return	55.90%	31.23%	27.77%	21.31%
Small Stocks Minimum Compound Return	−31.20%	−18.61%	−9.44%	1.36%
Small Stocks Maximum Compound Return	61.00%	37.29%	32.86%	24.13%

T A B L E 4-16

Best and Worst Average Annual Compound Returns over Period for Monthly Data 1963–2003

For Any	1-Year Period	3-Year Period	5-Year Period	10-Year Period
S&P 500 Minimum Compound Return	−38.93%	−16.10%	−4.15%	0.49%
S&P 500 Maximum Compound Return	61.01%	33.40%	29.72%	19.48%
Large Stocks Minimum Compound Return	−42.05%	−13.80%	−6.05%	−0.20%
Large Stocks Maximum Compound Return	68.49%	32.79%	28.65%	19.57%
Market Leaders Minimum Compound Return	−36.43%	−9.42%	−2.72%	2.26%

(continued on next page)

T A B L E 4-16

Best and Worst Average Annual Compound Returns over Period for Monthly Data 1963-2003
(Continued)

For Any	1-Year Period	3-Year Period	5-Year Period	10-Year Period
Market Leaders Maximum Compound Return	64.35%	35.52%	31.65%	21.07%
All Stocks Minimum Compound Return	−41.65%	−16.82%	−8.94%	0.68%
All Stocks Maximum Compound Return	81.51%	29.46%	27.02%	21.46%
Small Stocks Minimum Compound Return	−41.32%	−18.99%	−10.27%	1.41%
Small Stocks Maximum Compound Return	91.56%	34.61%	31.58%	23.97%

T A B L E 4-17

Average Annual Compound Rates of Return by Decade

Universe	1950s*	1960s	1970s	1980s	1990s	2000s**
S&P 500	17.33%	7.81%	5.86%	17.55%	18.20%	−5.34%
Large Stocks	15.33%	8.99%	6.99%	16.89%	15.34%	2.40%
Market Leaders	16.91%	9.50%	10.67%	19.46%	16.09%	3.93%
All Stocks	19.22%	11.09%	8.53%	15.85%	14.75%	5.91%
Small Stocks	20.04%	12.37%	9.69%	15.00%	14.42%	7.31%

*Returns for 1952-1959.
**Returns for 2000-2003.

T A B L E 4-18

Base Rates for Small Stocks versus All Stocks and Market Leaders versus Large Stocks, 1951–2003

Item	"Small Stocks" Beat "All Stocks"	Percent
Single-Year Return	30 out of 52	58%
Rolling Five-Year Compound Return	27 out of 48	56%
Rolling 10-Year Compound Return	29 out of 43	67%

Item	"Market Leaders" Beat "Large Stocks"	Percent
Single-Year Return	35 out of 52	67%
Rolling Five-Year Compound Return	41 out of 48	85%
Rolling 10-Year Compound Return	37 out of 43	86%

Although Small Stocks do beat All Stocks in the majority of all rolling five- and 10-year periods, they are not as overwhelmingly superior as Market Leaders are to both Large Stocks and the S&P 500. Looking at Table 4-16, you see that, regardless of the period, Market Leaders do consistently better than Large Stocks and the S&P 500. And when you compare the summary results featured in Table 4-12, you see that Market Leaders supplied double the return of Large Stocks at virtually the same level of risk.

But it's really when you compare them to other style-specific indexes that you see that using quantitative selection rules, like those followed here, might be a much better way to construct an index. The Russell Indexes are widely used capitalization and style-specific indexes created in 1979. Many institutional clients compare their managers to these indexes. Tables 4-19 and 4-20 compare the large-cap Russell 1000 and the S&P 500 with the Market Leaders universe.

T A B L E 4-19

Annual Performance of Market Leaders, Russell 1000, and Standard & Poor's 500

	Market Leaders	Russell 1000	S&P 500
Dec-79	24.8	22.31	18.44
Dec-80	30.2	31.88	32.42
Dec-81	1.2	-5.1	−4.91
Dec-82	24.7	20.3	21.41
Dec-83	29	22.13	22.51
Dec-84	2.6	4.75	6.27
Dec-85	33.7	32.27	32.16
Dec-86	22.9	17.87	18.47
Dec-87	8.9	2.94	5.23
Dec-88	21.2	17.23	16.81
Dec-89	25.5	30.42	31.49
Dec-90	−7.4	−4.16	−3.17
Dec-91	29.6	33.03	30.55
Dec-92	7.3	9.04	7.67
Dec-93	14.8	10.15	9.99
Dec-94	1.46	0.38	1.31
Dec-95	31.13	37.77	37.43
Dec-96	21.57	22.45	23.07
Dec-97	28.78	32.85	33.36
Dec-98	16.92	27.02	28.58
Dec-99	23.45	20.91	21.04
Dec-00	6.54	−7.79	−9.11
Dec-01	−5.81	−12.45	−11.88
Dec-02	−15.73	−21.65	−22.1
Dec-03	37.97	29.89	28.7
Average	16.61	14.98	15.03
Standard Deviation	14.14	16.12	15.99

In virtually every category, Market Leaders provide superior results to both the S&P 500 and Russell 1000 indexes. Between 1979 and 2003, Market Leaders provided nearly double the return of the other two large-cap indexes and did so with a lower standard deviation of return and significantly lower downside risk. The Market Leaders universe beta was lower than either index, and its Sharpe ratio was much higher.

T A B L E 4-20

Summary Return and Risk Results for Annual Data, Market Leaders, Russell 1000, and Standard & Poor's 500, December 31, 1978–December 31, 2003

	S&P 500	Russell 1000	Market Leaders
Arithmetic Average	15.03%	14.98%	16.61%
Geometric Average	13.83%	13.76%	15.70%
Median Return	18.47%	20.30%	21.57%
Standard Deviation of Return	16.32%	16.45%	14.43%
Downside Risk—lower is better	5.47%	5.40%	3.67%
Correlation with S&P 500	1.00	1.00	0.94
T-Statistic	4.60	4.55	5.76
Sharpe Ratio	0.53	0.52	0.70
Number of Positive Periods	20	20	22
Number of Negative Periods	5	5	3
Maximum Peak-to-Trough Decline (using monthly data series)	−44.73%	−45.06%	−28.06%
Beta	1.00	1.00	0.83
$10,000 becomes:	$255,020.00	$251,281.00	$383,047.00
Minimum Annual Return	−22.10%	−21.65%	−15.86%
Maximum Annual Return	37.43%	37.77%	43.19%
Minimum *Expected* Return*	−17.61%	−17.92%	−12.25%
Maximum *Expected* Return**	47.67%	47.88%	45.47%

*Minimum Expected Return is Arithmetic Return minus 2 times the standard deviation.
**Maximum Expected Return is Arithmetic Return plus 2 times the standard deviation.

Small Stocks also outperform the Russell 2000 Index, but not at the magnitude that the Market Leaders universe beats the Russell 1000 and S&P 500. Table 4-21 shows the annual results since the Russell 2000 was created, and Table 4-22 summarizes the return and risk results for Small Stocks and the Russell 2000.

I think these results demonstrate that creators of indexes can do a better job than the current committee selection structure that drives much of index creation. If firms that create broad indexes were to use more explicitly stated rules, they could both test the index historically and build a better index for investors who prefer a broad index to a style-specific or conventionally managed portfolio.

T A B L E 4-21

Annual Performance of Russell 2000 and Small Stocks, December 31, 1978–December 31, 2003

	Small Stocks	Russell 2000
Dec-79	39.10%	43.09%
Dec-80	32.10%	38.58%
Dec-81	2.50%	2.03%
Dec-82	24.60%	24.95%
Dec-83	31.40%	29.13%
Dec-84	−5.40%	−7.30%
Dec-85	29.60%	31.05%
Dec-86	7.80%	5.68%
Dec-87	−4.90%	−8.77%
Dec-88	22.90%	24.89%
Dec-89	18.10%	16.24%
Dec-90	−17.60%	−19.51%
Dec-91	44.70%	46.05%
Dec-92	16.50%	18.41%
Dec-93	17.40%	18.91%
Dec-94	−2.92%	−1.82%
Dec-95	28.61%	28.44%
Dec-96	18.93%	16.49%
Dec-97	22.65%	22.36%
Dec-98	−1.58%	−2.55%
Dec-99	31.63%	21.26%
Dec-00	−2.40%	−3.02%
Dec-01	7.00%	2.49%
Dec-02	−18.78%	−20.48%
Dec-03	56.31%	47.25%
Average	15.93%	14.95%
Standard Deviation	18.78%	19.13%

T A B L E 4-22

Summary Return and Risk Results for Annual Data, Russell 2000, and Small Stocks, December 31, 1978–December 31, 2003

	Russell 2000	Small Stocks
Arithmetic Average	14.95%	15.93%
Geometric Average	13.31%	14.37%
Median Return	18.41%	18.10%
Standard Deviation of Return	19.52%	19.17%
Downside Risk—lower is better	6.16%	5.41%
Correlation with S&P 500	0.75	0.74
T-Statistic	3.83	4.16
Sharpe Ratio	0.44	0.49
Number of Positive Periods	18	18

(continued on next page)

TABLE 4-22

Summary Return and Risk Results for Annual Data, Russell 2000, and Small Stocks, December 31, 1978–December 31, 2003 (Continued)

	Russell 2000	Small Stocks
Number of Negative Periods	7	7
Maximum Peak-to-Trough Decline (using monthly data series)	−35.55%	−33.67%
Beta	0.89	0.87
$10,000 becomes:	$227,110.00	$286,972.00
Minimum Annual Return	−20.48%	−18.78%
Maximum Annual Return	47.25%	56.31%
Minimum *Expected* Return*	−24.09%	−22.41%
Maximum *Expected* Return**	53.99%	54.27%

*Minimum Expected Return is Arithmetic Return minus 2 times the standard deviation.
**Maximum Expected Return is Arithmetic Return plus 2 times the standard deviation.

IMPLICATIONS FOR INVESTORS

Investors should be wary of small-stock strategies that promise high returns *simply* because they invest in smaller issues. The numbers show that the smallest stocks—those with market capitalizations below $25 million—account for the lion's share of the difference between small- and large-stock returns. They're impossible to buy and are therefore shunned by mutual funds and individual investors alike.

Small-cap stocks *do* outperform larger stocks on an absolute basis but are virtually indistinguishable when risk is taken into account, having Sharpe ratios similar to those of Large Stocks. (Remember that higher Sharpe ratios are better.)

The big surprise is the performance of Market Leaders. These large, well-known stocks outperformed All Stocks, Large Stocks, the S&P 500, and Small Stocks, while taking considerably less risk (Figure 4-5). They had the highest Sharpe ratio of all stocks that you can actually invest in and proved to be excellent performers over a variety of market cycles. They are superior to other large-cap indexes like the Russell 1000 and S&P 500, and they offer a lesson to the creators of index funds, demonstrating that they may wish to bring a more objective, quantitative screening process to bear when devising new indexes.

We'll see later that investors who want to beat the S&P 500 and are willing to take more risk should concentrate on all reasonably sized stocks—

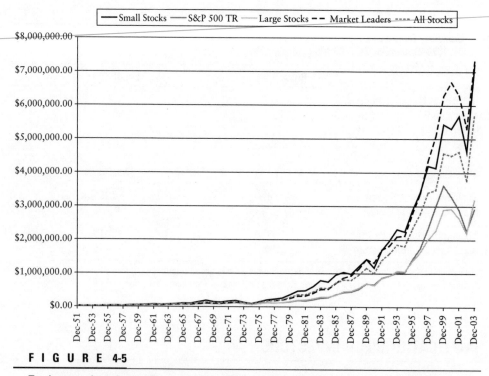

FIGURE 4-5

Total returns by universe, December 31, 1951–December 31, 2003. Year-end 1951=$10,000.

those in the All Stocks group with market capitalizations above $185 million—instead of focusing exclusively on just tiny or huge stocks. As of December 31, 2003, the All Stocks universe included 3,797 stocks, ranging from General Electric at the top to Sirenza Microdevices Inc. at the bottom. Their average market capitalization of $5.5 billion was considerably smaller than the Large Stocks universe, which had an average market capitalization of $17.6 billion.

OUR TWO BENCHMARKS

In each chapter to follow, we'll use the All Stocks and Large Stocks groups as benchmarks for all the strategies we study. Each provides an excellent indication of what you can achieve in each capitalization class. For tests that expressly begin with either the Market Leaders universe or the Small Stocks universe, we will include those as benchmarks as well.

5

C H A P T E R

PRICE-TO-EARNINGS RATIOS: SEPARATING THE WINNERS AND LOSERS

When it comes to making money, everyone is of the same religion.
—Voltaire

For many on Wall Street, buying stocks with low price-to-earnings (PE) ratios is the one true faith. You find a stock's current PE ratio by dividing the price by the current earnings per share. The higher the PE, the more investors are paying for earnings, and the larger the implied expectations for future earnings growth. A stock's PE ratio is the most common measurement of how cheap or expensive it is relative to other stocks. Many investors are willing to pay an above-average price for current earnings, because they believe the company can grow its way out of a higher multiple. Thus, most people equate high PE stocks with growth investing.

Investors who buy stocks with low PE ratios think they're getting a bargain. Generally, they believe that when a stock's PE ratio is high, investors have unrealistic expectations for the earnings growth of that stock. High hopes, the low PE investor reasons, are usually dashed, along with the price of the stock. Conversely, they believe the prices of low PE stocks are unduly discounted and, when earnings recover, the price of the stock will follow. These investors are usually referred to as value investors.

THE RESULTS

Remember that we look at two distinct groups—those with high and low PE ratios drawn from the All Stocks universe (all stocks with market capitalizations greater than a deflated $185 million) and those with high and low PE ratios drawn from the Large Stocks universe (those stocks with market capitalizations greater than the Compustat mean, usually the upper 15 percent of the database). We'll also be looking at the All Stocks and Large Stocks universes ranked by PE decile.

Let's look at low-PE stocks first. We start with $10,000 on December 31, 1951, and buy the 50 stocks with the highest earnings-to-price (EP) ratios from the All Stocks and Large Stocks universes. Due to Compustat's internal math, we must rank stocks by the 50 *highest* EP ratios (the EP is the reciprocal of the PE ratio). Remember that stocks with high EP ratios are low-PE stocks. We rebalance the portfolios annually to hold the 50 stocks with the lowest PE ratios in any given year. As with all the tests, the stocks are equally weighted and the earnings variable is time-lagged to avoid look-ahead bias.

Figure 5-1 shows the growth of $10,000 invested on December 31, 1951, and Tables 5-1 through 5-6 summarize the results for low-PE investing.

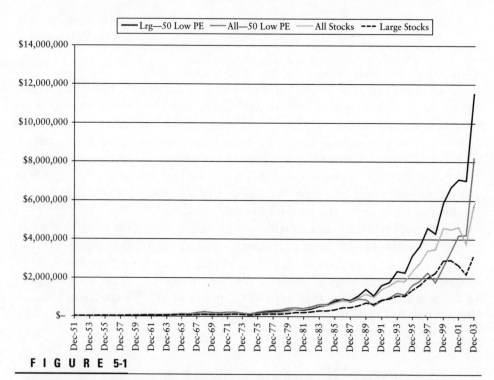

FIGURE 5-1

Returns on low-PE stocks versus All Stocks and Large Stocks, 1951–2003. Year-end 1951=$10,000.

T A B L E 5-1

Summary Return and Risk Results for Annual Data, All Stocks, and 50 Highest EP (Low PE) Stocks from All Stocks, December 31, 1951–December 31, 2003

	All Stocks	All Stocks, Top 50 Earnings/Price (Low PE)
Arithmetic Average	14.79%	16.87%
Geometric Average	13.00%	13.77%
Median Return	16.80%	16.50%
Standard Deviation of Return	20.11%	27.39%
Downside Risk—lower is better	7.17%	9.23%
Correlation with S&P 500	0.87	0.67
T-Statistic	5.30	4.44
Sharpe Ratio	0.46	0.41
Number of Positive Periods	39	37
Number of Negative Periods	13	15
Maximum Peak-to-Trough Decline (using monthly data series)	−50.12%	−50.76%
Beta	0.99	1.04
$10,000 becomes:	$5,743,706.00	$8,189,182.00
Minimum Annual Return	−27.90%	−36.30%
Maximum Annual Return	55.90%	94.81%
Minimum *Expected* Return*	−25.43%	−37.91%
Maximum *Expected* Return**	55.01%	71.65%

*Minimum Expected Return is Arithmetic Return minus 2 times the standard deviation.
**Maximum Expected Return is Arithmetic Return plus 2 times the standard deviation.

T A B L E 5-2

Summary Return and Risk Results for Annual Data, Large Stocks, and 50 Highest EP (Low PE) Stocks from Large Stocks, December 31, 1951–December 31, 2003

	Large Stocks	Large Stocks, Top 50 Earnings/Price (Low PE)
Arithmetic Average	12.99%	16.51%
Geometric Average	11.71%	14.51%
Median Return	15.75%	15.36%
Standard Deviation of Return	16.84%	21.93%
Downside Risk—lower is better	5.86%	6.20%
Correlation with S&P 500	0.95	0.80
T-Statistic	5.56	5.43
Sharpe Ratio	0.45	0.50
Number of Positive Periods	39	39
Number of Negative Periods	13	13
Maximum Peak-to-Trough Decline (using monthly data series)	−46.59%	−39.71%
Beta	0.89	1.00
$10,000 becomes:	$3,173,724.00	$11,502,432.00

(continued on next page)

T A B L E 5-2

Summary Return and Risk Results for Annual Data, Large Stocks, and 50 Highest EP (Low PE) Stocks from Large Stocks, December 31, 1951–December 31, 2003 *(Continued)*

	Large Stocks	Large Stocks, Top 50 Earnings/Price (Low PE)
Minimum Annual Return	-26.70%	-24.40%
Maximum Annual Return	45.07%	72.90%
Minimum *Expected* Return*	-20.69%	-27.35%
Maximum *Expected* Return**	46.67%	60.37%

*Minimum Expected Return is Arithmetic Return minus 2 times the standard deviation.
**Maximum Expected Return is Arithmetic Return plus 2 times the standard deviation.

T A B L E 5-3

Base Rates for All Stocks and 50 Highest EP (Low PE) Stocks from All Stocks Universe, 1951–2003

Item	50 low PE beat "All Stocks"	Percent
Single-Year Return	30 out of 52	58%
Rolling Five-Year Compound Return	27 out of 48	56%
Rolling 10-Year Compound Return	22 out of 43	51%

T A B L E 5-4

Base Rates for Large Stocks and 50 Highest EP (Low PE) Stocks from Large Stocks Universe, 1951–2003

Item	50 low PE beat "Large Stocks"	Percent
Single-Year Return	37 out of 52	71%
Rolling Five-Year Compound Return	35 out of 48	73%
Rolling 10-Year Compound Return	38 out of 43	88%

T A B L E 5-5

Worst-Case Scenarios: All 10 Percent or Greater Declines for 50 Stocks from All Stocks with Lowest PE, December 31, 1962–December 31, 2003

Peak Date	Peak Index Value	Trough Date	Trough Index Value	Recovery Date	Decline (%)	Decline Duration	Recovery Duration
Apr-65	1.84	Jun-65	1.65	Sep-65	−10	2	3
Jan-66	2.36	Sep-66	1.87	Feb-67	−20.58	8	5
Jan-69	4.36	Jun-70	2.62	Apr-71	−39.77	17	10
Apr-71	4.37	Dec-74	2.15	Apr-77	−50.76	44	28
Aug-78	7.02	Oct-78	5.47	Apr-79	−22.04	2	6
Aug-79	8.17	Oct-79	6.73	Jan-80	−17.65	2	3
Jan-80	8.25	Mar-80	6.91	Jul-80	−16.29	2	4

(continued on next page)

T A B L E 5-5

Worst-Case Scenarios: All 10 Percent or Greater Declines for 50 Stocks from All Stocks with Lowest PE, December 31, 1962–December 31, 2003 *(Continued)*

Peak Date	Peak Index Value	Trough Date	Trough Index Value	Recovery Date	Decline (%)	Decline Duration	Recovery Duration
Jun-81	10.19	Jul-82	8.71	Oct-82	−14.55	13	3
Aug-83	16.11	Jul-84	13.03	Dec-84	−19.13	11	5
Aug-87	33.22	Nov-87	21.24	Aug-89	−36.06	3	21
Aug-89	33.81	Oct-90	18.33	Feb-92	−45.79	14	16
Jan-94	50.34	Nov-94	43.90	May-95	−12.78	10	6
Mar-98	104.18	Feb-99	65.08	Jul-00	−37.53	11	17
Jan-01	160.45	Mar-01	143.25	May-01	−10.72	2	2
Jun-01	166.22	Sep-01	127.18	Feb-02	−23.49	3	5
Apr-02	196.59	Sep-02	139.00	Apr-03	−29.29	5	7
Average					−25.40	9.31	8.81

T A B L E 5-6

Worst-Case Scenarios: All 10 Percent or Greater Declines for 50 Stocks from Large Stocks with Lowest PE, December 31, 1962—December 31, 2003

Peak Date	Peak Index Value	Trough Date	Trough Index Value	Recovery Date	Decline (%)	Decline Duration	Recovery Duration
Jan-66	1.98	Sep-66	1.58	Apr-67	−20.37	8	7
Jan-69	3.02	Jun-70	1.97	Aug-72	−34.54	17	26
Nov-72	3.28	Dec-74	2.08	Dec-75	−36.42	25	12
Aug-78	6.36	Oct-78	5.43	Mar-79	−14.52	2	5
Aug-79	7.72	Oct-79	6.83	Jan-80	−11.49	2	3
Jan-80	7.93	Mar-80	6.78	Jul-80	−14.54	2	4
Jun-81	10.14	Jul-82	8.29	Oct-82	−18.22	13	3
Jan-84	14.37	Jul-84	12.27	Sep-84	−14.63	6	2
Aug-87	28.81	Nov-87	20.88	Jan-89	−27.54	3	14
Aug-89	35.91	Oct-90	21.65	Jan-92	−39.71	14	15
Mar-98	116.30	Aug-98	84.50	Apr-99	−27.34	5	8
Dec-99	130.25	Feb-00	115.96	May-00	−10.97	2	3
Jun-01	166.44	Sep-01	131.33	Mar-02	−21.09	3	6
Mar-02	174.85	Sep-02	146.29	May-03	−16.34	6	8
Average					−21.98	7.71	8.29

Fifty-two years of data show that, although low PE ratios are important for the smaller stocks that make up the All Stocks universe, they are much more important for larger stocks. The 50 lowest PE stocks from the All Stock universe turned $10,000 into $8,189,182, a compound rate of return of 13.77 percent a year. That return was better than both the All Stocks and Large Stocks universes. But with the low-PE All Stocks portfolio, risk was higher than the index, with a standard deviation of return of 27.39 percent. That hurts the overall Sharpe ratio, with the low-PE All Stocks portfolio Sharpe ratio coming in at 41, five points behind the All Stock group's score of 46. Analyzing the base rate information in Table 5-5, we see little more than chance at work in the number of years the strategy beats the universe, with all rolling five- and 10-year base rates similar to what you would get flipping a coin.

LARGE STOCKS ARE DIFFERENT

Large Stocks are entirely different. Here, an investment in the 50 stocks with the lowest PE ratios turned $10,000 into $11,502,432; more than triple the Large Stock universe's $3,173,724 return. The compound return of the 50 low-PE stocks was 14.51 percent, 2.80 percent better than the Large Stock's return of 11.71 percent a year. Remember, when you get 2.80 percent more per year over 52 years, the power of compounding drives up total return, something that is extremely important to keep in mind as you look at the performance of all the strategies featured here. In addition to this much better absolute return, the 50 low-PE stocks from Large Stocks had a better risk-adjusted return—sporting a Sharpe ratio of 50, compared to the Large Stocks universe's 45. Here, as Table 5-4 shows, base rates are not random. When looking at rolling 10-year rates of return from the 50 low-PE stocks, we see that they beat the Large Stocks group 88 percent of the time. This is important information for investors when they are deciding on which investment strategy to use. For example, we see that in all rolling 10-year periods over the last 52 years, low-PE Large Stocks beat the Large Stocks universe all but 12 percent of the time, and when they were beating Large Stocks, they added 2.13 percent annual compound return to the Large Stocks universe. This can make a significant difference in your terminal wealth.

Let's assume that two investors decide to invest in the equity markets, the first deciding on a pure index strategy like Large Stocks and the second investing in those 50 stocks from the Large Stocks universe with the lowest PE ratios. If the first investor earned the average compound return over all 10-year periods analyzed here (11.69 percent), after 10 years his $10,000 would be worth $30,206. If the second investor earned the average additional compound returns that low-PE stocks usually enjoy, her $10,000 would be worth $36,491—21 percent more than the first investor. But what if our second investor was unlucky, and her returns just happened to fall into the 12 percent of the time when large company stocks with low PEs underperformed Large Stocks? The average of the five 10-year periods when low-PE Large Stocks underperform the Large Stocks universe is a negative 0.86 percent. If she had a similar fate, her $10,000 would be worth $27,962—8.4 percent less wealth than the Large Stocks index investor. Even if she was *really* unlucky and got a return that matched the *worst* 10-year relative performance for low-PE versus Large Stocks, her $10,000 would be worth $25,656—15 percent less wealth than the Large Stocks index investor.

Although both the Large Stocks and All Stocks versions of the strategy had higher standard deviations of return than their universes, only the Large Stocks with low PE ratios compensated for the higher risk. We'll see in the Market Leaders chapter that you can improve returns even more by focusing on even larger, better known names with low PE ratios. The difference in returns for the large and small stock sections of the database is striking, but it makes sense. Small companies can have a string of spectacular earnings gains on their way to becoming large companies. It's sensible for investors to award them higher PE ratios. Indeed, whereas you would not want to buy small stocks with very high PE ratios, you might not want them too low, either. Because low PE ratios indicate lower investor expectations for earnings growth, a small company with a low PE might have very limited prospects. As companies grow, their ability to produce dazzling earnings gains decreases, as should the expectations of investors. On the other hand, we see investors consistently rewarding large stocks with lower PE ratios, possibly because their prices are more realistic in relation to their prospective growth rates.

We'll see that low PE ratios become even more important when you use multifactor models to select stocks, but their importance now for larger stocks is obvious from the data.

HIGH PE RATIOS ARE DANGEROUS

Buying high-PE stocks, regardless of their market capitalization, is a dangerous endeavor. You shouldn't let the flash of the latest glamor stock draw you into paying ridiculous prices for earnings, yet investors do so frequently. Witness investors pushing Polaroid's PE to 164 in 1961; Best Buy's to 712 in 1997, and Yahoo's to 4,921 in 1999. Figure 5-2 and Tables 5-7 through 5-12 catalog the damage.

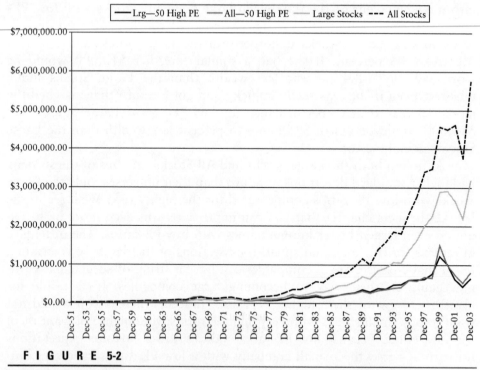

FIGURE 5-2

Returns on high-PE stocks versus All Stocks and Large Stocks, 1951–2003. Year-end 1951=$10,000.

TABLE 5-7

Summary Return and Risk Results for Annual Data, All Stocks, and 50 Lowest EP (High PE) Stocks from All Stocks, December 31, 1951–December 31, 2003

	All Stocks	All Stocks, Bottom 50 Earnings/Price (High PE)
Arithmetic Average	14.79%	12.97%
Geometric Average	13.00%	8.78%
Median Return	16.80%	9.80%
Standard Deviation of Return	20.11%	32.05%
Downside Risk—lower is better	7.17%	13.25%
Correlation with S&P 500	0.87	0.67
T-Statistic	5.30	2.92
Sharpe Ratio	0.46	0.24
Number of Positive Periods	39	37
Number of Negative Periods	13	15
Maximum Peak-to-Trough Decline (using monthly data series)	−50.12%	−75.06%
Beta	0.99	1.22

(continued on next page)

T A B L E 5-7

Summary Return and Risk Results for Annual Data, All Stocks, and 50 Lowest EP (High PE) Stocks from All Stocks, December 31, 1951–December 31, 2003 *(Continued)*

	All Stocks	All Stocks, Bottom 50 Earnings/Price (High PE)
$10,000 becomes:	$5,743,706.00	$793,558.00
Minimum Annual Return	−27.90%	−36.10%
Maximum Annual Return	55.90%	128.91%
Minimum *Expected* Return*	−25.43%	−51.13%
Maximum *Expected* Return**	55.01%	77.07%

*Minimum Expected Return is Arithmetic Return minus 2 times the standard deviation.
**Maximum Expected Return is Arithmetic Return plus 2 times the standard deviation.

T A B L E 5-8

Summary Return and Risk Results for Annual Data, Large Stocks, and 50 Lowest EP (High PE) Stocks from Large Stocks, December 31, 1951–December 31, 2003

	Large Stocks	Large Stocks, Bottom 50 Earnings/Price (High PE)
Arithmetic Average	12.99%	10.85%
Geometric Average	11.71%	8.31%
Median Return	15.75%	10.75%
Standard Deviation of Return	16.84%	23.20%
Downside Risk—lower is better	5.86%	11.22%
Correlation with S&P 500	0.95	0.77
T-Statistic	5.56	3.37
Sharpe Ratio	0.45	0.24
Number of Positive Periods	39	38
Number of Negative Periods	13	14
Maximum Peak-to-Trough Decline (using monthly data series)	−46.59%	−74.24%
Beta	0.89	1.02
$10,000 becomes:	$3,173,724.00	$635,293.00
Minimum Annual Return	−26.70%	−38.81%
Maximum Annual Return	45.07%	60.90%
Minimum *Expected* Return*	−20.69%	−35.55%
Maximum *Expected* Return**	46.67%	57.25%

*Minimum Expected Return is Arithmetic Return minus 2 times the standard deviation.
**Maximum Expected Return is Arithmetic Return plus 2 times the standard deviation.

T A B L E 5-9

Base Rates for All Stocks and 50 Highest PE Stocks from All Stocks Universe, 1951–2003

Item	50 High-PE beat "All Stocks"	Percent
Single-Year Return	18 out of 52	35%
Rolling Five-Year Compound Return	12 out of 48	25%
Rolling 10-Year Compound Return	5 out of 43	12%

T A B L E 5-10

Base Rates for Large Stocks and 50 Highest PE Stocks from Large Stocks Universe, 1951–2003

Item	50 High-PE beat "Large Stocks"	Percent
Single Year Return	22 out of 52	42%
Rolling Five-Year Compound Return	11 out of 48	23%
Rolling 10-Year Compound Return	8 out of 43	19%

T A B L E 5-11

Worst-Case Scenarios: All 10 Percent or Greater Declines for 50 Stocks from All Stocks with Highest PE, December 31, 1962–December 31, 2003

Peak Date	Peak Index Value	Trough Date	Trough Index Value	Recovery Date	Decline (%)	Decline Duration	Recovery Duration
Apr-66	1.94	Oct-66	1.51	Feb-67	−22.02	6	4
Dec-67	2.80	Feb-68	2.34	Apr-68	−16.43	2	2
Jan-69	3.40	Sep-74	1.00	Sep-80	−70.55	68	72
Nov-80	4.22	Jul-82	2.62	Apr-83	−37.96	20	9
Jun-83	4.91	Jul-84	3.19	Mar-86	−35.1	13	20
Jun-86	5.31	Sep-86	4.37	May-87	−17.76	3	8
Aug-87	5.86	Nov-87	3.60	Aug-89	−38.65	3	21
Sep-89	6.07	Oct-90	4.22	Jan-92	−30.42	13	15
Jan-92	6.22	Aug-92	5.26	Jan-93	−15.35	7	5
May-96	13.95	Apr-97	9.98	Sep-97	−28.48	11	5
Mar-98	15.23	Aug-98	10.51	Mar-99	−31.01	5	7
Jun-99	20.25	Sep-99	17.55	Nov-99	−13.35	3	2
Feb-00	41.22	Sep-02	10.28		−75.06	31	NA
Average					−33.24	14.23	14.17

T A B L E 5-12

Worst-Case Scenarios: All 10 Percent or Greater Declines for 50 Stocks from Large Stocks with Highest PE, December 31, 1962–December 31, 2003

Peak Date	Peak Index Value	Trough Date	Trough Index Value	Recovery Date	Decline (%)	Decline Duration	Recovery Duration
Apr-66	1.72	Sep-66	1.46	Feb-67	−15.02	5	5
Dec-67	2.13	Feb-68	1.78	May-68	−16.43	2	3
Nov-68	2.30	Jun-70	1.36	Feb-72	−40.74	19	20
May-72	2.64	Sep-74	0.98	Jul-80	−63.03	28	70
Nov-80	3.76	Jan-81	3.28	May-81	−12.59	2	4
May-81	3.80	Jul-82	2.53	Nov-82	−33.28	14	4
Jun-83	5.39	Jul-84	3.79	Feb-86	−29.7	13	19
Sep-87	8.08	Nov-87	5.62	Apr-89	−30.42	2	17
Aug-89	9.37	Oct-90	7.44	Mar-91	−20.52	14	5
Aug-94	15.75	Jan-95	13.89	Jul-95	−11.83	5	6
May-96	20.92	Apr-97	15.43	Feb-98	−26.24	11	10
Apr-98	23.12	Aug-98	17.97	Jan-99	−22.27	4	5
Feb-00	46.50	May-00	33.92	Aug-00	−27.06	3	3
Aug-00	46.84	Sep-02	12.06		−74.24	25	NA
Average					−30.24	10.50	13.15

Starting with the All Stocks universe, $10,000 invested in 1951 in the 50 stocks with the highest PE ratios and rebalanced annually grew to $793,558 by the end of 2003, $4,950,148 less than if you bought the All Stocks universe itself. The compound return of 8.78 percent was well behind All Stocks' 13.0 percent annual return. When you adjust for risk, the news is even grimmer. The 50 high-PE stocks' Sharpe ratio of 24 was nearly half that of the All Stocks universe. The high-PE stocks beat the All Stock group just 12 percent of the time in all rolling 10-year periods (Table 5-9).

T A B L E 5-13

Average Annual Compound Rates of Return by Decade

Portfolio	1950s*	1960s	1970s	1980s	1990s	2000s**
Large Stocks	15.33%	8.99%	6.99%	16.89%	15.34%	2.40%
50 High PE from Large Stocks	14.77%	10.94%	0.93%	14.11%	13.24%	−14.90%
50 Low PE from Large Stocks	16.12%	11.14%	12.64%	16.19%	15.38%	18.36%
All Stocks	19.22%	11.09%	8.53%	15.85%	14.75%	5.91%
50 High PE from All Stocks	19.27%	10.96%	2.26%	7.99%	16.99%	−14.73%
50 Low PE from All Stocks	21.84%	13.96%	8.89%	7.56%	11.44%	33.6%

*Returns for 1952–59
**Returns for 2000–2003

What's more, high-PE stocks show *extreme* volatility and concentration of returns, usually only running up in speculative markets heading toward their peaks. For example, an investor who got caught up in the frenzy of the Internet and technology boom of the late 1990s, and put all his money in the high-PE "story" stocks from the All Stocks universe at the end of 1997, would have seen his investment nearly *triple* in the 2.5 years heading into the market's peak in March 2000. If he had invested $10,000 in high-PE stocks on December 31, 1997, it would have been worth $29,416 in March 2000, a compound average annual return of 61.53 percent.

The price moves in these names were extraordinary. For example, look at the shares of Xcelera Inc., a technology–E-commerce company that made the high-PE list. On December 31, 1999, it was trading at $17.44 per share. By March 22, 2000, its price soared to $110. That's a move of over 530 percent in fewer than three months. Investors who lacked access to long-term data, like that featured here, based all their hopes on what they had witnessed over the last few years and kept on buying the stock. Lack of perspective cost these investors a bundle—the shares plunged to a low of $0.31 in August, before closing at $3.69 at the end of 2000.

Looking at Table 5-11, we see that the bad news just keeps getting worse for high-PE stocks. The worst-case scenario for high-PE stocks from All Stocks shows that high-PE stocks fell by more than 30 percent from peak to trough seven times; two of those were for *more than 70 percent!* Table 5-15 shows us that the best- and worst-case scenario for high-PE investors is decidedly limited, with the worst 10-year period serving up a loss of 8.17 percent per year, turning $10,000 into just $4,266 at the end of the 10 years, and the best 10 years providing a gain of 22.45 percent a year, turning $10,000 into $75,786—a few dollars more than you would receive from the best 10-year period for the All Stocks universe itself. Table 5-18 lists the terminal value of a $10,000 investment for the best- and worst-case scenarios featured for high and low-PE stocks.

T A B L E 5-14

Best and Worst Average Annual Compound Returns over Period for Annual Data 1951–2003

For Any	1-Year Period	3-Year Period	5-Year Period	10-Year Period
Large Stocks Minimum Compound Return	−26.70%	−11.93%	−4.37%	1.21%
Large Stocks Maximum Compound Return	45.07%	24.39%	22.40%	17.01%
Low PE Large Stocks Minimum Compound Return	−24.40%	−6.18%	−1.13%	3.71%
Low PE Large Stocks Maximum Compound Return	72.90%	34.87%	28.34%	20.20%
High PE Large Stocks Minimum Compound Return	−32.90%	−22.36%	−10.67%	−1.89%
High PE Large Stocks Maximum Compound Return	50.70%	29.18%	20.82%	14.74%

(continued on next page)

T A B L E 5-14

Best and Worst Average Annual Compound Returns over Period for Annual Data 1951–2003
(Continued)

For Any	1-Year Period	3-Year Period	5-Year Period	10-Year Period
All Stocks Minimum Compound Return	−27.90%	−16.48%	−7.81%	1.26%
All Stocks Maximum Compound Return	55.90%	31.23%	27.77%	21.31%
Low PE All Stocks Minimum Compound Return	−36.30%	−16.99%	−8.59%	2.28%
Low PE All Stocks Maximum Compound Return	94.81%	37.60%	36.06%	22.36%
High PE All Stocks Minimum Compound Return	−36.10%	−29.54%	−15.94%	−6.87%
High PE All Stocks Maximum Compound Return	128.91%	45.76%	32.58%	21.85%

T A B L E 5-15

Best and Worst Average Annual Returns over Period from Monthly Data 1962–2003

For Any	1-Year Period	3-Year Period	5-Year Period	10-Year Period
Large Stocks Minimum Compound Return	−42.05%	−13.80%	−6.05%	−0.20%
Large Stocks Maximum Compound Return	68.49%	32.79%	28.65%	19.57%
Low PE Large Stocks Minimum Compound Return	−35.29%	−9.72%	−3.18%	3.55%
Low PE Large Stocks Maximum Compound Return	69.40%	34.34%	29.25%	22.52%
High PE Large Stocks Minimum Compound Return	−69.22%	−35.40%	−14.73%	−5.10%
High PE Large Stocks Maximum Compound Return	110.57%	44.88%	31.40%	20.01%
All Stocks Minimum Compound Return	−41.65%	−16.82%	−8.94%	0.68%
All Stocks Maximum Compound Return	81.51%	29.46%	27.02%	21.46%
Low PE All Stocks Minimum Compound Return	−41.49%	−16.39%	−10.11%	3.09%
Low PE All Stocks Maximum Compound Return	94.81%	40.58%	36.06%	22.36%
High PE All Stocks Minimum Compound Return	−64.62%	−36.68%	−18.59%	−8.17%
High PE All Stocks Maximum Compound Return	193.45%	58.97%	36.83%	22.45%

LARGE STOCKS FARE NO BETTER

The high-PE damage is similar in the Large Stocks group. $10,000 invested in the 50 Large Stocks with the highest PE ratios on December 31, 1951 grows to $635,293 at the end of 2003, $2.5 million less than you'd earn with an investment in the Large Stocks universe itself. The Sharpe ratio of 24 pales in comparison to that of 45 for the Large Stocks universe. Worse yet, the 50 large stocks with the highest PE ratios beat the Large Stocks universe just 19 percent of the time over all rolling 10-year periods.

BEST- AND WORST-CASE RETURNS

Much like All Stocks, high-PE stocks from the Large Stocks universe exhibited horrible and terrifying worst-case scenario numbers, with five declines of more than 30 percent over the last 40 years, the most recent and largest being a 74 percent plunge between August 2000 and September 2002. As Table 5-15 shows, the best- and worst-case scenarios for high-PE stocks is even narrower than All Stocks, with an investor losing 5.10 percent a year over the worst 10 years and gaining 20.01 percent a year over the *best* 10-year period; this is very similar to the best 10-year gain for the Large Stocks universe itself. Table 5-18 lists the terminal value of a $10,000 investment for the best- and worst-case scenarios featured for high- and low-PE stocks.

Marrying together the base rates with worst- and best-case scenarios is a good way to test if a strategy is right for you. In the case of Large Stocks with high PE ratios, we see that the best they did in any 10-year period was a compound annual return of 20.01 percent. If we then marry that to the probability of their beating Large Stocks in any 10-year period (using the 10-year base rate as that probability), we see that we had a 19 percent chance to beat Large Stocks, and even if we did, we would have a maximum expected return over those 10 years equal to 20.01 percent, which is behind the maximum you could get from low-PE Large Stocks. All in all, these are bad odds for a mediocre payoff.

DECILES

Sorting the All Stocks and Large Stocks universes by decile paints a different picture, particularly in All Stocks. Here we see that the lowest four deciles by PE all outperformed an investment in All Stocks, whereas deciles five through 10 (with decile 10 being the 10 percent of stocks with the highest PE ratios) underperformed. Perhaps the 50 lowest PE stocks from All Stocks underperform the universe because their low PEs are indicative of more serious problems. As an investor, you'd be better off focusing on the second decile of low PE, rather than the lowest.

The Large Stocks universe paints a similar picture, with the lowest PE deciles outperforming Large Stocks and the highest underperforming the universe.

IMPLICATIONS

Figures 5-3 and 5-4 and Table 5-18 summarize what you can expect when buying stocks with the 50 lowest and highest PE ratios, whereas Figures 5-5 and 5-6 and Tables 5-16 and 5-17 summarize the results by decile. The results are striking. Both Large Stocks and All Stocks with high PE ratios perform substantially worse than the market. This is true both when focusing on the 50 highest PE stocks themselves and on the highest PE stocks by decile. Companies with the 50 lowest PE ratios from the Large Stocks universe do much better than the universe, and the three lowest PE deciles substantially outperform Large Stocks. The decile results from All Stocks show that investors using the All Stocks universe would be better off avoiding the 50 lowest PE stocks in favor of selecting more broadly from the four deciles having the lowest PE ratios. In both groups, *stocks with low PE ratios do much better than stocks with high PE ratios, both at the 50-stock extreme and when looking at the larger PE deciles.* Moreover, there's not much difference in risk. In the All Stocks universe, the standard deviation of return on the 50 low-PE stocks was 27.39 percent, whereas the 50 highest PE stocks had a standard deviation of 32.05 percent. In the Large Stocks universe, the low PE strategy had a standard deviation of 21.93 percent, whereas the high-PE strategy's standard deviation was 23.20 percent.

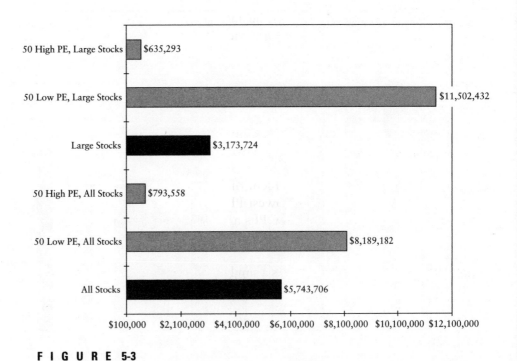

F I G U R E 5-3

December 31, 2003 value of $10,000 invested on December 31, 1951 and annually rebalanced.

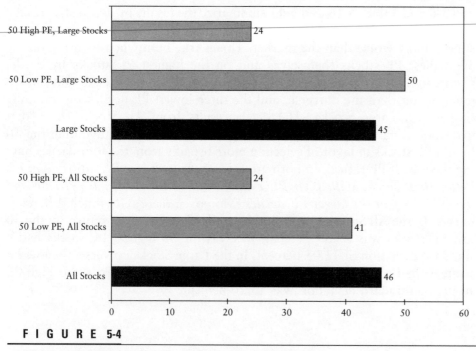

F I G U R E 5-4

Sharpe risk-adjusted return ratio, 1951–2003. (Higher is better.)

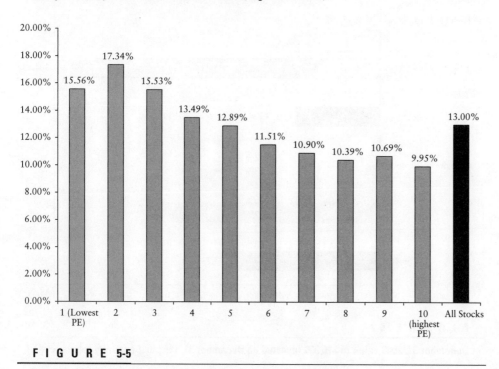

F I G U R E 5-5

Compound return by PE ratio decile, All Stocks universe, 1951–2003.

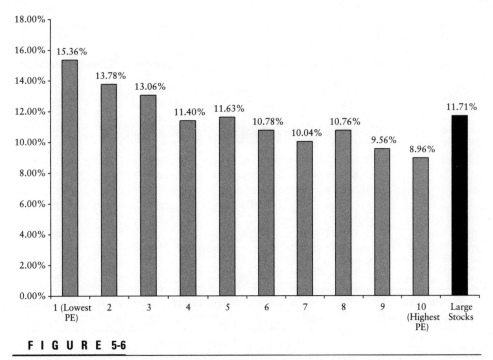

F I G U R E 5-6

Compound return by PE ratio decile, Large Stocks universe, 1951–2003.

T A B L E 5-16

Summary Results for PE Decile Analysis of All Stocks Universe, 1951–2003

Decile	$10,000 Grows to:	Average Return	Compound Return	Standard Deviation
1 (Lowest PE)	$18,472,507	17.96%	15.56%	23.60%
2	$40,917,583	19.32%	17.34%	21.49%
3	$18,171,765	17.13%	15.53%	19.29%
4	$7,204,836	15.14%	13.49%	19.62%
5	$5,477,493	14.36%	12.89%	17.83%
6	$2,882,201	13.02%	11.51%	18.00%
7	$2,167,761	12.42%	10.90%	17.67%
8	$1,711,045	12.03%	10.39%	18.62%
9	$1,966,515	12.65%	10.69%	20.23%
10 (Highest PE)	$1,384,190	12.93%	9.95%	25.52%
All Stocks	$5,743,706	14.79%	13.00%	20.11%

T A B L E 5-17

Summary Results for PE Decile Analysis of Large Stocks Universe, 1951–2003

Decile	$10,000 Grows to:	Average Return	Compound Return	Standard Deviation
1 (Lowest PE)	$16,867,165	17.33%	15.36%	21.68%
2	$8,213,178	15.39%	13.78%	19.22%
3	$5,926,873	14.47%	13.06%	18.13%
4	$2,743,438	12.60%	11.40%	16.38%
5	$3,057,427	12.86%	11.63%	16.49%
6	$2,048,297	11.88%	10.78%	15.31%
7	$1,448,276	11.34%	10.04%	16.63%
8	$2,033,622	12.05%	10.76%	16.44%
9	$1,154,264	11.24%	9.56%	18.52%
10 (Highest PE)	$868,029	11.43%	8.96%	22.69%
Large Stocks	$3,173,724	12.99%	11.71%	16.84%

T A B L E 5-18

Terminal Value of $10,000 Invested for Best and Worst Average Annual Compound Returns over Period for Monthly Data 1963–2003

For Any	1-Year Period	3-Year Period	5-Year Period	10-Year Period
Large Stocks Minimum $10,000 Value	$5,795.00	$6,405.04	$7,319.54	$9,801.79
Large Stocks Maximum $10,000 Value	$16,849.00	$23,415.11	$35,241.06	$69,737.00
Low PE Large Stocks Minimum $10,000 Value	$6,472.00	$7,359.00	$8,506.00	$14,171.00
Low PE Large Stocks Maximum $10,000 Value	$16,940.00	$24,246.00	$36,066.00	$76,191.00
High PE Large Stocks Minimum $10,000 Value	$3,078.00	$2,696.00	$4,662.00	$5,926.00
High PE Large Stocks Maximum $10,000 Value	$21,057.00	$24,246.00	$39,169.00	$61,979.00
All Stocks Minimum $10,000 Value	$5,835.00	$5,756.00	$6,260.00	$10,700.00
All Stocks Maximum $10,000 Value	$18,151.00	$21,680.00	$33,064.00	$69,868.00
Low PE All Stocks Minimum $10,000 Value	$5,851.00	$5,844.00	$5,870.00	$13,555.00
Low PE All Stocks Maximum $10,000 Value	$19,481.00	$27,782.00	$46,629.00	$75,024.00
High PE All Stocks Minimum $10,000 Value	$3,538.00	$2,539.00	$3,577.00	$4,266.00
High PE All Stocks Maximum $10,000 Value	$29,345.00	$40,171.00	$47,963.00	$75,786.00

FOLLOWING THIS ADVICE IN REAL TIME

Following this advice in real time can be trying, as any reader of the original edition of this book can attest. The first edition of *What Works on Wall Street* covered data from 1951 to 1994, and I gave the same advice then as I do now: Avoid stocks with the highest PE ratios if you want to do well. But long-term research is frequently ignored in the presence of the real behavior of stocks in the here and now. It can be very difficult to stick with your prudent low-PE stocks when risky high-PE stocks are soaring. Such was the case shortly after the first edition of this book was originally published. The market was beginning its frenzied speculative ascent that would lead to the huge bear market of 2000 to 2002. The speculative high-PE stocks were soaring near the height of the bubble, with the 50 highest PE stocks from All Stocks earning 128.91 percent in 1999. Obviously, that made it nearly impossible for investors to stand by their low-PE shares. Yet, those who did so would have been richly rewarded. An investor putting $10,000 into the 50 stocks with the lowest PE ratios from All Stocks in 1997 (when the book first appeared) would have seen that investment grow to $44,770 by the end of 2003, a compound return of 23.88 percent. Conversely, the same amount invested in the 50 highest PE stocks from All Stocks would have grown to just $10,461, an anemic compound return of 0.65 percent per year.

Thus, even though it was more than 60 years ago, Ben Graham and David Dodd's statement remains as true today as it was in their 1940 book *Security Analysis: Principles and Technique*: "People who habitually purchase common stocks at more than about 20 times their average earnings are likely to lose considerable money in the long run." Amen.

6 C H A P T E R

PRICE-TO-BOOK RATIOS: A BETTER GAUGE OF VALUE

Life can only be understood backwards; but it must be lived forwards.
—Soren Kierkgaard

In this chapter, I'll review stocks' price-to-book ratios. Many investors believe this is a more important ratio than price-to-earnings (PEs) when looking for a bargain. They argue that earnings can be easily manipulated by a clever chief financial officer, using an old joke as an example: A company wants to hire a new chief financial officer. Each candidate is asked just one question. "What does two plus two equal?" Each candidate answers four, with the exception of the one they hire. His answer was: "What number did you have in mind?"

You find the price-to-book ratio by dividing the current price of the stock by the book value per share. Here, we use the common equity liquidating value per share as a proxy for book value per share. Essentially, investors who buy stocks with low price-to-book ratios believe they are getting stocks at a price close to their liquidating value, and that they will be rewarded for not paying high prices for assets.

We'll look at both the high and low price-to-book ratio stocks from All Stocks and Large Stocks. We'll start on December 31, 1951, and buy those 50 stocks with the *highest* book-to-price ratios from the All Stocks universe. (Again, because of Compustat's ranking function, we must rank stocks by the 50 *highest* book-to-price ratios, the inverse of the price-to-book ratio.)

We'll also look at the All Stocks and Large Stocks universes segregated by decile.

THE RESULTS

Over the long-term, the market rewards stocks with low price-to-book ratios and punishes those with high ones. $10,000 invested on December 31, 1951 in the 50 stocks with the lowest price-to-book ratios from the All Stocks universe grew to $22,004,691 by December 31, 2003, a compound return of 15.95 percent a year. That's nearly four times the $5,743,706 you'd earn from an investment in All Stocks. Risk was fairly high. The standard deviation for the 50 low price-to-book stocks was 30.11 percent, considerably higher than the All Stocks universe's 20.11 percent (Table 6-1). But because of the higher returns, the Sharpe ratio for both the 50 low price-to-book stocks and the All Stocks universe was 46.

T A B L E 6-1

Summary Return and Risk Results for Annual Data, All Stocks, and 50 Highest Book-to-Price (Low P/Book) Stocks from All Stocks, December 31, 1951–December 31, 2003

	All Stocks	All Stocks, Top 50 Book/Price (Low P/Book)
Arithmetic Average	14.79%	19.39%
Geometric Average	13.00%	15.95%
Median Return	16.80%	16.16%
Standard Deviation of Return	20.11%	30.11%
Downside Risk—lower is better	7.17%	8.02%
Correlation with S&P 500	0.87	0.64
T-Statistic	5.30	4.64
Sharpe Ratio	0.46	0.46
Number of Positive Periods	39	37
Number of Negative Periods	13	15
Maximum Peak-to-Trough Decline (using monthly data series)	−50.12%	−48.55%
Beta	0.99	1.09
$10,000 becomes:	$5,743,706.00	$22,004,691.00
Minimum Annual Return	−27.90%	−34.50%
Maximum Annual Return	55.90%	133.55%
Minimum *Expected* Return*	−25.43%	−40.83%
Maximum *Expected* Return**	55.01%	79.61%

*Minimum Expected Return is Arithmetic Return minus 2 times the standard deviation.
**Maximum Expected Return is Arithmetic Return plus 2 times the standard deviation.

LARGE STOCKS ARE LESS VOLATILE

The 50 low price-to-book stocks from the Large Stocks universe did better on a risk-adjusted basis. Here, $10,000 invested in 1951 grew to $13,569,058 by the end of 2003, a compound return of 14.88 percent a year. That's more than three times the $3,173,058 you'd earn from $10,000 invested in the Large Stocks universe, but with a standard deviation of 21.60 percent. Although higher than the Large Stocks' 16.84 percent, it's much less volatile than the low price-to-book stocks from All Stocks. The Sharpe ratio here was 53, a strong showing from a single variable (Table 6-2).

T A B L E 6-2

Summary Return and Risk Results for Annual Data, Large Stocks, and 50 Highest Book-to-Price (Low P/Book) Stocks from Large Stocks, December 31, 1951–2003

	Large Stocks	Large Stocks, Top 50 Book/Price (Low P/Book)
Arithmetic Average	12.99%	16.85%
Geometric Average	11.71%	14.88%
Median Return	15.75%	17.55%
Standard Deviation of Return	16.84%	21.60%
Downside Risk—lower is better	5.86%	6.77%
Correlation with S&P 500	0.95	0.79
T-Statistic	5.56	5.63
Sharpe Ratio	0.45	0.53
Number of Positive Periods	39	43
Number of Negative Periods	13	9
Maximum Peak-to-Trough Decline (using monthly data series)	−46.59%	−42.84%
Beta	0.89	0.97
$10,000 becomes:	$3,173,724.00	$13,569,058.00
Minimum Annual Return	−26.70%	−31.70%
Maximum Annual Return	45.07%	68.94%
Minimum *Expected* Return*	−20.69%	−26.35%
Maximum *Expected* Return**	46.67%	60.05%

*Minimum Expected Return is Arithmetic Return minus 2 times the standard deviation.
**Maximum Expected Return is Arithmetic Return plus 2 times the standard deviation.

Base rates here are mixed. Although the 50 low price-to-book stocks from All Stocks beat the universe 58 percent of the time on a year-by-year basis and 72 percent of the time over all rolling 10-year periods, they beat the All Stocks group just 52 percent of the time on a rolling five-year basis (Tables 6-3 and 6-4). This suggests the low price-to-book group saw some wild rides on the way to beating the All Stocks universe. Indeed, when you look at the worst-case scenarios featured in Table 6-5, you see that low price-to-book stocks declined by more than 10 percent 18 times over the last 40 years, and seemed to be at odds with the overall market many times. For example, between August of 1989 and October of 1990, low price-to-book stocks declined by more than 48 percent, whereas over the same period, the All Stocks group was down 22.5 percent and the S&P 500 just 6.6 percent. These periods are important to keep in mind when thinking about using any strategy, because many investors would jettison the strategy after such a poor showing. For a strategy to be valuable, it must be consistent enough for investors to stick with it through rough patches.

T A B L E 6-3

Base Rates for All Stocks and 50 Highest Book/Price (Low P/Book) Stocks from All Stocks Universe, 1951–2003

Item	50 Low P/Book Beat "All Stocks"	Percent
Single-Year Return	30 out of 52	58%
Rolling Five-Year Compound Return	25 out of 48	52%
Rolling 10-Year Compound Return	31 out of 43	72%

T A B L E 6-4

Base Rates for Large Stocks and 50 Highest Book/Price (Low P/Book) Stocks from Large Stocks Universe, 1951–2003

Item	50 low P/Book Beat "Large Stocks"	Percent
Single-Year Return	34 out of 52	65%
Rolling Five-Year Compound Return	39 out of 48	81%
Rolling 10-Year Compound Return	39 out of 43	91%

T A B L E 6-5

Worst-Case Scenarios: All 10 Percent or Greater Declines for 50 Stocks from All Stocks with Lowest P/Book, December 31, 1962–December 31, 2003

Peak Date	Peak Index Value	Trough Date	Trough Index Value	Recovery Date	Decline (%)	Decline Duration	Recovery Duration
Jan-66	2.46	Sep-66	1.89	Jul-67	−23.32	8	10
Jan-69	3.88	Jun-70	2.09	Apr-75	−46.2	17	58
Jun-75	4.36	Sep-75	3.91	Jan-76	−10.51	3	4
Aug-78	10.10	Oct-78	7.73	Jun-79	−23.41	2	8
Aug-79	11.47	Mar-80	9.35	Jul-80	−18.46	7	4
May-81	14.99	Jul-82	11.60	Nov-82	−22.67	14	4
Jan-84	25.89	Jul-84	20.18	Jul-85	−22.05	6	12
Mar-86	29.24	Jul-86	23.97	Feb-87	−18.02	4	7

(continued on next page)

T A B L E 6-5

Worst-Case Scenarios: All 10 Percent or Greater Declines for 50 Stocks from All Stocks with Lowest P/Book, December 31, 1962–December 31, 2003 *(Continued)*

Peak Date	Peak Index Value	Trough Date	Trough Index Value	Recovery Date	Decline (%)	Decline Duration	Recovery Duration
Jul-87	38.57	Nov-87	24.11	Feb-89	−37.5	4	15
Aug-89	43.42	Oct-90	22.34	Feb-92	−48.55	14	16
Aug-94	76.56	Jan-95	66.40	May-95	−13.27	5	4
May-96	108.87	Jul-96	96.58	Jan-97	−11.29	2	6
Apr-98	145.96	Aug-98	102.11	Apr-99	−30.05	4	8
Jun-99	166.33	Oct-99	147.42	Dec-99	−11.37	4	2
Dec-99	171.91	Nov-00	138.84	Jan-01	−19.24	11	2
Jan-01	205.12	Mar-01	169.43	May-01	−17.4	2	2
May-01	208.61	Sep-01	154.97	Feb-02	−25.71	4	5
Apr-02	253.56	Sep-02	160.96	Apr-03	−36.52	5	7
Average					−24.20	6.44	9.67

LARGE STOCKS BASE RATES ARE MORE CONSISTENT

Base rates for the low price-to-book stocks from the Large Stocks universe are more consistent. Here, the low price-to-book stocks beat the Large Stocks universe a minimum of 65 percent of the time, with rolling 10-year returns showing the highest probability of beating the Large Stocks universe. The worst-case scenarios featured in Table 6.6 show a similar pattern to the All Stocks low price-to-book portfolio, with some fairly large losses occurring at times when the overall market was doing much better.

T A B L E 6-6

Worst-Case Scenarios: All 10 Percent or Greater Declines for 50 Stocks from Large Stocks with Lowest P/Book, December 31, 1962–December 31, 2003

Peak Date	Peak Index Value	Trough Date	Trough Index Value	Recovery Date	Decline (%)	Decline Duration	Recovery Duration
Jan-66	1.84	Sep-66	1.48	Apr-67	−19.2	8	7
Jan-69	2.67	Jun-70	1.63	Feb-72	−38.71	17	20
Nov-72	2.86	Jun-73	2.38	Jan-74	−16.69	7	7
Feb-74	2.99	Sep-74	2.13	Feb-75	−28.89	7	5
Aug-78	6.91	Oct-78	6.00	Mar-79	−13.07	2	5
Sep-79	7.95	Oct-79	7.13	Jan-80	−10.27	1	3
Jan-80	8.21	Mar-80	7.12	Jun-80	−13.22	2	3
May-81	11.18	Jul-82	9.62	Oct-82	−13.91	14	3

(continued on next page)

T A B L E 6-6

Worst-Case Scenarios: All 10 Percent or Greater Declines for 50 Stocks from Large Stocks with Lowest P/Book, December 31, 1962–December 31, 2003 *(Continued)*

Peak Date	Peak Index Value	Trough Date	Trough Index Value	Recovery Date	Decline (%)	Decline Duration	Recovery Duration
Jan-84	21.51	Jul-84	17.42	Jan-85	−19.02	6	6
Mar-86	30.70	Jul-86	25.58	Jan-87	−16.68	4	6
Jul-87	37.54	Nov-87	26.51	Sep-88	−29.37	4	10
Sep-89	49.61	Oct-90	30.84	Jan-92	−37.84	13	15
Apr-98	180.63	Aug-98	139.07	Apr-99	−23.01	4	8
Dec-99	231.44	Feb-00	204.53	May-00	−11.63	2	3
Jan-01	306.53	Mar-01	275.27	May-01	−10.2	2	2
May-01	314.67	Sep-02	179.86	Dec-03	−42.84	16	15
Average					−21.53	6.81	7.38

HIGH PRICE-TO-BOOK STOCKS—A WILD RIDE TO NOWHERE

Like high-PE stocks, stocks with high price-to-book ratios are generally bad investments. Figures 6-1 and 6-2 and Tables 6-7 through 6-12 summarize the results. $10,000 invested on December 31, 1951 in the 50 stocks with the highest price-to-book ratios drawn from the All Stocks universe grew to just $267,147 at the end of 2003, a mere fraction of the amount you would earn by investing in either the All Stocks Universe alone or the 50 stocks with low price-to-books from All Stocks. The standard deviation of 32.69 percent signifies a wild ride, verified by the results featured in the worst-case scenarios in Table 6-11. Imagine being an investor in the 50 stocks with the highest price-to-book ratios in the late 1960s through the 1970s. Between January 1969 and June 1970, you would have lost almost half the value of your portfolio, only to watch the stocks turn around and soar right back to the old high in May of 1972. Yet this was merely the eye of the storm. The high price-to-book stocks then plunged over 73 percent during the bear market of 1973–1974, a plunge from which they didn't recover for six years.

T A B L E 6-7

Summary Return and Risk Results for Annual Data, All Stocks, and 50 Lowest Book-to-Price (High P/Book) Stocks from All Stocks, December 31, 1951–December 31, 2003

	All Stocks	All Stocks, Bottom 50 Book/Price (High P/Book)
Arithmetic Average	14.79%	11.55%
Geometric Average	13.00%	6.52%

(continued on page 98)

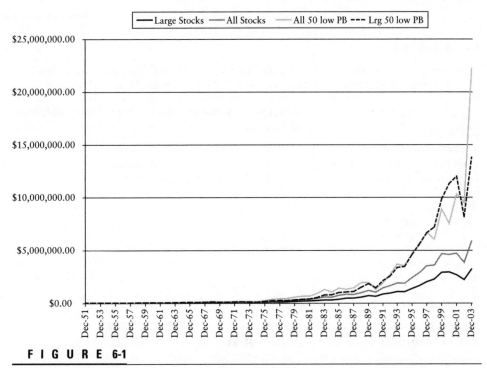

FIGURE 6-1

Returns on low P/Book stocks versus All Stocks and Large Stocks, 1951–2003. Year-end 1951=$10,000.

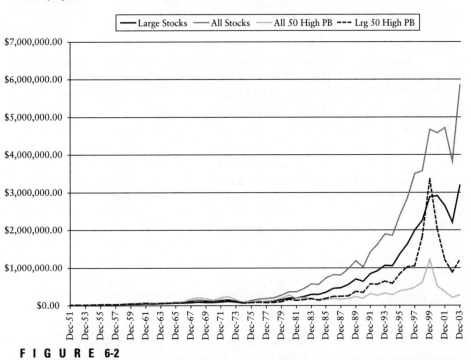

FIGURE 6-2

Returns on high P/Book stocks versus All Stocks and Large Stocks, 1951–2003. Year-end 1951=$10,000.

T A B L E 6-7

Summary Return and Risk Results for Annual Data, All Stocks, and 50 Lowest Book-to-Price
(High P/Book) Stocks from All Stocks, December 31, 1951–December 31, 2003 *(Continued)*

	All Stocks	All Stocks, Bottom 50 Book/Price (High P/Book)
Median Return	16.80%	14.46%
Standard Deviation of Return	20.11%	32.69%
Downside Risk—lower is better	7.17%	16.55%
Correlation with S&P 500	0.87	0.72
T-Statistic	5.30	2.55
Sharpe Ratio	0.46	0.19
Number of Positive Periods	39	36
Number of Negative Periods	13	16
Maximum Peak-to-Trough Decline (using monthly data series)	−50.12%	−89.19%
Beta	0.99	1.34
$10,000 becomes:	$5,743,706.00	$267,147.00
Minimum Annual Return	−27.90%	−57.75%
Maximum Annual Return	55.90%	100.62%
Minimum *Expected* Return*	−25.43%	−53.83%
Maximum *Expected* Return**	55.01%	76.93%

*Minimum Expected Return is Arithmetic Return minus 2 times the standard deviation.
**Maximum Expected Return is Arithmetic Return plus 2 times the standard deviation.

T A B L E 6-8

Summary Return and Risk Results for Annual Data, Large Stocks, and 50 Lowest Book-to-Price
(High P/Book) Stocks from Large Stocks, December 31, 1951–December 31, 2003

Large Stocks	Large Stocks, Bottom 50 Book/Price (High P/Book)	
Arithmetic Average	12.99%	13.22%
Geometric Average	11.71%	9.65%
Median Return	15.75%	11.20%
Standard Deviation of Return	16.84%	28.31%
Downside Risk—lower is better	5.86%	12.43%
Correlation with S&P 500	0.95	0.79
T-Statistic	5.56	3.37
Sharpe Ratio	0.45	0.28
Number of Positive Periods	39	38
Number of Negative Periods	13	14
Maximum Peak-to-Trough Decline (using monthly data series)	−46.59%	−80.78%
Beta	0.89	1.27
$10,000 becomes:	$3,173,724.00	$1,201,082.00
Minimum Annual Return	−26.70%	−39.81%

(continued on next page)

T A B L E 6-8

Summary Return and Risk Results for Annual Data, Large Stocks, and 50 Lowest Book-to-Price (High P/Book) Stocks from Large Stocks, December 31, 1951–December 31, 2003 *(Continued)*

Large Stocks	Large Stocks, Bottom 50 Book/Price (High P/Book)	
Maximum Annual Return	45.07%	83.51%
Minimum *Expected* Return*	−20.69%	−43.40%
Maximum *Expected* Return**	46.67%	69.84%

*Minimum Expected Return is Arithmetic Return minus 2 times the standard deviation.
**Maximum Expected Return is Arithmetic Return plus 2 times the standard deviation.

T A B L E 6-9

Base Rates for All Stocks and 50 Highest P/Book Stocks from All Stocks Universe, 1951–2003

Item	50 High P/Book Beat "All Stocks"	Percent
Single-Year Return	25 out of 52	48%
Rolling Five-Year Compound Return	16 out of 48	33%
Rolling 10-Year Compound Return	13 out of 43	30%

T A B L E 6-10

Base Rates for Large Stocks and 50 Highest P/Book Stocks from Large Stocks Universe, 1951–2003

Item	50 High P/Book Beat "Large Stocks"	Percent
Single-Year Return	20 out of 52	38%
Rolling Five-Year Compound Return	24 out of 48	50%
Rolling 10-Year Compound Return	19 out of 43	44%

T A B L E 6-11

Worst-Case Scenarios: All 10 Percent or Greater Declines for 50 Stocks from All Stocks with Highest P/Book, December 31, 1962–December 31, 2003

Peak Date	Peak Index Value	Trough Date	Trough Index Value	Recovery Date	Decline (%)	Decline Duration	Recovery Duration
Apr-66	1.90	Oct-66	1.48	Feb-67	−21.94	6	4
Dec-67	2.96	Mar-68	2.48	Apr-68	−16.35	3	1
Jan-69	3.59	Jun-70	1.69	Jan-72	−52.99	17	19
May-72	4.30	Sep-74	1.14	Sep-80	−73.38	28	72
Nov-80	5.49	Nov-84	2.48	Jul-87	−54.77	48	32
Jul-87	5.50	Oct-90	2.97	Dec-91	−46.01	39	14
Jan-92	6.43	Aug-92	4.44	Jul-95	−30.88	7	35
May-96	8.54	Mar-97	6.33	Sep-97	−25.84	10	6
Jun-98	9.99	Aug-98	7.60	Dec-98	−23.91	2	4

(continued on next page)

T A B L E 6-11

Worst-Case Scenarios: All 10 Percent or Greater Declines for 50 Stocks from All Stocks with Highest P/Book, December 31, 1962–December 31, 2003 *(Continued)*

Peak Date	Peak Index Value	Trough Date	Trough Index Value	Recovery Date	Decline (%)	Decline Duration	Recovery Duration
Feb-00	30.98	Mar-03	3.35		−89.19	37	NA
Average					−3.526	19.7	20.8

T A B L E 6-12

Worst-Case Scenarios: All 10 Percent or Greater Declines for 50 Stocks from Large Stocks with Highest P/Book, December 31, 1962–December 31, 2003

Peak Date	Peak Index Value	Trough Date	Trough Index Value	Recovery Date	Decline (%)	Decline Duration	Recovery Duration
Apr-66	1.79	Sep-66	1.48	Feb-67	−17.36	5	5
Sep-67	2.10	Feb-68	1.73	May-68	−17.74	5	3
Nov-68	2.22	Jul-69	1.89	Oct-69	−14.92	8	3
Oct-69	2.26	Jun-70	1.46	Sep-71	−35.49	8	15
May-72	3.00	Sep-74	1.06	Nov-80	−64.57	28	74
Nov-80	3.27	Jul-82	1.82	Mar-83	−44.55	20	8
Jun-83	3.97	May-84	2.51	Mar-86	−36.81	11	22
Jun-86	4.67	Sep-86	3.92	Jan-87	−16.18	3	4
Aug-87	5.63	Nov-87	3.64	Feb-91	−35.44	3	39
Dec-91	8.80	Jun-92	7.50	May-93	−14.8	6	11
Jan-94	10.47	Jun-94	8.63	Jun-95	−17.56	5	12
May-96	17.99	Mar-97	14.20	Sep-97	−21.04	10	6
Jun-98	23.55	Aug-98	18.41	Nov-98	−21.84	2	3
Feb-00	68.24	Sep-02	13.11		−80.78	31	NA
Average					−31.36	10.36	15.77

Common sense dictates that this stomach-turning performance would have investors avoiding high price-to-book stocks like the plague—but you'd be wrong. These were the very stocks that hapless investors plowed all their money into at the end of the speculative bubble, sending them up over 300 percent between August 1998 and February 2000. Needless to say, that ended very badly, with the group plummeting almost 90 percent between February 2000 and March 2003. And it wasn't just this list of high price-to-book stocks that got hammered: A visit to Morningstar's website finds that many of the most aggressive mutual funds investing in these much loved (at the time) high price-to-book stocks suffered similar fates, with quite a few of the aggressive technology and growth funds declining over 90 percent during the life of the bear market.

LARGE STOCKS ARE NO DIFFERENT

The 50 stocks with high price-to-book ratios from the Large Stocks group didn't fare much better. $10,000 invested on December 31, 1951 grows to $1,201,082 by the end of 2003, a compound return of 9.65 percent, less than half the return of the Large Stocks universe. The standard deviation was a bit lower—28.31 percent—but the Sharpe ratio of 28 was still dismal.

The base rates for the high price-to-book stocks are unusual. Although the longer-term numbers are overwhelmingly negative, high price-to-book stocks from the Large Stocks universe actually beat the group 50 percent of the time when reviewing rolling five-year returns. What's more, the compound returns in Table 6-13 show that the 50 large stocks with the highest price-to-book ratios did better than Large Stocks in both the 1950s and 1960s. In contrast, large stocks with high PE ratios failed to beat the universe in any of the decades from the 1950s to the 1990s. This teaches you to be careful when reviewing returns by decade. As Table 6-14 shows, you're better off looking at the best- and worst-case scenarios for a particular strategy over all rolling periods. You can see that the difference in the downside between Large Stocks with low price-to-book versus high price-to-book ratios is fairly extreme, with the worst five year period for low price-to-book stocks from Large Stocks showing a $10,000 initial investment just about breaking even at $9,760. Alternatively, the worst five years for high price-to-book Large Stocks reduces your $10,000 to a little over $4,000, nearly 60 percent less than you started with.

T A B L E 6-13

Average Annual Compound Rates of Return by Decade

Portfolio	1950s*	1960s	1970s	1980s	1990s	2000s**
Large Stocks	15.33%	8.99%	6.99%	16.89%	15.34%	2.40%
50 High Price-to-Book from Large Stocks	16.55%	11.30%	−0.60%	14.40%	24.87%	−22.38%
50 Low Price-to-Book from Large Stocks	15.41%	9.57%	13.95%	19.99%	18.28%	8.99%
All Stocks	19.22%	11.09%	8.53%	15.85%	14.75%	5.91%
50 High Price-to-Book from All Stocks	22.32%	13.13%	0.82%	1.97%	18.03%	−31.17%
50 Low Price-to-Book from All Stocks	21.84%	13.96%	8.89%	7.56%	16.21%	25.68%

*Returns for 1952–1959
**Returns for 2000–2003

T A B L E 6-14

Best and Worst Average Annual Compound Returns over Period for Annual Data 1951–2003

For Any	1-Year Period	3-Year Period	5-Year Period	10-Year Period
Large Stocks Minimum Compound Return	–26.70%	–11.93%	–4.37%	1.21%
Large Stocks Maximum Compound Return	45.07%	24.39%	22.40%	17.01%
Low P/Book Large Stocks Minimum Compound Return	–31.70%	–5.83%	1.18%	4.12%
Low P/Book Large Stocks Maximum Compound Return	68.94%	36.85%	27.52%	24.21%
High P/Book Large Stocks Minimum Compound Return	–39.81%	–36.07%	–12.72%	–2.34%
High P/Book Large Stocks Maximum Compound Return	83.51%	48.48%	42.24%	24.87%
All Stocks Minimum Compound Return	–27.90%	–16.48%	–7.81%	1.26%
All Stocks Maximum Compound Return	55.90%	31.23%	27.77%	21.31%
Low P/Book All Stocks Minimum Compound Return	–34.50%	–3.62%	–1.54%	7.09%
Low P/Book All Stocks Maximum Compound Return	133.55%	43.16%	33.20%	24.11%
High P/Book All Stocks Minimum Compound Return	–57.75%	–44.92%	–15.42%	–4.34%
High P/Book All Stocks Maximum Compound Return	100.62%	43.26%	34.43%	22.64%

BEST- AND WORST-CASE RETURNS

Tables 6-14, 6-15, and 6-18 show the compound annual best and worst returns for the strategies and relevant benchmarks. In all periods, buying stocks with the highest price-to-book puts investors at risk of losing nearly their entire investment when returns head south. The worst three-year period for the 50 stocks with the highest price-to-book from All Stocks saw an investment of $10,000 dwindle to slightly more than $1,000. That's a loss of nearly 90 percent. To put this in perspective, the worst decline that the S&P 500 ever turned in was a loss of 83.41 percent, and that was at the dawn of the Great Depression of the early 1930s.

The 50 stocks with the highest price-to-book from Large Stocks didn't fare much better, with the same $10,000 reduced to $1,985 over the worst three-year period. And for investors who place more emphasis on more recent events, remember these two worst periods were for the three years ending in March 2003.

The 50 stocks with low price-to-book ratios from each universe fared much better in all rolling periods. The worst cases there, while still painful, are decidedly more palatable than the near-fatal plunge that high price-to-book stocks inflicted on investors. The lesson is clear to the investors who thought that the end-of-millennium mania signified a new world order: It's no different this time.

T A B L E 6-15

Best and Worst Average Annual Compound Returns over Period for Monthly Data 1963–2003.

For Any	1-Year Period	3-Year Period	5-Year Period	10-Year Period
Large Stocks Minimum Compound Return	−42.05%	−13.80%	−6.05%	−0.20%
Large Stocks Maximum Compound Return	68.49%	32.79%	28.65%	19.57%
Low P/Book Large Stocks Minimum Compound Return	−33.53%	−6.05%	−0.49%	3.31%
Low P/Book Large Stocks Maximum Compound Return	103.78%	38.95%	31.29%	25.61%
High P/Book Large Stocks Minimum Compound Return	−71.24%	−41.66%	−16.02%	−4.77%
High P/Book Large Stocks Maximum Compound Return	122.93%	64.72%	48.09%	29.89%
All Stocks Minimum Compound Return	−41.65%	−16.82%	−8.94%	0.68%
All Stocks Maximum Compound Return	81.51%	29.46%	27.02%	21.46%
Low P/Book All Stocks Minimum Compound Return	−42.62%	−12.38%	−5.17%	5.16%
Low P/Book All Stocks Maximum Compound Return	133.55%	44.44%	32.76%	25.00%
High P/Book All Stocks Minimum Compound Return	−74.68%	−52.30%	−19.30%	−5.20%
High P/Book All Stocks Maximum Compound Return	172.55%	62.72%	42.93%	22.29%

DECILES

The decile results confirm our 50-stock findings. In both the All Stocks and Large Stocks universes, the low price-to-book deciles do better than both their benchmarks and the high price-to-book deciles. Indeed, in the All Stocks universe, the lowest decile did 29 times as well as the highest! Tables 6-16 and 6-17 as well as Figures 6-3 and 6-4 summarize the results.

T A B L E 6-16

Summary Results for Price-to-Book Decile Analysis of All Stocks Universe, 1951–2003

Decile	$10,000 Grows to:	Average Return	Compound Return	Standard Deviation
1 (Lowest P/Book)	$29,306,921	19.35%	16.59%	25.95%
2	$17,834,533	17.46%	15.48%	21.52%
3	$14,859,443	16.81%	15.08%	19.83%
4	$8,833,385	15.81%	13.93%	20.68%
5	$4,067,121	14.12%	12.25%	20.18%
6	$3,011,887	13.46%	11.60%	19.92%
7	$2,863,995	13.29%	11.49%	19.50%
8	$2,672,928	13.84%	11.35%	23.45%
9	$2,408,922	13.83%	11.12%	24.26%
10 (Highest P/Book)	$1,000,292	13.11%	9.26%	29.31%
All Stocks	$5,743,706	14.79%	13.00%	20.11%

T A B L E 6-17

Summary Results for Price-to-Book Decile Analysis of Large Stocks Universe, 1951–2003

Decile	$10,000 Grows to:	Average Return	Compound Return	Standard Deviation
1 (Lowest P/Book)	$21,000,941	17.73%	15.85%	21.16%
2	$5,236,475	14.26%	12.79%	18.28%
3	$3,807,346	13.41%	12.11%	17.12%
4	$2,543,392	12.52%	11.24%	16.83%
5	$2,674,408	12.60%	11.35%	16.66%
6	$2,093,122	12.32%	10.82%	17.86%
7	$1,331,521	11.32%	9.86%	17.50%
8	$1,794,366	12.03%	10.50%	18.05%
9	$1,748,474	12.43%	10.44%	20.46%
10 (Highest P/Book)	$1,319,374	12.89%	9.84%	25.41%
Large Stocks	$3,173,724	12.99%	11.71%	16.84%

T A B L E 6-18

Terminal Value of $10,000 Invested for Best and Worst Average Annual Compound Returns over Period for Monthly Data 1963–2003

For Any	1-Year Period	3-Year Period	5-Year Period	10-Year Period
Large Stocks Minimum $10,000 Value	$5,795.00	$6,405.04	$7,319.54	$9,801.79
Large Stocks Maximum $10,000 Value	$16,849.00	$23,415.11	$35,241.06	$69,737.00
Low P/Book Large Stocks Minimum $10,000 Value	$6,647.00	$8,292.00	$9,760.00	$13,854.00
Low P/Book Large Stocks Maximum $10,000 Value	$20,378.00	$26,828.00	$39,002.00	$97,780.00
High P/Book Large Stocks Minimum $10,000 Value	$2,876.00	$1,985.00	$4,178.00	$6,132.00
High P/Book Large Stocks Maximum $10,000 Value	$22,293.00	$44,690.00	$71,231.00	$136,649.00
All Stocks Minimum $10,000 Value	$5,835.00	$5,756.00	$6,260.00	$10,700.00
All Stocks Maximum $10,000 Value	$18,151.00	$21,680.00	$33,064.00	$69,868.00
Low P/Book All Stocks Minimum $10,000 Value	$5,738.00	$7,270.00	$7,671.00	$16,539.00
Low P/Book All Stocks Maximum $10,000 Value	$23,355.00	$30,134.00	$41,234.00	$93,156.00
High P/Book All Stocks Minimum $10,000 Value	$2,532.00	$1,085.00	$3,423.00	$5,865.00
High P/Book All Stocks Maximum $10,000 Value	$27,255.00	$43,088.00	$59,648.00	$74,797.00

IMPLICATIONS

Over the long-term, the market clearly rewards low price-to-book ratios and punishes high ones (Figures 6-5 and 6-6). Yet, the data shows why investors are willing to overlook high price-to-book ratios—for 20 years, between 1952 and 1972, the 50 large stocks with high price-to-book ratios did *better*

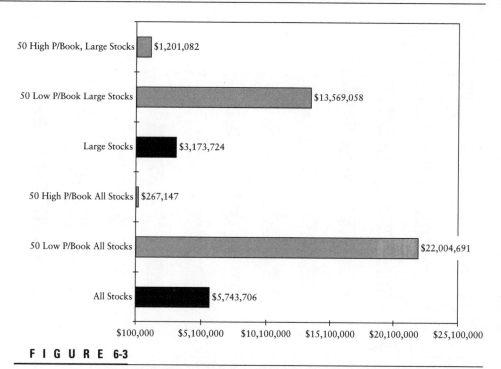

F I G U R E 6-3

December 31, 2003 value of $10,000 invested on December 31, 1951 and annually rebalanced.

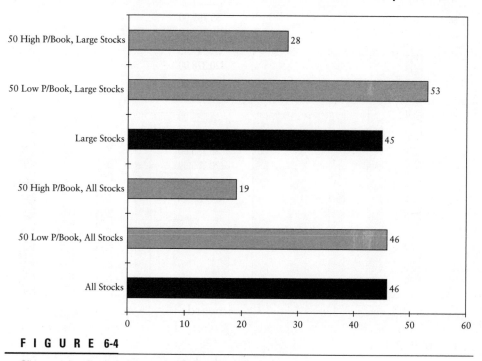

F I G U R E 6-4

Sharpe risk-adjusted return ratio, 1951–2003. (Higher is better.)

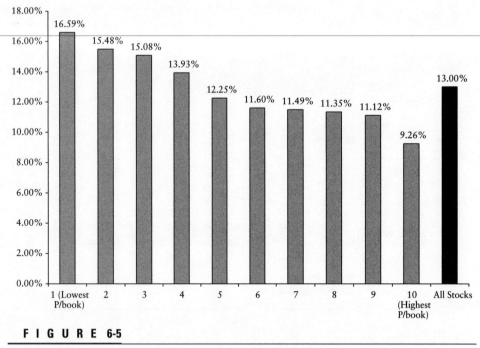

F I G U R E 6-5

Compound return by price-to-book ratio decile, All Stocks universe, 1951–2003.

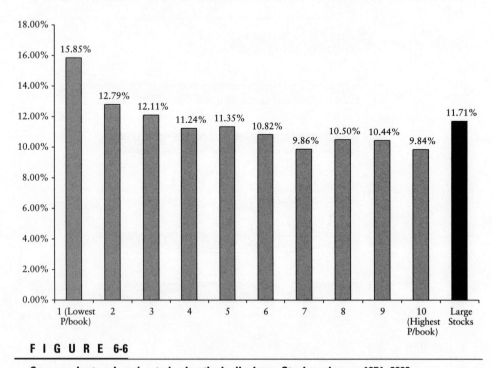

F I G U R E 6-6

Compound return by price-to-book ratio decile, Large Stocks universe, 1951–2003.

than the Large Stocks universe. A high price-to-book ratio is one of the hall-marks of a growth stock, so a somewhat high price-to-book ratio alone shouldn't keep you from buying a stock. But the long-term results should caution you against the highest price-to-book ratio stocks.

7

CHAPTER

PRICE-TO-CASHFLOW RATIOS: USING CASH TO DETERMINE VALUE

Losing an illusion makes you wiser than finding a truth.
—Ludwig Borne

The price-to-cashflow ratio is yet another measure of whether a stock is cheap or not. You find cashflow by adding depreciation and amortization to income (before extraordinary items). The price-to-cashflow ratio is the market value of the stock divided by total cashflow. We'll look at it on a per share basis.

Some value investors prefer using price-to-cashflow ratios to find bargain-priced stocks because cashflow is more difficult to manipulate than earnings. I exclude utility stocks here, since utilities show up frequently and I want to avoid bias to one industry.

As usual, I look at both the low- and high-price-to-cashflow ratio stocks from the All Stocks and Large Stocks universes. I'll also rank both All Stocks and Large Stocks by price-to-cashflow decile. (Again, due to Compustat's ranking function, I rank stocks by the 50 *highest* cashflow-to-price ratios, the inverse of the price-to-cashflow ratio.) The stocks are equally weighted, all variables except price are time-lagged to avoid look-ahead bias, and the portfolio is rebalanced annually.

THE RESULTS

As with the other value criteria, investors reward stocks with low price-to-cashflow ratios and punish those with high ones. Let's look at the returns of low price-to-cashflow ratio stocks first. $10,000 invested on December 31, 1951 in the 50 stocks with the lowest price-to-cashflow ratios from the All Stocks universe was worth $17,724,382 on December 31, 2003, a compound return of 15.47 percent a year, significantly better than the $5,743,706 you'd earn from the same investment in the All Stocks universe (Table 7-1). Risk was fairly high. The standard deviation of return for the 50 lowest price-to-cashflow stocks was 27.15 percent, higher than the All Stocks universe's 20.11 percent. Yet the low price-to-cashflow portfolio still managed to earn a higher Sharpe ratio than All Stocks, compensating investors for the higher level of risk. All base rates were positive, with the 50 stocks with the lowest price-to-cashflow from All Stocks beating the All Stocks universe 70 percent of the time over all rolling 10-year periods (Figures 7-1 and 7-2).

T A B L E 7-1

Summary Return and Risk Results for Annual Data, All Stocks, and 50 Highest Cashflow-to-Price (Low P/Cashflow) Stocks from All Stocks, December 31, 1951–December 31, 2003

	All Stocks	All Stocks, Top 50 Cashflow/ Price (Low P/Cashflow)
Arithmetic Average	14.79%	18.54%
Geometric Average	13.00%	15.47%
Median Return	16.80%	18.80%
Standard Deviation of Return	20.11%	27.15%
Downside Risk—lower is better	7.17%	8.58%
Correlation with S&P 500	0.87	0.74
T-Statistic	5.30	4.93
Sharpe Ratio	0.46	0.48
Number of Positive Periods	39	35
Number of Negative Periods	13	17
Maximum Peak-to-Trough Decline (using monthly data series)	−50.12%	−44.22%
Beta	0.99	1.13
$10,000 becomes:	$5,743,706.00	$17,724,382.00
Minimum Annual Return	−27.90%	−31.60%
Maximum Annual Return	55.90%	79.91%
Minimum *Expected* Return*	−25.43%	−35.76%
Maximum *Expected* Return**	55.01%	72.84%

*Minimum Expected Return is Arithmetic Return minus 2 times the standard deviation.
**Maximum Expected Return is Arithmetic Return plus 2 times the standard deviation.

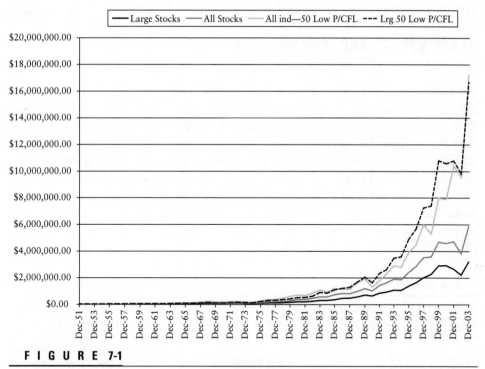

F I G U R E 7-1

Returns on low P/Cashflow stocks versus All Stocks and Large Stocks, 1951–2003. Year-end 1951=$10,000.

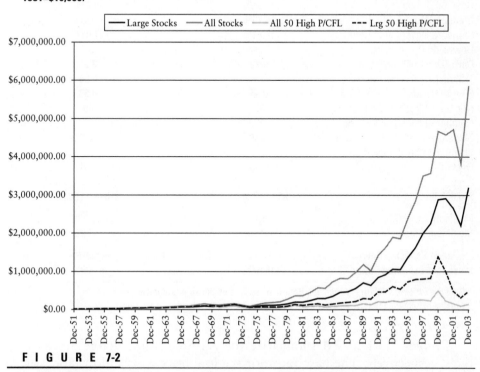

F I G U R E 7-2

Returns on high P/Cashflow stocks versus All Stocks and Large Stocks, 1951–2003. Year-end 1951=$10,000.

LARGE STOCKS ARE LESS VOLATILE

As we've seen with the other value factors, the 50 low price-to-cashflow stocks from the Large Stocks universe did much better on both an absolute and a risk-adjusted basis. The original $10,000 invested in 1951 grew to $16,060,150 at the end of 2003, a compound return of 15.25 percent a year. That's more than five times the $3,173,724 you'd earn from $10,000 invested in the Large Stocks universe alone. The standard deviation of return of 21.94 percent is higher than the Large Stocks' 16.84 percent, but considerably lower than the low price-to-cashflow stocks from the All Stocks category. The Sharpe ratio for the low price-to-cashflow stocks from Large Stocks was 53 (Table 7.2).

T A B L E 7-2

Summary Return and Risk Results for Annual Data, Large Stocks, and 50 Highest Cashflow-to-Price (Low P/Cashflow) Stocks from Large Stocks, December 31, 1951–December 31, 2003

	Large Stocks	Large Stocks, Top 50 Cashflow/ Price (Low P/Cashflow)
Arithmetic Average	12.99%	17.21%
Geometric Average	11.71%	15.25%
Median Return	15.75%	17.35%
Standard Deviation of Return	16.84%	21.94%
Downside Risk—lower is better	5.86%	5.55%
Correlation with S&P 500	0.95	0.81
T-Statistic	5.56	5.66
Sharpe Ratio	0.45	0.53
Number of Positive Periods	39	40
Number of Negative Periods	13	12
Maximum Peak-to-Trough Decline (using monthly data series)	−46.59%	−39.33%
Beta	0.89	1.01
$10,000 becomes:	$3,173,724.00	$16,060,150.00
Minimum Annual Return	−26.70%	−23.00%
Maximum Annual Return	45.07%	75.70%
Minimum *Expected* Return*	−20.69%	−26.67%
Maximum *Expected* Return**	46.67%	61.09%

*Minimum Expected Return is Arithmetic Return minus 2 times the standard deviation.
**Maximum Expected Return is Arithmetic Return plus 2 times the standard deviation.

Tables 7-3 and 7-4 summarize the All Stocks and Large Stocks base rates, respectively. The base rates for the low price-to-cashflow stocks from the Large Stocks universe are uniformly high. Over all rolling 10-year periods, the 50 lowest price-to-cashflow stocks from the Large Stocks group beat the universe 93 percent of the time. Using the long-term base rate as an indicator tells you that you have a 93 percent chance to beat the performance of the Large Stocks universe if you stick to large stocks with low price-to-cashflow ratios. Using the average over- and underperformance from all rolling 10-year periods, a portfolio falling during the 7 percent of the time that low price-to-cashflow large stocks underperform, the Large Stocks universe would be worth 12 percent less than one invested in the Large Stocks universe itself. However, if the 10-year period fell into the 93 percent of the times when low price-to-cashflow Large Stocks outperformed the Large Stocks universe, a portfolio would be worth 92 percent more than one invested in the Large Stocks universe. These great odds make it very compelling to stick with a low price-to-cashflow strategy.

T A B L E 7-3

Base Rates for All Stocks and 50 Highest Cashflow/Price (Low P/Cashflow) Stocks from All Stocks Universe, 1951–2003

Item	50 Low P/Cashflow Beat "All Stocks"	Percent
Single-Year Return	31 out of 52	60%
Rolling Five-Year Compound Return	29 out of 48	60%
Rolling 10-Year Compound Return	30 out of 43	70%

T A B L E 7-4

Base Rates for Large Stocks and 50 Highest Cashflow/Price (Low P/Cashflow) Stocks from Large Stocks Universe, 1951–2003

Item	50 Low P/Cashflow Beat "Large Stocks"	Percent
Single-Year Return	34 out of 52	65%
Rolling Five-Year Compound Return	34 out of 48	71%
Rolling 10-Year Compound Return	40 out of 43	93%

WORST-CASE SCENARIOS AND BEST AND WORST RETURNS

Looking at Tables 7-5, 7-6, and 7-7, we see that the worst-case scenario for low price-to-cashflow stocks from both the All Stocks and Large Stocks universes came in the bear market of 1969–1970, with the low price-to-cashflow stocks from All Stocks losing 44 percent and the low price-to-cashflow stocks from Large Stocks falling 39 percent over the period. The low price-to-cashflow stocks from All Stocks had six declines in excess of 30 percent, whereas the low price-to-cashflow stocks from Large Stocks had just three declines exceeding 30 percent, making them the better choice for more risk adverse investors.

T A B L E 7-5

Worst-Case Scenarios: All 10 Percent or Greater Declines for 50 Stocks from All Stocks with Lowest P/Cashflow, December 31, 1962–December 31, 2003

Peak Date	Peak Index Value	Trough Date	Trough Index Value	Recovery Date	Decline (%)	Decline Duration	Recovery Duration
Feb-66	2.45	Sep-66	1.98	Feb-67	−19.26	7	5
Jan-69	4.43	Jun-70	2.47	Jan-72	−44.22	17	19
Nov-72	4.58	Dec-74	2.91	Jan-76	−36.32	25	13
Aug-78	9.85	Oct-78	8.15	Jul-79	−17.26	2	9
Sep-79	10.52	Oct-79	9.22	Jan-80	−12.34	1	3
Jan-80	10.80	Mar-80	8.67	Jul-80	−19.72	2	4
Jun-81	13.64	Jul-82	10.71	Nov-82	−21.48	13	4
Jun-83	19.74	Jul-84	16.42	Jan-85	−16.82	13	6
May-86	29.69	Jul-86	26.48	Jan-87	−10.84	2	6
Aug-87	37.58	Nov-87	24.89	Jul-88	−33.77	3	8
Aug-89	48.40	Oct-90	29.74	Feb-92	−38.57	14	16
Aug-94	74.92	Dec-94	66.34	Apr-95	−11.45	4	4
Mar-98	169.52	Aug-98	110.94	Jun-99	−34.56	5	10
Aug-00	198.41	Nov-00	174.20	Jan-01	−12.2	3	2
May-01	262.02	Sep-01	202.48	Feb-02	−22.72	4	5
Apr-02	307.65	Sep-02	191.76	Aug-03	−37.67	5	11
Average					—24.32	7.5	7.81

T A B L E 7-6

Worst-Case Scenarios: All 10 Percent or Greater Declines for 50 Stocks from Large Stocks with Lowest P/Cashflow, December 1961–December 31, 2003

Peak Date	Peak Index Value	Trough Date	Trough Index Value	Recovery Date	Decline (%)	Decline Duration	Recovery Duration
Feb-66	1.98	Sep-66	1.66	Jan-67	−16.43	7	4
Jan-69	3.00	Jun-70	1.82	Jan-72	−39.33	17	19
Nov-72	3.38	Sep-74	2.20	Apr-75	−35	22	7
Jun-75	3.83	Sep-75	3.44	Jan-76	−10.36	3	4
Sep-78	6.92	Oct-78	6.02	Mar-79	−13.12	1	5
Aug-79	8.16	Oct-79	7.24	Jan-80	−11.34	2	3
Jan-80	8.24	Mar-80	7.05	Jul-80	−14.45	2	4
May-81	10.67	Jul-82	8.78	Oct-82	−17.72	14	3
Aug-87	35.38	Nov-87	23.66	Jan-89	−33.12	3	14
Aug-89	44.53	Oct-90	27.66	Dec-91	−37.88	14	14
Mar-98	156.20	Aug-98	118.89	Apr-99	−23.89	5	8

(continued on next page)

T A B L E 7-6

Worst-Case Scenarios: All 10 Percent or Greater Declines for 50 Stocks from Large Stocks with Lowest P/Cashflow, December 1961–December 31, 2003 *(Continued)*

Peak Date	Peak Index Value	Trough Date	Trough Index Value	Recovery Date	Decline (%)	Decline Duration	Recovery Duration
May-00	203.39	Nov-00	181.15	Jan-01	−10.93	6	2
May-01	227.58	Sep-02	166.64	Jul-03	−26.78	16	10
Average					−22.33	8.62	7.46

Table 7-7 shows the terminal value of a $10,000 investment comparing the best- and worst-case returns from the previous 40 years. An investor with a five-year time horizon should choose the 50 stocks from Large Stocks with the lowest price-to-cashflow ratios, because the worst-case return for these was above both the All Stocks and Large Stocks universes. Stretching the horizon to 10 years, we see that in both the All Stocks and Large Stocks universes, the stocks with low price-to-cashflow had positive returns even in the worst periods.

T A B L E 7-7

Terminal Value of $10,000 Invested for Best and Worst Average Annual Compound Returns over Period for Monthly Data 1963–2003

For Any	1-Year Period	3-Year Period	5-Year Period	10-Year Period
Large Stocks Minimum $10,000 Value	$5,795.00	$6,405.04	$7,319.54	$9,801.79
Large Stocks Maximum $10,000 Value	$16,849.00	$23,415.11	$35,241.06	$69,737.00
Low P/Cashflow Large Stocks Minimum $10,000 Value	$6,542.00	$7,870.00	$9,061.00	$14,874.00
Low P/Cashflow Large Stocks Maximum $10,000 Value	$18,162.00	$24,930.00	$39,941.00	$81,423.00
High P/Cashflow Large Stocks Minimum $10,000 Value	$1,937.00	$1,656.00	$3,167.00	$6,414.00
High P/Cashflow Large Stocks Maximum $10,000 Value	$22,440.00	$25,707.00	$34,540.00	$62,573.00
All Stocks Minimum $10,000 Value	$5,835.00	$5,756.00	$6,260.00	$10,700.00
All Stocks Maximum $10,000 Value	$18,151.00	$21,680.00	$33,064.00	$69,868.00
Low P/Cashflow All Stocks Minimum $10,000 Value	$6,481.00	$6,865.00	$8,256.00	$17,349.00
Low P/Cashflow All Stocks Maximum $10,000 Value	$18,272.00	$25,145.00	$35,569.00	$71,137.00
High P/Cashflow All Stocks Minimum $10,000 Value	$2,421.00	$1,276.00	$2,685.00	$4,222.00
High P/Cashflow All Stocks Maximum $10,000 Value	$26,768.00	$29,250.00	$34,298.00	$55,176.00

HIGH PRICE-TO-CASHFLOW RATIOS ARE DANGEROUS

As with the other value factors, we see that stocks with high price-to-cashflow ratios are usually bad investments. Tables 7-8 through 7-11 summarize the data and Tables 7-12 and 7-13 show the worst-case scenarios for high price-to-cashflow stocks. The 50 stocks with the highest price-to-cashflow ratios from All Stocks had 13 years in which they underperformed All Stocks by more than 15 percent, but only five years in which they beat it by 15 percent or more. They also exhibit concentrations of strong returns in brief periods, typically during speculative market environments. And, generally, great relative performance in any one year is followed by a plunge in the next. In the very speculative year of 1967, the high price-to-cashflow stocks did 26 percent better than All Stocks, but then dramatically underperformed during the next three years. And the three years that followed 1999's blowout return of 117 percent should serve as fair warning to any investor tempted to forget the odds and buy the hottest story stocks: In 2000, the 50 highest price-to-cashflow stocks from All Stocks lost 54 percent, in 2001 they lost 32 percent, and in 2002 they lost 44 percent.

T A B L E 7-8

Summary Return and Risk Results for Annual Data, All Stocks, and 50 Lowest Cashflow-to-Price (High P/Cashflow) Stocks from All Stocks, December 31, 1951–December 31, 2003

	All Stocks	All Stocks, Bottom 50 Cashflow/Price (High P/Cashflow)
Arithmetic Average	14.79%	10.05%
Geometric Average	13.00%	5.16%
Median Return	16.80%	8.42%
Standard Deviation of Return	20.11%	32.87%
Downside Risk—lower is better	7.17%	16.42%
Correlation with S&P 500	0.87	0.69
T-Statistic	5.30	2.20
Sharpe Ratio	0.46	0.15
Number of Positive Periods	39	35
Number of Negative Periods	13	17
Maximum Peak-to-Trough Decline (using monthly data series)	−50.12%	−88.19%
Beta	0.99	1.29
$10,000 becomes:	$5,743,706.00	$136,834.00
Minimum Annual Return	−27.90%	−54.43%
Maximum Annual Return	55.90%	117.23%
Minimum *Expected* Return*	−25.43%	−55.69%
Maximum *Expected* Return**	55.01%	75.79%

*Minimum Expected Return is Arithmetic Return minus 2 times the standard deviation.
**Maximum Expected Return is Arithmetic Return plus 2 times the standard deviation.

T A B L E 7-9

Summary Return and Risk Results for Annual Data, Large Stocks, and 50 Lowest Cashflow-to-Price (High P/Cashflow) Stocks from Large Stocks, December 31, 1951–December 31, 2003

	Large Stocks	Large Stocks, Bottom 50 Cashflow/Price (High P/Cashflow)
Arithmetic Average	12.99%	10.94%
Geometric Average	11.71%	7.64%
Median Return	15.75%	9.89%
Standard Deviation of Return	16.84%	26.30%
Downside Risk—lower is better	5.86%	13.12%
Correlation with S&P 500	0.95	0.75
T-Statistic	5.56	3.00
Sharpe Ratio	0.45	0.22
Number of Positive Periods	39	39
Number of Negative Periods	13	13
Maximum Peak-to-Trough Decline (using monthly data series)	−46.59%	−84.35%
Beta	0.89	1.12
$10,000 becomes:	$3,173,724.00	$459,556.00
Minimum Annual Return	−26.70%	−51.64%
Maximum Annual Return	45.07%	71.44%
Minimum *Expected* Return*	−20.69%	−41.66%
Maximum *Expected* Return**	46.67%	63.54%

*Minimum Expected Return is Arithmetic Return minus 2 times the standard deviation.
**Maximum Expected Return is Arithmetic Return plus 2 times the standard deviation.

T A B L E 7-10

Base Rates for All Stocks and 50 Highest P/Cashflow Stocks from All Stocks Universe, 1951–2003

Item	50 High P/Cashflow Beat "All Stocks"	Percent
Single-Year Return	22 out of 52	42%
Rolling Five-Year Compound Return	10 out of 48	21%
Rolling 10-Year Compound Return	1 out of 43	2%

T A B L E 7-11

Base Rates for Large Stocks and 50 Highest P/Cashflow Stocks from Large Stocks Universe, 1951–2003

Item	50 High P/Cashflow Beat "Large Stocks"	Percent
Single-Year Return	22 out of 52	42%
Rolling Five-Year Compound Return	21 out of 48	44%
Rolling 10-Year Compound Return	16 out of 43	37%

T A B L E 7-12

Worst-Case Scenarios: All 10 Percent or Greater Declines for 50 Stocks from All Stocks with Highest P/Cashflow, December 31, 1962–December 31, 2003

Peak Date	Peak Index Value	Trough Date	Trough Index Value	Recovery Date	Decline (%)	Decline Duration	Recovery Duration
Apr-66	1.83	Oct-66	1.48	Jan-67	−19.44	6	3
Dec-67	2.75	Feb-68	2.31	Apr-68	−15.82	2	2
Jan-69	3.60	Sep-74	1.17	Oct-80	−67.62	68	73
Nov-80	4.42	Jul-82	2.24	May-83	−49.3	20	10
Jun-83	4.75	Nov-84	2.94	Feb-87	−38.17	17	27
Aug-87	5.08	Oct-90	2.92	Dec-91	−42.54	38	14
Feb-92	5.58	Aug-92	4.85	Nov-92	−13.12	6	3
Oct-93	8.12	Jan-95	6.07	Apr-96	−25.33	15	15
May-96	9.75	Aug-98	5.69	Jun-99	−41.65	27	10
Feb-00	21.14	Sep-02	2.50		−88.19	31	NA
Average					−40.11	23	17.44

T A B L E 7-13

Worst-Case Scenarios: All 10 Percent or Greater Declines for 50 Stocks from Large Stocks with Highest P/Cashflow, December 31, 1962–December 31, 2003

Peak Date	Peak Index Value	Trough Date	Trough Index Value	Recovery Date	Decline (%)	Decline Duration	Recovery Duration
Apr-66	1.80	Sep-66	1.49	Jan-67	−16.79	5	4
Dec-67	2.31	Feb-68	1.93	May-68	−16.73	2	3
Nov-68	2.43	Jun-70	1.54	Dec-71	−36.79	19	18
May-72	3.21	Sep-74	1.17	Nov-80	−63.49	28	74
Nov-80	3.52	Jul-82	2.32	Nov-82	−34.05	20	4
Jun-83	4.82	Jul-84	3.13	May-86	−35.12	13	22
Jun-86	5.01	Sep-86	4.37	Jan-87	−12.72	3	4
Sep-87	6.58	Nov-87	4.54	Apr-89	−31.06	2	17
Aug-89	7.17	Sep-90	5.72	Jan-91	−20.18	13	4
Dec-91	11.02	Sep-92	8.77	Jun-93	−20.49	9	9
Jan-94	13.22	Jun-94	10.96	Jul-95	−17.09	5	13
May-96	19.13	Mar-97	14.40	Sep-97	−24.73	10	6
Sep-97	19.56	Jan-98	17.14	Mar-98	−12.37	4	2
Apr-98	20.02	Aug-98	14.36	Apr-99	−28.27	4	8
Feb-00	39.56	Sep-02	6.19		−84.35	31	NA
Average					−30.28	11.2	13.43

The same is true over the long-term. A $10,000 investment on December 31, 1951 in the 50 stocks with the highest price-to-cashflow ratios from All Stocks grew to just $136,834 by the end of 2003. That return is dwarfed by a simple investment in the All Stocks universe. The Sharpe ratio

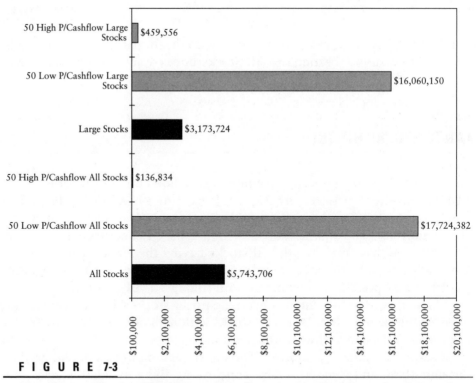

FIGURE 7-3

December 31, 2003 value of $10,000 invested on December 31, 1951 and annually rebalanced.

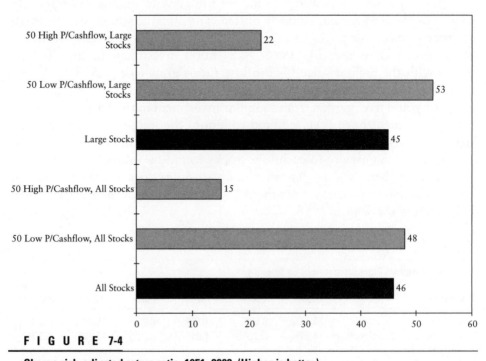

FIGURE 7-4

Sharpe risk-adjusted return ratio, 1951–2003. (Higher is better.)

119

is a dismal 15. All base rates are negative, with the 50 stocks having the highest price-to-cashflow beating the All Stocks universe just once in all rolling 10-year periods (Figures 7-3 and 7-4).

LARGE STOCKS HIT TOO

Large stocks with high price-to-cashflow ratios didn't fare much better. Here, $10,000 invested on December 31, 1951 grew to $459,556 by the end of 2003, $2.5 million less than what you'd earn from an investment in the Large Stocks universe. The Sharpe ratio was an anemic 22. Like their brethren in All Stocks, all base rates for the 50 stocks having the highest price-to-cashflow ratios from Large Stocks are negative, with the group beating Large Stocks just 37 percent of the time over all rolling 10-year periods.

Like many of our findings concerning pricey stocks with rich valuations, focusing on the returns of large-cap stocks with high price-to-cashflow ratios helps you understand why scrutinizing long-term results is the only way to understand the value of a strategy. The second edition of this book had data through 1996, and came to similar conclusions about avoiding stocks with high price-to-cashflow ratios.

Yet, if you only reviewed the data for the 10 years ending December 31, 1996, you'd have been dangerously misled. The 50 large stocks with the highest price-to-cashflow ratios handily *beat* the Large Stocks universe for the 10 years ending December 31, 1996. A $10,000 investment in the 50 large stocks with the highest price-to-cashflow ratios grew to $47,518 at the end of 1986, a compound return of 16.87 percent, $11,000 more than the $36,314 you'd have earned from a similar investment in the Large Stocks universe. You might have been tempted to ignore the long-term odds, particularly in a market that continued to reward speculative stocks. Looking at the base rates for high price-to-cashflow stocks found in Tables 7-10 and 7-11, you see that there is a 37 percent chance to outperform Large Stocks, but just a 2 percent chance if you use the All Stocks universe. Tables 7-10 through 7-16 catalog the woe.

T A B L E 7-14

Average Annual Compound Return by Decade

Portfolio	1950s*	1960s	1970s	1980s	1990s	2000s**
Large Stocks	15.33%	8.99%	6.99%	16.89%	15.34%	2.40%
50 High Price-to-Cashflow from Large Stocks	14.85%	12.35%	−1.85%	13.29%	17.21%	−23.76%

(continued on next page)

T A B L E 7-14

Average Annual Compound Return by Decade *(Continued)*

Portfolio	1950s*	1960s	1970s	1980s	1990s	2000s**
50 Low Price-to-Cashflow from Large Stocks	17.28%	10.36%	15.40%	17.31%	18.03%	11.46%
All Stocks	19.22%	11.09%	8.53%	15.85%	14.75%	5.91%
50 High Price-to-Cashflow from All Stocks	19.30%	8.02%	−3.03%	8.77%	12.77%	−27.77%
50 Low Price-to-Cashflow from All Stocks	18.71%	15.41%	13.57%	12.53%	15.62%	21.23%

*Returns for 1952–1959
**Returns for 2000–2003

T A B L E 7-15

Best and Worst Average Annual Compound Returns over Period for Annual Data 1951–2003

For Any	1-Year Period	3-Year Period	5-Year Period	10-Year Period
Large Stocks Minimum Compound Return	−26.70%	−11.93%	−4.37%	1.21%
Large Stocks Maximum Compound Return	45.07%	24.39%	22.40%	17.01%
Low P/Cashflow Large Stocks Minimum Compound Return	−23.00%	−3.19%	0.69%	5.77%
Low P/Cashflow Large Stocks Maximum Compound Return	75.70%	38.59%	28.89%	21.82%
High P/Cashflow Large Stocks Minimum Compound Return	−51.64%	−39.42%	−17.28%	−3.94%
High P/Cashflow Large Stocks Maximum Compound Return	71.44%	30.83%	23.28%	18.00%
All Stocks Minimum Compound Return	−27.90%	−16.48%	−7.81%	1.26%
All Stocks Maximum Compound Return	55.90%	31.23%	27.77%	21.31%
Low P/Cashflow All Stocks Minimum Compound Return	−31.60%	−14.37%	−6.04%	5.07%
Low P/Cashflow All Stocks Maximum Compound Return	79.91%	42.34%	35.25%	23.16%
High P/Cashflow All Stocks Minimum Compound Return	−54.43%	−44.21%	−19.46%	−9.51%
High P/Cashflow All Stocks Maximum Compound Return	117.23%	38.92%	23.72%	18.40%

T A B L E 7-16

Best and Worst Average Annual Compound Returns over Period for Monthly Data 1963–2003

For Any	1-Year Period	3-Year Period	5-Year Period	10-Year Period
Large Stocks Minimum Compound Return	–42.05%	–13.80%	–6.05%	–0.20%
Large Stocks Maximum Compound Return	68.49%	32.79%	28.65%	19.57%
Low P/Cashflow Large Stocks Minimum Compound Return	–34.58%	–7.67%	–1.95%	4.05%
Low P/Cashflow Large Stocks Maximum Compound Return	81.62%	35.59%	31.91%	23.33%
High P/Cashflow Large Stocks Minimum Compound Return	–80.63%	–45.08%	–20.54%	–4.34%
High P/Cashflow Large Stocks Maximum Compound Return	124.40%	36.99%	28.13%	20.13%
All Stocks Minimum Compound Return	–41.65%	–16.82%	–8.94%	0.68%
All Stocks Maximum Compound Return	81.51%	29.46%	27.02%	21.46%
Low P/Cashflow All Stocks Minimum Compound Return	–35.19%	–11.78%	–3.76%	5.66%
Low P/Cashflow All Stocks Maximum Compound Return	82.72%	35.98%	28.89%	21.68%
High P/Cashflow All Stocks Minimum Compound Return	–75.79%	–49.66%	–23.12%	–8.26%
High P/Cashflow All Stocks Maximum Compound Return	167.68%	43.01%	27.95%	18.62%

WORST-CASE SCENARIO AND BEST AND WORST RETURNS

Unlike the low price-to-cashflow stocks, returns here are abysmal. High price-to-cashflow stocks lost more than 30 percent from peak to trough six times, with bear market years being particularly brutal. In the bear market of the early 1970s, the high price-to-cashflow stocks from All Stocks lost 68 percent, whereas in the most recent bear market of 2000–2002, they lost a whopping 88 percent. Their best and worst case returns from the last 40 years put them well behind the All Stocks universe and dramatically behind the 50 stocks from All Stocks with the lowest price-to-cashflow ratios. Someone investing for a 10-year period and getting a return similar to the *worst* return over the prior 40 years would see $10,000 dwindle to just over $4,000. See Table 7-12 for details.

Large Stocks fared little better. The 50 stocks from the Large Stocks universe having the highest price-to-cashflow ratios also declined by more than

30 percent six times over the last 40 years and performed abysmally in the bear markets of 1973–1974 and 2000–2002. Both the best- and worst-case scenarios for the group lag the Large Stocks universe itself. They have very little to recommend them, with the exception of performing well in periods of speculative market frenzy. Table 7-19 shows the minimum and maximum returns on $10,000 for each strategy.

DECILES

The decile analysis of the All Stocks universe by price-to-cashflow conforms with what we've seen in previous chapters—stocks in the lowest deciles have much higher returns than stocks in the highest deciles. As we move from the lowest decile to the highest, risk skyrockets and returns plummet. The decile with the stocks having the lowest price-to-cashflows turned $10,000 invested in 1951 into $24,259,579 at the end of 2003, whereas the highest grew to just $478,296. What's more, the highest decile *took a greater risk than the lowest* when measured by the standard deviation of return.

The lowest decile from the Large Stocks universe generated even better returns. There, the lowest price-to-cashflow decile from the Large Stocks universe turned $10,000 into $30,377,718 by the end of 2003, nearly $27 million more than an investment in Large Stocks. Tables 7-17 and 7-18, as well as Figures 7-5 and 7-6 summarize the results.

T A B L E 7-17

Summary Results for Price-to-Cashflow Decile Analysis of All Stocks Universe, 1951–2003				
Decile	$10,000 Grows to:	Average Return	Compound Return	Standard Deviation
1 (Lowest P/Cashflow)	$24,259,579	18.54%	16.17%	23.72%
2	$21,588,654	17.67%	15.91%	20.42%
3	$9,038,589	15.70%	13.99%	19.73%
4	$3,680,472	13.25%	12.03%	16.53%
5	$4,292,974	13.79%	12.36%	17.60%
6	$5,508,016	14.38%	12.90%	17.73%
7	$2,708,954	12.58%	11.37%	16.12%
8	$1,387,613	11.85%	9.95%	19.80%
9	$1,440,372	12.03%	10.03%	20.41%
10 (Highest P/Cashflow)	$478,296	11.14%	7.72%	27.29%
All Stocks	$5,743,706	14.79%	13.00%	20.11%

T A B L E 7-18

Summary Results for Price-to-Cashflow Decile Analysis of Large Stocks Universe, 1951–2003

Decile	$10,000 Grows to:	Average Return	Compound Return	Standard Deviation
1 (Lowest P/Cashflow)	$30,377,718	18.49%	16.67%	21.06%
2	$6,640,167	14.66%	13.31%	17.52%
3	$3,546,509	13.14%	11.95%	16.21%
4	$3,437,088	13.10%	11.89%	16.48%
5	$2,930,327	12.58%	11.54%	15.19%
6	$1,723,912	11.62%	10.41%	16.09%
7	$2,969,013	12.82%	11.57%	16.39%
8	$1,357,041	11.39%	9.90%	17.69%
9	$1,150,822	11.21%	9.56%	18.59%
10 (Highest P/Cashflow)	$860,956	11.74%	8.95%	24.09%
Large Stocks	$3,173,724	12.99%	11.71%	16.84%

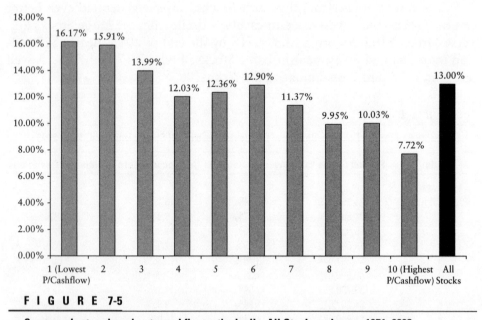

F I G U R E 7-5

Compound return by price-to-cashflow ratio decile, All Stocks universe, 1951–2003.

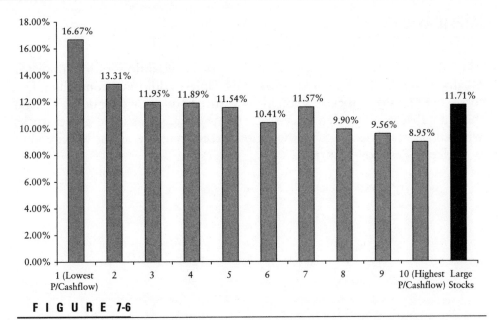

FIGURE 7-6

Compound return by price-to-cashflow ratio decile, Large Stocks universe, 1951–2003.

TABLE 7-19

Terminal Value of $10,000 Invested for Best and Worst Average Annual Compound Returns over Period for Monthly Data 1963–2003

For Any	1-Year Period	3-Year Period	5-Year Period	10-Year Period
Large Stocks Minimum $10,000 Value	$5,795.00	$6,405.04	$7,319.54	$9,801.79
Large Stocks Maximum $10,000 Value	$16,849.00	$23,415.11	$35,241.06	$69,737.00
Low P/Cashflow Large Stocks Minimum $10,000 Value	$6,542.00	$7,870.00	$9,061.00	$14,874.00
Low P/Cashflow Large Stocks Maximum $10,000 Value	$18,162.00	$24,930.00	$39,941.00	$81,423.00
High P/Cashflow Large Stocks Minimum $10,000 Value	$1,937.00	$1,656.00	$3,167.00	$6,414.00
High P/Cashflow Large Stocks Maximum $10,000 Value	$22,440.00	$25,707.00	$34,540.00	$62,573.00
All Stocks Minimum $10,000 Value	$5,835.00	$5,756.00	$6,260.00	$10,700.00
All Stocks Maximum $10,000 Value	$18,151.00	$21,680.00	$33,064.00	$69,868.00
Low P/Cashflow All Stocks Minimum $10,000 Value	$6,481.00	$6,865.00	$8,256.00	$17,349.00
Low P/Cashflow All Stocks Maximum $10,000 Value	$18,272.00	$25,145.00	$35,569.00	$71,137.00
High P/Cashflow All Stocks Minimum $10,000 Value	$2,421.00	$1,276.00	$2,685.00	$4,222.00
High P/Cashflow All Stocks Maximum $10,000 Value	$26,768.00	$29,250.00	$34,298.00	$55,176.00

IMPLICATIONS

The odds strongly favor stocks with low price-to-cashflow ratios. Both the 50-stock and the decile analysis prove this. Unless additional compelling factors exist (e.g., the stock is selected by a successful growth model's criteria that can absorb some high price-to-cashflow risk), you should avoid stocks with the highest price-to-cashflow ratios and concentrate on the lower end of the price-to-cashflow spectrum.

8
C H A P T E R

PRICE-TO-SALES RATIOS: THE KING OF THE VALUE FACTORS

For me the greatest beauty always lay in the greatest clarity.
—Gotthold Lessing

The final individual value ratio I'll review is also the best. A stock's price-to-sales ratio (PSR) is similar to its price-to-earning (PE) ratio, but measures the price of the company against annual sales instead of earnings. Like investors who favor low PE stocks, investors buy low PSR stocks because they believe they're getting a bargain. Ken Fisher says in his 1984 book *Super Stocks*, that a stock's PSR is "an almost perfect measure of popularity," warning that only hope and hype will increase the price of a stock with a high PSR.

I'll again look at both the 50 lowest PSR stocks and the 50 highest PSR stocks from both the All Stocks and Large Stocks universes. As with other ratios, I'll also look at how the two universes stack up when ranked by PSR deciles. All accounting data are time-lagged to avoid look-ahead bias, and the portfolios are rebalanced annually. Finally, because of Compustat's ranking function, I rank stocks by the 50 *highest* sales-to-price ratios (SPR), the inverse of the PSR ratio. I'll refer to them, however, as high and low PSR stocks throughout the chapter.

THE RESULTS

$10,000 invested on December 31, 1951 in the 50 lowest PSR stocks from the All Stocks universe grew to $22,012,919 by December 31, 2003, a compound return of 15.95 percent (Table 8-1). This dwarfs the $5,743,706 earned from the $10,000 invested in the All Stocks universe and beats the returns of each 50-stock value ratio I've studied. The strategy also performs well over time, with the low-PSR stocks from All Stocks beating the universe 88 percent of all rolling 10-year periods. The low-PSR stocks also do well on a risk-adjusted basis, with a Sharpe ratio of 50. Tables 8-1 and 8-2 summarize the returns of low-PSR stocks from the All Stocks and Large Stocks universes, and Table 8-3 compares the base rates for the strategy with All Stocks.

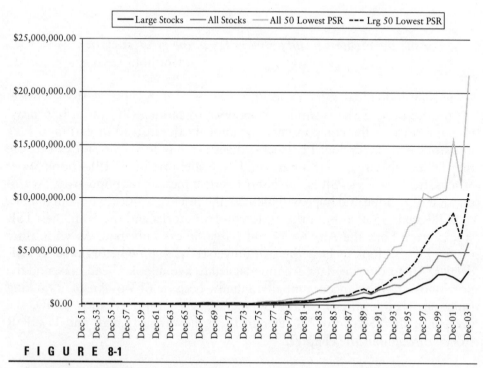

FIGURE 8-1

Returns on low PSR stocks versus All Stocks and Large Stocks, 1951–2003. Year-end 1951=$10,000.

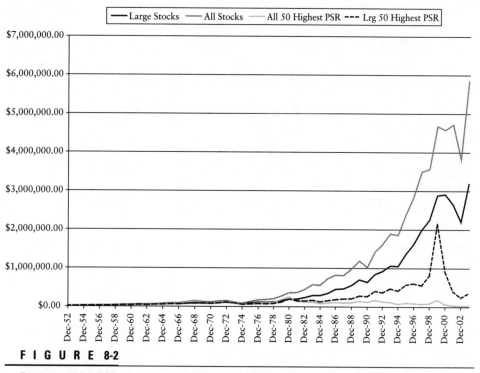

FIGURE 8-2

Returns on high PSR stocks versus All Stocks and Large Stocks, 1951–2003. Year-end 1951=$10,000.

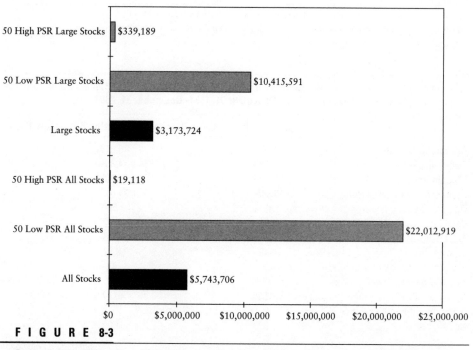

FIGURE 8-3

December 31, 2003 value of $10,000 invested on December 31, 1951 and annually rebalanced.

T A B L E 8-1

Summary Return and Risk Results for Annual Data, All Stocks, and 50 Highest Sales-to-Price (Low PSR) Stocks from All Stocks, December 31, 1951–December 31, 2003

	All Stocks	All Stocks, Top 50 Sales/Price (Low PSR)
Arithmetic Average	14.79%	19.01%
Geometric Average	13.00%	15.95%
Median Return	16.80%	13.55%
Standard Deviation of Return	20.11%	27.40%
Downside Risk—lower is better	7.17%	8.09%
Correlation with S&P 500	0.87	0.68
T-Statistic	5.30	5.00
Sharpe Ratio	0.46	0.50
Number of Positive Periods	39	40
Number of Negative Periods	13	12
Maximum Peak-to-Trough Decline (using monthly data series)	−50.12%	−52.15%
Beta	0.99	1.07
$10,000 becomes:	$5,743,706.00	$22,012,919.00
Minimum Annual Return	−27.90%	−28.80%
Maximum Annual Return	55.90%	87.56%
Minimum *Expected* Return*	−25.43%	−35.79%
Maximum *Expected* Return**	55.01%	73.81%

*Minimum Expected Return is Arithmetic Return minus 2 times the standard deviation.
**Maximum Expected Return is Arithmetic Return plus 2 times the standard deviation.

T A B L E 8-2

Summary Return and Risk Results for Annual Data, Large Stocks, and 50 Highest Sales-to-Price (Low PSR) Stocks from Large Stocks, December 31, 1951–December 31, 2003

	Large Stocks	Large Stocks, Top 50 Sales/Price (Low PSR)
Arithmetic Average	12.99%	16.31%
Geometric Average	11.71%	14.30%
Median Return	15.75%	15.60%
Standard Deviation of Return	16.84%	21.47%
Downside Risk—lower is better	5.86%	7.55%
Correlation with S&P 500	0.95	0.82
T-Statistic	5.56	5.48
Sharpe Ratio	0.45	0.51
Number of Positive Periods	39	42
Number of Negative Periods	13	10
Maximum Peak-to-Trough Decline (using monthly data series)	−46.59%	−40.71%
Beta	0.89	1.00

(continued on next page)

TABLE 8-2

Summary Return and Risk Results for Annual Data, Large Stocks, and 50 Highest Sales-to-Price (Low PSR) Stocks from Large Stocks, December 31, 1951–December 31, 2003 *(Continued)*

	Large Stocks	Large Stocks, Top 50 Sales/Price (Low PSR)
$10,000 becomes:	$3,173,724.00	$10,412,591.00
Minimum Annual Return	−26.70%	−26.76%
Maximum Annual Return	45.07%	66.05%
Minimum *Expected* Return*	−20.69%	−26.63%
Maximum *Expected* Return**	46.67%	59.25%

*Minimum Expected Return is Arithmetic Return minus 2 times the standard deviation.
**Maximum Expected Return is Arithmetic Return plus 2 times the standard deviation.

TABLE 8-3

Base Rates for All Stocks and 50 Highest Sales/Price (Low PSR) Stocks from All Stocks Universe, 1951–2003

Item	50 Low PSR Beat "All Stocks"	Percent
Single-Year Return	33 out of 52	63%
Rolling Five-Year Compound Return	31 out of 48	65%
Rolling 10-Year Compound Return	38 out of 43	88%

LARGE STOCKS WITH LOW PRICE-TO-SALES RATIOS DO WELL

Large stocks with low PSRs also beat the Large Stocks universe, but not by as much as those from the smaller-cap All Stocks universe. A $10,000 investment on December 31, 1951 was worth $10,412,591 at the end of 2003, a compound return of 14.30 percent. The return was considerably better than the $3,173,724 you'd earn if you invested $10,000 in the Large Stocks universe itself. We also see consistency here, and a high Sharpe ratio of 51. Compound return by decile is shown in Figure 8-4.

The rolling five- and 10-year base rates for both groups of low PSR stocks are outstanding—the best of all the value ratios. For all rolling 10-year periods, the Large Stocks group beat the universe 95 percent of the time, whereas the All Stocks group beat their universe 88 percent of the time. This consistency is rare—as you'll recall, several other low-ratio strategies exhibit far more erratic returns (Table 8-4).

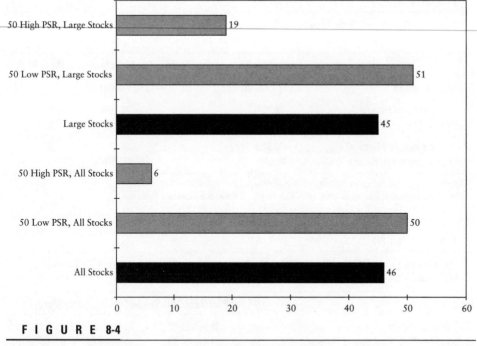

F I G U R E 8-4

Sharpe risk-adjusted return ratio, 1951–2003. (Higher is better.)

T A B L E 8-4

Base Rates for Large Stocks and 50 Highest Sales/Price (Low PSR) Stocks from Large Stocks Universe, 1951–2003

Item	50 Low PSR Beat "Large Stocks"	Percent
Single-Year Return	35 out of 52	67%
Rolling Five-Year Compound Return	35 out of 48	73%
Rolling 10-Year Compound Return	41 out of 43	95%

BEST- AND WORST-CASE SCENARIOS

Over the last 40 years, the lowest PSR stocks from All Stocks lost more than 30 percent from high to low on five occasions, and several of these declines came rapidly. Looking at Table 8-5, you see that the group lost more than 20 percent in just a few months five times. Anyone pursuing a low-PSR strategy should keep this in mind. As Table 8-6 shows, low-PSR stocks from the Large Stocks universe exhibit similar declines. During the worst five years, $10,000 invested in the 50 stocks with the lowest PSR from All Stocks declines to a little less than $6,000, whereas the low-PSR stocks from Large Stocks declined to slightly less than $8,000. Ten-year periods perform better, with both the low-PSR stocks from All Stocks and Large Stocks recording positive results during the worst 10-year periods. Table 8-18 shows the best- and worst-case returns for a $10,000 investment.

T A B L E 8-5

Worst-Case Scenarios: All 10 Percent or Greater Declines for 50 Stocks from All Stocks with Lowest PSR, December 31, 1962–December 31, 2003

Peak Date	Peak Index Value	Trough Date	Trough Index Value	Recovery Date	Decline (%)	Decline Duration	Recovery Duration
Jan-66	2.06	Nov-66	1.55	Jul-67	−24.68	10	8
Nov-68	3.27	Dec-74	1.57	Feb-76	−52.15	73	14
Aug-78	5.68	Oct-78	4.43	Mar-79	−21.94	2	5
Sep-79	7.00	Oct-79	6.26	Jan-80	−10.55	1	3
Jan-80	7.57	Mar-80	6.00	Aug-80	−20.77	2	5
May-81	9.91	Feb-82	7.87	Oct-82	−20.6	9	8
Jan-84	17.98	May-84	15.98	Sep-84	−11.16	4	4
Aug-87	43.99	Nov-87	28.17	Jan-89	−35.97	3	14
Aug-89	55.60	Oct-90	34.38	Aug-91	−38.16	14	10
Aug-91	55.87	Nov-91	49.82	Jan-92	−10.82	3	2
May-96	143.87	Jul-96	124.83	Jun-97	−13.24	2	11
Apr-98	206.51	Aug-98	141.75	Jan-01	−31.36	4	29
Jun-01	291.25	Oct-01	231.22	Mar-02	−20.61	4	5
Apr-02	317.57	Mar-03	163.96	Oct-03	−48.37	11	7
Average					−25.74	10.14	8.93

T A B L E 8-6

Worst-Case Scenarios: All 10 Percent or Greater Declines for 50 Stocks from Large Stocks with Lowest PSR, December 31, 1962–December 31, 2003

Peak Date	Peak Index Value	Trough Date	Trough Index Value	Recovery Date	Decline (%)	Decline Duration	Recovery Duration
Jan-66	1.93	Sep-66	1.61	Mar-67	−16.59	8	6
Jan-69	2.90	Jun-70	1.72	Nov-72	−40.71	17	29
Nov-72	2.93	Sep-74	1.91	May-75	−35.02	22	8
Jun-77	4.89	Oct-77	4.38	Apr-78	−10.32	4	6
Aug-78	5.85	Oct-78	4.99	Jun-79	−14.69	2	8
Aug-79	6.62	Mar-80	5.49	Jul-80	−17	7	4
May-81	8.45	Sep-81	7.17	Sep-82	−15.19	4	12
Jan-84	14.69	May-84	13.04	Sep-84	−11.22	4	4
Aug-87	32.50	Nov-87	21.49	Oct-88	−33.88	3	11
Aug-89	42.05	Oct-90	26.67	May-91	−36.58	14	7
Mar-98	177.43	Aug-98	144.08	Dec-98	−18.79	5	4

(continued on next page)

TABLE 8-6

Worst-Case Scenarios: All 10 Percent or Greater Declines for 50 Stocks from Large Stocks with Lowest PSR, December 31, 1962–December 31, 2003 *(Continued)*

Peak Date	Peak Index Value	Trough Date	Trough Index Value	Recovery Date	Decline (%)	Decline Duration	Recovery Duration
Jul-01	254.89	Sep-01	201.22	Mar-02	−21.06	2	6
Apr-02	257.88	Mar-03	158.08	Oct-03	−38.7	11	7
Average					−23.34	7.86	8.21

HIGH PSR STOCKS ARE TOXIC

The dubious honor of worst performance-to-date goes to those 50 stocks having the highest PSRs from the All Stocks universe: $10,000 invested on December 31, 1951, was worth just $19,118 at the end of 2003. You'd be vastly better off with T-bills, where the same $10,000 grows to $135,185! The Sharpe ratio is 6, the bottom of the barrel.

Let's catalog the carnage. The All Stocks universe beat the 50 highest PSR stocks 67 percent of the time in any given year. December 31, 1980 through December 31, 1984 is particularly gruesome: $10,000 invested in the All Stocks universe grew by more than 50 percent to $15,416, but an investment in the 50 stocks with the highest PSRs *fell* by 70 percent, turning $10,000 into $3,079. Unfortunately, such horrendous performance is not unique—the 50 stocks with the highest PSRs routinely underperform the All Stocks universe, regardless of what the market is doing. The only real exceptions are during extremely speculative markets. If you look at the annual data for the high-PSR stocks from All Stocks at www.whatworksonwallstreet.com, you'll see that their two best years were at the peak of the stock market bubbles in 1999 and 1967. In virtually all other market environments, these stocks are at the very bottom of the return barrel, rarely posting positive returns, whatever the stock market environment.

Looking at five-year rolling returns, the All Stocks universe beat the high-PSR stocks 87 percent of the time. On a rolling 10-year basis, the All Stocks universe beat high-PSR stocks 84 percent of the time. Yet, look at 1995 and 1999 at www.whatworksonwallstreet.com, two years during which the overhyped stocks that typically dominate the highest PSR group from All Stocks soared in value: In 1995, they gained 56 percent, swamping All Stocks' gain of 29 percent, whereas in 1999, they soared more than 112 percent, 80 percent better than All Stocks. Imagine how you would feel looking at the one-year performance of these sexy story stocks. The urge to join the bandwagon would be overwhelming, but the fullness of time shows how disastrous that decision would be. Indeed, 1996 and 1997 shows the group reverting to their base rate by *losing* roughly 15 percent in those bull market years. And finally, the high-PSR stocks' swan song: A loss of nearly 95 percent in the aftermath of the March 2000 market bubble.

LARGE STOCKS DO A LITTLE BETTER

Large Stocks paint only a slightly brighter picture. Here, $10,000 invested in the 50 stocks with the highest PSRs on December 31, 1951 grows to $339,189, a compound return of 7.01 percent. That's a fraction of what you'd earn from the Large Stocks universe, but much better than the 50 high-PSR stocks from All Stocks. The Sharpe ratio is 19, considerably below the Large Stocks universe's 45. All base rates are negative, with the 50 highest PSR stocks from Large Stocks underperforming the Large Stocks universe 70 percent of the time over all 10-year periods. Tables 8-7 through 8-12 summarize the damage. Compound returns are summarized in Tables 8-13 through 8-15.

T A B L E 8-7

Summary Return and Risk Results for Annual Data, All Stocks, and 50 Lowest SPR (High PSR) Stocks from All Stocks, December 31, 1951–December 31, 2003

	All Stocks	All Stocks, Bottom 50 Sales/ Price (High PSR)
Arithmetic Average	14.79%	7.20%
Geometric Average	13.00%	1.25%
Median Return	16.80%	8.35%
Standard Deviation of Return	20.11%	34.51%
Downside Risk—lower is better	7.17%	19.63%
Correlation with S&P 500	0.87	0.66
T-Statistic	5.30	1.50
Sharpe Ratio	0.46	0.06
Number of Positive Periods	39	33
Number of Negative Periods	13	19
Maximum Peak-to-Trough Decline (using monthly data series)	−50.12%	−95.94%
Beta	0.99	1.3
$10,000 becomes:	$5,743,706.00	$19,118.00
Minimum Annual Return	−27.90%	−65.14%
Maximum Annual Return	55.90%	112.16%
Minimum *Expected* Return*	−25.43%	−61.82%
Maximum *Expected* Return**	55.01%	76.22%

*Minimum Expected Return is Arithmetic Return minus 2 times the standard deviation.
**Maximum Expected Return is Arithmetic Return plus 2 times the standard deviation.

T A B L E 8-8

Summary Return and Risk Results for Annual Data, Large Stocks, and 50 Lowest SPR (High PSR) Stocks from Large Stocks, December 31, 1951–December 31, 2003

	Large Stocks	Large Stocks, Bottom 50 Sales/ Price (High PSR)
Arithmetic Average	12.99%	11.81%
Geometric Average	11.71%	7.01%
Median Return	15.75%	11.40%
Standard Deviation of Return	16.84%	33.81%
Downside Risk—lower is better	5.86%	15.09%
Correlation with S&P 500	0.95	0.61
T-Statistic	5.56	2.52
Sharpe Ratio	0.45	0.19
Number of Positive Periods	39	36
Number of Negative Periods	13	16
Maximum Peak-to-Trough Decline (using monthly data series)	−46.59%	−93.36%
Beta	0.89	1.18
$10,000 becomes:	$3,173,724.00	$339,189.00
Minimum Annual Return	−26.70%	−58.45%
Maximum Annual Return	45.07%	164.82%
Minimum *Expected* Return*	−20.69%	−55.81%
Maximum *Expected* Return**	46.67%	79.43%

*Minimum Expected Return is Arithmetic Return minus 2 times the standard deviation.
**Maximum Expected Return is Arithmetic Return plus 2 times the standard deviation.

T A B L E 8-9

Base Rates for All Stocks and 50 Highest PSR Stocks from All Stocks Universe, 1951–2003

Item	50 High PSR Beat "All Stocks"	Percent
Single-Year Return	17 out of 52	33%
Rolling Five-Year Compound Return	6 out of 48	13%
Rolling 10-Year Compound Return	7 out of 43	16%

T A B L E 8-10

Base Rates for Large Stocks and 50 Highest PSR Stocks from Large Stocks Universe, 1951–2003

Item	50 High PSR Beat "Large Stocks"	Percent
Single-Year Return	24 out of 52	46%
Rolling Five-Year Compound Return	18 out of 48	38%
Rolling 10-Year Compound Return	13 out of 43	30%

T A B L E 8-11

Worst-Case Scenarios: All 10 Percent or Greater Declines for 50 Stocks from All Stocks with Highest PSR, December 31, 1962–December 31, 2003

Peak Date	Peak Index Value	Trough Date	Trough Index Value	Recovery Date	Decline (%)	Decline Duration	Recovery Duration
Apr-66	1.67	Sep-66	1.39	Feb-67	−16.86	5	5
Jan-69	3.32	Feb-69	2.93	May-69	−11.71	1	3
May-69	3.37	Sep-74	1.24	Sep-79	−63.32	64	60
Feb-80	4.88	Mar-80	3.47	Aug-80	−28.89	1	5
Nov-80	6.37	Feb-03	0.26		−95.94	267	NA
Average					−43.34	67.6	18.25

T A B L E 8-12

Worst-Case Scenarios: All 10 Percent or Greater Declines for 50 Stocks from Large Stocks with Highest PSR, December 31, 1962–December 31, 2003

Peak Date	Peak Index Value	Trough Date	Trough Index Value	Recovery Date	Decline (%)	Decline Duration	Recovery Duration
Apr-66	1.62	Aug-66	1.39	Jan-67	−14.39	4	5
Dec-67	1.95	Feb-68	1.69	May-68	−12.88	2	3
Nov-68	2.15	Jul-69	1.85	Nov-69	−13.81	8	4
Nov-69	2.18	Jun-70	1.36	Feb-72	−37.68	7	20
Dec-72	2.60	Sep-74	1.14	Dec-79	−56.33	21	63
Feb-80	3.19	Mar-80	2.43	Jun-80	−23.64	1	3
Nov-80	4.83	Jul-82	2.36	Jun-83	−51.22	20	11
Jun-83	4.86	Jul-84	3.04	Jan-87	−37.33	13	30
Aug-87	6.75	Nov-87	4.73	Aug-89	−29.89	3	21
Dec-89	7.33	Oct-90	5.50	Feb-91	−24.92	10	4
Dec-91	9.95	Apr-92	7.88	Aug-93	−20.82	4	16
Jan-94	11.16	Jun-94	9.17	Jun-95	−17.83	5	12
May-96	15.74	Apr-97	11.82	Jun-98	−24.94	11	14
Jun-98	16.19	Aug-98	12.32	Nov-98	−23.89	2	3
Feb-00	74.34	Sep-02	4.93		−93.36	31	NA
Average					−32.2	9.47	14.93

T A B L E 8-13

Average Annual Compound Return by Decade

Portfolio	1950s*	1960s	1970s	1980s	1990s	2000s**
Large Stocks	15.33%	8.99%	6.99%	16.89%	15.34%	2.40%
50 High Price-to-Sales from Large Stocks	13.21%	11.73%	3.23%	9.54%	22.56%	−36.87%

(continued on next page)

T A B L E 8-13

Average Annual Compound Return by Decade *(Continued)*

Portfolio	1950s*	1960s	1970s	1980s	1990s	2000s**
50 Low Price-to-Sales from Large Stocks	16.39%	9.48%	10.90%	20.09%	17.19%	9.86%
All Stocks	19.22%	11.09%	8.53%	15.85%	14.75%	5.91%
50 High Price-to-Sales from All Stocks	14.96%	11.99%	5.82%	−2.02%	2.46%	−42.37%
50 Low Price-to-Sales from All Stocks	20.85%	11.15%	14.80%	20.43%	12.28%	19.94%

*Returns for 1952–1959
**Returns for 2000–2003

T A B L E 8-14

Best and Worst Average Annual Compound Returns over Period for Annual Data 1951–2003

For Any	1-Year Period	3-Year Period	5-Year Period	10-Year Period
Large Stocks Minimum Compound Return	−26.70%	−11.93%	−4.37%	1.21%
Large Stocks Maximum Compound Return	45.07%	24.39%	22.40%	17.01%
Low PSR Large Stocks Minimum Compound Return	−26.76%	−10.66%	−5.80%	1.75%
Low PSR Large Stocks Maximum Compound Return	66.05%	34.67%	27.53%	23.16%
High PSR Large Stocks Minimum Compound Return	−58.45%	−52.57%	−16.02%	−4.59%
High PSR Large Stocks Maximum Compound Return	164.82%	53.08%	39.36%	22.56%
All Stocks Minimum Compound Return	−27.90%	−16.48%	−7.81%	1.26%
All Stocks Maximum Compound Return	55.90%	31.23%	27.77%	21.31%
Low PSR All Stocks Minimum Compound Return	−28.80%	−12.63%	−7.65%	3.06%
Low PSR All Stocks Maximum Compound Return	87.56%	39.54%	36.97%	28.61%
High PSR All Stocks Minimum Compound Return	−65.14%	−57.68%	−28.35%	−20.04%
High PSR All Stocks Maximum Compound Return	112.16%	37.15%	29.75%	18.71%

T A B L E 8-15

Best and Worst Average Annual Compound Returns over Period for Monthly Data 1963–2003

For Any	1-Year Period	3-Year Period	5-Year Period	10-Year Period
Large Stocks Minimum Compound Return	−42.05%	−13.80%	−6.05%	−0.20%
Large Stocks Maximum Compound Return	68.49%	32.79%	28.65%	19.57%
Low PSR Large Stocks Minimum Compound Return	−38.69%	−10.48%	−4.99%	2.78%
Low PSR Large Stocks Maximum Compound Return	83.05%	37.45%	33.70%	22.93%
High PSR Large Stocks Minimum Compound Return	−84.29%	−58.35%	−19.38%	−4.91%
High PSR Large Stocks Maximum Compound Return	232.55%	78.15%	50.05%	27.12%

(continued on next page)

T A B L E   8-15

Best and Worst Average Annual Compound Returns over Period for Monthly Data 1963–2003
(Continued)

For Any	1-Year Period	3-Year Period	5-Year Period	10-Year Period
All Stocks Minimum Compound Return	−41.65%	−16.82%	−8.94%	0.68%
All Stocks Maximum Compound Return	81.51%	29.46%	27.02%	21.46%
Low PSR All Stocks Minimum Compound Return	−46.07%	−17.47%	−9.87%	0.63%
Low PSR All Stocks Maximum Compound Return	108.39%	44.97%	38.83%	28.15%
High PSR All Stocks Minimum Compound Return	−79.97%	−62.97%	−30.53%	−20.16%
High PSR All Stocks Maximum Compound Return	157.91%	45.16%	35.41%	13.42%

DECILES

The decile returns for PSRs are stunning. Look at Table 8-16 and Figure 8-5. Total returns march downhill, from a compound return of 17.46 percent for the decile of stocks having the lowest PSRs to an abysmal 3.12 percent for the decile of the stocks having the highest PSRs. A $10,000 investment in 1951, in the lowest PSR decile from the All Stocks universe, annually rebalanced, was worth $43.1 million at the end of 2003. Over the same period, a $10,000 investment in the highest PSR decile grew to a paltry $49,482. The PSR also shows the most consistent decile performance, with declining decile returns from low to high.

T A B L E   8-16

Summary Results for Price-to-Sales Decile Analysis of All Stocks Universe, 1951–2003

Decile	$10,000 Grows to:	Average Return	Compound Return	Standard Deviation
1 (Lowest PSR)	$43,132,389	19.35%	17.46%	21.28%
2	$26,169,902	17.98%	16.34%	19.47%
3	$24,450,379	17.89%	16.19%	19.79%
4	$18,231,032	17.20%	15.53%	19.38%
5	$8,772,840	15.76%	13.92%	20.12%
6	$5,955,426	14.84%	13.07%	19.58%
7	$2,797,020	13.18%	11.44%	19.07%
8	$1,343,886	11.52%	9.88%	18.46%
9	$301,863	9.04%	6.77%	21.54%
10 (Highest PSR)	$49,482	7.01%	3.12%	28.06%
All Stocks	$5,743,706	14.79%	13.00%	20.11%

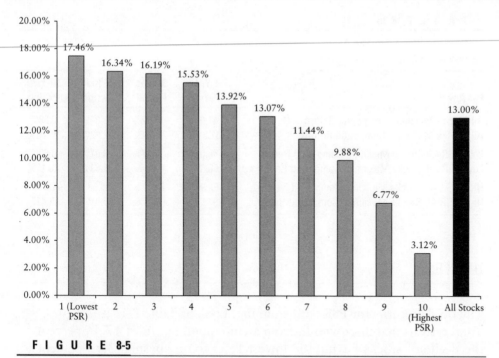

F I G U R E 8-5

Compound return by price-to-sales ratio decile, All Stocks universe, 1951–2003.

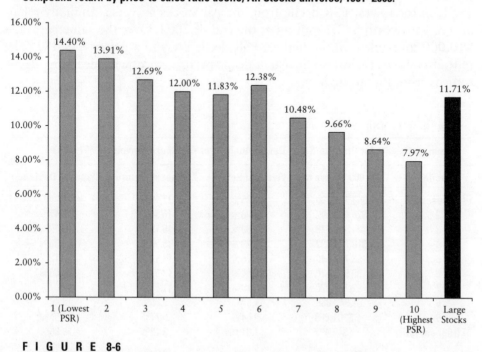

F I G U R E 8-6

Compound return by PSR decile, Large Stocks universe, 1951–2003.

Large Stocks show similar—although more muted—findings. Here, the bottom six PSR deciles outperformed the Large Stocks universe, whereas the higher PSR deciles (seven through ten) did significantly worse. Table 8-17 and Figure 8-6 summarize the findings for Large Stocks.

T A B L E 8-17

Summary Results for PSR Decile Analysis of Large Stocks Universe, 1951–2003

Decile	$10,000 Grows to:	Average Return	Compound Return	Standard Deviation
1 (Lowest PSR)	$10,917,903	16.30%	14.40%	20.71%
2	$8,721,233	15.55%	13.91%	19.62%
3	$4,981,062	14.03%	12.69%	17.20%
4	$3,626,432	13.18%	12.00%	16.11%
5	$3,352,285	13.14%	11.83%	16.88%
6	$4,325,377	13.56%	12.38%	16.10%
7	$1,785,171	11.60%	10.48%	15.45%
8	$1,211,504	10.76%	9.66%	15.09%
9	$743,314	10.15%	8.64%	17.56%
10 (Highest PSR)	$539,062	11.30%	7.97%	26.10%
Large Stocks	$3,173,724	12.99%	11.71%	16.84%

T A B L E 8-18

Terminal Value of $10,000 Invested for Best and Worst Average Annual Compound Returns over Period for Monthly Data 1963–2003

For Any	1-Year Period	3-Year Period	5-Year Period	10-Year Period
Large Stocks Minimum $10,000 Value	$5,795.00	$6,405.04	$7,319.54	$9,801.79
Large Stocks Maximum $10,000 Value	$16,849.00	$23,415.11	$35,241.06	$69,737.00
Low PSR Large Stocks Minimum $10,000 Value	$6,131.00	$7,174.00	$7,744.00	$13,154.00
Low PSR Large Stocks Maximum $10,000 Value	$18,305.00	$25,979.00	$42,716.00	$78,824.00
High PSR Large Stocks Minimum $10,000 Value	$1,571.00	$723.00	$3,406.00	$6,044.00
High PSR Large Stocks Maximum $10,000 Value	$33,255.00	$56,539.00	$76,071.00	$110,219.00
All Stocks Minimum $10,000 Value	$5,835.00	$5,756.00	$6,260.00	$10,700.00
All Stocks Maximum $10,000 Value	$18,151.00	$21,680.00	$33,064.00	$69,868.00
Low PSR All Stocks Minimum $10,000 Value	$5,393.00	$5,622.00	$5,948.00	$10,643.00
Low PSR All Stocks Maximum $10,000 Value	$20,839.00	$30,465.00	$51,565.00	$119,430.00
High PSR All Stocks Minimum $10,000 Value	$2,003.00	$508.00	$1,618.00	$1,052.00
High PSR All Stocks Maximum $10,000 Value	$25,791.00	$30,589.00	$45,526.00	$35,227.00

IMPLICATIONS

Low PSRs beat the market more than any other value ratio and do so more consistently, in both the 50-stock portfolios and decile returns. Low PSR stocks from both the All Stocks and Large Stocks groups beat their respective universes in every decade except the 1990s, during which the second half of the decade became one of the largest stock market bubbles in history. The only time both Large Stock and All Stock high-PSR stocks beat the benchmarks was in the 1960s, an era dominated by performance-obsessed managers who would pay any price for a stock with a good story. Indeed, 1967 was the second-best year for high PSR stocks drawn from All Stocks. In his book *101 Years on Wall Street*, John Dennis Brown calls 1967: "...a vintage year for speculators. About 45 percent of all issues listed at the NYSE would gain 50 percent or more." Thus, high-PSR stocks perform best in frothy, speculative markets but do poorly in all other years. Amazingly, during the speculative 1967 market, *low*-PSR stocks still did well.

The decile analysis confirms that of all the value ratios, PSR is the most consistent and best guide for future performance.

9
C H A P T E R

DIVIDEND YIELDS: BUYING AN INCOME

October. This is one of the peculiarly dangerous months to speculate in stocks. The others are July, January, September, April, November, May, March, June, December, August, and February.

—Mark Twain

Investors who find all months peculiarly dangerous often seek redemption in stocks with high dividend yields. Because dividends have historically accounted for more than half a stock's total return, they think it wise to concentrate on stocks paying high dividends. What's more, it's impossible to monkey with a dividend yield, because a company must either pay, defer, or cancel it.

You find a stock's dividend yield by dividing the indicated annual dividend rate by the current price of the stock. The result is then multiplied by 100 to make it a percentage. Thus, if a company pays an annual dividend of $1 and the current price of the stock is $10, the dividend yield is 10 percent.

We'll look at buying the 50 highest-yielding stocks from the All Stocks and Large Stocks universes. We're going to *exclude* utility stocks, because they would dominate the list if included.

143

THE RESULTS

As Tables 9-1 through 9-7 show, the effectiveness of investing in a 50-stock high dividend yield portfolio increases as the size of the companies you buy increases. Reviewing Tables 9-1 and 9-3, we see that the 50 high-yielding stocks drawn from All Stocks managed to beat the All Stocks Universe through 2003, something they failed to do in earlier editions of this book (Table 9-1). Over the last seven years, more Real Estate Investment Trusts (REITs) and American Depository Receipts (ADRs) have been added to the Compustat database, many of which had high dividend yields and went on to perform well.

T A B L E 9-1

Summary Return and Risk Results for Annual Data, All Stocks, and 50 Highest Dividend Yield Stocks from All Stocks, December 31, 1951–December 31, 2003

	All Stocks	All Stocks, Top 50 Dividend Yield
Arithmetic Average	14.79%	15.46%
Geometric Average	13.00%	13.35%
Median Return	16.80%	14.25%
Standard Deviation of Return	20.11%	21.81%
Downside Risk—lower is better	7.17%	7.99%
Correlation with S&P 500	0.87	0.74
T-Statistic	5.30	5.11
Sharpe Ratio	0.46	0.45
Number of Positive Periods	39	40
Number of Negative Periods	13	12
Maximum Peak-to-Trough Decline (using monthly data series)	−50.12%	−57.23%
Beta	0.99	0.91
$10,000 becomes:	$5,743,706.00	$6,752,640.00
Minimum Annual Return	−27.90%	−40.50%
Maximum Annual Return	55.90%	62.49%
Minimum *Expected* Return*	−25.43%	−28.16%
Maximum *Expected* Return**	55.01%	59.08%

*Minimum Expected Return is Arithmetic Return minus 2 times the standard deviation.
**Maximum Expected Return is Arithmetic Return plus 2 times the standard deviation.

T A B L E 9-2

Summary Return and Risk Results for Annual Data, Large Stocks, and 50 Highest Dividend Yield Stocks from Large Stocks, December 31, 1951–December 31, 2003

	Large Stocks	Large Stocks, Top 50 Dividend Yield
Arithmetic Average	12.99%	15.02%
Geometric Average	11.71%	13.64%
Median Return	15.75%	14.86%
Standard Deviation of Return	16.84%	18.19%
Downside Risk—lower is better	5.86%	4.42%
Correlation with S&P 500	0.95	0.79
T-Statistic	5.56	5.95
Sharpe Ratio	0.45	0.52
Number of Positive Periods	39	41
Number of Negative Periods	13	11
Maximum Peak-to-Trough Decline (using monthly data series)	−46.59%	−28.95%
Beta	0.89	0.81
$10,000 becomes:	$3,173,724.00	$7,715,190.00
Minimum Annual Return	−26.70%	−16.50%
Maximum Annual Return	45.07%	61.13%
Minimum *Expected* Return*	−20.69%	−21.36%
Maximum *Expected* Return**	46.67%	51.40%

*Minimum Expected Return is Arithmetic Return minus 2 times the standard deviation.
**Maximum Expected Return is Arithmetic Return plus 2 times the standard deviation.

T A B L E 9-3

Base Rates for All Stocks and 50 Highest Dividend Yield Stocks from All Stocks Universe, 1951–2003

Item	50 High Dividend Yield Stocks Beat "All Stocks"	Percent
Single-Year Return	27 out of 52	52%
Rolling Five-Year Compound Return	17 out of 48	40%
Rolling 10-Year Compound Return	12 out of 43	28%

T A B L E 9-4

Base Rates for Large Stocks and 50 Highest Dividend Yield Stocks from Large Stocks Universe, 1951–2003

Item	50 Highest Dividend Yield Stocks Beat "Large Stocks"	Percent
Single-Year Return	30 out of 52	58%
Rolling Five-Year Compound Return	32 out of 48	67%
Rolling 10-Year Compound Return	37 out of 43	86%

T A B L E 9-5

Worst-Case Scenarios: All 10 Percent or Greater Declines for 50 Stocks from All Stocks with Highest Dividend Yields, December 31, 1962–December 31, 2003

Peak Date	Peak Index Value	Trough Date	Trough Index Value	Recovery Date	Decline (%)	Decline Duration	Recovery Duration
Jan-66	1.89	Sep-66	1.54	Mar-67	−18.38	8	6
Jan-69	3.18	Jun-70	2.15	Apr-71	−32.54	17	10
Apr-71	3.24	Nov-71	2.87	Jan-72	−11.43	7	2
Nov-72	3.60	Dec-74	1.54	Apr-78	−57.23	25	40
Sep-78	4.07	Oct-78	3.63	Apr-79	−10.67	1	6
Aug-79	4.74	Mar-80	3.93	Jul-80	−17.07	7	4
Jan-84	9.34	Jul-84	8.30	Sep-84	−11.14	6	2
Jul-87	13.47	Oct-90	9.35	Aug-91	−30.56	39	10
Jul-98	53.12	Feb-99	45.43	Apr-99	−14.48	7	2
Apr-02	98.54	Sep-02	76.16	May-03	−22.71	5	8
Average					−22.62	12.2	9

T A B L E 9-6

Worst-Case Scenarios: All 10 Percent or Greater Declines for 50 Stocks from Large Stocks with Highest Dividend Yields, December 31, 1962–December 31, 2003

Peak Date	Peak Index Value	Trough Date	Trough Index Value	Recovery Date	Decline (%)	Decline Duration	Recovery Duration
Jan-66	1.68	Sep-66	1.34	Mar-67	−19.89	8	6
Jan-69	2.46	Jun-70	1.75	Feb-71	−28.95	17	8
Apr-71	2.65	Nov-71	2.35	Jan-72	−11.47	7	2
Nov-72	2.99	Sep-74	2.30	Feb-75	−23.11	22	5
Jun-75	3.64	Sep-75	3.24	Jan-76	−11.07	3	4
Aug-78	6.06	Oct-78	5.42	Mar-79	−10.57	2	5
Aug-79	7.13	Mar-80	6.30	Jun-80	−11.61	7	3
Mar-84	16.31	Jul-84	14.06	Sep-84	−13.81	4	2
Aug-87	32.48	Nov-87	23.76	Jan-89	−26.83	3	14
Aug-89	39.83	Oct-90	28.43	Jul-91	−28.63	14	9
May-92	47.13	Oct-92	41.97	Mar-93	−10.95	5	5
Mar-98	119.35	Aug-98	98.22	Apr-99	−17.71	5	8
Jun-01	162.45	Oct-01	140.23	Mar-02	−13.68	4	5
May-02	168.21	Sep-02	134.47	May-03	−20.06	4	8
Average					−17.74	7.5	6

T A B L E 9-7

Average Annual Compound Rates of Return by Decade

Portfolio	1950s*	1960s	1970s	1980s	1990s	2000s**
Large Stocks	15.33%	8.99%	6.99%	16.89%	15.34%	2.40%
50 Highest Dividend Yield from Large Stocks	15.20%	9.82%	11.44%	17.15%	13.89%	16.56%
All Stocks	19.22%	11.09%	8.53%	15.85%	14.75%	5.91%
50 Highest Dividend Yield from All Stocks	20.29%	10.54%	6.55%	11.20%	16.25%	23.17%

*Returns for 1952–1959.
**Returns for 2000–2003.

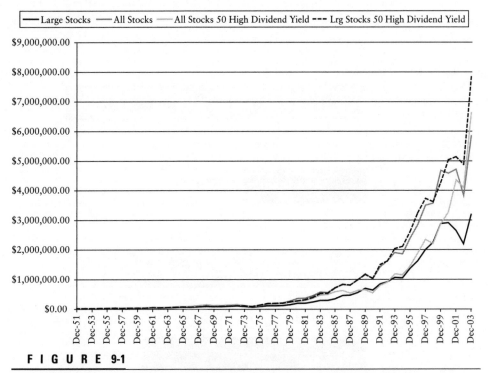

F I G U R E 9-1

Returns on high dividend stocks versus All Stocks and Large Stocks, 1951–2003. Year-end 1951=$10,000.

A \$10,000 investment in the 50 highest-yielding stocks from the All Stocks universe on December 31, 1951 was worth \$6,752,640 at the end of 2003, over \$1 million more than an investment in the All Stocks universe. However, the strategy has a lower Sharpe ratio than All Stocks, because it took more risk to generate the moderately better absolute performance. And, although the high dividend yielding stocks from All Stocks managed to come from behind over the last seven years, Table 9-3 shows that the strategy beat the universe only 28 percent of the time over all rolling 10-year periods, thus making it a poor strategy for investors over the long-term.

LARGE STOCKS ENTIRELY DIFFERENT

The returns of the 50 high-yielding large stocks are entirely different. Here, we see the 50 highest-yielding stocks perform twice as well as the Large Stock

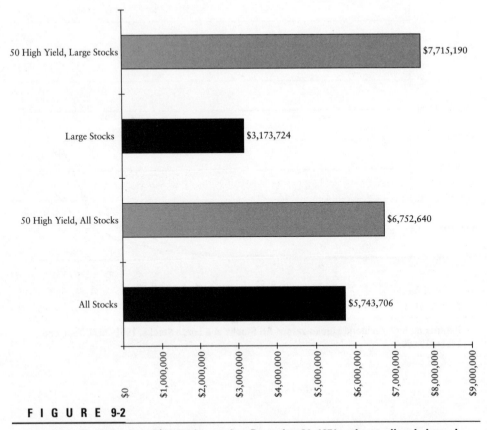

FIGURE 9-2

December 31, 2003 value of \$10,000 invested on December 31, 1951 and annually rebalanced.

universe, with virtually the same risk. A $10,000 investment in the 50 highest-yielding stocks from the Large Stocks universe on December 31, 1951 grew to $7,715,190 by the end of 2003 (Table 9-2). That's a compound return of 13.64 percent, some 1.93 percent better than the Large Stocks universe's return of 11.71 percent. The 50 highest-yielding stocks from Large Stocks had a standard deviation of return of 18.19 percent, slightly higher than the Large Stocks universe itself. This, coupled with the higher absolute return, accounts for the high Sharpe ratio of 52 (Figure 9-3). In absolute terms, the strategy is less risky than Large Stocks. The largest loss the strategy ever endured was a drop of 28.95 percent between January 1969 and June 1970, whereas the Large Stocks universe declined by 46.59 percent between November 1972 and September 1974.

The high-yield strategy is also far more consistent when used with Large Stocks. Here, the 50 highest-yielding stocks beat the universe 86 percent of the time over all rolling 10-year periods and never had a five-year period where they lost money. We'll see in Chapter 17 that dividend yield can be an even stronger strategy when combined with market-leading companies.

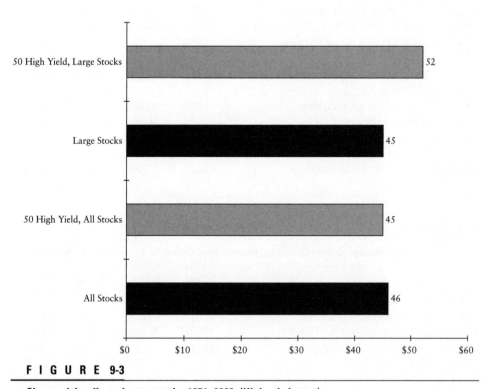

FIGURE 9-3

Sharpe risk-adjusted return ratio, 1951–2003. (Higher is better.)

149

WORST-CASE SCENARIOS

As we've seen before, the worst-case scenario for All Stocks is more frightening than for that of Large Stocks. The high-yielding stocks from the All Stocks universe suffered three declines exceeding 30 percent, with their worst showing a loss of over 57 percent during the bear market of the early 1970s. It then took them four years to regain their old highs (Tables 9-5 and 9-6). Looking at best- and worst-case scenarios on an annualized basis, the high-yielding stocks from All Stocks' worst five years turned $10,000 into just under $6,000 (Tables 9-8 and 9-9). This is hardly the type of return that a risk-averse investor would hope for, and it serves as a reminder that capitalization really matters when searching for returns through higher dividend yields.

T A B L E 9-8

Best and Worst Average Annual Compound Returns over Period for Annual Data 1951–2003

For Any	1-Year Period	3-Year Period	5-Year Period	10-Year Period
Large Stocks Minimum Compound Return	−26.70%	−11.93%	−4.37%	1.21%
Large Stocks Maximum Compound Return	45.07%	24.39%	22.40%	17.01%
High Dividend Yield Large Stocks Minimum Compound Return	−16.50%	−4.40%	0.48%	4.20%
High Dividend Yield Large Stocks Maximum Compound Return	61.13%	31.00%	22.67%	19.98%
All Stocks Minimum Compound Return	−27.90%	−16.48%	−7.81%	1.26%
All Stocks Maximum Compound Return	55.90%	31.23%	27.77%	21.31%
High Dividend Yield All Stocks Minimum Compound Return	−40.50%	−18.14%	−8.99%	0.67%
High Dividend Yield All Stocks Maximum Compound Return	62.49%	32.20%	24.75%	20.70%

T A B L E 9-9

Best and Worst Average Annual Compound Returns over Period for Monthly Data 1963–2003

For Any	1-Year Period	3-Year Period	5-Year Period	10-Year Period
Large Stocks Minimum Compound Return	−42.05%	−13.80%	−6.05%	−0.20%
Large Stocks Maximum Compound Return	68.49%	32.79%	28.65%	19.57%
High Dividend Yield Large Stocks Minimum Compound Return	−24.12%	−4.40%	0.63%	4.87%

(continued on next page)

TABLE 9-9

Best and Worst Average Annual Compound Returns over Period for Monthly Data 1963–2003
(Continued)

For Any	1-Year Period	3-Year Period	5-Year Period	10-Year Period
High Dividend Yield Large Stocks Maximum Compound Return	67.08%	32.22%	29.93%	21.66%
All Stocks Minimum Compound Return	−41.65%	−16.82%	−8.94%	0.68%
All Stocks Maximum Compound Return	81.51%	29.46%	27.02%	21.46%
High Dividend Yield All Stocks Minimum Compound Return	−46.79%	−21.20%	−9.91%	0.67%
High Dividend Yield All Stocks Maximum Compound Return	64.33%	36.92%	27.77%	21.88%

Large stocks with high dividend yields show a much smoother ride. Their single largest decline was a loss of 28.95 percent, which they recovered from in just six months. Although the high-yielding large stocks lost more than 20 percent from peak to trough five times, they also demonstrate the ability to snap back quickly from their losses. Looking at the best- and worst-case scenarios on an annualized basis, the high-yielding large stocks never had a five-year period during which they lost money, with their worst performance turning $10,000 into $10,317. They also had consistently better minimum and maximum returns over all time periods.

DECILES

The high-dividend yield decile analysis paints a somewhat different picture (Figures 9-4 and 9-5). Here, we see the top four deciles doing better than the All Stocks universe itself, whereas deciles five through ten—with lower dividend yields—didn't beat the benchmark. Contrasting this with the 50-stock portfolios we reviewed, you're better off simply selecting broadly from higher-yielding stocks from among All Stocks, rather than focusing on those stocks with the absolute highest yields.

The Large Stocks decile analysis shows that you're still better off focusing on the highest yielding stocks from the Large Stocks universe. Tables 9-10 and 9-11 and Figures 9-4 and 9-5 summarize the results.

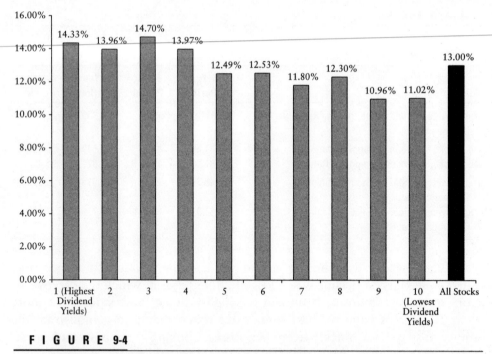

F I G U R E 9-4

Compound return by dividend yield decile, All Stocks universe, 1951–2003.

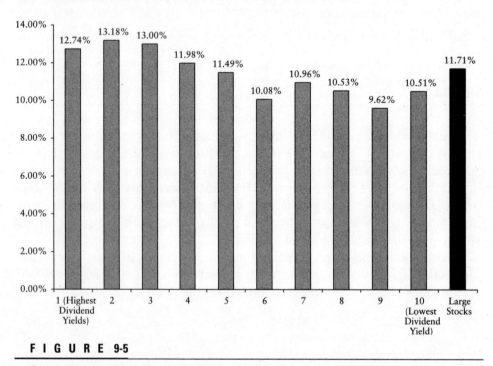

F I G U R E 9-5

Compound return by dividend yield decile, Large Stocks universe, 1951–2003.

T A B L E 9-10

Summary Results for Dividend Yield Decile Analysis of All Stocks Universe, 1951–2003

Decile	$10,000 Grows to:	Average Return	Compound Return	Standard Deviation
1 (Highest Dividend Yields)	$10,579,773	15.98%	14.33%	19.39%
2	$8,917,620	15.35%	13.96%	18.00%
3	$12,528,595	16.03%	14.70%	17.53%
4	$8,970,051	15.25%	13.97%	17.07%
5	$4,542,793	13.91%	12.49%	17.63%
6	$4,626,259	14.31%	12.53%	19.52%
7	$3,298,452	13.76%	11.80%	20.42%
8	$4,164,599	14.48%	12.30%	21.90%
9	$2,236,343	13.19%	10.96%	21.75%
10 (Lowest Dividend Yields)	$2,290,506	13.91%	11.02%	24.90%
All Stocks	$5,743,706	14.79%	13.00%	20.11%

T A B L E 9-11

Summary Results for Dividend Yield Decile Analysis of Large Stocks Universe, 1951–2003

Decile	$10,000 Grows to:	Average Return	Compound Return	Standard Deviation
1 (Highest Dividend Yields)	$5,100,693	14.31%	12.74%	19.52%
2	$6,263,690	14.45%	13.18%	17.01%
3	$5,756,331	14.14%	13.00%	16.11%
4	$3,598,092	13.00%	11.98%	14.96%
5	$2,852,907	12.58%	11.49%	15.45%
6	$1,475,245	11.37%	10.08%	16.52%
7	$2,232,663	12.49%	10.96%	18.00%
8	$1,825,011	12.34%	10.53%	19.26%
9	$1,185,812	11.90%	9.62%	23.03%
10 (Lowest Dividend Yield)	$1,805,002	13.12%	10.51%	23.66%
Large Stocks	$3,173,724	12.99%	11.71%	16.84%

IMPLICATIONS

From a market capitalization standpoint, the difference between the returns for high-yielding 50-stock portfolios is huge. Investors who want to use yield as a sole determinant should stick to large, better-known companies because these usually have the stronger balance sheets and longer operating histories that make higher dividends possible. Indeed, in coming chapters, we'll see that when you include other criteria, such as strong cashflows, large sales, and large numbers of shares outstanding, large stocks with high dividend yields offer the best risk-adjusted returns available. See Table 9-12 for best- and worst-case compound returns.

T A B L E 9-12

Terminal Value of $10,000 Invested for Best and Worst Average Annual Compound Returns over Period for Monthly Data 1963–2003

For Any	1-Year Period	3-Year Period	5-Year Period	10-Year Period
Large Stocks Minimum $10,000 Value	$5,795.00	$6,405.04	$7,319.54	$9,801.79
Large Stocks Maximum $10,000 Value	$16,849.00	$23,415.11	$35,241.06	$69,737.00
High Dividend Yield Large Stocks Minimum $10,000 Value	$8,074.00	$9,030.00	$10,317.00	$16,083.00
High Dividend Yield Large Stocks Maximum $10,000 Value	$16,689.00	$23,114.00	$37,027.00	$71,010.00
All Stocks Minimum $10,000 Value	$5,835.00	$5,756.00	$6,260.00	$10,700.00
All Stocks Maximum $10,000 Value	$18,151.00	$21,680.00	$33,064.00	$69,868.00
High Dividend Yield All Stocks Minimum $10,000 Value	$5,321.00	$4,894.00	$5,934.00	$10,361.00
High Dividend Yield All Stocks Maximum $10,000 Value	$16,433.00	$25,666.00	$31,465.00	$72,332.00

With the smaller-cap stocks from All Stocks, you're better off focusing on top deciles, and you should avoid buying those 50 stocks from All Stocks having the highest dividend yields. With these smaller stocks, such a huge yield may be signs of problems to come.

THE VALUE OF VALUE FACTORS

Discovery consists in seeing what everybody has seen and thinking what nobody has thought.

—Albert Szent-Gyorgyi

The past 52 years show that, rather than careening about like a drunken monkey, the stock market methodically rewards certain types of stocks while punishing others. What's more, had you simply read and followed the advice in the last edition of this book, you could have avoided the carnage that investors in the highest valued stocks suffered between 2000 and 2003. And even though this book has been in the public eye since 1997, nothing has changed regarding the longer term performance of overpriced companies: They do *horribly* over the long-term.

There's nothing random about Figure 10-1. Stocks with low price-to-book, low price-to-cashflow, and low price-to-sales ratios (PSRs) dramatically outperform the All Stocks universe. Just as important, those with high price-to-book, high price-to-cashflow, and high PSRs underperform dramatically. The symmetry is striking. What's more, the decile results continue to confirm our 50-stock portfolio findings. Investors putting money into the lowest deciles by price-to-earnings (PEs), price-to-book, price-to-cashflow, and PSRs did much better than those who invested in the broader market and *vastly* better than investors who invested in high-ratio stocks. Indeed, with the decile studies—particularly PSR—we see a continuum where returns fall and risk rises as you move from low- to high-ratio deciles.

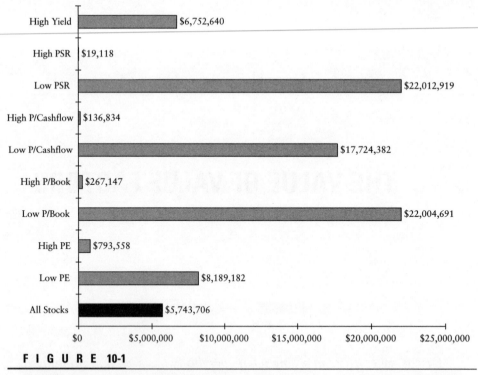

F I G U R E 10-1

December 31, 2003 value of $10,000 invested in various strategies using the All Stocks universe. Initial investment made December 31, 1951. 1951=$10,000.

RISK DOESN'T ALWAYS EQUAL REWARD

An important principle of the Capital Asset Pricing Model is that risk is compensated. It steers investors seeking higher returns to stocks with higher standard deviations. All the winning strategies I've covered thus far have higher standard deviations of return than the All Stocks universe. However, higher risk does not always lead to higher returns. As Figure 10-2 shows, the higher risk of the *high* PEs, price-to-book, price-to-cashflow, and PSRs went uncompensated. Indeed, each of the strategies significantly underperformed the All Stocks universe. Buying the 50 lowest PSR stocks turns $10,000 into $22,012,919, with a standard deviation of return of 27.40 percent, but buying the 50 stocks with the highest PSRs turns $10,000 into just $19,118, *with a higher standard deviation of return of 34.51 percent.* The same holds true in the decile analysis, with a $10,000 investment in the lowest PSR decile growing to $43,132,389, with a standard deviation of 21.28 percent and the same $10,000 invested in the highest PSR decile growing to $49,482, with a higher standard deviation of 28.06 percent.

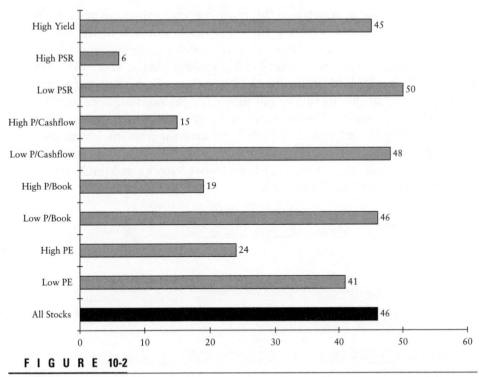

F I G U R E 10-2

Sharpe ratios for the various strategies applied to the All Stocks universe, 1951–2003. (Higher is better.)

IS IT WORTH THE RISK?

Risk is a powerful predator, culling the weak strategies from the herd. Buying the 50 stocks with the lowest PSRs and the 50 stocks with the lowest price-to-cashflow ratios were the only two strategies that beat the All Stocks universe on a risk-adjusted basis. The 50-stock low price-to-book portfolio matched the All Stocks' Sharpe ratio of 46; whereas the 50 stocks with the lowest PE ratios and highest dividend yields came in several points lower than the All Stocks universe. The Sharpe ratios for the deciles of these ratios shows that sticking with the lowest decile generally offers a higher Sharpe ratio than the 50-stock portfolio strategies. For example, the Sharpe ratios for decile one (the lowest) for both price-to-book and price-to-cashflow are 54 and 56, respectively.

Strategies that buy stocks with high PEs, price-to-book, price-to-cashflow, or PSRs have abysmal risk-adjusted returns. This is true both for the 50-stock portfolios and the decile analysis. It's like enduring a violent and stormy night at sea on a rickety ship, only to be dashed upon the rocks before reaching shore. Nothing demonstrated this more forcefully than the performance of the strategies since 1997. During the stock market bubble of the late 1990s, investors pushed the prices of richly valued stocks to unprecedented levels. An investor who believed the market-bubble mantra that it was "different this time," and who focused on buying the "story" stocks with no earnings, little sales, but *great* stories about a bright future (think Anything.com) would have done extraordinarily well in the three years after the revised edition of *What Works on Wall Street* came out in 1997. An investor who stuck with the time-tested strategies featured in my book would have felt like a fool comparing her portfolio's performance to the high-ratio "story" stocks in March of 2000, at the top of the stock market bubble.

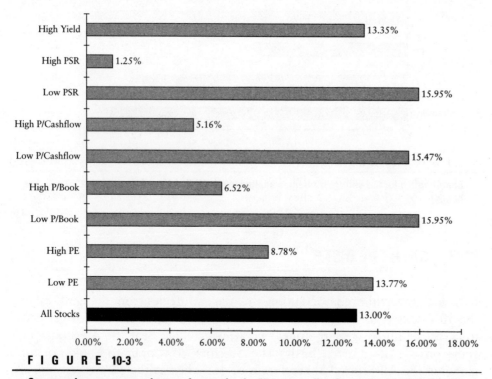

F I G U R E 10-3

Compound average annual rates of return for the 52 years ending December 31, 2003. Results of applying strategies on the All Stocks universe.

Between January 1, 1997 and March 31, 2000, the 50 stocks from the All Stocks universe with the highest PE ratios compounded at *46.69 percent per year*, turning $10,000 into $34,735 in three years and three months. Other speculative names did equally as well, with the 50 stocks from All Stocks with the highest price-to-book ratios growing a $10,000 investment into $33,248, a compound return of 44.72 percent. *All* the highest valuation stocks trounced All Stocks over that brief period, leaving those focusing on the shorter term to

T A B L E 10-1

Average Annual Compound Rates of Return by Decade, All Stocks Universe

Portfolio	1950s*	1960s	1970s	1980s	1990s	2000s**
All Stocks	19.22%	11.09%	8.53%	15.85%	14.75%	5.91%
50 low PE	21.84%	13.96%	8.89%	7.56%	13.58%	33.55%
50 high PE	19.27%	10.96%	2.26%	7.99%	16.99%	−14.73%
50 low price-to-book ratios	18.86%	11.49%	17.06%	13.15%	15.83%	25.68%
50 high price-to-book ratios	22.32%	13.13%	0.82%	1.97%	18.03%	−31.17%
50 low price-to-cashflow ratios	18.71%	15.41%	13.57%	12.53%	12.86%	21.23%
50 high price-to-cashflow ratios	19.30%	8.02%	−3.03%	8.77%	12.77%	−27.77%
50 low price-to-sales ratios	20.85%	11.15%	14.80%	20.43%	13.80%	19.94%
50 high price-to-sales ratios	14.96%	11.99%	5.82%	−2.02%	2.46%	−42.37%
50 highest-yielding stocks	20.29%	10.54%	6.55%	11.20%	16.25%	23.17%

*Returns for 1952–1959.
**Returns for 2000–2003.

think that maybe it really was different this time. But anyone familiar with past market bubbles knows that ultimately, the laws of economics reassert their grip on market activity. Investors back in 2000 would have done well to remember Horace's *Ars Poetica*, in which he states: "Many shall be restored that are now fallen, and many shall fall that now are in honor."

For fall they did, and they fell hard. A near-sighted investor entering the market at its peak in March of 2000 would face true devastation. A $10,000 investment in the 50 stocks with the highest PSRs from the All Stocks universe would have been worth a mere $526 at the end of March 2003; worth just $1,081 if invested in the highest price-to-book stocks; $1,293 invested in the highest price-to-cashflow stocks, and $2,549 if invested in the 50 stocks with the highest PE ratios. The devastation was so severe that even a $10,000 portfolio invested in 1997 and comprised of the highest price-to-book, price-to-cashflow, PSR, and PE stocks—while growing to $30,000 at the bubble's peak—would have been worth just $4,500 by March 2003.

You must *always* consider risk before investing in strategies that buy stocks significantly different from the market. Remember that high risk does not always mean high reward. All the higher-risk strategies are eventually dashed on the rocks, as Figure 10-5 makes plain.

EMBRACE CONSISTENCY

It's also important to keep the base rates of a strategy in mind. A strategy won't do you any good if you can't stick with it, so you must look for consistency over time. All the value strategies covered here beat the All Stocks universe more than 50 percent of the time over all rolling 10-year periods, yet the records are mixed. Buying the 50 stocks with the lowest price-to-book ratios and the 50 stocks with the lowest PSRs had identical returns of 15.95 percent between 1951 and 2003. Yet, if you bought the 50 lowest price-to-book stocks annually, you'd underperform the All Stocks universe during *48 percent* of all rolling five-year periods. Only the low PSR strategy shows enough consistency to be worth betting on. *All* the high ratio strategies have horrible peak-to-trough declines and should be avoided. Figures 10-4 and 10-5 summarize the results for the All Stocks universe.

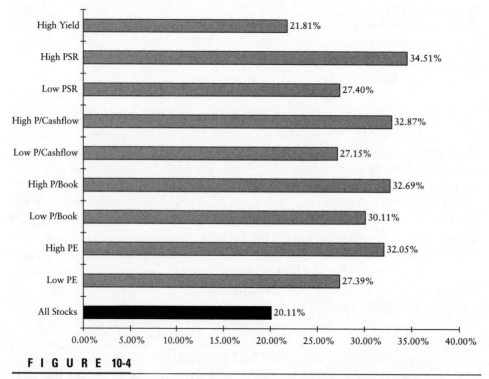

F I G U R E 10-4

Standard deviation of return for strategies from the All Stocks universe 1951–2003. (Higher is riskier.)

LARGE STOCKS ARE MORE CONSISTENT

When looking at the Large Stocks universe, we see the same results as for All Stocks. All the value strategies with low ratios beat the market, and all the

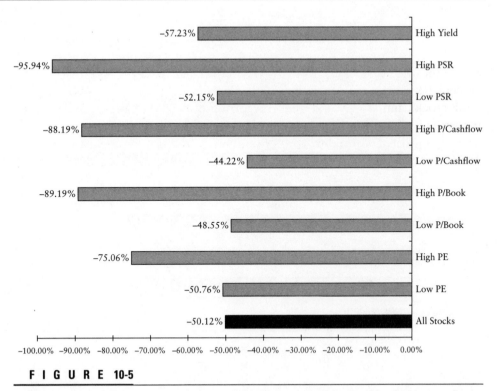

F I G U R E 10-5

Worst-case scenarios—maximum percentage decline for strategies from the All Stocks universe 1963–2003.

strategies with high ratios do considerably worse. All the high-ratio strategies had higher standard deviations of return than their low-ratio counterparts— and performed significantly worse. But the absolute amounts are more modest. With Large Stocks, the best-performing strategy is to buy those 50 stocks having the lowest price-to-cashflow ratios, with a $10,000 investment on December 31, 1951 growing to $16,060,150 by the end of 2003. We also see high dividend yield and low PE ratio stocks beating the Large Stocks universe by wide margins. Figure 10-6 shows the returns of $10,000 invested on December 31, 1951 in the various value strategies.

The base rates for the Large Stocks value strategies are far more consistent than for those in the All Stocks universe. All the Large Stocks value strategies beat the universe *at least* 86 percent of the time over the 43 rolling 10-year periods. All the high-ratio strategies fail to beat the Large Stocks universe a majority of the time over all rolling 10-year periods, with the most successful beating the Large Stocks universe just 44 percent of the time.

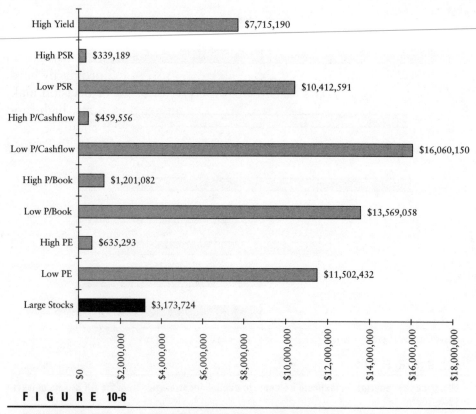

F I G U R E 10-6

December 31, 2003 value of $10,000 invested in the various strategies using the Large Stocks universe. Initial investment made December 31, 1951. 1951=$10,000.

T A B L E 10-2

Average Annual Compound Rates of Return by Decade, Large Stocks Universe

Portfolio	1950s*	1960s	1970s	1980s	1990s	2000s**
Large Stocks	15.33%	8.99%	6.99%	16.89%	15.34%	2.40%
50 low PE	16.12%	11.14%	12.64%	16.19%	15.38%	18.36%
50 high PE	14.77%	10.94%	0.93%	14.11%	13.24%	−14.90%
50 low price-to-book ratios	15.41%	9.57%	13.95%	19.99%	18.28%	8.99%
50 high price-to-book ratios	16.55%	11.30%	−0.60%	14.40%	24.87%	−22.38%
50 low price-to-cashflow ratios	17.28%	10.36%	15.40%	17.31%	18.03%	11.46%
50 high price-to-cashflow ratios	14.85%	12.35%	−1.85%	13.29%	17.21%	−23.76%
50 low price-to-sales ratios	16.39%	9.48%	10.90%	20.09%	17.19%	9.86%
50 high price-to-sales ratios	13.21%	11.73%	3.23%	9.54%	22.56%	−36.87%
50 highest-yielding stocks	15.20%	9.82%	11.44%	17.15%	13.89%	16.56%

*Returns for 1952–1959.
**Returns for 2000–2003.

IMPLICATIONS

Value strategies work, rewarding patient investors who stick with them through bull and bear. But it's sticking with them that's extraordinarily hard. Because we all filter today's market performance through our decision making process, it's almost always the glamorous, high-expectations, high-ratio stocks that grab our attention. They are the stocks we see zooming up in price, they are the ones that our friends and fellow investors talk about, and they are the ones on which investors focus their attention and buying power. Yet they are the very stocks that consistently disappoint investors over the long-term.

All the Large Stocks value strategies beat the Large Stocks universe on an absolute and risk-adjusted basis, and they did so at least 86 percent of the time over all rolling 10-year periods. That's an extraordinary track record. The decile analysis confirms our 50-stock findings, showing that you are almost always better confining your search for market-beating stocks to the lower deciles of each of the ratios. Figures 10-7 through 10-10 summarize the returns from the Large Stocks universe.

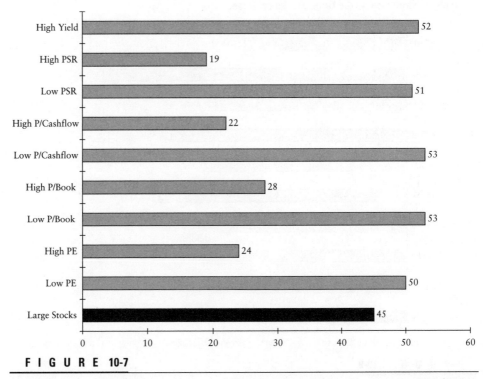

F I G U R E 10-7

Sharpe ratios for the various strategies applied to the Large Stocks universe, 1951–2003. (Higher is better.)

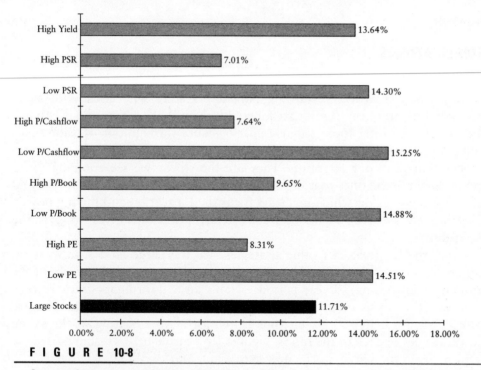

F I G U R E 10-8

Compound average annual rates of return for the 52 years ending December 31, 2003. Results of applying strategies on the Large Stocks universe.

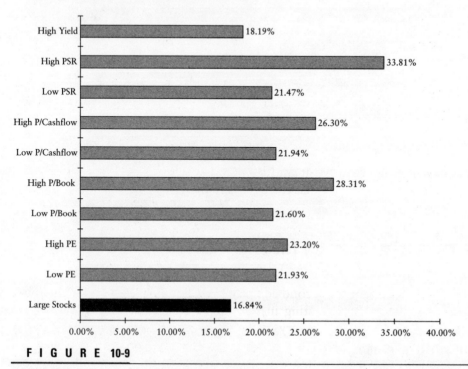

F I G U R E 10-9

Standard deviation of return for strategies from the Large Stocks universe, 1951–2003. (Higher is riskier.)

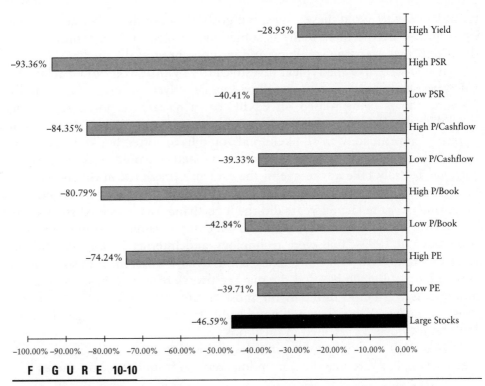

F I G U R E 10-10

Worst-case scenarios—maximum percentage decline for strategies from the Large Stocks universe, 1963–2003.

High-ratio strategies (e.g., high PE, high price-to-book, etc.) consistently underperform their universes over the long-term. They take more risk and offer less reward. This is true for both the 50-stock portfolios and the high-ratio deciles. They have some spectacular runs that encourage investors to pay unwarranted prices for the stocks with the best story or most sizzle. But they consistently disappoint and should be avoided unless *extremely compelling* strategic reasons exist for buying the stock.

LEARNING TO FOCUS ON THE LONG TERM

Let's say you bought the second edition of this book in 1998 and truly understood the dangers of investing in overvalued stocks. Yet, in real time, you would have watched those very stocks soar—month in and month out—for the next two years. Two years feels like an eternity to the average investor, and I believe that even armed with all this information, you would have had a tough time staying away from those high-flying story stocks. Yes, the long-term data say to avoid these issues, but gosh, they are the only ones moving up in price—maybe there really is something to this "new economy" paradigm shift that everyone is talking and writing about in the media.

If you were like the typical investor, little by little you would relax the rules, becoming more and more willing to take a flyer on some of the rapidly growing shares being touted on CNBC or in research reports. And then, much like the drug user who thinks he's just experimenting, you'd have been hooked. Unfortunately, in all likelihood you'd have gotten hooked nearer the end of the speculative market environment—and it would have cost you a fortune. To truly take advantage of the evidence presented in this book, you have to internalize this message and stay focused on the much longer term. In *no period* over the last 52 years did the high flying, richly valued stocks stay ahead over the long-term. They *always* ended up crashing and burning. The hot stocks of 1997–2000 were technology and Internet issues, but the hot stocks of tomorrow will quite likely come from a different industry with a new hot story. Remember that the market always reverts to basic economics and that it will be no different for those future hot stocks than it was for those in the past. Only then will you be able to take full advantage of all the long-term evidence presented in this book.

Now let's turn to growth variables and look for any compelling strategies that might overcome the horrendous returns from high-ratio stocks.

11
CHAPTER

DO HIGH EARNINGS GAINS MEAN HIGH PERFORMANCE?

It ain't so much what people know that hurts as what they know that ain't so.

—Artemus Ward

Now, let's look at factors commonly associated with growth investing. Generally, growth investors like high while value investors like low. Growth investors want high earnings and sales growth with prospects for more of the same. They usually don't care if a stock has a high PE ratio, reasoning that a company can grow its way out of short-term overvaluations. Growth investors often award high prices to stocks with rapidly increasing earnings.

Unfortunately, Compustat lacks long-term data on earnings forecasts. Many growth investors make substantial use of earnings forecasts when constructing their portfolios, so our inability to do a long-term test is somewhat limiting. However, some studies have found that forecasts are remarkably undependable. In the October 11, 1993 issue of *Forbes Magazine*, David Dreman recounts a study that used a sample of 67,375 analysts' quarterly estimates for New York and American Stock Exchange listed companies between 1973 and 1990. It found that analysts' average forecast error was 40 percent and that estimates were misleading (i.e., missed their mark by more than 10 percent) two-thirds of the time. Therefore, I'll look at actual earnings changes, not earnings forecasts.

EXAMINING ANNUAL EARNINGS CHANGES

First, we'll look at buying the 50 stocks with the best and the worst one-year earnings per share percentage changes from the All Stocks and Large Stocks universes. For the rankings to work smoothly, we eliminate stocks whose annual earnings went from positive to negative. Also, due to time-lag constraints, we must start the test on December 31, 1952. When comparing these returns to other strategies, keep in mind 1952 isn't included. We'll do the same for the decile tests, with decile one being the 10 percent of stocks from each universe that had the highest earnings gains, and decile 10 being the smallest.

First, let's look at the returns from buying the 50 stocks from the All Stocks universe having the best one-year earnings-per-share percentage gains (Figure 11-1). As usual, we start with $10,000 and rebalance the portfolio annually. As Tables 11-1 through 11-3 show, buying stocks with the best one-year earnings gains is like closing the barn door after the horse has left. $10,000 invested on December 31, 1952 in the top 50 one-year earnings

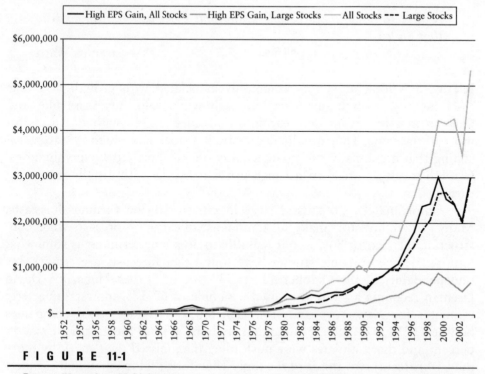

F I G U R E   11-1

Returns 50 stocks with highest one-year earnings gains versus All Stocks and Large Stocks, 1952–2003. Year-end 1952=$10,000.

gainers from All Stocks grew to $2,975,074 by the end of 2003. That's more than $2,000,000 shy of the $5,323,175 you'd earn with a similar investment in All Stocks. The 50 highest one-year earnings gainers also took considerably more risk—their standard deviation was 26.59 percent compared to All Stocks' 20.29 percent. The strategy has had some magnificent runs, however. Between December 31, 1962 and December 31, 1967, the strategy almost doubled the performance of the All Stocks universe, turning $10,000 into $38,546. It had another terrific streak between 1976 and 1980, but it lacks long-term consistency. Right after these great runs, it went on to do significantly worse than All Stocks. It's also interesting to look at the recent market bubble, when earnings really ceased to matter. Between 1997 and March 31, 2000, the stocks with the biggest gains in earnings only did modestly better than All Stocks, returning 21.74 percent per year, whereas All Stocks compounded at 19.45 percent. The base rates in Table 11-3 show that the strategy underperforms the All Stocks universe in each period.

T A B L E 11-1

Summary Return and Risk Results for All Stocks and 50 Stocks with Highest One-Year Earnings Gains from All Stocks Universe, December 31, 1952–December 31, 2003

	All Stocks	All Stocks, Top 50 One-Year Earnings Gains
Arithmetic Average	14.93%	14.90%
Geometric Average	13.10%	11.81%
Median Return	17.00%	17.50%
Standard Deviation of Return	20.29%	26.59%
Downside risk—lower is better	7.24%	10.62%
Correlation with S&P 500	0.87	0.80
T-Statistic	5.26	4.00
Sharpe Ratio	0.46	0.35
Number of Positive Periods	38	36
Number of Negative Periods	13	15
Maximum Peak-to-trough Decline (using Monthly data series)	−50.12%	−65.54%
Beta	0.99	1.1972
$10,000 becomes:	$5,323,175.00	$2,975,074.00
Minimum Annual Return	−27.90%	−32%
Maximum Annual Return	55.90%	81%
Minimum *Expected* Return*	−25.65%	−38.28%
Maximum *Expected* Return**	55.51%	68.08%

*Minimum Expected Return is Arithmetic Return minus 2 times the standard deviation.
**Maximum Expected Return is Arithmetic Return plus 2 times the standard deviation.

T A B L E 11-2

Summary Return and Risk Results for Large Stocks and 50 Stocks with Highest One-Year
Earnings Gains from Large Stocks Universe, December 31, 1952–December 31, 2003

	Large Stocks	Large Stocks, Top 50 One-Year Earnings Gains
Arithmetic Average	13.07%	10.64%
Geometric Average	11.76%	8.66%
Median Return	16.20%	12.23%
Standard Deviation of Return	17.00%	20.57%
Downside risk—lower is better	5.91%	9.25%
Correlation with S&P 500	0.95	0.85
T-Statistic	5.49	3.70
Sharpe Ratio	0.45	0.25
Number of Positive Periods	38	34
Number of Negative Periods	13	17
Maximum Peak-to-trough Decline (using Monthly data series)	−46.59%	−51.36%
Beta	0.90	0.99
$10,000 becomes:	$2,903,681.00	$692,600.00
Minimum Annual Return	−26.70%	−31.80%
Maximum Annual Return	45.07%	48.10%
Minimum *Expected* Return*	−20.93%	−30.50%
Maximum *Expected* Return**	47.07%	51.78%

*Minimum Expected Return is Arithmetic Return minus 2 times the standard deviation.
**Maximum Expected Return is Arithmetic Return plus 2 times the standard deviation.

T A B L E 11-3

Base Rates for All Stocks and 50 Stocks with Highest One-Year Earnings Gains from All Stocks
Universe, 1951–2003

Item	Top 50 One-Year Earnings Gains Beat "All Stocks"	Percent
Single-Year Return	24 out of 52	46%
Rolling Five-Year Compound Return	17 out of 47	36%
Rolling 10-Year Compound Return	17 out of 42	40%

LARGE STOCKS DO WORSE

The 50 stocks with the highest one-year earnings gains from the Large
Stocks universe did not perform as well, as Table 11-2 shows. Here, $10,000
invested on December 31, 1952 grew to $692,600 by the end of 2003, a
compound return of 8.66 percent. That's more than $2,000,000 less than
the $2,903,681 you'd earn investing $10,000 in the Large Stocks universe,

which had a return of 11.76 percent a year. The Sharpe ratio is a paltry 25, compared to Large Stocks' 45. All base rates are negative, with the 50 highest one-year earnings gainers beating Large Stocks just 10 percent of the time over all rolling 10-year periods. Tables 11-2 and 11-4 show the summary information as well as the base rates for the stocks from Large Stocks with the best one-year earnings gain.

T A B L E 11-4

Base Rates for Large Stocks and 50 Stocks with Highest One-Year Earnings Gains from Large Stocks Universe, 1951–2003

Item	Top 50 One-Year Earnings Gains Beat "Large Stocks"	Percent
Single-Year Return	18 out of 51	35%
Rolling Five-Year Compound Return	9 out of 47	19%
Rolling 10-Year Compound Return	4 out of 42	10%

The record shows that buying stocks with the highest one-year earnings gains rarely beats the market. This probably occurs because high expectations are hard to meet. Seduced by stellar earnings gains, investors bid the stocks to unsustainable levels. When earnings growth fails to continue, they become disenchanted and sell their shares in disgust.

BEST- AND WORST-CASE RETURNS

Between 1964 and 2003, the 50 stocks from the All Stocks universe having the highest earnings per share percentage gains lost more than 20 percent of their value nine times. The largest peak-to-trough decline was a loss of 65.54 percent. They also proved more volatile when stock prices are declining, with a downside risk of 10.62 percent, compared to 7.24 percent for All Stocks. Their best five-year return came at the end of the "soaring sixties," when they turned $10,000 into $46,245, an average annual compound return of 35.84 percent, whereas their worst five years reduced the same $10,000 to $4,312. Table 11-5 shows the worst-case scenario for the All Stocks universe.

Large Stocks with the highest one-year earnings gains lost more than 20 percent eight times between 1964 and 2003. Their largest peak-to-trough decline was between March 2000 and March 2003, during which time they lost 51.38 percent. Like their All Stocks counterparts, they also proved much more volatile than Large Stocks when prices are declining, with a downside risk of 9.25 percent compared to 5.91 for Large Stocks. Their best five-year return saw $10,000 grow to $31,340, a compound return of 25.67 percent per year, whereas their worst five years turned the same $10,000 into $5,909.

Table 11-6 shows the worst-case scenarios and Tables 11-15 and 11-18 the best and worst returns for all periods.

T A B L E 11-5

Worst-Case Scenarios: All 10 Percent or Greater Declines for 50 Stocks with Highest One-Year Earnings Gains from All Stocks Universe, December 31, 1963–December 31, 2003

Peak Date	Peak Index Value	Trough Date	Trough Index Value	Recovery Date	Decline (%)	Decline Duration	Recovery Duration
Apr-65	1.43	Jun-65	1.26	Sep-65	−11.88	2	3
Apr-66	2.17	Oct-66	1.6	Jan-67	−26.28	6	3
Dec-67	3.36	Feb-68	3.01	Apr-68	−10.4	2	2
Dec-68	4.62	Sep-74	1.59	Mar-79	−65.54	69	54
Sep-79	5.7	Oct-79	5.04	Dec-79	−11.67	1	2
Feb-80	7.52	Mar-80	5.69	Sep-80	−24.36	1	6
Nov-80	8.59	Jul-82	6.36	Nov-82	−25.98	20	4
Jun-83	14.04	Jul-84	9.09	Mar-86	−35.26	13	20
Jun-86	15.82	Sep-86	13.43	Jan-87	−15.06	3	4
Aug-87	20.46	Nov-87	14.05	Jan-89	−31.32	3	14
Sep-89	26.94	Jan-90	23.58	Jun-90	−12.47	4	5
Jun-90	27.55	Oct-90	21.41	Mar-91	−22.3	4	5
Jan-97	80.04	Mar-97	71.78	May-97	−10.32	2	2
Mar-98	110.32	Aug-98	76.71	Dec-99	−30.47	5	16
Feb-00	140.21	Mar-03	75.94		−45.84	37	NA
Average					−25.28	11.47	10.00

T A B L E 11-6

Worst-Case Scenarios: All 10 Percent or Greater Declines for 50 Stocks with Highest One-Year Earnings Gains from Large Stocks Universe, December 31, 1963–December 31, 2003

Peak Date	Peak Index Value	Trough Date	Trough Index Value	Recovery Date	Decline (%)	Decline Duration	Recovery Duration
Apr-66	1.75	Oct-66	1.35	Mar-67	−22.52	6	5
Dec-67	2.06	Feb-68	1.85	Apr-68	−10.43	2	2
Nov-68	2.52	Sep-74	1.29	Aug-78	−48.86	70	47
Sep-78	2.65	Oct-78	2.27	Mar-79	−14.46	1	5
Aug-79	3.17	Oct-79	2.83	Dec-79	−10.44	2	2
Feb-80	3.77	Mar-80	3.03	Jul-80	−19.72	1	4
Nov-80	4.85	Jul-82	3.56	Nov-82	−26.49	20	4
Jun-83	7.23	Jul-84	4.99	Feb-86	−31.08	13	19
Aug-87	11.15	Nov-87	7.54	Mar-89	−32.37	3	16
Aug-89	13.64	Oct-90	10.04	Jul-91	−26.36	14	9
May-96	29.05	Jul-96	25.64	Nov-96	−11.72	2	4
Apr-98	40.32	Aug-98	26.62	Dec-99	−33.97	4	16

(continued on next page)

T A B L E 11-6

Worst-Case Scenarios: All 10 Percent or Greater Declines for 50 Stocks with Highest One-Year Earnings Gains from Large Stocks Universe, December 31, 1962–December 31, 2003 *(Continued)*

Peak Date	Peak Index Value	Trough Date	Trough Index Value	Recovery Date	Decline (%)	Decline Duration	Recovery Duration
Mar-00	47.9	Mar-03	23.29		−51.38	36	NA
Average					−26.14	13.38	11.08

BUYING STOCKS WITH THE WORST EARNINGS CHANGES

Perhaps you'd be better off buying the 50 stocks with the worst annual earnings changes (Figure 11-2). At least expectations for these stocks are modest. Remember that we require stocks to have positive earnings, so although these stocks aren't losing money, they will have experienced substantial declines in earnings.

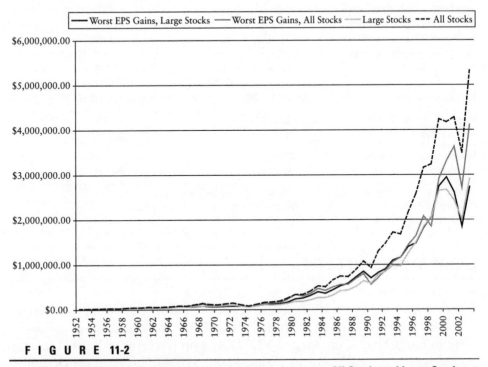

F I G U R E 11-2

Returns on 50 stocks with worst one-year earnings gains versus All Stocks and Large Stocks, 1952–2003. Year end 1952=$10,000.

A $10,000 investment on December 31, 1952 in those 50 stocks from the All Stocks universe having the worst one-year earnings changes grew to $4,109,473 by the end of 2003. That's better than the return from buying the best 50 earnings gainers, but it still falls short of the $5,323,175 you'd make investing the $10,000 in All Stocks alone. Risk was lower at 24.57 percent, but again, still higher than the All Stocks universe's 20.29 percent. Table 11-7 summarize the results.

T A B L E 11-7

Summary Return and Risk Results for Annual Data, All Stocks, and 50 Lowest Earnings-to-Price (High PE) Stocks from All Stocks, December 31, 1951–December 31, 2003

	All Stocks	All Stocks, Worst 50 1-yr Earnings Gains
Arithmetic Average	14.93%	15.22%
Geometric Average	13.10%	12.53%
Median Return	17.00%	16.20%
Standard Deviation of Return	20.29%	24.57%
Downside risk—lower is better	7.24%	9.57%
Correlation with S&P 500	0.87	0.75
T-Statistic	5.26	4.42
Sharpe Ratio	0.46	0.40
Number of Positive Periods	38	37
Number of Negative Periods	13	14
Maximum Peak-to-trough Decline (using Monthly data series)	−50.12%	−63.66%
Beta	0.99	1.039
$10,000 becomes:	$5,323,175.00	$4,109,473.00
Minimum Annual Return	−27.90%	−32.00%
Maximum Annual Return	55.90%	60.10%
Minimum *Expected* Return*	−25.65%	−33.92%
Maximum *Expected* Return**	55.51%	64.36%

*Minimum Expected Return is Arithmetic Return minus 2 times the standard deviation.
**Maximum Expected Return is Arithmetic Return plus 2 times the standard deviation.

LARGE STOCKS DO BETTER

$10,000 invested in those 50 stocks from the Large Stocks universe having the worst one-year earnings returned virtually the same amount as an investment in Large Stocks, growing to $2,721,463 on December 31, 2003, a compound return of 11.62 percent (Table 11-8). $10,000 invested on December 31, 1952 in Large Stocks grew to $2,903,681, a return of 11.76 percent a year. The Sharpe ratio for Large Stocks was 45 and 41 for the 50 stocks hav-

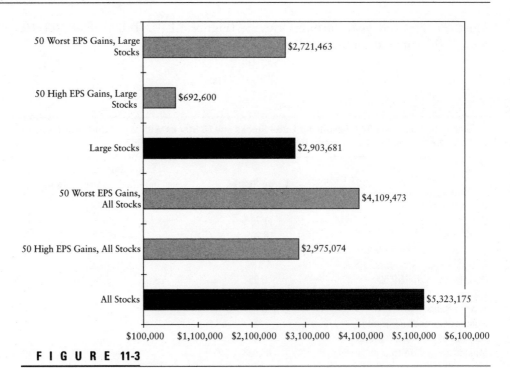

FIGURE 11-3

December 31, 2003 value of $10,000 invested on December 31, 1951 and annually rebalanced.

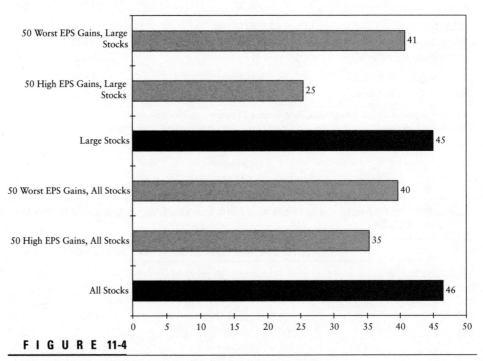

FIGURE 11-4

Sharpe risk-adjusted return ratio, 1951–2003. (Higher is better.)

ing the worst one-year earnings change (Figure 11-4). Tables 11-8, 11-10, and 11-12 summarize the results.

T A B L E 11-8

Summary Return and Risk Results for Large Stocks and 50 Stocks with Worst One-Year Earnings Gains from Large Stocks Universe, December 31, 1951–December 31, 2003

	Large Stocks	Large Stocks, Worst 50 One-Year Earnings Gains
Arithmetic Average	13.07%	13.30%
Geometric Average	11.76%	11.62%
Median Return	16.20%	15.90%
Standard Deviation of Return	17.00%	19.45%
Downside risk—lower is better	5.91%	7.26%
Correlation with S&P 500	0.95	0.86
T-Statistic	5.49	4.88
Sharpe Ratio	0.45	0.41
Number of Positive Periods	38	38
Number of Negative Periods	13	13
Maximum Peak-to-trough Decline (using Monthly data series)	−46.59%	−44.07%
Beta	0.90	0.9398
$10,000 becomes:	$2,903,681.00	$2,721,463.00
Minimum Annual Return	−26.70%	−29.49%
Maximum Annual Return	45.07%	57.40%
Minimum *Expected* Return*	−20.93%	−25.60%
Maximum *Expected* Return**	47.07%	52.20%

*Minimum Expected Return is Arithmetic Return minus 2 times the standard deviation.
**Maximum Expected Return is Arithmetic Return plus 2 times the standard deviation.

T A B L E 11-9

Base Rates for All Stocks and 50 Stocks with Worst One-Year Earnings Gains from All Stocks Universe, 1951–2003

Item	Worst 50 One-Year Earnings Gains Beat "All Stocks"	Percent
Single-Year Return	25 out of 51	49%
Rolling Five-Year Compound Return	22 out of 47	47%
Rolling 10-Year Compound Return	12 out of 42	29%

T A B L E 11-10

Base Rates for Large Stocks and 50 Stocks with Worst One-Year Earnings Gains from Large Stocks Universe, 1951–2003

Item	Worst 50 One-Year Earnings Gains Beat "Large Stocks"	Percent
Single-Year Return	30 out of 51	59%
Rolling Five-Year Compound Return	21 out of 47	45%
Rolling 10-Year Compound Return	18 out of 42	43%

T A B L E 11-11

Worst-Case Scenarios: All 10 Percent or Greater Declines for 50 Stocks with Worst One-Year Earnings Gains from All Stocks Universe, December 31, 1963–December 31, 2003

Peak Date	Peak Index Value	Trough Date	Trough Index Value	Recovery Date	Decline (%)	Decline Duration	Recovery Duration
Apr-66	1.67	Oct-66	1.4	Jan-67	−15.7	6	3
Nov-68	2.61	Dec-74	0.95	Aug-78	−63.65	73	44
Sep-78	2.73	Oct-78	2.23	Mar-79	−18.36	1	5
Sep-79	3.47	Oct-79	3.06	Dec-79	−11.83	1	2
Feb-80	3.94	Mar-80	3.03	Jul-80	−23.05	1	4
May-81	5.14	Jun-82	3.86	Nov-82	−24.83	13	5
Jul-83	7.45	Jul-84	6.3	Jan-85	−15.44	12	6
May-85	8.13	Sep-85	7.28	Nov-85	−10.48	4	2
May-86	9.83	Sep-86	8.05	Feb-87	−18.1	4	5
Aug-87	11.23	Nov-87	7.2	Mar-89	−35.89	3	16
Aug-89	13.5	Oct-90	8.07	Dec-92	−40.19	14	26
May-96	25.64	Jul-96	22.47	Dec-96	−12.38	2	5
Mar-98	36.4	Aug-98	25.08	Jun-99	−31.11	5	10
Jun-99	38.89	Oct-99	34.44	Dec-99	−11.44	4	2
Aug-00	58.93	Nov-00	45.9	May-01	−22.12	3	6
May-01	61.54	Sep-02	39.61	Dec-03	−35.64	16	15
Average					−24.39	10.13	9.75

T A B L E 11-12

Worst-Case Scenarios: All 10 Percent or Greater Declines for 50 Stocks with Worst One-Year Earnings Gains from Large Stocks Universe, December 31, 1963–December 31, 2003

Peak Date	Peak Index Value	Trough Date	Trough Index Value	Recovery Date	Decline (%)	Decline Duration	Recovery Duration
Jan-66	1.3	Sep-66	1.06	Mar-67	−18.29	8	6
Sep-67	1.48	Mar-68	1.32	May-68	−10.57	6	2
Nov-68	1.75	Jun-70	1.01	Feb-72	−42.12	19	20
Nov-72	1.85	Sep-74	1.08	Jun-75	−41.91	22	9
Jun-75	1.94	Sep-75	1.67	Nov-75	−13.94	3	2

(continued on next page)

T A B L E 11-12

Worst-Case Scenarios: All 10 Percent or Greater Declines for 50 Stocks with Worst One-Year Earnings Gains from All Stocks Universe, December 31, 1962–December 31, 2003 *(Continued)*

Peak Date	Peak Index Value	Trough Date	Trough Index Value	Recovery Date	Decline (%)	Decline Duration	Recovery Duration
Dec-76	2.54	Feb-78	2.19	Jul-78	−13.74	14	5
Sep-78	2.59	Oct-78	2.25	Mar-79	−13.08	1	5
Jan-80	3.3	Mar-80	2.81	Jun-80	−14.77	2	3
May-81	4.56	Jun-82	3.47	Nov-82	−24	13	5
Nov-83	6.25	Jul-84	5.28	Jan-85	−15.52	8	6
May-86	7.47	Jul-86	6.49	Jan-87	−13.18	2	6
Jul-87	10.16	Nov-87	6.53	May-89	−35.73	4	18
Dec-89	10.93	Oct-90	7.85	Feb-92	−28.15	10	16
Apr-98	29.72	Aug-98	23.27	Apr-99	−21.69	4	8
Jan-01	42.2	Sep-02	23.61		−44.06	20	NA
Average					−23.38	9.07	7.93

BEST- AND WORST-CASE SCENARIOS

Between 1964 and 2003, those 50 stocks from the All Stocks Universe having the biggest annual drop in earnings per share declined by more than 20 percent from peak to trough eight times. The largest decline was a loss of 63.65 percent. Like the 50 stocks from All Stocks having the biggest earnings per share gains, the 50 having the worst were also more volatile when stock prices were declining, with a downside risk of 14.41 percent versus 7.24 percent for All Stocks. The best five-year period for the 50 stocks having the worst earnings per share changes turned $10,000 into $39,233, a compound return of 31.44 percent per year. The worst five-year period saw the same $10,000 decline to $5,113.

Those 50 stocks from the Large Stocks Universe having the worst earnings per share declines dropped more than 20 percent seven times, with the largest decline from peak to trough being a loss of 44.06 percent. Like the 50 Large Stocks with the best earnings gains, those with the worst were riskier when stock prices were declining, with a downside risk of 11.48 percent, versus 5.91 percent for Large Stocks. The best five-year return for the group turned $10,000 into $29,169, a compound return of 23.88 percent. The worst five-year period saw the same $10,000 decline to $8,062. Tables 11-12 and 11-15 catalog the worst-case scenarios and best- and worst-case returns over all time periods.

T A B L E 11-13

Average Annual Compound Rates of Return by Decade

Portfolio	1950s*	1960s	1970s	1980s	1990s	2000s**
Large Stocks	16.21%	8.99%	6.99%	16.89%	15.34%	2.40%
50 High EPS Gains, Large Stocks	15.05%	10.03%	4.13%	9.33%	13.55%	−6.45%
50 Worst EPS Gains, Large Stocks	18.43%	6.46%	9.77%	18.39%	12.53%	−0.1%
All Stocks	20.94%	11.09%	8.53%	15.85%	14.75%	5.91%
50 High EPS Gains, All Stocks	21.33%	12.52%	8.42%	8.67%	16.52%	−0.18%
50 Worst EPS Gains, All Stocks	19.06%	9.42%	10.44%	13.33%	13.97%	9.01%

*Returns for 1953–1959.
**Returns for 2000–2003.

T A B L E 11-14

Best and Worst Average Annual Compound Returns over Period for Annual Data 1953–2003

For Any	1-Year Period	3-Year Period	5-Year Period	10-Year Period
Large Stocks Minimum Compound Return	−26.70%	−11.93%	−4.37%	1.21%
Large Stocks Maximum Compound Return	45.07%	24.39%	22.40%	17.01%
50 High EPS Gains, Large Stocks Minimum Compound Return	−31.80%	−19.70%	−11.32%	−1.27%
50 High EPS Gains, Large Stocks Maximum Compound Return	48.10%	32.02%	23.01%	14.94%
50 Worst EPS Gains, Large Stocks Minimum Compound Return	−29.49%	−12.47%	−1.42%	1.98%
50 Worst EPS Gains, Large Stocks Maximum Compound Return	57.40%	27.71%	26.60%	19.91%
All Stocks Minimum Compound Return	−27.90%	−16.48%	−7.81%	1.26%
All Stocks Maximum Compound Return	55.90%	31.23%	27.77%	21.31%
50 High EPS Gains, All Stocks Minimum Compound Return	−32.00%	−18.20%	−13.02%	0.01%
50 High EPS Gains, All Stocks Maximum Compound Return	81.00%	38.77%	34.45%	24.03%
50 Worst EPS Gains, All Stocks Minimum Compound Return	−32.00%	−14.58%	−9.37%	1.24%
50 Worst EPS Gains, All Stocks Maximum Compound Return	60.10%	34.66%	32.51%	22.37%

T A B L E 11-15

Best and Worst Average Annual Compound Returns over Period for Monthly Data 1963–2003

For Any	1-Year Period	3-Year Period	5-Year Period	10-Year Period
Large Stocks Minimum Compound Return	−42.04%	−13.79%	−6.05%	−0.20%
Large Stocks Maximum Compound Return	68.49%	32.78%	28.65%	19.57%
50 High EPS Gains, Large Stocks Minimum Compound Return	−42.02%	−21.37%	−9.99%	−0.66%
50 High EPS Gains, Large Stocks Maximum Compound Return	97.17%	33.10%	25.67%	18.47%
50 Worst EPS Gains, Large Stocks Minimum Compound Return	−39.64%	−15.83%	−4.22%	−0.73%
50 Worst EPS Gains, Large Stocks Maximum Compound Return	79.34%	28.88%	23.88%	18.80%
All Stocks Minimum Compound Return	−41.65%	−16.82%	−8.94%	0.68%
All Stocks Maximum Compound Return	81.51%	29.46%	27.02%	21.46%
50 High EPS Gains, All Stocks Minimum Compound Return	−54.63%	−21.25%	−15.48%	−2.02%
50 High EPS Gains, All Stocks Maximum Compound Return	116.96%	46.76%	35.84%	21.81%
50 Worst EPS Gains, All Stocks Minimum Compound Return	−49.67%	−18.96%	−12.56%	−1.93%
50 Worst EPS Gains, All Stocks Maximum Compound Return	90.92%	32.82%	31.44%	22.29%

DECILES

The decile analysis shows that earnings gains aren't a very good variable to use when selecting stocks (Figures 11-5 and 11-6). As we found in the 50-stock portfolios, concentrating on those stocks having the best earnings per share gains is a losing proposition, probably because investors have unrealistic expectations for them and have pushed up their PE ratios and PSRs. The decile analysis confirms the 50-stock findings that one-year earnings changes are an unreliable tool for making security selections (Tables 11-16 and 11-17).

IMPLICATIONS

Buying stocks simply because they had great earnings gains is a losing proposition. Investors get overly excited about companies with dramatic earnings

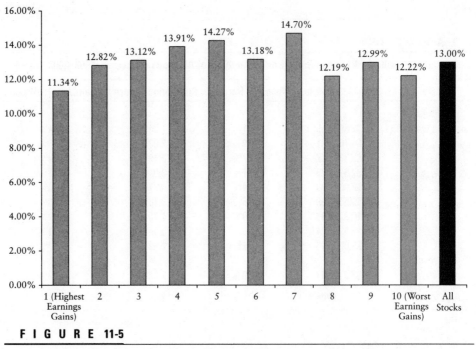

F I G U R E 11-5

Compound return by earnings gains decile, All Stocks universe, 1952–2003.

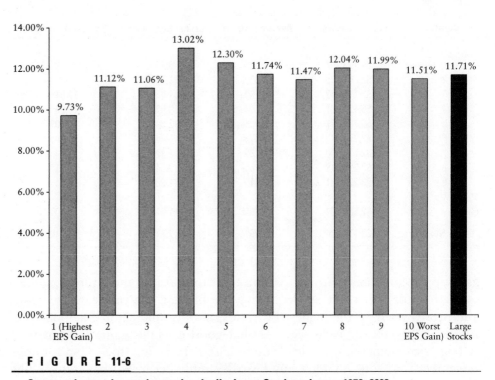

F I G U R E 11-6

Compound return by earnings gains decile, Large Stocks universe, 1952–2003.

T A B L E 11-16

Summary Results for Earnings Gains Decile Analysis of All Stocks Universe, 1952–2003

Decile	$10,000 Grows to:	Average Return	Compound Return	Standard Deviation
1 (Highest Earnings Gains)	$2,392,155	14.01%	11.34%	24.44%
2	$4,703,991	15.29%	12.82%	23.30%
3	$5,371,947	15.07%	13.12%	20.56%
4	$7,674,083	15.51%	13.91%	18.61%
5	$9,008,196	15.74%	14.27%	18.10%
6	$5,518,298	14.66%	13.18%	17.90%
7	$10,920,985	16.20%	14.70%	18.37%
8	$3,529,224	13.66%	12.19%	17.91%
9	$5,080,765	14.67%	12.99%	19.17%
10 (Worst Earnings Gains)	$3,575,567	14.39%	12.22%	21.82%
All Stocks	$5,743,706	14.79%	13.00%	20.11%

T A B L E 11-17

Summary Results for Earnings per Share Change Decile Analysis of Large Stocks Universe, 1952–2003

Decile	$10,000 Grows to:	Average Return	Compound Return	Standard Deviation
1 (Highest Earnings Gains)	$1,139,201	11.69%	9.73%	20.29%
2	$2,167,629	12.93%	11.12%	19.88%
3	$2,110,043	12.50%	11.06%	17.81%
4	$5,128,891	14.19%	13.02%	15.95%
5	$3,704,477	13.72%	12.30%	17.80%
6	$2,873,813	12.97%	11.74%	16.24%
7	$2,539,690	12.78%	11.47%	17.04%
8	$3,298,719	13.20%	12.04%	16.03%
9	$3,222,381	13.61%	11.99%	19.04%
10 (Worst Earnings Gains)	$2,586,309	13.06%	11.51%	18.50%
Large Stocks	$3,173,724	12.99%	11.71%	16.84%

gains, projecting these earnings assumptions too far into the future. It's interesting to note that those stocks having the highest one-year earnings gains almost always have the highest PE ratios, another indicator that poor performance lies ahead. We'll see later that good earnings gains coupled with strong price momentum will lead you to high-performing stocks; but for now, remember that you shouldn't buy a stock simply because it has outstanding one-year earnings gains.

You're not much better off buying stocks with the worst earnings changes. Although their returns are slightly higher than those with the best earnings changes, no compelling reason to buy them exists. History suggests you should not make investment decisions based on either one of these variables. Table 11-18 summarizes compound returns.

T A B L E 11-18

Terminal Value of $10,000 Invested for Best and Worst Average Annual Compound Returns over Period for Monthly Data 1963–2003

For Any	1-Year Period	3-Year Period	5-Year Period	10-Year Period
Large Stocks Minimum $10,000 Value	$5,796.00	$6,407.27	$7,319.54	$9,801.79
Large Stocks Maximum $10,000 Value	$16,849.00	$23,409.82	$35,241.06	$59,734.10
50 High EPS Gains, Large Stocks Minimum $10,000 Value	$5,798.00	$4,861.44	$5,908.18	$9,359.26
50 High EPS Gains, Large Stocks Maximum $10,000 Value	$19,717.00	$23,579.48	$31,344.26	$54,460.78
50 Worst EPS Gains, Large Stocks Minimum $10,000 Value	$6,036.00	$5,963.10	$8,060.73	$9,293.52
50 Worst EPS Gains, Large Stocks Maximum $10,000 Value	$17,934.00	$21,407.04	$29,174.67	$55,996.95
All Stocks Minimum $10,000 Value	$5,835.00	$5,755.15	$6,260.92	$10,701.19
All Stocks Maximum $10,000 Value	$18,151.00	$21,697.36	$33,064.39	$69,876.76
50 High EPS Gains, All Stocks Minimum $10,000 Value	$4,537.00	$4,883.73	$4,313.18	$8,154.07
50 High EPS Gains, All Stocks Maximum $10,000 Value	$21,696.00	$31,609.90	$46,252.84	$71,916.65
50 Worst EPS Gains, All Stocks Minimum $10,000 Value	$5,033.00	$5,322.29	$5,111.53	$8,229.28
50 Worst EPS Gains, All Stocks Maximum $10,000 Value	$19,092.00	$23,430.98	$39,231.76	$74,801.35

CASE STUDY: DO SALES INCREASES WORK BETTER THAN EARNINGS GAINS?

After the original version of *What Works on Wall Street* was published, I received many questions about whether stocks having the best annual increases of sales did better than stocks having the greatest earnings gains. The question seemed rational to many readers who saw that PSRs worked so much better than PE ratios.

In reality, I've found that buying stocks with the best one-year sales increases actually perform considerably *worse* than those with the highest earnings gains. Those 50 stocks from the All Stocks universe having the best one-year increase in revenues have among the worst performance we've seen with any of the single-factor strategies. For the period between December 31, 1952 and December 31, 2003, the group had a compound average annual return of just 2.68 percent, turning $10,000 into just $38,542, considerably worse than a similar investment in U.S. Treasury bills. Its Sharpe ratio was an abysmal 12. Risk, as measured by the standard deviation of return, and downside ratio, was off the charts, coming in at 41.52 and 19.86 percent, respectively. The performance was absolutely dreadful, with the exception of the two stock market bubbles in the late 1960s and late 1990s. The 50 stocks with the largest gains in annual sales had great performance in the "go-go" sixties, with 1967 coming in as the second-best year in annual performance, soaring 83.20 percent in that year alone. But that also marked a peak for the group that they would not reclaim until 1999. That year marked the best performance for the group over the 51 years for which we have data. In 1999, the group soared 167.84 percent. It then peaked again in early 2000 and went on to plunge 91.39 percent in the most recent bear market of 2000 through 2003. As for base rates, they were uniformly negative, with the group beating All Stocks in only *one* 10-year period, those 10 years ending in 1999.

Thus, we see that, along with all the other high-ratio stocks, those with high one-year sales and earnings serve as an excellent proxy for stock market excess. They do well only when investors get really excited about new issues with dramatically improving sales and without the more dispassionate and rational view that stocks eventually have to make money to make money for their investors. Whenever they are doing inordinately well, investors should take a very careful look at the overall market environment, as these stocks *only* do well in excessively speculative markets.

Large Stocks having the highest annual sales gains fared little better, turning $10,000 into $257,667, a compound return of 6.58 percent. Risk, as measured by both standard deviation and by the downside ratio was huge, coming in at 29.03 and 14.76 percent, respectively. The Sharpe ratio came in at a low 18. Like the All Stocks group, all base rates were uniformly negative, with the group beating Large Stocks in just 12 percent of all rolling 10-year periods. Like the group from All Stocks, the best 10-year period was the 10 years ending in 1999.

Thus, good performance from this group seems to only occur when we're at the end of a speculative market bubble, and this should caution us to what might come afterward.

12 CHAPTER

FIVE-YEAR EARNINGS-PER-SHARE PERCENTAGE CHANGES

The same thing happened today that happened yesterday, only to different people.

—Walter Winchell

Some analysts believe that a one-year change in earnings is meaningless, and we would be better off focusing on five-year growth rates. This, they argue, is enough time to separate the one-trick pony from the true thoroughbred. Let's see if they are right by examining the results to buying stocks based on their five-year earnings per share changes.

THE RESULTS

Unfortunately, five years of big earnings gains doesn't help us pick thoroughbreds either. Starting on December 31, 1954 (we need five years of data to compute the compound five-year earnings growth rate), $10,000 invested in the 50 stocks from the All Stocks universe with the highest five-year compound earnings-per-share growth rates grew to $1,287,685 by the end of 2003, a compound return of 10.42 percent (Table 12-1). A $10,000 investment in the All Stocks universe on December 31, 1954 was worth $3,519,152 on December 31, 2003, a return of 12.71 percent a year.

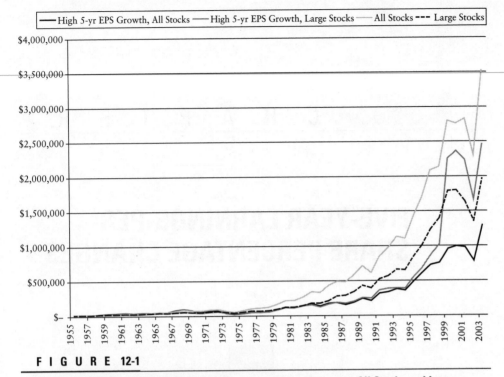

F I G U R E 12-1

Returns on high five-year compound earnings growth stocks versus All Stocks and Large Stocks, 1954–1996. Year-end 1954=$10,000.

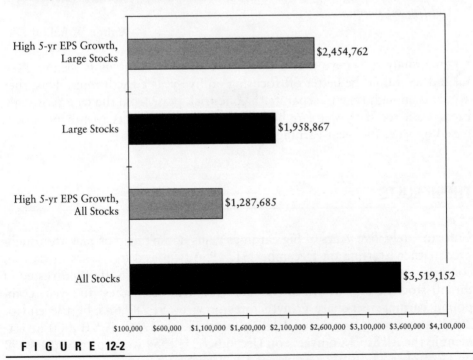

F I G U R E 12-2

December 31, 2003 value of $10,000 invested on December 31, 1954 and annually rebalanced.

Much like the 50 stocks with the highest one-year earnings gains, investors get dazzled by high five-year earnings growth rates and bid prices to unsustainable levels. When the future earnings are lower than expected, investors punish their former darlings and prices swoon.

The 50 stocks from All Stocks with the highest compound five-year earnings growth rates were also risky—their standard deviation of return was 26.80 percent, significantly higher than All Stocks' 20.10 percent. High risk coupled with poor return accounts for the Sharpe ratio of 30 (Figure 12-3). Over the same period, the Sharpe ratio for All Stocks was 44.

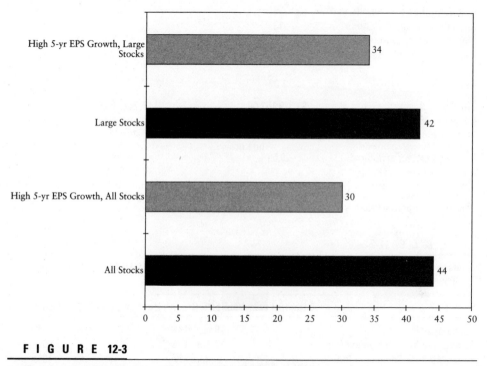

F I G U R E 12-3

Sharpe risk-adjusted return ratio, 1951–2003. (Higher is better.)

All the base rates for the strategy are horrible, with the 50 stocks with the highest five-year compound earnings growth rates beating All Stocks just 13 percent of the time over all rolling 10-year periods. Tables 12-1, 12-2, and 12-3 summarize the results.

T A B L E 12-1

Summary Return and Risk Results for Annual Data, All Stocks, and 50 Highest Five-Year EPS Growth from All Stocks, December 31, 1954–December 31, 2003

	All Stocks	All Stocks, 50 Highest Five-Year EPS Growth
Arithmetic Average	14.52%	13.71%
Geometric Average	12.71%	10.42%
Median Return	17.00%	19.20%
Standard Deviation of Return	20.10%	26.80%
Downside risk—lower is better	7.39%	11.91%
Correlation with S&P 500	0.86	0.80
T-Statistic	5.06	3.58
Sharpe Ratio	0.44	0.30
Number of Positive Periods	36	35
Number of Negative Periods	13	14
Maximum Peak-to-trough Decline (using Monthly data series)	−50.12%	−84.72%
Beta	1.02	1.26
$10,000 becomes:	$3,519,152.00	$1,287,685.00
Minimum Annual Return	−27.90%	−45.90%
Maximum Annual Return	55.90%	78.90%
Minimum *Expected* Return*	−25.68%	−39.89%
Maximum *Expected* Return**	54.72%	67.31%

*Minimum Expected Return is Arithmetic Return minus 2 times the standard deviation.
**Maximum Expected Return is Arithmetic Return plus 2 times the standard deviation.

T A B L E 12-2

Base Rates for All Stocks and 50 Highest Five-Year EPS Growth from All Stocks Universe, 1954–2003

Item	50 Highest Five-Year EPS Growth Beat "All Stocks"	Percent
Single-Year Return	19 out of 49	39%
Rolling Five-Year Compound Return	17 out of 45	38%
Rolling 10-Year Compound Return	5 out of 40	13%

T A B L E 12-3

Worst-Case Scenarios: All 10 Percent or Greater Declines for 50 Stocks with Highest Five-Year EPS Growth from All Stocks Universe, December 31, 1962–December 31, 2003

Peak Date	Peak Index Value	Trough Date	Trough Index Value	Recovery Date	Decline (%)	Decline Duration	Recovery Duration
Apr-65	1.56	Jun-65	1.38	Aug-65	−11.18	2	2
Apr-66	2.20	Oct-66	1.73	Jan-67	−21.31	6	3

(continued on next page)

T A B L E 12-3

Worst-Case Scenarios: All 10 Percent or Greater Declines for 50 Stocks with Highest Five-Year EPS Growth from All Stocks Universe, December 31, 1962–December 31, 2003 *(Continued)*

Peak Date	Peak Index Value	Trough Date	Trough Index Value	Recovery Date	Decline (%)	Decline Duration	Recovery Duration
Dec-67	2.94	Mar-68	2.53	Apr-68	−13.75	3	1
Nov-68	3.52	Sep-74	0.54	Apr-83	−84.72	70	103
Jun-83	4.08	Jul-84	2.73	Jan-86	−33.03	13	18
Jun-86	5.31	Sep-86	4.21	Feb-87	−20.78	3	5
Feb-87	5.79	Nov-87	3.31	Apr-89	−42.86	9	17
Sep-89	6.64	Jan-90	5.75	May-90	−13.34	4	4
Jun-90	6.71	Oct-90	5.05	Feb-91	−24.74	4	4
Feb-92	8.79	Aug-92	7.77	Dec-92	−11.6	6	4
Feb-94	10.27	Jun-94	8.65	Apr-95	−15.76	4	10
May-96	14.45	Jul-96	12.80	Sep-96	−11.47	2	2
Jan-97	16.97	Mar-97	15.26	May-97	−10.09	2	2
Sep-97	21.31	Aug-98	14.08	Apr-99	−33.93	11	8
Aug-00	30.22	Sep-02	18.13	Oct-03	−40.01	25	13
Average					−25.90	10.93	13.07

LARGE STOCKS SLIGHTLY OUTPERFORM UNIVERSE

Large stocks with outstanding five-year earnings gains perform slightly better than an investment in the Large Stocks universe. Starting on December 31, 1954, $10,000 invested in the 50 stocks from Large Stocks with the highest five-year compound earnings growth rates grew to $2,454,762 at the end of 2003, a compound annual return of 11.89 percent. $10,000 invested in the Large Stocks universe grew to $1,958,867, an annual return of 11.37 percent. But the 50 stocks with the high earnings gains were much riskier than Large Stocks, having a standard deviation of return of 26.91 percent, well ahead of Large Stocks' 16.66 percent.

The base rates are better than for All Stocks, with the strategy beating the Large Stocks universe 38 percent of the time over all rolling 10-year periods. The overall returns to the 50 stocks from Large Stocks were improved by excellent performance during the bubble years of the last half of the 1990s. During that period, large capitalization growth stocks did particularly well, and stocks with the highest five-year earnings gains are an excellent proxy for large cap growth. Tables 12-4, 12-5, and 12-6 summarize the returns for Large Stocks. Table 12-7 shows returns by decade.

T A B L E 12-4

Summary Return and Risk Results for Annual Data, Large Stocks, and 50 Highest Five-Year EPS Growth from Large Stocks, December 31, 1954–December 31, 2003

	Large Stocks	Large Stocks, 50 Highest Five-Year EPS Growth
Arithmetic Average	12.64%	14.78%
Geometric Average	11.37%	11.89%
Median Return	16.20%	13.20%
Standard Deviation of Return	16.66%	26.91%
Downside risk—lower is better	6.03%	9.38%
Correlation with S&P 500	0.93	0.75
T-Statistic	5.31	3.84
Sharpe Ratio	0.42	0.34
Number of Positive Periods	36	35
Number of Negative Periods	13	14
Maximum Peak-to-trough Decline (using Monthly data series)	−46.59%	−64.10%
Beta	0.91	1.18
$10,000 becomes:	$1,958,867.00	$2,454,762.00
Minimum Annual Return	−26.70%	−31.90%
Maximum Annual Return	45.07%	121.25%
Minimum *Expected* Return*	−20.68%	−39.04%
Maximum *Expected* Return**	45.96%	68.60%

*Minimum Expected Return is Arithmetic Return minus 2 times the standard deviation.
**Maximum Expected Return is Arithmetic Return plus 2 times the standard deviation.

T A B L E 12-5

Base Rates for Large Stocks and 50 Highest Five-Year EPS Growth Stocks from Large Stocks Universe, 1954–2003

Item	50 Highest Five-Year EPS Growth Beat "Large Stocks"	Percent
Single-Year Return	27 out of 49	55%
Rolling Five-Year Compound Return	23 out of 45	51%
Rolling 10-Year Compound Return	15 out of 40	38%

T A B L E 12-6

Worst-Case Scenarios: All 10 Percent or Greater Declines for 50 Stocks with Highest Five-Year EPS Growth from Large Stocks Universe, December 31, 1962–December 31, 2003

Peak Date	Peak Index Value	Trough Date	Trough Index Value	Recovery Date	Decline (%)	Decline Duration	Recovery Duration
Apr-66	2.04	Sep-66	1.64	Feb-67	−19.7	5	5
Sep-67	2.45	Feb-68	2.10	May-68	−14.19	5	3

(continued on next page)

T A B L E 12-6

Worst-Case Scenarios: All 10 Percent or Greater Declines for 50 Stocks with Highest Five-Year EPS Growth from Large Stocks Universe, December 31, 1962–December 31, 2003 *(Continued)*

Peak Date	Peak Index Value	Trough Date	Trough Index Value	Recovery Date	Decline (%)	Decline Duration	Recovery Duration
Nov-68	2.77	Sep-74	0.99	Jan-80	−64.1	70	64
Feb-80	2.92	Mar-80	2.49	Jun-80	−14.68	1	3
Nov-80	4.30	Jan-81	3.86	Apr-81	−10.02	2	3
May-81	4.55	Jul-82	3.22	Nov-82	−29.22	14	4
Jun-83	6.43	Jul-84	4.44	Dec-85	−30.89	13	17
Jun-86	8.32	Sep-86	6.87	Feb-87	−17.46	3	5
Aug-87	9.75	Nov-87	6.14	Aug-89	−37.03	3	21
May-90	10.00	Oct-90	7.76	Jan-91	−22.48	5	3
Jan-94	15.48	Jun-94	13.82	Feb-95	−10.72	5	8
May-96	24.31	Jul-96	21.30	Sep-96	−12.37	2	2
Apr-98	37.63	Aug-98	27.03	Dec-98	−28.16	4	4
Aug-00	110.67	Sep-02	58.30		−47.32	25	NA
Average					−25.60	11.21	10.92

T A B L E 12-7

Average Annual Compound Rates of Return by Decade

Portfolio	1950s*	1960s	1970s	1980s	1990s	2000s**
Large Stocks	14.07%	8.99%	6.99%	16.89%	15.34%	2.40%
Large Stocks, 50 Highest Five-Year EPS Growth	16.39%	8.24%	5.28%	12.34%	24.44%	2.20%
All Stocks	20.12%	11.09%	8.53%	15.85%	14.75%	5.91%
All Stocks, 50 Highest Five-Year EPS Growth	26.02%	8.77%	0.91%	11.60%	14.69%	7.83%

*Returns for 1955–1959.
**Returns for 2000–2003.

BEST- AND WORST-CASE RETURNS

The 50 stocks with the highest five-year earnings per share growth rates from All Stocks had eight declines exceeding 20 percent over the last 40 years, three of which exceeded 40 percent. The worst-case scenario was a drop of 84.72 percent following the 1968 peak, from which it took them more than 10 years to recover. They were also almost twice as risky when stock prices are declining, with a downside ratio of 11.91 percent, compared to 7.39 percent for All Stocks. The best five-year period grew a $10,000 investment into

$33,397, a compound return of 27.27 percent. On the downside, the same $10,000 fell to just $2,156, a five-year compound loss of 26.43 percent.

Over the last 40 years, the 50 stocks with the highest five-year earnings per share growth rates from Large Stocks had seven declines exceeding 20 percent. The worst-case scenario was a drop of 64.09 percent. They were more risky when stock prices were falling, with a downside ratio of 9.38 percent versus 6.03 percent for the Large Stocks universe. The 50 stocks from Large Stocks with the highest five-year earnings per share growth rates also showed extremely concentrated and spiky returns. For example, between August 1998 and August 2000, the end of the stock market bubble, they gained an amazing 76.08 *percent* per year, turning $10,000 into $32,501 in two years. They then went on to lose over half their value in the ensuing bear market of 2000–2003. Extending the time frame to five years, the best return came from the five years ending March 2000, with $10,000 growing to over $60,521, an average annual return of 43.34 percent. The worst five-year return, ending on September 31, 1974, saw the same $10,000 sink to $4,734, a compound average annual loss of 13.89 percent over those five years. Tables 12-3 and 12-6 detail the worst-case scenarios for each as well as Table 12-8, which shows the minimum and maximum returns.

T A B L E 12-8

Best and Worst Average Annual Compound Returns over Period for Annual Data 1954–2003				
For Any	**1-Year Period**	**3-Year Period**	**5-Year Period**	**10-Year Period**
Large Stocks Minimum Compound Return	−26.70%	−11.93%	−4.37%	1.21%
Large Stocks Maximum Compound Return	45.07%	24.39%	22.40%	17.01%
Large Stocks, 50 Highest Five-Year EPS Growth Minimum Compound Return	−31.90%	−18.41%	−10.51%	−0.95%
Large Stocks, 50 Highest Five-Year EPS Growth Maximum Compound Return	121.25%	49.35%	42.36%	25.50%
All Stocks Minimum Compound Return	−27.90%	−16.48%	−7.81%	1.26%
All Stocks Maximum Compound Return	55.90%	31.23%	27.77%	21.31%
All Stocks, 50 Highest Five-Year EPS Growth Minimum Compound Return	−45.90%	−28.21%	−19.93%	−5.56%
All Stocks, 50 Highest Five-Year EPS Growth Maximum Compound Return	78.90%	37.43%	28.38%	19.73%

DECILES

The decile analysis for All Stocks suggests that you could be somewhat better off focusing not on the upper 10 percent of the database by five-year earn-

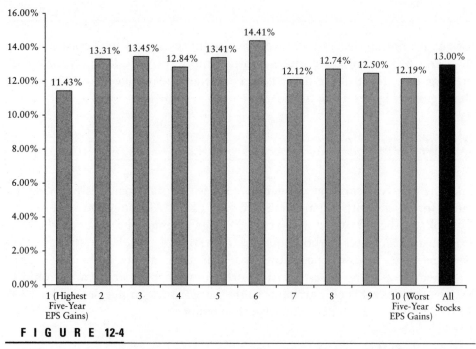

FIGURE 12-4

Compound return by five-year earnings gains decile, All Stocks universe, 1954–2003.

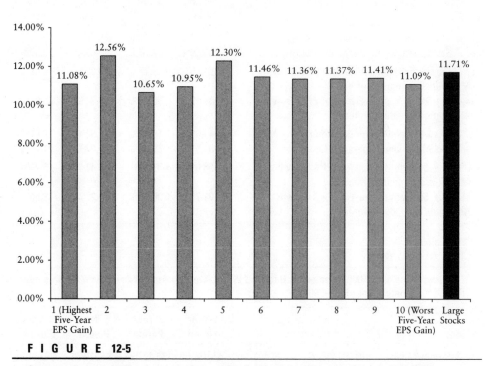

FIGURE 12-5

Compound return by five-year earnings gains decile, Large Stocks universe, 1954–2003.

ings gains, but on deciles two through six. But we see no such consistency in the Large Stocks universe, where returns simply show you're best off *avoiding* that 10 percent of the database having the highest five-year earnings per share gains (Figures 12-4 and 12-5).

IMPLICATIONS

Like the one-year earnings winners, we see investors consistently paying too much for stocks with outstanding five-year gains. Although we were unable to look at the 50 worst five-year earnings changes because of the way Compustat calculates the compound returns, they are probably similar to the one-year tests. The evidence shows that it is a mistake to get overly excited by big earnings gains. Investors pay a premium for these stocks and would be better off indexing their portfolios to the Large Stocks universe. Tables 12-9, 12-10, 12-11, and 12-12 summarize the results.

T A B L E 12-9

Best and Worst Average Annual Compound Returns over Period for Monthly Data 1954–2003

For Any	1-Year Period	3-Year Period	5-Year Period	10-Year Period
Large Stocks Minimum Compound Return	−42.04%	−13.79%	−6.05%	−0.20%
Large Stocks Maximum Compound Return	68.49%	32.78%	28.65%	19.57%
Large Stocks, 50 Highest Five-Year EPS Growth Minimum Compound Return	−54.35%	−23.32%	−13.90%	−4.58%
Large Stocks, 50 Highest Five-Year EPS Growth Maximum Compound Return	137.19%	56.95%	43.34%	30.03%
All Stocks Minimum Compound Return	−41.65%	−16.82%	−8.94%	0.68%
All Stocks Maximum Compound Return	81.51%	29.46%	27.02%	21.46%
All Stocks, 50 Highest Five-Year EPS Growth Minimum Compound Return	−56.01%	−33.94%	−26.43%	−10.23%
All Stocks, 50 Highest Five-Year EPS Growth Maximum Compound Return	101.70%	36.95%	27.27%	19.40%

T A B L E 12-10

Terminal Value of $10,000 Invested for Best and Worst Average Annual Compound Returns over Period for Monthly Data 1963–2003

For Any	1-Year Period	3-Year Period	5-Year Period	10-Year Period
Large Stocks Minimum $10,000 Value	$5,796.00	$6,407.27	$7,319.54	$9,801.79

(continued on next page)

T A B L E 12-10

Terminal Value of $10,000 Invested for Best and Worst Average Annual Compound Returns over Period for Monthly Data 1963–2003 *(Continued)*

For Any	1-Year Period	3-Year Period	5-Year Period	10-Year Period
Large Stocks Maximum $10,000 Value	$16,849.00	$23,409.82	$35,241.06	$59,734.10
Highest Five-Year EPS Large Stocks Minimum $10,000 Value	$4,565.00	$4,508.65	$4,731.68	$6,257.40
Highest Five-Year EPS Large Stocks Maximum $10,000 Value	$23,719.00	$38,661.97	$60,511.37	$138,176.96
All Stocks Minimum $10,000 Value	$5,835.00	$5,755.15	$6,260.92	$10,701.19
All Stocks Maximum $10,000 Value	$18,151.00	$21,697.36	$33,064.39	$69,876.76
Highest Five-Year EPS All Stocks Minimum $10,000 Value	$4,399.00	$2,882.81	$2,155.28	$3,398.70
Highest Five-Year EPS All Stocks Maximum $10,000 Value	$20,170.00	$25,685.39	$33,391.06	$58,890.23

T A B L E 12-11

Summary Results for Five-Year Earnings Gains Decile Analysis of All Stocks Universe, 1954–2003

Decile	$10,000 Grows to:	Average Return	Compound Return	Standard Deviation
1 (Highest Five-Year Earnings Gains)	$2,012,924	14.84%	11.43%	26.86%
2	$4,553,632	15.79%	13.31%	23.05%
3	$4,856,356	15.20%	13.45%	19.45%
4	$3,723,460	14.38%	12.84%	18.01%
5	$4,756,859	14.74%	13.41%	17.11%
6	$7,317,598	15.86%	14.41%	18.21%
7	$2,713,461	13.31%	12.12%	16.18%
8	$3,561,722	14.01%	12.74%	16.77%
9	$3,203,971	13.82%	12.50%	16.87%
10 (Worst Five-Year Earnings Gains)	$2,802,055	14.09%	12.19%	20.46%
All Stocks	$5,743,706	14.79%	13.00%	20.11%

T A B L E 12-12

Summary Results for Five-Year Earnings per Share Change Decile Analysis of Large Stocks Universe, 1954–2003

Decile	$10,000 Grows to:	Average Return	Compound Return	Standard Deviation
1 (Highest Five-Year Earnings Gains)	$1,725,221	13.81%	11.08%	24.76%
2	$3,288,092	14.57%	12.56%	21.00%
3	$1,425,623	11.99%	10.65%	16.74%
4	$1,627,508	12.33%	10.95%	17.13%
5	$2,937,095	13.51%	12.30%	16.29%
6	$2,040,212	12.48%	11.46%	14.78%
7	$1,950,415	12.62%	11.36%	16.53%
8	$1,956,385	12.40%	11.37%	15.08%
9	$1,989,846	12.37%	11.41%	14.37%
10 (Worst Five-Year Earnings Gains)	$1,726,703	12.32%	11.09%	16.55%
Large Stocks	$3,173,724	12.99%	11.71%	16.84%

PROFIT MARGINS: DO INVESTORS PROFIT FROM CORPORATE PROFITS?

I am a strong believer that as one moves toward the future, the strongest and clearest way to do it is if you have a good sense of your past. You cannot have a very tall tree without deep roots.

—Cesar Pelli

Net profit margins are an excellent gauge of a company's operating efficiency and ability to compete successfully with other firms in its field. Many believe that firms with high profit margins are better investments, because they are the leaders in their industries. You find net profit margins by dividing income before extraordinary items (a company's income after all expenses but before provisions for dividends) by net sales. This is then multiplied by 100 to make it a percentage.

THE RESULTS

I'll test this strategy by buying those 50 stocks from the All Stocks and Large Stocks universes with the highest profit margins. Here, we're able to start the test on December 31, 1951, so we're again looking at the full 52 years of data. As usual, all the accounting data is time-lagged to avoid look-ahead bias, and the portfolio is rebalanced annually.

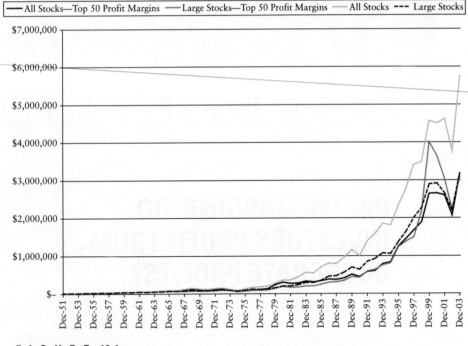

F I G U R E 13-1

Returns on high profit margin stocks versus All Stocks and Large Stocks, 1951–2003. Year-end 1951=$10,000.

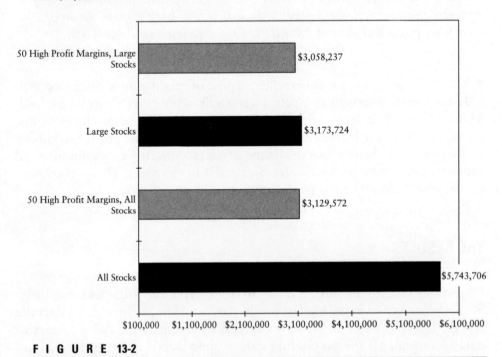

F I G U R E 13-2

December 31, 2003 value of $10,000 invested on December 31, 1951 and annually rebalanced.

198

As Table 13-1 shows, a $10,000 investment on December 31, 1951 in the 50 stocks from the All Stocks universe with the highest profit margins grew to $ 3,129,572 by the end of 2003, a compound return of 11.68 percent. That's 2.6 million dollars less than you'd earn investing in the All Stocks universe alone. There, $10,000 grew to $5,743,706, a return of 13 percent a year.

The 50 high profit margin stocks' risk was virtually the same as the All Stocks universe, with a standard deviation of return of 21.51 percent, slightly higher than All Stocks' 20.11 percent. Downside risk was also close to the All Stocks Universe, coming in at 8.29 percent, compared to 7.17 percent for All Stocks. All of the base rates for the 50 stocks with the highest profit margins were negative, with the strategy beating All Stocks just 30 percent of the time over all rolling ten-year periods. Tables 13-1, 13-3 and 13-5 summarize the returns for the All Stocks version of the strategy.

LARGE STOCKS DO BETTER

On a comparative basis, those 50 stocks with the highest profit margins from the Large Stocks universe do better than the All Stocks group. Here, $10,000 invested on December 31, 1951 grows to $3,058,237 by the end of 2003. That's about $100,000 less than the $3,173,724 you'd earn investing the money in the Large Stocks universe. Here, the 50 stocks with the highest profit margins were actually more risky than the Large Stocks universe, with a standard deviation of 20.95 percent compared to 16.84 percent for Large Stocks. The Sharpe ratio for the strategy was 39, compared to 45 for the Large Stocks universe. All base rates are negative, with the 50 stocks with the highest profit margins beating the Large Stocks universe 44 percent of the time over all rolling ten-year periods. Tables 13-2, 13-4 and 13-6 summarize the returns for the high profit margin stocks from Large Stocks.

T A B L E 13-1

Summary Return and Risk Results for Annual Data, All Stocks and 50 Highest Profit Margins from All Stocks, December 31, 1951–December 31, 2003

	All Stocks	All Stocks—Top 50 Profit Margins
Arithmetic Average	14.79%	13.73%
Geometric Average	13.00%	11.68%
Median Return	16.80%	12.43%
Standard Deviation of Return	20.11%	21.51%
Downside risk—lower is better	7.17%	8.29%
Correlation with S&P 500	0.87	0.73
T-Statistic	5.30	4.60

(continued on next page)

T A B L E 13-1

Summary Return and Risk Results for Annual Data, All Stocks and 50 Highest Profit Margins from All Stocks, December 31, 1951–December 31, 2003 *(Continued)*

	All Stocks	All Stocks—Top 50 Profit Margins
Sharpe Ratio	0.46	0.39
Number of Positive Periods	39	40
Number of Negative Periods	13	12
Maximum Peak-to-trough Decline (using Monthly data series)	−50.12%	−67.26%
Beta	0.99	0.89
$10,000 becomes:	$5,743,706.00	$3,129,572.00
Minimum Annual Return	−27.90%	−45.70%
Maximum Annual Return	55.90%	85.10%
Minimum *Expected* Return*	−25.43%	−29.29%
Maximum *Expected* Return**	55.01%	56.75%

*Minimum Expected Return is Arithmetic Return minus 2 times the standard deviation.
**Maximum Expected Return is Arithmetic Return plus 2 times the standard deviation.

T A B L E 13-2

Summary Return and Risk Results for Annual Data, All Stocks and 50 Highest Profit Margins from All Stocks, December 31, 1951–December 31, 2003

	Large Stocks	Large Stocks—Top 50 Profit Margins
Arithmetic Average	12.99%	13.47%
Geometric Average	11.71%	11.63%
Median Return	15.75%	9.35%
Standard Deviation of Return	16.84%	20.95%
Downside risk—lower is better	5.86%	6.92%
Correlation with S&P 500	0.95	0.77
T-Statistic	5.56	4.64
Sharpe Ratio	0.45	0.39
Number of Positive Periods	39	42
Number of Negative Periods	13	10
Maximum Peak-to-trough Decline (using Monthly data series)	−46.59%	−57.17%
Beta	0.89	0.92
$10,000 becomes:	$3,173,724.00	$3,058,237.00
Minimum Annual Return	−26.70%	−31.70%
Maximum Annual Return	45.07%	83.86%
Minimum Expected Return*	−20.69%	−28.43%
Maximum Expected Return**	46.67%	55.37%

*Minimum Expected Return is Arithmetic Return minus 2 times the standard deviation.
**Maximum Expected Return is Arithmetic Return plus 2 times the standard deviation.

T A B L E 13-3

Base Rates for All Stocks and 50 Highest Profit Margin Stocks from All Stocks Universe, 1951–2003

Item	Top 50 by High Margins Beat "All Stocks"	Percent
Single-Year Return	22 out of 52	42%
Rolling Five-Year Compound Return	22 out of 48	46%
Rolling 10-Year Compound Return	13 out of 43	30%

T A B L E 13-4

Base Rates for Large Stocks and 50 Highest Profit Margin Stocks from Large Stocks Universe, 1951–2003

Item	Top 50 by High Margins Beat "Large Stocks"	Percent
Single-Year Return	24 out of 52	46%
Rolling Five-Year Compound Return	23 out of 48	48%
Rolling 10-Year Compound Return	19 out of 43	44%

T A B L E 13-5

Worst-Case Scenarios: All 10 Percent or Greater Declines for 50 Stocks from All Stocks with Highest Profit Margins, December 31, 1962–December 31, 2003

Peak Date	Peak Index Value	Trough Date	Trough Index Value	Recovery Date	Decline (%)	Decline Duration	Recovery Duration
Jan-66	1.46	Sep-66	1.18	Mar-67	−19.31	8	6
May-69	2.31	Jun-70	1.62	Mar-71	−29.94	13	9
Dec-72	2.96	Dec-74	0.97	Jan-80	−67.26	24	61
Jan-80	3.14	Mar-80	2.58	Jun-80	−17.86	2	3
May-81	4.3	Jul-82	3.25	Nov-82	−24.43	14	4
Jun-83	5.97	Jul-84	4.28	Dec-85	−28.3	13	17
Aug-87	9.59	Nov-87	6.75	Dec-89	−29.56	3	25
Jun-90	10.5	Oct-90	8.14	Feb-91	−22.53	4	4
Jan-92	15.6	Jun-92	13.55	Dec-92	−13.13	5	6
Jan-94	18.41	Jun-94	16.09	Dec-94	−12.6	5	6
May-96	31.85	Jul-96	27.45	Sep-96	−13.81	2	2
Jan-97	34.56	Mar-97	28.83	Jul-97	−16.59	2	4
Apr-98	41.05	Aug-98	30.88	Dec-98	−24.77	4	4
Jan-99	43.33	Apr-99	38.97	Jun-99	−10.04	3	2
Feb-00	70.84	Sep-02	41.16		−41.9	31	NA
Average					−24.80	8.87	10.93

T A B L E 13-6

Worst-Case Scenarios: All 10 Percent or Greater Declines for 50 Stocks from All Stocks with Highest Profit Margins, December 31, 1962–December 31, 2003

Peak Date	Peak Index Value	Trough Date	Trough Index Value	Recovery Date	Decline (%)	Decline Duration	Recovery Duration
Jan-66	1.51	Sep-66	1.27	Jan-67	−15.82	8	4
Nov-68	2.3	May-70	1.71	Feb-71	−25.37	18	9
Dec-72	3.27	Sep-74	1.46	Jan-80	−55.22	21	64
Feb-80	3.36	Mar-80	2.89	Jun-80	−13.88	1	3
May-81	4.57	Jul-82	3.81	Oct-82	−16.76	14	3
Jun-83	6.68	May-84	5.37	Feb-85	−19.64	11	9
Jun-86	11.82	Sep-86	10.6	Jan-87	−10.35	3	4
Aug-87	15.87	Nov-87	10.7	May-89	−32.6	3	18
Jun-90	21.56	Oct-90	18.94	Dec-90	−12.15	4	2
Dec-91	35.32	Sep-92	29.39	Jan-94	−16.78	9	16
May-96	61.25	Jul-96	55.11	Nov-96	−10.03	2	4
Jun-98	86.36	Aug-98	67.59	Nov-98	−21.74	2	3
Feb-00	211.42	Sep-02	90.54		−57.17	31	NA
Average					−23.65	9.77	11.58

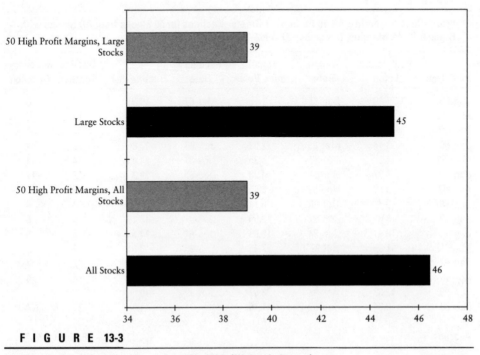

F I G U R E 13-3

Sharpe risk-adjusted return ratio, 1951–2003. (Higher is better.)

BEST AND WORST CASE RETURNS

The worst-case scenario tables show us that buying stocks with the highest profit margins, especially Large Stocks, doesn't have as much potential for dramatic declines as many of the other strategies we've looked at. Over the last 40 years, the 50 high margin stocks from the All Stocks universe lost more than 30 percent from peak to trough two times, both during times when stocks in general were in a bear market. Their biggest loss was 67 percent during the bear market of 1973 through 1974. Looking at Table 13-10, we see that for their best five-year period the high margin stocks would have turned $10,000 into $35,848, whereas the worst five years reduced the same $10,000 to $4,574.

The high-margin stocks from Large Stocks had three drops exceeding 30 percent, with the largest, 57 percent, coming during the bear market of 2000 through 2002. The best five-year period saw $10,000 growing to $53,380, with the worst five reducing it to $6,206. Tables 13-5, 13-6 and 13-10 show the worst-case scenarios as well as the best and worst returns for one-, three-, five-, and ten-year periods.

T A B L E 13-7

Average Annual Compound Rates of Return by Decade

Portfolio	1950s*	1960s	1970s	1980s	1990s	2000s**
Large Stocks	15.33%	8.99%	6.99%	16.89%	15.34%	2.40%
Large Stocks—Top 50 Profit Margins	14.70%	8.24%	7.26%	12.66%	24.72%	−6.48%
All Stocks	19.22%	11.09%	8.53%	15.85%	14.75%	5.91%
All Stocks—Top 50 Profit Margins	15.02%	13.02%	8.14%	8.16%	18.12%	4.37%

*Returns for 1952–1959.
**Returns for 2000–2003.

T A B L E 13-8

Best and Worst Average Annual Compound Returns Over Period for Annual Data 1951–2003

For Any	1-Year Period	3-Year Period	5-Year Period	10-Year Period
Large Stocks Minimum Compound Return	−26.70%	−11.93%	−4.37%	1.21%
Large Stocks Maximum Compound Return	45.07%	24.39%	22.40%	17.01%
Large Stocks Top 50 by High Margins Minimum Compound Return	−31.70%	−17.96%	−4.83%	−1.41%
Large Stocks Top 50 by High Margins Maximum Compound Return	83.86%	42.84%	37.86%	24.72%

(continued on next page)

T A B L E 13-8

Best and Worst Average Annual Compound Returns Over Period for Annual Data 1951–2003
(Continued)

For Any	1-Year Period	3-Year Period	5-Year Period	10-Year Period
All Stocks Minimum Compound Return	−27.90%	−16.48%	−7.81%	1.26%
All Stocks Maximum Compound Return	55.90%	31.23%	27.77%	21.31%
All Stocks Top 50 by High Margins Minimum Compound Return	−45.70%	−20.81%	−12.79%	−2.12%
All Stocks Top 50 by High Margins Maximum Compound Return	85.10%	40.02%	34.36%	19.84%

T A B L E 13-9

Best and Worst Average Annual Compound Returns Over Period for Monthly Data 1962–2003

For Any	1-Year Period	3-Year Period	5-Year Period	10-Year Period
Large Stocks Minimum Compound Return	−42.04%	−13.79%	−6.05%	−0.20%
Large Stocks Maximum Compound Return	68.49%	32.78%	28.65%	19.57%
Large Stocks Top 50 by High Margins Minimum Compound Return	−52.37%	−21.98%	−9.10%	0.19%
Large Stocks Top 50 by High Margins Maximum Compound Return	103.80%	50.62%	39.79%	27.93%
All Stocks Minimum Compound Return	−41.65%	−16.82%	−8.94%	0.68%
All Stocks Maximum Compound Return	81.51%	29.46%	27.02%	21.46%
All Stocks Top 50 by High Margins Minimum Compound Return	−58.63%	−26.76%	−14.48%	−2.48%
All Stocks Top 50 by High Margins Maximum Compound Return	81.70%	32.71%	29.09%	23.51%

T A B L E 13-10

Terminal Value of $10,000 Invested for Best and Worst Average Annual Compound Returns Over Period for Monthly Data 1963-2003

For Any	1-Year Period	3-Year Period	5-Year Period	10-Year Period
Large Stocks Minimum $10,000 Value	$5,796.00	$6,407.27	$7,319.54	$9,801.79
Large Stocks Maximum $10,000 Value	$16,849.00	$23,409.82	$35,241.06	$59,734.10
50 High Profit Margin Large Stocks Minimum $10,000 Value	$4,763.00	$4,749.17	$6,206.11	$10,191.63
50 High Profit Margin Large Stocks Maximum $10,000 Value	$20,380.00	$34,170.23	$53,380.24	$117,415.11

(continued on next page)

T A B L E 13-10

Terminal Value of $10,000 Invested for Best and Worst Average Annual Compound Returns Over Period for Monthly Data 1963-2003 *(Continued)*

For Any	1-Year Period	3-Year Period	5-Year Period	10-Year Period
All Stocks Minimum $10,000 Value	$5,835.00	$5,755.15	$6,260.92	$10,701.19
All Stocks Maximum $10,000 Value	$18,151.00	$21,697.36	$33,064.39	$69,876.76
50 High Profit Margin All Stocks Minimum $10,000 Value	$4,137.00	$3,928.67	$4,574.45	$7,779.24
50 High Profit Margin All Stocks Maximum $10,000 Value	$18,170.00	$23,372.81	$35,847.84	$82,607.83

DECILES

The decile analysis of profit margins confirms the 50-stock results—it's not a good idea to buy a stock simply because it has a high profit margin. The decile analysis shows quite the opposite, with stocks in the some of the lowest profit margin deciles outperforming those in the top (the exception is the tenth decile). For example, $10,000 invested in the ten percent of stocks with the highest profit margins from All Stocks grew to $3,419,441, well behind All Stocks and *considerably* behind those in the eighth decile! The same holds true with Large Stocks, where we see lower margin deciles outperforming higher deciles.

IMPLICATIONS

History shows using high profit margins as the only determinant in buying a stock leads to disappointing results. Indeed, with the decile results, we see that if an investor were to use profit margin as a factor at all, it should simply be to avoid those stocks with the highest margins.

T A B L E 13-11

Summary Results for Profit Margin Decile Analysis of All Stocks Universe, 1951–2003

Decile	$10,000 Grows to:	Average Return	Compound Return	Standard Deviation
1 (Highest Profit Margins)	$3,419,441	13.30%	11.87%	17.54%
2	$4,539,454	13.61%	12.49%	15.65%

(continued on next page)

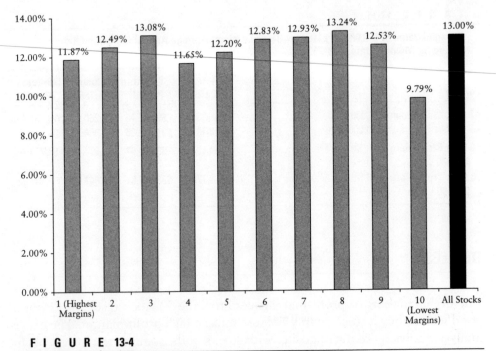

Compound return by profit margin decile, All Stocks universe, 1951–2003.

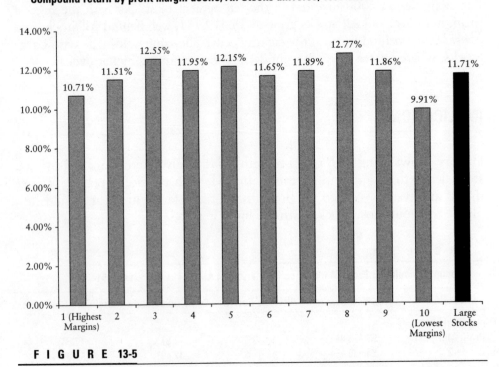

F I G U R E 13-5

Compound return by profit margin decile, Large Stocks universe, 1951–2003.

T A B L E 13-11

Summary Results for Profit Margin Decile Analysis of All Stocks Universe, 1951–2003
(Continued)

Decile	$10,000 Grows to:	Average Return	Compound Return	Standard Deviation
3	$5,966,562	14.38%	13.08%	16.82%
4	$3,083,435	12.89%	11.65%	16.70%
5	$3,978,661	13.88%	12.20%	18.82%
6	$5,332,421	14.71%	12.83%	20.21%
7	$5,583,233	14.96%	12.93%	20.82%
8	$6,430,318	15.41%	13.24%	21.87%
9	$4,635,006	15.17%	12.53%	24.10%
10 (Lowest Profit Margins)	$1,286,721	14.41%	9.79%	31.82%
All Stocks	$5,743,706	14.79%	13.00%	20.11%

T A B L E 13-12

Summary Results for Profit Margin Decile Analysis of Large Stocks Universe, 1951–2003

Decile	$10,000 Grows to:	Average Return	Compound Return	Standard Deviation
1 (Highest Profit Margin)	$1,983,207	11.97%	10.71%	16.69%
2	$2,880,784	12.57%	11.51%	15.19%
3	$4,686,774	13.60%	12.55%	14.97%
4	$3,537,168	13.18%	11.95%	16.56%
5	$3,884,299	13.44%	12.15%	16.65%
6	$3,081,715	12.95%	11.65%	16.79%
7	$3,438,303	13.39%	11.89%	18.22%
8	$5,166,443	14.30%	12.77%	18.26%
9	$3,395,347	13.49%	11.86%	18.98%
10 (Lowest Profit Margin)	$1,360,873	13.38%	9.91%	26.07%
Large Stocks	$3,173,724	12.99%	11.71%	16.84%

14

CHAPTER

RETURN ON EQUITY

I'd rather see folks doubt what's true than accept what isn't.
—Frank A. Clark

High return on equity is a hallmark of a growth stock. You find return on equity by dividing common stock equity into income before extraordinary items (a company's income after all expenses, but before provisions for dividends.) You then multiply by 100 to express the term as a percentage. Here, we use common liquidating equity (called CEQL in Compustat) as a proxy for common equity.

Like high profit margins, many believe that a high return on equity (ROE) is an excellent gauge of how effectively a company invests shareholders' money. The higher the ROE, the better the company's ability to invest your money, and presumably, the better an investment the stock will be.

THE RESULTS

We'll look at the results for high-ROE stocks drawn from both the All Stocks and Large Stocks universes. We start on December 31, 1951 with a $10,000 investment in the 50 stocks from All Stocks having the highest ROE. We'll also look at ROE by deciles for both All Stocks and Large Stocks. As usual,

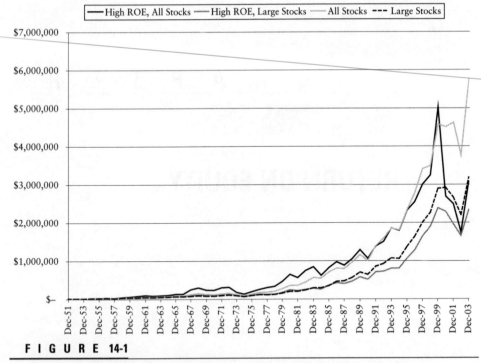

F I G U R E 14-1

Returns on high-ROE stocks versus All Stocks and Large Stocks, 1951–2003. Year-end 1951=$10,000.

we'll rebalance the portfolio annually and time lag all accounting data to avoid look-ahead bias.

As of December 31, 2003, $10,000 invested in those 50 stocks having the highest ROE is worth $3,063,447, $2.6 million less than the $5,743,706 you'd earn investing the money in All Stocks (Table 14-1). And while earning less money, you'd take a lot more risk—the 50 stocks with the highest ROE had a standard deviation of return of 28.94 percent, considerably higher than All Stocks' 20.11 percent. The 50 stocks with the highest ROE were twice as risky as All Stocks, with a downside of 12.31 percent, compared to 7.17 percent for All Stocks. This risk accounts for the 50 highest ROE stocks' Sharpe ratio of 34, 12 points behind the All Stocks ratio of 46 (Figure 14-3).

All base rates are negative. The 50 highest ROE stocks beat the All Stocks universe 48 percent of the time in any one-year period, 42 percent of the time in rolling five-year periods, and 35 percent of the time in rolling 10-year periods. The 50 highest ROE stocks from All Stocks lost more than 20 percent from peak to trough nine times, whereas All Stocks lost more than20 percent just six times. And the worst-case scenario for the 50 highest ROE stocks was considerably worse than All Stocks, declining 74.82 percent between February 2000 and September 2002. The worst drop for All Stocks

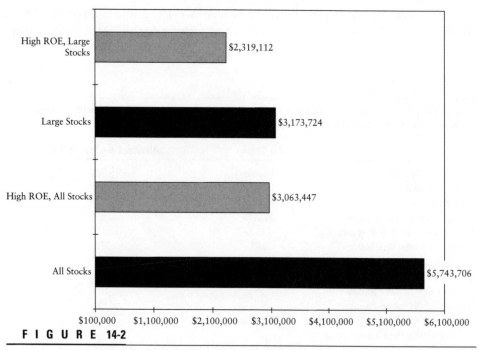

F I G U R E 14-2

December 31, 2003 value of $10,000 invested on December 31, 1951 and annually rebalanced.

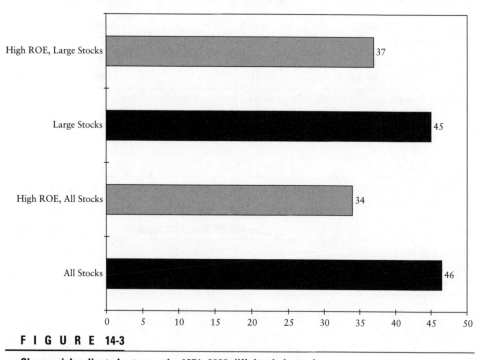

F I G U R E 14-3

Sharpe risk-adjusted return ratio, 1951–2003. (Higher is better.)

was a loss of 50.12 percent between November 1972 and September 1974. Tables 14-1, 14-2, and 14-3 summarize the returns for the All Stocks group.

T A B L E 14-1

Summary Return and Risk Results for Annual Data, All Stocks, and 50 Stocks with Highest Return on Equity from All Stocks, December 31, 1951–December 21, 2003

	All Stocks	All Stocks—Top 50 ROE
Arithmetic Average	14.79%	15.38%
Geometric Average	13.00%	11.64%
Median Return	16.80%	18.35%
Standard Deviation of Return	20.11%	28.94%
Downside Risk—lower is better	7.17%	12.31%
Correlation with S&P 500	0.87	0.76
T-Statistic	5.30	3.83
Sharpe Ratio	0.46	0.34
Number of Positive Periods	39	37
Number of Negative Periods	13	15
Maximum Peak-to-Trough Decline (using monthly data series)	−50.12%	−74.83%
Beta	0.99	1.25
$10,000 becomes:	$5,743,706.00	$3,063,447.00
Minimum Annual Return	−27.90%	−46.80%
Maximum Annual Return	55.90%	96.30%
Minimum *Expected* Return*	−25.43%	−42.50%
Maximum *Expected* Return**	55.01%	73.26%

*Minimum Expected Return is Arithmetic Return minus 2 times the standard deviation.
**Maximum Expected Return is Arithmetic Return plus 2 times the standard deviation.

T A B L E 14-2

Base Rates for All Stocks and 50 Stocks with Highest Return on Equity from All Stocks Universe, 1951–2003

Item	Top 50 ROE Beat "All Stocks"	Percent
Single-Year Return	25 out of 52	48%
Rolling Five-Year Compound Return	20 out of 48	42%
Rolling 10-Year Compound Return	15 out of 43	35%

T A B L E 14-3

Worst-Case Scenarios: All 10 Percent or Greater Declines for 50 Stocks from All Stocks with Highest Return on Equity, December 31, 1962–December 31, 2003

Peak Date	Peak Index Value	Trough Date	Trough Index Value	Recovery Date	Decline (%)	Decline Duration	Recovery Duration
Apr-66	1.97	Oct-66	1.52	Jan-67	−22.74	6	3
Dec-67	2.94	Mar-68	2.46	May-68	−16.06	3	2
Nov-68	3.36	Jun-70	1.67	Dec-71	−50.48	19	18
May-72	4.17	Sep-74	1.12	Dec-79	−73.15	28	63
Feb-80	4.59	Mar-80	3.66	Jul-80	−20.3	1	4
Nov-80	6.52	Jul-82	4.60	Nov-82	−29.42	20	4
Jun-83	9.87	Jul-84	6.05	May-86	−38.75	13	22
Jun-86	10.66	Sep-86	8.71	Feb-87	−18.32	3	5
Mar-87	11.98	Nov-87	6.97	Dec-91	−41.84	8	49
Feb-92	13.21	Aug-92	11.22	Jan-93	−15.08	6	5
Jan-94	16.33	Jun-94	13.40	Jul-95	−17.94	5	13
Apr-96	21.79	Jul-96	19.06	Sep-96	−12.55	3	2
Jan-97	22.37	Apr-97	18.52	Jun-97	−17.19	3	2
Apr-98	30.01	Aug-98	20.57	Mar-99	−31.45	4	7
Apr-99	36.67	Sep-99	30.42	Dec-99	−17.04	5	3
Feb-00	50.45	Sep-02	12.70		−74.83	31	NA
Average					−31.07	9.88	13.47

LARGE STOCKS ARE THE SAME

The 50 highest ROE stocks from the Large Stocks universe do just about as badly as those from the All Stocks universe. Here, $10,000 grows to $2,319,112 at the end of 2003, a compound return of 11.04 percent a year. That's worse than the $3,173,724 you'd make investing the money in the Large Stocks universe itself. The 50 highest ROE stocks from Large Stocks were also riskier—their standard deviation of return was 20.02 percent, compared to 16.84 percent for the Large Stocks universe. Because of its lower return and higher risk, the 50 highest ROE stocks had a Sharpe ratio of 37, eight points behind the Large Stocks universe's 45.

Base rates for the Large Stocks group are similar to All Stocks, with the 50 highest ROE stocks beating the Large Stocks universe 46 percent of the time in any one-year period, 42 percent of the time in rolling five-year periods, and 35 percent of the time in rolling 10-year periods. Tables 14-4, 14-5, and 14-6 summarize the returns for the Large Stocks group. Table 14-7 shows returns for both groups by decade.

T A B L E 14-4

Summary Return and Risk Results for Annual Data, Large Stocks, and 50 Stocks with Highest Return on Equity from Large Stocks, December 31, 1951–December 21, 2003

	Large Stocks	Large Stocks—Top 50 ROE
Arithmetic Average	12.99%	12.87%
Geometric Average	11.71%	11.04%
Median Return	15.75%	13.85%
Standard Deviation of Return	16.84%	20.02%
Downside Risk—lower is better	5.86%	7.96%
Correlation with S&P 500	0.95	0.93
T-Statistic	5.56	4.64
Sharpe Ratio	0.45	0.37
Number of Positive Periods	39	37
Number of Negative Periods	13	15
Maximum Peak-to-Trough Decline (using monthly data series)	−46.59%	−61.89%
Beta	0.89	1.06
$10,000 becomes:	$3,173,724.00	$2,319,112.00
Minimum Annual Return	−26.70%	−32.40%
Maximum Annual Return	45.07%	56.20%
Minimum *Expected* Return*	−20.69%	−27.17%
Maximum *Expected* Return**	46.67%	52.91%

*Minimum Expected Return is Arithmetic Return minus 2 times the standard deviation.
**Maximum Expected Return is Arithmetic Return plus 2 times the standard deviation

T A B L E 14-5

Base Rates for Large Stocks and 50 Stocks with Highest Return on Equity from Large Stocks Universe, 1951–2003

Item	Top 50 ROE Beat "Large Stocks"	Percent
Single-Year Return	24 out of 52	46%
Rolling Five-Year Compound Return	20 out of 48	42%
Rolling 10-Year Compound Return	15 out of 43	35%

T A B L E 14-6

Worst-Case Scenarios: All 10 Percent or Greater Declines for 50 Stocks from Large Stocks with Highest Return on Equity, December 31, 1962–December 31, 2003

Peak Date	Peak Index Value	Trough Date	Trough Index Value	Recovery Date	Decline (%)	Decline Duration	Recovery Duration
Apr-66	1.94	Sep-66	1.59	Feb-67	−18.32	5	5
Sep-67	2.27	Feb-68	1.91	Sep-68	−15.8	5	7

(continued on next page)

T A B L E 14-6

Worst-Case Scenarios: All 10 Percent or Greater Declines for 50 Stocks from Large Stocks with Highest Return on Equity, December 31, 1962–December 31, 2003 *(Continued)*

Peak Date	Peak Index Value	Trough Date	Trough Index Value	Recovery Date	Decline (%)	Decline Duration	Recovery Duration
Nov-68	2.46	Jun-70	1.63	Apr-71	−33.84	19	10
May-72	3.25	Sep-74	1.24	Jul-80	−61.89	28	70
Nov-80	4.22	Jul-82	2.52	Apr-83	−40.26	20	9
Jun-83	4.95	Jul-84	3.31	Dec-85	−33.19	13	17
Jun-86	6.93	Sep-86	5.95	Jan-87	−14.13	3	4
Aug-87	8.52	Nov-87	5.31	Jul-89	−37.73	3	20
Jul-90	8.93	Oct-90	7.62	Feb-91	−14.67	3	4
Jan-94	14.91	Jun-94	13.17	Feb-95	−11.67	5	8
Jun-98	34.12	Aug-98	27.57	Jan-99	−19.2	2	5
Mar-00	46.40	Sep-02	27.13		−41.54	30	NA
Average					−28.52	11.33	14.45

T A B L E 14-7

Average Annual Compound Rates of Return by Decade

Portfolio	1950s*	1960s	1970s	1980s	1990s	2000s**
Large Stocks	15.33%	8.99%	6.99%	16.89%	15.34%	2.40%
Large Stocks—Top 50 ROE	17.71%	10.22%	5.30%	13.29%	15.35%	−0.57%
All Stocks	19.22%	11.09%	8.53%	15.85%	14.75%	5.91%
All Stocks—Top 50 ROE	24.36%	14.96%	6.98%	10.97%	14.63%	−11.62%

*Returns for 1952–1959.
**Returns for 2000–2003.

WORST-CASE SCENARIOS AND BEST AND WORST RETURNS

As Tables 14-3, 14-6, and 14-8 show, a great deal of volatility is present in stocks with high ROE. The worst drop for high-ROE All Stocks came in the recent bear market of 2000–2002, during which time they fell 75 percent from peak to trough. They had a similar drop in the bear market of the early 1970s. Indeed, there were six separate times when the 50 stocks with the highest ROE from All Stocks dropped by more than 30 percent, and three times when they fell by more than 50 percent. Looking at Table 14-8, you see the best five years for the high ROE stocks turned $10,000 into $43,853, whereas the worst five years reduced the $10,000 to $3,792.

The 50 stocks having the highest ROE from Large Stocks were slightly less volatile. Their worst decline was 62 percent during the 1970s bear market. Like their All Stocks brethren, they fell by more than 30 percent from peak to trough six times, although only one drop exceeded 50 percent. An investment during the best five-year period turned $10,000 into $32,947, whereas the worst five years reduced $10,000 to $5,531. Generally speaking, high-ROE stocks offer mediocre best-case scenarios.

T A B L E 14-8

Terminal Value of $10,000 Invested for Best and Worst Average Annual Compound Returns over Period for Monthly Data 1963–2003

For Any	1-Year Period	3-Year Period	5-Year Period	10-Year Period
Large Stocks Minimum $10,000 Value	$5,796.00	$6,407.27	$7,319.54	$9,801.79
Large Stocks Maximum $10,000 Value	$16,849.00	$23,409.82	$35,241.06	$59,734.10
High ROE Large Stocks Minimum $10,000 Value	$4,596.00	$4,811.53	$5,530.93	$8,071.23
High ROE Large Stocks Maximum $10,000 Value	$18,833.00	$25,065.88	$32,947.42	$55,667.88
All Stocks Minimum $10,000 Value	$5,835.00	$5,755.15	$6,260.92	$10,701.19
All Stocks Maximum $10,000 Value	$18,151.00	$21,697.36	$33,064.39	$69,876.76
High ROE All Stocks Minimum $10,000 Value	$4,164.00	$2,658.48	$3,791.80	$7,940.26
High ROE All Stocks Maximum $10,000 Value	$21,209.00	$27,919.04	$43,852.70	$60,943.96

DECILE

The decile analysis of ROE paints a somewhat different picture—here, we see that an investor who concentrated on the higher ROE stocks that made up deciles two and three would have done nearly twice as well as someone investing in the benchmark. $10,000 invested in the second decile by ROE from All Stocks (the second highest group by ROE) would have grown to $13,551,914, a compound return of 14.88 percent. That's considerably better than All Stocks' 13 percent compound return. But the standard deviation of 25.20 percent pushed the Sharpe ratio to 48, one point above All Stocks 47. Tables 14-9 and 14-10, as well as Figures 14-4 and 14-5 summarize the results.

T A B L E 14-9

Best and Worst Average Annual Compound Returns over Period for Annual Data 1951–2003

For Any	1-Year Period	3-Year Period	5-Year Period	10-Year Period
Large Stocks Minimum Compound Return	−26.70%	−11.93%	−4.37%	1.21%
Large Stocks Maximum Compound Return	45.07%	24.39%	22.40%	17.01%

(continued on page 218)

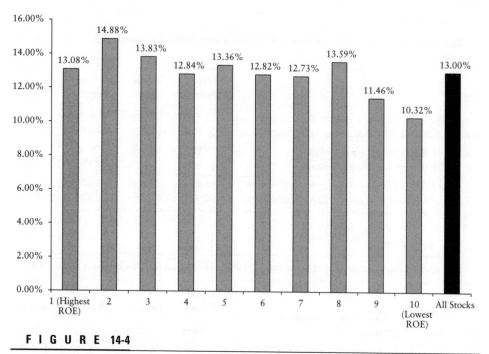

F I G U R E 14-4

Compound return by ROE decile, All Stocks universe, 1951–2003.

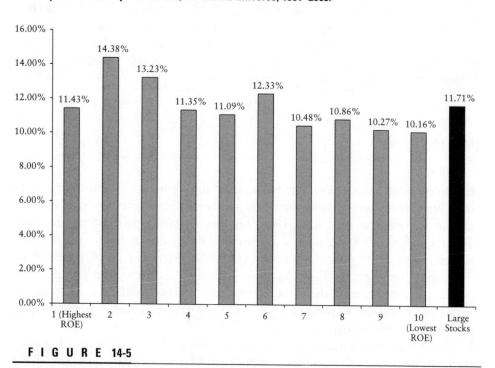

F I G U R E 14-5

Compound return by ROE decile, Large Stocks universe, 1951–2003.

T A B L E 14-9

Best and Worst Average Annual Compound Returns over Period for Annual Data 1951–2003
(Continued)

For Any	1-Year Period	3-Year Period	5-Year Period	10-Year Period
Large Stocks Top 50 ROE Minimum Compound Return	–32.40%	–18.86%	–7.99%	1.38%
Large Stocks Top 50 ROE Maximum Compound Return	56.20%	31.45%	24.47%	17.65%
All Stocks Minimum Compound Return	–27.90%	–16.48%	–7.81%	1.26%
All Stocks Maximum Compound Return	55.90%	31.23%	27.77%	21.31%
All Stocks Top 50 ROE Minimum Compound Return	–46.80%	–29.91%	–11.57%	1.28%
All Stocks Top 50 ROE Maximum Compound Return	96.30%	43.21%	30.43%	25.67%

T A B L E 14-10

Best and Worst Average Annual Compound Returns over Period for Monthly Data 1962–2003

For Any	1-Year Period	3-Year Period	5-Year Period	10-Year Period
Large Stocks Minimum Compound Return	–42.04%	–13.79%	–6.05%	–0.20%
Large Stocks Maximum Compound Return	68.49%	32.78%	28.65%	19.57%
Large Stocks Top 50 ROE Minimum Compound Return	–54.04%	–21.64%	–11.17%	–2.12%
Large Stocks Top 50 ROE Maximum Compound Return	88.33%	35.84%	26.93%	18.73%
All Stocks Minimum Compound Return	–41.65%	–16.82%	–8.94%	0.68%
All Stocks Maximum Compound Return	81.51%	29.46%	27.02%	21.46%
All Stocks Top 50 ROE Minimum Compound Return	–58.36%	–35.70%	–17.63%	–2.28%
All Stocks Top 50 ROE Maximum Compound Return	112.09%	40.81%	34.40%	19.81%

IMPLICATIONS

Return on equity is an excellent example of the importance of looking at the long-term when judging a strategy's effectiveness. Imagine a young investor just out of college at the end of 1964. He lands a job on Wall Street and studies how stocks with high ROE perform. The evidence from the previous decade is very encouraging—between December 31, 1951 and December 31, 1959, the 50 highest ROE stocks from both the All Stocks and Large Stocks universes outperformed their respective benchmarks, with the 50 from All Stocks returning 24.36 percent a year and the 50 from Large Stocks returning 17.71 percent a year.

Both the evidence and the story make sense. Buy companies that do a good job managing shareholder's money and let them manage yours. It's a simple and sensible thing to do. But our young investor is skeptical. He needs to see the evidence with his own eyes before he'll believe it.

And so, he watches. In 1965, the 50 highest ROE stocks from All Stocks return 26 percent, better than the 23 percent from All Stocks. Although the next year is a bear market for All Stocks, with the group losing 5 percent, the 50 stocks with the highest ROE eked out a gain of .02 percent. Our young investor is encouraged.

Then comes 1967. The 50 stocks with the highest ROE from All Stocks soar, gaining 96 percent, 55 percent more than the All Stocks universe. Our investor is hooked. He has both the results of the last decade and the personal experience of the last three years to prove he's *really* on to something.

He'll go on believing that high-ROE stocks are great investments for many years, yet they manage to do a bit *worse* than the market year-in, year-out. With access to studies that looked at the 1930s and 1940s, he probably would have seen what we see—the 50 stocks with highest ROE are only a good investment 50 percent of the time.

The decile analysis tells a somewhat different tale, revealing that it's really only that 10 percent of stocks having the highest ROE (decile one) that are mediocre investments. Deciles two and three from both All Stocks and Large Stocks do considerably better than their benchmarks on an absolute basis, but only the Large Stocks second decile beats its benchmark on a risk-adjusted basis. In both instances, however, the decile performance lacks the consistency we found when looking at ratios such as price-to-sales. Tables 14-11 and 14-12 summarize the ROE decile analyses.

T A B L E 14-11

Summary Results for ROE Decile Analysis of All Stocks Universe, 1951–2003

Decile	$10,000 Grows to:	Average Return	Compound Return	Standard Deviation
1 (Highest ROE)	$5,977,442	15.72%	13.08%	24.50%
2	$13,551,914	17.40%	14.88%	25.20%
3	$8,407,958	15.94%	13.83%	21.58%
4	$5,335,015	14.47%	12.84%	18.80%
5	$6,778,222	15.19%	13.36%	19.94%
6	$5,309,137	14.69%	12.82%	20.19%
7	$5,075,079	14.44%	12.73%	19.25%
8	$7,530,104	15.54%	13.59%	20.78%
9	$2,824,751	13.93%	11.46%	23.44%
10 (Lowest ROE)	$1,649,017	14.37%	10.32%	29.89%
All Stocks	$5,743,706	14.79%	13.00%	20.11%

T A B L E 14-12

Summary Results for ROE Decile Analysis of Large Stocks Universe, 1951–2003

Decile	$10,000 Grows to:	Average Return	Compound Return	Standard Deviation
1 (Highest ROE)	$2,775,652	13.42%	11.43%	20.94%
2	$10,820,336	16.00%	14.38%	18.94%
3	$6,394,664	14.72%	13.23%	18.04%
4	$2,679,466	12.65%	11.35%	16.72%
5	$2,371,457	12.43%	11.09%	17.07%
6	$4,224,881	13.77%	12.33%	17.69%
7	$1,782,487	11.77%	10.48%	16.66%
8	$2,133,084	12.23%	10.86%	17.32%
9	$1,612,662	11.86%	10.27%	18.49%
10 (Lowest ROE)	$1,532,300	12.83%	10.16%	23.24%
Large Stocks	$3,173,724	12.99%	11.71%	16.84%

15 CHAPTER

RELATIVE PRICE STRENGTH: WINNERS CONTINUE TO WIN

It may be that the race is not always to the swift, nor the battle to the strong—but that's the way to bet.

—Damon Runyon

"Don't fight the tape."
"Make the trend your friend."
"Cut your losses and let your winners run."

These Wall Street maxims all mean the same thing—bet on price momentum. Of all the beliefs on Wall Street, price momentum makes efficient market theorists howl the loudest. The defining principle of their theory is that you *cannot* use past prices to predict future prices. A stock may triple in a year, but according to efficient market theory, that will not affect next year. Efficient market theorists also hate price momentum because it is independent of all accounting variables. If buying winning stocks works, then stock prices have "memories" and carry useful information about the future direction of a stock.

In his book, *The Wisdom of Crowds: Why the Many Are Smarter than the Few and How Collective Wisdom Shapes Business, Economies, Societies and Nations*, James Surowiecki argues that "under the right circumstances, groups are remarkably intelligent, and are often smarter than the smartest people in them." Surowiecki says that if four conditions are met, a crowd's "collective intelligence" will prove superior to the judgments of a smaller

221

group of experts. The four conditions are (1) diversity of opinion; (2) independence of members from one another; (3) decentralization; and (4) a good method for aggregating opinions. He then goes on to list several accounts in which crowds were far more accurate than any individual member trying to make a correct forecast.

Generally speaking, these four conditions are present in market-based price auctions, with the final price of a stock serving as an aggregator of all market opinion about the prospects for that stock. The only times this is not true is when markets are either in a bubble or a bust. At these market extremes, a uniformity of opinion occurs that impairs the ability of a group to offer good collective judgment.

Conversely, another school of thought says you should buy stocks that have been *most* battered by the market. This is the argument of Wall Street's bottom fishers, who use absolute price change as their guide, buying issues after they've performed poorly. If Surowiecki is correct, this type of approach would only work after a bubble or bust, when the collective wisdom got the answer wrong. Let's see who is right.

THE RESULTS

We'll look at buying those 50 stocks having the *best* and the *worst* one-year price changes from both the All Stocks and Large Stocks universes. This will contrast the results of buying last year's biggest winners with last year's biggest losers. We'll also separate the stocks by decile for both universes. Let's look at the winners first. (In this and future chapters, I'll use the terms "relative strength" and "price appreciation" interchangeably. Stocks with the best relative strength are the biggest winners in terms of their previous year's price appreciation.) Starting on December 31, 1951, we'll buy those 50 stocks having the largest price appreciation from the previous year (Figure 15-2). I arrive at this number by dividing this year's closing price by that from the previous 12 months. Thus, if XYZ closed this year at 10 and last year at 2, it would have a gain of 400 percent and a price index of 5 (10 divided by 2).

A $10,000 investment on December 31, 1951 in those 50 stocks from All Stocks having the best one-year price appreciation is worth $4,814,164 at the end of 2003, a compound return of 12.61 percent a year (Table 15-1). This is the first fairly significant reversal of a factor's performance since the publication of this book in 1997. Originally, buying the stocks with the best performance from the All Stocks universe did better than All Stocks, but with much higher volatility. Due to the market bubble in 2000, and the three horrible years that ensued, we see them faring slightly worse than the 13 percent

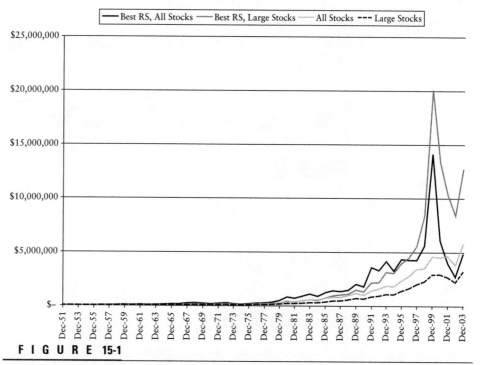

F I G U R E 15-1

Returns on best relative strength stocks versus All Stocks and Large Stocks, 1951–2003. Year-end 1951=$10,000.

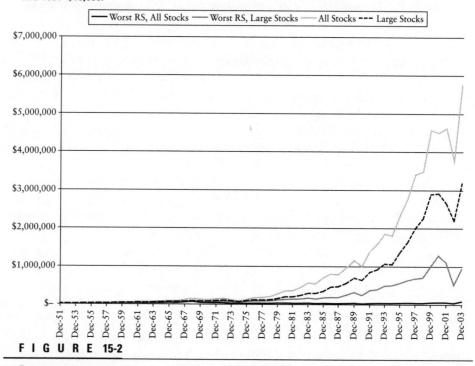

F I G U R E 15-2

Returns on worst relative strength stocks versus All Stocks and Large Stocks, 1951–2003. Year-end 1951=$10,000.

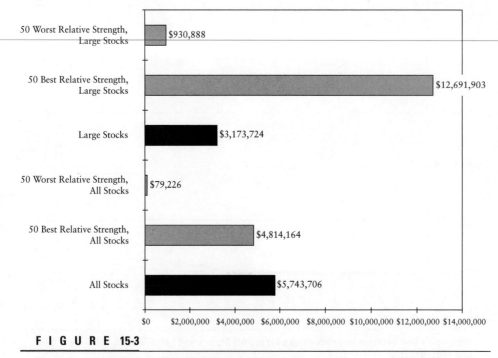

F I G U R E 15-3

December 31, 2003 value of $10,000 invested on December 31, 1951 and annually rebalanced.

return from the All Stocks universe. The volatility over the period since I last published this book was extraordinary—from February 1997 through February 2000, the 50 stocks having the best one-year price appreciation soared by nearly 500 percent, only to turn around and plunge over 89 percent during the next three years!

The performance of those 50 stocks from All Stocks having the best one-year price appreciation also had extraordinarily high risk. The standard deviation of return for the 50 best one-year price performers was 37.82 percent, the highest we've seen for an individual factor. The enormous risk pushed the Sharpe ratio to 35, well below All Stocks' 46 (Figure 15-4). When examining deciles, we'll see that performance is increased and risk is reduced when focusing on the top 10 percent of stocks by price appreciation.

I cannot overstate how difficult it can be to stick with volatile strategies such as this one. Investors are drawn to these strategies by outstanding relative performance, as when the 50 stocks with the best relative strength from All Stocks gained 101 percent in 1991 and an eye-popping 152 percent in 1999. And while people *think* they can cope with volatility when a strategy is doing well, they have the wind knocked out of them when their volatile strategy declines 30 percent in a bull market. The emotional toll this takes is enormous, and you must understand it before embracing a highly volatile

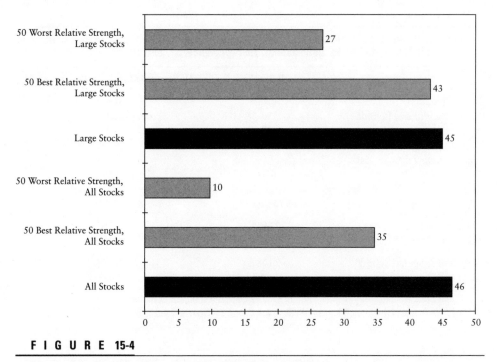

F I G U R E 15-4

Sharpe risk-adjusted return ratio, 1951–2003. (Higher is better.)

strategy. As I make clear later in the book, you should have *some* exposure to volatile strategies, but it should never comprise the majority of your portfolio. Very few have the stomach for the roller coaster ride.

The base rates for those 50 stocks having the best one-year relative strength are all positive, with the strategy beating the market 67 percent of the time over all rolling 10-year periods. Tables 15-1, 15-2, and 15-3 summarize the returns for the All Stocks group.

T A B L E 15-1

Summary Return and Risk Results for Annual Data, All Stocks, and 50 Stocks with Best Relative Strength (RS) from All Stocks, December 31, 1951–December 31, 2003

	All Stocks	All Stocks—Top 50 by One-Year RS
Arithmetic Average	14.79%	18.39%
Geometric Average	13.00%	12.61%
Median Return	16.80%	21.30%
Standard Deviation of Return	20.11%	37.82%
Downside Risk—lower is better	7.17%	14.18%
Correlation with S&P 500	0.87	0.70
T-Statistic	5.30	3.51

(continued on next page)

T A B L E 15-1

Summary Return and Risk Results for Annual Data, All Stocks, and 50 Stocks with Best Relative Strength (RS) from All Stocks, December 31, 1951–December 31, 2003 *(Continued)*

	All Stocks	All Stocks—Top 50 by One-Year RS
Sharpe Ratio	0.46	0.35
Number of Positive Periods	39	34
Number of Negative Periods	13	18
Maximum Peak-to-Trough Decline (using monthly data series)	−50.12%	−89.40%
Beta	0.99	1.51
$10,000 becomes:	$5,743,706.00	$4,814,164.00
Minimum Annual Return	−27.90%	−57%
Maximum Annual Return	55.90%	152.25%
Minimum *Expected* Return*	−25.43%	−57.25%
Maximum *Expected* Return**	55.01%	94.03%

*Minimum Expected Return is Arithmetic Return minus 2 times the standard deviation.
**Maximum Expected Return is Arithmetic Return plus 2 times the standard deviation.

T A B L E 15-2

Base Rates for All Stocks and 50 Best Relative Strength (RS) Stocks from All Stocks Universe, 1951–2003

Item	Top 50 by One-Year Relative Strength Beat "All Stocks"	Percent
Single-Year Return	30 out of 52	58%
Rolling Five-Year Compound Return	28 out of 48	58%
Rolling 10-Year Compound Return	29 out of 43	67%

T A B L E 15-3

Worst-Case Scenarios: All 10 Percent or Greater Declines for 50 Stocks from All Stocks with Best One-Year Relative Strength, December 31, 1963–December 31, 2003

Peak Date	Peak Index Value	Trough Date	Trough Index Value	Recovery Date	Decline (%)	Decline Duration	Recovery Duration
Apr-65	1.35	Jun-65	1.20	Sep-65	−11.29	2	3
Apr-66	2.15	Oct-66	1.50	Feb-67	−30.32	6	4
Dec-67	3.32	Mar-68	2.73	Apr-68	−17.78	3	1
Dec-68	4.43	Sep-74	1.67	Apr-78	−62.33	69	43
Aug-78	6.63	Oct-78	4.81	Apr-79	−27.41	2	6
Feb-80	9.18	Mar-80	6.62	Jul-80	−27.89	1	4
Nov-80	14.45	Feb-82	9.96	Nov-82	−31.09	15	9
Jun-83	22.83	May-84	13.83	Mar-86	−39.42	11	22
Jun-86	26.43	Dec-86	21.40	Feb-87	−19.01	6	2

(continued on next page)

T A B L E 15-3

Worst-Case Scenarios: All 10 Percent or Greater Declines for 50 Stocks from All Stocks with Best One-Year Relative Strength, December 31, 1963–December 31, 2003 *(Continued)*

Peak Date	Peak Index Value	Trough Date	Trough Index Value	Recovery Date	Decline (%)	Decline Duration	Recovery Duration
Aug-87	29.53	Nov-87	18.19	Aug-89	−38.42	3	21
Sep-89	32.14	Jan-90	26.46	May-90	−17.65	4	4
May-90	35.76	Oct-90	24.92	Mar-91	−30.3	5	5
Jan-92	59.27	Aug-92	41.98	Sep-93	−29.17	7	13
Oct-93	61.14	Jan-95	42.84	Jul-95	−29.92	15	6
Sep-95	68.81	Jan-96	57.25	Apr-96	−16.8	4	3
May-96	77.40	Mar-97	48.73	Dec-98	−37.04	10	21
Apr-99	126.83	May-99	113.13	Jun-99	−10.8	1	1
Jun-99	134.78	Jul-99	116.88	Nov-99	−13.28	1	4
Feb-00	317.01	Mar-03	33.59		−89.4	37	NA
Average					−30.49	10.63	9.56

LARGE STOCKS DO BETTER

Those 50 stocks from the Large Stocks universe having high relative strength actually do much better than those from All Stocks, more than tripling the return of an investment in the Large Stocks universe. A $10,000 investment on December 31, 1951 in those 50 stocks from the Large Stocks universe having the best one-year price performance in the previous year grew to $12,691,903, more than three times the $3,173,724 you'd earn investing in the Large Stocks universe. Risk here is also high, with the 50 best price performers showing a standard deviation of return of 29.58 percent, 12.74 percent higher than the Large Stocks' 16.84 percent. Because the risk was so much higher, the Sharpe ratio for this portfolio came in at 43, compared to 45 for Large Stocks.

All the base rates are positive, with the 50 best relative strength stocks from Large Stocks beating the universe 91 percent of the time over all rolling 10-year periods. Tables 15-4, 15-5, and 15-6 summarize the results for Large Stocks.

T A B L E 15-4

Summary Return and Risk Results for Annual Data, Large Stocks, and 50 Stocks with Best Relative Strength (RS) from Large Stocks, December 31, 1951–December 31, 2003

	Large Stocks	Large Stocks—Top 50 by One-Year RS
Arithmetic Average	12.99%	18.09%
Geometric Average	11.71%	14.73%

(continued on next page)

T A B L E 15-4

Summary Return and Risk Results for Annual Data, Large Stocks, and 50 Stocks with Best Relative Strength (RS) from Large Stocks, December 31, 1951–December 31, 2003 *(Continued)*

	Large Stocks	Large Stocks—Top 50 by One-Year RS
Median Return	15.75%	19.90%
Standard Deviation of Return	16.84%	29.58%
Downside Risk—lower is better	5.86%	9.06%
Correlation with S&P 500	0.95	0.73
T-Statistic	5.56	4.41
Sharpe Ratio	0.45	0.43
Number of Positive Periods	39	39
Number of Negative Periods	13	13
Maximum Peak-to-Trough Decline (using monthly data series)	−46.59%	−71.51%
Beta	0.89	1.23
$10,000 becomes:	$3,173,724.00	$12,691,903.00
Minimum Annual Return	−26.70%	−33.51%
Maximum Annual Return	45.07%	139.94%
Minimum *Expected* Return*	−20.69%	−41.07%
Maximum *Expected* Return**	46.67%	77.25%

*Minimum Expected Return is Arithmetic Return minus 2 times the standard deviation.
**Maximum Expected Return is Arithmetic Return plus 2 times the standard deviation.

T A B L E 15-5

Base Rates for Large Stocks and 50 Best Relative Strength (RS) Stocks from Large Stocks Universe, 1951–2003

Item	Top 50 by One-Year Relative Strength Beat "Large Stocks"	Percent
Single-Year Return	29 out of 52	56%
Rolling Five-Year Compound Return	41 out of 48	85%
Rolling 10-Year Compound Return	39 out of 43	91%

T A B L E 15-6

Worst-Case Scenarios: All 10 Percent or Greater Declines for 50 Stocks from Large Stocks with Best One-Year Relative Strength, December 31, 1963–December 31, 2003

Peak Date	Peak Index Value	Trough Date	Trough Index Value	Recovery Date	Decline (%)	Decline Duration	Recovery Duration
Apr-66	1.71	Oct-66	1.33	Mar-67	−22.08	6	5
Dec-67	2.04	Feb-68	1.69	May-68	−17.17	2	3
Nov-68	2.23	Jun-70	1.26	Mar-72	−43.64	19	21
May-72	2.45	Sep-74	1.20	May-78	−51.14	28	44

(continued on next page)

T A B L E 15-6

Worst-Case Scenarios: All 10 Percent or Greater Declines for 50 Stocks from Large Stocks with Best One-Year Relative Strength, December 31, 1963–December 31, 2003 *(Continued)*

Peak Date	Peak Index Value	Trough Date	Trough Index Value	Recovery Date	Decline (%)	Decline Duration	Recovery Duration
Aug-78	2.86	Oct-78	2.41	Mar-79	−15.87	2	5
Aug-79	3.24	Oct-79	2.88	Dec-79	−11.26	2	2
Feb-80	4.12	Mar-80	3.09	Jul-80	−24.92	1	4
Nov-80	6.39	Feb-82	4.28	Nov-82	−32.9	15	9
Jun-83	9.74	Jul-84	6.29	Nov-85	−35.45	13	16
Jun-86	13.86	Sep-86	11.67	Jan-87	−15.76	3	4
Aug-87	16.94	Nov-87	11.95	Apr-89	−29.42	3	17
Sep-89	20.75	Jan-90	18.32	May-90	−11.71	4	4
May-90	20.86	Oct-90	16.33	Jan-91	−21.71	5	3
Dec-91	32.54	Jun-92	27.86	Nov-92	−14.39	6	5
Jan-94	45.15	Jun-94	40.12	Oct-94	−11.14	5	4
Oct-94	45.60	Jan-95	40.90	Mar-95	−10.31	3	2
May-96	74.93	Jul-96	58.29	Jul-97	−22.21	2	12
Jun-98	100.79	Aug-98	74.12	Dec-98	−26.46	2	4
Feb-00	378.98	Sep-02	107.98		−71.51	31	NA
Average					−25.74	8.00	9.11

WHY PRICE PERFORMANCE WORKS WHILE OTHER MEASURES DO NOT

Price momentum, particularly with large capitalization stocks, conveys different information about the prospects of a stock and is a much better indicator than factors such as earnings growth rates. Many look at the disappointing results of buying stocks with the highest earnings gains and wonder why they differ from the best one-year price performers. First, price momentum is the market putting its money where its mouth is. Second, the common belief that stocks with strong relative strength also have the highest price-to-earnings (PE) ratios or earnings growth is incorrect. When you look at the top one-year performers over time, you find they usually have PE ratios 30 to 50 percent higher than the market, but are *rarely* the highest in the market. The same is true for five-year earnings-per-share growth rates and one-year earnings-per-share growth rates. As a group, they usually are higher than the market, but not by extraordinary amounts. Also, Surowiecki's concept of "wise crowds" is proved in the longer-term data for price momentum, with price movement being an excellent measure of what the overall market opinion is of the current price.

WORST-CASE SCENARIOS AND BEST AND WORST RETURNS

Looking at Tables 15-3, 15-6, and 15-18, we see that for both All Stocks and Large Stocks, the biggest drawdown for those 50 stocks from All Stocks having the best one-year price appreciation came in the recent bear market of 2000–2002. The 50 stocks from All Stocks plummeted more than 89 percent between February 2000 and March 2003, whereas the 50 stocks from Large Stocks lost 71 percent over the same period. You have to go back to the last great bear market of the early 1970s to find plunges nearly as frightening.

Between 1964 and 2003, the All Stocks group lost more than 30 percent from peak to trough eight times, with two of them exceeding 60 percent. The Large Stocks group lost more than 30 percent five times, with two drops exceeding 50 percent.

Extreme upside volatility also occurred with both the All Stocks group and the Large Stocks group, with those 50 stocks having the best one-year price appreciation from each compounding at *more than 80 percent per year* between March of 1997 and February 2000. Looking at Table 15-18, we see that for the All Stocks group, the best five-year period turned $10,000 into $71,248, and into $86,870 for the Large Stocks group. Conversely, the worst five-year period for the All Stocks group saw $10,000 drop to $4,745 for the best performers from All Stocks and $6,587 for the gainers from Large Stocks. You can examine all the tables for the best and worst one-, five-, and 10-year returns. Remember to note the disparity between best- and worst-case scenarios and consider the magnitude of the worst-case scenarios before using one-year relative strength on its own.

BUYING THE WORST PERFORMING STOCKS

If you're looking for a great way to underperform the market, look no further. A $10,000 investment on December 31, 1951, in those 50 stocks from the All Stocks universe having the worst one-year price performance, was worth just $79,226 at the end of 2003, a compound return of 4.06 percent a year. Only those 50 stocks having the highest price-to-sales ratios did worse. The standard deviation of return for the 50 losers was 32.63 percent, considerably higher than All Stocks' 20.11 percent. With such abysmal returns, *any* risk will wreak havoc with the Sharpe ratio, and here it's a pathetic 10. Base rates are atrocious, with the 50 losers beating All Stocks in only 14 of the 52 years reviewed. The rolling five-year returns are even worse. The 50 losers beat All Stocks only twice in 48 five-year periods. And the *magnitude* of all rolling five-year losses was huge as well, with those 50 stocks having the worst performance on average almost 10 percent behind the average return for All Stocks in any five-year period. But the booby prize goes to the 10-year returns, in which the losers *never* beat the All Stocks universe. The magnitude of the underperformance is staggering—over all 10-year periods, the 50 biggest losers had an average annual compound return that was 10 percent *less* than All Stocks. Tables 15-7, 15-8, and 15-9 detail the grim news.

T A B L E 15-7

Summary Return and Risk Results for Annual Data, All Stocks, and 50 Stocks Worst Relative Strength (RS) from All Stocks, December 31, 1951–December 31, 2003

	All Stocks	All Stocks—Worst 50 by One-Year RS
Arithmetic Average	14.79%	8.43%
Geometric Average	13.00%	4.06%
Median Return	16.80%	5.97%
Standard Deviation of Return	20.11%	32.63%
Downside Risk—lower is better	7.17%	14.71%
Correlation with S&P 500	0.87	0.65
T-Statistic	5.30	1.86
Sharpe Ratio	0.46	0.10
Number of Positive Periods	39	32
Number of Negative Periods	13	20
Maximum Peak-to-Trough Decline (using monthly data series)	−50.12%	−87.03%
Beta	0.99	1.20
$10,000 becomes:	$5,743,706.00	$79,226.00
Minimum Annual Return	−27.90%	−48.90%
Maximum Annual Return	55.90%	142.63%
Minimum *Expected* Return*	−25.43%	−56.83%
Maximum *Expected* Return**	55.01%	73.69%

*Minimum Expected Return is Arithmetic Return minus 2 times the standard deviation.
**Maximum Expected Return is Arithmetic Return plus 2 times the standard deviation.

T A B L E 15-8

Base Rates for All Stocks and 50 Worst Relative Strength (RS) Stocks from All Stocks Universe, 1951–2003

Item	50 Worst by One-Year Relative Strength Beat "All Stocks"	Percent
Single-Year Return	14 out of 52	27%
Rolling Five-Year Compound Return	2 out of 45	4%
Rolling 10-Year Compound Return	0 out of 40	0%

T A B L E 15-9

Worst-Case Scenarios: All 10 Percent or Greater Declines for 50 Stocks with Worst Relative Strength from All Stocks, December 31, 1963–December 31, 2003

Peak Date	Peak Index Value	Trough Date	Trough Index Value	Recovery Date	Decline (%)	Decline Duration	Recovery Duration
Jan-66	1.67	Sep-66	1.35	Jan-67	−18.93	8	4
Nov-68	2.52	Dec-74	0.33		−87.03	73	NA
Average					−52.98	40.5	4

LARGE STOCKS ALSO HIT

Large stocks also suffer, but the results aren't fatal. A $10,000 investment in those 50 stocks having the worst one-year price performance from the Large Stocks universe on December 31, 1951 grew to $930,888 by the end of 2003, a compound return of 9.11 percent a year. That's much worse than the $3,173,724 you'd earn from $10,000 invested in the Large Stocks universe, but not as damaging to your wealth as the biggest losers from All Stocks. The risk was higher than Large Stocks, with the standard deviation for the 50 losers at 24.32 percent. The Sharpe ratio was a fairly low 27.

The base rates are better here over the short-term, but equally grim over the long-term. The 50 biggest losers beat the Large Stocks universe 46 percent of the time over any single year; 33 percent over five-year periods, and only once over all 10-year periods. Tables 15-10, 15-11, and 15-12 summarize the results for the 50 Large Stocks losers.

T A B L E 15-10

Summary Return and Risk Results for Annual Data, Large Stocks, and 50 Stocks Worst Relative Strength (RS) from Large Stocks, December 31, 1951–December 31, 2003

	Large Stocks	Large Stocks Worst 50 by One-Year RS
Arithmetic Average	12.99%	11.84%
Geometric Average	11.71%	9.11%
Median Return	15.75%	11.10%
Standard Deviation of Return	16.84%	24.32%
Downside Risk—lower is better	5.86%	11%
Correlation with S&P 500	0.95	0.74
T-Statistic	5.56	3.51
Sharpe Ratio	0.45	0.27
Number of Positive Periods	39	38

(continued on next page)

T A B L E 15-10

Summary Return and Risk Results for Annual Data, Large Stocks, and 50 Stocks Worst Relative Strength (RS) from Large Stocks, December 31, 1951–December 31, 2003 *(Continued)*

	Large Stocks	Large Stocks Worst 50 by One-Year RS
Number of Negative Periods	13	14
Maximum Peak-to-Trough Decline (using monthly data series)	−46.59%	−77.00%
Beta	0.89	1.03
$10,000 becomes:	$3,173,724.00	$930,888.00
Minimum Annual Return	−26.70%	−53.80%
Maximum Annual Return	45.07%	83.75%
Minimum *Expected* Return*	−20.69%	−36.80%
Maximum *Expected* Return**	46.67%	60.48%

*Minimum Expected Return is Arithmetic Return minus 2 times the standard deviation.
**Maximum Expected Return is Arithmetic Return plus 2 times the standard deviation.

T A B L E 5-11

Base Rates for Large Stocks and 50 Worst Relative Strength (RS) Stocks from Large Stocks Universe, 1951–2003

Item	50 Worst by One-Year Relative Strength Beat "Large Stocks"	Percent
Single-Year Return	24 out of 52	46%
Rolling Five-Year Compound Return	15 out of 45	33%
Rolling 10-Year Compound Return	1 out of 40	3%

T A B L E 15-12

Worst-Case Scenarios: All 10 Percent or Greater Declines for 50 Stocks with Worst Relative Strength from Large Stocks, December 31, 1962–December 31, 2003

Peak Date	Peak Index Value	Trough Date	Trough Index Value	Recovery Date	Decline (%)	Decline Duration	Recovery Duration
Nov-65	1.40	Sep-66	1.13	Jan-67	−19.19	10	4
Sep-67	1.66	Mar-68	1.46	Jul-68	−12.11	6	4
Nov-68	1.96	Sep-74	0.78	Mar-79	−60.19	70	54
Jan-80	2.21	Mar-80	1.95	May-80	−11.49	2	2
May-81	2.82	Jul-82	1.88	Apr-83	−33.19	14	9
Aug-83	3.35	Jul-84	2.43	May-86	−27.42	11	22
May-86	3.44	Jul-86	2.93	Jan-87	−14.99	2	6
Aug-87	4.55	Nov-87	2.84	May-89	−37.41	3	18
Dec-89	5.18	Oct-90	3.41	May-91	−34.2	10	7
Jan-94	8.16	Jun-94	7.26	May-95	−11.08	5	11
Apr-96	10.37	Jul-96	9.14	May-97	−11.91	3	10

(continued on next page)

T A B L E 15-12

Worst-Case Scenarios: All 10 Percent or Greater Declines for 50 Stocks with Worst Relative
Strength from Large Stocks, December 31, 1962–December 31, 2003 *(Continued)*

Peak Date	Peak Index Value	Trough Date	Trough Index Value	Recovery Date	Decline (%)	Decline Duration	Recovery Duration
Apr-98	12.15	Aug-98	8.17	Apr-99	−32.76	4	8
Dec-99	15.72	Feb-00	13.64	May-00	−13.28	2	3
Jan-01	26.43	Sep-02	6.08		−77	20	NA
Average					−28.30	11.57	12.15

BEST- AND WORST-CASE RETURNS

Looking at Tables 15-9, 15-12, and 15-18, we see a very unattractive picture.
Those 50 stocks having the worst one-year performance from All Stocks
peaked back in November 1968, and have yet to recover that old high. The
drawdown of more than 87 percent means that had you—or more likely your
parents—started buying the 50 biggest losers from All Stocks once a year and
slavishly rebalanced the portfolio to always hold the biggest 50 losers, your
$10,000 would be worth $1,300, before inflation! If you really want to get
depressed, keep in mind that the 20-year bull market ending in March of
2000 was the biggest bull market of the last 100 years. When you look at the
best- and worst-case returns for any five-year period, what you don't see on
the surface is that over all rolling five-year periods between 1964 and 2003,
the *absolute return* for the 50 stocks was negative nearly half the time. On a
relative basis, the news is even more depressing: The 50 biggest losers from
All Stocks only beat the All Stocks universe in 14 of 421 monthly observations, and only six times by more than 10 percent. Here, the best case isn't
great—and it doesn't happen very often.

T A B L E 15-13

Average Annual Compound Rates of Return by Decade

Portfolio	1950s*	1960s	1970s	1980s	1990s	2000s**
Large Stocks	17.70%	8.99%	6.99%	16.89%	15.34%	2.40%
50 Best One-Year RS from Large Stocks	19.81%	13.27%	6.90%	19.89%	29.86%	−10.82%
50 Worst One-Year RS from Large Stocks	17.49%	6.58%	6.34%	11.19%	12.25%	−1.6%
All Stocks	22.26%	11.09%	8.53%	15.85%	14.75%	5.91%

(continued on next page)

T A B L E 15-13

Average Annual Compound Rates of Return by Decade *(Continued)*

Portfolio	1950s*	1960s	1970s	1980s	1990s	2000s**
50 Best One-Year RS from All Stocks	28.60%	13.00%	9.28%	15.35%	21.59%	−23.59%
50 Worst One-Year RS from All Stocks	13.49%	4.31%	−3.52%	0.06%	6.27%	13.54%

*Returns for 1952–1959.
**Returns for 2000–2003.

DECILES

The decile results show that you're actually much better off focusing on the upper 10 percent (decile one) than on just the 50 best-performing stocks from both All Stocks and Large Stocks universes. A $10,000 investment in the 10 percent of stocks having the best price appreciation over the previous year from All Stocks grew to $17,098,154 by the end of 2003, a compound return of 15.39 percent. The risk was less than the 50-stock portfolio, coming in at 28.49 percent. The higher absolute return coupled with the lower risk improved the risk-adjusted rate of return as well. In the Large Stocks universe, we see a similar superiority to focusing on the upper 10 percent by price appreciation, with the first decile compounding at 14.92 percent per year and with a lower standard deviation of 24.80 percent. We see a great symmetry to the decile analysis of stocks ranked by relative strength, much like that we saw with price-to-sales ratios, with returns uniformly declining as you move from decile one to 10. Tables 15-14 and 15-15 as well as Figures 15-5 and 15-6 summarize the results of the decile studies.

T A B L E 15-14

Best and Worst Average Annual Compound Returns over Period for Annual Data 1951–2003

For Any	1-Year Period	3-Year Period	5-Year Period	10-Year Period
Large Stocks Minimum Compound Return	−26.70%	−11.93%	−4.37%	1.21%
Large Stocks Maximum Compound Return	45.07%	24.39%	22.40%	17.01%
Large Stocks Top 50 by Relative Strength Minimum Compound Return	−33.51%	−25.25%	−5.03%	2.60%
Large Stocks Top 50 by Relative Strength Maximum Compound Return	139.94%	64.79%	45.94%	29.86%

(continued on next page)

T A B L E 15-14

Best and Worst Average Annual Compound Returns over Period for Annual Data 1951–2003
(Continued)

For Any	1-Year Period	3-Year Period	5-Year Period	10-Year Period
Large Stocks Worst 50 by Relative Strength Minimum Compound Return	−53.80%	−20.05%	−7.05%	−1.70%
Large Stocks Worst 50 by Relative Strength Maximum Compound Return	83.75%	27.23%	22.63%	18.61%
All Stocks Minimum Compound Return	−27.90%	−16.48%	−7.81%	1.26%
All Stocks Maximum Compound Return	55.90%	31.23%	27.77%	21.31%
All Stocks Top 50 by Relative Strength Minimum Compound Return	−57.00%	−42.42%	−9.33%	−1.90%
All Stocks Top 50 by Relative Strength Maximum Compound Return	152.25%	49.32%	37.06%	24.06%
All Stocks Worst 50 by Relative Strength Minimum Compound Return	−48.90%	−32.11%	−24.95%	−11.33%
All Stocks Worst 50 by Relative Strength Maximum Compound Return	142.63%	23.28%	22.30%	13.13%

T A B L E 15-15

Best and Worst Average Annual Compound Returns over Period for Monthly Data 1964–2003

For Any	1-Year Period	3-Year Period	5-Year Period	10-Year Period
Large Stocks Minimum Compound Return	−42.04%	−13.79%	−6.05%	−0.20%
Large Stocks Maximum Compound Return	68.49%	32.78%	28.65%	19.57%
Large Stocks Top 50 by Relative Strength Minimum Compound Return	−58.24%	−32.53%	−8.01%	−0.32%
Large Stocks Top 50 by Relative Strength Maximum Compound Return	180.75%	84.26%	54.09%	35.14%
Large Stocks Worst 50 by Relative Strength Minimum Compound Return	−55.04%	−25.63%	−12.24%	−3.68%
Large Stocks Worst 50 by Relative Strength Maximum Compound Return	111.18%	34.58%	22.82%	20.64%
All Stocks Minimum Compound Return	−41.65%	−16.82%	−8.94%	0.68%
All Stocks Maximum Compound Return	81.51%	29.46%	27.02%	21.46%
All Stocks Top 50 by Relative Strength Minimum Compound Return	−79.27%	−52.33%	−13.85%	−4.29%
All Stocks Top 50 by Relative Strength Maximum Compound Return	240.33%	81.64%	48.10%	27.16%
All Stocks Worst 50 by Relative Strength Minimum Compound Return	−54.32%	−32.18%	−26.24%	−13.34%
All Stocks Worst 50 by Relative Strength Maximum Compound Return	279.99%	33.56%	27.97%	17.98%

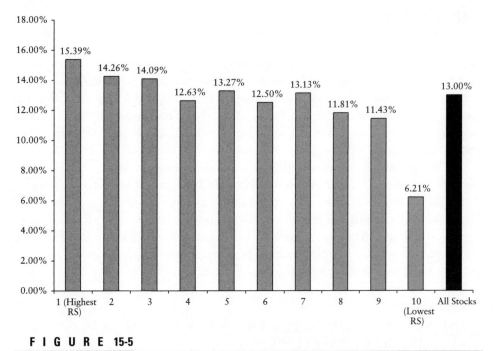

F I G U R E   15-5

Compound return by price appreciation (relative strength [RS]) decile, All Stocks universe, 1951–2003.

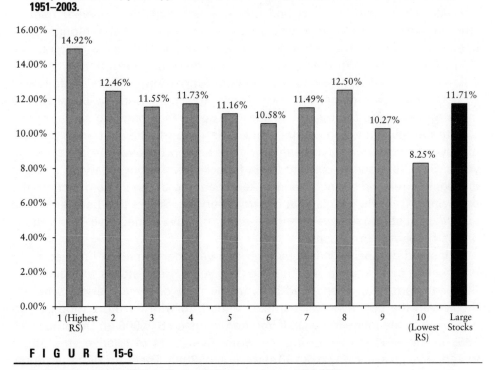

F I G U R E   15-6

Compound return by ROE decile, Large Stocks universe, 1951–2003.

IMPLICATIONS

Runyon's quote is apt. Over one-year periods, winners generally continue to win and losers continue to lose. Remember that when we say losers, we're not talking about stocks that lost some ground last year, but about the 50 *worst* casualties from the entire universe. Yet, the decile analysis shows that investors are best avoiding stocks in the lowest deciles for last year's price performance.

The advice is simple—unless financial ruin is your goal, avoid the biggest one-year losers. Buy stocks with the *best* one-year relative strength, but understand that their volatility will continually test your emotional endurance. In coming chapters, we will see how relative strength is an excellent factor to use in conjunction with other factors to help us avoid the most richly valued stocks. For now, we see that relative strength is among the only pure growth factors that actually beat the market.

CASE STUDY: HOW WELL DOES LONGER-TERM RELATIVE STRENGTH WORK?

The data clearly support that both positive and negative one-year relative strength persists into the following year's results. But what about longer periods of time? One of the central tendencies of financial data series is regression to the longer-term mean, where outstanding long-term performance is followed by more modest returns, and poor longer-term results are followed by better than average performance. The longer the period you consider, the more regression to the mean you see. We do, in fact, begin to see a regression to the mean after about five years. This supports the contrarian practice of buying stocks that have been seriously beaten up over the past several years. So, although the performance of stocks with strong one-year positive or negative relative strength tend to keep heading in the same direction, the opposite is true when looking at five-year periods. Stocks that have exhibited five years of strong relative strength—either positive or negative—are usually on the brink of a turnaround.

Instead of ranking stocks by their one-year performance, I ranked them on absolute performance over the prior five years. Here, stocks with the *worst* five-year performance snapped back in the next one-year period, whereas those with the *best* five-year numbers ended up with far more modest performance in the following year. If you had invested $10,000 on December 31, 1955 in those 50 stocks having the worst five years of relative strength, it would have grown to $17,037,790 at the end of 2003. That's an average annual compound return of 16.77 percent, vastly ahead of the return to the All Stocks universe itself. With the All Stocks universe, the same $10,000 grew to $2,915,619, an average annual compound return of 12.55 percent. The standard deviation of return for those 50 stocks having the worst five-year performance was 28.04 percent, versus 20.30 percent for the All Stocks universe, but the downside risk was virtually the same, with the 50 stocks having the worst five-year results coming in at 7.86 percent, versus 7.46 percent for the All Stocks universe. This demonstrates that, when markets are declining, this strategy is no riskier than an investment in the All Stocks universe itself. Looking at the annual data, the biggest loss the strategy suffered was 32 percent, much better than the 48 percent loss in the All Stocks universe. The Sharpe ratio was also better, coming in at 50, versus 43 for the All Stocks universe. All base rates were positive, with the 50 stocks having the worst five-year price performance beating All Stocks 63 percent of the time in any one-year period, 70 percent in any five-year period, and 74 percent in any 10-year period.

Large Stocks behaved in a similar manner. Investing $10,000 in those 50 stocks from the Large Stocks universe having the worst five-year price performance at the end of 1955 grew to $5,764,305, a compound average annual return of 14.16 percent. A similar investment in Large Stocks grew to $1,616,227, a compound return of 11.18 percent. The standard deviation for the 50 stocks from Large Stocks with the worst five-year performance was 21.45 percent, versus 16.79 percent for Large Stocks; the downside risk actually came in lower at 5.85 percent, versus 6.09 percent for Large Stocks. This demonstrates that, when prices are declining, this strategy is actually less risky than an investment in Large Stocks. Looking at the annual data, the maximum decline for the strategy was a loss of 33 percent compared to a loss of 41 percent for Large Stocks. The Sharpe ratio was 48 versus 41 for the Large Stocks universe, and as with the All Stocks group, all base rates were positive, with the strategy beating the Large Stocks universe 65 percent of the time in any one-year period, 80 percent in any five-year period, and 79 percent in any 10-year period.

BEST FIVE-YEAR PERFORMERS SHOW STRONG MEAN REGRESSION

Unlike stocks with great one-year price appreciation, those with the best five-year performance clearly drop off the performance train by year six. A $10,000 investment in those 50 stocks having the best five-year price appreciation from the All Stocks universe on December 31, 1955 would be worth just $244,670, an average annual compound return of 6.89 percent. That's $2.6 million *less* than the $2,915,619 you'd have if you invested in the All Stocks universe. The standard deviation of return was nine points higher, coming in at 29.02 percent, compared to 20.30 percent for All Stocks; the downside risk was nearly double All Stocks' at 14 percent, compared to 7.46 percent for All Stocks. That much riskier number is borne out in the maximum decline: The worst decline that the 50 stocks with the best five-year price performance ever had was a loss of 72 percent, compared to 48 percent for All Stocks. The Sharpe ratio was a low 18 compared to 43 for All Stocks, and all base rates were negative, with the strategy beating All Stocks just 33 percent of the time in any one-year period, 18 percent in any five-year period, and only once in all 10-year periods.

LARGE STOCKS ALSO REVERT TO THOSE LONG-TERM MEAN

Large Stocks saw similar results, with the 50 stocks from Large Stocks having the best five-year price performance, turning $10,000 invested at the end of 1955 into $422,427 at the end of 2003, well behind the $1,616,227 you'd have earned with an investment in the Large Stocks universe. Like their brethren from All Stocks, the 50 stocks from Large Stocks with the best five-year price performance had a much higher standard deviation of return—26.57 percent versus 16.79 for Large Stocks. The downside risk for the group was 12.25 percent, more than double Large Stocks' 6.09 percent. As was the case with All Stocks, the high downside risk is reflected in the worst-case scenario for the group, which plunged more than 71 percent from peak to trough. All this volatility is reflected in the group's low Sharpe ratio of 22. All base rates are negative, with the 50 stocks having the best five-year price performance from Large Stocks beating the Large Stocks universe just 26 percent of the time in all rolling 10-year periods.

RESULTS FAVOR SHORTER-TERM RELATIVE STRENGTH

Thus, our results show that although winners over the previous year continue to win in the next year, the reverse is true when you look at longer-term price appreciation. Short-term relative strength is one of the most powerful of the growth factors, especially—as we will see in coming chapters—when married to other factors. Longer term, you're much better off using a contrarian strategy that selects from the group of stocks with the *worst* five-year price appreciation from both All Stocks and Large Stocks. Tables 15-16, 15-17, and 15-18 summarize the results.

T A B L E 15-16

Summary Results for Price Appreciation (Relative Strength) Decile Analysis of All Stocks Universe, 1951–2003

Decile	$10,000 Grows to:	Average Return	Compound Return	Standard Deviation
1 (Highest Price Appreciation)	$17,098,154	18.91%	15.39%	28.49%
2	$10,252,541	16.11%	14.26%	20.12%
3	$9,486,225	15.63%	14.09%	18.35%
4	$4,849,266	13.98%	12.63%	17.11%
5	$6,520,534	14.61%	13.27%	17.00%
6	$4,570,374	13.87%	12.50%	17.26%
7	$6,109,507	14.73%	13.13%	18.89%
8	$3,317,639	13.36%	11.81%	18.42%
9	$2,782,388	13.46%	11.43%	21.24%
10 (Lowest Price Appreciation)	$229,418	9.48%	6.21%	26.63%
All Stocks	$5,743,706	14.79%	13.00%	20.11%

T A B L E 15-17

Summary Results for Price Appreciation (Relative Strength) Decile Analysis of Large Stocks Universe, 1951–2003

Decile	$10,000 Grows to:	Average Return	Compound Return	Standard Deviation
1 (Highest Price Appreciation)	$13,812,074	17.56%	14.92%	24.80%
2	$4,495,266	14.06%	12.46%	18.72%
3	$2,942,577	12.91%	11.55%	17.14%
4	$3,191,245	12.82%	11.73%	15.49%
5	$2,449,084	12.33%	11.16%	15.91%
6	$1,862,986	11.69%	10.58%	15.40%
7	$2,855,392	12.63%	11.49%	15.65%
8	$4,571,073	13.75%	12.50%	16.84%
9	$1,612,061	11.67%	10.27%	17.45%
10 (Lowest Price Appreciation)	$617,977	10.73%	8.25%	23.02%
Large Stocks	$3,173,724	12.99%	11.71%	16.84%

T A B L E 15-18

Terminal Value of $10,000 Invested for Best and Worst Average Annual Compound Returns over Period for Monthly Data 1964–2003

For Any	1-Year Period	3-Year Period	5-Year Period	10-Year Period
Large Stocks Minimum $10,000 Value	$5,796.00	$6,407.27	$7,319.54	$9,801.79
Large Stocks Maximum $10,000 Value	$16,849.00	$23,415.11	$35,241.06	$59,734.10
Large Stocks Top 50 by Relative Strength Minimum $10,000 Value	$4,176.00	$3,071.37	$6,587.23	$10,324.65
Large Stocks Top 50 by Relative Strength Maximum $10,000 Value	$28,075.00	$62,559.49	$86,870.49	$203,160.44
Large Stocks Worst 50 by Relative Strength Minimum $10,000 Value	$4,496.00	$4,113.33	$5,205.75	$6,873.29
Large Stocks Worst 50 by Relative Strength Maximum $10,000 Value	$21,118.00	$24,374.83	$27,947.66	$65,300.02
All Stocks Minimum $10,000 Value	$5,835.00	$5,755.15	$6,260.92	$10,701.19
All Stocks Maximum $10,000 Value	$18,151.00	$21,682.28	$33,064.39	$69,876.76
All Stocks Top 50 by Relative Strength Minimum $10,000 Value	$2,073.00	$1,083.27	$4,745.44	$6,450.20
All Stocks Top 50 by Relative Strength Maximum $10,000 Value	$34,033.00	$59,928.65	$71,248.43	$110,536.37
All Stocks Worst 50 by Relative Strength Minimum $10,000 Value	$4,568.00	$3,119.42	$2,183.26	$2,388.84
All Stocks Worst 50 by Relative Strength Maximum $10,000 Value	$37,999.00	$23,824.80	$34,319.49	$52,249.71

16
CHAPTER

USING MULTIFACTOR MODELS TO IMPROVE PERFORMANCE

It is not who is right, but what is right, that is important.
—Thomas Huxley

Thus far, I've only looked at individual factors, such as low price-to-sales ratios (PSRs) or outstanding relative strength. Now, we'll look at building portfolios using two or more criteria. Using several factors allows you to dramatically enhance performance or substantially reduce risk, depending on your goal. Let's look at how adding factors can improve the performance of the 50 best-performing stocks from the All Stocks universe.

ADDING VALUE FACTORS

Ben Graham said anyone paying more than 20 times earnings for a stock should prepare to lose money in the long run. What happens if we remove high price-to-earnings (PE) ratio stocks from the All Stocks universe and then buy the 50 biggest winners? Instead of just buying the top 50 relative strength stocks, let's also require that stocks have PE ratios between zero and 20. Thus, we start with the All Stocks universe and screen out stocks with negative PE ratios or PE ratios above 20, *then* buy those 50 stocks having the best one-year price appreciation.

If you invested $10,000 on December 31, 1951 in those 50 stocks from the All Stocks universe having the best price appreciation from the previous year and PE ratios below 20, your investment would grow to $51,501,774 by the end of 2003 (Figure 16-1). Simply by refusing to overpay for earnings, you add $46,687,610 to what you would earn by just buying the 50 stocks from All Stocks with the best relative strength. What's more, this two-factor portfolio has a standard deviation of 24.23 percent, *much lower* than the 50 All Stocks winners' 37.82 percent. The Sharpe ratio for this two-factor strategy is 61, compared to 35 for the 50 best-performing stocks from All Stocks (Figure 16-2). The downside risk is well below that faced by the best performers alone, coming in at 6.4 percent, compared to 14.18 percent for the top 50 from All Stocks with the best one-year price appreciation. The maximum decline (using the monthly data) for the low-PE stocks with strong price appreciation was nearly half that of the winners alone, with a decline of 53 percent from peak to trough, compared to an 89 percent drop for those 50 stocks from All Stocks having the best one-year price appreciation.

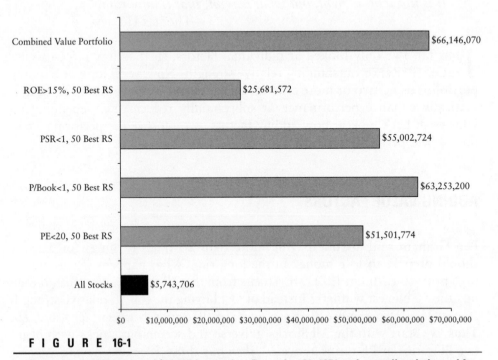

F I G U R E   16-1

December 31, 2003 value of $10,000 invested on December 31, 1951 and annually rebalanced for different multifactor relative strength (RS) models using All Stocks as the universe.

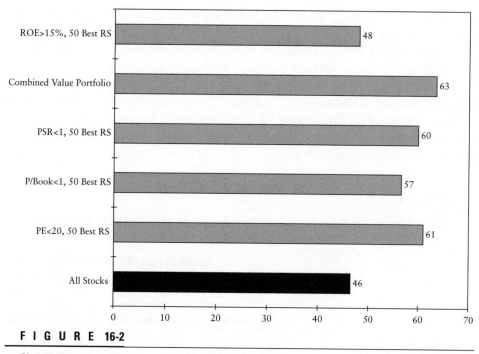

F I G U R E 16-2

Sharpe risk-adjusted return ratios for different multifactor relative strength (RS) models using All Stocks as the universe, 1951–2003. (Higher is better.)

BASE RATES IMPROVE

Risk and return aren't the only things enhanced by this model—the base rates are better as well. The 50 biggest winners from All Stocks having PE ratios below 20 beat the All Stocks universe in 38 of the 52 years of the study, or 73 percent of the time. Long-term, the results get better, with this strategy outperforming All Stocks in 43 of the 48 rolling five-year periods and all the 43 rolling 10-year periods. It doesn't get much better than that!

WHAT ABOUT OTHER VALUE FACTORS?

Adding low-PE ratios is just one way to improve performance. Other factors work as well. For example, if you take stocks from the All Stocks universe having price-to-book ratios below one and then buy those 50 stocks having the highest one-year price appreciation, a $10,000 investment made on December 31, 1951 grows to $63,253,200 by the end of 2003, a compound return of 18.33 percent. Risk is higher than with the low-PE strategy, with a standard deviation of return of 28.57 percent. Downside risk is also higher, coming in at 8.71 percent, whereas the maximum decline was similar, with a 50 percent loss from peak to trough. The higher risk translates to a lower Sharpe ratio of 57 for the strategy. Base rates are slightly worse, with the strategy beating All Stocks in 37 of the 52 years of the study; 43 of the 48 rolling five-year periods, and 42 of the 43 rolling 10-year periods. That's 97 percent of the time over all rolling 10-year periods. Table 16-1 summarizes the results for these two strategies.

T A B L E 16-1

Summary Results for Buying Best One-Year Price Appreciation Stocks with PE Ratios below 20 or Price-to-Book Ratios below One from All Stocks Universe. December 31, 1951–December 31, 2003

	All Stocks	50 Stocks with PE Ratios Below 20 (Earnings Yields >5%) and Best One-Year Price Appreciation	50 Stocks with Price-to-Book Ratios Below One and Best One-Year Price Appreciation
$10,000 Becomes:	$5,743,706.00	$51,501,774.00	$63,253,200.00
Average Annual Compound Return	13.00%	17.86%	18.33%
Arithmetic Average	14.79%	20.29%	21.65%
Standard Deviation of Return	20.11%	24.23%	28.57%
Downside Risk—lower is better	7.17%	6.40%	8.71%
Maximum Decline	−50.12%	−53.00%	−50.00%
Sharpe Ratio	46	61	57
Percent of Rolling 10-Year Periods Beats All Stocks	NA	100.00%	97.00%

One point is worth highlighting with these strategies—they can have significant deviations from both the All Stocks universe *and each other* when you examine the annual data. For example, in 1999, the height of the stock market bubble, buying those 50 stocks from All Stocks having PE ratios less than 20 and the best price appreciation returned 12.65 percent, compared to 31.16 percent for All Stocks. Yet in that same year, the 50 stocks from All Stocks having price-to-book ratios less than one and the best price appreciation gained 76 percent. That's quite a difference for similar strategies in the same year. Conversely, in 2000, the low-PE stocks having good price appreciation gained 15.83 percent, compared to a loss of more than 35 percent for those low price-to-book stocks having good price appreciation. We'll see later how combining these strategies actually improves returns while lowering risk, but for now, keep in mind that great variation in returns is possible when you look at the annual data.

PRICE-TO-SALES HAS SIMILAR RETURNS

Price-to-sales (PSR) also performs beautifully when joined with relative strength. If you start December 31, 1951 with the All Stocks universe and only consider stocks having PSRs below one and *then* buy those 50 having the best one-year price appreciation, $10,000 grows to $55,002,724 at the end of 2003, a compound rate of return of 18.01 percent. That's about 10 times better than the $5,743,706 you'd earn from an investment in All Stocks. The standard deviation of return of 25.22 percent is higher than All Stocks' 20.11 percent, but like the other value-oriented relative strength strategies, much lower than the 50 best-performer's 37.82 percent. The Sharpe ratio is 60 for this strategy, well ahead of All Stocks' 46. Downside risk was 8.18 percent, and the worst-case scenario was a drop of 53.40 percent. Table 16-2 compares this strategy to the All Stocks universe.

T A B L E 16-2

Summary Return and Risk Results for Annual Data for All Stocks and 50 Stocks with PSR <1 and Best Relative Strength, December 31, 1951–December 31, 2003

	All Stocks	All Stocks, PSR <1, Top 50 by Relative Strength
Arithmetic Average	14.79%	20.79%
Geometric Average	13.00%	18.01%
Median Return	16.80%	26.35%
Standard Deviation of Return	20.11%	25.22%
Downside Risk—lower is better	7.17%	8.18%
Correlation with S&P 500	0.87	0.76
T-Statistic	5.30	5.95
Sharpe Ratio	0.46	0.60
Number of Positive Periods	39	39
Number of Negative Periods	13	13
Maximum Peak-to-Trough Decline (using monthly data series)	−50.12%	−53.40%
Beta	0.99	1.08
$10,000 becomes:	$5,743,706.00	$55,002,724.00
Minimum Annual Return	−27.90%	−33.60%
Maximum Annual Return	55.90%	67.50%
Minimum *Expected* Return*	−25.43%	−29.65%
Maximum *Expected* Return**	55.01%	71.23%

*Minimum Expected Return is Arithmetic Return minus 2 times the standard deviation.
**Maximum Expected Return is Arithmetic Return plus 2 times the standard deviation.

The strategy is very consistent, beating All Stocks in 39 of the 52 years of the test, or 75 percent of the time. For rolling five-year periods, it beats the

All Stocks universe in 45 of 48 periods, or 93.75 percent of the time. Long-term, the record can't get any better—it beat the All Stocks universe 100 percent of the time over all rolling 10-year periods. Table 16-3 shows the base rates.

T A B L E 16-3

Base Rates for All Stocks and 50 Stocks with PSRs below One and Best One-Year Price Appreciation from All Stocks, 1951–2003

Item	Stocks with PSR <1 and Best One-Year RS Beat All Stocks	Percent
Single-Year Return	39 out of 52	75%
Rolling Five-Year Compound Return	43 out of 48	94%
Rolling 10-Year Compound Return	43 out of 43	100%

COMBINING THE THREE STRATEGIES

I noted earlier that a great deal of variation existed between the strategies on an annual basis, with some years having one of the strategies soaring while the others swooned. Indeed, the low-PE, high price appreciation strategy actually has a lower correlation to the low price-to-book, high price appreciation strategy than it has with the S&P 500. What if we were to put them together, buying all the stocks from each of the strategies? Here, we will assume that if a stock appears in two of the three strategies, it will be double weighted, if in all three, triple weighted, etc. We'll assume we begin each year with each of the three strategies awarded a one-third weighting of the overall portfolio, and we'll rebalance the portfolio annually.

Table 16-4 shows the results. By using the three strategies together, we obtain a compound average annual return that is virtually the same as the highest individual strategies, while keeping the overall standard deviation of return near that of the least volatile of the three strategies. We also keep downside risk near that of the *least* risky strategy. Finally, we see that we also increase the number of years of positive performance. The base rates improve as well, with the combined portfolio beating All Stocks 75 percent of the time in all one-year periods, 92 percent of the time in all rolling five-year periods, and 100 percent of the time in all rolling 10-year periods. Table 16-10 lists the worst-case scenarios for this combined strategy.

T A B L E 16-4

Summary Return and Risk Results for Annual Data for All Stocks and Portfolio that Combines the Three Value/Relative Strength Strategies, December 31, 1951–December 31, 2003

	All Stocks	Portfolio Combining Three Value/ Relative Strength Strategies
Arithmetic Average	14.79%	20.91%
Geometric Average	13.00%	18.43%
Median Return	16.80%	25.92%
Standard Deviation of Return	20.11%	24.29%
Downside risk—lower is better	7.17%	6.72%
Correlation with S&P 500	0.87	0.81
T-Statistic	5.30	6.22
Sharpe Ratio	0.46	0.63
Number of Positive Periods	39	40
Number of Negative Periods	13	12
Maximum Peak-to-trough Decline (using Monthly data series)	−50.12%	−47.79%
Beta	0.99	1.12
$10,000 becomes:	$5,743,706.00	$66,146,070.00
Minimum Annual Return	−27.90%	−25.07%
Maximum Annual Return	55.90%	72.72%
Minimum *Expected* Return*	−25.43%	−27.67%
Maximum *Expected* Return**	55.01%	69.49%

*Minimum Expected Return is Arithmetic Return minus 2 times the standard deviation.
**Maximum Expected Return is Arithmetic Return plus 2 times the standard deviation.

TEST FOR DEVIATION FROM BENCHMARK

The magnitude of how much a strategy could lag the All Stocks universe is also dampened with the combined portfolio. Looking at the annual data for the three separate strategies, we saw some one-year periods when a strategy could be as much as 43 percent *behind* the return for All Stocks universe. With the combined portfolio, the worst one-year lag was −11.3 percent, a vast improvement compared to the strategies individually. When you extend the holding period to all rolling five-year periods, the worst the combined portfolio ever lagged All Stocks was by −0.95 percent. Looking at 10 years, performance was always positive when compared with All Stocks.

Looking at how much a strategy lags its benchmark can be very helpful when determining whether or not an investor is likely to stick with a strategy. To take the research even further, it's worth looking at the monthly year-over-year data. This strategy, for example, had one 12-month period during which it was 11.63 percent behind the All Stocks universe. That figure is reasonably low and would probably not shake an investor's confidence enough to make him abandon the strategy.

But how about the stand-alone strategies? Here, the numbers are decidedly different. Despite doing extraordinarily better than All Stocks over the entire period, some very bumpy passages occurred—the low price-to-book, high relative strength strategy had one 12-month period out of the 469 observations during which it was *42 percent* behind the All Stocks universe. It doesn't matter that it was the 12 months ending January 2001, when this occurred. Had an investor actually been experiencing this shortfall in real time, I highly doubt if she could have stuck with the strategy. It is only with hindsight that we can identify this as the tail end of the speculative bubble and that the strategy would go on to massively outperform All Stocks in the ensuing bear market. Thus, looking at the maximum shortfall against the relevant benchmark can help you avoid strategies that will ultimately get the better of your emotions.

Thus, we've seen that you can *significantly* enhance returns by using more than one factor. Generally, combining a value factor with a growth factor leads to the most improvement, but we'll see later in this chapter that using multifactor models with pure growth characteristics leads to excellent performance as well.

ADDITIONAL FACTORS ADD LESS TO LARGE STOCKS

Using multifactor models on the Large Stocks universe does not enhance performance as much as it does with All Stocks. Starting on December 31, 1951, requiring stocks from the Large Stocks universe to have PE ratios below 20, and then buying those 50 having the best one-year price performance, $10,000 grows to $13,652,039 at the end of 2003, a 14.89 percent compound annual return (Table 16-5). Risk is relatively low—the standard deviation of 19.92 percent led to a high Sharpe ratio of 56 (Figure 16-4).

Base rates for the strategy are reasonably high, beating the Large Stocks universe in 33 of the 52 years of the study, or 63 percent of the time over any one-year period. The longer term looks even better, with the strategy beating the universe in 37 of the 48 rolling five-year periods, and in 42 of the 43 rolling 10-year periods, or 97 percent of the time.

I was unable to run a test on Large Stocks using price-to-book ratios because Large Stocks rarely trade at price-to-book ratios, below one.

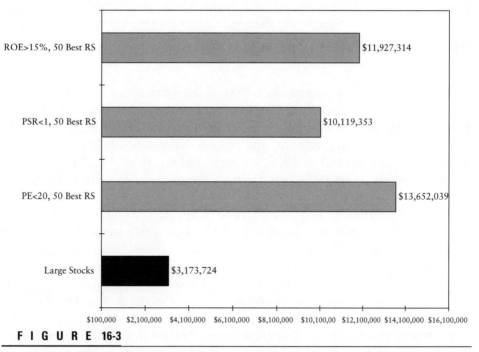

F I G U R E 16-3

December 31, 2003 value of $10,000 invested on December 31, 1951 and annually rebalanced for different multifactor relative strength (RS) models using Large Stocks as the universe.

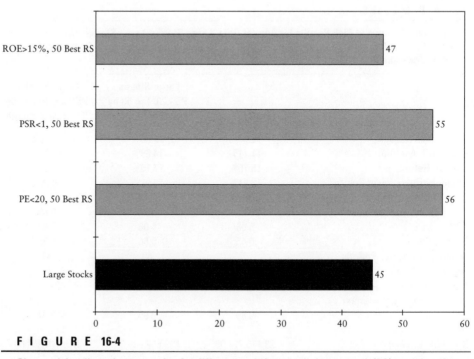

F I G U R E 16-4

Sharpe risk-adjusted return ratios for different multifactor relative strength (RS) models using Large Stocks as the universe, 1951–2003. (Higher is better.)

251

PRICE-TO-SALES RATIOS DO WELL, TOO

When looking at the Large Stocks universe, the marriage of low price-to-sales ratios to relative strength does about the same as buying stocks with PE ratios below 20. $10,000 invested in those 50 stocks from Large Stocks having the best one-year price appreciation and price-to-sales ratios below one grew to $10,119,353 by the end of 2003, a compound return of 14.23 percent. The standard deviation of 19.26 was virtually the same as the stocks having PE ratios below 20, possibly because you end up with many of the same stocks in the two portfolios. The Sharpe ratio was 55, considerably better than Large Stocks' 45 and one point behind the best price performers with PE ratios below 20.

Here, the base rates are not as good as the relative strength stocks with PE ratios below 20. This strategy beat the Large Stocks universe in 34 of 52 one-year periods, 34 out of 48 rolling five-year periods, and 38 out of 43 rolling 10-year periods. Both of these strategies outperform Large Stocks, yet have lower downside risk, smaller maximum declines, and lower betas. That's unusual with strategies that use relative strength as the final factor. Table 16-5 compares the two strategies to Large Stocks.

T A B L E 16-5

Summary Return and Risk Results for Annual Data, Large Stocks, Large Stocks With PE <20, 50 Best Relative Strength, and Large Stocks, PSR <1, 50 Best Relative Strength, December 31, 1951–December 31, 2003

	Large Stocks	Large Stocks, PE <20, Top 50 by Relative Strength	Large Stocks, PSR <1, Top 50 by Relative Strength
Arithmetic Average	12.99%	16.56%	15.81%
Geometric Average	11.71%	14.89%	14.23%
Median Return	15.75%	17.15%	17.75%
Standard Deviation of Return	16.84%	19.92%	19.26%
Downside Risk—lower is better	5.86%	5.05%	4.84%
Correlation with S&P 500	0.95	0.84	0.86
T-Statistic	5.56	6.00	5.92
Sharpe Ratio	0.45	0.56	0.55
Number of Positive Periods	39	40	37
Number of Negative Periods	13	12	14
Maximum Peak-to-Trough Decline (using monthly data series)	−46.59%	−39.48%	−37.73%
Beta	0.89	0.95	0.94
$10,000 becomes:	$3,173,724.00	$13,652,039.00	$10,119,353.00

(continued on next page)

T A B L E 16-5

Summary Return and Risk Results for Annual Data, Large Stocks, Large Stocks With PE <20, 50 Best Relative Strength, and Large Stocks, PSR <1, 50 Best Relative Strength. December 31, 1951–December 31, 2003 *(Continued)*

	Large Stocks	Large Stocks, PE <20, Top 50 by Relative Strength	Large Stocks, PSR <1, Top 50 by Relative Strength
Minimum Annual Return	−26.70%	−25.20%	−21.10%
Maximum Annual Return	45.07%	66.90%	54.10%
Minimum *Expected* Return*	−20.69%	−23.28%	−22.71%
Maximum *Expected* Return**	46.67%	56.40%	54.33%

*Minimum Expected Return is Arithmetic Return minus 2 times the standard deviation.
**Maximum Expected Return is Arithmetic Return plus 2 times the standard deviation.

WHAT ABOUT GROWTH FACTORS?

Growth factors work with relative strength too, but the returns are less consistent. For example, if you took those stocks from the Large Stocks universe having PE ratios below 20 *and* positive earnings gains for the year, and then bought the 50 with the best one-year price performance, you would actually earn $4,509,956 *less* than if you bought the low PE, high relative strength stocks alone. In this instance, the addition of positive earnings gains hurt performance.

Conversely, adding the higher earnings requirement to the Large Stocks portfolio having PSRs less than one and good one-year price appreciation actually helped performance. Simply requiring that the low-PSR Large Stocks with good price appreciation have positive earnings gains added over $3 million to the terminal value of a $10,000 investment relative to the original strategy. Higher earnings requirements seem to work better with low price-to-sales stocks than with low PE stocks, and we'll see in Chapter 20 that higher earnings can help even more when used within the All Stocks universe. For now, understand that more factors do not necessarily mean better performance.

TWO GROWTH MODELS

While buying stocks with the best one-year earnings gains doesn't beat All Stocks (see Chapter 11), buying stocks with strong one-year earnings gains *and* strong relative price strength does beat the All Stocks universe. A two-factor model that requires stocks from All Stocks to have one-year earnings gains exceeding 25 percent and then selects the 50 with the best one-year price performance turns $10,000 invested on December 31, 1952 (we need the extra year to determine the earnings growth rate) into $8,230,906 by the end of 2003 (Figure 16-5). That's a compound return of 14.07 percent a year, slightly ahead of All Stocks' 13.10 percent a year. But beware, risk is sky high—the standard deviation for the strategy is 34.77 percent, much higher than All Stocks' 20.29 percent. The other risk statistics are even scarier, with a downside risk of 12.40 percent and a maximum decline of a whopping 84 percent. So, although this strategy improves the overall return of buying stocks with large earnings gains, it also illustrates the dangers of following a "growth at any cost" strategy. The strategy got absolutely hammered in the bear market of 2000–2003, falling 51.65 percent in 2000, 18.62 percent in 2001, and 25.82 percent in 2002. Of course, prior to this fall, it would have seduced investors with a gain of 120.90 percent in 1999, the last year of the bubble market. Once again, these results emphasize why it is so important to look at maximum declines and base rates before deciding on any investment strategy.

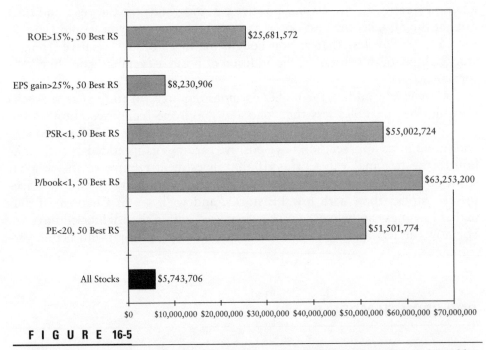

FIGURE 16-5

December 31, 2003 value of $10,000 invested on December 31, 1951 and annually rebalanced for different multifactor relative strength (RS) models using All Stocks as the universe.

RETURN ON EQUITY DOES BETTER

Other growth variables work better. In Chapter 14, we saw that buying those 50 stocks from the All Stocks universe having the best ROE didn't beat the market, but adding a high ROE factor to a relative strength model enhances returns much more than the earnings gains model.

By starting on December 31, 1951 and requiring stocks from the All Stocks universe to have a return on equity above 15, then buying the 50 with the best one-year price performance, $10,000 grows to $25,681,572 by the end of 2003, a compound return of 16.30 percent. Although that's a much better performance than buying the stocks with high earnings gains, it's still well behind the returns from buying the 50 best-performing stocks having PE ratios below 20.

This strategy is riskier than strategies that buy cheap stocks having strong relative strength, with a standard deviation of 30.50 percent. The Sharpe ratio of 56 is similar to buying the best-performing low-PE stocks. All base rates are positive, with the rolling 10-year returns beating the All Stocks universe 93 percent of the time. Tables 16-6 and 16-7 summarize the findings.

T A B L E 16-6

Summary Return and Risk Results for Annual Data for All Stocks and 50 Stocks with ROE >15 and Best Relative Strength, December 31, 1951–December 31, 2003

	All Stocks	All Stocks, ROE >15, Top 50 by Relative Strength
Arithmetic Average	14.79%	20.04%
Geometric Average	13.00%	16.30%
Median Return	16.80%	21.40%
Standard Deviation of Return	20.11%	30.50%
Downside Risk—lower is better	7.17%	9.42%
Correlation with S&P 500	0.87	0.72
T-Statistic	5.30	4.74
Sharpe Ratio	0.46	0.48
Number of Positive Periods	39	37
Number of Negative Periods	13	15
Maximum Peak-to-Trough Decline (using monthly data series)	−50.12%	−65.82%
Beta	0.99	1.25
$10,000 becomes:	$5,743,706.00	$25,681,572.00
Minimum Annual Return	−27.90%	−34.60%
Maximum Annual Return	55.90%	105.71%
Minimum *Expected* Return*	−25.43%	−40.96%
Maximum *Expected* Return**	55.01%	81.04%

*Minimum Expected Return is Arithmetic Return minus 2 times the standard deviation.
**Maximum Expected Return is Arithmetic Return plus 2 times the standard deviation.

T A B L E 16-7

Base Rates for All Stocks and 50 Stocks with ROE Greater than 15 and Best One-Year Price Appreciation from All Stocks, 1951–2003

Item	Stocks with ROE >15 and Best One-Year RS Beat All Stocks	Percent
Single-Year Return	31 out of 52	60%
Rolling Five-Year Compound Return	36 out of 48	75%
Rolling 10-Year Compound Return	40 out of 43	93%

LARGE STOCKS LESS DRAMATIC

The results are less striking for Large Stocks. Here, buying the 50 best one-year price performers that also have a return on equity higher than 15 turns $10,000 invested on December 31, 1951 into $11,927,314, a compound return of 14.59 percent a year. That's more than three times Large Stocks' return over the same period. The standard deviation for the strategy was 25.3 percent, and the Sharpe ratio of 47 was slightly better than Large Stocks. The downside risk was 7.47 percent, and the maximum decline was a drop of 51.57 percent. Base rates were fairly weak short-term, with the strategy beating Large Stocks just 56 percent of all one-year periods. They improve over the longer term, with the strategy beating Large Stocks 88 percent of all rolling 10-year periods. Tables 16-8 and 16-9 show the details.

T A B L E 16-8

Summary Return and Risk Results for Annual Data, Large Stocks, Large Stocks with ROE >15, 50 Best Relative Strength, December 31, 1951–December 31, 2003

	Large Stocks	Large Stocks, ROE >15, Top 50 by Relative Strength
Arithmetic Average	12.99%	17.18%
Geometric Average	11.71%	14.59%
Median Return	15.75%	16.25%
Standard Deviation of Return	16.84%	25.30%
Downside Risk—lower is better	5.86%	7.47%
Correlation with S&P 500	0.95	0.81
T-Statistic	5.56	4.90
Sharpe Ratio	0.45	0.47
Number of Positive Periods	39	39
Number of Negative Periods	13	13
Maximum Peak-to-Trough Decline (using monthly data series)	−46.59%	−51.57%
Beta	0.89	1.17

(continued on next page)

T A B L E 16-8

Summary Return and Risk Results for Annual Data, Large Stocks, Large Stocks with ROE >15, 50 Best Relative Strength, December 31, 1951–December 31, 2003

	Large Stocks	Large Stocks, ROE >15, Top 50 by Relative Strength
$10,000 becomes:	$3,173,724.00	$11,927,314.00
Minimum Annual Return	−26.70%	−34.90%
Maximum Annual Return	45.07%	98.68%
Minimum Expected Return*	−20.69%	−33.42%
Maximum Expected Return**	46.67%	67.78%

*Minimum Expected Return is Arithmetic Return minus 2 times the standard deviation.
**Maximum Expected Return is Arithmetic Return plus 2 times the standard deviation.

T A B L E 16-9

Base Rates for Large Stocks and 50 Stocks with ROE Greater than 15 and Best One-Year Price Appreciation from Large Stocks, 1951–2003

Item	Stocks with ROE >15 and Best One-Year RS Beat Large Stocks	Percent
Single-Year Return	29 out of 52	56%
Rolling Five-Year Compound Return	39 out of 48	81%
Rolling 10-Year Compound Return	38 out of 43	88%

IMPLICATIONS

Using multifactor models dramatically enhances returns. Whether your focus is All Stocks or Large Stocks, you're better off using several factors to choose stocks. Buying those 50 stocks from the All Stocks universe having price-to-sales ratios below one and the best price performance from the previous year actually has a slightly lower standard deviation than buying the 50 stocks from All Stocks having the lowest price-to-sales ratios, yet earns $17 million more over 52 years!

I believe that adding relative strength to a value portfolio dramatically increases performance because it picks stocks just after investors have recognized that they are bargains and are buying them once again. All the value factors that make them good buys are still in place, but the addition of relative strength helps pinpoint when investors believe the stocks have been oversold. We'll see in Chapter 22 that more recent research shows you can improve returns even further by adding shorter-term relative strength to the mix.

Adding relative strength also helps growth stocks, but the results aren't uniform. Adding some growth factors actually reduces the gains from relative strength and should be avoided whereas others, such as return on equity above 15, are helpful.

T A B L E 16-10

Worst-Case Scenarios: All 10 Percent or Greater Declines for Combined Value Strategies, December 31, 1963–December 31, 2003

Peak Date	Peak Index Value	Trough Date	Trough Index Value	Recovery Date	Decline (%)	Decline Duration	Recovery Duration
Apr-66	1.93	Oct-66	1.5	Feb-67	−22.5	6	4
Nov-68	3.75	Jun-70	2.1	Feb-72	−43.93	19	20
Apr-72	4.08	Sep-74	2.13	Feb-76	−47.79	29	17
Aug-78	8.58	Oct-78	6.34	Apr-79	−26.12	2	6
Aug-79	9.74	Oct-79	8.54	Dec-79	−12.39	2	2
Feb-80	11.41	Mar-80	8.51	Jul-80	−25.44	1	4
May-81	17.53	Sep-81	13.87	Sep-82	−20.87	4	12
Jun-83	32.46	May-84	24.4	Apr-85	−24.84	11	11
Jun-86	52.35	Sep-86	44.79	Feb-87	−14.44	3	5
Aug-87	59.25	Nov-87	38.45	Mar-89	−35.11	3	16
Sep-89	74.22	Oct-90	49.55	May-91	−33.24	13	7
Jan-94	145.35	Jun-94	129.55	Jun-95	−10.87	5	12
May-96	206.7	Jul-96	184.38	Nov-96	−10.79	2	4
Jun-98	332.86	Aug-98	243.77	May-99	−26.77	2	9
Feb-00	451.53	May-00	389.29	Aug-00	−13.78	3	3
Aug-00	468.67	Nov-00	369.31	Mar-02	−21.2	3	16
Apr-02	530.5	Feb-03	375.1	Jul-03	−29.29	10	5
Average					−24.67	6.94	9.00

DISSECTING THE MARKET LEADERS UNIVERSE: RATIOS THAT ADD THE MOST VALUE

Numbers serve to discipline rhetoric. Without them it is too easy to follow flights of fancy, to ignore the world as it is, and to remold it nearer the heart's desire.

—Ralph Waldo Emerson

We saw in the last chapter how building a model portfolio using several factors can lead to much better returns with lower risk. In this chapter, I'll take a look at the Market Leaders universe—a multifactor model itself—and then apply single factors or groups of factors to enhance its performance. You will recall from Chapter 4 that the Market Leaders universe is a bit like the S&P 500 on steroids, and that these large, well-known stocks outperformed All Stocks, Large Stocks, the S&P 500, and Small Stocks while taking considerably less risk. Market Leaders had the highest Sharpe ratio of all the broader-based, indexlike portfolios (that you can actually invest in) and proved to be an excellent performer over a variety of market cycles. Market Leaders also outperformed other large-cap indexes like the Russell 1000.

Market Leading companies are nonutility stocks with greater than average market capitalization, shares outstanding, cashflows, and sales of 50 percent greater than the average stock. Applying these factors to the Compustat database leaves just 6 percent of the stocks qualifying as Market Leaders. It is important to note that Market Leaders allow the inclusion of American Depository Receipts (ADRs), which are dollar-denominated overseas shares that trade in the United States. Thus, giant companies like Germany's Deutsche Telekom, Japan's NTT, and the United Kingdom's British Petroleum are available for consideration. This is an important distinction, especially when comparing performance with the S&P 500, which is made up of only U.S. companies. In the new global economy, the ability to purchase shares of companies domiciled outside the United States might be an advantage. Indeed, the number of ADRs in the Market Leaders universe has grown considerably over time—in 1995, they made up approximately 20 percent of the universe, whereas at the end of 2003, they accounted for 35 percent. Also important to note is that the Market Leaders universe is equally weighted, whereas the S&P 500 is cap-weighted, giving far greater weight to the largest companies in the index. Over longer periods, equal-weighted indexes have outperformed cap-weighted indexes, an important fact when comparing the S&P 500 to Market Leaders. Table 17-1 offers a refresher on how the Market Leaders universe compared to All Stocks, Large Stocks, Small Stocks, and the S&P 500 over the entire period of this study.

T A B L E 17-1

Summary Return and Risk Results for Annual Data, Large Stocks, Standard & Poor's 500, All Stocks, Market Leaders, and Small Stocks, December 31, 1952–December 31, 2003

	Market Leaders	Large Stocks	S&P 500	All Stocks	Small Stocks
Arithmetic Average	14.82%	12.99%	12.92%	14.79%	15.66%
Geometric Average	13.52%	11.71%	11.52%	13.00%	13.49%
Median Return	18.35%	15.75%	15.40%	16.80%	17.75%
Standard Deviation of Return	17.37%	16.84%	17.61%	20.11%	22.16%
Downside Risk—lower is better	4.94%	5.86%	6.33%	7.17%	8.00%
Correlation with S&P 500	0.94	0.95	1.00	0.87	0.82
T-Statistic	6.16	5.56	5.29	5.30	5.02
Sharpe Ratio	0.54	0.45	0.43	0.46	0.46
Number of Positive Periods	41	39	39	39	38
Number of Negative Periods	11	13	13	13	14
Maximum Peak-to-Trough Decline (using monthly data series)	−38.98%	−46.59%	−44.73%	−50.12%	−53.82%
Beta	0.92	0.89	1.00	0.99	1.03
$10,000 becomes:	$7,316,665.00	$3,173,724.00	$2,896,700.00	$5,743,706.00	$7,202,765.00
Minimum Annual Return	−21.40%	−26.70%	−26.47%	−27.90%	−31.20%
Maximum Annual Return	66.00%	45.07%	52.62%	55.90%	66.00%
Minimum *Expected* Return*	−19.92%	−20.69%	−22.30%	−25.43%	−28.66%
Maximum *Expected* Return**	49.56%	46.67%	48.14%	55.01%	59.98%

*Minimum Expected Return is Arithmetic Return minus 2 times the standard deviation.
**Maximum Expected Return is Arithmetic Return plus 2 times the standard deviation.

NEW PERIOD EXAMINED

Because we will look at some strategies that use three- and six-month price appreciation, in this chapter, I use the monthly data from 1963 forward—which still gives us 40 years of data. Because I am using monthly data, many more rolling one-, five-, and 10-year periods are available to use for base rates (each year now yields 12 observations as opposed to one).

Table 17-2 shows the results for Market Leaders, the S&P 500, Large Stocks, All Stocks, and Small Stocks between 1963 and 2003. The basic data are similar to that in Table 17-1, with the exception of the number of both positive and negative returns and the final value of a $10,000 investment. The number of positive versus negative returns changes because here we are looking at positive and negative months rather than years. Typically, large, broad-based indexes like the S&P 500 and the other universes featured here have positive monthly returns about 61 percent of the time, with negative returns accounting for the balancing 39 percent. Interestingly, that figure tends to persist whatever long period you look at—for example, for all

T A B L E 17-2

Summary Return and Risk Results for Monthly Data, Large Stocks, Standard & Poor's 500, All Stocks, Market Leaders, and Small Stocks, December 31, 1963–December 31, 2003

	Market Leaders	Large Stocks	S&P 500	All Stocks	Small Stocks
Arithmetic Average	14.05%	12.63%	11.87%	13.82%	14.69%
Geometric Average	12.77%	11.20%	10.61%	12.02%	12.57%
Median Return	14.05%	13.16%	12.45%	15.23%	16.87%
Standard Deviation of Return	17.06%	17.96%	16.82%	20.23%	22.02%
Downside Risk—lower is better	9.20%	10.15%	9.43%	11.53%	12.50%
Correlation with S&P 500	0.97	0.95	1.00	0.89	0.84
T-Statistic	5.55	4.72	4.72	4.61	4.53
Sharpe Ratio	0.49	0.39	0.37	0.40	0.41
Number of Positive Periods (months)	297	289	295	286	290
Number of Negative Periods (months)	183	191	185	194	190
Maximum Peak-to-Trough Decline (using monthly data series)	−38.98%	−46.59%	−44.73%	−50.12%	−53.82%
Beta	0.96	1.01	1.00	1.05	1.07
$10,000 becomes:	$1,225,022.00	$697,718.00	$564,584.00	$936,071.00	$1,139,641.00
Minimum Rolling Annual Return	−36.46%	−42.05%	−38.93%	−41.65%	−41.32%
Maximum Rolling Annual Return	64.42%	68.49%	61.01%	81.51%	91.56%
Minimum *Expected* Return*	−20.07%	−23.29%	−22.30%	−26.64%	−29.35%
Maximum *Expected* Return**	48.17%	48.55%	48.14%	54.28%	58.73%

*Minimum Expected Return is Arithmetic Return minus 2 times the standard deviation.
**Maximum Expected Return is Arithmetic Return plus 2 times the standard deviation.

monthly returns for the S&P 500 between January 1, 1926 and May 31, 2004, about 61 percent are positive and 39 percent are negative. If you choose to look at the market only after World War II, the figure barely budges, moving up to 63 percent positive and 37 percent negative. And if you look at the dismal 1926 through 1944 time period—dominated by the Great Depression of the 1930s—you would still see that 58 percent of all monthly returns for the S&P 500 were positive. Keep in mind that the terminal value of a $10,000 portfolio is much lower here, simply because we are missing more than a decade of compounding. Einstein was probably right when he said that compounding was the most miraculous mathematical formula he had ever seen.

SUMMARY RESULTS FOR VARIOUS MARKET LEADERS STRATEGIES

Here, I confine myself to reviewing the summary data on each strategy, because my goal is to show you that what holds true for the broad All Stocks and Large Stocks universes is equally as compelling within the Market Leaders universe. Table 17-3 illustrates this. Notice that the high ratio factors are not as devastating to Market Leaders as they are to All Stocks and Large Stocks, primarily because of the sheer size of these market-leading companies.

Yet, even here, the difference between high and low is extraordinary. The best strategy, buying the 50 Market Leaders with the lowest price-to-book ratios, turned $10,000 into over $4.7 million, whereas the worst, buying the 50 Market Leaders with the highest price-to-cashflow ratios, saw it grow to just $296,750. The low price-to-book strategy performs 15 times better. A $10,000 investment in the Market Leaders universe itself grew to $1.2 million over the same period.

I've sorted the strategies by average annual compound returns and, much like the returns seen in the All Stocks and Large Stocks universes, the highest returns are awarded to those market-leading companies having the lowest price-to-book, price-to-earnings, price-to-sales, and price-to-cashflow ratios, whereas the lowest returns are awarded to those market-leading companies having the highest price-to-book, price-to-earnings, price-to-sales, and price-to-cashflow ratios. Here we see the same symmetry that we found in our review of all the value factors in Chapter 10.

A $10,000 investment in either those 50 stocks from Market Leaders having the lowest price-to-book or price-to-earnings (PE) grew to over $4 million, whereas the same amount invested in those 50 stocks from Market Leaders having the highest price-to-cashflow ratio or price-to-sales ratio (PSR) was worth approximately $300,000! The chasm separating the strategies is huge and very similar to those we've seen for All Stocks and Large Stocks.

T A B L E 17-3

Summary Results for Various Strategies Applied to Market Lenders Universe (Standard & Poor's 500 Included for Comparison), December 31, 1963–December 31, 2003 (Strategies Sorted by Compound Return)

Strategy	Geometric Average	Arithmetic Average	Standard Deviation (%)	T-Stat	Ending Value	Sharpe Ratio	Downside Risk	Beta
Market Leaders, 50 Low P/Book	16.63	18.51	21.21	6	$4,705,461	0.62	10.53	1.04
Market Leaders, 50 Low PE	16.55	18.36	20.83	6.06	$4,571,422	0.62	10.29	1.02
Market Leaders, PSR<Average, Top 50 by Rel Str	16.21	17.92	20.07	6.12	$4,078,153	0.62	10.2	1.02
Market Leaders, 50 Low PSR	16.15	17.93	20.52	5.99	$3,981,957	0.61	10.67	1.01
Market Leaders, 50 Low PCFL	16.09	17.83	20.37	6	$3,906,209	0.61	10.23	1
Market Leaders, 50 Best 1-yr Rel Str	14.75	16.63	21.03	5.4	$2,452,387	0.53	11.13	1.06
Market Leaders, PCF<Avg, Top 50 by 3,6,12 Month Rel Str	14.53	16.25	19.98	5.54	$2,275,626	0.54	10.72	1.02
Market Leaders, 50 Best 5-yr EPS Gains	14.52	16.61	22.27	5.1	$2,267,445	0.5	11.31	1.17
Market Leaders, PSR<Avg, Top 50 by 3,6,12 Month Rel Str	14.14	16.01	20.85	5.23	$1,983,979	0.5	11.31	1.06
Market Leaders, 50 Worst Profit Margin	13.63	15.35	19.93	5.23	$1,659,290	0.49	10.91	1.04
Market Leaders, 50 Worst 5-yr EPS Change	13.62	15.15	18.77	5.47	$1,651,414	0.51	10.02	0.99
Market Leaders, Best 50 Yield, Sector Relative	13.51	14.89	17.84	5.65	$1,587,313	0.52	9.41	0.93
Market Leaders, ROE>Avg, Top 50 by 3,6,12 Month Rel Str	13.13	14.97	20.65	4.92	$1,390,238	0.46	11.23	1.07
Market Leaders	**12.77**	**14.05**	**17.06**	**5.55**	**$1,225,022**	**0.49**	**9.2**	**0.96**
Market Leaders, 50 Best Profit Margin	12.63	13.98	17.56	5.37	$1,166,320	0.48	9.31	0.97
Market Leaders, 50 High ROE	12.63	14.14	18.63	5.13	$1,165,770	0.46	10.05	1.02
Market Leaders, 50 Worst 1-yr EPS Change	12.51	14.26	20.09	4.8	$1,114,960	0.43	10.8	1.05
Market Leaders, 50 Low ROE	12.51	14.23	19.87	4.84	$1,114,342	0.43	10.84	1.03
Market Leaders, 50 Best 1-yr EPS Change	11.94	13.64	19.6	4.69	$1,225,022	0.41	11.03	1.05
S&P 500	10.61	11.87	16.82	4.72	$564,584	0.37	9.43	1
Market Leaders, 50 Worst 1-yr Rel Str	10.52	12.55	21.57	3.91	$545,735	0.32	11.83	1.08
Market Leaders, 50 High P/Book	10.35	11.97	19.2	4.18	$513,783	0.33	10.64	1.06
Market Leaders, 50 High PE	9.16	10.85	19.49	3.72	$332,875	0.26	11.29	1.07
Leaders, 50 High PSR	8.9	10.43	18.56	3.74	$302,226	0.25	10.64	1.05
Market Leaders, 50 High PCFL	8.85	10.46	18.96	3.67	$296,750	0.25	11.02	1.05

MULTIFACTOR STRATEGIES ALSO DO WELL

The same multifactor strategies we looked at in the last chapter also perform well with Market Leaders. The best strategy buys those 50 stocks from Market Leaders having PSRs less than the Market Leaders average and which also had the best 12-month price appreciation. In Chapter 20, we'll see that you can earn even better absolute returns using this strategy on a smaller capitalization universe; here, we see that it provided excellent overall returns, with the lowest maximum decline and an almost perfect 10-year base rate. This type of strategy essentially buys cheap stocks on the mend. You never pay more than the average for every dollar of sales, and you buy them when their prices are heading up. This type of momentum strategy almost always works best when you include a value factor in the model.

For example, if you consult Table 17-3, you see that a pure growth strategy of focusing on the stocks from Market Leaders with return on equity greater than average and then buying the 50 with the best three-, six-, and 12-month price, appreciation does considerably worse than focusing on cheaper stocks with great relative strength. It still beats the Market Leaders universe, but barely. It is also less consistent over longer periods and has a larger maximum decline.

BASE RATES

When we examine the strategies' underlying base rates, we see that they sort in a similar manner to compound return. The strategies with the best average annual compound return have the highest long-term base rates, and those with the lowest average annual compound return have the worst. The top five performing strategies all had 10-year base rates of 95 percent or better, with two strategies beating the Market Leaders universe over all 10-year periods. Of the five worst-performing strategies, only one managed a double-digit 10-year base rate, with the other four beating Market Leaders over any 10-year period between just 2 and 8 percent of the time. As we saw with the Large Stocks and All Stocks universes, over time, the underlying base rate gets stronger using the winning strategies and weaker using the losing ones.

Some of the strategies that beat the Market Leaders during the 40 years covered were marked by erratic returns within the period. For example, buying those 50 stocks from the Market Leaders universe having the best five-year earnings growth rates compounded at 14.52 percent per year, yet earned much of that between December 1996 and March 2000, when it compounded at more than 34 percent per year. This strategy's erratic behavior and tendency towards huge, concentrated run-ups can be seen when looking at its 10-year base rate—despite its good overall returns, it beat the Market Leaders universe in just 46 percent of all rolling 10-year periods. This illustrates why you must look at not just *overall* return, but the long-term consistency of those returns as well.

WORST-CASE SCENARIOS

Consistent with what we found with base rates, we find that the strategies with the worst overall performance and consistency also delivered the worst declines to investors. The stocks with the highest price-to-earnings, price-to-cashflow, and price-to-sales ratios suffered declines exceeding 55 percent. And, if that's not bad enough, there are many times within the 40-year period when investors got taken for a wild ride. For example, the 50 stocks from the Market Leaders universe having the highest price-to-cashflow ratios had three other declines during which they lost more than 25 percent.

Conversely, the stocks with the strongest and most consistent overall returns also had the lowest maximum decline. Most of the best performing strategies had maximum declines less that the Market Leaders universe itself. The best—buying those 50 stocks from Market Leaders having price-to-sales ratios below average and the best price appreciation—dropped a mild 31 percent from top to bottom.

IMPLICATIONS

In the Market Leaders universe we see exactly the same thing that we see in the broader All Stocks and Large Stocks universes—focusing on the most expensive, popular stocks delivers the worst overall return, whereas consistently concentrating on the cheapest stocks delivers the best returns. Moreover, the strategies that provided the best overall compound return also did so with the highest degree of consistency. They also tended to have the lowest overall maximum declines.

The strategies with the worst overall returns also had the worst Sharpe ratios, downside risks, and maximum declines. The best strategies, while having higher downside risks than the Market Leaders universe, all had much better Sharpe ratios. Finally, in Market Leaders, we also see that using models that marry growth and value characteristics provide excellent overall returns at reasonable levels of risk. Tables 17-4 and 17-5 summarize the performance of these methods.

T A B L E 17-4

Summary Base Rate Information for all Rolling One-, Five-, and 10-Year Periods. December 31, 1963–December 31, 2003. Strategies Ranked by Average Annual Compound Return

Strategy Beats Market Leaders Over Any	1-Year	5-Year	10-Year	Percent of the Time
Market Leaders, 50 Low P/Book	67%	90%	100%	
Market Leaders, 50 Low PE	69%	78%	95%	
Market Leaders, PSR<Average, Top 50 by Rel Str	72%	84%	99%	
Market Leaders, 50 Low PSR	68%	83%	100%	
Market Leaders, 50 Low PCFL	64%	76%	98%	
Market Leaders, 50 Best 1-yr Rel Str	62%	88%	95%	
Market Leaders, PCF<Avg, Top 50 by 3,6,12 Month Rel Str	58%	67%	87%	
Market Leaders, 50 Best 5-yr EPS Gains	51%	46%	46%	
Market Leaders, PSR<Avg, Top 50 by 3,6,12 Month Rel Str	65%	76%	89%	
Market Leaders, 50 Worst Profit Margin	57%	71%	85%	
Market Leaders, 50 Worst 5-yr EPS Change	52%	72%	75%	
Market Leaders, Best 50 Yield, Sector Relative	54%	77%	79%	
Market Leaders, ROE>Avg, Top 50 by 3,6,12 Month Rel Str	56%	62%	71%	
Market Leaders	**0%**	**0%**	**0%**	
Market Leaders, 50 Best Profit Margin	47%	61%	49%	
Market Leaders, 50 High ROE	53%	55%	48%	
Market Leaders, 50 Worst 1-yr EPS Change	49%	51%	71%	
Market Leaders, 50 Low ROE	47%	48%	62%	
Market Leaders, 50 Best 1-yr EPS Change	46%	39%	35%	
S&P 500	32%	20%	16%	
Market Leaders, 50 Worst 1-yr Rel Str	40%	22%	2%	
Market Leaders, 50 High P/Book	46%	29%	23%	
Market Leaders, 50 High PE	36%	17%	3%	
Leaders, 50 High PSR	32%	22%	8%	
Market Leaders, 50 High PCFL	35%	23%	7%	

T A B L E 17-5

Summary Average and Maximum Declines for Declines of 10 Percent or Greater for Market Leaders Strategies, December 31, 1963–December 31, 2003 (Sorted by Maximum Decline)

Strategy	Number of Drawdowns	Average Decline (%)	Maximum Decline (%)	Average Decline Duration	Average Recovery Duration	Average Drawdown Duration
Market Leaders, 50 High PCFL	10	−26.18	−61.83	10	14	22
Market Leaders, 50 High PSR	10	−26.05	−59.06	10	14	23
Market Leaders, 50 High PE	10	−27.02	−57.7	11	14	23
Market Leaders, 50 Worst 1-yr RS	15	−24.49	−54.94	10	6	16
Market Leaders, 50 Worst Profit Margin	12	−23.67	−52.22	9	6	14

(continued on next page)

T A B L E 17-5

Summary Average and Maximum Declines for Declines of 10 Percent or Greater for Market Leaders Strategies, December 31, 1963–December 31, 2003 (Sorted by Maximum Decline) *(Continued)*

Strategy	Number of Drawdowns	Average Decline (%)	Maximum Decline (%)	Average Decline Duration	Average Recovery Duration	Average Drawdown Duration
Market Leaders, 50 Low ROE	13	−22.82	−50.37	8	7	14
Market Leaders, Worst 50 by PBK	11	−24.71	−50.01	10	12	21
Market Leaders, 50 High ROE	13	−20.36	−50	9	8	16
Market Leaders, 50 Worst 1-yr EPS	15	−22	−48.9	8	6	14
Market Leaders, ROE>Avg, 50 by 3,6,12 Month Rel Str	14	−22.64	−48.63	7	8	14
Market Leaders, 50 Best 5-yr EPS Change	13	−23.25	−46.47	8	10	17
Market Leaders, PSR<Avg, 50 by 3,6,12 Month Rel Str	16	−20.23	−45.23	7	7	13
S&P 500	9	−24.77	−44.73	13	8	20
Market Leaders, 50 Best 1-yr Rel Str	16	−20.23	−41.19	6	7	12
Market Leaders, 50 Low PCF	14	−20.24	−39.15	7	7	14
Market Leaders, 50 Best 1-yr EPS	12	−23.1	−39.04	12	7	18
Market Leaders	**11**	**−20.15**	**−38.98**	**10**	**7**	**17**
Market Leaders, 50 Best Profit Margin	12	−19.76	−38.51	9	7	16
Market Leaders, 50 Low P/Book	14	−21.14	−37.08	6	7	13
Market Leaders, 50 Low PE	15	−19.95	−35.13	7	5	13
Market Leaders, 50 Low PSR	13	−22.18	−35.07	7	6	14
Market Leaders, PCFL<Avg, 50 by 3,6,12 Month Rel Str	15	−19.05	−34.73	8	6	13
Market Leaders, 50 Worst 5-yr EPS Change	13	−19.89	−32.82	6	8	15
Market Leaders, Best 50 Div Yield, Sector Relative	12	−19.73	−32.65	9	7	16
Market Leaders, PSR<Avg, Top 50 by Rel Str	15	−18.22	−31.11	7	6	14

BEST OF MARKET LEADERS FOUND IN CHAPTER 19

I've left one Market Leaders strategy out of this chapter—the strongest one. Offering the best overall return, lowest risk, excellent base rates, low maximum declines, and the highest Sharpe ratio, it deserves its own chapter. You can read about it in Chapter 19, *Searching for the Ideal Value Stock Investment Strategy.*

18

DISSECTING THE SMALL STOCKS UNIVERSE: RATIOS THAT ADD THE MOST VALUE

The degree of one's emotions varies inversely with one's knowledge of the facts—the less you know, the hotter you get.

—Bertrand Russell

Let's now turn our attention to the Small Stocks universe and dissect it much as we did the Market Leaders universe. You'll recall from Chapter 4 that the smallest capitalization stocks often are almost impossible to buy due to their lack of liquidity. The smallest stocks in the Compustat database provided the best overall returns mainly because their prices were essentially a mirage.

For this reason, we define our Small Stocks universe as any company within the Compustat universe having a market capitalization greater than an inflation-adjusted $185 million but less than the database average. Unlike Market Leaders, whose constraints lead us to just a handful of stocks, the Small Stocks universe is much larger. As of December 31, 2003, there were 2,915 stocks in the Small Stocks universe, with a weighted market capitalization of $1.5 billion and a median market capitalization of $607 million. By way of contrast, the median market capitalization of the 1,215 mutual funds in Morningstar's equity small-cap category was $967 million on December 31, 2003, thus making the market capitalization of our Small Stocks universe roughly $360 million less than that of Morningstar's small-cap category.

Table 18-1 will refresh your memory on how the Small Stocks universe compares with the All Stocks universe. Recall that the All Stocks universe includes every company in the Compustat database with market capitalizations exceeding an inflation-adjusted $185 million. Thus, All Stocks includes many large companies that Small Stocks explicitly excludes. Because both are equal-weighted indexes, their returns are closer than you might expect, with the far more numerous small cap stocks in the All Stocks universe driving much of the performance.

T A B L E 18-1

Summary Return and Risk Results for Annual Data, All Stocks, and Small Stocks, December 31, 1951–December 31, 2003

	All Stocks	Small Stocks
Arithmetic Average	14.79%	15.66%
Geometric Average	13.00%	13.49%
Median Return	16.80%	17.75%
Standard Deviation of Return	20.11%	22.16%
Downside Risk—lower is better	7.17%	8.00%
Correlation with S&P 500	0.87	0.82
T-Statistic	5.30	5.02
Sharpe Ratio	0.46	0.46
Number of Positive Periods	39	38
Number of Negative Periods	13	14
Maximum Peak-to-Trough Decline (using monthly data series)	−50.12%	−53.82%
Beta	0.99	1.03
$10,000 becomes:	$5,743,706.00	$7,202,765.00
Minimum Annual Return	−27.90%	−31.20%
Maximum Annual Return	55.90%	66.00%
Minimum *Expected* Return*	−25.43%	−28.66%
Maximum *Expected* Return**	55.01%	59.98%

*Minimum Expected Return is Arithmetic Return minus 2 times the standard deviation.
**Maximum Expected Return is Arithmetic Return plus 2 times the standard deviation.

MONTHLY DATA REVIEWED, SUMMARY DATA ACCESSED

As with Market Leaders, I focus on the monthly data over the last 40 years for the tests I run in this chapter. Table 18-2 shows the results for Small Stocks versus All Stocks over the last 40 years, and Table 18-3 lists the various strategies by compound average annual return. Although the order is similar to what we find with the various other universes we've examined, the magnitude is quite a bit larger than what we saw with Market Leaders.

T A B L E 18-2

Summary Return and Risk Results for Monthly Data, All Stocks, and Small Stocks, December 31, 1963–December 31, 2003

	All Stocks	Small Stocks
Arithmetic Average	13.82%	14.69%
Geometric Average	12.02%	12.57%
Median Return	15.23%	16.87%
Standard Deviation of Return	20.23%	22.02%
Downside Risk—lower is better	11.53%	12.50%
Correlation with S&P 500	0.89	0.84
T-Statistic	4.61	4.53
Sharpe Ratio	0.40	0.41
Number of Positive Periods (months)	286	290
Number of Negative Periods (months)	194	190
Maximum Peak-to-Trough Decline (using monthly data series)	−50.12%	−53.82%
Beta	1.05	1.07
$10,000 becomes:	$936,071.00	$1,139,641.00
Minimum Rolling Annual Return	−41.65%	−41.32%
Maximum Rolling Annual Return	81.51%	91.56%
Minimum *Expected* Return*	−26.64%	−29.35%
Maximum *Expected* Return**	54.28%	58.73%

*Minimum Expected Return is Arithmetic Return minus 2 times the standard deviation.
**Maximum Expected Return is Arithmetic Return plus 2 times the standard deviation.

With Small Stocks, the single best strategy buys cheap stocks on the mend. I determine that they are cheap by refusing to pay more than $1 for each dollar of sales. By requiring a PSR of 1.0 or less, we wind up, on average, paying approximately 60 cents for every dollar of sales. This gives us a group of stocks in which the expectations are so low that *any* good news should have an excellent effect on the stock price. We use three-, six-, and 12-month relative strength because these indicate that investors are putting their money where their mouth is, buying the shares and driving up their prices.

This is a very powerful formula, particularly with smaller capitalization stocks. Here, we see a $10,000 investment on December 31, 1963 growing to over $9.2 million at the end of 2003. That's a compound return of 18.62 percent per year, vastly greater than the 12.57 percent we would earn investing in the broader Small Stocks universe. And, although the strategy is riskier than the Small Stocks universe, that risk was well compensated, with the strategy delivering the highest Sharpe ratio of all strategies tested.

Ranking next in performance we find our usual suspects: those 50 stocks having the lowest price-to-earnings (PE), price-to-sales, price-to-book,

T A B L E 18-3

Summary Results for Various Strategies Applied to Small Stocks Universe, December 31, 1963–December 31, 2003 (Strategies Sorted by Compound Return)

Strategy	Geometric Average	Arithmetic Average	Standard Deviation (%)	T-Stat	Ending Value	Sharpe Ratio	Downside Risk	Beta
Small Stocks, PSR<1, 50 by Highest 3, 6, and 12 Month Rel Str	18.62	21.79	27.74	5.49	$9,249,548	0.6	14.45	1.17
Small Stocks, 50 Low PCFL	16.82	19.94	27.7	5	$5,023,916	0.53	13.78	1.17
Small Stocks, 50 Low PE	16.31	19	25.5	5.15	$4,214,230	0.53	13.03	1.07
Small Stocks, ROE>Avg. 50 by Highest 3, 6, and 12 Month Rel Str	15.8	20.15	32.63	4.31	$3,530,758	0.46	17.48	1.33
Small Stocks, 50 Low PSR	15.38	18.36	26.9	4.71	$3,051,506	0.48	13.81	1.11
Small Stocks, PSR<Avg, 50 by Highest 3, 6, and 12 Month Rel Str	15.08	19.44	32.45	4.17	$2,757,808	0.43	17.61	1.26
Small Stocks, 50 Low P/Book	14.97	18.35	28.92	4.39	$2,654,859	0.45	14.31	1.17
Small Stocks, 50 Best 1-yr EPS Growth	14.16	17.43	27.83	4.31	$1,995,556	0.43	15.4	1.23
Small Stocks, PCF<Avg. 50 by Highest 3, 6, and 12 Month Rel Str	13.97	18.69	33.64	3.86	$1,865,835	0.4	18.5	1.27
Small Stocks, 50 Worst 5-yr EPS Change	13.25	15.64	23.41	4.55	$1,449,185	0.43	13.41	1.05
Small Stocks	**12.57**	**14.69**	**22.02**	**4.53**	**$1,139,641**	**0.41**	**12.5**	**1.07**
All Stocks	12.02	13.82	20.23	4.61	$936,071	0.4	11.53	1.05
Small Stocks, 50 Best 1-yr RS	10.21	16.03	37.29	2.98	$487,995	0.28	21.25	1.47
Small Stocks, 50 best 5-yr EPS Change	9.53	12.8	27.31	3.17	$381,829	0.26	15.87	1.3
Small Stocks, 50 Best Profit Margins	9.4	11.03	18.91	3.89	$363,389	0.28	11.67	0.83
Small Stocks, 50 Best ROE	9.15	13.28	30.78	2.93	$331,915	0.25	18.25	1.37
Small Stocks, 50 High PE	7.72	11.48	29.23	2.65	$195,864	0.2	17.5	1.29
Small Stocks, 50 Worst 1-yr EPS Growth	5.73	9.78	30.37	2.16	$92,979	0.13	18.11	1.38
Small Stocks, 50 High P/Book	3.42	8.35	33.18	1.69	$38,375	0.07	21.03	1.44
Small Stocks, 50 High PCFL	3.12	7.74	31.89	1.62	$34,173	0.06	20.58	1.46
Small Stocks, 50 Worst 1-yr Rel Str	2.11	7.3	34.97	1.4	$23,071	0.04	20.23	1.48
Small Stocks, 50 High PSR	−2.16	2.18	30.18	0.47	$4,182	−0.13	21.05	1.29
Small Stocks, 50 Worst Profit Margins	−2.73	2.03	31.81	0.42	$3,299	−0.13	21.77	1.36

and price-to-cashflow ratios. All beat the Small Stocks universe and all came in with Sharpe ratios better than the universe. Several of the multifactor models that marry lower than average price-to-sales and price-to-cashflow ratios with relative strength also beat the universe by healthy margins.

We also find the usual suspects at the bottom of the list, but here again, we find a larger magnitude of difference—the two worst strategies actually *lost* money over the last 40 years. Moreover, the seven worst-performing strategies all returned less than T-bills over the same period. For the 40 years ending December 31, 2003, an investor in T-bills would have seen his investment compound at 6.03 percent per year, turning the $10,000 into $103,893. All seven of the worst performing strategies did drastically worse than the no-risk T-bill investment. As you'll see in the base rate section, they also were very consistent in their underperformance, with the bottom three never having a rolling 10-year period during which they beat the Small Stocks universe.

The worst two strategies, buying stocks from Small Stocks with the worst profit margins or the highest price-to-sales ratios (PSRs), both lost more than 2 percent per year over the last 40 years, reducing a $10,000 investment to $3,299 and $4,182 respectively. With small cap stocks, it appears that having horrible profit margins can essentially wipe you out. This makes sense. Smaller companies tend to be single- or dual-line business models and, if the margins are awful, you don't have much of a business. PSR remains an excellent litmus test for small cap stocks, with the highest PSR stocks performing the worst and lowest PSR stocks performing the best. Generally, however, we see exactly the same thing in the Small Stocks universe that we saw in the Market Leaders universe—low-ratio stocks do vastly better than high, and multifactor relative strength models that marry value with growth end up at or near the top of the performance tables.

BASE RATES

Two Small Stock strategies stand out for their long-term consistency—buying the 50 stocks with low PSRs and strong relative strength, and buying the 50 stocks with the lowest price-to-cashflow. Each beat the Small Stocks universe by more than 85 percent over all rolling five-year periods while beating the Small Stocks universe by 99 and 100 percent of all rolling 10-year periods, respectively. The odds are clearly in favor of these two strategies. Buying stocks with low PSRs or PEs from Small Stocks also managed to beat the Small Stocks universe by wide margins over the longer term, but did not perform quite as well. Remember that our mantra is to focus not only on absolute performance, but also on the consistency of that performance. Great performance alone is not enough: You must marry it to consistency if you want a strategy that you can actually stick with through all the market's gyrations.

Take a look at buying those 50 stocks from Small Stocks having the lowest price-to-book ratios. Longer term, this investment does significantly better than an investment in Small Stocks; it compounds at 14.97 percent per year and turns a $10,000 investment into $2,654,859 at the end of 2003—$1 million more than a similar investment in Small Stocks. But look at the base rates: We see that it actually *underperformed* the Small Stocks universe in all rolling five-year periods, and beat the universe just 57 percent of the time over all rolling 10-year periods. This shows us that this strategy's performance comes in intense spurts, running up rapidly before settling back to a more mediocre pace alongside Small Stocks. This is not a strategy you would be likely to stick with if you found yourself in one of the majority of five-year periods when the strategy underperformed the Small Stocks universe. Again, always marry great absolute returns with the high consistency of excellent base rates.

Yet again, the worst performing strategies have awful base rates. The three worst performing strategies never had a rolling 10-year period in which they beat the Small Stocks universe, and they had pathetic five-year base rates as well. Almost every strategy that underperformed the Small Stocks universe did so consistently, so you'll want to carefully review where any small-cap stock you are considering for purchase falls in the continuum. The worst-case offenders are the usual group—stocks with the highest price-to-earnings, price-to-cashflow, price-to-book, and price-to-sales ratios, plus the biggest decliners from the previous year. Avoid them like the plague.

WORST-CASE SCENARIOS

Table 18-4 lists maximum declines and the number of declines exceeding 10 percent. The first thing you notice is that, with the exception of buying those 50 stocks from Small Stocks having the highest dividend yield, *all* the Small Stocks strategies had maximum declines exceeding 50 percent. As we saw with average annual returns and base rates, the biggest losses accrue to the riskiest strategies. Small Stocks with the worst profit margins, highest price-to-sales ratios, worst return on equity, and highest price-to-book ratios all experienced declines exceeding 92 percent from peak to trough.

T A B L E 18-4

Summary Average and Maximum Declines for Declines of 10 Percent or Greater for Small Stocks Strategies, December 31, 1963–December 31, 2003 (Sorted by Maximum Decline)

Strategy	Number of Drawdowns	Average Decline (%)	Maximum Decline (%)	Average Decline Duration	Average Recovery Duration	Average Drawdown Duration
Small Stocks, 50 Worst Margins	5	−45.9	−95.55	67	19	39
Small Stocks, 50 High PSR	5	−43.41	−95.23	68	17	36
Small Stocks, 50 Worst ROE	10	−41.99	−92.96	25	15	40
Small Stocks, 50 High PBK	11	−38.05	−92.49	14	23	35
Small Stocks, 50 Best 1-yr RS	20	−30.84	−91.18	8	10	17
Small Stocks, PCF<Avg Top 50 by 3, 6, and 12 Month Rel Str	19	−28.17	−87.48	9	7	15

(continued on next page)

T A B L E 18-4

Summary Average and Maximum Declines for Declines of 10 Percent or Greater for Small Stocks Strategies, December 31, 1963–December 31, 2003 (Sorted by Maximum Decline) *(Continued)*

Strategy	Number of Drawdowns	Average Decline (%)	Maximum Decline (%)	Average Decline Duration	Average Recovery Duration	Average Drawdown Duration
Small Stocks, 50 High PCFL	11	−32.41	−86.4	13	26	37
Small Stocks, 50 Worst 1-yr Rel Str	2	−52.39	−85.46	40	4	12
Small Stocks, 50 best 5-yr EPS Change	14	−28.7	−84.91	12	12	25
Small Stocks, PSR<Avg Top 50 by 3, 6, and 12 Month Rel Str	20	−27.52	−76.71	7	8	14
Small Stocks, 50 Best ROE	18	−30.17	−75.93	11	9	19
Small Stocks, 50 Worst 1-yr EPS Growth	11	−34.18	−74.17	20	15	35
Small Stocks, ROE>Avg. Top 50 by 3, 6, and 12 Month Rel Str	19	−29.31	−70.56	8	8	15
Small Stocks, 50 High PE	13	−32.59	−70.39	15	13	28
Small Stocks, 50 best 1-yr EPS Growth	17	−25	−66.78	10	9	18
Small Stocks, 50 Best Margins	10	−26.57	−59.53	13	16	30
Small Stocks, 50 Low PCFL	16	−27.33	−55.73	8	8	17
Small Stocks	**14**	**−22.29**	**−53.82**	**12**	**8**	**21**
Small Stocks, PSR<1, Top 50 by 3, 6, and 12 Month Rel Str	20	−24.27	−53.14	6	8	15
Small Stocks, 50 Low PSR	15	−25.75	−52.87	9	10	20
Small Stocks, 50 Low PE	14	−25.84	−52.13	11	8	20
Small Stocks, 50 Worst 5-yr EPS Change	14	−23.82	−52.04	7	13	20
Small Stocks, 50 Low P/Book	18	−24.69	−52	7	10	17
All Stocks	11	−26.37	−50.12	11	10	22
Small Stocks, 50 High Div Yld	16	−19.09	−49.29	7	7	15

Even great strategies can have breathtaking declines. The strategy of buying stocks with price-to-cashflow ratios less than average and good price appreciation was a winner over time, yet plunged 87 percent from peak to trough between February 2000 and February 2003. Even the best performing small cap strategy—buying stocks with price-to-sales ratios less than one and good price performance—had a maximum decline of over 53 percent. Study Table 18-4 very carefully. Small capitalization stocks are inherently more volatile than larger cap stocks—a very important thing to remember when embarking on a small-cap strategy.

IMPLICATIONS

Over the past 40 years, the best performing small-cap strategy performed nine times as well as the Small Stocks universe, and many of the commonly successful strategies, such as buying stocks with the lowest PEs, price-to-cashflow, or price-to-sales ratios significantly enhance the returns of a small capitalization strategy. The best performing strategies also perform consistently, with excellent base rates over all rolling five- and 10-year periods.

A red flag is raised here, however. Even the best strategies have suffered 50 percent declines, a reality all small-cap investors must face. If you don't think you can take that, consider using the more tranquil Market Leaders or Large Stocks strategies. If you can take the roller coaster ride, however, small-cap strategies can play an important role in diversifying your portfolio while greatly enhancing overall performance. Table 18-5 summarizes the various strategies.

T A B L E 18-5

Summary Base Rate Information for All Rolling One-, Five-, and 10-Year Periods—December 31, 1963–December 31, 2003 (Strategies Ranked by Average Annual Compound Return)

Strategy Beats Small Stocks over Any	1-Year	5-Year	10-Year	Percent of the Time
Small Stocks, PSR<1, 50 by Highest 3, 6, and 12 Month Rel Str	73%	91%	100%	
Small Stocks, 50 Low PCFL	64%	86%	99%	
Small Stocks, 50 Low PE	60%	77%	77%	
Small Stocks, ROE>Avg. 50 by Highest 3, 6, and 12 Month Rel Str	67%	73%	89%	
Small Stocks, 50 Low PSR	62%	70%	87%	
Small Stocks, PSR<Avg, 50 by Highest 3, 6, and 12 Month Rel Str	66%	86%	89%	
Small Stocks, 50 Low P/Book	56%	46%	57%	
Small Stocks, 50 Best 1-yr EPS Growth	56%	67%	84%	
Small Stocks, PCF<Avg. 50 by Highest 3, 6, and 12 Month Rel Str	64%	69%	66%	
Small Stocks, 50 Worst 5-yr EPS Change	55%	56%	68%	
Small Stocks, 50 Highest Dividend Yiled	43%	43%	31%	
Small Stocks	**0%**	**0%**	**0%**	
All Stocks	45%	53%	45%	
Small Stocks, 50 Best 1-yr Rel Str	51%	57%	54%	
Small Stocks, 50 best 5-yr EPS Change	42%	31%	11%	
Small Stocks, 50 Best Profit Margins	38%	20%	4%	
Small Stocks, 50 Best ROE	42%	25%	5%	
Small Stocks, 50 High PE	33%	21%	3%	
Small Stocks, 50 Worst 1-yr EPS Growth	30%	8%	4%	
Small Stocks, 50 Worst ROE	35%	14%	1%	
Small Stocks, 50 High P/Book	39%	26%	12%	
Small Stocks, 50 High PCFL	29%	6%	2%	
Small Stocks, 50 Worst 1-yr Rel Str	16%	2%	0%	
Small Stocks, 50 High PSR	28%	10%	0%	
Small Stocks, 50 Worst Profit Margins	30%	4%	0%	

Finally, think very carefully about volatility before using a more concentrated version of these small-cap strategies—concentration enhances both return and volatility, but it is the volatility that you should think about most deeply. Many an investor has been lured by performance, only to crack and throw in the towel when the strategy takes a dive. Always look at the worst-case scenario for any strategy before you take the leap.

CASE STUDY: A NOTE ON SMALL-CAP CONCENTRATED INVESTING

Many investors have asked me if more concentrated portfolios do better than the 50-stock versions featured in this book. The short answer is yes—*but*. Yes, using the strategies to invest in portfolios with fewer securities generally leads to much better absolute performance over time, but the strategies also exhibit much greater volatility and a potential for serious declines. For example, the best performing 50-stock portfolio from Small Stocks buys stocks with price-to-sales ratios less than one and great three-, six-, and 12-month price appreciation. What if you focused on even smaller-cap stocks (to take full advantage of the "small-cap effect") and then concentrated the portfolio to 10 or 25 stocks? The argument is often made that, whereas institutional investors need adequate liquidity to invest their huge portfolios, individuals should be able to put much smaller sums—say, $10,000—to work in even the smallest issues.

So, let's take a look. I tested a strategy of buying stocks with market capitalizations between a deflated $25 million and $250 million, requiring price-to-sales ratios less than one and then buying those 10 or 25 stocks having the best one-year price appreciation. As you might expect, total returns soared, with the 10-stock portfolio compounding at 21.18 percent and the 25-stock portfolio growing at 24.32 percent per year. Those extra returns helped drive a $10,000 investment made on December 31, 1963 in the 10-stock group to over $22 million at the end of 2003 and to $60.5 million in the 25-stock portfolio. Pretty impressive—*but*—look at the standard deviation of returns: For the 10-stock portfolio, it is a whopping *43.28 percent!* And although the 25-stock portfolio's standard deviation was a somewhat more reasonable 36.35 percent, we're still looking at stratospheric volatility.

Consider the 10-stock portfolio. With a standard deviation of 43.28 percent, 95 percent of all returns over any 12-month period would vary from −58.39 percent to +114.73 percent. Imagine if you started a concentrated strategy like this, and 12 months later found yourself with a portfolio worth less than half of what you started with. Do you think that you could stick with the strategy? The honest answer is, no, absolutely not! And the monthly returns show just what our expected rate of returns shows—a seriously wild ride. What's more, with the 10-stock portfolio, the maximum decline was a loss of 86.04 percent, which rivals some of the declines we saw among the *worst* performing strategies I've covered.

Although the Small Stocks universe only dropped by more than 40 percent from peak to trough once over the last 40 years, the 10-stock version of this strategy dropped more than 40 percent six times. Between January 1, 1994 and March 31, 1995, the 10-stock version was down 46 percent, turning $10,000 into just $5,891. Over the same period, the Small Stocks universe itself *gained* more than 1.33 percent on an annual basis, turning the $10,000 into $10,167. More recently, between January 1, 1998 and December 31, 2000—a time when the broad market was soaring into the final stages of a speculative bubble—the 10-stock portfolio lost 86 percent, turning $10,000 into just $1,958. And if that's not enough to scare you, consider the monthly performance. This strategy has declined by 39 percent in a single month!

Granted, the 10-stock strategy has had some thrilling increases—in its best month, it soared by more than 40 percent—but it is the downside that is the deal-breaker. Thus, although the long-term performance of this 10-stock portfolio is stunning, I do not recommend it. Few investors could weather the intense short-term volatility.

25-STOCK VERSION PREFERRED

The 25-stock version of this small-cap strategy is worth considering, however. Its returns are much better than the 10-stock version, and its volatility is lower. While it too has periods when it is totally out of sync with the overall market or the Small Stocks universe, the extremes are much less pronounced. It's still much riskier than the Small Stocks universe, suffering four peak-to-trough declines of over 40 percent. It also had 20 separate declines exceeding 10 percent, and like the 10-stock version, falls when the general market is rising. For example, for much of the raging bull market between 1998 and 2000, this strategy soared and crashed repeatedly, yet wound up basically going nowhere.

CAUTION ADVISED

Thus, although this 25-stock strategy is much less volatile than the 10-stock version, I still urge extreme caution. Yes, over the last 40 years they both would have outperformed 50-stock versions, and yes, 25 stocks are easier to buy and follow, but I cannot overemphasize the hazards of higher volatility. Everyone thinks they are ready to withstand it, and perhaps intellectually they are, but you have to watch out for emotions when the going gets rough. Think hard about how you might react if your portfolio lost 25 percent in a month while the general market edged higher. If you honestly believe you could stay the course, then a more concentrated strategy might be right for you.

19

C H A P T E R

SEARCHING FOR THE IDEAL VALUE STOCK INVESTMENT STRATEGY

The best way to manage anything is by making use of its own nature.
—Lao Tzu

All the data I have presented thus far have pointed to the overwhelming superiority of single value factors. This is true for all the separate universes that we have examined—All Stocks, Small Stocks, Large Stocks, and Market Leaders—as well as for both the monthly and annual data. When examined on a single-factor basis, buying those stocks from any universe having the lowest price-to-earnings (PE), price-to-sales, price-to-book, and price-to-cashflow ratios consistently beat either buying stocks with the best single growth factors (i.e., return on equity, relative strength, and earnings gains) or buying the universe itself.

Yet, using single factors also led to problems. The greatest of these is volatility—although many single-factor strategies ended up vastly ahead of their universes over the full period of the study, significant volatility was present along the way. Many had huge underperformance over some of the rolling 12-month periods. This makes it difficult, if not impossible, for investors to stick with the strategy in real time, and more important, with real money. Watching these strategies perform over the last seven years has confirmed this for me. Many investors are uncomfortable with any strategy that possesses risks or performance significantly different from indexes like the Dow Jones Industrial Average, the S&P 500, or the Russell 2000. They'd love to outperform the indexes, but cannot stomach the volatility that is the inevitable by-product. They can't stand seeing their portfolio lose money when the market is up, much less own stocks that do well in bull markets, but get crushed in bear markets. These jittery investors frequently end up in index funds, unable to stomach the higher volatility that goes with higher returns.

FOCUSING ON DOWNSIDE RISK AND RETURN

Therefore, when searching for the ideal value strategy, it is imperative to find a strategy that offers outstanding returns while minimizing the downside risk. In addition to looking for strategies with the smallest maximum declines and downside risk, I try to identify strategies that never strayed too far from the performance of their underlying benchmark. In this chapter, I look at multi-factor value strategies from the All Stocks and Market Leaders universes to see if we can identify those with limited risk levels that still generate excess returns. I look at both the annual and monthly data when examining the efficacy of each strategy.

A SUPERIOR ALL-STOCKS VALUE STRATEGY

You'll recall from Chapter 16 that it is almost always better to use multiple factors when looking for superior strategies. What about using *all* the superior value factors within a single strategy? Instead of sorting on just low PE or price-to-book, what about combining them to cover all the value bases? That's the idea behind this first multifactor value strategy.

Here, I begin with the All Stocks universe, and I require that the following conditions are met:

- Price-to-book ratios are below 1.5 (or, as Compustat will calculate it, book-to-price ratios are above .66)
- Dividend yield must exceed the Compustat database average
- PE ratio must be below the Compustat database average
- Buy the 50 stocks with the lowest price-to-cashflow ratios

With this strategy, I'm combining traditional value factors, yet also requiring that dividend payout is not only present, but greater than that of the average stock. Table 19-1 shows the results of this strategy. (I'm using 51 years of data here to keep this strategy's annual returns consistent with a Market Leaders strategy that I present later in this chapter.) You can see that, for the 51 years of data between December 31, 1952 and December 31, 2003,

T A B L E 19-1

Summary Return and Risk Results for Annual Data, All Stocks, and Multifactor All Stocks Value Strategy, December 31, 1952–December 31, 2003

	All Stocks	Multifactor Value Strategy, All Stocks
Arithmetic Average	14.93%	20.05%
Geometric Average	13.10%	17.54%
Median Return	17.00%	17.12%
Standard Deviation of Return	20.29%	25.46%
Downside Risk—lower is better	7.24%	5.81%
Correlation with S&P 500	0.87	0.75
T-Statistic	5.25	5.62
Sharpe Ratio	0.46	0.56
Number of Positive Periods	38	41
Number of Negative Periods	13	10
Maximum Peak-to-Trough Decline (using monthly data series)	−50.12%	−42.59%
Beta	0.99	1.07
$10,000 becomes:	$5,323,175.00	$37,991,316.00
Minimum Annual Return	−27.90%	−21.20%
Maximum Annual Return	55.90%	89.09%
Minimum *Expected* Return*	−25.65%	−30.87%
Maximum *Expected* Return**	55.51%	70.97%

*Minimum Expected Return is Arithmetic Return minus 2 times the standard deviation.
**Maximum Expected Return is Arithmetic Return plus 2 times the standard deviation.

this multifactor value strategy adds significant value to the single-factor value strategies already reviewed. A $10,000 investment on December 31, 1952 grew to $37,991,316 at the end of 2003, a compound average annual return of 17.54 percent. That's dramatically higher than the $5,323,175 it would have grown to invest in the All Stocks universe over the same period. Risk, as measured by the standard deviation of return, was considerably higher than All Stocks, coming in at 25.46 percent for the strategy and 20.29 percent for All Stocks. But now we see why looking at downside risk is so important—this strategy had a *lower* downside risk than All Stocks, coming in at 5.81 percent, compared to 7.24 percent for All Stocks. Thus, when stock returns were negative, this strategy was actually less risky than All Stocks. This is also apparent when you look at the maximum decline—the largest drop this strategy ever had was a loss of 42.59 percent, compared to a drop of 50.12 percent for All Stocks. The strategy had seven separate losses exceeding 20 percent, whereas All Stocks had six.

Thus, the strategy does significantly better than single-factor value strategies applied to the All Stocks universe. But it fails to deliver the absolute upside that those simple mixed value and growth strategies featured in

Chapter 16 offered. Simply buying the 50 stocks with the best price appreciation and price-to-sales lower than one performed significantly better, without much higher risk. What's more, the base rates for the growth–value strategy were better than those we see here. Finally, when we dig deep in the monthly data and analyze the 481 monthly observations of 12-month returns, we see that the strategy had one instance where it lagged the All Stocks universe by 27 percent.

For investors seeking lower risk, this might not be the best strategy to use. Let's see if we do better using the larger-cap and more stable stocks from the Market Leaders universe.

MARKET LEADERS BY DIVIDEND AND SHAREHOLDER VALUE

In the original edition of *What Works on Wall Street*, I found that the best long-term Market Leaders strategy was buying those 50 stocks having the highest dividend yield from that universe. In earlier editions of the book, I dubbed this strategy Cornerstone Value, demonstrating that it could serve as a cornerstone of your investment portfolio. Let's review the updated numbers for that strategy before we move on to an improved version. If we focused exclusively on the 50 stocks from Market Leaders having the highest dividend yield and invested $10,000 on December 31, 1952, $10,000 would grow to $17,567,144, a compound average annual return of 15.78 percent per year. That was significantly higher than the $6,345,763 you'd earn with a similar investment in the Market Leaders universe itself.

Cornerstone Value's distinguishing feature was that it offered these returns at risk levels *less* than those of the Market Leaders universe itself. The standard deviation of return of 17.77 percent was indistinguishable from Market Leaders' 17.54 percent, and the 3.99 percent downside risk was a full point lower than that of the Market Leaders universe. Moreover, the maximum decline of 28.18 percent was a full 10 points better than Market Leaders' maximum drop of 39 percent.

Even more important for risk-adverse investors, the worst five-year period for the Cornerstone Value strategy—the one ending on May 31, 1970—saw $10,000 grow to $11,337, a gain of 2.54 percent per year. In other words, the strategy *never had a five-year period when it lost money*. The strategy also stayed quite close to its underlying Market Leaders benchmark. Cornerstone Value was truly a strategy that offered excellent risk-adjusted returns, as its high Sharpe ratio of 65 makes plain. Table 19-2 shows the summary return data, whereas Tables 19-3 and 19-4 show base rates and worst-case scenarios for the strategy.

T A B L E 19-2

Summary Return and Risk Results for Annual Data, Large Stocks, Standard & Poor's 500, All Stocks, Market Leaders, and Small Stocks, December 31, 1952–December 31, 2003

	Market Leaders	Cornerstone Value	S&P 500
Arithmetic Average	14.82%	17.10%	12.81%
Geometric Average	13.49%	15.78%	11.39%
Median Return	18.40%	17.60%	14.31%
Standard Deviation of Return	17.54%	17.77%	17.76%
Downside Risk—lower is better	4.99%	3.99%	6.39%
Correlation with S&P 500	0.94	0.86	1.00
T-Statistic	6.03	6.87	5.15
Sharpe Ratio	0.53	0.65	0.42
Number of Positive Periods	40	42	38
Number of Negative Periods	11	9	13
Maximum Peak-to-Trough Decline (using monthly data series)	−38.98%	−28.18%	−44.73%
Beta	0.93	0.86	1.00
$10,000 becomes:	$6,345,763.00	$17,567,144.00	$2,447,210.00
Minimum Annual Return	−21.40%	−15.00%	−26.47%
Maximum Annual Return	66.00%	58.20%	52.62%
Minimum *Expected* Return*	−20.26%	−18.44%	−22.30%
Maximum *Expected* Return**	49.90%	52.64%	48.14%

*Minimum Expected Return is Arithmetic Return minus 2 times the standard deviation.
**Maximum Expected Return is Arithmetic Return plus 2 times the standard deviation.

T A B L E 19-3

Base Rates for Cornerstone Value and Market Leaders, 1952–2003

Item	Cornerstone Value Beat Market Leaders	Percent
Single-Year Return	35 out of 51	69%
Rolling Five-Year Compound Return	38 out of 37	81%
Rolling 10-Year Compound Return	40 out of 42	95%

T A B L E 19-4

Worst-Case Scenarios: All 10 Percent or Greater Declines for Cornerstone Value, December 31, 1962–December 31, 2003

Peak Date	Peak Index Value	Trough Date	Trough Index Value	Recovery Date	Decline (%)	Decline Duration	Recovery Duration
Jan-66	1.6	Sep-66	1.32	Mar-67	−17.55	8	6
Jan-69	2.22	Jun-70	1.63	Jan-71	−26.69	17	7
Nov-72	2.85	Aug-73	2.56	Jan-74	−10.27	9	5

(continued on next page)

T A B L E 19-4

Worst-Case Scenarios: All 10 Percent or Greater Declines for Cornerstone Value, December 31, 1962–December 31, 2003 *(Continued)*

Peak Date	Peak Index Value	Trough Date	Trough Index Value	Recovery Date	Decline (%)	Decline Duration	Recovery Duration
Feb-74	2.95	Sep-74	2.23	Feb-75	−24.57	7	5
Jan-80	7.29	Mar-80	6.48	May-80	−11.14	2	2
Jun-81	10.17	Sep-81	9.04	Aug-82	−11.06	3	11
Jan-84	17.25	Jul-84	15.36	Sep-84	−10.94	6	2
Aug-87	40.1	Nov-87	29.78	Jan-89	−25.73	3	14
Dec-89	52.41	Oct-90	37.64	May-91	−28.18	10	7
Mar-98	190.08	Aug-98	153.17	Mar-99	−19.42	5	7
Dec-99	247.17	Feb-00	217.96	Aug-00	−11.81	2	6
May-01	308.96	Sep-01	265.07	Mar-02	−14.21	4	6
May-02	325	Mar-03	251.52	Jul-03	−22.61	10	4
Average					−18.01	6.62	6.31

IMPROVING ON THE BEST

Trying to improve my original strategies is an important part of my ongoing research. I was able to improve Cornerstone Value by including *shareholder yield*. This concept requires a brief explanation. Companies have two basic ways to make payments to shareholders. The first is paying cash *dividends* as a distribution of their share of the company's profits. But companies can also support their stock prices by buying up their own stock, thereby reducing the number of shares outstanding and shoring up the company's stock price.

Thus, to create shareholder yield, you add the current dividend yield of the stock to any net buyback activity the company has engaged in over the prior year. If, for example, a company trading at $40 a share is paying an annual dividend of $1, the company would have a dividend yield of 2.5 percent. If that same company engaged in no stock buybacks over the year, its shareholder yield would equal 2.5 percent, the same as the dividend yield. If, however, the company had 1,000,000 shares outstanding at the beginning of the year and 900,000 at the end of the year, the company's buyback yield would be 10 percent. Adding this to the dividend yield of 2.5 percent, you would get a total shareholder yield of 12.5 percent. This formula allows us to capture all of a company's "payments" to shareholders, and it is indifferent as to whether those payments come in the form of cash dividends or buyback activity. This is important because, like all other things in life, trends come in and out of favor on Wall Street. There are times when buybacks are all the rage, and times when cash dividends are in favor. Shareholder yield captures them both.

Using shareholder yield improves the original Cornerstone Value strategy. Table 19-5 shows the summary results for the improved strategy that incorporates shareholder yield, along with Market Leaders and the original Cornerstone Value. A $10,000 investment on December 31, 1952 grew to $24,071,481 at the end of 2003, a compound average annual return of 16.49 percent. Simply including a company's buyback activity adds more than $6 million of value to the original Cornerstone Value strategy. Better yet, the standard deviation of return goes down, coming in at 17.47, lower than that of the Market Leaders universe. This excellent performance married to the lower standard deviation pushes the Sharpe ratio of the improved Cornerstone Value strategy up to 71. The downside risk remains lower than that of Market Leaders at 4.01 percent and similar to the downside risk of the original Cornerstone Value. The worst one-year drop is a smaller 12.90 percent, whereas the maximum decline was similar to Cornerstone Value, coming in at 29.05 percent. Like the original, the shareholder yield strategy never had a five-year period when it lost money.

T A B L E 19-5

Summary Return and Risk Results for Annual Data, Market Leaders, Cornerstone Value, and Market Leaders, Shareholder Yield, December 31, 1952–December 31, 2003

	Market Leaders	Cornerstone Value	Market Leaders, Shareholder Yield
Arithmetic Average	14.82%	17.10%	17.78%
Geometric Average	13.49%	15.78%	16.49%
Median Return	18.40%	17.60%	17.72%
Standard Deviation of Return	17.54%	17.77%	17.47%
Downside Risk—lower is better	4.99%	3.99%	4.01%
Correlation with S&P 500	0.94	0.86	0.87
T-Statistic	6.03	6.87	7.27
Sharpe Ratio	0.53	0.65	0.71
Number of Positive Periods	40	42	43
Number of Negative Periods	11	9	8
Maximum Peak-to-Trough Decline (using monthly data series)	−38.98%	−28.18%	−29.05%
Beta	0.93	0.86	0.86
$10,000 becomes:	$6,345,763.00	$17,567,144.00	$24,071,481.00
Minimum Annual Return	−21.40%	−15.00%	−12.90%
Maximum Annual Return	66.00%	58.20%	54.94%
Minimum *Expected* Return*	−20.26%	−18.44%	−22.30%
Maximum *Expected* Return**	49.90%	52.64%	48.14%

*Minimum Expected Return is Arithmetic Return minus 2 times the standard deviation.
**Maximum Expected Return is Arithmetic Return plus 2 times the standard deviation.

All base rates are positive, and the five-year base rate is slightly better than that of the original Cornerstone Value. Additionally, we see worst-case scenario returns similar to those for Cornerstone Value. Tables 19-6 and 19-7 cover base rates and worst-case scenarios.

T A B L E 19-6

Base Rates for Market Lenders, Shareholder Yield, and Market Leaders, 1952–2003

Item	Market Leaders, Shareholder Yield Beat Market Leaders	Percent
Single-Year Return	34 out of 51	67%
Rolling Five-Year Compound Return	40 out of 37	85%
Rolling 10-Year Compound Return	38 out of 42	90%

T A B L E 19-7

Worst-Case Scenarios: All 10 Percent or Greater Declines for New Cornerstone Value (Market Leaders, High Shareholder Yield), December 31, 1962–December 31, 2003

Peak Date	Peak Index Value	Trough Date	Trough Index Value	Recovery Date	Decline (%)	Decline Duration	Recovery Duration
Jan-66	1.6	Sep-66	1.33	Mar-67	−16.9	8	6
Apr-69	2.32	Jun-70	1.72	Jan-71	−25.71	14	7
Nov-72	2.98	Sep-74	2.21	Mar-75	−25.64	22	6
Sep-78	6.28	Oct-78	5.63	Mar-79	−10.38	1	5
Jan-80	7.73	Mar-80	6.85	May-80	−11.42	2	2
Jun-81	10.48	Sep-81	9.34	Aug-82	−10.93	3	11
Aug-87	48.6	Nov-87	34.48	Oct-88	−29.05	3	11
Aug-89	65.13	Oct-90	49.48	Mar-91	−24.03	14	5
Apr-98	303.28	Aug-98	255.29	Dec-98	−15.82	4	4
Jun-99	377.92	Feb-00	323.12	Aug-00	−14.5	8	6
Jul-01	470.03	Oct-01	420.79	Dec-01	−10.48	3	2
May-02	524.08	Mar-03	408.14	Jul-03	−22.12	10	4
Average					−18.08	7.67	5.75

DIGGING DEEPER

Using the monthly data and generating a series of 481 observations of rolling 12-month rates of return, we see that the worst the strategy ever underperformed its benchmark was for the 12 months ending November 1980, when the strategy returned 21.23 percent and the Market Leaders universe gained 34.54 percent. Much more important, in the 111 periods between 1963 and 2003, when the S&P 500 had negative 12-month returns, the strategy outperformed its benchmark by an average of 7.42 percent. Moreover, when the S&P 500 was declining, the strategy underperformed its benchmark just 15 percent of the time. In other words, this is the perfect strategy for investors nervous about how a strategy does in declining markets. It offers excellent overall returns while giving investors a far gentler ride when markets get rocky.

REAL-TIME PERFORMANCE

After publishing this research in 1996, I began using the strategies featured in the book to manage actual portfolios. I have run a mutual fund for the Royal Bank of Canada since 1997, called RBC O'Shaughnessy US Value, first using the original Cornerstone Value formula and then the enhanced shareholder yield version. As of September 1, 2004, it was awarded 5 stars by Morningstar and ranked in the first quartile of performance (as ranked by Morningstar) over the previous one-, three-, and five-year periods. You can examine all returns for the fund at Morningstar's Canadian site located at www.morningstar.ca or at RBC Funds located at www.rbcfunds.com.

INVESTING IN A MORE CONCENTRATED PORTFOLIO

Now let's look at the 10-stock version of the enhanced Cornerstone Value strategy. Much like the concentrated small-stock portfolios, using a more concentrated version of Market Leaders with high shareholder yield leads to substantially higher returns, but it also leads to higher levels of risk. To compare apples to apples, we must review the monthly data between 1963 and 2003. A $10,000 investment in the Market Leaders universe would grow to $1,507,652 at the end of 2003, a compound average annual return of 13.01 percent. The same amount invested in the 50-stock Market Leaders, high shareholder yield portfolio would grow to $6,446,281, a compound average annual return of 17.09 percent. Risk levels were similar for each, with the 50-stock Market Leaders, high shareholder yield portfolio sporting a downside risk of 8.57 percent, versus 9.1 percent for the Market Leaders universe.

Now, look at the performance of the 10-stock version. Investing $10,000 in those 10 stocks from Market Leaders having the highest shareholder yield on December 31, 1962 would grow to $10,040,890 by the end of 2003, a compound average annual return of 18.36 percent. But—no surprise here—your risk would go up as well. The standard deviation of return jumps to 21.2 percent, downside risk climbs to 10.24 percent, and the maximum decline grows to a loss of 38.27 percent, similar to what we saw for the Market Leaders universe. Because the risks are higher, the Sharpe ratio declines to 71, two points lower than that of the 50-stock portfolio.

Yet again, the 25-stock portfolio comes out on top. Here, a $10,000 investment grows to $9,553,947, a compound average annual return of 18.22 percent. Although the standard deviation of return is higher, the downside risk still comes in at 9.06, less than the Market Leaders universe. The good risk versus reward characteristics pushes the Sharpe ratio up to 76, among the highest for all our strategies. Long-term base rates actually improve with both the 10-stock and 25-stock versions of the strategy, beating Market Leaders in all rolling 10-year periods between 1963 and 2003.

But there is a price that investors in more concentrated portfolios have to pay—these strategies deviate from their benchmarks more than the 50-stock versions do. The 10-stock portfolio had one 12-month period when it earned 34.49 percent less than the Market Leaders universe, whereas the 25-stock version had one 12-month period when it earned 21.26 percent less. As I've stressed earlier, before using one of these concentrated portfolios, envision how you would respond to those sorts of declines in real time. Table 19-8 summarizes the results.

T A B L E 19-8

Summary Return and Risk Results for Monthly Data, Market Leaders, Market Leaders, Shareholder Yield by Various Levels of Portfolio Concentration, December 31, 1962–December 31, 2003

	Market Leaders	Market Leaders, Shareholder Yield 50-Stock	Market Leaders, Shareholder Yield 25-Stock	Market Leaders, Shareholder Yield 10-Stock
Arithmetic Average	14.27%	18.44%	19.73%	20.22%
Geometric Average	13.01%	17.09%	18.22%	18.36%
Median Return	17.34%	18.36%	21.60%	21.93%
Standard Deviation of Return	16.98%	17.96%	19.09%	21.20%
Downside Risk—lower is better	9.10%	8.57%	9.06%	10.24%
Correlation with S&P 500	0.97	0.88	0.86	0.8
T-Statistic	5.75	7.13	7.22	6.68
Sharpe Ratio	0.51	0.73	0.76	0.71
Number of Positive Periods	304	315	315	316
Number of Negative Periods	188	177	177	176
Maximum Peak-to-Trough Decline (using monthly data series)	−38.98%	−29.05%	−32.22%	−38%
Beta	0.96	0.90	0.92	0.95
$10,000 becomes:	$1,507,652.00	$6,446,281.00	$9,553,947.00	$10,040,890.00
Minimum Annual Return (All Rolling 12-Month Periods)	−36.43%	−22.39%	−22.69%	−27.94%

(continued on next page)

T A B L E 19-8

Summary Return and Risk Results for Monthly Data, Market Leaders, Market Leaders, Shareholder Yield by Various Levels of Portfolio Concentration, December 31, 1962–December 31, 2003 *(Continued)*

	Market Leaders	Market Leaders, Shareholder Yield 50-Stock	Market Leaders, Shareholder Yield 25-Stock	Market Leaders, Shareholder Yield 10-Stock
Maximum Annual Return (All Rolling 12-Month Periods)	64.42%	65.29%	66.29%	83.79%
Minimum *Expected* Return*	−19.69%	−17.48%	−18.45%	−22.18%
Maximum *Expected* Return**	48.23%	54.36%	57.91%	62.62%

*Minimum Expected Return is Arithmetic Return minus 2 times the standard deviation.
**Maximum Expected Return is Arithmetic Return plus 2 times the standard deviation.

IMPLICATIONS

Many investors want portfolios that do much better than the S&P 500 and the Dow Jones Industrial Average, but cannot stomach doing *much worse* over any 12-month period. They become especially anxious when markets are falling, and ample evidence supports the fact that they will not stick with their strategy if their portfolios are well behind their benchmarks. The smaller-cap value stocks found in the All Stocks universe all offered outstanding total returns over the full 52 years of our study, but they did so with much greater volatility and deviations from their benchmark. They are only appropriate for investors who understand that greater reward comes with greater risk.

Unfortunately, most investors can't tolerate the high risk or large deviations from a benchmark. For these investors, I highly recommend using the larger-cap Market Leaders stocks with the highest shareholder yield.

This strategy is more appealing for risk-averse investors for a number of reasons. The strategy sticks to large, well-known companies, yet does four times as well as the Market Leaders universe while taking *less* risk. It has the highest risk-adjusted return of all pure value strategies examined. It has more positive years than Market Leaders, a lower downside risk, and a maximum decline much lower than the Market Leaders universe. The strategy's actual minimum and maximum annual returns are outstanding, with the worst year showing a loss of 12.90 percent and the best a gain of 54.94 percent. And, while we've seen that more concentrated versions of the strategy offer better total returns, you should only use them if you can stomach a much greater variation from the underlying benchmark.

Finally, the 50-stock strategy's high returns, low risk, and persistence of returns make it a natural replacement for an S&P 500 index fund or other large-cap index. Tables 19-9 through 19-12 summarize the performance of this strategy.

T A B L E 19-9

Base Rates for All Stocks and 50-Stock Multifactor Value Model from All Stocks, 1952–2003

Item	Multifactor Value Model Beat All Stocks	Percent
Single-Year Return	35 out of 51	69%
Rolling Five-Year Compound Return	38 out of 37	81%
Rolling 10-Year Compound Return	39 out of 42	93%

T A B L E 19-10

Worst-Case Scenarios: All 10 Percent or Greater Declines for 50 Stocks from All Stocks Meeting Multifactor Criteria, December 31, 1962–December 31, 2003

Peak Date	Peak Index Value	Trough Date	Trough Index Value	Recovery Date	Decline (%)	Decline Duration	Recovery Duration
Jan-66	2.1	Sep-66	1.65	Apr-67	−21.28	8	7
Jan-69	3.55	Jun-70	2.04	Jan-72	−42.59	17	19
Nov-72	3.67	Dec-74	2.54	Apr-75	−30.85	25	4
Jun-75	4.29	Sep-75	3.83	Jan-76	−10.65	3	4
Sep-78	8.44	Oct-78	7.1	Mar-79	−15.86	1	5
Aug-79	10.76	Mar-80	9.12	Jul-80	−15.26	7	4
Aug-87	49.31	Nov-87	37.37	Jul-88	−24.21	3	8
Aug-89	62.76	Oct-90	41.35	Aug-91	−34.11	14	10
Apr-98	235.66	Aug-98	195.29	Apr-99	−17.13	4	8
Jun-01	507	Sep-01	403.03	Mar-02	−20.51	3	6
Apr-02	512.43	Sep-02	367.95	May-03	−28.2	5	8
Average					−23.7	8.18	7.55

T A B L E 19-11

Best and Worst Average Annual Compound Returns over Period for Monthly Data 1963–2003

For Any	1-Year Period	3-Year Period	5-Year Period	10-Year Period
Large Stocks Minimum Compound Return	−42.04%	−13.79%	−6.05%	−0.20%
Large Stocks Maximum Compound Return	68.49%	32.78%	28.65%	19.57%
Original CSV Minimum Compound Return	−24.58%	−1.99%	2.54%	4.61%
Original CSV Maximum Compound Return	69.89%	36.57%	33.62%	23.03%
Improved CSV (Mkt Ldrs, High Shareholder Yield) Minimum Compound Return	−22.39%	−4.04%	1.58%	4.55%

(continued on next page)

T A B L E 19-11

Best and Worst Average Annual Compound Returns over Period for Monthly Data 1963–2003 *(Continued)*

For Any	1-Year Period	3-Year Period	5-Year Period	10-Year Period
Improved CSV (Mkt Ldrs, High Shareholder Yield) Maximum Compound Return	65.29%	40.64%	37.39%	24.50%

T A B L E 19-12

Terminal Value of $10,000 Invested for Best and Worst Average Annual Compound Returns over Period for Monthly Data 1963–2003

For Any	1-Year Period	3-Year Period	5-Year Period	10-Year Period
Large Stocks Minimum $10,000 Value	$5,796.00	$6,407.27	$7,319.54	$9,801.79
Large Stocks Maximum $10,000 Value	$16,849.00	$23,409.82	$35,241.06	$59,734.10
Original CSV Minimum Compound Return	$7,542.00	$9,414.80	$11,336.18	$15,693.94
Original CSV Maximum Compound Return	$16,989.00	$25,472.17	$42,594.87	$79,452.99
Improved CSV (Mkt Ldrs, High Shareholder Yield) Minimum Compound Return	$7,761.00	$8,836.31	$10,815.36	$15,604.16
Improved CSV (Mkt Ldrs, High Shareholder Yield) Maximum Compound Return	$16,529.00	$27,818.04	$48,952.58	$89,473.31

SEARCHING FOR THE IDEAL GROWTH STRATEGY

Facts do not cease to exist because they are ignored.
—Aldous Huxley

In the first edition of this book, the Cornerstone Growth strategy emerged as the best performing of all the growth strategies I tested. Here, I'll review the performance of the original strategy, look at why it does better than strategies built around traditional growth factors, and then review some improvements made to the strategy over the last several years. I'll also review growth strategies from the other universes we've looked at. You'll see that the same growth factors that work in the All Stocks universe work in the other universes as well. First, I'll review and update the annual performance of the original Cornerstone Growth strategy, then look at the monthly data, because one of the improvements includes shorter-term relative strength.

ORIGINAL CORNERSTONE GROWTH STRATEGY REVISITED

We saw earlier that relative strength alone was the best-performing growth factor and that it could be enhanced by marrying it to other growth factors, such as high earnings growth, high return on equity, and profit margins. Yet, I found that you could do dramatically better by adding a value factor to a growth strategy. By doing this, you focus on cheap stocks on the mend. *Cheap* because the inclusion of a value factor, such as low price-to-sales ratios, ensured that you were not paying the moon for a stock, and *on the mend* because earnings and price appreciation were moving in the right direction.

We found in an earlier chapter that marrying low PSR to relative strength was a winning strategy, but also found that you could improve it further by requiring that earnings per share be higher than in the previous year. The result was the original Cornerstone Growth strategy. Here it is:

- Market capitalization must be greater than a deflated $200 million
- Price-to-sales ratio must be less than 1.5
- Earnings must be higher than in the previous year
- Buy the 50 stocks with the greatest one-year price appreciation

This simple strategy proved to be one of the best I've found, and its great performance has persisted over the last seven years. Table 20-1 shows summary results for the annual data, and Tables 20-2 and 20-3 cover base rates and worst-case scenario drops of more than 10 percent. Examining the data, we see that, much like classic Coke, the original version of Cornerstone Growth continues to do well. A $10,000 investment on December 31, 1951 grew to $53 million at the end of 2003, a compound average annual return of 18.31 percent. Downside risk was a reasonable 8.28 percent, and the maximum decline the strategy ever suffered was a loss of 60.13 percent. That's a bit steeper than All Stocks' maximum decline of 50.12 percent, but is still reasonable given the strategy's vastly better long-term performance. All base rates for the strategy are positive, with the Cornerstone Growth strategy beating All Stocks 73 percent of the time in any one-year period, 89 percent of any five-year periods, and 100 percent of all 10-year periods. What's more, the strategy continued to outperform the All Stocks universe in real time. During the original 1952–1996 period, the strategy compounded at 18.74 percent, versus 13.44 percent for All Stocks, thus creating a delta over All Stocks of 5.3 percent per year. Between 1997 and 2003, the strategy compounded at 15.64 percent, versus 11 percent for All Stocks, for a delta of 4.64 percent per year. Keep in mind how atypical that time period was: It included the huge market bubble of 1997 to 2000 and the ferocious bear market that followed.

T A B L E 20-1

Summary Return and Risk Results for All Stocks and Original Cornerstone Growth Strategy from All Stocks Universe, December 31, 1952–December 31, 2003

	All Stocks	Original Cornerstone Growth
Arithmetic Average	14.79%	21.14%
Geometric Average	13.00%	18.31%

(continued on next page)

T A B L E 20-1

Summary Return and Risk Results for All Stocks and Original Cornerstone Growth Strategy from All Stocks Universe, December 31, 1952–December 31, 2003 *(Continued)*

	All Stocks	Original Cornerstone Growth
Median Return	16.80%	24.30%
Standard Deviation of Return	20.11%	25.59%
Downside risk—lower is better	7.17%	8.28%
Correlation with S&P 500	0.87	0.75
T-Statistic	5.30	5.90
Sharpe Ratio	0.46	0.61
Number of Positive Periods	39	37
Number of Negative Periods	13	14
Maximum Peak-to-trough Decline (using Monthly data series)	−50.12%	−60.13%
Beta	0.99	1.08
$10,000 becomes:	$5,743,706.00	$53,023,961.00
Minimum Annual Return	−27.90%	−29.10%
Maximum Annual Return	55.90%	83.30%
Minimum *Expected* Return*	−25.43%	−30.04%
Maximum *Expected* Return**	55.01%	72.32%

*Minimum Expected Return is Arithmetic Return minus 2 times the standard deviation.
**Maximum Expected Return is Arithmetic Return plus 2 times the standard deviation.

T A B L E 20-2

Base Rates for All Stocks and Original Cornerstone Growth (CSG) All Stocks Universe, 1952–2003

Item	Original CSG Beat "All Stocks"	Percent
Single-Year Return	37 out of 51	73%
Rolling Five-Year Compound Return	42 out of 47	89%
Rolling 10-Year Compound Return	42 out of 42	100%

T A B L E 20-3

Worst-Case Scenarios: All 10 Percent or Greater Declines for Original Cornerstone Growth Strategy, December 31, 1963–December 31, 2003

Peak Date	Peak Index Value	Trough Date	Trough Index Value	Recovery Date	Decline (%)	Decline Duration	Recovery Duration
Apr-65	1.46	Jun-65	1.3	Sep-65	−10.61	2	3
Apr-66	2.05	Oct-66	1.49	Feb-67	−27.51	6	4
Nov-68	4.55	Jun-70	2.4	Jan-72	−47.38	19	19
Apr-72	5.29	Sep-74	2.11	Aug-77	−60.13	29	35
Aug-78	9.25	Oct-78	6.85	Mar-79	−25.9	2	5

(continued on next page)

T A B L E 20-3

Worst-Case Scenarios: All 10 Percent or Greater Declines for Original Cornerstone Growth Strategy, December 31, 1963–December 31, 2003 *(Continued)*

Peak Date	Peak Index Value	Trough Date	Trough Index Value	Recovery Date	Decline (%)	Decline Duration	Recovery Duration
Aug-79	10.5	Oct-79	8.97	Jan-80	−14.49	2	3
Feb-80	11.85	Mar-80	9.01	Jul-80	−23.97	1	4
Nov-80	19.57	Feb-81	17.05	May-81	−12.89	3	3
May-81	19.92	Sep-81	15.06	Oct-82	−24.38	4	13
Jun-83	39.35	May-84	26.18	Nov-85	−33.46	11	18
Jun-86	54.79	Sep-86	46.27	Feb-87	−15.54	3	5
Aug-87	63.08	Nov-87	39.92	Mar-89	−36.72	3	16
Sep-89	75.77	Jan-90	61.68	May-90	−18.59	4	4
May-90	82.95	Oct-90	58.86	Mar-91	−29.04	5	5
Feb-92	120.72	Jun-92	104.6	Oct-92	−13.35	4	4
Jan-94	180.51	Jan-95	151.76	Jul-95	−15.93	12	6
May-96	242.64	Jul-96	204.83	Nov-96	−15.58	2	4
Sep-97	355.4	Jan-98	306.41	Apr-98	−13.78	4	3
Apr-98	363.14	Aug-98	246.32	Nov-99	−32.17	4	15
Aug-00	521.17	Nov-00	449.92	Apr-01	−13.67	3	5
Jul-01	524.33	Sep-01	459.81	Jan-02	−12.3	2	4
Apr-02	618.39	Feb-03	409.9	Aug-03	−33.71	10	6
Average					−24.14	6.14	8.36

Two of my mutual funds replicated these results in real time: the RBC O'Shaughnessy U.S. Growth Fund (which first used this version of the strategy and later an improved version that we discuss later in this chapter) and the O'Shaughnessy Cornerstone Growth Fund, renamed the Hennessy Cornerstone Growth Fund after my firm sold it to Hennessy Advisors in June of 2000. (The fund still uses the Cornerstone Growth strategy to select securities.) You can get information on the RBC O'Shaughnessy U.S. Growth Fund at www.rbcfunds.com or at Morningstar's independent research site found at www.morningstar.ca and on the Hennessy Cornerstone Growth Fund at www.hennessyfunds.com.

TRADITIONAL GROWTH FACTORS WORK, BUT PROVIDE LOWER OVERALL RETURN

Now let's review strategies that just use traditional growth factors. While they do improve upon the performance of a pure relative-strength strategy, they fall short of strategies that combine the best value and growth factors.

First, I'll test a typical group of growth factors coupled with relative strength. We'll call this Growth Model One and require stocks to:

- Come from the All Stocks Universe
- Have five-year earnings-per-share growth rates exceeding the Compustat mean
- Have profit margins exceeding the Compustat mean
- Have earnings higher than the previous year
- We'll then buy the 50 stocks with the best one-year relative strength

I begin the test on December 31, 1954, in order to capture the five-year earnings per share growth rate. Thus, $10,000 invested on that date grows to $33,703,070 by the end of 2003, a compound growth rate of 17.09 percent per year. Although that is less than what we would have earned using the original Cornerstone Growth strategy, it does provide these excellent returns with lower levels of risk. Here, the standard deviation is 21.90 percent, and the downside risk is 6.36 percent, which is actually *below* All Stocks' 7.39 percent. The lower risk accounts for the high Sharpe ratio of 61. The strategy has lower base rates than the original Cornerstone Growth, beating All Stocks 65 percent of the time in all one-year periods, 87 percent of all five-year periods, and 95 percent of all 10-year periods. For the 468 rolling one-year periods we observe in the monthly data, the greatest one-year underperformance it had versus All Stocks was –21.84 percent, whereas the greatest overperformance was 49.83 percent.

Even though it does not do as well as the Cornerstone Growth strategy, this is an excellent pure growth strategy. It can be useful when used in conjunction with a pure value strategy, such as those found in Chapter 16. I'll feature such a mixture in the next chapter, which details the benefits of using value and growth strategies together.

LARGE STOCKS CORNERSTONE GROWTH STRATEGY WORKS WELL, TOO

Investors daunted by the rather large maximum decline and higher risk of the original Cornerstone Growth strategy drawn from All Stocks should consider using the same strategy on the Large Stocks universe. Tables 20-4, 20-5, and 20-6 cover the summary data for the annual data, base rates, and worst-case scenarios for the strategy used on the Large Stocks universe. The strategy turns $10,000 invested on December 31, 1952 into $13,201,788 at the end of 2003, a compound average annual rate of return of 15.13 percent, and it delivers these returns with less risk than the Large Stocks universe. Large Stocks' downside risk is 5.91 percent, whereas for this strategy, it's a lower 5.01 percent. Base rates aren't as good, but are all still positive, with the strategy beating the Large Stocks universe in 95 percent of all rolling 10-year periods.

T A B L E 20-4

Summary Return and Risk Results for Large Stocks and Original Cornerstone Growth Strategy from Large Stocks Universe, December 31, 1952–December 31, 2003

	Large Stocks	Original Cornerstone Growth, Large Stocks Universe
Arithmetic Average	13.07%	16.52%
Geometric Average	11.76%	15.13%
Median Return	16.20%	17.94%
Standard Deviation of Return	17.00%	17.84%
Downside Risk—lower is better	5.91%	5.01%
Correlation with S&P 500	0.94	0.88
T-Statistic	5.49	6.61
Sharpe Ratio	0.45	0.63
Number of Positive Periods	38	40
Number of Negative Periods	13	11
Maximum Peak-to-Trough Decline (using monthly data series)	−46.59%	−51.60%
Beta	0.90	0.88
$10,000 becomes:	$2,903,681.00	$13,201,788.00
Minimum Annual Return	−26.70%	−24.20%
Maximum Annual Return	45.07%	55.50%
Minimum *Expected* Return*	−20.93%	−19.16%
Maximum *Expected* Return**	47.07%	52.20%

*Minimum Expected Return is Arithmetic Return minus 2 times the standard deviation.
**Maximum Expected Return is Arithmetic Return plus 2 times the standard deviation.

T A B L E 20-5

Base Rates for Large Stocks and Original Cornerstone Growth (CSG) from Large Stocks Universe, 1952–2003

Item	Large Stocks CSG Beat "Large Stocks"	Percent
Single-Year Return	35 out of 51	69%
Rolling Five-Year Compound Return	39 out of 47	83%
Rolling 10-Year Compound Return	40 out of 42	95%

T A B L E 20-6

Worst-Case Scenarios: All 10 Percent or Greater Declines for Original Large Stocks Cornerstone Growth Strategy, December 31, 1963–December 31, 2003

Peak Date	Peak Index Value	Trough Date	Trough Index Value	Recovery Date	Decline (%)	Decline Duration	Recovery Duration
Jan-66	1.41	Aug-66	1.21	Jan-67	−13.76	7	5
Sep-67	1.71	Feb-68	1.53	Apr-68	−10.52	5	2
Nov-68	1.99	Jun-70	1.42	Feb-71	−28.64	19	8
Dec-72	2.64	Sep-74	1.28	Jul-78	−51.6	21	46
Aug-78	2.89	Oct-78	2.51	Jul-79	−13.36	2	9
Feb-80	3.63	Mar-80	3.19	Jun-80	−11.98	1	3
Nov-80	5.47	Sep-81	4.36	Oct-82	−20.21	10	13
Jun-83	7.99	May-84	6.78	Sep-84	−15.25	11	4
Jun-86	16.59	Sep-86	14.36	Feb-87	−13.43	3	5
Aug-87	18.35	Nov-87	13.68	Apr-89	−25.45	3	17
Jun-90	23.1	Oct-90	18.07	Feb-91	−21.79	4	4
Mar-98	86.12	Aug-98	70.24	Dec-98	−18.43	5	4
Apr-99	100.67	Feb-00	76.02	Dec-00	−24.49	10	10
Jul-01	115.41	Sep-01	98.26	Dec-01	−14.86	2	3
Apr-02	125.52	Sep-02	97.11	Aug-03	−22.63	5	11
Average					−20.43	7.2	9.6

IMPROVING THE ORIGINAL STRATEGY

As we began using the Cornerstone Growth strategy in real time to manage the O'Shaughnessy Cornerstone Growth Fund and separate accounts for high net-worth individuals, we saw that one of the problems that presented itself was not evident when you looked only at annual data. Namely, stocks can have excellent one-year price appreciation, yet perform horribly over the shorter-term. In many instances, the annual price appreciation was extraordinarily high—putting the stock on our 50-stock list—yet in the shorter-term, the stock might have *declined* by 30 or 40 percent. This seemed inconsistent with the strategy of looking for cheap stocks on the mend, so we added shorter-term price momentum screens as well. The new version of the Cornerstone Growth strategy includes the requirement that three- and six-month price appreciation also exceed the database average.

The new Cornerstone Growth strategy looks like this:

- Market capitalization must be greater than a deflated $200 million
- Price-to-sales ratio must be below 1.5 at time of purchase
- Earnings must be higher than in the previous year
- Three-month price appreciation must exceed the database average

- Six-month price appreciation must exceed the database average
- Buy the 50 stocks with the highest one-year price appreciation

Remember that, because we are using three- and six-month price movements, we will use the monthly database. Table 20-7 shows the summary results for this strategy versus the original strategy. As you can see, you significantly improve the strategy's returns by keeping shorter-term relative strength positive. A $10,000 investment in the original Cornerstone Growth strategy on December 31, 1963 grew to a little under $7 million at the end of 2003, a compound average annual return of 17.77 percent. The strategy's Sharpe ratio was 55, and it had a downside risk of 14.8 percent. The worst-case scenario saw the strategy losing 60 percent from peak to trough. Simply by adding the requirement that short-term relative strength also be positive, we see the $10,000 grow to $18.9 million at the end of 2003, a compound average annual return of 20.75 percent. The Sharpe ratio improves to 67, and downside risk and maximum decline actually go *down* to 14.1 percent and a loss of 55 percent respectively. That's a great improvement from the simple addition of short-term relative strength to the strategy.

T A B L E 20-7

Summary Return and Risk Results for Monthly Data, All Stocks, Original Cornerstone Growth (CSG), and Improved Version, December 31, 1963–December 31, 2003

	All Stocks	Original CSG	Improved CSG
Arithmetic Average	13.82%	21.16%	23.97%
Geometric Average	12.02%	17.77%	20.75%
Median Return	17.96%	19.28%	24.61%
Standard Deviation of Return	20.23%	28.74%	28.31%
Downside Risk—lower is better	11.53%	14.80%	14.10%
Correlation with S&P 500	0.89	0.77	0.78
T-Statistic	4.61	5.14	5.97
Sharpe Ratio	0.40	0.55	0.67
Number of Positive Periods	286	277	296
Number of Negative Periods	194	203	184
Maximum Peak-to-Trough Decline (using monthly data series)	−50.12%	−60.13%	−55.25%
Beta	1.05	1.21	1.19
$10,000 becomes:	$936,071.00	$6,950,741.00	$18,860,926.00
Minimum 12-month Return	−41.65%	−49.29%	−47.38%
Maximum 12-month Return	81.51%	133.41%	138.68%
Minimum *Expected* Return*	−26.64%	−36.32%	−32.65%
Maximum *Expected* Return**	54.28%	78.64%	80.59%

*Minimum Expected Return is Arithmetic Return minus 2 times the standard deviation.
**Maximum Expected Return is Arithmetic Return plus 2 times the standard deviation.

BASE RATES ALSO IMPROVE

As Table 20-8 illustrates, the base rates of the new strategy improve as well. Because we are using monthly data, we can create many more observations of all 12-, 60-, and 120-month trailing returns. Here, we see that the strategy beats the All Stocks universe in 78 percent of all rolling 12-month periods, 98 percent of all rolling 60-month periods, and 100 percent of all rolling 120-month periods. All in all, a dramatic improvement.

T A B L E 20-8

Base Rates for All Stocks and Original Cornerstone Growth, Improved Cornerstone Growth (CSD), and All Stocks Universe, Monthly Data 1963–2003

Item	Original CSG Beat "All Stocks"	Percent
Rolling 12-Month Returns	310 out of 469	66%
Rolling 5-Year Compound Return	358 out of 421	85%
Rolling 10-Year Compound Return	361 out of 361	100%
Item	Improved CSG Beat "All Stocks"	Percent
Rolling 12-Month Returns	364 out of 469	78%
Rolling 5-Year Compound Return	414 out of 421	98%
Rolling 10-Year Compound Return	361 out of 361	100%

Table 20-9 covers the worst-case scenarios for the improved Cornerstone Growth strategy. As we saw with the original version, investors using this method of stock selection have to prepare themselves for more volatility than they would get with an investment in All Stocks. This strategy declined by more than 20 percent from peak to trough 12 times over the last 40 years, compared to six times for All Stocks. Short, sharp corrections happen often within this strategy, and not only when the general stock market is declining. For example, the summer of 1998 saw the strategy decline by more than 30 percent, at a time when the S&P 500 was down half as much. Because the strategy tends toward smaller-cap stocks, you'll want to remember that you will face *both* strategy risk and the more general risk from investing in smaller-cap stocks. Always review a strategy's downside before proceeding—it makes no sense for investors to put a lot of money into a strategy that they will ultimately abandon when the going gets rough.

IMPLICATIONS

If you can tolerate higher risk, you can handily beat the market using the improved Cornerstone Growth strategy. It's worth noting that our best

T A B L E 20-9

Worst-Case Scenarios: All 10 Percent or Greater Declines for Improved Cornerstone Growth Strategy, December 31, 1963–December 31, 2003

Peak Date	Peak Index Value	Trough Date	Trough Index Value	Recovery Date	Decline (%)	Decline Duration	Recovery Duration
Apr-65	1.5	Jun-65	1.35	Sep-65	−10.05	2	3
Apr-66	2.04	Oct-66	1.48	Feb-67	−27.44	6	4
Nov-68	4.69	Jun-70	2.73	Dec-71	−41.88	19	18
May-72	5.99	Sep-74	2.68	Jun-77	−55.25	28	33
Aug-78	11.72	Oct-78	8.69	Aug-79	−25.82	2	10
Feb-80	16.01	Mar-80	12.39	Jul-80	−22.58	1	4
Nov-80	26.73	Feb-81	23.63	Apr-81	−11.6	3	2
May-81	27.59	Sep-81	20.96	Sep-82	−24.01	4	12
Jun-83	59.04	May-84	39.63	Jun-85	−32.88	11	13
Jun-86	89.1	Sep-86	73.84	Feb-87	−17.13	3	5
Aug-87	107.62	Nov-87	70.93	Mar-89	−34.09	3	16
Sep-89	145.98	Jan-90	121.81	May-90	−16.56	4	4
May-90	154.68	Oct-90	116.75	Feb-91	−24.52	5	4
Feb-92	239.96	Jun-92	208.69	Oct-92	−13.03	4	4
Feb-94	385.35	Jun-94	331.82	Jul-95	−13.89	4	13
May-96	537.7	Jul-96	458.16	Nov-96	−14.79	2	4
Sep-97	842.86	Jan-98	739.02	Mar-98	−12.32	4	2
Jun-98	936.43	Aug-98	645.38	Jun-99	−31.08	2	10
Mar-00	1324.82	May-00	1189.47	Aug-00	−10.22	2	3
Aug-00	1439.74	Jan-01	1064.21	Apr-02	−26.08	5	15
Apr-02	1502.33	Feb-03	1137.3	Jun-03	−24.3	10	4
Average					−23.31	5.90	8.71

growth strategy includes a low price-to-sales requirement, traditionally a value factor. The best time to buy growth stocks is when they are cheap, not when the investment herd is clamoring to buy. This strategy will never buy a Netscape, Cybercash, or Polaroid at 165 times earnings. That's why it works so well. It forces you to buy stocks just when the market realizes the companies have been overlooked. That's the beauty of using relative strength as your final factor. It gets you to buy just as the market is embracing the stocks, while the price-to-sales constraint assures they are still reasonably priced. Indeed, the evidence in this book shows that *all* the most successful strategies include at least one value factor, thus keeping investors from paying too much for a stock. Tables 20-10 through 20-14 summarize the performance of this strategy.

T A B L E 20-10

Summary Return and Risk Results for All Stocks and Growth Model One from All Stocks Universe, December 31, 1954–December 31, 2003

	All Stocks	Growth Model One
Arithmetic Average	14.52%	19.16%
Geometric Average	12.71%	17.09%
Median Return	17.00%	22.20%
Standard Deviation of Return	20.10%	21.90%
Downside Risk—lower is better	7.39%	6.36%
Correlation with S&P 500	0.86	0.82
T-Statistic	5.06	6.12
Sharpe Ratio	0.44	0.61
Number of Positive Periods	36	35
Number of Negative Periods	13	14
Maximum Peak-to-Trough Decline (using monthly data series)	−50.12%	−50.93%
Beta	1.02	1.05
$10,000 becomes:	$3,519,152.00	$33,703,070.00
Minimum Annual Return	−27.90%	−30.80%
Maximum Annual Return	55.90%	74.40%
Minimum *Expected* Return*	−25.68%	−24.64%
Maximum *Expected* Return**	54.72%	62.96%

*Minimum Expected Return is Arithmetic Return minus 2 times the standard deviation.
**Maximum Expected Return is Arithmetic Return plus 2 times the standard deviation.

T A B L E 20-11

Base Rates for All Stocks and Growth Model One from All Stocks Universe, Monthly Data 1954–2003

Item	Growth Model One Beat "All Stocks"	Percent
Single-Year Return	32 out of 49	65%
Rolling Five-Year Compound Return	39 out of 45	87%
Rolling 10-Year Compound Return	38 out of 40	95%

T A B L E 20-12

Worst-Case Scenarios: All 10 Percent or Greater Declines for Growth Model One, December 31, 1963–December 31, 2003

Peak Date	Peak Index Value	Trough Date	Trough Index Value	Recovery Date	Decline (%)	Decline Duration	Recovery Duration
Apr-66	1.43	Sep-66	1.17	Jan-67	−18.52	5	4
Dec-67	1.89	Feb-68	1.7	Apr-68	−10	2	2

(continued on next page)

T A B L E 20-12

Worst-Case Scenarios: All 10 Percent or Greater Declines for Growth Model One, December 31, 1963–December 31, 2003 *(Continued)*

Peak Date	Peak Index Value	Trough Date	Trough Index Value	Recovery Date	Decline (%)	Decline Duration	Recovery Duration
Nov-68	2.48	Jun-70	1.73	Mar-71	−30.23	19	9
Dec-72	3.94	Sep-74	1.94	Nov-77	−50.93	21	38
Aug-78	5.42	Oct-78	4.41	Mar-79	−18.7	2	5
Feb-80	7.63	Mar-80	6.49	May-80	−14.88	1	2
Nov-80	12.67	Feb-81	11.33	Apr-81	−10.55	3	2
May-81	13.54	Sep-81	10.24	Oct-82	−24.33	4	13
Jun-83	21.68	May-84	16.86	Feb-85	−22.24	11	9
Jun-86	40.36	Sep-86	34.15	Jan-87	−15.38	3	4
Aug-87	52.48	Nov-87	35.55	May-89	−32.25	3	18
Jun-90	60.09	Oct-90	47.6	Feb-91	−20.79	4	4
Jan-94	103.99	Jun-94	91.46	Mar-95	−12.05	5	9
Jun-98	264.08	Aug-98	213.23	Nov-98	−19.25	2	3
Aug-00	475.87	Mar-01	341.37	Oct-03	−28.26	7	31
Average					−21.89	6.13	10.2

T A B L E 20-13

Best and Worst Average Annual Compound Returns over Period for Monthly Data 1963–2003

For Any	1-Year Period	3-Year Period	5-Year Period	10-Year Period
Original CSG Minimum Compound Return	−49.29%	−19.63%	−10.14%	5.13%
Original CSG Maximum Compound Return	133.41%	51.88%	42.78%	30.62%
Improved CSG Minimum Compound Return	−47.38%	−16.40%	−6.45%	7.33%
Improved CSG Maximum Compound Return	138.68%	55.82%	44.46%	33.31%

T A B L E 20-14

Terminal Value of $10,000 Invested for Best and Worst Average Annual Compound Returns over Period for Monthly Data 1963–2003

For Any	1-Year Period	3-Year Period	5-Year Period	10-Year Period
Original CSG Minimum Compound Return	$5,071.00	$5,191.37	$5,859.12	$16,491.75
Original CSG Maximum Compound Return	$23,341.00	$35,034.97	$59,338.54	$144,576.20
Improved CSG Minimum Compound Return	$5,262.00	$5,842.77	$7,165.05	$20,286.69
Improved CSG Maximum Compound Return	$23,868.00	$37,832.90	$62,912.66	$177,266.75

CASE STUDY: USING MORE CONCENTRATED VERSIONS OF THE GROWTH STRATEGY

As we saw with small stocks in Chapter 18, using a more concentrated version of the improved version of Cornerstone Growth might make sense for investors with smaller portfolios. But, just as we found with the micro-cap and small-cap versions of the strategy, the price you pay is an increase in overall risk. You don't want to get *too* concentrated. Using 10 stocks with this strategy actually does about the same as the 25-stock version, but does so with higher risk. If you're considering a more concentrated portfolio, the smallest I would recommend is 25 stocks.

With 25 stocks, we see an improvement in the overall compound average annual return and, even though overall risk goes up, the increase is not drastic. A $10,000 investment in the 25-stock improved Cornerstone Growth strategy grew to $21 million at the end of 2003, a compound average annual return of 21.08 percent. The standard deviation increased to 32.55, and the downside risk increased to 15.7 percent. The maximum decline also increased to a total loss of 59.33 percent. Thus, you can slightly improve results using this more concentrated version of the strategy.

ADDITIONAL FACTOR HELPS CONCENTRATED STRATEGY

You can mitigate risk by adding stocks with excellent profit margins to the concentrated Cornerstone Growth strategy. A Cornerstone Growth strategy tailor-made for a more concentrated portfolio looks like this:

- Market capitalization exceeds a deflated $185 million
- Price-to-sales ratio is less than 1.5 at time of purchase
- Earnings higher than in previous year
- Three-month price appreciation greater than average
- Six-month price appreciation greater than average
- *Allow only the top 100 stocks when ranked by profit margin*
- Buy the 25 stocks with the highest one-year price appreciation

When the additional profit margin criterion is added, $10,000 grows to $17 million, a compound average annual return of 20.41 percent. But it's on the risk side where this concentrated strategy shines. Standard deviation declines to 24.94 percent, downside risk declines to 12.11 percent, and the worst maximum decline is a loss of 48.46 percent. Thus, you get virtually the same returns for much less risk. If you really want to use a more concentrated version of the strategy, I recommend this one.

21 CHAPTER

UNITING STRATEGIES FOR THE BEST RISK-ADJUSTED PERFORMANCE

What we learn from history is that we do not learn from history.
—Benjamin Disraeli

Thus far, we've only looked at the results of one style or a single strategy. Yet the most effective way to diversify your portfolio and enhance risk-adjusted returns is to unite growth and value strategies. Joining growth with value substantially reduces the volatility of growth strategies while increasing the capital appreciation potential of the less volatile value strategies. It also ensures a diversified portfolio, giving you the chance to perform well regardless of what style is in favor on Wall Street.

Let's look at the returns of a portfolio that unites our improved Cornerstone Growth and Cornerstone Value (Market Leaders with high shareholder yield) strategies. We'll use the monthly data, start on December 31, 1963, and split a $10,000 investment between the improved Cornerstone Growth and Value strategies, investing $5,000 in each. We'll rebalance the portfolio annually so it always reflects a fifty-fifty split between growth and value. Although I recommend that investors nearing retirement should allocate less money to the growth strategy and younger investors should allocate more, the fifty-fifty mix is a good example to study. This gives us a portfolio of 100 stocks, half featuring smaller-cap stocks from All Stocks with low price-to-sales and high price momentum, and half coming from the large-cap Market Leaders universe. We'll also look at using the 25-stock versions of each strategy for a more concentrated 50-stock portfolio. In each instance, we will compare the portfolios to a benchmark that is 50 percent invested in the All Stocks universe and 50 percent invested in the Market Leaders universe. This customized benchmark will also be annually recalculated to reflect a fifty-fifty asset allocation. This allows us to do apples to apples comparisons of the portfolios with the benchmarks from which they are drawn.

THE RESULTS

With both the 100-stock and 50-stock versions of the strategy, we see performance that is dramatically better than the benchmark. A $10,000 investment in the 50 percent All Stocks and 50 percent Market Leaders benchmark grew to $1,097,513 over the 40 years ending December 31, 2003. That's a compound average annual return of 12.46 percent per year. That return compares quite favorably to the S&P 500, where the same $10,000 grew to $564,584, a compound average annual return of 10.61 percent. The custom benchmark nevertheless had a high correlation of .94 with the S&P 500, as well as similar maximum declines and downside risks. The maximum declines of the benchmark and the S&P 500 were virtually identical, with the benchmark declining 44.51 percent and the S&P 500 declining 44.73 percent.

With the 100-stock strategy that invests in the improved Cornerstone Growth and Value strategies, $10,000 invested on December 31, 1963 grows to $11,275,830 at the end of 2003, a compound average annual return of 19.21 percent. Yet even with this significant performance increase, the strategy's standard deviation is 21.46 percent, pushing the Sharpe ratio up to 74. The downside risk for the 100-stock strategy is 10.74 percent— barely more than that of the benchmark—and the maximum decline of 38.82 is several points *below* the maximum decline for the benchmark. The strategy has more positive periods than the benchmark, with 311 positive observations versus 169 negative. Better yet, the worst the 100-stock strategy ever performed against the benchmark for all rolling 12-month periods was -6.45 percent, whereas in its best 12-month period, it was 27.94 percent ahead of the benchmark.

The base rates for the 100-stock combined portfolio are among the highest we've seen, with the portfolio beating the benchmark 91 percent of all rolling 12-month periods and 100 percent of all five- and 10-year rolling periods. This combined strategy is truly a vast improvement over a simple combination of the All Stocks and Market Leaders universes.

The united 100-stock strategy does so well because, if one strategy is coasting, the other is often soaring. Consider 1967, a frothy, speculative year. Had you invested only in the new Cornerstone Value strategy, you'd have gained 26.29 percent. That beat the Market Leaders return of 24.70 percent, but didn't do nearly as well as All Stocks, which gained 39.16 percent for the year. Yet, by adding the 50 stocks from the improved Cornerstone Growth Strategy, which soared 78.52 percent that year, you were able to bring the combined portfolio's performance up to 52.40 percent, which beat *all* the other benchmarks. That's with *half* your portfolio safely invested in large, conservative market-leading companies paying high dividends.

Conversely, when growth stocks are getting clobbered, the conservative, high-yielding stocks from Cornerstone Value buffer the portfolio's performance. The improved Cornerstone Growth suffered during the bear market of 1973–1975, but the new Cornerstone Value fared much better. Having an investment in both strategies allowed you to do better than both the Large and All Stocks universes during the two-year debacle.

More recently, the combined strategies allowed you to participate in the market during the bubble years, but, far more important, protected you during the bear market years of 2000 through 2002. Had you invested $10,000 in the combined 100-stock portfolio on December 31, 1996, your portfolio would have grown to $21,007 by the end of March 2000, a compound average annual return of 25.66 percent. Over those same bubble years, $10,000 invested in the S&P 500 would have gained 26.07 percent per year, turning the $10,000 into $21,233. Thus, for even the most extreme years of the bubble, you would have kept pace with the sizzling S&P 500.

Far more important is how much of your investment you would have held in the ensuing bear market. If you had the misfortune of putting $10,000 in the S&P 500 on March 31, 2000—the end of the bubble—your investment would have declined to $6,696 at the end of 2002, a compound average annual return of -13.2 percent per year. Yet, the same investment in the 100-stock combined strategy actually grew 4.23 percent over that time, turning $10,000 into $11,246. Over the entire period between December 31, 1996 and December 31, 2002, an investment in the S&P 500 would have turned $10,000 into $12,950, a gain of 4.40 percent per year, whereas an investment in the 100-stock combined portfolio would have more than doubled to $21,906, a gain of 13.96 per year. Even in one of the most volatile markets of the last 40 years, the strategy continued to provide good, steady returns.

50-STOCK VERSION WORKS WELL, TOO

For investors preferring a more concentrated portfolio, a combined strategy investing in the 25 stocks from the improved Cornerstone Growth strategy and 25 stocks from the new Cornerstone Value strategy works even better on an absolute return basis, albeit with higher risk and lower base rates than the 100-stock version. As Table 21-1 shows, $10,000 invested in the 50-stock combined strategy grows to $15.5 million by the end of 2003, a compound average annual return of 20.17 percent. The standard deviation increases to 23.38 percent, and downside risk increases to 11.46 percent, whereas the maximum decline increases only slightly, to a loss of 40.52 percent. Base rates, although still strong, decline to 83 percent of any 12-month rolling periods, 99 percent of any five-year rolling periods, and 100 percent of all rolling 10-year periods. Nevertheless, for smaller investors desiring fewer stocks to look after, this strategy remains a strong contender versus any of the single stock strategies we have examined.

T A B L E 21-1

Summary Return and Risk Results for Monthly Data, Benchmarks, and Combined Strategies, December 31, 1963–December 31, 2003

	50 Percent Market Leaders/ 50 Percent All Stocks	50 Percent Improved CSG/50 Percent ML, High Shareholder Yield	50 Percent Improved 25-Stock CSG/50 Percent ML, 25-Stock High Shareholder Yield
Arithmetic Average	13.93%	21.12%	22.40%
Geometric Average	12.46%	19.21%	20.17%
Median Return	18.24%	23.71%	25.02%
Standard Deviation of Return	18.28%	21.46%	23.38%
Downside Risk—lower is better	10.18%	10.74%	11.46%
Correlation with S&P 500	0.94	0.88	0.85
T-Statistic	5.15	6.83	6.69
Sharpe Ratio	0.45	0.74	0.74
Number of Positive Periods	293	311	295
Number of Negative Periods	187	169	185
Maximum Peak-to-Trough Decline (using monthly data series)	−44.51%	−38.82%	−40.52%
Beta	1.00	1.05	1.08
$10,000 becomes:	$1,097,513.00	$11,275,830.00	$15,542,562.00
Minimum 12-Month Return	−38.92%	−34.86%	−36.63%
Maximum 12-Month Return	72.81%	100.75%	105.60%
Minimum *Expected* Return*	−22.63%	−21.12%	−24.36%
Maximum *Expected* Return**	50.49%	63.36%	69.16%

*Minimum Expected Return is Arithmetic Return minus 2 times the standard deviation.
**Maximum Expected Return is Arithmetic Return plus 2 times the standard deviation.

A BROADER APPROACH

The combined Cornerstone Growth and Value strategies give you fairly good diversification, with half of your assets committed to market-leading stocks having high shareholder yield and half to smaller-cap stocks with low price-to-sales ratios and strong price momentum. But what about a strategy that explicitly covers small-, mid-, and large-capitalization stocks with both value and growth characteristics? Might we be able to get an even higher level of risk-adjusted return from a more comprehensive portfolio?

I sorted the various strategies by compound average annual return and selected a group of strategies from both value and growth that would cover all the various capitalization categories. I'll use three growth strategies and four value strategies. On the growth side, I'll use the following:

- A micro-cap 25-stock growth strategy that invests in stocks with market capitalizations between $25 million and $250 million
- A mid-cap 25-stock improved Cornerstone Growth Strategy
- A large-cap 25-stock Market Leaders strategy that buys market-leading companies with price-to-sales below average and good 3-, 6-, and 12-month price appreciation

On the value side, I'll use the following four strategies:

- A small-cap 50-stock strategy from Small Stocks with low price-to-cashflow ratios
- A mid-cap 50-stock strategy from All Stocks that buys stocks with price-to-book ratios below 1.5, dividend yield above the average, price-to-earnings (PE) below the average, and then buys the stocks with the lowest price-to-cashflow ratios
- A large-cap 25-stock Market Leaders strategy with high shareholder yield
- A large-cap 10-stock Market Leaders strategy with the lowest price-to-cashflow ratios

I equally weight the value and growth allocations and rebalance the portfolio annually. Thus, on the growth side, each strategy will receive a 16.67 percent allocation and on the value side, each strategy will receive a 12.5 percent allocation. This is truly an all-cap, all-style portfolio, split between value and growth. The benchmark I use for this strategy is comprised of Small Stocks, All Stocks, Large Stocks, and Market Leaders, all with a 25 percent allocation. Table 21-2 shows the results.

T A B L E 21-2

Summary Return and Risk Results for Monthly Data, All-Cap Benchmarks, and Combined Strategies, December 31, 1963–December 31, 2003

	Custom Benchmark	All-Cap, Value Growth Portfolio
Arithmetic Average	13.81%	22.60%
Geometric Average	12.23%	20.34%
Median Return	16.88%	27.33%
Standard Deviation of Return	18.93%	23.50%
Downside Risk—lower is better	10.66%	11.66%
Correlation with S&P 500	0.92	0.86
T-Statistic	4.92	6.72
Sharpe Ratio	0.43	0.74
Number of Positive Periods	290	304
Number of Negative Periods	190	176
Maximum Peak-to-Trough Decline (using monthly data series)	−46.75%	−40.69%
Beta	1.02	1.10
$10,000 becomes:	$1,010,683.00	$16,469,954.00
Minimum 12-Month Return	−40.21%	−36.55%
Maximum 12-Month Return	76.31%	109.54%
Minimum *Expected* Return*	−24.05%	−24.40%
Maximum *Expected* Return**	51.67%	69.60%

*Minimum Expected Return is Arithmetic Return minus 2 times the standard deviation.
**Maximum Expected Return is Arithmetic Return plus 2 times the standard deviation.

Generally speaking, results are very similar to the 50-stock Cornerstone Value and Growth portfolio examined earlier. A $10,000 investment on December 31, 1963 grows to $16,469,954, a compound average annual return of 20.34 percent. Downside risk and maximum decline are very similar to the 50-stock portfolio, and the Sharpe ratio is an identical 74. Base rates, too, are nearly identical to the simpler 50-stock portfolio. Thus, although this strategy offers an extremely broad level of diversification, it hardly seems worth the trouble. The simpler 50-stock portfolio captures very similar returns with far fewer stocks to watch. Tables 21-3 through 21-5 show worst-case scenarios for the portfolio and its benchmark as well as base rates against benchmark.

T A B L E 21-3

Base Rates for All-Cap Value and Growth Portfolio and Custom Benchmark, Monthly Data 1963–2003

Item	All-Cap Value Growth Portfolio Beats Benchmark	Percent
Rolling 12-Month Returns	397 out of 469	85%
Rolling Five-Year Compound Return	421 out of 421	100%
Rolling 10-Year Compound Return	361 out of 361	100%

T A B L E 21-4

Worst-Case Scenarios: All 10 Percent or Greater Declines for Custom Benchmark, December 31, 1963–December 31, 2003

Peak Date	Peak Index Value	Trough Date	Trough Index Value	Recovery Date	Decline (%)	Decline Duration	Recovery Duration
Jan-66	1.47	Sep-66	1.24	Jan-67	−15.54	8	4
Nov-68	2.25	Jun-70	1.39	Jan-72	−38.43	19	19
Nov-72	2.45	Sep-74	1.3	Jun-76	−46.75	22	21
Aug-78	3.45	Oct-78	2.93	Apr-79	−15.06	2	6
Jan-80	4.31	Mar-80	3.65	Jun-80	−15.3	2	3
May-81	5.9	Jul-82	4.9	Oct-82	−16.83	14	3
Jun-83	8.8	Jul-84	7.67	Jan-85	−12.83	13	6
Aug-87	17.56	Nov-87	12.18	Apr-89	−30.65	3	17
Aug-89	20.27	Oct-90	15.73	Mar-91	−22.39	14	5
Apr-98	68.27	Aug-98	51.88	Apr-99	−24.01	4	8
Aug-00	89.2	Nov-00	78.53	Jan-01	−11.96	3	2
Jan-01	89.96	Sep-02	63.96	Oct-03	−28.91	20	13
Average					−23.22	10.33	8.92

T A B L E 21-5

Worst-Case Scenarios: All 10 Percent or Greater Declines for All-Cap Value Growth Strategy, December 31, 1963–December 31, 2003

Peak Date	Peak Index Value	Trough Date	Trough Index Value	Recovery Date	Decline (%)	Decline Duration	Recovery Duration
Apr-66	2.02	Oct-66	1.64	Feb-67	−18.69	6	4
Jan-69	4.28	Jun-70	2.54	Apr-71	−40.69	17	10
Apr-71	4.37	Nov-71	3.85	Jan-72	−11.84	7	2
Apr-72	5.17	Sep-74	3.16	May-75	−38.76	29	8
Aug-78	13.49	Oct-78	10.68	Apr-79	−20.82	2	6
Sep-79	15.93	Oct-79	14.18	Dec-79	−10.93	1	2
Jan-80	17.52	Mar-80	14.48	Jul-80	−17.36	2	4
May-81	26.38	Sep-81	22.15	Sep-82	−16.04	4	12
Jun-83	49.14	Jul-84	42.65	Jan-85	−13.2	13	6

(continued on next page)

TABLE 21-5

Worst-Case Scenarios: All 10 Percent or Greater Declines for All-Cap Value Growth Strategy, December 31, 1963–December 31, 2003 *(Continued)*

Peak Date	Peak Index Value	Trough Date	Trough Index Value	Recovery Date	Decline (%)	Decline Duration	Recovery Duration
Aug-87	104.94	Nov-87	69.36	Feb-89	−33.91	3	15
Sep-89	134.98	Oct-90	96.11	Feb-91	−28.8	13	4
Jan-94	282.75	Jan-95	252.44	May-95	−10.72	12	4
May-96	413.9	Jul-96	368.07	Nov-96	−11.07	2	4
Apr-98	687.67	Aug-98	524.63	Apr-99	−23.71	4	8
Aug-00	877.73	Nov-00	729.69	Apr-01	−16.87	3	5
May-01	930.89	Sep-01	768.63	Dec-01	−17.43	4	3
Apr-02	1091.33	Sep-02	844.21	May-03	−22.64	5	8
Average					−20.79	7.47	6.18

IMPLICATIONS

Uniting growth and value stocks is the best way to diversify your portfolio and improve your risk-adjusted return. The fifty-fifty split is most appropriate for younger investors with average risk tolerance. As retirement approaches, you should reduce the amount of money you allocate to the growth strategy and increase the allocation to the more conservative stocks from Market Leaders with high shareholder yield. Other than for investors very near retirement, all investors benefit from diversifying their investments by style. Even the most aggressive younger investors should have some money in the Cornerstone Value strategy, which bolsters the portfolio during the inevitable periods when larger stocks outperform their smaller brethren from Cornerstone Growth.

The most important thing style diversification does is deliver higher returns with lower risk. Wall Streeters often joke that you should decide based on whether you want to eat well or sleep well. Splitting your portfolio between growth and value strategies lets you do both, because it provides vastly higher absolute returns than the market at similar levels of risk.

And for investors who want to get returns close to the market with much less risk, consider marrying the fifty-fifty growth and value portfolios with either intermediate-term bonds or T-bills. A portfolio that allocates 60 percent to the 100-stock value–growth combination, 40 percent to intermediate-term government bonds, and annually rebalances to maintain that 60/40 split turned $10,000 invested on December 31, 1963 into $2,691,420, a compound return of 15.01 percent a year. That's vastly better than the S&P

500, which turned $10,000 into $565,584, a compound average annual return of 10.61 percent. Yet, because 40 percent of the portfolio is in bonds, the risk fell dramatically—the standard deviation was 13.13 percent, well below the S&P 500's 16.82 percent. Because of the lower risk, the Sharpe ratio improved to 78, versus 37 for the S&P 500. What's more, the downside risk fell to 6.55 percent, and the maximum decline the portfolio ever suffered was a loss of 22 percent. For risk-adverse investors, mixing these style-specific equity models with bonds is a great way to get better-than-index results with dramatically lower volatility and risk. Tables 21-6, 21-7, and 21-8 summarize the results of this strategy.

T A B L E 21-6

Base Rates for Combined Value and Growth 50- and 25-Stock Strategies versus Combined Market Leaders and All Stocks Benchmark, Monthly Data 1963–2003

Item	Combined 100-Stock Portfolio Beats Benchmark	Percent
Rolling 12-Month Returns	427 out of 469	91%
Rolling Five-Year Compound Return	421 out of 421	100%
Rolling 10-Year Compound Return	361 out of 361	100%
Item	Combined 50-Stock Portfolio Beats Benchmark	Percent
Rolling 12-Month Returns	389 out of 469	83%
Rolling Five-Year Compound Return	417 out of 421	99%
Rolling 10-Year Compound Return	361 out of 361	100%

T A B L E 21-7

Worst-Case Scenarios: All 10 Percent or Greater Declines for Combined 100-Stock Strategy, December 31, 1963–December 31, 2003

Peak Date	Peak Index Value	Trough Date	Trough Index Value	Recovery Date	Decline (%)	Decline Duration	Recovery Duration
Apr-66	1.62	Oct-66	1.33	Feb-67	−18.11	6	4
Nov-68	3.07	Jun-70	2.03	Mar-71	−33.76	19	9
May-72	3.78	Sep-74	2.32	Jun-75	−38.82	28	9
Aug-78	8.29	Oct-78	6.7	Apr-79	−19.22	2	6
Feb-80	10.59	Mar-80	8.87	Jun-80	−16.26	1	3
May-81	16.69	Sep-81	13.87	Aug-82	−16.86	4	11
Jun-83	31.05	May-84	26.28	Jan-85	−15.36	11	8
Jun-86	55.08	Sep-86	49	Jan-87	−11.04	3	4
Aug-87	71.97	Nov-87	49.22	Jan-89	−31.6	3	14
Sep-89	96.38	Jan-90	83.82	May-90	−13.03	4	4
May-90	98.33	Oct-90	75.76	Feb-91	−22.95	5	4
Jun-98	537.55	Aug-98	411.08	Apr-99	−23.53	2	8
Jul-01	773.27	Oct-01	688.59	Dec-01	−10.95	3	2

(continued on next page)

T A B L E 21-7

Worst-Case Scenarios: All 10 Percent or Greater Declines for Combined 100-Stock Strategy, December 31, 1963–December 31, 2003 *(Continued)*

Peak Date	Peak Index Value	Trough Date	Trough Index Value	Recovery Date	Decline (%)	Decline Duration	Recovery Duration
Apr-02	902.16	Feb-03	701.81	Jul-03	−22.21	10	5
Average					−20.98	7.21	6.50

T A B L E 21-8

Worst-Case Scenarios: All 10 Percent or Greater Declines for Combined 50-Stock Strategy, December 31, 1963–December 31, 2003

Peak Date	Peak Index Value	Trough Date	Trough Index Value	Recovery Date	Decline (%)	Decline Duration	Recovery Duration
Apr-66	1.8	Oct-66	1.4	Feb-67	−22.43	6	4
Nov-68	3.85	Jun-70	2.43	Aug-71	−36.79	19	14
May-72	4.75	Sep-74	2.83	Jun-75	−40.52	28	9
Aug-78	11.36	Oct-78	9	Apr-79	−20.76	2	6
Feb-80	14.64	Mar-80	12.21	Jun-80	−16.57	1	3
May-81	24.26	Sep-81	20.14	Aug-82	−16.99	4	11
Jun-83	45.42	May-84	38.39	Jan-85	−15.49	11	8
Jun-86	76.96	Sep-86	68.58	Jan-87	−10.89	3	4
Aug-87	100.82	Nov-87	65.41	Mar-89	−35.13	3	16
Sep-89	137.78	Oct-90	103.29	Feb-91	−25.03	13	4
Jan-94	320.46	Jun-94	285.56	Apr-95	−10.89	5	10
Sep-97	757.79	Jan-98	672.07	Mar-98	−11.31	4	2
Jun-98	827.18	Aug-98	632.78	Apr-99	−23.5	2	8
Aug-00	1083.08	Nov-00	929.71	Mar-02	−14.16	3	16
Apr-02	1218.16	Feb-03	960.32	Jun-03	−21.17	10	4
Average					−21.44	7.60	7.93

22 CHAPTER

NEW RESEARCH INITIATIVES

The difficulty lies not so much in developing new ideas as in escaping old ones.

—John M. Keynes

Much has changed since I did the original research for *What Works on Wall Street* in the early 1990s. While I can now use FactSet's Alpha Tester and Backtester, which are automated programs that can quickly test any strategy for any period, in the early 1990s, the Compustat database was accessible only via a DOS program, lacking any automation. Back then, I was forced to do my tests by hand, year-by-year, analyzing each year as I went. It was an extremely laborious task, but exhilarating nevertheless. To have access to a huge database with decades of returns on simple factors was a vast improvement over using either the Dow Jones Industrial Average alone (as I did with my Dogs of the Dow research) or looking at a larger universe of stocks, but over a much shorter period of time.

My Dogs of the Dow research led me to believe that I would find similar relationships across a much larger universe, and I was correct. Yet in hindsight, much of my original research was rudimentary. In trying to decide how to approach so many variables, I opted for a simple approach that looked at the most extreme sections of the universe, separating thousands of stocks into those 50 stocks having the lowest and highest readings for any particular variable. As a result, much of my original research was a look at extremes. This

319

was one of the legitimate criticisms of the first edition of *What Works on Wall Street*, with critics pointing out that I had successfully identified what happens at opposite ends of the spectrum but ignored what went on in the middle.

In the second edition, I attempted to rectify this using decile analysis. Here, the various universes are separated into 10-percent groupings, with, for example, the stocks having the lowest price-to-sales ratios in decile one, the next 10 percent in decile two, etc., to see if a performance relationship exists beyond what the extremes showed. For the most part, the decile analysis confirmed what I had found with the 50-stock portfolios—generally, what works at the 50-stock extreme also works when the universe is grouped by decile.

LIMITED STATISTICS

The first two editions of this book featured limited statistics. In part, that was intentional, because I wanted to cover a great deal of ground and didn't want to inundate readers with a complicated statistical analysis of all the raw data. For this edition, I have included many of the relevant statistics that the most popular analysis programs like the Ibbotson EnCorr Analyzer use to generate statistics.

But I also left many out—my goal is to inform as broad a class of readers as possible without burying them under a mountain of data. For example, I currently use statistics like Jensen's Alpha, which is the difference between a data series' realized or expected rate of return and its expected position on the security market line given its risk level. The purpose of Jensen's Alpha is to see if a strategy is positioned above the security market line and therefore outperforming what the Capital Asset Pricing Model (CAPM) would predict its performance to be. But I strongly believe that its inclusion here would more likely confuse readers than lead them to any greater understanding. In addition to the potential for confusion, there is serious debate today about the validity of the CAPM and all its assumptions.

A slew of additional statistics exist, such as the Treynor ratio, M-Squared, the Sortino ratio, and others that are also based on the validity of the CAPM. I leave them out because again, the intention of this book is not to engage the reader in theoretical debates around financial data series but to inform—from the point of view of a practitioner. I find the statistics featured in the summary tables—such as maximum decline, downside risk, and number of drawdowns—to be much more relevant to both the average and professional investor.

One of the greatest mistakes many investors make is to assume that short-term conditions will continue to prevail over the long-term and that they will be able to bounce back from any setback they may endure in the market. One look at the maximum decline tables for many of the strategies featured here should disabuse them of these beliefs. Thus, my goal with all the statistics that I did include was to give investors a framework that would allow them to make better long-term decisions. A slew of unfamiliar and confusing statistics may do more harm than good.

SEASONAL ANALYSIS

My ongoing research into various factor combinations has evolved considerably in the past seven years. In my original research, as well as for the research presented in this book, portfolios are generated on a December 31 to December 31 basis. For the most part, this gives investors an adequate description of what to expect from a strategy. But since I began managing money exclusively in accordance with these strategies, I wanted to dig deeper. I now routinely create "composite" backtests, generating a new portfolio with the strategy every month and following each through to its relevant rebalance date. This allows us to test for a strategy's seasonal effects and creates a more realistic data series about what an investor should expect from a strategy, regardless of the month they begin investing.

Table 22-1 illustrates how this is accomplished. In this example, the composite return was created for an annually rebalanced strategy. Each of the returns shown is the monthly return for the portfolio that was generated exactly 12 months earlier. The different returns are then summed up at the bottom to show the annualized returns for each of the monthly seasonalities. This is to see if the "average" experience of an investor would differ substantially from that of an investor who always started and rebalanced his portfolio at the end of December. In this instance, the composite average investor would have earned an average annual return of 19.51 percent per year, with a standard deviation of return of 23.44 percent. For this strategy, little variation occurs across all the start dates, and therefore also little difference in what the average investor can expect to earn.

The point of this exercise is twofold. First, it's important to see if a strategy exhibits extreme seasonal differences. If the December data showed a return of 22 percent with a standard deviation of 21 percent, but the average composite return showed a return of 16 percent with a standard deviation of 23 percent, that strategy would exhibit extreme seasonality and may not be appropriate for investors starting in months other than December. A strategy that exhibits strong seasonality means that it is somewhat unstable, and you should be cautious about using it. The second reason to create a composite return is that you are able to get a truer sense of what most investors will experience with the strategy, regardless of their start date.

T A B L E 22-1

Seasonality Research and the Creation of a Composite Return across Rebalancing Cycles, Data beginning December 31, 1965 and ending December 31, 2003—Data Are Truncated to Fit on Page

	December	January	February	March	April	May	June	July	August	September	October	November	Composite
1/31/1965		3.64											
2/28/1965		0.86	1.52										
3/31/1965		6.58	5.26	7.82									
4/30/1965		1.15	3.37	3.86	2.35								
5/31/1965		−9.41	−10.93	−10.96	−10.41	−10.97							
6/30/1965		5.70	5.33	6.85	6.89	6.72	5.77						
7/31/1965		11.08	13.36	8.95	9.41	13.32	9.33	9.60					
8/31/1965		13.08	11.73	19.02	16.73	14.78	6.45	11.06	14.31				
9/30/1965		7.27	7.02	2.91	2.08	4.99	5.58	4.21	7.40	7.45			
10/31/1965		8.50	8.45	11.73	12.28	12.71	8.85	9.53	10.83	10.91	12.32		
11/30/1965		2.83	2.23	3.69	2.37	1.87	1.95	2.97	3.59	2.28	3.70	1.99	
12/31/1965	**4.04**	**2.63**	**3.10**	**6.21**	**6.34**	**7.40**	**9.87**	**6.77**	**5.33**	**8.45**	**5.68**	**7.08**	**6.08**
1/31/1966	4.40	4.23	8.49	4.39	4.66	8.69	4.21	6.20	5.77	5.37	6.42	2.54	5.45
2/28/1966	−4.22	−4.50	−3.24	−4.77	−4.94	−3.73	−2.57	−4.04	−4.65	−3.64	−2.64	−4.09	−3.92
3/31/1966	9.36	6.13	5.43	6.65	16.69	13.97	5.16	6.46	15.91	11.19	10.08	9.21	9.69
4/30/1966	−10.02	−10.13	−10.08	−11.47	−12.70	−15.05	−11.96	−12.79	−13.41	−13.65	−12.54	−9.98	−11.98
5/31/1966	0.69	0.76	1.47	0.94	2.13	3.03	1.10	2.34	2.58	1.95	2.36	−0.17	1.60
6/30/1966	−1.33	−3.81	−2.46	−1.72	−2.28	−2.32	−2.98	−1.34	−4.00	−3.88	−4.67	−4.52	−2.94
7/31/1966	−7.26	−8.54	−8.55	−7.90	−8.07	−8.37	−7.22	−7.37	−5.35	−5.60	−5.26	−7.41	−7.24
8/31/1966	−2.84	−4.20	−3.30	−2.84	−2.89	−2.43	−1.88	−0.33	−0.81	−5.43	−2.45	−5.03	−2.87
9/30/1966	−2.80	−1.84	−1.30	−1.14	−1.35	−1.12	−2.47	−3.03	−2.77	−2.30	−11.41	−6.62	−3.18
10/31/1966	**12.13**	**7.84**	**7.25**	**9.58**	**9.40**	**7.84**	**7.39**	**6.58**	**5.85**	**5.49**	**3.51**	**14.39**	**8.11**
11/30/1966	0.70	2.61	3.32	2.76	1.29	2.79	3.24	1.37	1.32	1.90	1.16	2.41	2.07
12/31/1966	13.65	16.14	15.61	14.28	14.99	13.82	13.44	12.77	13.10	12.13	11.81	13.42	13.76
1/31/1967	2.36	3.57	1.31	2.31	2.50	1.59	2.16	0.96	2.29	2.13	1.61	2.73	2.13
2/28/1967	8.16	7.66	8.52	8.39	7.87	8.77	9.18	8.34	7.39	6.53	7.19	8.04	8.00
3/31/1967	6.04	5.75	5.37	5.05	4.75	6.51	4.58	4.86	4.38	2.87	4.69	3.97	4.90
4/30/1967	−2.01	−1.43	−0.47	−1.01	−1.11	−1.25	−1.58	−0.76	0.10	0.47	−1.21	−0.99	−0.94

(continued on next page)

T A B L E 22-1

Seasonality Research and the Creation of a Composite Return across Rebalancing Cycles, Data beginning December 31, 1965 and ending December 31, 2003—Data Are Truncated to Fit on Page *(Continued)*

	December	January	February	March	April	May	June	July	August	September	October	November	Composite
5/31/1967	10.63	9.83	9.90	10.55	12.59	10.53	6.25	5.75	7.35	6.03	8.97	9.79	9.01
6/30/1967	6.27	7.91	8.89	9.33	9.14	7.83	9.67	4.38	5.16	4.85	4.43	5.94	6.98
7/31/1967	−1.75	−0.29	−0.47	−1.19	−0.51	−0.09	−1.41	−1.59	0.43	−0.05	0.44	−0.18	−0.56
8/31/1967	5.37	3.59	3.13	3.06	4.38	2.59	6.02	4.36	5.63	7.19	6.81	5.09	4.77
9/30/1967	−1.19	−1.30	−3.25	−3.94	−1.94	−1.12	−0.52	−0.94	−0.01	−0.46	−2.07	−2.87	−1.63
10/31/1967	2.02	3.33	1.69	1.35	1.98	0.21	0.03	1.60	1.09	1.67	3.63	1.37	1.67
11/30/1967	4.78	6.48	7.38	7.20	5.75	6.24	7.17	7.16	8.05	8.75	8.22	9.65	7.24
12/31/1967	1.34	−5.27	−4.63	−4.02	−2.29	−1.62	−1.57	−0.43	−0.61	−3.16	−0.07	1.22	−1.76
12/31/2003	0.29	3.60	5.08	3.91	3.61	1.97	5.05	5.46	0.93	1.18	2.13	−0.03	2.77
Return	**20.68%**	**19.98%**	**17.71%**	**19.41%**	**18.96%**	**19.52%**	**20.55%**	**19.75%**	**19.18%**	**16.78%**	**19.00%**	**20.32%**	**19.51%**
STD	**23.88%**	**23.75%**	**24.29%**	**23.97%**	**24.39%**	**24.39%**	**24.41%**	**24.18%**	**24.38%**	**24.40%**	**23.80%**	**23.96%**	**23.44%**

TESTING HOLDING PERIODS

For all the strategies featured in this book, I use a one-year holding period. This simplifies the data and is particularly relevant for investors in taxable portfolios. Any securities that are held for a more than a year (it can be just 366 days) are taxed as long-term capital gains, a tax with significantly lower rates than ordinary income tax rates for most investors. Yet, I also want to know the ideal holding period for a strategy when taxes are not an issue. Therefore, my team and I create composites and look at holding periods from one month to two years and more. For most of the strategies, the one-year holding period remains optimal, but for many, such as the price momentum growth strategies and many of the smaller capitalization strategies, more frequent rebalancing is better. For example, most of the smaller-cap strategies featured in Chapter 18 earn higher compound returns when they are rebalanced quarterly, as opposed to annually.

Table 22-2 shows a summary of a small-cap strategy requiring market capitalization at time of purchase to be between $200 million and $2 billion; price-to-sales ratios less than 1.5; earnings higher than in the previous year; three- and six-month price appreciation to be above the database average; and then it buys those 50 stocks having the highest one-year price appreciation. Even after assuming transaction costs and market impact of 1 percent, a nontaxable investor would be better off rebalancing the portfolio either semiannually or quarterly. Obviously, if you reduce trading and market impact costs, the more frequent rebalancing will look even more attractive. That said, I now have extensive experience trading these smaller issues and believe that the 1 percent figure is accurate. I now conduct these tests on all strategies used to manage portfolios, while always keeping the tax status of the investor in mind.

T A B L E 22-2

Seasonally Adjusted Rebalance Test for a Small-Cap Growth Strategy, December 31, 1964–May 31, 2004—Assumes Trading Costs Equal 1 Percent

Small Cap Growth Seasonality/Rebalance Analysis
Market Cap 200-2B (adjusted for inflation), with 3/6 Month Relative Strength

Item	Annual	Semi-Annual	Quarterly	Monthly
Seasonally Adjusted Return	19.51%	22.76%	24.84%	26.04%
Seasonally Adjusted STD	23.44%	23.57%	23.71%	23.84%
Annualized Turnover (both ways)	174%	302%	510%	990%
Turnover Cost (per 100% turnover)	1.00%			
Net Return	17.77%	19.74%	19.74%	16.15%

RANDOMIZATION OF IN-SAMPLE DATA AND TESTING STRATEGIES ON OTHER DATABASES

Although the real-time results for the period 1994–2003 serve as a forward test of all the strategies I tested for the original edition of this book, 10 years of data is not enough to prove anything. While it is edifying to see the strategies perform in line with their historical returns, I now also do in-sample randomization of the data. I perform these additional tests to verify the validity of the long-term results. If they aren't random, they should work equally as well on one half of the database as the other. You can achieve this randomization of the database in a variety of ways, from splitting the database up alphabetically (running the test only on stocks whose ticker symbols begin with a letter from the first half of the alphabet and then checking to see if you get similar results from the second half) to random number generation, assigning half of the database randomly to one group and the other half randomly to another. You can also split the database by periods, to make certain that each subperiod conforms to what you see over the full period.

I also routinely test the strategies on other databases. I use the Value Line Investment Survey database most frequently. The caveat here is that they only have data available electronically from 1984 on, but it still adds value to see that those strategies tested on the Compustat show similar returns when using Value Line.

Finally, I also have begun testing the strategies in other countries. If the strategies work in the United States, they should also work in other developed country markets. My first test outside the United States was in the Canadian market, where I submanage three mutual funds for the Royal Bank of Canada. One is devoted to Canadian securities, with half the fund buying growth stocks having low price-to-sales ratios and good price appreciation and half buying market-leading companies having high shareholder value. Both the backtest and the forward results for the fund show that these strategies work just as well in Canada as they do in the United States. The fund is called the RBC O'Shaughnessy Canadian Equity Fund. As of September 1, 2004, Morningstar has awarded the fund five stars, and it is in the upper quartile (as ranked by Morningstar) for the last one-, three-, and five-year period. You can get current information on the fund from Morningstar's Canadian website at www.morningstar.ca. My preliminary research on European and Asian stock markets finds that the strategies perform in those markets much as they do in the United States; I began managing the RBC O'Shaughnessy International Fund in January 2005 as a result of this research.

SECTOR-SPECIFIC ANALYSIS

My team and I now also conduct in-depth research at the sector level, to see which sectors are the most responsive to the various factors. The database is broken down into 10 economic sectors, and the factor analysis is conducted at the sector level. The research suggests, for example, that high price-to-earnings (PE) ratios are most damaging in the Energy Sector and least damaging to the Utility Sector. A common criticism of my work is that focusing on low price-to-sales will eliminate many stocks from the Information Technology and Healthcare Sectors. Yet, when we do a sector-specific test, we see that buying the decile of highest price-to-sales from each sector consistently loses money over time. Even within these higher priced sectors, a high price-to-sales ratio

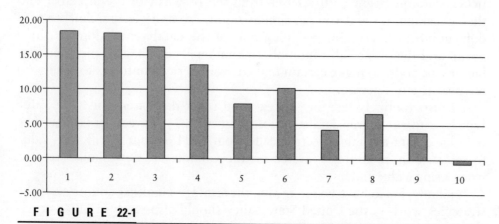

F I G U R E 22-1

Compound average annual return for price-to-sales ratio deciles, Information Technology Sector, December 31, 1975–July 31, 2004.

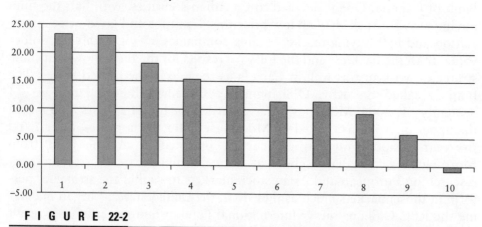

F I G U R E 22-2

Compound average annual return for price-to-sales ratio deciles, Health Care Sector, December 31, 1975–July 31, 2004.

remains toxic. Figures 22-1 and 22-2 show the compound returns by price-to-sales ratio for the Information Technology and Health Care sectors.

The sector work is another way of validating my broader research. Because all the ratios work at the sector level, using particular factors like low price-to-sales married to high price appreciation does not lead you to a certain anomalous portfolio that only buys low-margin stocks from a certain sector. Strategies drawn from the broad All Stocks and Large Stocks universes are equally effective at the sector level.

SUMMATION MODELS

One of the more recent additions to my toolkit is the use of factor summation models, rather than the traditional funnel approach used for many of the strategies covered here. Using a factor summation model, rather than put inordinate weight on a single factor—like many of the growth strategies here do when using price appreciation as the final screen— you award an ordinal rank to each factor that has proven itself efficacious in identifying future excess return. For example, price-to-sales and price appreciation have proven to be strong predictors of future price appreciation, with low price-to-sales ratios leading to strong price performance and high price-to-sales leading to price declines. The same is true for high and low price appreciation. But rather than screen for the 50 "best" from either of these categories, we now have models that award an ordinal rank, in which each stock falls on a continuum for each variable. Thus, if a stock was in the first percentile by price-to-sales, it would get an ordinal rank of 100 for that variable. If it was in the fiftieth percentile, a 50, and so on all the way up to the highest price-to-sales percentile, which would be awarded a score of 1.

By ranking each relevant factor this way, you can then sum up the ordinal ranks for a portfolio of stocks that scored best on *all* the relevant factors. This allows you to keep a stock in the portfolio that might score poorly on one factor, but is at the top for all the others. If, for example, a stock scores 100 for price appreciation, working capital, and price-to-cashflow, but has a 20 for PE ratio or price-to-sales ratio, it could still be included in the portfolio. Using the funnel approach would have knocked the stock out of consideration. I've found that using the two types of models together leads to the best overall performance.

CORRELATION MATRIX ANALYSIS

I now have monthly performance data on hundreds of stock selection strategies. One of the tenets of asset allocation is that you should build a portfolio of stocks that cover different styles of investing and different market capitalizations. The theory behind this is that you always want to have some part of your portfolio invested in a style that is currently working well. In the recent bear market, we all witnessed how poorly investors could do by refusing to diversify by style. Many investors had overconcentrated their portfolios in technology and large-cap growth stocks, with virtually no exposure to small- and mid-cap stocks or to stocks with value characteristics. Along came the bear market, and the very styles that people had shunned—small- and mid-cap growth and value and large-cap value—performed extremely well while most large-cap growth approaches crashed and burned.

One reason diversification works so well is that the underlying strategies have lower correlations with one another than they do with other portfolios that nevertheless adhere to the same investment style. Table 22-3 illustrates that this is true over a long period. The Fama-French data series serve as proxies for value and growth investing by splitting the universe by price-to-book ratios, with the high price-to-book stocks assigned to the growth category and the low price-to-book stocks assigned to the value category. You can see that, whereas the Fama-French small-cap value strategy correlates at .95 with small-cap stocks in general, it has a much lower correlation of .84 with the S&P 500 and virtually none with U.S. intermediate term bonds. It also has only a .78 correlation with the Fama-French Large Growth series. Because they are investing in very different stocks, the correlation goes down.

What works over long periods using broad categories also works at the strategy level and *within* a particular universe. Table 22-4 shows several of the strategies featured in *What Works on Wall Street* and how they correlate with one another. You see that the Market Leaders universe has correlations above .80 with all but the micro-cap low price-to-sales, high price apprecia-

T A B L E 22-3

Long-Term Annual Correlations between Various Asset Classes and Equity Style, July 1927–December 2003

Index	S&P 500	U.S. Small Stk	U.S. LT Gvt Bond	U.S. IT Gvt Bond	Fama-French Small Growth	Fama-French Large Growth	Fama-French Large Value	Fama-French Small Value
S&P 500 TR	1	0.82	0.14	0.1	0.84	0.97	0.9	0.84
U.S. Small Stk TR	0.82	1	0.07	0.04	0.93	0.8	0.85	0.95
U.S. LT Gvt TR	0.14	0.07	1	0.85	0.09	0.15	0.11	0.08
U.S. IT Gvt TR	0.1	0.04	0.85	1	0.05	0.1	0.07	0.05
Fama-French Small Growth TR	0.84	0.93	0.09	0.05	1	0.85	0.8	0.89
Fama-French Large Growth TR	0.97	0.8	0.15	0.1	0.85	1	0.82	0.78
Fama-French Large Value TR	0.9	0.85	0.11	0.07	0.8	0.82	1	0.92
Fama-French Small Value TR	0.84	0.95	0.08	0.05	0.89	0.78	0.92	1

Source: Ibbotson EnCorr Analyzer

tion strategy. Indeed, that strategy has a low correlation with all the other strategies. By marrying strategies from different capitalization categories with different styles, you can substantially reduce the volatility of any of the sub-strategies.

T A B L E 22-4

Strategy Correlations, December 31, 1963–December 31, 2003

Strategy	Market Leaders	25-Stock Micro-Cap by Rel Str	50-Stock ML by Shareholder Value	10-Stock ML by Shareholder Value	10-Stock ML, by Low PCFL
Market Leaders	1	0.67	0.94	0.83	0.8
25-Stock Micro-Cap by Rel Str	0.67	1	0.61	0.59	0.57
50-Stock ML by Shareholder Value	0.94	0.61	1	0.89	0.82
10-Stock ML by Shareholder Value	0.83	0.59	0.89	1	0.77
10-Stock ML, by Low PCFL	0.8	0.57	0.82	0.77	1

Table 22-5 illustrates what can be accomplished. You'd need a risk tolerance that was off the charts to ever use the 25-stock version of the micro-cap low price-to-sales, high price appreciation strategy on its own—the standard deviation of 36.35 percent makes it off limits to all but the most aggressive investors. Yet, if you marry that strategy to those having a low correlation with it, you can dramatically reduce overall risk while seriously improving performance. For example, if you look at a 50/50 portfolio that invests 50 percent of the portfolio in the Market Leaders universe and 50 percent in the 25-stock micro-cap portfolio, you see that you can raise both the total return and Sharpe ratio and lower downside risk declines to an acceptable 12.41 percent. That's a lot of benefit gained by joining two strategies that have a .67 correlation.

Notice that, in Table 22-4, the 50-stock Market Leaders, high shareholder value portfolio (new Cornerstone Value) actually has a *lower* correlation of .61 with the micro-cap strategy. By combining those two, you push the compound average annual return up to 21.73 percent, reduce the standard deviation to 24.6 percent, and reduce the downside risk to 11.98. You also produce the highest Sharpe ratio of 77 with a portfolio that has an overall beta of 1.04. I've also included the two strategies with the lowest correlation, the 10-stock Market Leaders portfolio with the lowest price-to-cashflow and the micro-cap strategy. You can get even more bang for your buck using this combination, provided you are willing to take on a little additional risk.

Finally, we see that you can use very similar stocks that nevertheless have a low correlation to improve overall returns. By marrying the 10-stock Market Leaders high shareholder yield portfolio with the 10-stock Market

T A B L E 22-5

Return and Risk Characteristics for Various Strategies and Combinations, December 31, 1963–December 31, 2003

Strategy	Geometric Mean	Arithmetic Mean	Standard Deviation	T-Stat	Ending Index Value	Sharpe Ratio	N Positive Periods	N Negative Periods	Down-side Risk	Maximum Decline (%)	Beta
25-Stock Small-Cap Microcap Growth $25mm–$250mm	24.32	29.3	36.35	5.82	$60,580,240.29	0.67	304	176	16.99	–55.6	1.19
50 Percent 10-Stock ML, Low PCFL/ 50 Percent Microcap Growth	23.27	26.42	28.32	6.63	$43,139,512.75	0.76	312	168	13.46	–49.1	1.15
50 Percent 50-Stock ML, High ShareholderYld/50 Percent Microcap Growth	21.73	24.16	24.6	6.91	$26,047,911.41	0.77	313	167	11.98	–41.33	1.04
ML, TOP 10 BY LOW P/CFL	19.96	22.88	27.29	5.88	$14,504,404.48	0.65	300	180	12.38	–45.15	1.11
50 Percent Market Leaders/50 Percent Microcap Growth	19.62	22.09	24.55	6.28	$12,957,175.97	0.69	310	170	12.41	–46.34	1.08
50 Percent 10-Stock ML, Low PCFL/ 50 Percent 10-Stock ML, High Shareholder YLD	19.25	21.36	22.85	6.5	$11,418,583.81	0.7	308	172	10.83	–36.96	1.03
Market Leaders—10-Stock High Shareholder Yld	18.1	19.98	21.31	6.48	$7,772,433.39	0.69	309	171	10.35	–38.27	0.95
50-Stock Market Leaders, High Shareholder Yld	17.02	18.39	18.09	6.97	$5,368,550.70	0.72	308	172	8.66	–29.05	0.9
Market Leaders	12.77	14.05	17.06	5.55	$1,225,022.10	0.49	297	183	9.2	–38.98	0.96

Leaders low price-to-cashflow portfolio, you are investing entirely in large, well-known companies with a value bent, yet improving on the returns of Market Leaders itself by a factor of 11. The maximum decline of the portfolio is actually *less* than that of Market Leaders, with a downside risk only slightly higher. Therefore, even within style and capitalization categories, you can substantially improve performance by uniting strategies with relatively low correlations to one another.

REGRESSION TO LONG-TERM MEAN WITHIN STRATEGIES

Regression to the long-term mean is one of the hallmarks of financial data series. If you look at the S&P 500, small-cap stocks, and value and growth stocks, over the last 79 years, you see that, over long spans of time, they regress to their long-term mean. This allows insights on where markets might be headed over time. For example, if you analyze the S&P 500's returns on a rolling 20-year basis, you'll see that between 1926 and 2003, the average real rate of return (subtracting inflation) for any 20-year period was around 7.1 percent. Interestingly, this is also the real return of the S&P 500 over the full 1926–2003 period. Indeed, it's the return over *all* major periods of time. According to Jeremy Siegel's superb book *Stocks for the Long Run*, the real rate of return to U.S. stocks between 1802 and 1997 was 7.0 percent, between 1871 and 1997, also 7 percent. If you break it down to the 1800s versus the 1900s, you still get the same 7 percent. Therefore, that 7 percent figure exerts a very strong gravitational pull—when the returns for the last 20 years get substantially below or above it, they spend the next 20 years reverting to the 7 percent mean.

I've also found that a shorter-term regression to mean occurs, not just at the broad index level, but at the strategy level as well. In one current project, I am engaged in examining all monthly returns of the strategies over time, creating a longer-term average and then examining where the strategy's current returns are relative to the longer-term. I've found that when a strategy is currently well above or below its long-term average, it changes course and reverts either up or down to the longer-term mean over the next three to five years. This can give you meaningful guidance about which strategies you should emphasize and which you should avoid. It also provides very counterintuitive advice—most people flock to a strategy when its shorter-term performance is very strong, whereas this methodology has you do the opposite. The important thing to know is where the strategy's return is, relative to its longer-term mean.

A variant on this theme can help you decide which broad mutual fund categories you might want to invest in over any three- to five-year period. It uses the same assumption of regression to mean. If you go to Morningstar's website at www.morningstar.com and choose the funds category, you can select category returns from the mutual fund performance tab. Sort these by five-year return and then examine the top two or three categories and the bottom two or three categories. The regression-to-the-mean data suggest that you buy the bottom two or three categories and sell (if you own them) the top three categories.

I've informally done this for years, first using Morningstar's CD OnDisc and then using their website. It's amazing how well this works. For example, at the end of 1999, it would have had you *sell* technology and large-cap growth funds and *buy* small-cap value and growth funds—a very counterintuitive, yet ultimately very profitable move. Currently, it would have you do the opposite, selling real estate specialty funds and small-cap value funds and buying technology and large-cap growth funds. It is a fairly simple and easy way to keep your emotions in check, and I recommend it for anyone using mutual funds as their investment vehicles.

FUTURE PROJECTS

Quantitative researchers have come a long way from doing simple backtests by hand, but we still have further to go. Some of the projects that I'm working on now involve decomposing multifactor models in an attempt to isolate which factor or group of factors offers the purest "signal" to the rest of the information's "noise." Many times, factors overlap, with stocks having low price-to-sales also having low price-to-cashflow ratios, PE ratios, and so on. Current research is attempting to discover which factor is the most relevant to a variety of different stocks or sectors. This research is being conducted in concert with the sector research and may ultimately lead to different models being used to pick stocks from different sectors or different overall subgroups. It's a bit like drug companies attempting to develop drugs that are targeted to individuals of a certain subset of people, with certain variants of the drug working much better on certain subsets of the population.

I'm also looking at building intersection portfolios, in which all the stocks must be contained in a variety of deciles to be included in a portfolio. An example of this is a strategy that requires membership in value deciles and then, if the resultant stocks are more than 50, it sorts the remaining names by one-year price appreciation. The strategy would look like this:

- Stock must be in the bottom three deciles by price-to-sales ratio (the 30 percent of the database with the lowest price-to-sales ratios)
- Stock must also be in the bottom three deciles by price-to-cashflow
- Stock must also be in the top three deciles by dividend yield

- If more than 50 stocks are left, buy the top 50 by one-year price appreciation

Table 22-6 shows the results of this strategy. A $10,000 investment on December 31, 1963 grew to $6.7 million by the end of 2003, a compound average annual return of 17.69. But the amazing thing about this intersection strategy is that it achieved these results with very low levels of risk. The strategy's standard deviation was 18.38 percent, nearly 2 percent less than the All Stocks benchmark. The downside risk of 9.10 percent was also over 2 percent less than the benchmark, and the maximum decline was a very modest 28.57 percent. The biggest problem this strategy had was its deviation from its benchmark—in one 12-month period, it was 51 percent below the All Stocks universe. Nevertheless, this type of strategy, where you earn excellent returns at low levels of risk, makes an excellent component of larger, lower-risk portfolios.

T A B L E 22-6

Summary Return and Risk Results for Monthly Data, All Stocks, and Decile Intersection Strategy, December 31, 1963–December 31. 2003

	All Stocks	Decile Intersection Portfolio
Arithmetic Average	13.82%	19.11%
Geometric Average	12.02%	17.69%
Median Return	17.96%	24.30%
Standard Deviation of Return	20.23%	18.38%
Downside Risk—lower is better	11.53%	9.10%
Correlation with S&P 500	0.89	0.81
T-Statistic	4.61	7.15
Sharpe Ratio	0.40	0.75
Number of Positive Periods	286	316
Number of Negative Periods	194	164
Maximum Peak-to-Trough Decline (using monthly data series)	−50.12%	−37.68%
Beta	1.05	0.83
$10,000 becomes:	$936,071.00	$6,754,726.00
Minimum 12-Month Return	−41.65%	−28.57%
Maximum 12-Month Return	81.51%	69.76%
Minimum Expected Return*	−26.64%	−17.65%
Maximum Expected Return**	54.28%	55.87%

*Minimum Expected Return is Arithmetic Return minus 2 times the standard deviation.
**Maximum Expected Return is Arithmetic Return plus 2 times the standard deviation.

I'm also attempting to build all-style, all-cap portfolios that, when used in concert with other asset classes such as bonds and commodities, have unusual characteristics like never having a 12-month period when they lose more than 10 percent, low to zero correlations with the S&P 500 and other major market indices, and very low downside risk. The search for the best absolute return portfolio is tailor-made to quantitative financial engineering, because we can use a variety of combinations to fine-tune things like downside risk, number of drawdowns, and maximum decline.

As part of this effort, we also have developed shorting strategies. As you might expect, doing the inverse of what works well on the long side ends up providing you with stocks that are excellent shorting candidates. For example, the inverse of our strongest growth theme, buying stocks with low price-to-sales, earnings higher than in the previous year, and excellent three-, six-, and 12-month price appreciation leads to a bounty of poorly performing stocks. Here, you would look only for stocks with the *highest* price-to-sales, *deteriorating* earnings, and price declines to boot. That strategy identified a portfolio that declined 11.26 percent per year during one of the biggest bull markets in history! Between December 31, 1985 and December 31, 2003, that strategy turned $10,000 into just $1,164, whereas a similar investment in All Stocks turned $10,000 into $82,681, a compound average annual return of 12.45 percent. These strategies can be *very* useful when identifying which stocks to short.

By marrying shorting strategies like this with the best long strategies, and then including asset classes outside of equities such as fixed income, commodities, futures, and foreign shares, you can develop portfolios with extremely high Sharpe ratios, very low downside risk, and low maximum declines. I believe that most quantitative research will now focus on developing these lower-risk, higher-return absolute performance strategies.

23 C H A P T E R

RANKING THE STRATEGIES

I know of no way of judging of the future but by the past.
—Patrick Henry

It's time to rank all the strategies' returns on both an absolute and a risk-adjusted basis. To present an apples to apples comparison, I rank the strategies using the monthly return data between December 31, 1963 and December 31, 2003. This allows me to include all the strategies featured in various sections of the book. These 40 years of data also cover every type of market environment, save the Great Depression. Booms, busts, manias, speculative fervor, a market crash, the biggest bull market in 70 years, and two wicked bear markets are all woven into the market's tapestry of the last 40 years.

We begin with the market at the end of 1963. Still reeling from the horrible events of November, when the market was forced into an emergency closing because of the panic that swept the exchanges following the assassination of President John F. Kennedy, the Dow Jones Industrial Average closed the year at 762.95, up 17 percent for the year. Many of the huge gainers from the 1950s were still dominating trading, with Xerox, Polaroid, IBM, and Control Data still years away from the speculative highs they would achieve on their way to becoming members of the "nifty-fifty." NASDAQ did not exist. Total volume had finally surpassed that of 1929. Computers still used punch cards, and even the most advanced lacked a fraction of the power we take for granted today. A tiny percentage of U.S. households owned stocks or mutual funds, and many a market participant vividly and personally recalled the crash of 1929 and the ensuing depression of the 1930s.

We end in 2003, a new millennium to be sure, but not a new market. Although our world today looks little like the one of 1963 when we began, human beings, the agents of change in the marketplace, remain very much the same. We learned that first-hand with the speculative blow-off of the late 1990s and the resulting bear market of 2000–2002, when the reality of the marketplace ferociously reasserted itself. In the end, it is our consistent refusal to learn from history that condemns us to repeat it. Although our situation and circumstances might change dramatically, *we* do not. It's that very fact that makes long-term data especially useful. By examining how investment strategies perform in many different market environments, we prepare ourselves for what might come in the future. No doubt the names of the securities and the industries they are in will change in future years, but the underlying persistence of what works and what doesn't will continue. I have no idea what the *names* of the winning and losing stocks of tomorrow will be, yet I have a very good idea of what factors will define them.

We also see little variation in return when the 1951–2003 annual data are compared to the 1963–2003 monthly data. The strategies' ranking by monthly data is consistent with that of the strategies ranked on an annual data basis. For example, when we sort the annual data by compound return, the same strategies occupy the top and bottom positions as do the monthly data. And, if you really want to get your hands on every stitch of data, you can find all the annual results at www.whatworksonwallstreet.com.

THE RESULTS

Forty years of monthly data prove that the market follows a purposeful stride, not a random walk. The stock market consistently rewards some strategies and consistently punishes others. The strategies found near the top or the bottom of our list possess similar attributes that are easily identified. Each of the 10 best-performing strategies, for example, includes relative strength criteria. Yet it is *always* tied to another factor, usually one requiring the stocks to be modestly priced in terms of how much you are paying for every dollar of sales. All the 10 worst-performing strategies buy stocks that investors have bid to unsustainable prices, giving them astronomical price-to-earnings, price-to-book, price-to-sales, or price-to-cashflow ratios, or are last year's biggest losers. With the exception of the disastrous performance of last year's biggest losers, all these factors usually reflect high hopes on the part of investors. History shows that high hopes are usually dashed and that investors are better off buying reasonably priced stocks with good relative strength.

Most of the best-performing strategies are riskier than the market as a whole, but a handful do much better than the market while taking only slightly more risk. Most of the worst performing strategies are actually riskier than the best performing strategies. The results prove that the market doesn't always award high returns to portfolios having higher risk. Indeed, you see when we sort the strategies by either downside risk or maximum decline, the riskiest strategies also have the highest downside risk and maximum decline, whereas many of the lowest downside risks belong to strategies that have historically done very well. Buying the 25 stocks from Market Leaders with the highest Shareholder Yield is a good example: It has the second highest Sharpe ratio of all the single strategies featured, as well as one of the lowest downside risks and a smaller maximum decline than Market Leaders, yet it has done seven times as well as the Market Leaders universe over the last 40 years.

ABSOLUTE RETURNS

Table 23-1 ranks all the strategies by absolute return, and Figures 23-1 and 23-2 show the five best and worst performers. All but one of the top strategies use relative price appreciation as a final screen, with the majority marrying it to low price-to-sales. The best performing strategy buys those 25 stocks having market capitalizations between $25 million and $250 million, price-to-sales ratios below one, and excellent relative strength. It turned $10,000 invested on December 31, 1963 into over $60 million at the end of 2003, a compound average annual rate of return of 24.32 percent. Awesome numbers, but awesome numbers are usually accompanied by awesome risk. This was the case with this strategy—the standard deviation of 36.35 percent is off the charts, indicating that investors considering the strategy should anticipate that 95 percent of potential returns in the future will likely fall between a gain of 102 percent and a loss of *43.4 percent*. You could drive several trucks through a hole that big. This huge disparity of potential returns should warn off virtually all investors from putting money into it—yes, the upside can be enormous, but so can the downside. Imagine putting your hard-earned money into these 25 names only to watch them plunge by over 55 percent over the next 12 months (as they did in one of the 12-month time periods in the study). I honestly doubt that there is an investor alive who could live with that type of performance, which is one of the reasons I'm passionate about looking at strategies from all perspectives: absolute return, risk-adjusted return, the potential for volatility while stock prices are declining (downside risk), and the

T A B L E 23-1

All Strategies for Monthly Data Series, December 31, 1963–December 31, 2003—Strategies Sorted by Compound Average Annual Return

Strategy	Geometric Mean	Arithmetic Mean	Standard Deviation	T-Stat	Ending Index Value	Sharpe Ratio	Pos Periods	Neg Periods	Downside Risk	Maximum Decline	Beta	Median
Cap Bx. $25mm, $250mm, PSR<1, Top 25 Stocks by 1-Yr Rel Str	24.32	29.3	36.35	5.82	$60,580,240	0.67	304	176	16.99	−55.6	1.19	32.14
Cap Bx. $25mm, $250, PSR<1, 3/6 Mth Price Chg Pos, Top 25 Stocks by High 1-Yr Rel Str	22.7	27.58	35.8	5.53	$35,738,548	0.63	299	181	17.04	−61.29	1.15	35.88
Cap Bx. $25mm, $250, PSR<1, 3/6 Mth Price Chg Pos, Top 50 Stocks by High 1-Yr Rel Str	21.21	25.03	30.98	5.73	$21,983,019	0.64	305	175	15.58	−54.75	1.15	33.73
Cap Bx. $25mm, $250, PSR<1, 3/6 Mth Price Chg Pos, Top 10 Stocks by High 1-Yr Rel Str	21.18	28.17	43.28	4.72	$21,707,627	0.54	281	199	20.6	−86.04	1.19	28.51
Improved CSG, Top 25 Stocks	21.08	25.23	32.55	5.51	$21,055,793	0.62	290	190	15.7	−59.33	1.24	27.16
Improved CSG, Top 50 Stocks	20.75	23.97	28.31	5.97	$18,860,926	0.67	296	184	14.1	−55.25	1.19	24.61
CSG Top 100 Pmargin, Pos 3/6 Mth Price Chg, Top 25 Stocks by 1-Yr Rel Str	20.41	22.91	24.94	6.43	$16,818,255	0.71	313	167	12.11	−48.46	1.07	27.18
50-Stock Value-Growth Portfolio	20.17	22.4	23.38	6.69	$15,543,562	0.74	295	185	11.46	−40.52	1.08	25.02
Market Leaders, 10 Stocks by Low PCFL	19.96	22.88	27.29	5.88	$14,504,404	0.65	300	180	12.38	−45.15	1.11	20.23
100-Stock Value-Growth Portfolio	19.21	21.12	21.46	6.83	$11,275,830	0.74	311	169	10.74	−38.82	1.05	23.71
Original CSG, Top 25 Stocks by 1-Yr Rel Str	19.02	23.24	32.56	5.04	$10,575,472	0.56	283	197	16.26	−60.85	1.24	25.21
Small Stocks, PSR<1, 3/6 Mth Price Chg Pos, Top 50 Stocks by 1-Yr Rel Str	18.62	21.79	27.74	5.49	$9,249,548	0.6	291	189	14.45	−53.14	1.17	21.61
Original CSG, Top 100 Pmargin, Top 10 Stocks by 1-Yr Rel Str	18.61	21.15	24.9	5.91	$9,221,276	0.64	284	196	12.45	−37.6	0.94	21.97
Small Stocks, PSR<1, 3/6 Mth Price Chg Pos, Top 25 Stocks by 1-Yr Rel Str	18.55	22.51	31.29	5.06	$9,040,439	0.55	291	189	16.08	−52.82	1.22	28.85
Improved CSG, Top 100 Pmargin, Top 25 Stocks by 1-Yr Rel Str	18.24	21.01	26	5.63	$8,127,684	0.61	300	180	13.3	−43.8	1.11	25.81
Improved CSG, Top 100 Pmargin, Top 50 Stocks by 1-Yr Rel Str	18.14	20.22	22.36	6.26	$7,855,317	0.67	308	172	11.66	−39.56	1.02	23.46
Market Leaders, Top 10 Stocks by Shareholder Yield	18.1	19.98	21.31	6.48	$7,772,433	0.69	309	171	10.35	−38.27	0.95	21.74

(continued on next page)

T A B L E 23-1

All Strategies for Monthly Data Series, December 31, 1963–December 31, 2003—Strategies Sorted by Compound Average Annual Return *(Continued)*

Strategy	Geometric Mean	Arithmetic Mean	Standard Deviation	T-Stat	Ending Index Value	Sharpe Ratio	Pos Periods	Neg Periods	Downside Risk	Maximum Decline	Beta	Median
Market Leaders, Top 25 Stocks by Shareholder Yield	18.05	19.58	19.22	7.03	$7,632,140	0.74	308	172	9.16	−32.22	0.92	21.6
Original Cornerstone Growth	17.77	21.16	28.74	5.14	$6,950,741	0.55	277	203	14.8	−60.13	1.21	19.28
Value Decile Intersection, 50 Stocks	17.69	19.11	18.38	7.15	$6,754,726	0.75	316	164	9.1	−37.68	0.83	24.3
All—P/Book<1—Top 50 Stocks by 1-Yr Rel Str	17.68	20.28	24.97	5.64	$6,737,675	0.6	298	182	13.09	−49.66	1.04	23.39
All—Good Value—50 Stocks by Low PCFL	17.53	19.47	21.84	6.16	$6,395,835	0.65	300	180	10.13	−42.59	0.92	20.06
All—Earn Yld>5%—Top 50 Stocks by 1-Yr Rel Str	17.49	20.61	27.44	5.23	$6,305,425	0.56	288	192	14.38	−53.09	1.18	22.84
All—Low PE,EPS Up—Top 50 Stocks by 1-Yr Rel Str	17.49	19.33	20.99	6.35	$6,305,417	0.67	310	170	10.66	−49.58	0.99	21.56
Al—5-Yr Payout<50 Percent, Top 50 Stocks by Div Yld	17.08	18.58	19.02	6.71	$5,483,629	0.69	305	175	9.19	−44.16	0.84	20.1
All Stocks, 5-Yr EPS > Avg, Net Mrg > Avg, EPS > EPS—1-Yr, Top 50 Stocks by 1-Yr Rel Str	17.02	19.71	25.53	5.35	$5,380,301	0.56	293	187	13	−48.12	1.17	21.8
Market Leaders, Top 50 Stocks by Shareholder Yield	17.02	18.39	18.09	6.97	$5,368,551	0.72	308	172	8.66	−29.05	0.9	18.36
All—Str Earn—Top 50 Stocks by 1-Yr Rel Str	16.94	19.15	23.03	5.74	$5,238,626	0.6	291	189	11.71	−50.93	1.12	20.29
All—EPS up 5 Yrs—Top 50 Stocks by 1-Yr Rel Str	16.91	19.39	24.41	5.49	$5,179,460	0.58	299	181	12.59	−52.73	1.16	23.85
Market Leaders, 10 Stocks by Low PSR	16.9	19.3	24.12	5.53	$5,159,969	0.58	295	185	12.07	−50.31	0.99	18.65
Small Stocks, 50 Stocks by Low PCFL	16.82	19.94	27.7	5	$5,023,916	0.53	285	195	13.78	−55.73	1.17	17.92
All—PSR<1—Top 50 Stocks by 1-Yr Rel Str	16.75	19.92	27.54	5.02	$4,909,077	0.53	281	199	14.69	−53.4	1.17	23.3
Market Leaders, 50 Stocks by Low P/Book	16.63	18.51	21.21	6	$4,705,461	0.62	296	184	10.53	−37.08	1.04	17.72
Market Leaders, 50 Stocks by Low PE	16.55	18.36	20.83	6.06	$4,571,422	0.62	297	183	10.29	−35.13	1.02	17.56
Market Leaders, PSR<Avg, Top 25 Stocks by 1-Yr Rel Str	16.54	18.47	21.44	5.93	$4,561,805	0.61	304	176	10.93	−32.2	1.03	23.61
Market Leaders, 25 Stocks by Low PSR	16.41	18.28	21.07	5.96	$4,362,020	0.61	301	179	10.89	−43.34	0.99	19.94

(continued on next page)

339

T A B L E 23-1

All Strategies for Monthly Data Series, December 31, 1963–December 31, 2003—Strategies Sorted by Compound Average Annual Return *(Continued)*

Strategy	Geometric Mean	Arithmetic Mean	Standard Deviation	T-Stat	Ending Index Value	Sharpe Ratio	Pos Periods	Neg Periods	Downside Risk	Maximum Decline	Beta	Median
Small Stocks, 50 Stocks by Low PE	16.31	19	25.5	5.15	$4,214,230	0.53	297	183	13.03	−52.13	1.07	19.23
All, PSR<1, Top 25 Stocks by 1-Yr Rel Str	16.24	20.19	31	4.54	$4,118,890	0.48	288	192	16.27	−57.73	1.22	19.87
CSV, top 25 Stocks by Div Yield	16.24	17.72	18.82	6.45	$4,111,429	0.65	303	177	8.93	−28.5	0.85	17
Market Leaders, PSR<Avg, Top 50 Stocks by 1-Yr Rel Str	16.21	17.92	20.07	6.12	$4,078,153	0.62	304	176	10.2	−31.11	1.02	21.42
Market Leaders, 50 Stocks by Low PSR	16.15	17.93	20.52	5.99	$3,981,957	0.61	307	173	10.67	−35.07	1.01	19.18
Market Leaders, 50 Stocks by Low PCFL	16.09	17.83	20.37	6	$3,906,209	0.61	305	175	10.23	−39.15	1	20.92
Small Stocks, ROE>Avg. 3/6 Mth Price Chg Pos, Top 50 Stocks by 1-Yr Rel Str	15.8	20.15	32.63	4.31	$3,530,758	0.46	295	185	17.48	−70.56	1.33	25.77
Cornerstone Value	15.76	17.14	18.13	6.45	$3,481,988	0.64	301	179	8.74	−28.18	0.89	17.57
CSV, Top 10 Stocks by Dividend Yield	15.67	17.36	20.18	5.89	$3,378,075	0.59	293	187	9.47	−29.7	0.81	16.72
All—50 Stocks by Low P/Book	15.66	18.98	28.8	4.57	$3,365,965	0.47	287	193	13.96	−48.55	1.17	18.13
All—Yld, Price up-50 Stocks by Low PSR	15.62	17.25	19.51	6.05	$3,318,667	0.6	306	174	10.48	−43.94	0.89	22.07
Market Leaders, PSR<Avg, Top 10 Stocks by 1-Yr Rel Str	15.6	17.77	22.74	5.37	$3,299,346	0.54	298	182	11.66	−38.21	0.96	18.38
All Industrials—50 Stocks by Low PCFL	15.53	17.89	23.7	5.19	$3,223,752	0.52	297	183	12.29	−44.22	1.05	18.73
All—50 Stocks by Low PSR	15.38	18.2	26.13	4.8	$3,054,908	0.49	283	197	13.33	−52.15	1.09	20.77
Small Stocks, 50 Stocks by Low PSR	15.38	18.36	26.9	4.71	$3,051,506	0.48	290	190	13.81	−52.87	1.11	21.59
Small Stocks, Value Model 2	15.28	17.05	20.2	5.77	$2,954,941	0.57	301	179	11.03	−47.53	0.9	21.05
Large CSG, with 3/6 Mth Price Chg Pos, Top 50 Stocks by 1-Yr Rel Str	15.16	16.96	20.59	5.63	$2,831,275	0.56	303	177	10.83	−39.56	1	20.97
Small Stocks, PSR<Avg, 3/6 Mth Price Chg Pos, Top 50 Stocks by 1-Yr Rel Str	15.08	19.44	32.45	4.17	$2,757,808	0.43	289	191	17.61	−76.71	1.26	21.04
Small Stocks, 50 Stocks by Low P/Book	14.97	18.35	28.92	4.39	$2,654,859	0.45	279	201	14.31	−52	1.17	18.46
All—50 Stocks by Low PE	14.89	17.45	24.75	4.84	$2,581,104	0.48	288	192	12.83	−50.76	1.07	16.9
Lrg—50 Stocks by Low P/Book	14.87	16.84	21.67	5.32	$2,562,423	0.53	298	182	10.96	−42.84	1.01	18.07
Large Industrial—50 Stocks by Low PCFL	14.77	16.69	21.21	5.38	$2,476,539	0.53	294	186	11.17	−39.33	1.04	19.86
Market Leaders, Top 50 Stocks by 1-Yr Rel Str	14.75	16.63	21.03	5.4	$2,452,387	0.53	301	179	11.13	−41.19	1.06	19.8
Large—EPS up—PE<20—Top 50 Stocks by 1-Yr Rel Str	14.67	16.64	21.39	5.31	$2,391,513	0.52	296	184	11.54	−40.11	1.04	20.72
Large—50 Stocks by Low PSR	14.64	16.58	21.29	5.32	$2,364,710	0.52	297	183	11.39	−40.71	1.03	16.52

(continued on next page)

T A B L E 23-1

All Strategies for Monthly Data Series, December 31, 1963–December 31, 2003—Strategies Sorted by Compound Average Annual Return *(Continued)*

Strategy	Geometric Mean	Arithmetic Mean	Standard Deviation	T-Stat	Ending Index Value	Sharpe Ratio	Pos Periods	Neg Periods	Downside Risk	Maximum Decline	Beta	Median
Large—PE<20—50 Stocks by High 1-Yr Rel Str	14.63	16.66	21.74	5.24	$2,353,621	0.51	303	177	11.86	−39.48	1.06	21.35
Large Stocks CSG 25 Stocks	14.61	16.92	23.34	4.97	$2,340,370	0.49	290	190	12.41	−46.13	1.11	20.05
Market Leaders, PCFL<Avg, 3/6 Mth Price Chg Pos, Top 50 Stocks by 1-Yr Rel Str	14.53	16.25	19.98	5.54	$2,275,626	0.54	301	179	10.72	−34.73	1.02	19.18
Market Leaders, 50 Stocks by Best 5-Yr EPS Gain	14.52	16.61	22.27	5.1	$2,267,445	0.5	288	192	11.31	−46.47	1.17	17.16
Large—50 Stocks by Low PE	14.31	16.04	20.16	5.42	$2,103,738	0.52	293	187	10.58	−39.71	0.96	17.57
Large—Strong Earn—Top 50 Stocks by 1-Yr Rel Str	14.16	15.98	20.68	5.26	$1,997,588	0.51	285	195	10.71	−49.32	1.08	17.06
Small Stocks—50 Stocks by Best 1-Yr EPS Growth	14.16	17.43	27.83	4.31	$1,995,556	0.43	287	193	15.4	−66.78	1.23	20.19
Market Leaders, PSR<Avg, 3/6 Mth Price Chg Pos, Top 50 Stocks by 1-Yr Rel Str	14.14	16.01	20.85	5.23	$1,983,979	0.5	296	184	11.31	−45.23	1.06	20
All—ROE>15—Top 50 Stocks by 1-Yr Rel Str	14.13	18.65	33.18	3.91	$1,975,512	0.4	280	200	17.88	−65.82	1.39	24.96
Large Stock CSG 50 Stocks	14.12	16.06	21.26	5.15	$1,970,929	0.5	298	182	11.4	−41.03	1.05	18.49
Large—Low PE-EPS Up—Top 50 Stocks by 1-Yr Rel Str	14.06	15.57	18.76	5.64	$1,931,668	0.54	303	177	9.75	−47.96	0.95	13.76
Large—ROE>15—Top 50 Stocks by 1-Yr Rel Str	14.05	16.95	26.27	4.43	$1,920,627	0.44	285	195	14	−51.57	1.21	17.2
Large Industrials—50 Stocks by High Dividend Yield	14.01	15.28	17.29	5.99	$1,892,183	0.56	300	180	8.55	−28.95	0.81	15.83
Small Stocks, PCFL<Avg. 3/6 Mth Price Chg Pos, Top 50 Stocks by 1-Yr Rel Str	13.97	18.69	33.64	3.86	$1,865,835	0.4	291	189	18.5	−87.48	1.27	22.06
All—Pmargin>20 -50 Stocks by 1-Yr Rel Str	13.9	19.6	37.7	3.64	$1,825,902	0.38	287	193	19.95	−81.66	1.44	20.73
Dow 10 Stocks by High Dividend Yield (Dogs of the Dow)	13.89	15.33	18.36	5.67	$1,817,710	0.53	291	189	9.21	−30.23	0.87	13.6
Lrg—5-Yr Payout<50 Percent—50 Stocks by High Dividend Yield	13.89	15.51	19.41	5.43	$1,816,627	0.51	294	186	10.19	−46.01	0.94	16.92

(continued on next page)

341

T A B L E 23-1

All Strategies for Monthly Data Series, December 31, 1963–December 31, 2003—Strategies Sorted by Compound Average Annual Return *(Continued)*

Strategy	Geometric Mean	Arithmetic Mean	Standard Deviation	T-Stat	Ending Index Value	Sharpe Ratio	Pos Periods	Neg Periods	Downside Risk	Maximum Decline	Beta	Median
Large—50 Stocks by Best 1-Yr Rel Str	13.87	17.44	29.36	4.1	$1,805,450	0.41	280	200	15.56	−71.51	1.27	20.17
Large—PSR<1—50 Stocks by 1-Yr Rel Str	13.64	15.56	21.04	5.03	$1,666,318	0.48	295	185	11.5	−37.73	1.03	16.09
Market Leaders, 50 Stocks by Worst Pmargin	13.63	15.35	19.93	5.23	$1,659,290	0.49	296	184	10.91	−52.22	1.04	17.24
Market Leaders, 50 Stocks by Worst 5-Yr EPS Gain	13.62	15.15	18.77	5.47	$1,651,414	0.51	291	189	10.02	−32.82	0.99	18.03
Small Stocks—50 Stocks by Worst 5-Yr EPS Gain	13.25	15.64	23.41	4.55	$1,449,185	0.43	295	185	13.41	−52.04	1.05	19.5
All—EPS Chg>25—50 Stocks by 1-Yr Rel Str	13.2	18.68	36.74	3.55	$1,424,187	0.36	288	192	19.94	−83.88	1.4	23.31
Market Leaders, ROE>Avg, 3/6 Mth Price Chg Pos, Top 50 Stocks by 1-Yr Rel Str	13.13	14.97	20.65	4.92	$1,390,238	0.46	287	193	11.23	−48.63	1.07	17.45
Large—Low PSR-EPS Up—50 Stocks by 1-Yr Rel Str	13.12	14.7	19.11	5.21	$1,385,160	0.48	290	190	10.12	−51.6	0.98	15.38
All—50 Stocks by Percentage 1-Yr EPS Gain	12.77	15.8	26.54	4.07	$1,225,226	0.39	287	193	15.02	−65.54	1.2	19.82
Market Leaders	**12.77**	**14.05**	**17.06**	**5.55**	**$1,225,022**	**0.49**	**297**	**183**	**9.2**	**−38.98**	**0.96**	**17.02**
Large—50 Stocks by High Pmargin	12.69	14.86	22.53	4.48	$1,188,767	0.41	286	194	12.01	−57.17	1.13	11.22
Small Stocks 50 Stocks by High Dividend Yield	12.64	14.12	18.5	5.16	$1,166,914	0.46	296	184	9.92	−49.29	0.8	14.51
Market Leaders, 50 Stocks by High Pmargin	12.63	13.98	17.56	5.37	$1,166,320	0.48	297	183	9.31	−38.51	0.97	16.73
Market Leaders, 50 Stocks by High ROE	12.63	14.14	18.63	5.13	$1,165,770	0.46	289	191	10.05	−50	1.02	15.26
Small Stocks	**12.57**	**14.69**	**22.02**	**4.53**	**$1,139,641**	**0.41**	**290**	**190**	**12.5**	**−53.82**	**1.07**	**18.55**
Large—50 Stocks by High Dividend Yield	12.52	13.61	16	5.73	$1,121,835	0.5	294	186	7.53	−32.97	0.61	10.82
Market Leaders, 50 Stocks by Worst 1-Yr EPS Change	12.51	14.26	20.09	4.8	$1,114,960	0.43	295	185	10.8	−48.9	1.05	14.65
Market Leaders, 50 Stocks by Low ROE	12.51	14.23	19.87	4.84	$1,114,342	0.43	293	187	10.84	−50.37	1.03	14.23
All Industrials—50 Stocks by High Dividend Yield	12.49	13.87	17.89	5.23	$1,107,592	0.46	298	182	9.42	−57.23	0.72	12.83

(continued on next page)

342

T A B L E 23-1

All Strategies for Monthly Data Series, December 31, 1963–December 31, 2003—Strategies Sorted by Compound Average Annual Return *(Continued)*

Strategy	Geometric Mean	Arithmetic Mean	Standard Deviation	T-Stat	Ending Index Value	Sharpe Ratio	Pos Periods	Neg Periods	Downside Risk	Maximum Decline	Beta	Median
All Stocks	**12.02**	**13.82**	**20.23**	**4.61**	**$936,071**	**0.4**	**286**	**194**	**11.53**	**-50.12**	**1.05**	**17.96**
Large—50 Stocks by 1-Yr Percentage Sales Decline	11.96	13.89	21	4.47	$917,141	0.39	285	195	11.49	-45.39	1.07	12.29
Market Leaders, 50 Stocks by Best 1-Yr EPS Gains	11.94	13.64	19.6	4.69	$911,483	0.41	290	190	11.03	-39.04	1.05	16.06
Large—50 Stocks by Best 5-Yr EPS Growth	11.42	14.18	25.42	3.79	$755,599	0.34	275	205	13.9	-64.09	1.3	11.66
Large Stocks	**11.2**	**12.63**	**17.96**	**4.72**	**$697,718**	**0.39**	**289**	**191**	**10.15**	**-46.59**	**1.01**	**15.23**
All—50 Stocks by Best 1-Yr Rel Str	11.13	16.88	37.44	3.13	$681,201	0.3	281	199	20.61	-89.4	1.47	18.68
All—50 Stocks by Percentage 1-Yr EPS Decline	11	13.79	25.39	3.68	$651,005	0.32	288	192	14.41	-63.65	1.19	15.31
All—50 Stocks by High Pmargins	10.71	13.03	23.02	3.82	$585,378	0.32	281	199	13.11	-67.26	1.06	15.53
S&P 500	**10.61**	**11.87**	**16.82**	**4.72**	**$564,584**	**0.37**	**295**	**185**	**9.43**	**-44.73**	**1**	**13.53**
Market Leaders, 50 Stocks by Worst 1-Yr Rel Str	10.52	12.55	21.57	3.91	$545,735	0.32	273	207	11.83	-54.94	1.08	12.09
Market Leaders, 50 Stocks by High P/Book	10.35	11.97	19.2	4.18	$513,783	0.33	274	206	10.64	-50.01	1.06	14.82
Small Stocks—50 Stocks by High 1-Yr Rel Str	10.21	16.03	37.29	2.98	$487,995	0.28	280	200	21.25	-91.18	1.47	21.05
Small Stocks—50 Stocks by High 5-Yr EPS Gain	9.53	12.8	27.31	3.17	$381,829	0.26	277	203	15.87	-84.91	1.3	14.24
Large—50 Stocks by Percentage 1-Yr EPS Decline	9.47	11.32	20.46	3.7	$372,662	0.27	271	209	11.48	-44.06	1.07	10.18
Small Stocks—50 Stocks by Best PMargins	9.4	11.03	18.91	3.89	$363,389	0.28	295	185	11.67	-59.53	0.83	13.3
Large—50 Stocks by High ROE	9.38	11.52	21.91	3.53	$360,686	0.26	280	200	12.99	-61.89	1.16	12.98
Large—50 Stocks by 1-Yr Percentage EPS Gain	9.3	11.51	22.19	3.48	$350,153	0.26	283	197	13.28	-51.38	1.14	13.04
Market Leaders, 50 Stocks by High PE	9.16	10.85	19.49	3.72	$332,875	0.26	288	192	11.29	-57.7	1.07	15.83
Small Stocks, 50 Stocks by High ROE	9.15	13.28	30.78	2.93	$331,915	0.25	278	202	18.25	-75.93	1.37	17.87
Market Leaders, 50 Stocks by High PSR	8.9	10.43	18.56	3.74	$302,226	0.25	283	197	10.64	-59.06	1.05	13.84
Market Leaders, 50 Stocks by High PCFL	8.85	10.46	18.96	3.67	$296,750	0.25	283	197	11.02	-61.83	1.05	11.27
All—50 Stocks by High 5-Yr EPS Growth	8.65	11.83	26.84	2.97	$276,665	0.23	271	209	15.85	-84.72	1.34	13.96

(continued on next page)

343

T A B L E 23-1

All Strategies for Monthly Data Series, December 31, 1963–December 31, 2003—Strategies Sorted by Compound Average Annual Return *(Continued)*

Strategy	Geometric Mean	Arithmetic Mean	Standard Deviation	T-Stat	Ending Index Value	Sharpe Ratio	Pos Periods	Neg Periods	Downside Risk	Maximum Decline	Beta	Median
All—50 Stocks by 1-Yr Percentage Sales Decrease	8.25	11.64	27.85	2.82	$238,130	0.21	272	208	16.25	–75	1.23	9.38
All—50 Stocks by High ROE	7.94	11.74	29.31	2.71	$212,800	0.2	271	209	17.71	–74.82	1.34	13.85
U.S. Long-Term Corp Bonds	**7.76**	**8.18**	**9.58**	**5.61**	**$198,948**	**0.24**	**302**	**178**	**4.96**	**–22.37**	**0.19**	**6.41**
Inter. Term U.S. Gov't Bonds	**7.72**	**7.89**	**5.96**	**8.66**	**$196,030**	**0.33**	**338**	**141**	**2.72**	**–8.89**	**0.07**	**6.42**
Small Stocks, 50 Stocks by High PE	7.72	11.48	29.23	2.65	$195,864	0.2	278	202	17.5	–70.39	1.29	16.73
U.S. Long-Term Gov't Bonds	**7.53**	**8.07**	**10.91**	**4.86**	**$182,136**	**0.2**	**281**	**198**	**5.69**	**–20.97**	**0.17**	**5.28**
Large—50 Stocks by High P/Book	7.24	10.79	28.45	2.55	$163,772	0.18	271	209	16.74	–80.78	1.34	11.92
Large—50 Stocks by High PE	7.15	10.31	26.69	2.59	$158,626	0.17	274	206	15.9	–74.24	1.28	11.08
Large—50 Stocks by Worst 1-Yr Rel Str	6.96	9.99	26.26	2.55	$147,620	0.16	266	214	15.18	–77	1.25	6.35
All—50 Stocks by High PE	6.62	10.53	29.69	2.39	$130,076	0.16	277	203	18.08	–75.06	1.34	12.69
U.S. 30-Day Tbill	**6.03**	**6.03**	**0.81**	**48.43**	**$103,893**	**NA**	**480**	**0**	**0**	**0**	**0**	**5.46**
Small Stocks—50 Stocks by Worst 1-Yr EPS Growth	5.73	9.78	30.37	2.16	$92,979	0.13	264	216	18.11	–74.17	1.38	13.84
Large Industrials, 50 Stocks by High PCFL	5.39	9.23	29.25	2.11	$81,697	0.12	274	206	18.03	–84.35	1.38	10.23
Large—50 Stocks by High PSR	4.96	9.21	30.87	2	$69,365	0.11	272	208	19	–93.36	1.34	12.14
Large—50 Stocks by 1-Yr Percentage Sales Increase	4.87	8.39	27.81	2.01	$67,087	0.09	271	209	17.56	–89.45	1.37	12.18
U.S. Inflation	**4.57**	**4.57**	**1.16**	**25.53**	**$59,686**	**NA**	**432**	**28**	**0.18**	**–0.94**	**–0.01**	**3.85**
Small Stocks, 50 Stocks by Worst ROE	3.77	8.79	33.74	1.75	$43,983	0.09	270	210	20.86	–92.96	1.46	14.33
All, 50 Stocks by High P/Book	3.48	7.87	31.11	1.69	$39,229	0.06	264	216	19.89	–89.19	1.43	9.63
All Industrials, 50 Stocks by High PCFL	3.42	7.86	31.24	1.68	$38,397	0.06	276	204	20.07	–88.19	1.47	14.05
Small Stocks, 50 Stocks by High P/Book	3.42	8.35	33.18	1.69	$38,375	0.07	269	211	21.03	–92.49	1.44	11.91
Small Stocks, 50 Stocks by High PCFL	3.12	7.74	31.89	1.62	$34,173	0.06	270	210	20.58	–86.4	1.46	12.95
Small Stocks, 50 Stocks by Worst 1-Yr Rel Str	2.11	7.3	34.97	1.4	$23,071	0.04	243	237	20.23	–85.46	1.48	2.45
All—50 Stocks by Worst 1-Yr Rel Str	1.98	7.09	34.57	1.37	$21,898	0.03	243	237	20.1	–87.03	1.49	1.94
All—50 Stocks by 1-Yr Percentage Sales Increase	–0.17	4.78	32.74	0.96	$9,327	–0.04	255	225	21.72	–91.39	1.55	6.33
Small Stocks, 50 Stocks by High PSR	–2.16	2.18	30.18	0.47	$4,182	–0.13	262	218	21.05	–95.23	1.29	8.67
All—50 Stocks by High PSR	–2.66	1.71	30.2	0.37	$3,400	–0.15	259	221	21.29	–95.94	1.33	6.88
Small Stocks—50 Stocks by Worst PMargins	–2.73	2.03	31.81	0.42	$3,299	–0.13	253	227	21.77	–95.55	1.36	5.28

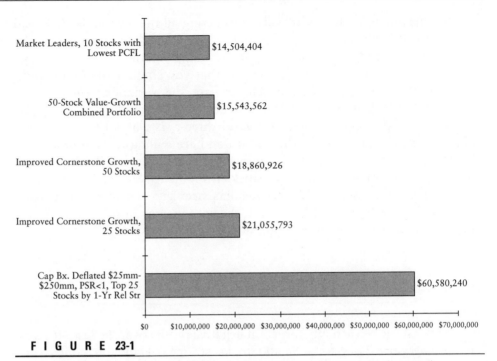

F I G U R E 23-1

The five strategies with the highest absolute returns (duplicate strategies eliminated), 1963–2003.

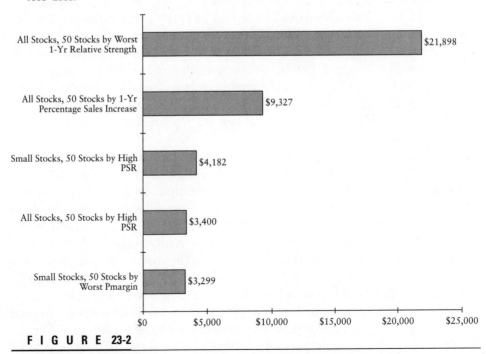

F I G U R E 23-2

The five strategies with the worst absolute performance, 1963–2003.

absolute maximum decline. Carefully considering all these variables will lead us to strategies that we can actually stick with, rather than being enticed by absolute returns and bushwhacked by the resulting volatility.

The first strategies on the list—those that you could actually use without putting yourself in constant danger—are the variations on the best growth strategies featured in Chapter 20, generally buying low price-to-sales stocks with improving earnings and good three-, six-, and 12-month price appreciation. If you want a higher return and are willing to take more risk, you can focus on small-cap stocks with these characteristics; if you want to bring risk down, focus on the larger stocks from the All Stocks universe. Also high on the list are several Market Leaders strategies where risk is reasonable—buying the 10 Market Leaders stocks with the lowest price-to-cashflow ratio, or the 25 stocks with the highest shareholder yield.

THE DOWNSIDE

Four of the strategies actually turned in negative results over the last 40 years! The booby prize goes to a Small Stocks strategy. Had you consistently invested in the 50 stocks from Small Stocks with the worst profit margins, you would have turned $10,000 invested in 1963 into $3,299, a loss of 2.73 percent per year. You also would have had to face the ignominy of a maximum decline of 96 percent. When I first saw this figure, my hypothesis was that it was due to the rash of junk initial public offerings (IPOs) that came to market in the 1980s and 1990s. Yet, when you analyze all the subperiods between 1963 and 2003, you see that this strategy consistently lands at the bottom of the list. Horrible margins lead to unsustainable business models—which lead to bankruptcy court. Thus, beware any small-cap stock where the margins are shaky.

The balance of the bottom 10 are the usual suspects in our rogues gallery of underperformance—the stocks with the richest valuations by price-to-sales, price-to-book, and price-to-cashflow ratios. All 10 underperformed a riskless investment in 30-day T-bills. For each capitalization category, these stocks always end up near the bottom of the absolute return list and at the top of the risk and maximum decline lists. In virtually every market environment save the most speculative ones, these are the toxic strategies you *must* avoid. Also at the bottom of the list are stocks with the worst one-year price appreciation and stocks from All Stocks with the best one-year gain in sales. All these should serve as red flags, helping you to weed out stocks you own or are considering as an investment. Now that we have seven years of real-time returns showing us the same performance seen in the original backtests, there is simply no legitimate reason for you to ever allow yourself to buy the most richly priced stocks. The prospects for such stocks are about as bad as the story is good. Investors who buy these stocks always brag about the handful that work out and conveniently forget the majority that don't. The evidence is painfully clear—if you habitually buy stocks with good stories but the highest multiples, you'll do much worse than the market.

In the absence of stories, investors look at the base rates. But let one dot.com stock in the door at the end of the 1990s, and many investors will jettison common sense and sound research, believing it's different this time. It isn't. I said this in the 1997 edition of this book, and my advice is the same today—tomorrow's hot "story" stocks may not be Internet darlings or large-cap tech stocks, but they share one thing in common—they will crash and burn.

RISK-ADJUSTED RETURNS

Table 23-2 ranks the strategies by risk-adjusted return (Sharpe ratio), and Figures 23-3 and 23-4 show the five strategies with the highest and lowest risk-adjusted returns. This is a much more appropriate table for most investors to look at when trying to decide which strategy is right for them. When you look only at absolute return, you're blind to how rocky the road was getting there. In a perfect world, investors would simply stick with long-term strategies that had the best returns with the highest base rates, but we all know that we don't live in that world. Risk matters.

In the real world, many investors check their portfolio's value daily and let the daily ups and downs inform their decisions, usually for the worse. In the real world, investors are far more frightened of short-term volatility than any rational economic model would suggest, but that very real fear must be accounted for in determining which strategy will be right for you. I have watched investors' reactions to short-term volatility over the last eight years, and I can tell you that it is far more predictable than markets. The example that follows—using one of the best-performing strategies—is illuminating.

A near perfect storm for small-cap stocks was brewing at the end of July in 1998—Asian markets were roiling, Russia was nearing default on its sovereign debt, and a giant hedge fund called Long-Term Capital Management was imploding. All those ingredients made for a bitter brew, and small-cap stocks were hit especially hard. In August 1998, the Russell 2000, a small-cap index, declined 19.42 percent and the O'Shaughnessy Cornerstone Growth Fund, a mutual fund that used the Cornerstone Growth Strategy to select its stocks, declined 26.60 percent. That was the worst decline in any single month the strategy ever experienced, save the market crash of October 1987.

T A B L E 23-2

All Strategies for Monthly Data Series, December 31, 1963–December 31, 2003—Strategies Sorted by Risk-Adjusted Return (Sharpe Ratio)

Strategy	Geometric Mean	Arithmetic Mean	Standard Deviation	T-Stat	Ending Index Value	Sharpe Ratio	Pos Periods	Neg Periods	Downside Risk	Maximum Decline	Beta	Median
Value Decile Intersection, 50 Stocks	17.69	19.11	18.38	7.15	$6,754,726	0.75	316	164	9.1	−37.68	0.83	24.3
100—Stock Value, Growth Portfolio	19.21	21.12	21.46	6.83	$11,275,830	0.74	311	169	10.74	−38.82	1.05	23.71
50—Stock Value, Growth Portfolio	20.17	22.4	23.38	6.69	$15,543,562	0.74	295	185	11.46	−40.52	1.08	25.02
Market Leaders, Top 25 Stocks by Shareholder Yield	18.05	19.58	19.22	7.03	$7,632,140	0.74	308	172	9.16	−32.22	0.92	21.6
Market Leaders, Top 50 Stocks by Shareholder Yield	17.02	18.39	18.09	6.97	$5,368,551	0.72	308	172	8.66	−29.05	0.9	18.36
CSG Top 100 Pmargin, Pos 3/6 Mth Price Chg, Top 25 Stocks by 1-Yr Rel Str	20.41	22.91	24.94	6.43	$16,818,255	0.71	313	167	12.11	−48.46	1.07	27.18
Market Leaders, Top 10 Stocks by Shareholder Yield	18.1	19.98	21.31	6.48	$7,772,433	0.69	309	171	10.35	−38.27	0.95	21.74
All—5-Yr Payout<50 Percent, Top 50 Stocks by Div Yld	17.08	18.58	19.02	6.71	$5,483,629	0.69	305	175	9.19	−44.16	0.84	20.1
Cap Bx. $25mm-$250mm, PSR<1, Top 25 Stocks by 1-Yr Rel Str	24.32	29.3	36.35	5.82	$60,580,240	0.67	304	176	16.99	−55.6	1.19	32.14
Improved CSG, Top 50 Stocks	20.75	23.97	28.31	5.97	$18,860,926	0.67	296	184	14.1	−55.25	1.19	24.61
Improved CSG, Top 100 Pmargin, Top 50 Stocks by 1-Yr Rel Str	18.14	20.22	22.36	6.26	$7,855,317	0.67	308	172	11.66	−39.56	1.02	23.46
All—Low PE,EPS Up—Top 50 Stocks by 1-Yr Rel Str	17.49	19.33	20.99	6.35	$6,305,417	0.67	310	170	10.66	−49.58	0.99	21.56
Market Leaders,10 Stocks by Low PCFL	19.96	22.88	27.29	5.88	$14,504,404	0.65	300	180	12.38	−45.15	1.11	20.23
All—Good Value, 50 Stocks by Low PCFL	17.53	19.47	21.84	6.16	$6,395,835	0.65	300	180	10.13	−42.59	0.92	20.06
CSV, Top 25 Stocks by Div Yield	16.24	17.72	18.82	6.45	$4,111,429	0.65	303	177	8.93	−28.5	0.85	17
Cap Bx. $25mm—$250, PSR<1, 3/6 Mth Price Chg Pos, Top 50 Stocks by High 1-Yr Rel Str	21.21	25.03	30.98	5.73	$21,983,019	0.64	305	175	15.58	−54.75	1.15	33.73
Original CSG, Top 100 Pmargin, Top 10 Stocks by 1-Yr Rel Str	18.61	21.15	24.9	5.91	$9,221,276	0.64	284	196	12.45	−37.6	0.94	21.97
Cornerstone Value	15.76	17.14	18.13	6.45	$3,481,988	0.64	301	179	8.74	−28.18	0.89	17.57
Cap Bx. $25mm-$250, PSR<1, 3/6 Mth Price Chg Pos, Top 25 Stocks by High 1-Yr Rel Str	22.7	27.58	35.8	5.53	$35,738,548	0.63	299	181	17.04	−61.29	1.15	35.88
Improved CSG, Top 25 Stocks	21.08	25.23	32.55	5.51	$21,055,793	0.62	290	190	15.7	−59.33	1.24	27.16

(continued on next page)

T A B L E 23-2

All Strategies for Monthly Data Series, December 31, 1963–December 31, 2003—Strategies Sorted by Risk-Adjusted Return (Sharpe Ratio) *(Continued)*

Strategy	Geometric Mean	Arithmetic Mean	Standard Deviation	T-Stat	Ending Index Value	Sharpe Ratio	Pos Periods	Neg Periods	Downside Risk	Maximum Decline	Beta	Median
Market Leaders, 50 Stocks by Low P/Book	16.63	18.51	21.21	6	$4,705,461	0.62	296	184	10.53	−37.08	1.04	17.72
Market Leaders, 50 Stocks by Low PE	16.55	18.36	20.83	6.06	$4,571,422	0.62	297	183	10.29	−35.13	1.02	17.56
Market Leaders, PSR<Avg, Top 50 Stocks by 1-Yr Rel Str	16.21	17.92	20.07	6.12	$4,078,153	0.62	304	176	10.2	−31.11	1.02	21.42
Improved CSG, Top 100 Pmargin, Top 25 Stocks by 1-Yr Rel Str	18.24	21.01	26	5.63	$8,127,684	0.61	300	180	13.3	−43.8	1.11	25.81
Market Leaders, PSR<avg, Top 25 Stocks by 1-Yr Rel Str	16.54	18.47	21.44	5.93	$4,561,805	0.61	304	176	10.93	−32.2	1.03	23.61
Market Leaders, 25 Stocks by Low PSR	16.41	18.28	21.07	5.96	$4,362,020	0.61	301	179	10.89	−43.34	0.99	19.94
Market Leaders, 50 Stocks by Low PSR	16.15	17.93	20.52	5.99	$3,981,957	0.61	307	173	10.67	−35.07	1.01	19.18
Market Leaders, 50 Stocks by Low PCFL	16.09	17.83	20.37	6	$3,906,209	0.61	305	175	10.23	−39.15	1	20.92
Small Stocks, PSR<1, 3/6 Mth Price Chg Pos, Top 50 Stocks by 1-Yr Rel Str	18.62	21.79	27.74	5.49	$9,249,548	0.6	291	189	14.45	−53.14	1.17	21.61
All, P/Book<1, Top 50 Stocks by 1-Yr Rel Str	17.68	20.28	24.97	5.64	$6,737,675	0.6	298	182	13.09	−49.66	1.04	23.39
All, Str Earn, Top 50 Stocks by 1-Yr Rel Str	16.94	19.15	23.03	5.74	$5,238,626	0.6	291	189	11.71	−50.93	1.12	20.29
All, Yld, Price up-50 Stocks by Low PSR	15.62	17.25	19.51	6.05	$3,318,667	0.6	306	174	10.48	−43.94	0.89	22.07
CSV, Top 10 Stocks by Dividend Yield	15.67	17.36	20.18	5.89	$3,378,075	0.59	293	187	9.47	−29.7	0.81	16.72
All, EPS Up 5 Yrs—Top 50 Stocks by 1-Yr Rel Str	16.91	19.39	24.41	5.49	$5,179,460	0.58	299	181	12.59	−52.73	1.16	23.85
Market Leaders, 10 Stocks by Low PSR	16.9	19.3	24.12	5.53	$5,159,969	0.58	295	185	12.07	−50.31	0.99	18.65
Small Stocks, Value Model 2	15.28	17.05	20.2	5.77	$2,954,941	0.57	301	179	11.03	−47.53	0.9	21.05
Original CSG, Top 25 Stocks by 1-Yr Rel Str	19.02	23.24	32.56	5.04	$10,575,472	0.56	283	197	16.26	−60.85	1.24	25.21
All-Earn Yld>5%—Top 50 Stocks by 1-Yr Rel Str	17.49	20.61	27.44	5.23	$6,305,425	0.56	288	192	14.38	−53.09	1.18	22.84
All Stocks, 5-yr EPS > Avg, Net Mrg > Avg, EPS > EPS—1-Yr, Top 50 Stocks by 1-Yr Rel Str	17.02	19.71	25.53	5.35	$5,380,301	0.56	293	187	13	−48.12	1.17	21.8
Large CSG, with 3/6 Mth Price Chg Pos, Top 50 Stocks by 1-Yr Rel Str	15.16	16.96	20.59	5.63	$2,831,275	0.56	303	177	10.83	−39.56	1	20.97

(continued on next page)

349

T A B L E 23-2

All Strategies for Monthly Data Series, December 31, 1963–December 31, 2003—Strategies Sorted by Risk-Adjusted Return (Sharpe Ratio) *(Continued)*

Strategy	Geometric Mean	Arithmetic Mean	Standard Deviation	T-Stat	Ending Index Value	Sharpe Ratio	Pos Periods	Neg Periods	Downside Risk	Maximum Decline	Beta	Median
Large Industrials, 50 Stocks by High Dividend Yield	14.01	15.28	17.29	5.99	$1,892,183	0.56	300	180	8.55	−28.95	0.81	15.83
Small Stocks, PSR<1, 3/6 Mth Price Chg Pos, Top 25 Stocks by 1-Yr Rel Str	18.55	22.51	31.29	5.06	$9,040,439	0.55	291	189	16.08	−52.82	1.22	28.85
Original Cornerstone Growth	17.77	21.16	28.74	5.14	$6,950,741	0.55	277	203	14.8	−60.13	1.21	19.28
Cap Bx. $25mm-$250, PSR<1, 3/6 Mth Price Chg Pos, Top 10 Stocks by High 1-Yr Rel Str	21.18	28.17	43.28	4.72	$21,707,627	0.54	281	199	20.6	−86.04	1.19	28.51
Market Leaders, PSR<Avg, Top 10 Stocks by 1-Yr Rel Str	15.6	17.77	22.74	5.37	$3,299,346	0.54	298	182	11.66	−38.21	0.96	18.38
Market Leaders, PCFL<Avg, 3/6 Mth Price Chg Pos, Top 50 Stocks by 1-Yr Rel Str	14.53	16.25	19.98	5.54	$2,275,626	0.54	301	179	10.72	−34.73	1.02	19.18
Large—Low PE—EPS Up—Top 50 Stocks by 1-Yr Rel Str	14.06	15.57	18.76	5.64	$1,931,668	0.54	303	177	9.75	−47.96	0.95	13.76
Small Stocks, 50 Stocks by Low PCFL	16.82	19.94	27.7	5	$5,023,916	0.53	285	195	13.78	−55.73	1.17	17.92
All, PSR<1, Top 50 Stocks by 1-Yr Rel Str	16.75	19.92	27.54	5.02	$4,909,077	0.53	281	199	14.69	−53.4	1.17	23.3
Small Stocks, 50 Stocks by Low PE	16.31	19	25.5	5.15	$4,214,230	0.53	297	183	13.03	−52.13	1.07	19.23
Lrg, 50 Stocks by Low P/Book	14.87	16.84	21.67	5.32	$2,562,423	0.53	298	182	10.96	−42.84	1.01	18.07
Large Industrial, 50 Stocks by Low PCFL	14.77	16.69	21.21	5.38	$2,476,539	0.53	294	186	11.17	−39.33	1.04	19.86
Market Leaders, Top 50 Stocks by 1-Yr Rel Str	14.75	16.63	21.03	5.4	$2,452,387	0.53	301	179	11.13	−41.19	1.06	19.8
Dow 10 Stocks by High Dividend Yield (Dogs of the Dow)	13.89	15.33	18.36	5.67	$1,817,710	0.53	291	189	9.21	−30.23	0.87	13.6
All Industrials, 50 Stocks by Low PCFL	15.53	17.89	23.7	5.19	$3,223,752	0.52	297	183	12.29	−44.22	1.05	18.73
Large, EPS up, PE<20—Top 50 Stocks by 1-Yr Rel Str	14.67	16.64	21.39	5.31	$2,391,513	0.52	296	184	11.54	−40.11	1.04	20.72
Large, 50 Stocks by Low PSR	14.64	16.58	21.29	5.32	$2,364,710	0.52	297	183	11.39	−40.71	1.03	16.52
Large, 50 Stocks by Low PE	14.31	16.04	20.16	5.42	$2,103,738	0.52	293	187	10.58	−39.71	0.96	17.57
Large, PE<20—50 Stocks by High 1-Yr Rel Str	14.63	16.66	21.74	5.24	$2,353,621	0.51	303	177	11.86	−39.48	1.06	21.35
Large, Strong Earn, Top 50 Stocks by 1-Yr Rel Str	14.16	15.98	20.68	5.26	$1,997,588	0.51	285	195	10.71	−49.32	1.08	17.06

(continued on next page)

T A B L E 23-2

All Strategies for Monthly Data Series, December 31, 1963–December 31, 2003—Strategies Sorted by Risk-Adjusted Return (Sharpe Ratio) *(Continued)*

Strategy	Geometric Mean	Arithmetic Mean	Standard Deviation	T-Stat	Ending Index Value	Sharpe Ratio	Pos Periods	Neg Periods	Downside Risk	Maximum Decline	Beta	Median
Lrg, 5-Yr payout<50 Percent—50 Stocks by High Dividend Yield	13.89	15.51	19.41	5.43	$1,816,627	0.51	294	186	10.19	–46.01	0.94	16.92
Market Leaders, 50 Stocks by Worst 5-Yr EPS Gain	13.62	15.15	18.77	5.47	$1,651,414	0.51	291	189	10.02	–32.82	0.99	18.03
Market Leaders, 50 Stocks by Best 5-Yr EPS Gain	14.52	16.61	22.27	5.1	$2,267,445	0.5	288	192	11.31	–46.47	1.17	17.16
Market Leaders, PSR<Avg, 3/6 Mth Price Chg Pos, Top 50 Stocks by 1-Yr Rel Str	14.14	16.01	20.85	5.23	$1,983,979	0.5	296	184	11.31	–45.23	1.06	20
Large Stock CSG 50 Stocks	14.12	16.06	21.26	5.15	$1,970,929	0.5	298	182	11.4	–41.03	1.05	18.49
Large, 50 Stocks by High Dividend Yield	12.52	13.61	16	5.73	$1,121,835	0.5	294	186	7.53	–32.97	0.61	10.82
All, 50 Stocks by Low PSR	15.38	18.2	26.13	4.8	$3,054,908	0.49	283	197	13.33	–52.15	1.09	20.77
Large Stocks CSG 25 Stocks	14.61	16.92	23.34	4.97	$2,340,370	0.49	290	190	12.41	–46.13	1.11	20.05
Market Leaders, 50 Stocks by Worst Pmargin	13.63	15.35	19.93	5.23	$1,659,290	0.49	296	184	10.91	–52.22	1.04	17.24
Market Leaders	**12.77**	**14.05**	**17.06**	**5.55**	**$1,225,022**	**0.49**	**297**	**183**	**9.2**	**–38.98**	**0.96**	**17.02**
All, PSR<1, Top 25 Stocks by 1-Yr Rel Str	16.24	20.19	31	4.54	$4,118,890	0.48	288	192	16.27	–57.73	1.22	19.87
Small Stocks, 50 Stocks by Low PSR	15.38	18.36	26.9	4.71	$3,051,506	0.48	290	190	13.81	–52.87	1.11	21.59
All, 50 Stocks by Low PE	14.89	17.45	24.75	4.84	$2,581,104	0.48	288	192	12.83	–50.76	1.07	16.9
Large, PSR<1—50 Stocks by 1-Yr Rel Str	13.64	15.56	21.04	5.03	$1,666,318	0.48	295	185	11.5	–37.73	1.03	16.09
Large, Low PSR-EPS Up—50 Stocks by 1-Yr Rel Str	13.12	14.7	19.11	5.21	$1,385,160	0.48	290	190	10.12	–51.6	0.98	15.38
Market Leaders, 50 Stocks by High Pmargin	12.63	13.98	17.56	5.37	$1,166,320	0.48	297	183	9.31	–38.51	0.97	16.73
All, 50 Stocks by Low P/Book	15.66	18.98	28.8	4.57	$3,365,965	0.47	287	193	13.96	–48.55	1.17	18.13
Small Stocks, ROE>Avg. 3/6 Mth Price Chg Pos, Top 50 Stocks by 1-Yr Rel Str	15.8	20.15	32.63	4.31	$3,530,758	0.46	295	185	17.48	–70.56	1.33	25.77
Market Leaders, ROE>Avg, 3/6 Mth Price Chg Pos, Top 50 Stocks by 1-Yr Rel Str	13.13	14.97	20.65	4.92	$1,390,238	0.46	287	193	11.23	–48.63	1.07	17.45
Small Stocks 50 Stocks by High Dividend Yield	12.64	14.12	18.5	5.16	$1,166,914	0.46	296	184	9.92	–49.29	0.8	14.51
Market Leaders, 50 Stocks by High ROE	12.63	14.14	18.63	5.13	$1,165,770	0.46	289	191	10.05	–50	1.02	15.26
All Industrials, 50 Stocks by High Dividend Yield	12.49	13.87	17.89	5.23	$1,107,592	0.46	298	182	9.42	–57.23	0.72	12.83

(continued on next page)

351

T A B L E 23-2

All Strategies for Monthly Data Series, December 31, 1963–December 31, 2003—Strategies Sorted by Risk-Adjusted Return (Sharpe Ratio) (Continued)

Strategy	Geometric Mean	Arithmetic Mean	Standard Deviation	T-Stat	Ending Index Value	Sharpe Ratio	Pos Periods	Neg Periods	Downside Risk	Maximum Decline	Beta	Median
Small Stocks, 50 Stocks by Low P/Book	14.97	18.35	28.92	4.39	$2,654,859	0.45	279	201	14.31	-52	1.17	18.46
Large, ROE>15, Top 50 Stocks by 1-Yr Rel Str	14.05	16.95	26.27	4.43	$1,920,627	0.44	285	195	14	-51.57	1.21	17.2
Small Stocks, PSR<Avg, 3/6 Mth Price Chg Pos, Top 50 Stocks by 1-Yr Rel Str	15.08	19.44	32.45	4.17	$2,757,808	0.43	289	191	17.61	-76.71	1.26	21.04
Small Stocks, 50 Stocks by Best 1-Yr EPS Growth	14.16	17.43	27.83	4.31	$1,995,556	0.43	287	193	15.4	-66.78	1.23	20.19
Small Stocks, 50 Stocks by Worst 5-Yr EPS Gain	13.25	15.64	23.41	4.55	$1,449,185	0.43	295	185	13.41	-52.04	1.05	19.5
Market Leaders, 50 Stocks by Worst 1-Yr EPS Change	12.51	14.26	20.09	4.8	$1,114,960	0.43	295	185	10.8	-48.9	1.05	14.65
Market Leaders, 50 Stocks by Low ROE	12.51	14.23	19.87	4.84	$1,114,342	0.43	293	187	10.84	-50.37	1.03	14.23
Large, 50 Stocks by Best 1-Yr Rel Str	13.87	17.44	29.36	4.1	$1,805,450	0.41	280	200	15.56	-71.51	1.27	20.17
Large, 50 Stocks by High Pmargin	12.69	14.86	22.53	4.48	$1,188,767	0.41	286	194	12.01	-57.17	1.13	11.22
Small Stocks	**12.57**	**14.69**	**22.02**	**4.53**	**$1,139,641**	**0.41**	**290**	**190**	**12.5**	**-53.82**	**1.07**	**18.55**
Market Leaders, 50 Stocks by Best 1-Yr EPS Gains	11.94	13.64	19.6	4.69	$911,483	0.41	290	190	11.03	-39.04	1.05	16.06
All, ROE>15, Top 50 Stocks by 1-Yr Rel Str	14.13	18.65	33.18	3.91	$1,975,512	0.4	280	200	17.88	-65.82	1.39	24.96
Small Stocks, PCFL<Avg. 3/6 Mth Price Chg Pos, Top 50 Stocks by 1-Yr Rel Str	13.97	18.69	33.64	3.86	$1,865,835	0.4	291	189	18.5	-87.48	1.27	22.06
All Stocks	**12.02**	**13.82**	**20.23**	**4.61**	**$936,071**	**0.4**	**286**	**194**	**11.53**	**-50.12**	**1.05**	**17.96**
All, 50 Stocks by Percentage 1-Yr EPS Gain	12.77	15.8	26.54	4.07	$1,225,226	0.39	287	193	15.02	-65.54	1.2	19.82
Large, 50 Stocks by 1-Yr Percentage Sales Decline	11.96	13.89	21	4.47	$917,141	0.39	285	195	11.49	-45.39	1.07	12.29
Large Stocks	**11.2**	**12.63**	**17.96**	**4.72**	**$697,718**	**0.39**	**289**	**191**	**10.15**	**-46.59**	**1.01**	**15.23**
All, Pmargin>20—50 Stocks by 1-Yr Rel Str	13.9	19.6	37.7	3.64	$1,825,902	0.38	287	193	19.95	-81.66	1.44	20.73
S&P 500	**10.61**	**11.87**	**16.82**	**4.72**	**$564,584**	**0.37**	**295**	**185**	**9.43**	**-44.73**	**1**	**13.53**
All, EPS Chg>25—50 Stocks by 1-Yr Rel Str	13.2	18.68	36.74	3.55	$1,424,187	0.36	288	192	19.94	-83.88	1.4	23.31

(continued on next page)

352

T A B L E 23-2

All Strategies for Monthly Data Series, December 31, 1963–December 31, 2003—Strategies Sorted by Risk-Adjusted Return (Sharpe Ratio) *(Continued)*

Strategy	Geometric Mean	Arithmetic Mean	Standard Deviation	T-Stat	Ending Index Value	Sharpe Ratio	Pos Periods	Neg Periods	Downside Risk	Maximum Decline	Beta	Median
Large, 50 Stocks by Best 5-Yr EPS Growth	11.42	14.18	25.42	3.79	$755,599	0.34	275	205	13.9	−64.09	1.3	11.66
Market Leaders, 50 Stocks by High P/Book	10.35	11.97	19.2	4.18	$513,783	0.33	274	206	10.64	−50.01	1.06	14.82
Inter. Term U.S. Gov't Bonds	**7.72**	**7.89**	**5.96**	**8.66**	**$196,030**	**0.33**	**338**	**141**	**2.72**	**−8.89**	**0.07**	**6.42**
All, 50 Stocks by Percentage 1-Yr EPS decline	11	13.79	25.39	3.68	$651,005	0.32	288	192	14.41	−63.65	1.19	15.31
All, 50 Stocks by High Pmargins	10.71	13.03	23.02	3.82	$585,378	0.32	281	199	13.11	−67.26	1.06	15.53
Market Leaders, 50 Stocks by Worst 1-Yr Rel Str	10.52	12.55	21.57	3.91	$545,735	0.32	273	207	11.83	−54.94	1.08	12.09
All, 50 Stocks by Best 1-Yr Rel Str	11.13	16.88	37.44	3.13	$681,201	0.3	281	199	20.61	−89.4	1.47	18.68
Small Stocks, 50 Stocks by High 1-Yr Rel Str	10.21	16.03	37.29	2.98	$487,995	0.28	280	200	21.25	−91.18	1.47	21.05
Small Stocks, 50 Stocks by Best PMargins	9.4	11.03	18.91	3.89	$363,389	0.28	295	185	11.67	−59.53	0.83	13.3
Large, 50 Stocks by Percentage 1-Yr EPS Decline	9.47	11.32	20.46	3.7	$372,662	0.27	271	209	11.48	−44.06	1.07	10.18
Small Stocks, 50 Stocks by High 5-Yr EPS Gain	9.53	12.8	27.31	3.17	$381,829	0.26	277	203	15.87	−84.91	1.3	14.24
Large, 50 Stocks by High ROE	9.38	11.52	21.91	3.53	$360,686	0.26	280	200	12.99	−61.89	1.16	12.98
Large, 50 Stocks by 1-Yr Percentage EPS Gain	9.3	11.51	22.19	3.48	$350,153	0.26	283	197	13.28	−51.38	1.14	13.04
Market Leaders, 50 Stocks by High PE	9.16	10.85	19.49	3.72	$332,875	0.26	288	192	11.29	−57.7	1.07	15.83
Small Stocks, 50 Stocks by High ROE	9.15	13.28	30.78	2.93	$331,915	0.25	278	202	18.25	−75.93	1.37	17.87
Market Leaders, 50 Stocks by High PSR	8.9	10.43	18.56	3.74	$302,226	0.25	283	197	10.64	−59.06	1.05	13.84
Market Leaders, 50 Stocks by High PCFL	8.85	10.46	18.96	3.67	$296,750	0.25	283	197	11.02	−61.83	1.05	11.27
U.S. Long-Term Corp Bonds	**7.76**	**8.18**	**9.58**	**5.61**	**$198,948**	**0.24**	**302**	**178**	**4.96**	**−22.37**	**0.19**	**6.41**
All, 50 Stocks by High 5-Yr EPS Growth	8.65	11.83	26.84	2.97	$276,665	0.23	271	209	15.85	−84.72	1.34	13.96
All, 50 Stocks by 1-Yr Percentage Sales Decrease	8.25	11.64	27.85	2.82	$238,130	0.21	272	208	16.25	−75	1.23	9.38
All, 50 Stocks by High ROE	7.94	11.74	29.31	2.71	$212,800	0.2	271	209	17.71	−74.82	1.34	13.85
Small Stocks, 50 Stocks by High PE	7.72	11.48	29.23	2.65	$195,864	0.2	278	202	17.5	−70.39	1.29	16.73
U.S. Long-Term Gov't Bonds	**7.53**	**8.07**	**10.91**	**4.86**	**$182,136**	**0.2**	**281**	**198**	**5.69**	**−20.97**	**0.17**	**5.28**

(continued on next page)

353

T A B L E 23-2

All Strategies for Monthly Data Series, December 31, 1963–December 31, 2003—Strategies Sorted by Risk-Adjusted Return (Sharpe Ratio) *(Continued)*

Strategy	Geometric Mean	Arithmetic Mean	Standard Deviation	T-Stat	Ending Index Value	Sharpe Ratio	Pos Periods	Neg Periods	Downside Risk	Maximum Decline	Beta	Median
Large, 50 Stocks by High P/Book	7.24	10.79	28.45	2.55	$163,772	0.18	271	209	16.74	−80.78	1.34	11.92
Large, 50 Stocks by High PE	7.15	10.31	26.69	2.59	$158,626	0.17	274	206	15.9	−74.24	1.28	11.08
Large, 50 Stocks by Worst 1-Yr Rel Str	6.96	9.99	26.26	2.55	$147,620	0.16	266	214	15.18	−77	1.25	6.35
All, 50 Stocks by High PE	6.62	10.53	29.69	2.39	$130,076	0.16	277	203	18.08	−75.06	1.34	12.69
Small Stocks, 50 Stocks by Worst 1-Yr EPS Growth	5.73	9.78	30.37	2.16	$92,979	0.13	264	216	18.11	−74.17	1.38	13.84
Large Industrials, 50 Stocks by High PCFL	5.39	9.23	29.25	2.11	$81,697	0.12	274	206	18.03	−84.35	1.38	10.23
Large, 50 Stocks by High PSR	4.96	9.21	30.87	2	$69,365	0.11	272	208	19	−93.36	1.34	12.14
Large, 50 Stocks by 1-Yr Percentage Sales Increase	4.87	8.39	27.81	2.01	$67,087	0.09	271	209	17.56	−89.45	1.37	12.18
Small Stocks, 50 Stocks by Worst ROE	3.77	8.79	33.74	1.75	$43,983	0.09	270	210	20.86	−92.96	1.46	14.33
Small Stocks, 50 Stocks by High P/Book	3.42	8.35	33.18	1.69	$38,375	0.07	269	211	21.03	−92.49	1.44	11.91
All, 50 Stocks by High P/Book	3.48	7.87	31.11	1.69	$39,229	0.06	264	216	19.89	−89.19	1.43	9.63
All Industrials, 50 Stocks by High PCFL	3.42	7.86	31.24	1.68	$38,397	0.06	276	204	20.07	−88.19	1.47	14.05
Small Stocks, 50 Stocks by High PCFL	3.12	7.74	31.89	1.62	$34,173	0.06	270	210	20.58	−86.4	1.46	12.95
Small Stocks, 50 Stocks by Worst 1-Yr Rel Str	2.11	7.3	34.97	1.4	$23,071	0.04	243	237	20.23	−85.46	1.48	2.45
All, 50 Stocks by Worst 1-Yr Rel Str	1.98	7.09	34.57	1.37	$21,898	0.03	243	237	20.1	−87.03	1.49	1.94
All, 50 Stocks by 1-Yr Percentage Sales Increase	−0.17	4.78	32.74	0.96	$9,327	−0.04	255	225	21.72	−91.39	1.55	6.33
Small Stocks, 50 Stocks by High PSR	−2.16	2.18	30.18	0.47	$4,182	−0.13	262	218	21.05	−95.23	1.29	8.67
Small Stocks, 50 Stocks by Worst PMargins	−2.73	2.03	31.81	0.42	$3,299	−0.13	253	227	21.77	−95.55	1.36	5.28
All, 50 Stocks by High PSR	−2.66	1.71	30.2	0.37	$3,400	−0.15	259	221	21.29	−95.94	1.33	6.88
U.S. 30-Day Tbill	**6.03**	**6.03**	**0.81**	**48.43**	**$103,893**	**NA**	**480**	**0**	**0**	**0**	**0**	**5.46**
U.S. Inflation	**4.57**	**4.57**	**1.16**	**25.53**	**$59,686**	**NA**	**432**	**28**	**0.18**	**−0.94**	**−0.01**	**3.85**

354

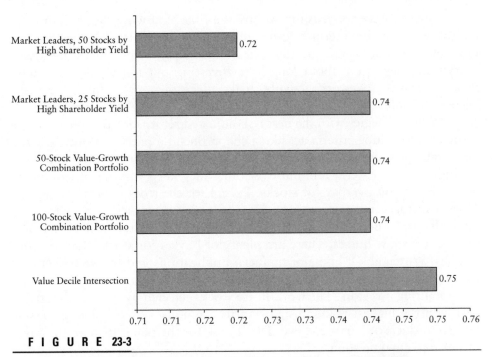

F I G U R E 23-3

The five strategies with the highest risk-adjusted return (Sharpe ratio), 1963–2003.

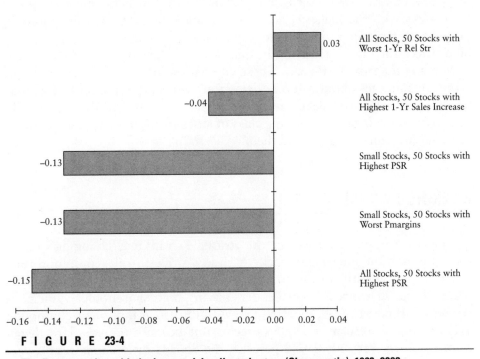

F I G U R E 23-4

The five strategies with the lowest risk-adjusted return (Sharpe ratio), 1963–2003.

Now, did investors rush in to buy the fund, knowing that the strategy had an excellent long-term return and excellent base rates? Nope. For the most part, they sold. Because that *one month* was horrible, investors tossed everything they knew about long-term investing out the window. Because that's the way investors actually make decisions, risk-adjusted returns become far more relevant for the average investor than absolute returns.

All the strategies with the best risk-adjusted returns include one or more value criteria. Value criteria act like a chaperone at a party, making sure you don't fall for some sexy stock with a great story. They may keep you from having some short-term fun, but over time, they keep you out of trouble by never letting you overpay for stocks. Except for the stocks selected from the Market Leaders universe, most of the stocks picked by these top-performing strategies aren't household names. Value criteria choose stocks that are work-horses, not show-horses. There are plenty of buyers for stocks that are continually written about in major financial publications and whose officers are treated like celebrities. That's what pushes their prices to levels that end up disappointing investors. The work-horse stocks selected by most of the strategies with the highest risk-adjusted returns are nonsexy issues like Riverside Forest Products or Smart & Final. Don't look for their chairman on the cover of *Fortune* anytime soon.

You will, however, probably find magazine features on companies with the worst risk-adjusted returns. Four of the five worst performing strategies buy stocks with the highest price-to-sales, price-to-cashflow, price-to-book, or price-to-earnings ratios. These glamour stocks command unreasonably high prices for their underlying businesses, and their investors believe that trees really *do* grow to the sky. These companies' prices are based on hope, greed, or fantasies about a future that rarely comes to pass. KFX, Inc. may be a great provider of "clean energy" technology, but is it really worth 4,411 times revenues? *It* may be, but the class of stocks with these characteristics is *not*, and investors should avoid them.

RANKING BY SHARPE RATIO

Sorting by Sharpe ratio, we see the strategie's rankings changing quite a bit. Although the micro-cap stocks with low price-to-sales and good relative strength are still in the top 10, they have been elbowed out of first place by the 25-stock Market Leaders having high shareholder value. The strategy turned $10,000, invested in 1963, into $7.6 million, a compound average annual return of 18.05 percent. But because the standard deviation of return was only 19.22 percent, the Sharpe ratio came in at a very high 74. In other words, this low-volatility strategy provided the most bang for the risk buck. The rest of the list continues to be dominated by strategies that marry low price-to-sales ratios to high relative strength. We also find an All Stocks value strategy here, comprised of stocks with dividend payout less than 50 percent and then those with the highest dividend yield.

THE WORST RISK-ADJUSTED RETURNS

No surprises here—the strategies with the worst risk-adjusted returns also had the worst absolute returns. Because they took such huge risks to deliver their horrible numbers, they land at the bottom of the list. Place on the list has been swapped, with the highest price-to-sales ratios stocks from All Stocks now earning the bottom of the risk-adjusted barrel. But it's the same rogues' gallery, all to be avoided at all costs.

DOWNSIDE RISK

What immediately jumps out at you when you look at the strategies ranked by downside risk is how high the broader indexes score. Only six strategies had lower downside risk than the Market Leaders universe, and all but one of them are derived from Market Leaders itself. All of them include either dividend yield or shareholder yield. This is not surprising. Cash dividend payments and share buyback programs cushion investors against the ups and downs of share price, so it makes sense that they all had lower downside risk than the broader Market Leaders universe. Investors who are concerned about a portfolio's downside should study this list very carefully, while keeping in mind that, when portfolios have low downside risk, they often have more limited upside potential. Thankfully, that was not the case with all but one of the top strategies ranked by downside risk.

The lowest downside risk was found in buying the 50 stocks from the Large Stocks universe (including utility stocks) having the highest dividend yield. Given that dividend yield is the final factor, this portfolio is usually loaded up with utility stocks, which are historically very low in volatility. But the lower volatility also led to returns lower than the Market Leaders universe itself, with the strategy compounding at 12.52 percent per year compared to 12.77 percent for Market Leaders. It was nevertheless ahead of the returns for the S&P 500, Large Stocks, All Stocks, and Small Stocks. All the other strategies with the lowest downside risk also provided excellent overall returns. Table 23-3 summarizes the downside ratios for these portfolios.

T A B L E 23-3

All Strategies for Monthly Data Series, December 31, 1963–December 31, 2003—Strategies Sorted by Downside Ratio, Least Risky to Most

Strategy	Geometric Mean	Arithmetic Mean	Standard Deviation	T-Stat	Ending Index Value	Sharpe Ratio	Pos Periods	Neg Periods	Downside Risk	Maximum Decline	Beta	Median
U.S. 30-Day Tbill	**6.03**	**6.03**	**0.81**	**48.43**	**$103,893**	**NA**	**480**	**0**	**0**	**0**	**0**	**5.46**
U.S. Inflation	**4.57**	**4.57**	**1.16**	**25.53**	**$59,686**	**NA**	**432**	**28**	**0.18**	**-0.94**	**-0.01**	**3.85**
Inter. Term U.S. Gov't Bonds	**7.72**	**7.89**	**5.96**	**8.66**	**$196,030**	**0.33**	**338**	**141**	**2.72**	**-8.89**	**0.07**	**6.42**
U.S. Long-Term Corp Bonds	**7.76**	**8.18**	**9.58**	**5.61**	**$198,948**	**0.24**	**302**	**178**	**4.96**	**-22.37**	**0.19**	**6.41**
U.S. Long-Term Gov't Bonds	**7.53**	**8.07**	**10.91**	**4.86**	**$182,136**	**0.2**	**281**	**198**	**5.69**	**-20.97**	**0.17**	**5.28**
Large, 50 Stocks by High Dividend Yield	12.52	13.61	16	5.73	$1,121,835	0.5	294	186	7.53	-32.97	0.61	10.82
Large Industrials, 50 Stocks by High Dividend Yield	14.01	15.28	17.29	5.99	$1,892,183	0.56	300	180	8.55	-28.95	0.81	15.83
Market Leaders, Top 50 Stocks by Shareholder Yield	17.02	18.39	18.09	6.97	$5,368,551	0.72	308	172	8.66	-29.05	0.9	18.36
Cornerstone Value	15.76	17.14	18.13	6.45	$3,481,988	0.64	301	179	8.74	-28.18	0.89	17.57
CSV, Top 25 Stocks by Div Yield	16.24	17.72	18.82	6.45	$4,111,429	0.65	303	177	8.93	-28.5	0.85	17
Value Decile Intersection, 50 Stocks	17.69	19.11	18.38	7.15	$6,754,726	0.75	316	164	9.1	-37.68	0.83	24.3
Market Leaders, Top 25 Stocks by Shareholder Yield	18.05	19.58	19.22	7.03	$7,632,140	0.74	308	172	9.16	-32.22	0.92	21.6
All, 5-Yr Payout-50 Percent, Top 50 Stocks by Div Yld	17.08	18.58	19.02	6.71	$5,483,629	0.69	305	175	9.19	-44.16	0.84	20.1
Market Leaders	**12.77**	**14.05**	**17.06**	**5.55**	**$1,225,022**	**0.49**	**297**	**183**	**9.2**	**-38.98**	**0.96**	**17.02**
Dow 10 Stocks by High Dividend Yield (Dogs of the Dow)	13.89	15.33	18.36	5.67	$1,817,710	0.53	291	189	9.21	-30.23	0.87	13.6
Market Leaders, 50 Stocks by High Pmargin	12.63	13.98	17.56	5.37	$1,166,320	0.48	297	183	9.31	-38.51	0.97	16.73
All Industrials, 50 Stocks by High Dividend Yield	12.49	13.87	17.89	5.23	$1,107,592	0.46	298	182	9.42	-57.23	0.72	12.83
S&P 500	**10.61**	**11.87**	**16.82**	**4.72**	**$564,584**	**0.37**	**295**	**185**	**9.43**	**-44.73**	**1**	**13.53**
CSV, Top 10 Stocks by Dividend Yield	15.67	17.36	20.18	5.89	$3,378,075	0.59	293	187	9.47	-29.7	0.81	16.72
Large, Low PE-EPS Up—Top 50 Stocks by 1-Yr Rel Str	14.06	15.57	18.76	5.64	$1,931,668	0.54	303	177	9.75	-47.96	0.95	13.76
Small Stocks 50 Stocks by High Dividend Yield	12.64	14.12	18.5	5.16	$1,166,914	0.46	296	184	9.92	-49.29	0.8	14.51
Market Leaders, 50 Stocks by Worst 5-Yr EPS Gain	13.62	15.15	18.77	5.47	$1,651,414	0.51	291	189	10.02	-32.82	0.99	18.03
Market Leaders, 50 Stocks by High ROE	12.63	14.14	18.63	5.13	$1,165,770	0.46	289	191	10.05	-50	1.02	15.26

(continued on next page)

T A B L E 23-3

All Strategies for Monthly Data Series, December 31, 1963–December 31, 2003—Strategies Sorted by Downside Ratio, Least Risky to Most *(Continued)*

Strategy	Geometric Mean	Arithmetic Mean	Standard Deviation	T-Stat	Ending Index Value	Sharpe Ratio	Pos Periods	Neg Periods	Downside Risk	Maximum Decline	Beta	Median
Large, Low PSR-EPS Up—50 Stocks by 1-Yr Rel Str	13.12	14.7	19.11	5.21	$1,385,160	0.48	290	190	10.12	-51.6	0.98	15.38
All, Good Value—50 Stocks by Low PCFL	17.53	19.47	21.84	6.16	$6,395,835	0.65	300	180	10.13	-42.59	0.92	20.06
Large Stocks	**11.2**	**12.63**	**17.96**	**4.72**	**$697,718**	**0.39**	**289**	**191**	**10.15**	**-46.59**	**1.01**	**15.23**
Lrg, 5-Yr Payout-50 Percent-50 Stocks by High Dividend Yield	13.89	15.51	19.41	5.43	$1,816,627	0.51	294	186	10.19	-46.01	0.94	16.92
Market Leaders, PSR<Avg, Top 50 Stocks by 1-Yr Rel Str	16.21	17.92	20.07	6.12	$4,078,153	0.62	304	176	10.2	-31.11	1.02	21.42
Market Leaders, 50 Stocks by Low PCFL	16.09	17.83	20.37	6	$3,906,209	0.61	305	175	10.23	-39.15	1	20.92
Market Leaders, 50 Stocks by Low PE	16.55	18.36	20.83	6.06	$4,571,422	0.62	297	183	10.29	-35.13	1.02	17.56
Market Leaders, Top 10 Stocks by Shareholder Yield	18.1	19.98	21.31	6.48	$7,772,433	0.69	309	171	10.35	-38.27	0.95	21.74
All, Yld, Price up-50 Stocks by Low PSR	15.62	17.25	19.51	6.05	$3,318,667	0.6	306	174	10.48	-43.94	0.89	22.07
Market Leaders, 50 Stocks by Low P/Book	16.63	18.51	21.21	6	$4,705,461	0.62	296	184	10.53	-37.08	1.04	17.72
Large, 50 Stocks by Low PE	14.31	16.04	20.16	5.42	$2,103,738	0.52	293	187	10.58	-39.71	0.96	17.57
Market Leaders, 50 Stocks by High P/Book	10.35	11.97	19.2	4.18	$513,783	0.33	274	206	10.64	-50.01	1.06	14.82
Market Leaders, 50 Stocks by High PSR	8.9	10.43	18.56	3.74	$302,226	0.25	283	197	10.64	-59.06	1.05	13.84
All, Low PE, EPS Up—Top 50 Stocks by 1-Yr Rel Str	17.49	19.33	20.99	6.35	$6,305,417	0.67	310	170	10.66	-49.58	0.99	21.56
Market Leaders, 50 Stocks by Low PSR	16.15	17.93	20.52	5.99	$3,981,957	0.61	307	173	10.67	-35.07	1.01	19.18
Large, Strong Earn, Top 50 Stocks by 1-Yr Rel Str	14.16	15.98	20.68	5.26	$1,997,588	0.51	285	195	10.71	-49.32	1.08	17.06
Market Leaders, PCFL<Avg, 3/6 Mth Price Chg Pos, Top 50 Stocks by 1-Yr Rel Str	14.53	16.25	19.98	5.54	$2,275,626	0.54	301	179	10.72	-34.73	1.02	19.18
100-Stock Value-Growth Portfolio	19.21	21.12	21.46	6.83	$11,275,830	0.74	311	169	10.74	-38.82	1.05	23.71
Market Leaders, 50 Stocks by Worst 1-Yr EPS Change	12.51	14.26	20.09	4.8	$1,114,960	0.43	295	185	10.8	-48.9	1.05	14.65
Large CSG, with 3/6 Mth Price Chg Pos, Top 50 Stocks by 1-Yr Rel Str	15.16	16.96	20.59	5.63	$2,831,275	0.56	303	177	10.83	-39.56	1	20.97
Market Leaders, 50 Stocks by Low ROE	12.51	14.23	19.87	4.84	$1,114,342	0.43	293	187	10.84	-50.37	1.03	14.23

(continued on next page)

359

T A B L E 23-3

All Strategies for Monthly Data Series, December 31, 1963–December 31, 2003—Strategies Sorted by Downside Ratio, Least Risky to Most *(Continued)*

Strategy	Geometric Mean	Arithmetic Mean	Standard Deviation	T-Stat	Ending Index Value	Sharpe Ratio	Pos Periods	Neg Periods	Downside Risk	Maximum Decline	Beta	Median
Market Leaders, 25 Stocks by Low PSR	16.41	18.28	21.07	5.96	$4,362,020	0.61	301	179	10.89	–43.34	0.99	19.94
Market Leaders, 50 Stocks by Worst Pmargin	13.63	15.35	19.93	5.23	$1,659,290	0.49	296	184	10.91	–52.22	1.04	17.24
Market Leaders, PSR<Avg, Top 25 Stocks by 1-Yr Rel Str	16.54	18.47	21.44	5.93	$4,561,805	0.61	304	176	10.93	–32.2	1.03	23.61
Lrg, 50 Stocks by Low P/Book	14.87	16.84	21.67	5.32	$2,562,423	0.53	298	182	10.96	–42.84	1.01	18.07
Market Leaders, 50 Stocks by High PCFL	8.85	10.46	18.96	3.67	$296,750	0.25	283	197	11.02	–61.83	1.05	11.27
Small Stocks, Value Model 2	15.28	17.05	20.2	5.77	$2,954,941	0.57	301	179	11.03	–47.53	0.9	21.05
Market Leaders, 50 Stocks by Best 1-Yr EPS Gains	11.94	13.64	19.6	4.69	$911,483	0.41	290	190	11.03	–39.04	1.05	16.06
Market Leaders, Top 50 Stocks by 1-Yr Rel Str	14.75	16.63	21.03	5.4	$2,452,387	0.53	301	179	11.13	–41.19	1.06	19.8
Large Industrial, 50 Stocks by Low PCFL	14.77	16.69	21.21	5.38	$2,476,539	0.53	294	186	11.17	–39.33	1.04	19.86
Market Leaders, ROE>Avg, 3/6 Mth Price Chg Pos, Top 50 Stocks by 1-Yr Rel Str	13.13	14.97	20.65	4.92	$1,390,238	0.46	287	193	11.23	–48.63	1.07	17.45
Market Leaders, 50 Stocks by High PE	9.16	10.85	19.49	3.72	$332,875	0.26	288	192	11.29	–57.7	1.07	15.83
Market Leaders, 50 Stocks by Best 5-Yr EPS Gain	14.52	16.61	22.27	5.1	$2,267,445	0.5	288	192	11.31	–46.47	1.17	17.16
Market Leaders, PSR<Avg, 3/6 Mth Price Chg Pos, Top 50 Stocks by 1-Yr Rel Str	14.14	16.01	20.85	5.23	$1,983,979	0.5	296	184	11.31	–45.23	1.06	20
Large, 50 Stocks by Low PSR	14.64	16.58	21.29	5.32	$2,364,710	0.52	297	183	11.39	–40.71	1.03	16.52
Large Stock CSG 50 Stocks	14.12	16.06	21.26	5.15	$1,970,929	0.5	298	182	11.4	–41.03	1.05	18.49
50-Stock Value-Growth Portfolio	20.17	22.4	23.38	6.69	$15,543,562	0.74	295	185	11.46	–40.52	1.08	25.02
Large, 50 Stocks by Percentage 1-Yr EPS Decline	9.47	11.32	20.46	3.7	$372,662	0.27	271	209	11.48	–44.06	1.07	10.18
Large, 50 Stocks by 1-Yr Percentage Sales Decline	11.96	13.89	21	4.47	$917,141	0.39	285	195	11.49	–45.39	1.07	12.29
Large, PSR<1—50 Stocks by 1-Yr Rel Str	13.64	15.56	21.04	5.03	$1,666,318	0.48	295	185	11.5	–37.73	1.03	16.09
All Stocks	**12.02**	**13.82**	**20.23**	**4.61**	**$936,071**	**0.4**	**286**	**194**	**11.53**	**–50.12**	**1.05**	**17.96**
Large, EPS Up—PE<20 - Top 50 Stocks by 1-Yr Rel Str	14.67	16.64	21.39	5.31	$2,391,513	0.52	296	184	11.54	–40.11	1.04	20.72
Improved CSG, Top 100 Pmargin, Top 50 Stocks by 1-Yr Rel Str	18.14	20.22	22.36	6.26	$7,855,317	0.67	308	172	11.66	–39.56	1.02	23.46

(continued on next page)

360

T A B L E 23-3

All Strategies for Monthly Data Series, December 31, 1963–December 31, 2003—Strategies Sorted by Downside Ratio, Least Risky to Most *(Continued)*

Strategy	Geometric Mean	Arithmetic Mean	Standard Deviation	T-Stat	Ending Index Value	Sharpe Ratio	Pos Periods	Neg Periods	Downside Risk	Maximum Decline	Beta	Median
Market Leaders, PSR<Avg, Top 10 Stocks by 1-Yr Rel Str	15.6	17.77	22.74	5.37	$3,299,346	0.54	298	182	11.66	−38.21	0.96	18.38
Small Stocks, 50 Stocks by Best PMargins	9.4	11.03	18.91	3.89	$363,389	0.28	295	185	11.67	−59.53	0.83	13.3
All, Str Earn, Top 50 Stocks by 1-Yr Rel Str	16.94	19.15	23.03	5.74	$5,238,626	0.6	291	189	11.71	−50.93	1.12	20.29
Market Leaders, 50 Stocks by Worst 1-Yr Rel Str	10.52	12.55	21.57	3.91	$545,735	0.32	273	207	11.83	−54.94	1.08	12.09
Large, PE<20 -50 Stocks by High 1-Yr Rel Str	14.63	16.66	21.74	5.24	$2,353,621	0.51	303	177	11.86	−39.48	1.06	21.35
Large, 50 Stocks by High Pmargin	12.69	14.86	22.53	4.48	$1,188,767	0.41	286	194	12.01	−57.17	1.13	11.22
Market Leaders, 10 Stocks by Low PSR	16.9	19.3	24.12	5.53	$5,159,969	0.58	295	185	12.07	−50.31	0.99	18.65
CSG Top 100 Pmargin, Pos 3/6 Mth Price Chg, Top 25 Stocks by 1-Yr Rel Str	20.41	22.91	24.94	6.43	$16,818,255	0.71	313	167	12.11	−48.46	1.07	27.18
All Industrials, 50 Stocks by Low PCFL	15.53	17.89	23.7	5.19	$3,223,752	0.52	297	183	12.29	−44.22	1.05	18.73
Market Leaders,10 Stocks by Low PCFL	19.96	22.88	27.29	5.88	$14,504,404	0.65	300	180	12.38	−45.15	1.11	20.23
Large Stocks CSG 25 Stocks	14.61	16.92	23.34	4.97	$2,340,370	0.49	290	190	12.41	−46.13	1.11	20.05
Original CSG, Top 100 Pmargin, Top 10 Stocks by 1-Yr Rel Str	18.61	21.15	24.9	5.91	$9,221,276	0.64	284	196	12.45	−37.6	0.94	21.97
Small Stocks	**12.57**	**14.69**	**22.02**	**4.53**	**$1,139,641**	**0.41**	**290**	**190**	**12.5**	**−53.82**	**1.07**	**18.55**
All, EPS Up 5 Yrs, Top 50 Stocks by 1-Yr Rel Str	16.91	19.39	24.41	5.49	$5,179,460	0.58	299	181	12.59	−52.73	1.16	23.85
All, 50 Stocks by Low PE	14.89	17.45	24.75	4.84	$2,581,104	0.48	288	192	12.83	−50.76	1.07	16.9
Large, 50 Stocks by High ROE	9.38	11.52	21.91	3.53	$360,686	0.26	280	200	12.99	−61.89	1.16	12.98
All Stocks, 5yr EPS > Avg, Net Mrg > Avg, EPS > EPS—1yr, Top 50 Stocks by 1-yr Rel Str	17.02	19.71	25.53	5.35	$5,380,301	0.56	293	187	13	−48.12	1.17	21.8
Small Stocks, 50 Stocks by Low PE	16.31	19	25.5	5.15	$4,214,230	0.53	297	183	13.03	−52.13	1.07	19.23
All, P/Book<1, Top 50 Stocks by 1-Yr Rel Str	17.68	20.28	24.97	5.64	$6,737,675	0.6	298	182	13.09	−49.66	1.04	23.39
All, 50 Stocks by High Pmargins	10.71	13.03	23.02	3.82	$585,378	0.32	281	199	13.11	−67.26	1.06	15.53
Large, 50 Stocks by 1-Yr Percentage EPS Gain	9.3	11.51	22.19	3.48	$350,153	0.26	283	197	13.28	−51.38	1.14	13.04

(continued on next page)

361

T A B L E 23-3

All Strategies for Monthly Data Series, December 31, 1963–December 31, 2003—Strategies Sorted by Downside Ratio, Least Risky to Most *(Continued)*

Strategy	Geometric Mean	Arithmetic Mean	Standard Deviation	T-Stat	Ending Index Value	Sharpe Ratio	Pos Periods	Neg Periods	Downside Risk	Maximum Decline	Beta	Median
Improved CSG, Top 100 Pmargin, Top 25 Stocks by 1-Yr Rel Str	18.24	21.01	26	5.63	$8,127,684	0.61	300	180	13.3	–43.8	1.11	25.81
All, 50 Stocks by Low PSR	15.38	18.2	26.13	4.8	$3,054,908	0.49	283	197	13.33	–52.15	1.09	20.77
Small Stocks, 50 Stocks by Worst 5-Yr EPS Gain	13.25	15.64	23.41	4.55	$1,449,185	0.43	295	185	13.41	–52.04	1.05	19.5
Small Stocks, 50 Stocks by Low PCFL	16.82	19.94	27.7	5	$5,023,916	0.53	285	195	13.78	–55.73	1.17	17.92
Small Stocks, 50 Stocks by Low PSR	15.38	18.36	26.9	4.71	$3,051,506	0.48	290	190	13.81	–52.87	1.11	21.59
Large, 50 Stocks by Best 5-Yr EPS Growth	11.42	14.18	25.42	3.79	$755,599	0.34	275	205	13.9	–64.09	1.3	11.66
All, 50 Stocks by Low P/Book	15.66	18.98	28.8	4.57	$3,365,965	0.47	287	193	13.96	–48.55	1.17	18.13
Large, ROE>15—Top 50 Stocks by 1-Yr Rel Str	14.05	16.95	26.27	4.43	$1,920,627	0.44	285	195	14	–51.57	1.21	17.2
Improved CSG, Top 50 Stocks	20.75	23.97	28.31	5.97	$18,860,926	0.67	296	184	14.1	–55.25	1.19	24.61
Small Stocks, 50 Stocks by Low P/Book	14.97	18.35	28.92	4.39	$2,654,859	0.45	279	201	14.31	–52	1.17	18.46
All, Earn Yld>5%—Top 50 Stocks by 1-Yr Rel Str	17.49	20.61	27.44	5.23	$6,305,425	0.56	288	192	14.38	–53.09	1.18	22.84
All, 50 Stocks by Percentage 1-Yr EPS Decline	11	13.79	25.39	3.68	$651,005	0.32	288	192	14.41	–63.65	1.19	15.31
Small Stocks, PSR<1, 3/6 Mth Price Chg Pos, Top 50 Stocks by 1-Yr Rel Str	18.62	21.79	27.74	5.49	$9,249,548	0.6	291	189	14.45	–53.14	1.17	21.61
All, PSR<1, Top 50 Stocks by 1-Yr Rel Str	16.75	19.92	27.54	5.02	$4,909,077	0.53	281	199	14.69	–53.4	1.17	23.3
Original Cornerstone Growth	17.77	21.16	28.74	5.14	$6,950,741	0.55	277	203	14.8	–60.13	1.21	19.28
All, 50 Stocks by Percentage 1-Yr EPS Gain	12.77	15.8	26.54	4.07	$1,225,226	0.39	287	193	15.02	–65.54	1.2	19.82
Large, 50 Stocks by Worst 1-Yr Rel Str	6.96	9.99	26.26	2.55	$147,620	0.16	266	214	15.18	–77	1.25	6.35
Small Stocks, 50 Stocks by Best 1-Yr EPS Growth	14.16	17.43	27.83	4.31	$1,995,556	0.43	287	193	15.4	–66.78	1.23	20.19
Large, 50 Stocks by Best 1-Yr Rel Str	13.87	17.44	29.36	4.1	$1,805,450	0.41	280	200	15.56	–71.51	1.27	20.17
Cap Bx. $25mm-$250, PSR<1, 3/6 Mth Price Chg Pos, Top 50 Stocks by High 1-Yr Rel Str	21.21	25.03	30.98	5.73	$21,983,019	0.64	305	175	15.58	–54.75	1.15	33.73
Improved CSG, Top 25 Stocks	21.08	25.23	32.55	5.51	$21,055,793	0.62	290	190	15.7	–59.33	1.24	27.16
All, 50 Stocks by High 5-Yr EPS Growth	8.65	11.83	26.84	2.97	$276,665	0.23	271	209	15.85	–84.72	1.34	13.96

(continued on next page)

T A B L E 23-3

All Strategies for Monthly Data Series, December 31, 1963–December 31, 2003—Strategies Sorted by Downside Ratio, Least Risky to Most *(Continued)*

Strategy	Geometric Mean	Arithmetic Mean	Standard Deviation	T-Stat	Ending Index Value	Sharpe Ratio	Pos Periods	Neg Periods	Downside Risk	Maximum Decline	Beta	Median
Small Stocks, 50 Stocks by High 5-Yr EPS Gain	9.53	12.8	27.31	3.17	$381,829	0.26	277	203	15.87	−84.91	1.3	14.24
Large, 50 Stocks by High PE	7.15	10.31	26.69	2.59	$158,626	0.17	274	206	15.9	−74.24	1.28	11.08
Small Stocks, PSR<1, 3/6 Mth Price Chg Pos, Top 25 Stocks by 1-Yr Rel Str	18.55	22.51	31.29	5.06	$9,040,439	0.55	291	189	16.08	−52.82	1.22	28.85
All, 50 Stocks by 1-Yr Percentage Sales Decrease	8.25	11.64	27.85	2.82	$238,130	0.21	272	208	16.25	−75	1.23	9.38
Original CSG, Top 25 Stocks by 1-Yr Rel Str	19.02	23.24	32.56	5.04	$10,575,472	0.56	283	197	16.26	−60.85	1.24	25.21
All, PSR<1, Top 25 Stocks by 1-Yr Rel Str	16.24	20.19	31	4.54	$4,118,890	0.48	288	192	16.27	−57.73	1.22	19.87
Large, 50 Stocks by High P/Book	7.24	10.79	28.45	2.55	$163,772	0.18	271	209	16.74	−80.78	1.34	11.92
Cap Bx. $25mm–$250mm, PSR<1, Top 25 Stocks by 1-Yr Rel Str	24.32	29.3	36.35	5.82	$60,580,240	0.67	304	176	16.99	−55.6	1.19	32.14
Cap Bx. $25mm–$250, PSR<1, 3/6 Mth Price Chg Pos, Top 25 Stocks by High 1-Yr Rel Str	22.7	27.58	35.8	5.53	$35,738,548	0.63	299	181	17.04	−61.29	1.15	35.88
Small Stocks, ROE>Avg. 3/6 Mth Price Chg Pos, Top 50 Stocks by 1-Yr Rel Str	15.8	20.15	32.63	4.31	$3,530,758	0.46	295	185	17.48	−70.56	1.33	25.77
Small Stocks, 50 Stocks by High PE	7.72	11.48	29.23	2.65	$195,864	0.2	278	202	17.5	−70.39	1.29	16.73
Large, 50 Stocks by 1-Yr Percentage Sales Increase	4.87	8.39	27.81	2.01	$67,087	0.09	271	209	17.56	−89.45	1.37	12.18
Small Stocks, PSR<Avg, 3/6 Mth Price Chg Pos, Top 50 Stocks by 1-Yr Rel Str	15.08	19.44	32.45	4.17	$2,757,808	0.43	289	191	17.61	−76.71	1.26	21.04
All, 50 Stocks by High ROE	7.94	11.74	29.31	2.71	$212,800	0.2	271	209	17.71	−74.82	1.34	13.85
All, ROE>15, Top 50 Stocks by 1-Yr Rel Str	14.13	18.65	33.18	3.91	$1,975,512	0.4	280	200	17.88	−65.82	1.39	24.96
Large Industrials, 50 Stocks by High PCFL	5.39	9.23	29.25	2.11	$81,697	0.12	274	206	18.03	−84.35	1.38	10.23
All, 50 Stocks by High PE	6.62	10.53	29.69	2.39	$130,076	0.16	277	203	18.08	−75.06	1.34	12.69
Small Stocks, 50 Stocks by Worst 1-Yr EPS Growth	5.73	9.78	30.37	2.16	$92,979	0.13	264	216	18.11	−74.17	1.38	13.84

(continued on next page)

363

T A B L E 23-3

All Strategies for Monthly Data Series, December 31, 1963–December 31, 2003—Strategies Sorted by Downside Ratio, Least Risky to Most *(Continued)*

Strategy	Geometric Mean	Arithmetic Mean	Standard Deviation	T-Stat	Ending Index Value	Sharpe Ratio	Pos Periods	Neg Periods	Downside Risk	Maximum Decline	Beta	Median
Small Stocks, 50 Stocks by High ROE	9.15	13.28	30.78	2.93	$331,915	0.25	278	202	18.25	−75.93	1.37	17.87
Small Stocks, PCFL<Avg. 3/6 Mth Price Chg Pos, Top 50 Stocks by 1-Yr Rel Str	13.97	18.69	33.64	3.86	$1,865,835	0.4	291	189	18.5	−87.48	1.27	22.06
Large, 50 Stocks by High PSR	4.96	9.21	30.87	2	$69,365	0.11	272	208	19	−93.36	1.34	12.14
All, 50 Stocks by High P/Book	3.48	7.87	31.11	1.69	$39,229	0.06	264	216	19.89	−89.19	1.43	9.63
All, EPS Chg>25—50 Stocks by 1-Yr Rel Str	13.2	18.68	36.74	3.55	$1,424,187	0.36	288	192	19.94	−83.88	1.4	23.31
All, Pmargin>20—50 Stocks by 1-Yr Rel Str	13.9	19.6	37.7	3.64	$1,825,902	0.38	287	193	19.95	−81.66	1.44	20.73
All Industrials, 50 Stocks by High PCFL	3.42	7.86	31.24	1.68	$38,397	0.06	276	204	20.07	−88.19	1.47	14.05
All, 50 Stocks by Worst 1-Yr Rel Str	1.98	7.09	34.57	1.37	$21,898	0.03	243	237	20.1	−87.03	1.49	1.94
Small Stocks, 50 Stocks by Worst 1-Yr Rel Str	2.11	7.3	34.97	1.4	$23,071	0.04	243	237	20.23	−85.46	1.48	2.45
Small Stocks, 50 Stocks by High PCFL	3.12	7.74	31.89	1.62	$34,173	0.06	270	210	20.58	−86.4	1.46	12.95
Cap Bx. $25mm-$250, PSR<1, 3/6 Mth Price Chg Pos, Top 10 Stocks by High 1-Yr Rel Str	21.18	28.17	43.28	4.72	$21,707,627	0.54	281	199	20.6	−86.04	1.19	28.51
All, 50 Stocks by Best 1-Yr Rel Str	11.13	16.88	37.44	3.13	$681,201	0.3	281	199	20.61	−89.4	1.47	18.68
Small Stocks, 50 Stocks by Worst ROE	3.77	8.79	33.74	1.75	$43,983	0.09	270	210	20.86	−92.96	1.46	14.33
Small Stocks, 50 Stocks by High P/Book	3.42	8.35	33.18	1.69	$38,375	0.07	269	211	21.03	−92.49	1.44	11.91
Small Stocks, 50 Stocks by High PSR	−2.16	2.18	30.18	0.47	$4,182	−0.13	262	218	21.05	−95.23	1.29	8.67
Small Stocks, 50 Stocks by High 1-Yr Rel Str	10.21	16.03	37.29	2.98	$487,995	0.28	280	200	21.25	−91.18	1.47	21.05
All, 50 Stocks by High PSR	−2.66	1.71	30.2	0.37	$3,400	−0.15	259	221	21.29	−95.94	1.33	6.88
All, 50 Stocks by 1-Yr Percentage Sales Increase	−0.17	4.78	32.74	0.96	$9,327	−0.04	255	225	21.72	−91.39	1.55	6.33
Small Stocks, 50 Stocks by Worst PMargins	−2.73	2.03	31.81	0.42	$3,299	−0.13	253	227	21.77	−95.55	1.36	5.28

Another sensible thing for risk-averse investors to consider is where the strategy stands against the All Stocks universe, as this is the broadest of all of the large universes I investigated. This would give you a greater number of strategies to choose from, while still investing in a portfolio that had a lower downside risk than the average stock. See Figures 23-5 and 23-6.

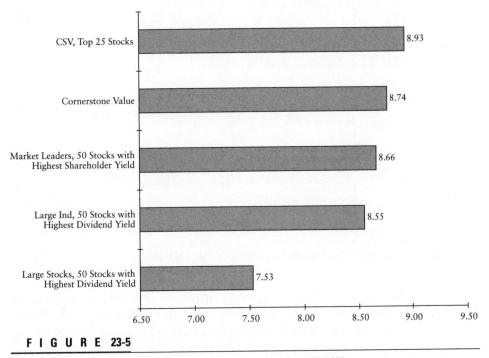

F I G U R E 23-5

The five equity strategies with the lowest downside risk, 1963–2003.

THE DOWNSIDE

It should come as no surprise that, much like the bad child frequently found waiting outside the principal's office, we see that those strategies with the highest downside risk also have the worst returns and worst risk-adjusted returns. At least they are *consistently* bad! All these strategies should be avoided, because the risk is just too high. You should never use a strategy with a downside risk much higher than the overall market's downside risk unless its performance is so fantastic that it pushes the Sharpe ratio into the stratosphere as well. Unless the potential rewards are vastly higher than the market, the emotional toll of high-risk strategies outweighs their benefits. No one should invest their entire portfolio in the riskiest strategies, no matter how good their absolute return. You'll capitulate to your fears, usually near

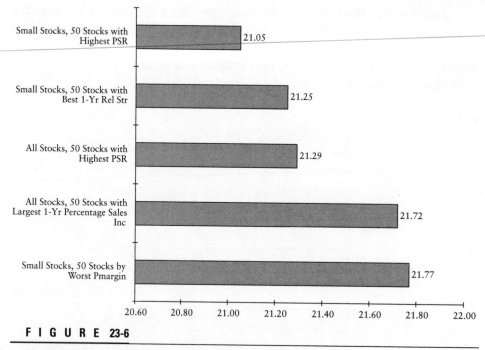

F I G U R E 23-6

The five equity strategies with the highest downside risk, 1963–2003.

a strategy's bottom. This brings nothing but misery and will probably send you into the arms of the nearest S&P 500 index fund. The best use of high-risk strategies is to blend them with lower risk ones, bringing overall risk to acceptable levels.

MAXIMUM DECLINE

The final ranking of the list is by a strategy's maximum decline over the last 40 years. Remember that virtually every type of market, except a prolonged depression, is covered during this period, so these figures give us a good sense for how bad things might get. Not surprisingly, the strategies with the smallest maximum declines come from either the Large Stocks or Market Leaders universes. Large-cap stocks tend to be less volatile than smaller-cap stocks, so it's natural to find them here.

The strategy that buys those 50 stocks from Market Leaders having the highest dividend yield, the original Cornerstone Value strategy, comes out on top of this list. Its maximum decline over the entire 40 years was a drop of 28.18 percent, much better than any of the broader market indexes. Its return of 15.76 percent per year turned $10,000, invested in 1963, into $3.5 million, and it never had a five-year period when it lost money. Also on the list are several strategies from the Market Leaders universe that had compound average annual rates of return exceeding 18 percent, like buying the stocks with the highest shareholder yield. This strategy turned $10,000 into $7.6 million and *also* never had a five-year period when it lost money. Note that, to get that higher return, you had to be willing to have a higher potential maximum decline. All in all, a great number of strategies had lower maximum declines than All Stocks, so if you're using this as one of your selection criteria, you've got a much broader group of strategies from which to choose.

THE DOWNSIDE

Surprise! All the worst-performing strategies also wind up at the bottom of the barrel here, with eight strategies turning in maximum declines exceeding 90 percent. They are the usual suspects—stocks with the highest price-to-sales and price-to-book ratios, and those with the worst margins, all have maximum declines exceeding 90 percent. The worst decline in a broad universe came from Small Stocks, which experienced a drop of nearly 54 percent. I would recommend that you use that as your drop-dead point. Only consider strategies with maximum declines less than that experienced by this most volatile of broad universes. Even when you eliminate strategies with maximum declines over 54 percent, you still have many strategies to choose from, but you avoid those that are too volatile to stick with.

BLENDED STRATEGIES

Table 23-4 and Figures 23-7 and 23-8 show the results of using several of these single strategies together. You see immediately that you can improve the risk-adjusted rate of return, downside risk, and the number of months when you earn positive returns by using the strategies together. As we saw in Chapter 21, most investors are best with portfolios that are diversified by investment style and capitalization. Because you never know ahead of time which strategy will shine, it's best to have exposure to both value and growth and large and small stocks. The only exception to this would be for the most conservative investors who want to limit their equity exposure to large, well-known stocks with lower volatility.

T A B L E 23-4

All Strategies for Monthly Data Series, December 31, 1963–December 31, 2003—Strategies Sorted by Maximum Decline, Smallest to Largest

Strategy	Geometric Mean	Arithmetic Mean	Standard Deviation	T-Stat	Ending Index Value	Sharpe Ratio	Pos Periods	Neg Periods	Downside Risk	Maximum Decline	Beta	Median
U.S. 30-Day Tbill	**6.03**	**6.03**	**0.81**	**48.43**	**$103,893**	**NA**	**480**	**0**	**0**	**0**	**0**	**5.46**
U.S. Inflation	**4.57**	**4.57**	**1.16**	**25.53**	**$59,686**	**NA**	**432**	**28**	**0.18**	**-0.94**	**-0.01**	**3.85**
Inter. Term U.S. Gov't Bonds	**7.72**	**7.89**	**5.96**	**8.66**	**$196,030**	**0.33**	**338**	**141**	**2.72**	**-8.89**	**0.07**	**6.42**
U.S. Long-Term Gov't Bonds	**7.53**	**8.07**	**10.91**	**4.86**	**$182,136**	**0.2**	**281**	**198**	**5.69**	**-20.97**	**0.17**	**5.28**
U.S. Long-Term Corp Bonds	**7.76**	**8.18**	**9.58**	**5.61**	**$198,948**	**0.24**	**302**	**178**	**4.96**	**-22.37**	**0.19**	**6.41**
Cornerstone Value	15.76	17.14	18.13	6.45	$3,481,988	0.64	301	179	8.74	-28.18	0.89	17.57
CSV, Top 25 Stocks by Div Yield	16.24	17.72	18.82	6.45	$4,111,429	0.65	303	177	8.93	-28.5	0.85	17
Large Industrials, 50 Stocks by High Dividend Yield	14.01	15.28	17.29	5.99	$1,892,183	0.56	300	180	8.55	-28.95	0.81	15.83
Market Leaders, Top 50 Stocks by Shareholder Yield	17.02	18.39	18.09	6.97	$5,368,551	0.72	308	172	8.66	-29.05	0.9	18.36
CSV, Top 10 Stocks by Dividend Yield	15.67	17.36	20.18	5.89	$3,378,075	0.59	293	187	9.47	-29.7	0.81	16.72
Dow 10 Stocks by High Dividend Yield (Dogs of the Dow)	13.89	15.33	18.36	5.67	$1,817,710	0.53	291	189	9.21	-30.23	0.87	13.6
Market Leaders, PSR<Avg, Top 50 Stocks by 1-Yr Rel Str	16.21	17.92	20.07	6.12	$4,078,153	0.62	304	176	10.2	-31.11	1.02	21.42
Market Leaders, PSR<Avg, Top 25 Stocks by 1-Yr Rel Str	16.54	18.47	21.44	5.93	$4,561,805	0.61	304	176	10.93	-32.2	1.03	23.61
Market Leaders, Top 25 Stocks by Shareholder Yield	18.05	19.58	19.22	7.03	$7,632,140	0.74	308	172	9.16	-32.22	0.92	21.6
Market Leaders, 50 Stocks by Worst 5-Yr EPS Gain	13.62	15.15	18.77	5.47	$1,651,414	0.51	291	189	10.02	-32.82	0.99	18.03
Large, 50 Stocks by High Dividend Yield	12.52	13.61	16	5.73	$1,121,835	0.5	294	186	7.53	-32.97	0.61	10.82
Market Leaders, PCFL<Avg, 3/6 Mth Price Chg Pos, Top 50 Stocks by 1-Yr Rel Str	14.53	16.25	19.98	5.54	$2,275,626	0.54	301	179	10.72	-34.73	1.02	19.18
Market Leaders, 50 Stocks by Low PSR	16.15	17.93	20.52	5.99	$3,981,957	0.61	307	173	10.67	-35.07	1.01	19.18
Market Leaders, 50 Stocks by Low PE	16.55	18.36	20.83	6.06	$4,571,422	0.62	297	183	10.29	-35.13	1.02	17.56
Market Leaders, 50 Stocks by Low P/Book	16.63	18.51	21.21	6	$4,705,461	0.62	296	184	10.53	-37.08	1.04	17.72
Original CSG, Top 100 Pmargin, Top 10 Stocks by 1-Yr Rel Str	18.61	21.15	24.9	5.91	$9,221,276	0.64	284	196	12.45	-37.6	0.94	21.97
Value Decile Intersection, 50 Stocks	17.69	19.11	18.38	7.15	$6,754,726	0.75	316	164	9.1	-37.68	0.83	24.3
Large, PSR<1—50 Stocks by 1-Yr Rel Str	13.64	15.56	21.04	5.03	$1,666,318	0.48	295	185	11.5	-37.73	1.03	16.09

(continued on next page)

T A B L E 23-4

All Strategies for Monthly Data Series, December 31, 1963–December 31, 2003—Strategies Sorted by Maximum Decline, Smallest to Largest *(Continued)*

Strategy	Geometric Mean	Arithmetic Mean	Standard Deviation	T-Stat	Ending Index Value	Sharpe Ratio	Pos Periods	Neg Periods	Downside Risk	Maximum Decline	Beta	Median
Market Leaders, PSR<Avg, Top 10 Stocks by 1-Yr Rel Str	15.6	17.77	22.74	5.37	$3,299,346	0.54	298	182	11.66	−38.21	0.96	18.38
Market Leaders, Top 10 Stocks by Shareholder Yield	18.1	19.98	21.31	6.48	$7,772,433	0.69	309	171	10.35	−38.27	0.95	21.74
Market Leaders, 50 Stocks by High Pmargin	12.63	13.98	17.56	5.37	$1,166,320	0.48	297	183	9.31	−38.51	0.97	16.73
100-Stock Value-Growth Portfolio	19.21	21.12	21.46	6.83	$11,275,830	0.74	311	169	10.74	−38.82	1.05	23.71
Market Leaders	**12.77**	**14.05**	**17.06**	**5.55**	**$1,225,022**	**0.49**	**297**	**183**	**9.2**	**−38.98**	**0.96**	**17.02**
Market Leaders, 50 Stocks by Best 1-Yr EPS Gains	11.94	13.64	19.6	4.69	$911,483	0.41	290	190	11.03	−39.04	1.05	16.06
Market Leaders, 50 Stocks by Low PCFL	16.09	17.83	20.37	6	$3,906,209	0.61	305	175	10.23	−39.15	1	20.92
Large Industrial, 50 Stocks by Low PCFL	14.77	16.69	21.21	5.38	$2,476,539	0.53	294	186	11.17	−39.33	1.04	19.86
Large, PE<20—50 Stocks by High 1-Yr Rel Str	14.63	16.66	21.74	5.24	$2,353,621	0.51	303	177	11.86	−39.48	1.06	21.35
Large CSG, with 3/6 Mth Price Chg Pos, Top 50 Stocks by 1-Yr Rel Str	15.16	16.96	20.59	5.63	$2,831,275	0.56	303	177	10.83	−39.56	1	20.97
Improved CSG, Top 100 Pmargin, Top 50 Stocks by 1-Yr Rel Str	18.14	20.22	22.36	6.26	$7,855,317	0.67	308	172	11.66	−39.56	1.02	23.46
Large, 50 Stocks by Low PE	14.31	16.04	20.16	5.42	$2,103,738	0.52	293	187	10.58	−39.71	0.96	17.57
Large, EPS up- PE<20 -Top 50 Stocks by 1-Yr Rel Str	14.67	16.64	21.39	5.31	$2,391,513	0.52	296	184	11.54	−40.11	1.04	20.72
50-Stock Value-Growth Portfolio	20.17	22.4	23.38	6.69	$15,543,562	0.74	295	185	11.46	−40.52	1.08	25.02
Large, 50 Stocks by Low PSR	14.64	16.58	21.29	5.32	$2,364,710	0.52	297	183	11.39	−40.71	1.03	16.52
Large Stock CSG 50 Stocks	14.12	16.06	21.26	5.15	$1,970,929	0.5	298	182	11.4	−41.03	1.05	18.49
Market Leaders, Top 50 Stocks by 1-Yr Rel Str	14.75	16.63	21.03	5.4	$2,452,387	0.53	301	179	11.13	−41.19	1.06	19.8
All, Good Value—50 Stocks by Low PCFL	17.53	19.47	21.84	6.16	$6,395,835	0.65	300	180	10.13	−42.59	0.92	20.06
Lrg, 50 Stocks by Low P/Book	14.87	16.84	21.67	5.32	$2,562,423	0.53	298	182	10.96	−42.84	1.01	18.07
Market Leaders, 25 Stocks by Low PSR	16.41	18.28	21.07	5.96	$4,362,020	0.61	301	179	10.89	−43.34	0.99	19.94
Improved CSG, Top 100 Pmargin, Top 25 Stocks by 1-Yr Rel Str	18.24	21.01	26	5.63	$8,127,684	0.61	300	180	13.3	−43.8	1.11	25.81
All, Yld, Price Up—50 Stocks by Low PSR	15.62	17.25	19.51	6.05	$3,318,667	0.6	306	174	10.48	−43.94	0.89	22.07

(continued on next page)

T A B L E 23-4

All Strategies for Monthly Data Series, December 31, 1963–December 31, 2003—Strategies Sorted by Maximum Decline, Smallest to Largest *(Continued)*

Strategy	Geometric Mean	Arithmetic Mean	Standard Deviation	T-Stat	Ending Index Value	Sharpe Ratio	Pos Periods	Neg Periods	Downside Risk	Maximum Decline	Beta	Median
Large, 50 Stocks by Percentage 1-Yr EPS Decline	9.47	11.32	20.46	3.7	$372,662	0.27	271	209	11.48	−44.06	1.07	10.18
All, 5-Yr Payout<50 Percent, Top 50 Stocks by Div Yld	17.08	18.58	19.02	6.71	$5,483,629	0.69	305	175	9.19	−44.16	0.84	20.1
All Industrials, 50 Stocks by Low PCFL	15.53	17.89	23.7	5.19	$3,223,752	0.52	297	183	12.29	−44.22	1.05	18.73
S&P 500	**10.61**	**11.87**	**16.82**	**4.72**	**$564,584**	**0.37**	**295**	**185**	**9.43**	**−44.73**	**1**	**13.53**
Market Leaders, 10 Stocks by Low PCFL	19.96	22.88	27.29	5.88	$14,504,404	0.65	300	180	12.38	−45.15	1.11	20.23
Market Leaders, PSR<Avg, 3/6 Mth Price Chg Pos, Top 50 Stocks by 1-Yr Rel Str	14.14	16.01	20.85	5.23	$1,983,979	0.5	296	184	11.31	−45.23	1.06	20
Large, 50 Stocks by 1-Yr Percentage Sales Decline	11.96	13.89	21	4.47	$917,141	0.39	285	195	11.49	−45.39	1.07	12.29
Lrg, 5-Yr Payout<50 Percent—50 Stocks by High Dividend Yield	13.89	15.51	19.41	5.43	$1,816,627	0.51	294	186	10.19	−46.01	0.94	16.92
Large Stocks CSG 25 Stocks	14.61	16.92	23.34	4.97	$2,340,370	0.49	290	190	12.41	−46.13	1.11	20.05
Market Leaders, 50 Stocks by Best 5-Yr EPS Gain	14.52	16.61	22.27	5.1	$2,267,445	0.5	288	192	11.31	−46.47	1.17	17.16
Large Stocks	**11.2**	**12.63**	**17.96**	**4.72**	**$697,718**	**0.39**	**289**	**191**	**10.15**	**−46.59**	**1.01**	**15.23**
Small Stocks, Value Model 2	15.28	17.05	20.2	5.77	$2,954,941	0.57	301	179	11.03	−47.53	0.9	21.05
Large, Low PE-EPS Up—Top 50 Stocks by 1-Yr Rel Str	14.06	15.57	18.76	5.64	$1,931,668	0.54	303	177	9.75	−47.96	0.95	13.76
All Stocks, 5-yr EPS > Avg, Net Mrg > Avg, EPS > EPS—1yr, Top 50 Stocks by 1-Yr Rel Str	17.02	19.71	25.53	5.35	$5,380,301	0.56	293	187	13	−48.12	1.17	21.8
CSG Top 100 Pmargin, Pos 3/6 Mth Price Chg, Top 25 Stocks by 1-Yr Rel Str	20.41	22.91	24.94	6.43	$16,818,255	0.71	313	167	12.11	−48.46	1.07	27.18
All, 50 Stocks by Low P/Book	15.66	18.98	28.8	4.57	$3,365,965	0.47	287	193	13.96	−48.55	1.17	18.13
Market Leaders, ROE>Avg, 3/6 Mth Price Chg Pos, Top 50 Stocks by 1-Yr Rel Str	13.13	14.97	20.65	4.92	$1,390,238	0.46	287	193	11.23	−48.63	1.07	17.45
Market Leaders, 50 Stocks by Worst 1-Yr EPS Change	12.51	14.26	20.09	4.8	$1,114,960	0.43	295	185	10.8	−48.9	1.05	14.65
Small Stocks 50 Stocks by High Dividend Yield	12.64	14.12	18.5	5.16	$1,166,914	0.46	296	184	9.92	−49.29	0.8	14.51

(continued on next page)

T A B L E 23-4

All Strategies for Monthly Data Series, December 31, 1963–December 31, 2003—Strategies Sorted by Maximum Decline, Smallest to Largest (Continued)

Strategy	Geometric Mean	Arithmetic Mean	Standard Deviation	T-Stat	Ending Index Value	Sharpe Ratio	Pos Periods	Neg Periods	Downside Risk	Maximum Decline	Beta	Median
Large, Strong Earn, Top 50 Stocks by 1-Yr Rel Str	14.16	15.98	20.68	5.26	$1,997,588	0.51	285	195	10.71	−49.32	1.08	17.06
All, Low PE,EPS Up—Top 50 Stocks by 1-Yr Rel Str	17.49	19.33	20.99	6.35	$6,305,417	0.67	310	170	10.66	−49.58	0.99	21.56
All, P/Book<1, Top 50 Stocks by 1-Yr Rel Str	17.68	20.28	24.97	5.64	$6,737,675	0.6	298	182	13.09	−49.66	1.04	23.39
Market Leaders, 50 Stocks by High ROE	12.63	14.14	18.63	5.13	$1,165,770	0.46	289	191	10.05	−50	1.02	15.26
Market Leaders, 50 Stocks by High P/Book	10.35	11.97	19.2	4.18	$513,783	0.33	274	206	10.64	−50.01	1.06	14.82
All Stocks	**12.02**	**13.82**	**20.23**	**4.61**	**$936,071**	**0.4**	**286**	**194**	**11.53**	**−50.12**	**1.05**	**17.96**
Market Leaders, 10 Stocks by Low PSR	16.9	19.3	24.12	5.53	$5,159,969	0.58	295	185	12.07	−50.31	0.99	18.65
Market Leaders, 50 Stocks by Low ROE	12.51	14.23	19.87	4.84	$1,114,342	0.43	293	187	10.84	−50.37	1.03	14.23
All, 50 Stocks by Low PE	14.89	17.45	24.75	4.84	$2,581,104	0.48	288	192	12.83	−50.76	1.07	16.9
All, Str Earn, Top 50 Stocks by 1-Yr Rel Str	16.94	19.15	23.03	5.74	$5,238,626	0.6	291	189	11.71	−50.93	1.12	20.29
Large, 50 Stocks by 1-Yr Percentage EPS Gain	9.3	11.51	22.19	3.48	$350,153	0.26	283	197	13.28	−51.38	1.14	13.04
Large, ROE>15—Top 50 Stocks by 1-Yr Rel Str	14.05	16.95	26.27	4.43	$1,920,627	0.44	285	195	14	−51.57	1.21	17.2
Large, low PSR-EPS Up—50 Stocks by 1-Yr Rel Str	13.12	14.7	19.11	5.21	$1,385,160	0.48	290	190	10.12	−51.6	0.98	15.38
Small Stocks, 50 Stocks by Low P/Book	14.97	18.35	28.92	4.39	$2,654,859	0.45	279	201	14.31	−52	1.17	18.46
Small Stocks, 50 Stocks by Worst 5-Yr EPS Gain	13.25	15.64	23.41	4.55	$1,449,185	0.43	295	185	13.41	−52.04	1.05	19.5
Small Stocks, 50 Stocks by Low PE	16.31	19	25.5	5.15	$4,214,230	0.53	297	183	13.03	−52.13	1.07	19.23
All, 50 Stocks by Low PSR	15.38	18.2	26.13	4.8	$3,054,908	0.49	283	197	13.33	−52.15	1.09	20.77
Market Leaders, 50 Stocks by Worst Pmargin	13.63	15.35	19.93	5.23	$1,659,290	0.49	296	184	10.91	−52.22	1.04	17.24
All, EPS up 5 Yrs—Top 50 Stocks by 1-Yr Rel Str	16.91	19.39	24.41	5.49	$5,179,460	0.58	299	181	12.59	−52.73	1.16	23.85
Small Stocks, PSR<1, 3/6 Mth Price Chg Pos, Top 25 Stocks by 1-Yr Rel Str	18.55	22.51	31.29	5.06	$9,040,439	0.55	291	189	16.08	−52.82	1.22	28.85
Small Stocks, 50 Stocks by Low PSR	15.38	18.36	26.9	4.71	$3,051,506	0.48	290	190	13.81	−52.87	1.11	21.59

(continued on next page)

371

T A B L E 23-4

All Strategies for Monthly Data Series, December 31, 1963–December 31, 2003—Strategies Sorted by Maximum Decline, Smallest to Largest *(Continued)*

Strategy	Geometric Mean	Arithmetic Mean	Standard Deviation	T-Stat	Ending Index Value	Sharpe Ratio	Pos Periods	Neg Periods	Downside Risk	Maximum Decline	Beta	Median
All, Earn Yld>5%—Top 50 Stocks by 1-Yr Rel Str	17.49	20.61	27.44	5.23	$6,305,425	0.56	288	192	14.38	−53.09	1.18	22.84
Small Stocks, PSR<1, 3/6 Mth Price Chg Pos, Top 50 Stocks by 1-Yr Rel Str	18.62	21.79	27.74	5.49	$9,249,548	0.6	291	189	14.45	−53.14	1.17	21.61
All, PSR<1, Top 50 Stocks by 1-Yr Rel Str	16.75	19.92	27.54	5.02	$4,909,077	0.53	281	199	14.69	−53.4	1.17	23.3
Small Stocks	**12.57**	**14.69**	**22.02**	**4.53**	**$1,139,641**	**0.41**	**290**	**190**	**12.5**	**−53.82**	**1.07**	**18.55**
Cap Bx. $25mm-$250, PSR<1, 3/6 Mth Price Chg Pos, Top 50 Stocks by High 1-Yr Rel Str	21.21	25.03	30.98	5.73	$21,983,019	0.64	305	175	15.58	−54.75	1.15	33.73
Market Leaders, 50 Stocks by Worst 1-Yr Rel Str	10.52	12.55	21.57	3.91	$545,735	0.32	273	207	11.83	−54.94	1.08	12.09
Improved CSG, Top 50 Stocks	20.75	23.97	28.31	5.97	$18,860,926	0.67	296	184	14.1	−55.25	1.19	24.61
Cap Bx. $25mm-$250mm, PSR<1, Top 25 Stocks by 1-Yr Rel Str	24.32	29.3	36.35	5.82	$60,580,240	0.67	304	176	16.99	−55.6	1.19	32.14
Small Stocks, 50 Stocks by Low PCFL	16.82	19.94	27.7	5	$5,023,916	0.53	285	195	13.78	−55.73	1.17	17.92
Large, 50 Stocks by High Pmargin	12.69	14.86	22.53	4.48	$1,188,767	0.41	286	194	12.01	−57.17	1.13	11.22
All Industrials, 50 Stocks by High	12.49	13.87	17.89	5.23	$1,107,592	0.46	298	182	9.42	−57.23	0.72	12.83
Market Leaders, 50 Stocks by High PE	9.16	10.85	19.49	3.72	$332,875	0.26	288	192	11.29	−57.7	1.07	15.83
All, PSR<1, Top 25 Stocks by 1-Yr Rel Str	16.24	20.19	31	4.54	$4,118,890	0.48	288	192	16.27	−57.73	1.22	19.87
Market Leaders, 50 Stocks by High PSR	8.9	10.43	18.56	3.74	$302,226	0.25	283	197	10.64	−59.06	1.05	13.84
Improved CSG, Top 25 Stocks	21.08	25.23	32.55	5.51	$21,055,793	0.62	290	190	15.7	−59.33	1.24	27.16
Small Stocks, 50 Stocks by Best PMargins	9.4	11.03	18.91	3.89	$363,389	0.28	295	185	11.67	−59.53	0.83	13.3
Original Cornerstone Growth	17.77	21.16	28.74	5.14	$6,950,741	0.55	277	203	14.8	−60.13	1.21	19.28
Original CSG, Top 25 Stocks by 1-Yr Rel Str	19.02	23.24	32.56	5.04	$10,575,472	0.56	283	197	16.26	−60.85	1.24	25.21
Cap Bx. $25mm-$250, PSR<1, 3/6 Mth Price Chg Pos, Top 25 Stocks by High 1-Yr Rel Str	22.7	27.58	35.8	5.53	$35,738,548	0.63	299	181	17.04	−61.29	1.15	35.88
Market Leaders, 50 Stocks by High PCFL	8.85	10.46	18.96	3.67	$296,750	0.25	283	197	11.02	−61.83	1.05	11.27
Large, 50 Stocks by High ROE	9.38	11.52	21.91	3.53	$360,686	0.26	280	200	12.99	−61.89	1.16	12.98

(continued on next page)

T A B L E 23-4

All Strategies for Monthly Data Series, December 31, 1963–December 31, 2003—Strategies Sorted by Maximum Decline, Smallest to Largest *(Continued)*

Strategy	Geometric Mean	Arithmetic Mean	Standard Deviation	T-Stat	Ending Index Value	Sharpe Ratio	Pos Periods	Neg Periods	Downside Risk	Maximum Decline	Beta	Median
All, 50 Stocks by Percentage 1-Yr EPS Decline	11	13.79	25.39	3.68	$651,005	0.32	288	192	14.41	−63.65	1.19	15.31
Large, 50 Stocks by Best 5-Yr EPS Growth	11.42	14.18	25.42	3.79	$755,599	0.34	275	205	13.9	−64.09	1.3	11.66
All, 50 Stocks by Percentage 1-Yr EPS Gain	12.77	15.8	26.54	4.07	$1,225,226	0.39	287	193	15.02	−65.54	1.2	19.82
All, ROE>15, Top 50 Stocks by 1-Yr Rel Str	14.13	18.65	33.18	3.91	$1,975,512	0.4	280	200	17.88	−65.82	1.39	24.96
Small Stocks, 50 Stocks by Best 1-Yr EPS Growth	14.16	17.43	27.83	4.31	$1,995,556	0.43	287	193	15.4	−66.78	1.23	20.19
All, 50 Stocks by High Pmargins	10.71	13.03	23.02	3.82	$585,378	0.32	281	199	13.11	−67.26	1.06	15.53
Small Stocks, 50 Stocks by High PE	7.72	11.48	29.23	2.65	$195,864	0.2	278	202	17.5	−70.39	1.29	16.73
Small Stocks, ROE>Avg. 3/6 Mth Price Chg Pos, Top 50 Stocks by 1-Yr Rel Str	15.8	20.15	32.63	4.31	$3,530,758	0.46	295	185	17.48	−70.56	1.33	25.77
Large, 50 Stocks by Best 1-Yr Rel Str	13.87	17.44	29.36	4.1	$1,805,450	0.41	280	200	15.56	−71.51	1.27	20.17
Small Stocks, 50 Stocks by Worst 1-Yr EPS Growth	5.73	9.78	30.37	2.16	$92,979	0.13	264	216	18.11	−74.17	1.38	13.84
Large, 50 Stocks by High PE	7.15	10.31	26.69	2.59	$158,626	0.17	274	206	15.9	−74.24	1.28	11.08
All, 50 Stocks by High ROE	7.94	11.74	29.31	2.71	$212,800	0.2	271	209	17.71	−74.82	1.34	13.85
All, 50 Stocks by 1-Yr Percentage Sales Decrease	8.25	11.64	27.85	2.82	$238,130	0.21	272	208	16.25	−75	1.23	9.38
All, 50 Stocks by High PE	6.62	10.53	29.69	2.39	$130,076	0.16	277	203	18.08	−75.06	1.34	12.69
Small Stocks, 50 Stocks by High ROE	9.15	13.28	30.78	2.93	$331,915	0.25	278	202	18.25	−75.93	1.37	17.87
Small Stocks, PSR<Avg. 3/6 Mth Price Chg Pos, Top 50 Stocks by 1-Yr Rel Str	15.08	19.44	32.45	4.17	$2,757,808	0.43	289	191	17.61	−76.71	1.26	21.04
Large, 50 Stocks by Worst 1-Yr Rel Str	6.96	9.99	26.26	2.55	$147,620	0.16	266	214	15.18	−77	1.25	6.35
Large, 50 Stocks by High P/Book	7.24	10.79	28.45	2.55	$163,772	0.18	271	209	16.74	−80.78	1.34	11.92
All- Pmargin>20—50 Stocks by 1-Yr Rel Str	13.9	19.6	37.7	3.64	$1,825,902	0.38	287	193	19.95	−81.66	1.44	20.73
All-EPS Chg>25—50 Stocks by 1-Yr Rel Str	13.2	18.68	36.74	3.55	$1,424,187	0.36	288	192	19.94	−83.88	1.4	23.31
Large Industrials, 50 Stocks by High PCFL	5.39	9.23	29.25	2.11	$81,697	0.12	274	206	18.03	−84.35	1.38	10.23
All, 50 Stocks by High 5-Yr EPS Growth	8.65	11.83	26.84	2.97	$276,665	0.23	271	209	15.85	−84.72	1.34	13.96

(continued on next page)

373

T A B L E 23-4

All Strategies for Monthly Data Series, December 31, 1963–December 31, 2003—Strategies Sorted by Maximum Decline, Smallest to Largest *(Continued)*

Strategy	Geometric Mean	Arithmetic Mean	Standard Deviation	T-Stat	Ending Index Value	Sharpe Ratio	Pos Periods	Neg Periods	Downside Risk	Maximum Decline	Beta	Median
Small Stocks, 50 Stocks by High 5-Yr EPS Gain	9.53	12.8	27.31	3.17	$381,829	0.26	277	203	15.87	−84.91	1.3	14.24
Small Stocks, 50 Stocks by Worst 1-Yr Rel Str	2.11	7.3	34.97	1.4	$23,071	0.04	243	237	20.23	−85.46	1.48	2.45
Cap Bx. $25mm–$250, PSR<1, 3/6 Mth Price Chg Pos, Top 10 Stocks by High 1-Yr Rel Str	28.17	28.17	43.28	4.72	$21,707,627	0.54	281	199	20.6	−86.04	1.19	28.51
Small Stocks, 50 Stocks by High PCFL	3.12	7.74	31.89	1.62	$34,173	0.06	270	210	20.58	−86.4	1.46	12.95
All, 50 Stocks by Worst 1-Yr Rel Str	1.98	7.09	34.57	1.37	$21,898	0.03	243	237	20.1	−87.03	1.49	1.94
Small Stocks, PCFL<Avg. 3/6 Mth Price Chg Pos, Top 50 Stocks by 1-Yr Rel Str	13.97	18.69	33.64	3.86	$1,865,835	0.4	291	189	18.5	−87.48	1.27	22.06
All Industrials, 50 Stocks by High PCFL	3.42	7.86	31.24	1.68	$38,397	0.06	276	204	20.07	−88.19	1.47	14.05
All, 50 Stocks by High P/Book	3.48	7.87	31.11	1.69	$39,229	0.06	264	216	19.89	−89.19	1.43	9.63
All, 50 Stocks by Best 1-Yr Rel Str	11.13	16.88	37.44	3.13	$681,201	0.3	281	199	20.61	−89.4	1.47	18.68
Large, 50 Stocks by 1-Yr Percentage Sales Increase	4.87	8.39	27.81	2.01	$67,087	0.09	271	209	17.56	−89.45	1.37	12.18
Small Stocks, 50 Stocks by High 1-Yr Rel Str	16.03	16.03	37.29	2.98	$487,995	0.28	280	200	21.25	−91.18	1.47	21.05
All, 50 Stocks by 1-Yr Percentage Sales Increase	−0.17	4.78	32.74	0.96	$9,327	−0.04	255	225	21.72	−91.39	1.55	6.33
Small Stocks, 50 Stocks by High P/Book	3.42	8.35	33.18	1.69	$38,375	0.07	269	211	21.03	−92.49	1.44	11.91
Small Stocks, 50 Stocks by Worst ROE	3.77	8.79	33.74	1.75	$43,983	0.09	270	210	20.86	−92.96	1.46	14.33
Large, 50 Stocks by High PSR	4.96	9.21	30.87	2	$69,365	0.11	272	208	19	−93.36	1.34	12.14
Small Stocks, 50 Stocks by High PSR	−2.16	2.18	30.18	0.47	$4,182	−0.13	262	218	21.05	−95.23	1.29	8.67
Small Stocks, 50 Stocks by Worst PMargins	−2.73	2.03	31.81	0.42	$3,299	−0.13	253	227	21.77	−95.55	1.36	5.28
All, 50 Stocks by High PSR	−2.66	1.71	30.2	0.37	$3,400	−0.15	259	221	21.29	−95.94	1.33	6.88

374

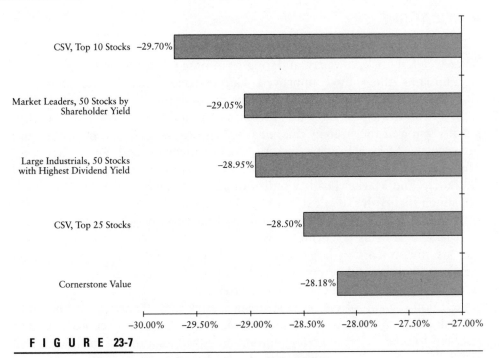

The five strategies with the lowest maximum decline, 1963–2003.

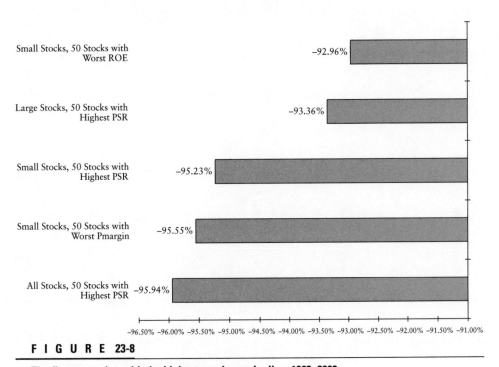

The five strategies with the highest maximum decline, 1963–2003.

IMPLICATIONS

After weighing risk, rewards, and long-term base rates, the best overall strategy remains the united improved Cornerstone Growth and improved Cornerstone Value portfolios. This is true for both the 50- and 100-stock versions of the strategies. Over the 40 years of monthly data studied, the 100-stock version of the strategy does nearly 11 times as well as a portfolio split between the Market Leaders and All Stocks universes, with an annual compound return of 19.21 percent, about 6.75 percent higher than the combined All Stocks and Market Leaders return of 12.46 percent a year. Yet the risk is not much higher. It's also extraordinarily consistent, beating the market the majority of all five-year rolling periods and all 10-year rolling periods.

It achieves this performance with a portfolio diversified by style, with half its investments in large, market-leading stocks having high dividend yields and half in stocks from All Stocks having persistent earnings gains, low price-to-sales ratios, and good relative strength.

If you use any of the other strategies, stick with those having the highest risk-adjusted returns and *always* look at the historical record if you're tempted to take a chance on a glamour stock trading at high multiples. I will remind you again: Most of those stocks crash and burn.

24 CHAPTER

GETTING THE MOST OUT OF YOUR EQUITY INVESTMENTS

To think is easy. To act is difficult. To act as one thinks is the most difficult of all.

—Johann Wolfgang von Goethe

Investors can learn much from the Taoist concept of *wu wei*. Taoism is one of the three schools of Chinese philosophy that have guided thinkers for thousands of years. Literally, wu wei means "to act without action," but in spirit, it means to let things occur as they are meant to occur. Don't try to put square pegs into round holes. Understand the essence of a circle and use it as nature intended. The closest Western equivalent is Wittgenstein's maxim: "Don't look for the meaning: Look for the use!"

For investors, this means letting good strategies work. Don't second-guess them. Don't try to outsmart them. Don't abandon them because they're experiencing a rough patch. Understand the nature of what you're using and let it work. This is the hardest assignment of all. It's virtually impossible not to insert our ego into decisions, yet it is only by being dispassionate that you can beat the market over time.

We've had tumultuous markets since the last edition of this book was published. A stock market bubble—the likes of which we had not seen since the late 1960s—led many investors to throw out the investing rule book. The more insanely overvalued a company, the more it soared. Everyone talked of "the New Economy" and how it *really* was different this time. Sticking with

377

time-tested investment strategies during the stock market orgy was close to impossible. Month in, month out, you had to stand on the sidelines, watching your reasonably priced stocks do nothing while the overpriced "story" stocks soared. And, as often happens with stock market bubbles, just as the last sane investors capitulated and learned to love the stocks with the craziest valuations, along came the reckoning—all gravity-defying stocks came crashing back to Earth. Fortunes were lost, and millions of investors lost their faith in the long-term potential of stocks.

In feverishly speculative markets, believing in Occam's razor—that the simplest theory is usually the best—is almost impossible. We love to make the simple complex, follow the crowd, get seduced by some hot "story" stock, let our emotions dictate decisions, buy and sell on tips and hunches, and approach each investment decision on a case-by-case basis, with no underlying consistency or strategy. Even seven years after this book was first published—showing decade upon decade of the results of all the various types of strategies—people were more than willing to throw it all out the window because of short-term events. No wonder the S&P 500 beats 80 percent of traditionally managed mutual funds over the long-term!

A Taoist story is illuminating: One day a man was standing at the edge of a pool at the bottom of a huge waterfall when he saw an old man being tossed about in the turbulent water. He ran to rescue him, but before he got there, the old man had climbed out onto the bank and was walking alone, singing to himself. The man was astonished and rushed up to the old man, questioning him about the secret of his survival. The old man said that it was nothing special. "I began to learn while very young, and grew up practicing it. Now, I'm certain of success. I go down with the water and come up with the water. I follow it and forget myself. The only reason I survive is because I don't struggle against the water's superior power."

The market is like the water, overpowering all who struggle against it and giving those who work with it a wonderful ride. But swimming lessons are in order. You can't just jump in: You need guidelines. Our study of the last 52 years suggests that to do well in the market, you must do the following:

ALWAYS USE STRATEGIES

You'll get nowhere buying stocks just because they have a great story. Usually, these are the very companies that have been the *worst* performers over the last 52 years. They're the stocks everyone talks about and wants to own. They often have sky-high price-to-earnings, price-to-book, and price-to-sales ratios. They're very appealing in the short-term, but deadly over the long haul. You *must* avoid them. Always think in terms of overall strategies and not individual stocks. One company's data is meaningless, yet can be very convincing. If you can't use strategies, and are inexorably drawn to the stock of the day, your returns suffer horribly in the long run. Remind yourself of what happens to these stocks by looking at charts of all the dot.com high flyers between 1998 and 2002. If, try as you might, you can't stick to a strategy, put the majority of your money in an index fund and treat the small amount you invest in story stocks as an entertainment expense.

IGNORE THE SHORT-TERM

Investors who look only at how a strategy has performed recently can be seriously misled and end up either ignoring a great long-term strategy that has recently underperformed or piling into a mediocre strategy that has recently been on fire. I witnessed this first-hand when my former firm, O'Shaughnessy Capital Management, decided to sell our mutual funds so that we might concentrate on separately managed accounts. No sooner had we announced the sale, *being very clear that we were doing so because we were changing our strategic focus to separately managed accounts*, than the negative press started pouring in, focusing, of course, on just a few years of history.

BusinessWeek got the ball rolling with an article on June 5, 2000 titled "What Happens when the Wizard Vanishes?" saying: "Yet the way I see it, O'Shaughnessy's investors have every right to cry like orphans. That is, for those who haven't been crying already. The author of *What Works on Wall Street* has had it tough getting his time-tested strategies to work in the funds."

A June 12, 2000 article in *U.S. News & World Reports* entitled "What Doesn't Work On Wall Street" chided: "If you write a book called *What Works On Wall Street* and launch mutual funds based on your theories, you'd better deliver some market-beating results. But James O'Shaughnessy didn't. Now he is selling his Cornerstone Growth and Cornerstone Value funds, which have a paltry $200 million in combined assets."

Money Magazine followed up in July of 2000, with a similarly titled "What Doesn't Work on Wall Street" (come on guys, at least think up a different title!) with a similar jab: "Too bad O'Shaughnessy hadn't launched his funds in 1950 rather than late 1996, because his formula *doesn't seem to work anymore*" (emphasis added).

Perhaps the most dismaying attack for me came under the imprimatur of the legendary Benjamin Graham, the father of modern securities analysis whom I have quoted elsewhere in this book. Of course, it wasn't Graham making the attack, since he died in 1976. Rather, it was made in the most recent edition of Graham's classic book, *The Intelligent Investor*, by Jason Zweig, a *Money Magazine* staff writer who was hired to add commentaries to Graham's original text. Much like the writers of the other magazine articles, and under the heading "What Used to Work on Wall Street," Zweig graphed the returns for various strategies featured in this book from November 1996 through August 2000, claiming that "But *What Works on Wall Street* stopped working right after O'Shaughnessy published it...O'Shaughnessy's shareholders might have been less upset if he had given his book a more precise title—for instance, *What Used to Work on Wall Street...Until I Wrote This Book.*"

Keep in mind that all these judgments were made based on *three and a half years* of data. The speculative fever on Wall Street was in full swing, and the small-cap and value stocks that the funds were largely invested in were having a hard time keeping up with the technology and growth stocks dominating the big-cap S&P 500.

For the record, these writers were primarily attacking the Cornerstone Growth Fund. When most of these articles began appearing, the fund had an average annual return between December 31, 1996 and May 31, 2000 of 19.05 percent, whereas the S&P 500's return over the same period was 22.37 percent. The small-cap Russell 2000, the fund's appropriate benchmark, had an average annual return of just 9.66 percent over the same period.

Because the magazine writers were focusing on a very short period and extrapolating those returns far into the future, they came to what ultimately proved to be very misguided conclusions. Had they spent any time reading the first editions of this book, they would have seen that historically, between 1951 and 1996, the strategy they were attacking had a 30 percent chance of underperforming the All Stocks benchmark in any given year, and a 10 percent chance of doing so over any five-year period. Of course, since then, the strategy has come roaring back and is again handily beating its benchmarks. But that's not the point. The point is that, at some other time in the future, any of the strategies in this book will underperform the market, and it is only those investors who can keep their focus on the very long-term results who will be able to stick with them and reap the rewards of a long-term commitment. Nevertheless, you should always guard against letting what the market is doing today influence the long-term investment decisions you make.

USE ONLY STRATEGIES PROVEN OVER THE LONG-TERM

Always focus on strategies whose effectiveness is proven over a variety of market environments. The more periods you can analyze, the better your odds of finding a strategy that has withstood a variety of stock market environments. Buying stocks with high price-to-book ratios appeared to work for as long as 15 years, but the fullness of time proves that it is not effective.

Many years of data help you understand the peaks and valleys of a strategy. Attempting to use strategies that have not withstood the test of time will lead to great disappointment. Stocks change. Industries change. But the underlying reasons certain stocks are good investments remain the same. Only the fullness of time reveals which are the most sound. Remember how alluring all the dot.com stocks were in the late 1990s? Don't let the investment mania *de jour* suck you in—insist on long-term data that support your investment philosophy. Remember that there will always be current market fads. In the 1990s, it was Internet and technology stocks, tomorrow it might be nanotechnology or emerging markets, but *all* bubbles get popped.

DIG DEEP

If you're a professional investor, make certain to test any strategy over as much time and as many seasons as possible. Look for the worst-case scenario, the time it took to recover from that loss, and how consistent the strategy was against its relevant benchmark. Note the largest downside deviation it had against the benchmark, and be very wary of any strategy that has a wide downside deviation from it. Most investors can't stomach being far behind the benchmark for long.

If you're an individual investor, insist that your advisor conduct such a study on your behalf, or do it yourself. Many websites now exist where you can do this research. The best of them, Jamie Gritton's www.backtest.org, allows you to run tests similar to those in this book. The website uses a different database and only has data from 1985 forward, but it allows for fairly robust tests. It allows you to pick your starting month, how frequently you want the portfolio rebalanced, and then shows you the monthly returns. With all the tools now available to individual investors, there is simply no excuse for not doing your homework. Check the links at www.whatworksonwallstreet.com for any new sites that might appear to aid you in your research.

INVEST CONSISTENTLY

Consistency is the hallmark of great investors, separating them from everyone else. If you use even a mediocre strategy *consistently*, you'll beat almost all investors who jump in and out of the market, change tactics in midstream, and forever second-guess their decisions. Look at the S&P 500. We've shown that it is a simple strategy that buys large capitalization stocks. Yet this one-factor, rather mediocre strategy still manages to beat 80 percent of all actively managed funds because *it never leaves its strategy*. Realistically consider your risk tolerance, plan your path, and then stick to it. You may have fewer stories to tell at parties, but you'll be among the most successful long-term investors. Successful investing isn't alchemy: It's a simple matter of consistently using time-tested strategies and letting compounding work its magic.

ALWAYS BET WITH THE BASE RATE

Base rates are boring, dull, and *very worthwhile*. Knowing how often and by how much a strategy beats the market is among the most useful information available to investors, yet few take advantage of it. Base rates are essentially the odds of beating the market over the period when you plan to invest. If you have a 10-year time horizon and understand base rates, you'll see that picking stocks with the highest multiples of earnings, cashflow, or sales has very bad odds. If you pay attention to the odds, you can put them on your side. You now have the numbers. Use them. Don't settle for strategies that may have done very well recently but have poor overall batting averages. Chances are you'll be getting in just as those long-term base rates are getting ready to reassert themselves.

NEVER USE THE RISKIEST STRATEGIES

There is no point in using the riskiest strategies. They will sap your will, and you will undoubtedly abandon them, usually at their low. Given the number of highly effective strategies, always concentrate on those with the highest risk-adjusted returns.

ALWAYS USE MORE THAN ONE STRATEGY

Unless you're near retirement and investing only in low-risk strategies, always diversify your portfolio by investing in several strategies. How much you allocate to each is a function of risk tolerance, but you should always have some growth and some value guarding you from the inevitable swings of fashion on Wall Street. Once you have exposure to both styles of investing, make sure you have exposure to the various market capitalizations as well. A simple rule of thumb for investors with 10 years or more to go until they need the money is to use the market's weights as guidelines. Currently, 75 percent of the market is large-cap and 25 percent is small- and mid-cap. That's a good starting point for the average investor. Unite strategies so that your portfolio can do much better than the overall market without taking more risk.

USE MULTIFACTOR MODELS

The single-factor models show that the market rewards certain characteristics while punishing others. Yet, you're much better off using several factors to build your portfolios. Returns are higher and risk is lower. You should always make a stock pass several hurdles before investing in it.

INSIST ON CONSISTENCY

If you don't have the time to build your own portfolios and prefer investing in mutual funds or separately managed accounts, buy only those that stress consistency of style. Many managers follow a hit-or-miss, intuitive method of stock selection. They have no mechanism to rein in their emotions or ensure that their good ideas work. All too often, their picks are based on hope rather than experience. You have no way to *really* know exactly how they are managing your money, or if their past performance is due to a hot hand unguided by a coherent underlying strategy.

Don't bet with them. Buy one of the many funds based on solid, rigorous strategies. If your fund doesn't clearly define its investment style, insist that they do. You should expect nothing less.

THE STOCK MARKET IS NOT RANDOM

Finally, the data prove the stock market takes purposeful strides. Far from chaotic, random movement, the market consistently rewards specific strategies while punishing others. And these purposeful strides have continued to persist well after they were first identified. We now have not only what Ben Graham requested—the historical behavior of securities with defined characteristics—we also have a seven-year period during which we've witnessed their continued performance in real time. We must let history be our guide, using only those time-tested methods that have proved successful. We know what is valuable, and we know what works on Wall Street. All that remains is to act upon this knowledge.

APPENDIX

As a rule, I always look for what others ignore.
　　　　　　　　—Marshall McLuhan

RESEARCH METHODOLOGY

I. Data

Annual, quarterly, and monthly data from Standard & Poor's Compustat database, including the Research data file. The research file contains information on all companies removed from the database. Compustat PC Plus designates these files *C and *R. All data from 1950 through 1974 were uploaded to O'Shaughnessy Capital Management PCs from Compustat Mainframe. We accessed subsequent years using various Compustat PC plus dataplates on CD. For the period from 1950 through 1994, we used the Research Insight backtesting tool to generate results. For the period from 1994 through 2003, as well as for all monthly testing back to 1963, we used the FactSet Alpha Testing application.

II. Time Horizon

We examined the 52 years from December 31, 1950 to December 31, 2003. The use of time-lags (to avoid look-ahead bias) forced us to start most tests as of December 31, 1951. Tests with five-year inputs, such as five-year earnings per share growth rates, required a starting point of December 31, 1954. After 1994, we are using the FactSet Alpha Testing engine, which allows monthly and quarterly data, thus allowing for closer time lags of 45 or 90 days, depending on the codes used.

III. Universe

We include only stocks that could actually be purchased without a tremendous liquidity problem. We review both the "average" stock in the universe and large stocks in the universe. We set a market capitalization of $150 million as a minimum (in 1995 dollars) for all stocks after consulting with institutional traders. Inflation has caused a tremendous shift in nominal values since 1950, so we deflated the current value of $150 million back to 1950. We used a five-average of the deflated value of $150 million in each year and switched it every five years. Thus, these were the capitalization minimums:

- December 31, 1951–December 31, 1954: $27 million
- December 31, 1955–December 31, 1958: $27 million
- December 31, 1959–December 31, 1963: $28 million
- December 31, 1964–December 31, 1968: $31 million
- December 31, 1969–December 31, 1973: $34 million
- December 31, 1974–December 31, 1978: $44 million
- December 31, 1979–December 31, 1983: $64 million
- December 31, 1984–December 31, 1988: $97 million
- December 31, 1989–December 31, 1993: $117 million
- December 31, 1994–December 31, 1996: $150 million

All stocks with a deflated market capitalization in excess of $150 million are included and are designated "All Stocks" in the book.

We also wanted to look at returns where large stocks—the group from which many money managers select—were the universe. A simple way to achieve this was to require that a stock's market capitalization exceed the mean in any given year ("Large Stocks"). Generally, stocks with market capitalization in excess of the mean accounted for the upper 16 percent of the database by market capitalization, and stocks with market capitalization in excess of a deflated $150 million accounted for the upper 50 percent of the database.

IV. Returns

Returns are calculated annually using the following formula:

Total Return=(PRCC[1y]/PRCC)+(DVPSX[1y]/PRCC)

where:

- PRCC[1y]=year-end price of stock one year ahead of date of test
- PRCC=price of stock at beginning of period when it qualified for inclusion in the portfolio
- DVPSX[1y]=dividend actually paid in year of test

As an example, consider a stock, XYZ, that qualified for a low PE screen on December 31, 1960. Total return for the period December 31, 1960 through December 31, 1961 would be calculated thus:

PRCC (Price on December 31, 1960): $10.00

PRCC[1y] (Price on December 31, 1961): $15.00

DVPSX[1y] (Dividend *actually* paid in 1961): $1.00

Thus, ($15.00/$10.00-1)+($1.00/$10.00)=0.5+0.1=0.60, or a gain of 60 percent for the year.

For 1994 forward, we use the actual total return as calculated by Compustat's total return function within Factset (MRET). Returns were done on either a monthly or year-by-year basis, and each year of the series was inspected for outliers. All portfolios, except in Chapter Four, contain 50 stocks. If a return for an individual stock was extreme or inconsistent with other data, it was removed. Because the dividend was not reinvested monthly for the 1951–1994 period, returns are slightly understated.

All stocks were equally weighted by dollar amount. Thus, if IBM was one selected stock and Terra Industries another, each would have the same amount of dollars invested (i.e., if we bought 10 stocks and invested a total of $100,000, $10,000 would be invested in each). Portfolios were not adjusted for any factor such as beta, industry, or geographical location.

Returns differ somewhat depending upon which Compustat dataplate (CD) you use. This happens because Standard & Poor's Compustat continually updates the data. A study to see if any material difference in returns occurred because of this irregularity found that over time, it was a wash.

V. Data Definitions

Annual data were lagged a minimum of 11 months to account for reporting delays and to avoid look-ahead bias. We used periods ranging from 11 months to 15 months due to the year-end, calendar nature of our data. This also allows the inclusion of stocks with fiscal years that are not based on December 31. Because we were only making trading decisions each December 31, we had to decide what data were available *at that time*. Using several current Compustat data CDs, we studied when information became available in real time and applied it to the historical record. Each data item's time-lag is consistent with what we found examining current databases. Since 1994, the use of monthly and quarterly data with Factset's Alpha Testing application allowed the use of tighter data lags of either 45 or 90 days.

Here are the definitions of items, followed in parenthesis by their Compustat descriptor and time-lag information for the 1951–1994 period. For all years after 1994, the same Compustat data items were used within Factset, with the addition of the monthly and quarterly code equivalents, where available:

- **Sales:** Annual net sales, time-lagged by 15 months (SALE[@yr(-15m)]).
- **Common Shares Outstanding:** Represents the net number of all common shares outstanding at year-end, excluding treasury shares and scrip. Adjusted for splits, lagged by 15 months (CSHO[@yr(-15m)]).
- **Common Equity Liquidating Value:** Represents the common shareholders' interest in a company in the event of liquidation of company assets. Common equity is adjusted by the preferred stockholders' legal claims against the company. Time-lagged by 15 months. (CEQL[@yr(-15m)]). We used this as a proxy for book value.
- **Income before Extra Items:** Represents the income of a company after all expenses, including special items, income taxes, and minority interest but before provisions for common and/or preferred dividends. Does not reflect discontinued operations. Time-lagged in larger formulas (IB).

Annual dividend per share by ex-date, lagged by 11 months. DVPSX represents the cash dividends per share adjusted for all stock splits and stock dividends. This item excludes payments in preferred stock. All extra dividends are included. The current sources for the data are Interactive Data Service, Inc. and Standard & Poor's *Dividend Record* (DVPSX[@yr(-11m)]).

Annual earnings per share, excluding extraordinary items. Not restated, but adjusted by the adjustment factor for each year. Represents primary earnings per share before extraordinary items and discontinued operations. Time-lagged by 15 months (EPSPX[@yr(-15m)]).

Calendar year closing price, not lagged (PRCC).

Pretax Income, represents operating and nonoperating income before provisions for income tax and minority interest. Specifically excludes income from extraordinary items and discontinued operations. Annual, lagged in larger formulas (PI).

Adjustment factor: Ratio used to adjust all share data for splits (AJEX).

Depreciation-amortization: Noncash charges for obsolescence and wear and tear on property. Annual figure (DP).

VI. Formulas

All formulas use the above items as well as common ranking and averaging techniques. Most common formulas establish an average or rank items in descending order. Here are the definitions:

- **Averages:** Established using the @CAVG(X,SET) function. The function calculates the average value of an item or expression (x) over a set. This function returns a decimal. Thus to obtain, for example, the average market capitalization of all the stocks in the Compustat database, the formula would be: @CAVG((PRCC*CSHO[@yr(-15m)])), @SET(*C+*R,@ISVALUE((PRCC*CSHO[@yr(0m)]))). This tells the computer to calculate the average market capitalization for all items in the active (*C) and research (*R) databases that have a value for market capitalization; that is, determines whether data exist for an item (@ISVALUE). The same @CAVG, @SET, and @ISVALUE formula is used to find the database average for all items, such as price-to-earnings, price-to-book, and the like. Similar functions and expressions are employed using Factset's methodology and Alpha Testing application.
- **Ranking Items:** Such as the top 50 by dividend yield or the top 50 by sales-to-price ratio is accomplished using Compustat's @RANK(X,SET) function. This function determines the relative rank of an entity in any item or expression (X) in a set. Entities are ranked in descending order. This function returns an integer. Thus, to get the top 50 stocks by price appreciation, the formula would read: @RANK((PRCC/PRCC[-1y]), @SET(*C+*R)<51.

The @SET(Base set, condition) select entities for a set within an expression by analyzing a set (Base set) according to the predetermined criterion.

Sample Formula. Here's a sample formula that returns the 50 best-performing stocks from All Stocks that also have price-to-sales ratios below 1:

@IF(PSR1#AND#MK1#AND#@RANK((PRCC/PRCC[-1]),
@SET(*C+*R,PSR1#AND#MK1))<51,1.0,.0)

where:

- PSR1=(PRCC/(SALE/CSHO)[@yr(15m)])<1 establishes a price-to-sales ratio less than 1 and
- MK1=(PRCC*CSHO[@YR(-15m)])>117 establishes that all market capitalizations must exceed 117 million.

The 1.0,.0 at the end simply tells the program to include a stock if it meets all the criteria and exclude it if not. The <51 says we just want the top 50 by price appreciation.

Here are the formula definitions, followed by the code written for Compustat PC Plus:

- **Market Capitalization:** 12/31/yy price times common shares outstanding, lagged by 15 months (PRCC*CSHO[@yr(-15m)]).
- **Return on Equity:** 100 times (IB divided by CEQL), lagged by 15 months (100*(IB/CEQL)) used as (ROE[@yr(-15m)]).
- **Annual Indicated Dividend Yield:** DVPSX, lagged 11 months divided by PRCC (DVPSX[@yr(-11m)]/PRCC).
- **Pretax Profit Margin:** 100 times (PI divided by SALE), lagged by 15 months, called PPM (PPM[@yr(-15m)]).
- **Sales-to-Price Ratio:** Annual sales per share, lagged by 15 months, divided by year-end price ((SALE/CSHO)[@yr(-15m)]/PRCC).
- **Price-to-Sales Ratio:** Year-end price, divided by annual sales data per share, lagged by 15 months ((PRCC/(SALE/CSHO)[@yr(-15m)])).
- **One-Year Earnings per Share Gain:** Change in earning per share compared to the year earlier figure, lagged by 15 months. (EPSPX/EPSPX[-1y])[@yr(-15m)]. Worst earnings per share changes where found using the inverse: (EPSPX[-1y]/EPSPX)[@yr(-15m)].
- **Earnings-to-Price Ratio:** The inverse of the price-to-earnings ratio, with earnings lagged by 15 months (EPSPX[@yr(-15m)]/PRCC).
- **Price-to-Earnings Ratio:** (PRCC/EPSPX[@yr(-15m)]).
- **Book-to-Price Ratio:** The inverse of the price-to-book ratio, with book value lagged by 15 months. A simple book value was calculated by dividing common equity liquidating value (CEQL) by common shares outstanding ((CEQL/CSHO)[@yr(-15m)]/PRCC).
- **Price-to-Book Ratio:** ((PRCC/(CEQL/CSHO)[@yr(-15m)])).
- **Cash Flow:** Income before extraordinary gains, which represents the income of a company after all expenses except provisions for common and preferred dividends plus depreciation, lagged by 15 months, called CFL (CFL=(IB+DP), CFL[@yr(-15m)]).

- **Cashflow/Price:** Cashflow, from above, divided by common shares outstanding, divided by price ((CFL/CSHO)[@yr(-15m)]/PRCC).
- **Price/Cashflow:** ((PRCC/(CFL/CSHO[@yr(-15m)]).
- **One-Year Sales Gain:** Change in sales compared to the year earlier figure, lagged by 15 months. (SALE/SALE[-1y])[@yr(-15m)]. Worst one-year sales gains were obtained using (SALE[-1y]/SALE)[@yr(-15m)].
- **Five-Year Compound Growth Rate for Earnings-per-Share:** Uses a Compustat function—@CGR—to calculate the five-year compound growth rate for earnings per share. The function returns a percent. The first and last observations must be positive ((@CGR(EPSPX,-5,0)[@yr(-15m)]).
- **Five-Year Compound Growth Rate for Sales:** Uses a Compustat function—@CGR—to calculate the five-year compound growth rate for sales. The function returns a percent. The first and last observations must be positive ((@CGR(SALE,-5,0)[@yr(-15m)]).
- **Annual Relative Strength:** Excludes dividends and uses simple share price appreciation. (PRCC/PRCC[-1y]). Worst annual price appreciation is obtained by dividing this year's closing price by the previous year (PRCC[-1y]/PRCC).

VII. Taxes, Commissions, and Market Impact Costs

These are not included, but a real-time use of the strategies reveals that market impact and commissions are minimal. Taxes would reduce the returns according to the tax rate faced. Because all the strategies are rebalanced annually, a taxable investor would pay at the 15 percent capital gains tax rate on all gains and would presumably sell all losses for short-term capital losses to be reported against ordinary income.

BIBLIOGRAPHY

Ambachtsheer, Keith P. "The Persistence of Investment Risk," *The Journal of Portfolio Management,* Fall 1989, pp. 69–72.

Arnott, Robert D., Kelso, Charles M., Jr., Kiscadden, Stephan, and Macedo, Rosemary. "Forecasting Factor Returns: An Intriguing Possibility," *The Journal of Portfolio Management,* Fall, 1990, pp. 28–35.

Banz, R., and Breen, W. "Sample-Dependent Results Using Accounting and Market Data: Some Evidence," *Journal of Finance,* September, 1986, pp. 779–793.

Barach, Roland. *Mind Traps: Mastering the Inner World of Investing,* Homewood, Ill.: Dow Jones-Irwin, 1988.

Basu, S. "The Relationship between Earnings Yield, Market Value and Return for NYSE Common Stocks: Further Evidence," *Journal of Financial Economics,* June, 1983, pp. 129–156.

Bell, David E., Raiffa, Howard, and Tversky, Amos. *Decision Making: Descriptive, Normative, and Prescriptive Interactions,* Cambridge, England: Cambridge University Press, 1988.

Belsky, Gary, and Gilovich, Thomas. *Why Smart People Make Big Money Mistakes and How to Correct Them: Lessons From the New Science of Behavioral Economics,* New York: Simon & Schuster; 1 Fireside edition, 2000.

Bernstein, Peter L. *Capital Ideas: The Improbable Origins of Modern Wall Street*. New York: The Free Press, 1992.

Bjerring, James H., Lakonishok, Josef, and Vermaelen, Theo. "Stock Prices and Financial Analysts' Recommendations," *The Journal of Finance*, March 1983, pp. 187–204.

Blakney, R. B. *The Way of Life: A New Translation of Tao Te Ching*. New York: New American Library Publishing, 1983.

Bogle, John C. *Bogle on Mutual Funds: New Perspectives for the Intelligent Investor*. New York: Irwin Professional Publishing, 1994.

Brandes, Charles H. *Value Investing Today*. Homewood, Ill.: Dow Jones-Irwin, 1989.

Brealey, Richard A. *An Introduction to Risk and Return from Common Stocks*. Second Edition. Cambridge, MA: MIT Press, 1993.

Brealey, Richard A. Portfolio Theory versus Portfolio Practice," *The Journal of Portfolio Management*, Summer 1990, pp. 6–10.

Brock, William, Lakonishok, Josef, and LeBaron, Blake. "Simple Technical Trading Rules and the Stochastic Properties of Stock Returns," *The Journal of Finance*, December 1992, pp. 1731–1764.

Brown, John Dennis. *101 Years on Wall Street: An Investor's Almanac*. Englewood Cliffs, NJ: Prentice Hall, 1991.

Brown, Stephen J., and Kritzman, Mark P. *Quantitative Methods for Financial Analysis*. Homewood, Ill.: Dow-Jones-Irwin, 1987.

Brown, Stephen J., and Goetzmann, William N. "Performance Persistence," *Journal of Finance*, 1995.

Brush, John S., and Boles, Keith E. "The Predictive Power in Relative Strength & CAPM," *The Journal of Portfolio Management*, Summer 1983, pp. 20–23.

Brush, John S. "Eight Relative Strength Models Compared," *The Journal of Portfolio Management*, Fall 1986, pp. 21–28.

Casti, John L. *COMPLEX-ification, Explaining a Paradoxical World through the Science of Surprise*. New York: HarperCollins Publishers, 1994.

Chan, Louis K., Hamao, Yasushi, and Lakonishok, Josef. "Fundamentals and Stock Returns in Japan," *The Journal of Finance*, December 1991, pp. 1739–1764.

Chan, Louis, K.C., and Lakonishok, Josef. "Are the Reports of Beta's Death Premature?" *The Journal of Portfolio Management,* Summer 1993, pp. 51–62.

Chopra, Navin, Lakonishok, Josef, and Ritter, Jay R. "Measuring Abnormal Performance: Do Stocks Overreact?" *Journal of Financial Economics,* November 1992, pp. 235–268.

Cottle, Sidney, Murray, Roger F., and Block, Frank E. *Graham and Dodd's Security Analysis,* 5th ed. New York: McGraw-Hill, 1988.

Coulson, Robert D. *The Intelligent Investor's Guide to Profiting from Stock Market Inefficiencies.* Chicago: Probus Publishing Company, 1987.

Damodaran, Aswath. *Investment Philosophies: Successful Strategies and the Investors Who Made Them Work.* Hoboken, NJ: John Wiley & Sons, 2003.

Dawes, Robyn M. *House of Cards: Psychology and Psychotherapy Built on Myth.* New York: The Free Press, 1994.

Dewdney, A.K. *200% of Nothing: An Eye-Opening Tour through the Twists and Turns of Math Abuse and Innumeracy.* New York: John Wiley & Sons, Inc., 1993.

Dimson, Elroy, Marsh, Paul, and Staunton, Mike. *Triumph of the Optimists: 101 Years of Global Investment Returns.* Princeton, NJ: Princeton University Press, 2002.

Dreman, David N. *Psychology and the Stock Market,* New York: Warner Books, 1977.

Dreman, David N. *The New Contrarian Investment Strategy.* New York: Random House, 1980.

Dreman, David N. *Contrarian Investment Strategies. The Next Generation,* New York: Simon & Schuster, 1998.

Dreman, David N. "Good-bye EMH," *Forbes Magazine,* June 20, 1994, p. 261.

Dreman, David N. "Nasty Surprises," *Forbes Magazine,* July 19, 1993, p. 246.

Dreman, David N. "Choronically Clouded Crystal Balls," *Forbes Magazine,* October 11, 1993, p. 178.

Dunn, Patricia C., and Theisen, Rolf D. "How Consistently Do Active Managers Win?" *The Journal of Portfolio Management,* Summer 1983, pp. 47–50.

Ellis, Charles D., and Vertin, James R. *Classics: An Investor's Anthology.* Homewood, Ill.: Dow Jones-Irwin 1989.

Ellis, Charles D., and Vertin, James R. *Classics II: Another Investor's Anthology.* Homewood, Ill.: Dow Jones-Irwin, 1991.

Fabozzi, Frank J., Fogler, H. Russell, Harrington, Diana R. *The New Stock Market, A Complete Guide to the Latest Research, Analysis and Performance.* Chicago: Probus Publishing Company, 1990.

Fabozzi, Frank J. *Pension Fund Investment Management.* Chicago: Probus Publishing Company, 1990.

Fabozzi, Frank J., and Zarb, Frank G. *Handbook of Financial Markets: Securities, Options and Futures.* Homewood, Ill.: Dow Jones-Irwin, 1986.

Faust, David. *The Limits of Scientific Reasoning.* Minneapolis: University of Minnesota Press, 1984.

Feinberg, Mortimer. *Why Smart People Do Dumb Things: Lessons from the New Science of Behavioral Economics.* Fireside, NY: 1995.

Ferguson, Robert. "The Trouble with Performance Measurement," *The Journal of Portfolio Management,* Spring 1986, pp. 4–9.

Ferguson, Robert. "The Plight of the Pension Fund Officer," *Financial Analysts Journal,* May/June, 1989, pp. 8–9.

Fisher, Kenneth L. *Super Stocks.* Homewood, Ill.: Dow Jones-Irwin, 1984.

Fogler, H. Russell. "Common Stock Management in the 1990s," *The Journal of Portfolio Management,* Winter 1990, pp. 26–34.

Freeman, John D. "Behind the Smoke and Mirrors: Gauging the Integrity of Investment Simulations," *Financial Analysts Journal,* November/December 1992, pp. 26–31.

Fridson, Martin S. *Investment Illusions.* New York: John Wiley & Sons, Inc., 1993.

Givoly, Dan, and Lakonishok, Josef. "Financial Analysts' Forecasts of Earnings: Their Value to Investors," *Journal of Banking and Finance,* December 1979, pp. 221–233.

Gleick, James. *Chaos: Making A New Science.* New York: Viking Penguin, 1987.

Graham, Benjamin, and Zweig, Jason. *The Intelligent Investor, Revised Edition.* New York: HarperBusiness, 2003.

Guerard, John, and Vaught, H.T. *The Handbook of Financial Modeling.* Chicago: Probus Publishing Co., 1989.

Hackel, Kenneth S., and Livnat, Joshua. *Cash Flow and Security Analysis.* Homewood, Ill.: Business-One Irwin, 1992.

Hagin, Bob. "What Practitioners Need to Know About T-Tests," *Financial Analysts Journal*, May/June 1990, pp. 17–20.

Harrington, Diana R., Fabozzi, Frank J., and Fogler, H. Russell. *The New Stock Market*. Chicago: Probus Publishing Company, 1990.

Haugen, Robert A., and Baker, Nardin L. "Dedicated Stock Portfolios," *The Journal of Portfolio Management*, Summer 1990, pp. 17–22.

Hoff, Benjamin. *The Tao of Pooh*. New York: Penguin Books, 1982.

Ibbotson Associates. *Stocks, Bonds, Bills, and Inflation 1995 Yearbook*. Chicago: Ibbotson Associates, 1995.

Ibbotson, Roger G., and Brinson, Gary P. *Gaining the Performance Advantage: Investment Markets*. New York: McGraw-Hill, 1987.

Ikenberry, David, Lakonishok, Josef, and Vermaelen, Theo. "Market Under Reaction to Open Market Share Repurchases," July 1994, unpublished.

Jacobs, Bruce J., and Levy, Kenneth N. "Disentangling Equity Return Regularities: New Insights and Investment Opportunities," *Financial Analysts Journal*, May/June 1988, pp. 18–38.

Jeffrey, Robert H. "Do Clients Need So Many Portfolio Managers?" *The Journal of Portfolio Management*, Fall 1991, pp. 13–19.

Kahneman, Daniel, and Riepe, Mark W. "The Psychology of the Non-Professional Investor," *Preliminary Draft,* September 1997.

Kahn, Ronald N. "What Practitioners Need to Know About Back Testing," *Financial Analysts Journal*, July/August 1990, pp. 17–20.

Keane, Simon M. "Paradox in the Current Crisis in Efficient Market Theory," *The Journal of Portfolio Management*, Winter 1991, pp. 30–34.

Keepler, A. Michael. "Further Evidence on the Predictability of International Equity Returns," *The Journal of Portfolio Management*, Fall 1991, pp. 48–53.

Keppler, A. Michael. "The Importance of Dividend Yields in Country Selection," *The Journal of Portfolio Management*, Winter 1991, pp. 24–29.

Klein, Robert A., Lederman, Jess. *Small Cap Stocks, Investment and Portfolio Strategies for the Institutional Investor*. Chicago: Probus Publishing Company, 1993.

Knowles, Harvey C. III, and Petty, Damon H. *The Dividend Investor*. Chicago: Probus Publishing Company, 1992.

Kritzman, Mark. "How To Detect Skill in Management Performance," *The Journal of Portfolio Management*, Winter 1986, pp. 16–20.

Kuhn, Thomas, S. *The Copernican Revolution: Planetary Astronomy in the Development of Western Thought*. Cambridge, MA: Harvard University Press, 1957.

Kuhn, Thomas S. *The Structure of Scientific Revolutions*. Chicago: University of Chicago Press, 1970.

Lakonishok, Josef, Shleifer, Andrei, and Vishny, Robert W. "Contrarian Investment, Extrapolation, and Risk," working paper, June 1994.

Lee, Wayne Y. "Diversification and Time: Do Investment Horizons Matter?" *The Journal of Portfolio Management*, Spring 1990, pp. 21–26.

Lerner, Eugene M., and Theerathorn, Pochara. "The Returns of Different Investment Strategies," *The Journal of Portfolio Management*, Summer 1983, pp. 26–28.

Lewis, Michael. *Moneyball: The Art of Winning an Unfair Game*. New York: W.W. Norton & Company, 2003.

Lo, Andrew W., and Mackinlay, A. Craig. *A Non-Random Walk Down Wall Street*. Princeton, NJ: Princeton University Press, 1999.

Lofthouse, Stephen. *Equity Investment Mangement, How to Select Stocks and Markets*. Chichester, England: John Wiley & Sons, 1994.

Lorie, James H., Dodd, Peter, and Kimpton, Mary Hamilton. *The Stock Market: Theories and Evidence*. Homewood, Ill.: Dow Jones-Irwin, 1985.

Lowe, Janet. *Benjamin Graham on Value Investing, Lessons from the Dean of Wall Street*. Chicago: Dearborn Financial Publishing Inc., 1994.

Lowenstein, Louis. *What's Wrong with Wall Street*. New York: Addison-Wesley, 1988.

Maital, Shloml. *Minds Markets & Money: Psychological Foundation of Economic Behavior*. New York: Basic Books, 1982.

Malkiel, Burton G. "Returns from Investing in Equity Mutual Funds 1971-1991," *Princeton University*, 1994.

Mandelbrot, Benoit, and Hudson, Richard L. *The (Mis)behavior of Markets: A Fractal View of Risk, Ruin, and Reward*. New York: Basic Books, 2004.

Martin, Linda J. "Uncertain? How Do You Spell Relief?" *The Journal of Portfolio Management*, Spring 1985, pp. 5–8.

Marcus, Alan J. "The Magellan Fund and Market Efficiency," *The Journal of Portfolio Management*, Fall 1990, pp. 85–88.

Mattlin, Everett. "Reliability Math: Manager Selection by the Numbers," *Institutional Investor,* January 1993, pp. 141–142.

Maturi, Richard J. *Stock Picking: The 11 Best Tactics for Beating the Market.* New York: McGraw-Hill, 1993.

McElreath, Robert B., Jr., and Wiggins C. Donald. "Using the COMPUSTAT Tapes in Financial Research: Problems and Solutions," *Financial Analysts Journal,* January/February 1984, pp. 71–76.

Melnikoff, Meyer. *"Anomaly Investing,"* in *The Financial Analyst's Handbook,* edited by Sumner N. Levine. Homewood, Ill.: Dow Jones-Irwin, 1988, pp. 699-721.

Montier, James. *Behavioral Finance: Insights into Irrational Minds and Markets.* West Sussex, England: John Wiley & Sons, Ltd., 2002.

Murphy, Joseph E., Jr. *Revised Edition: Stock Market Probability.* Chicago: Probus Publishing Company, 1994.

Newbold, Gerald D., and Poon, Percy S. "Portfolio Risk, Portfolio Performance and the Individual Investor," *The Journal of Finance,* Summer 1996.

Nisbett, Richard, and Ross, Lee. *Human Inference: Strategies and Shortcomings of Social Judgement.* Englewood Cliffs, NJ: Prentice-Hall, 1980.

O'Barr, William M., and Conley, John M. *Fortune & Folly: The Wealth & Power of Institutional Investing.* Homewood, Ill.: Business-One Irwin, 1992.

O'Hanlon, John, and Ward, Charles W.R. "How to Lose at Winning Strategies," *The Journal of Portfolio Management,* Spring 1986.

Oppenheimer, Henry R. "A Test of Ben Graham's Stock Selection Criteria," *Financial Analysts Journal,* September/October 1984, pp. 68–74.

O'Shaughnessy, James P. "Quantitative Models as an Aid in Offsetting Systematic Errors in Decision Making," St. Paul, MN, 1988, unpublished.

O'Shaughnessy, James P. *Invest Like the Best: Using Your Computer to Unlock the Secrets of the Top Money Managers.* New York: McGraw-Hill, 1994.

O'Shaughnessy, James P. *How To Retire Rich.* New York: Broadway Books, 1998.

Paulos, John Allen. *Innumeracy: Mathematical Illiteracy and Its Consequences.* New York: Hill and Wang, 1989.

Paulos, John Allen. *A Mathematician Plays the Stock Market.* New York: Basic Books, 2003.

Perritt, Gerald, W. *Small Stocks, Big Profit.* Chicago: Dearborn Financial Publishing, Inc., 1993.

Perritt, Gerald W., and Lavine, Alan. *Diversify Your Way To Wealth: How to Customize Your Investment Portfolio to Protect and Build Your Net Worth.* Chicago: Probus Publishing Company, 1994.

Peter, Edgar E. *Chaos and Order in the Capital Markets: A New View of Cycles, Prices, and Market Volatility.* New York: John Wiley & Sons, 1991.

Peters, Donald J. *A Contrarian Strategy for Growth Stock Investing: Theoretical Foundations & Empirical Evidence.* Westport, CT: Quorum Books, 1993.

Pettengill, Glenn N., and Jordan, Bradford D. "The Overreaction Hypothesis, Firm Size, and Stock Market Seasonality," *The Journal of Portfolio Management,* Spring 1990, pp. 60–64.

Reinganum, M. "Misspecificaiton of Capital Asset Pricing: Empirical Anomalies Based on Earnings' Yields and Market Values," *The Journal of Financial Economics*, March 1981, pp. 19–46.

Schwager, Jack D. *Market Wizards: Interviews with Top Traders.* New York: Simon & Schuster, 1992.

Schwager, Jack D. *The New Market Wizards.* New York: Harper-Collins Publishers, 1992.

Schleifer, Andrei. *Inefficient Markets: An Introduction to Behavioral Finance.* Oxford, England: Oxford University Press, 2000.

Sharp, Robert M. *The Lore and Legends of Wall Street.* Homewood, Ill.: Dow Jones-Irwin, 1989.

Shefrin, Hersh. *Beyond Greed and Fear: Understanding Behavioral Finance and the Psychology of Investing.* Boston, MA: Harvard Business School Press, 2000.

Shiller, Robert J. *Market Volatility.* Cambridge, MA: The MIT Press, 1989.

Shiller, Robert J. *Irrational Exuberance.* New York: Broadway Books, 2001.

Siegel, Jeremy J. *Stocks for the Long Run: Second Edition, Revised and Expanded.* New York: McGraw-Hill, 1998.

Siegel, Laurence B. *Stocks, Bonds, Bills and Inflation 1994 Yearbook.* Chicago: Ibbotson Associates, 1994.

Singal, Vijay. *Beyond the Random Walk: A Guide to Stock Market Anomalies and Low Risk Investing.* New York: Oxford University Press, 2004.

Smullyan, Raymond M. *The Tao Is Silent.* New York: Harper and Row, 1977.

Speidell, Lawrence S. "The New Wave Theory," *Financial Analysts Journal,* July/August 1988, pp. 9–12.

Speidell, Lawrence S. "Embarrassment and Riches: The Discomfort of Alternative Investment Strategies," *The Journal of Portfolio Management,* Fall 1990, pp. 6–11.

Stumpp, Mark, and Scott, James. "Does Liquidity Predict Stock Returns?" *The Journal of Portfolio Management,* Winter 1991, pp. 35–40.

Surowiecki, James. *The Wisdom of Crowds: Why the Many Are Smarter Than the Few and How Collective Wisdom Shapes Business, Economies, Societies and Nations.* New York: Doubleday, 2004.

Taleb, Nassim Nicholas. *Fooled by Randomness: The Hidden Role of Chance in the Markets and in Life.* Texere, NY, 2001.

Thaler, Richard H. *The Winner's Curse: Paradoxes and Anomalies of Economic Life.* Princeton, NJ: Princeton University Press, 1994.

Thomas, Dana L. *The Plungers and the Peacocks: An Update of the Classic History of the Stock Market.* New York: William Morrow, 1989.

Tierney, David E., and Winston, Kenneth. "Using Generic Benchmarks to Present Manager Styles," *The Journal of Portfolio Management,* Summer 1991, pp. 33–36.

Train, John. *The Money Masters.* New York: Harper & Row Publishers, 1985.

Train, John. *Famous Financial Fiascos.* New York: Clarkson N. Potter, 1985.

Train, John. *The New Money Masters: Winning Investment Strategies of: Soros, Lynch, Steinhardt, Rogers, Neff, Wanger, Michaelis, Carret.* New York: Harper & Row Publishers, 1989.

Treynor, Jack L. "Information-Based Investing," *Financial Analysts Journal,* May/June 1989, pp. 6–7.

Treynor, Jack L. "The 10 Most Important Questions to Ask in Selecting a Money Manager," *Financial Analysts Journal,* May/June, 1990, pp. 4–5.

Trippe, Robert R., and Lee, Jae K. *State-of-the-Art Portfolio Selection: Using Knowledge-Based Systems to Enhance Investment Performance.* Chicago: Probus Publishing Company, 1992

Tsetsekos, George P., and DeFusco, Richard. "Portfolio Performance, Managerial Ownership, and the Size Effect," *The Journal of Portfolio Management,* Spring 1990, pp. 33–39.

Twark, Allan, and D'Mello, James P. "Model Indexation: A Portfolio Management Tool," *The Journal of Portfolio Management,* Summer 1991, pp. 37–40.

Valentine, Jerome, L. "Investment Analysis and Capital Market Theory," *The Financial Analysts,* Occasional Paper Number 1, 1975.

Valentine, Jerome L., and Mennis, Edmund A. *Quantitative Techniques for Financial Analysis.* Homewood, Ill.: Richard D. Irwin, Inc., 1980.

Vandell, Robert F., and Parrino, Robert. "A Purposeful Stride Down Wall Street," *The Journal of Portfolio Management,* Winter 1986, pp. 31–39.

Vince, Ralph. *The Mathematics of Money Management.* New York: John Wiley & Sons, 1992.

Vishny, Robert W., Shleifer, Andrei, and Lakonishok, Josef. "The Structure and Performance of the Money Management Industry," in the *Brookings Papers on Economic Activity, Microeconomics 1992.*

Watzlawick, Paul. *How Real Is Real? Confusion, Disinformation, Communication.* New York: Vintage Books, 1977.

Wilcox, Jarrod W. *Investing by the Numbers.* New Hope, PA: Frank J. Fabozzi Associates, 1999.

Williams, John Burr. "Fifty Years of Investment Analysis," *The Financial Analysts Research Foundation,* 1979.

Wood, Arnold S. "Fatal Attractions for Money Managers," *Financial Analysts Journal,* May/June 1989, pp. 3–5.

Zeikel, Arthur. "Investment Management in the 1990s," *Financial Analysts Journal,* September/October 1990, pp. 6–9.

INDEX

NOTE: Boldface numbers indicate tables and illustrations.

absolute returns, 44, 337–346,
  338–345
active management investing, 1, 2,
  3
actuarial approach to decision
  making, 14–15
All Stocks universe, 155, **156**, 386
  absolute returns in, 337–346,
    338–345
  average annual compound rates
    of return by decade for, 51,
    52, 65
  average annual compound return
    by decile in, 56–57, **57**
  base rates for, 55, **55, 65**
  benchmarks in, 70
  best and worst average annual
    compound returns for, 52–53,
    52, 53, 64, 64–65
  consistent performance of,
    160–162, **161, 162**
  dividend yields and, 143,
    144–147
    decile analysis using, 151–153,
      152, 153
    worst-case scenarios using,
      150–151, **150–151**
  downside risk in, 346–347,
    357–366, **358–365, 366,** 357

All Stocks universe *(continued)*
  earnings gains and, 184
    best- and worst-case returns
      using, 171–173, **172–173,**
      178–180, **179, 180**
    changes in, 168–170, **168, 169,**
      170
    decile analysis using, 180, **181,**
      182
    worst changes in, 173–174,
      173, 174
  earnings per share percentage
    changes and, 185, **186–189**
    base rates for, 187, **188–189**
    best- and worst-case returns
      using, 191–192, **192**
    decile analysis using, 192–194,
      193
    Sharpe ratio and, 187, **187**
  growth investing and, 253–254,
    254, 295, 305
  maximum decline in, **161**
  Market Leaders universe vs.,
    annual data, 260, **260**
  Market Leaders universe vs.,
    monthly data, 261–262, **261**
  multifactor models and
    deviation from benchmark test-
      ing in, 249–250

All Stocks universe *(continued)*
  growth models using, 253–254,
    254
  P/E, P/B, and PSR combined in,
    248, **249**
  return on equity (ROE) and,
    255, 256, **255, 256, 257**
  value factors added to,
    243–244, **244, 245**
  price-to-book ratios and,
    245–246, **246,** 245
    best- and worst-case returns by,
      102, **103, 104**
    decile analysis by, 103, **103,**
      104
    high P/B stocks and, 96–100,
      96–98, 99, 99–100
    low P/B stocks and, 92–96, **92,**
      94–95
    overall peformance using,
      104–107, **105, 106**
  price-to-cashflow ratios and,
    best and worst returns using,
      113–115, **114, 115, 122–123**
    high P/C stocks and, 109, 110,
      110, 111, 116–120, **116, 117,**
      118
    low P/C stocks and, 109, 110,
      110, 111, 113

All Stocks universe *(continued)*
price-to-earnings (PE) ratios and, 243–244, **244**
high-PE stocks vs. 78–83, **78–83**
low PE stocks vs., 72–76, **72–75**
summary of performance using, 85–88, **85–88**
price-to-sales ratios (PSR) and, 128–131, **128–131**, 247–248, **247, 248**
best- and worst-case scenarios using, 132–134, **133–134**
decile analysis and, 139–141, **139–141**
high PSR stocks and, 134–139, **135–139**
low PSR stocks and, 128–131, **128–131**, 132–134–**134**
profit margins and, 197–207, **198, 199**–202
best- and worst-case returns using, 203, **203–205**
decile analysis using, 205, **205–207**
Sharpe ratio and, **202**
worst-case scenarios in, **201, 202**, 203, **203–205**
relative price strength and, 222–225, **223, 224, 225–227,** 222
base rates and, 225, **226**
best and worst returns using, 230–231, **231–234**, 234, **234–235, 236–237**
decile analysis using, 235, **237**
over longer-term, 239–240, **241–242**
Sharpe ratios and, **224**
over shorter term, 240, **241, 242**
worst-case scenarios and, **226–227**, 230–232, **231–234**
return on equity (ROE) and, 209–212, **210–213**, 255, 256, **255, 256, 257**
base rates and, 210, 212, **212**
best and worst returns using, 215–216, **216**
decile analysis using, 216, **217, 218, 219, 220**
Sharpe ratio and, **211**
worst-case scenarios using, **213, 214–215**, 215–216, **216**
risk assessment in, 156–159
risk-adjusted performance strategies for, 309–318, **312–318**, 347–357, **348–355**

All Stocks universe *(continued)*
S&P vs., 49–51, **50, 51**
small-cap stocks and, 56–57, **57**
summary return and risk results for, **62–63**
total returns by universe in, 69–70, **70**
value investing and, 281–293, **283, 292**
worst-case scenarios for, 53–55, **53, 54, 55, 161**
Alpha, Jensen's, 320
American Depository Receipts (ADRs), 43, 144, 259–260
anecdotal evidence in investing, 34–35
annual indicated dividend yield, 390
annual performance of Market Leaders universe, @, Russell 1000, 66–67, **66**
annual relative strength, 391
arithmetic average, 45
Asian market crisis, 25–27, **27**, 347
AT&T, 8
average annual compound rates of return by decade, 51, **52, 65**
averages, 389

Barber, Brad M., 20
Barron's, 46
base rates, 17–18, 55, **55**, 159–160, **160**, 382
All Stocks universe, **65**
earnings per share percentage changes and, 187, **188–189**
growth investing and, 303, **303, 305**
Market Leaders universe and, **65**, 264–265, **266**
multifactor models and, 245
price-to-book ratios and, 93–94, **94**, 159–160, **160**
price-to-cashflow ratios and, 112–113, **113**, 159–160, **160**
price-to-earnings (PE) and, 159–160, **160**
price-to-sales ratios (PSR) and, 131, 159–160, **160**
relative price strength and, 225, **226**
return on equity (ROE) and, 210, 212, **212**
Small Stocks universe and, **65**, 273–274, **276**
value investing and, **292**
Bavelas, Alex, 20–21

Bear Stearns Asset Management, 30, 37
behavioral economics theory, 4
Behavioral Finance, 4
benchmarking, 70, 249–381
best and worst average annual compound returns, 52–53, **52, 53, 64, 64–65**
Best Buy, 77
bias, 36, 38, 42, 388
bonds, 333–334
absolute returns in, 337–346, **338–345**
correlation matrix analysis in, **328**
downside risk in, 357–366, **358–365, 366**, 357
risk-adjusted returns in, 347–357, **348–355**
book-to-price ratio, 390
booms and busts, 335
Borne, Ludwig, 109
Brealey, Richard, 32
British Petroleum, 260
Brown, John Dennis, 142
bubble markets, 28–29, 30, 33–34, 377–378
price-to-book ratios and, 100
price-to-earnings (PE) ratios and, 89
price-to-sales ratios (PSR) and, 142
risk assessment and, 158–159, **158, 159**
bull markets, 335
BusinessWeek, 379

Canadian markets, 325
Capital Asset Pricing Model (CAPM), 156, 320
cash flow, 390
cashflow-to-price ratio, 391
clinical approach to decision making, 13–15
Clinical versus Statistical Prediction , 14
collective intelligence theory, 221–222
commission, 391
commodities, 333–334
common liquidating equity, 209. *See also* return on equity
compound and average returns by market capitalization, 58–59, **58**
compound rates of return by decade, 51, **52**

Compustat, 5, 7, 35, 38–39, , 42, 43, 385–391
computer analysis of investment strategies, 7, 33
consistency in investing, 4, 8, 159–162, **161, 162**, 377–383
Contrarian Investment, Extrapolation and Risk, 32
Control Data, 335
Cornerstone Growth Fund, 26–27, **27**, 380
  absolute returns in, 337–346, **338–345**
  downside risk in, 357–366, **358–365, 366**, 357
  growth investing and, 295–307, **296–298**
  risk-adjusted performance strategies for, 309–318, **312–318**, 347–357, **348–355**
  value investing and, 284, **285–286**, 289–290, **290–291**
correlation matrix analysis, 327–331, **328–330**
correlation with S&P, 45
costs, 46–47, 381
Courage of Misguided Convictions, The, 20
Cybercash, 304

data definitions used in book, 388–389
data mining, 7, 36
data sources used in book, 35, 385
Dawes, Robert, 15
decile analysis
  dividend yields and, 151–153, **152, 153**
  earnings gains and, 180, **181, 182**
  earnings per share percentage changes and, 192–194, **193**
  intersection portfolios and, 332–333, **333**
  price-to-book ratios and, 103, **103, 104**
  price-to-cashflow ratios and, 123–125, **123, 124, 125**
  price-to-earnings (PE) ratios and, 84
  price-to-sales ratios (PSR) and, 139–141, **139–141**
  profit margins and, 205, **205–207**
  relative price strength and, 235, 237
  return on equity (ROE) and, 216, **217, 218, 219, 220**

decision making, 13–15
Deutsche Telekon, 260
Dimson, Elroy, 32
discipline in investing, 7–8, 46
Disraeli, Benjamin, 309
dividend yields, 143–154, **144–147**
  All Stocks universe, 143, **144–147**
    decile analysis using, 151–153, **152, 153**
    worst-case scenarios using, 150–151, **150–151**
  decile analysis using, 151–153, **152, 153**
  implications for investing and, 153–154, **154**
  Large Stocks universe, 143, **144–147**, 148–149, **149**
    decile analysis using, 151–153, **152, 153**
    Sharpe ratio and, 149, **149**
    worst-case scenarios using, 150–151, **150–151**
  Sharpe ratio and, 149, **149**
  value investing and, 286
  worst-case scenarios using, 150–151, **150–151**
Dodd, David, 89
Dogs of the Dow, 7, 9–12, **10, 11, 12**, , 24–25, 319–320
Dow Jones Industrial Average, 319
  absolute returns in, 337–346, **338–345**
  Dogs of Dow and, 7, 9–12, **10, 11, 12**, 319–320
  downside risk in, 357–366, **358–365, 366**, 357
  risk-adjusted returns in, 347–357, **348–355**
  Roaring Twenties and, 33–34
  S&P 500 vs., 6–7
  value investing strategies for, 281–293
downside risk, 44, 45, 282, 346–347, 357–366, **358–365, 366**
Dreman, David, 167

earnings gains, 167–184
  All Stocks universe, 184
    best- and worst-case returns using, 171–173, **172–173**, 178–180, **179, 180**
    changes in, 168–170, **168, 169, 170**
    decile analysis using, 180, **181, 182**

earnings gains *(continued)*
    worst changes in, 173–174, **173, 174**
  best- and worst-case returns using, 171–173, **172–173**, 178–180, **179, 180**
  case study in, 183–184
  changes in, 168–170, **168, 169, 170**
  decile analysis using, 180, **181, 182**
  growth investing and, 167
  implications for investing and, 180–183, **183**
  Large Stocks universe, 184
    best- and worst-case returns using, 171–173, **172–173**, 178–180, **179, 180**
    changes in, 168–171, **168, 169, 170, 171**
    decile analysis using, 180, **181, 182**
    worst changes in, 173–178, **173, 174, 175–178**
  price-to-sales ratios (PSR) and, 183–184
  sales increases vs., 183–184
  worst changes in, 173–174, **173, 174**
earnings per share percentage changes (5-year), 185–196, **186–189**
  All Stocks universe, 185, **186–189**
    base rates for, 187, **188–189**
    best- and worst-case returns using, 191–192, **192**
    decile analysis using, 192–194, **193**
    Sharpe ratio and, 187, **187**
  base rates for, 187, **188–189**
  best- and worst-case returns using, 191–192, **192**
  decile analysis using, 192–194, **193**
  five-year compound growth rate for, 391
  implications for investing and, 194, **194–196**
  Large Stocks universe, **186**, 189, **190–191**
    base rates for, 187, **188–189**
    best- and worst-case returns using, 191–192, **192**
    decile analysis using, 192–194, **193**
    Sharpe ratio and, 187, **187**

earnings per share percentage changes (5-year) *(continued)*
relative price strength and, 229
Sharpe ratio and, 187, **187**
earnings-to-price ratio, 390
EnCorr Analyzer, 320
Exchange Traded Funds (ETFs), 2
expected returns, minimum vs. maximum, 44–45
explicit nature of investment strategy, 35
exposure, 382–383
Exxon, 46

FactSet Alpha Tester, 35, 42, 319
Fairchild Camera, 34
Fama, Eugene, 32
Fama-French data series, 328, **328–330**
Faust, David, 14
Financial Analysts Journal, 20
First Trust Value Line Fund, 17
Fisher, Ken, 127
five-year compound growth rate, 391
five-year earnings per share percentage changes. *See* earnings per share percentage changes (5-year)
Forbes Magazine, 167
foreign stocks, 43
formulas used in book, 389–391
Fortune & Folly, 22
French, Ken, 32

geometric average, 45
Goethe, 9, 377
Goldberg, L., 15
Gorbachev, Mikhail, 9
Graham, Ben, 31–32, 89, 243, 379
Great Depression, 27, 335
Greenspan, Alan, 6
Gritton, Jamie, 381
growth factors, multifactor models and, 253
growth investing, 1, 167, 295–307
  All Stocks universe, 295, **305**
  base rates in, 303, **303, 305**
  best and worst average annual returns in, **306**
  concentrated versions of, 307
  Cornerstone Growth Strategy in, 295–307, **296–298**
  earnings gains and, 167
  Hennessy Cornerstone Growth Fund and, 298

growth investing *(continued)*
  implications of, 303–304, **304, 305, 306**
  improved strategies for (Cornerstone), 301–302, **302**
  Large Stocks universe, 299–300, **300–301**
  multifactor models and, 253–254, **254,** 307
  O'Shaughnessy Cornerstone Growth Fund and, 298
  RBC O'Shaughnessy U.S. Growth Fund and, 298
  risk-adjusted performance and, 309–318, **312–318**
  summary return and risk results for, **305**
  traditional growth factors in, vs. newer strategies, 298–299
  worst-case scenarios in, **304, 306,** 306
growth investing, 295–307

Haloid-Xerox, 34
Hennessy Cornerstone Growth Fund, 298
Henry, Patrick, 335
heuristics, 14
hindsight bias, 16
history as guide in decision making, 22–23
holding period analysis, 324, **324**
holdout periods, out-of-sample, 38–39
House of Cards, 15
Huxley, Aldous, 295
Huxley, Thomas, 243

Ibbotson EnCorr Analyzer, 320
IBM, 34, 335
In Defense of Man's Best Friend, 24–25
indexing, index funds, 2, 5–7, 66
individual vs. group in decision making, 18–19
inefficiency of market, 3–4
inflation, **39–40**
  absolute returns and, 337–346, **338–345**
  downside risk in, 357–366, **358–365, 366,** 357
  risk-adjusted returns and, 347–357, **348–355**
ING Corporate Leaders Trust, 8–9, 8
initial public offerings (IPOs), 346

Intelligent Investor, The, 379–380
Internet Contrarian, The, 29–30
Internet market bubble, 29–30
intersection portfolios, 332–333, **333**
intuitive approach to decision making, 13–15
Invest Like the Best, 8
investment strategies, 335–376, 377–383
  absolute returns in, 337–346, **338–345**
  annual rebalancing in, 42–43
  base rates and, 159–160, **160,** 382
  benchmarks in, 381
  characteristics of, 35
  consistency in, 159–160, 378–383
  downside risk in, 44, 346–347, 357–366, **358–365, 366**
  expected returns in, minimum vs. maximum, 44–45
  growth investing in, 295–307
  long-term data and, 165–166, 335–337, 380–381
  look-ahead bias and, 42
  market capitalization in, 39–42, **39–42,** 49–70
  maximum decline in, 366–367, **368–375**
  multifactor models in, 383
  multiple or blended strategies in, 367, 382–383
  number of stocks in portfolio in, 45–46
  pitfalls of, 35–38
  ranking of, 335–376
  returns calculation in, risk-adjusted vs. absolute, 44, **44**
  risk assessment in, 156–159, **158, 159,** 337, 382
  risk-adjusted returns in, 347–357, **348–355.** *See also* Sharpe ratios
  rules for, in book, 38–47
  Sharpe ratio in, 44, 356–357
  short-term data and, 379–380
  summary statistics provided for, 45
  transaction costs in, 46–47
  universes of stocks in, 38–39
  value investing, 281–293
  worst-case scenarios in, 381

Jensen's Alpha, 320
judgment, limits of, 14–15

Kahneman, Daniel, 16–17
Kennedy, John F., 335
Keynes, John M., 319
KFX Inc., 356
Kierkgaard, Soren, 91

Lakonishok, Josef, 32
Large Stocks universe, **40–42**, 386
  absolute returns in, 337–346,
    338–345, 337
  average annual compound rates
    of return by decade for, 51,
    52, 162
  base rates for, 55, **55**
  benchmarks in, 70
  best and worst average annual
    compound returns for, 52–53,
    52, 53, 64, 64–65
  compound average annual rates
    of return in, **164**
  consistent performance of,
    160–162, **161, 162**
  dividend yields and, 143,
    144–147, 148–149, 149
  decile analysis using, 151–153,
    152, 153
  Sharpe ratio and, 149, **149**
  worst-case scenarios using,
    150–151, **150–151**
  downside risk in, 357–366,
    358–365, 366, 357
  earnings gains and, 184
  best- and worst-case returns
    using, 171–173, **172–173,**
    178–180, **179**
  changes in, 168–171, **168, 169,
    170, 171**
  decile analysis using, 180, **181,
    182**
  worst changes in, 173–178,
    173, 174, 175–178
  earnings per share percentage
    changes and, **186, 189,
    190–191**
  base rates for, **187–189**
  best- and worst-case returns
    using, 191–192, **192**
  decile analysis using, 192–194,
    193
  Sharpe ratio and, 187, **187**
  growth investing and, 299–300,
    300–301
  maximum decline in, **165**
  multifactor models and, 250, **251**
  price-to-sales ratios (PSR) and,
    252, **252–253**

Large Stocks universe *(continued)*
  return on equity (ROE), 256, **257**
  price-to-book ratios and
  best- and worst-case returns by,
    102, **103, 104**
  decile analysis by, 103, **103,
    104**
  high P/B stocks and, 96–102,
    97, 98–99, 100, 101, 102
  low P/B stocks and, 93–96, **93,
    94, 95–96**
  overall peformance using,
    104–107, **105, 106**
  price-to-cashflow ratios and, 109
  high P/C stocks and, 109, 110,
    110, 111
  best and worst returns using,
    113–115, **114, 115**, 122–123
  high P/C stocks and, **117, 118,**
    120–122, **120–121**
  low P/C stocks and, 109, 110,
    112–113, **110, 111, 112, 113**
  price-to-earnings (PE) ratios and
  high-PE stocks vs. 78–83,
    78–83
  low PE stocks vs., 72–77, **72–75**
  summary of performance using,
    85–88, **85–88**
  price-to-sales ratios (PSR) and,
    128–131, **128–131**, 252,
    252–253
  best- and worst-case scenarios
    using, 132–134, **133–134**
  decile analysis and, 139–141,
    139–141
  high PSR stocks and, 134–139,
    135–139
  low PSR stocks and, 128–132,
    128–131, 132, 132–134,
    133–134
  profit margins and, 197–207, **198**
  best- and worst-case returns
    using, 203, **203–205**
  decile analysis using, 205,
    205–207
  Sharpe ratio and, **202**
  relative price strength and,
    222–225, **223, 224, 225–227,**
    227, **227–229**
  base rates and, 225, **226**
  best and worst returns using,
    230–231, **231–234**, 234,
    234–235, 236–237
  decile analysis using, 235, **237**
  over longer term, 239–240,
    241–242

Large Stocks universe *(continued)*
  Sharpe ratios and, 224
  over shorter term, 240, **241, 242**
  worst-case scenarios and,
    226–227, 230–232, **231–234**
  return on equity (ROE),
    209–212, **210–213**, 256, **257**
  base rates and, 210, 212, **212**
  best and worst returns using,
    215–216, **216**
  decile analysis using, 216, **217,
    218, 219, 220**
  Sharpe ratio and, **211**
  worst-case scenarios using,
    214–215, 215–216, **216**
  risk-adjusted returns in,
    347–357, **348–355**
  S&P vs., 4–6, **6**, 49–51, **50, 51**
  Sharpe ratios for, 163, **163**
  standard deviation of return in,
    164
  summary return and risk results
    for, **62–63**
  total returns by universe in,
    69–70, **70**
  value investing strategies for,
    281–293
  worst-case scenarios for, 53–55,
    53, 54, 55, 165
Lehman Brothers, 37
Lessing, Gotthold, 127
*Limits of Scientific Reasoning,
  The*, 14
Long-Term Capital Management,
  25–27, **27**, 347
long-term data in decision making,
  24–30, 165–166, 335–337,
  380–381
look-ahead bias, 38, 42, 388
Looking Back-to-the Future, 28–29
LSV Asset Management, 32
Lynch, Peter, 8

Magellan, 8
mania in markets, 30, 335
Mann, Thomas, 49
market capitalization, 39–42,
  39–42, 49–70, 390
  All Stocks universe and, 49–51,
    50, 51
  benchmarks in, 70
  best and worst average annual
    compound returns in, **64,
    64–65**
  compound and average returns
    by, 58–59, **58**

market capitalization *(continued)*
  implications for investor and,
    69–70
  Large Stocks universe and,
    49–51, **50, 51**
  Market Leaders universe in,
    59–69
  micro-cap stocks in, 58
  reviewing stocks by size for,
    57–59
  Sharpe risk-adjusted return by,
    58–59, **59**
  Small Stocks universe in, 59–69
  small-cap stocks and, 55–57, **56,**
    60
  total returns by universe in,
    69–70, **70**
  universes of stocks used in book
    and, 386
  worst-case scenarios in, 51–55
market impact costs, 391
Market Leaders universe, 59–69,
    259–267, 284–291, **285–286**
  All Stocks universe vs., annual
    data, 260, **260**
  All Stocks universe vs., monthly
    data, 261–262, **261**
  absolute returns in, 337–346,
    338–345
  American Depository Receipts
    (ADRs) in, 259–260
  annual data, summary return and
    risk results for, 260, **260**
  annual performance of, 66–67, **66**
  average annual compound rates
    of return by decade, **65**
  base rates and, **65,** 264–265, **266**
  benchmarks in, 70
  best and worst average annual
    compound returns in, **64,**
    64–65
  best of, 267
  correlation matrix analysis in,
    329, 330
  downside risk in, 357–366,
    358–365, 366
  implications for investing in, 265
  maximum decline in, 265,
    266–267
  monthly data, summary return
    and risk results for, 261–262,
    261
  multifactor models and, 264
  price-to-book ratios and, 262, **263**
  price-to-cashflow ratio and, 262,
    263

Market Leaders universe *(continued)*
  price-to-earnings (PE) ratios and,
    262, **263**
  price-to-sales ratios (PSR) and,
    262, **263**
  risk-adjusted performance strate-
    gies for, 309–318, **312–318**
  risk-adjusted returns in,
    347–357, **348–355**
  S&P 500 vs., annual data, 260,
    260
  S&P 500 vs., monthly data,
    261–262, **261**
  Sharpe ratio and, 259, 356–357
  Small Stocks universe vs., 260,
    260, 261–262, **261**
  stocks included in, 259–260
  summary return and risk results
    for, **62–63,** 67, **67,** 262, , **263**
  total returns by universe in,
    69–70, **70**
  value investing strategies for,
    281–293
  worst-case scenarios and, **63,** 265
Marsh, Paul, 32
maximum decline rankings,
    366–367, **368–375**
  All Stocks universe, **161, 165**
  Market Leaders universe and,
    265, **266–267**
  Small Stocks universe and,
    274–275, **274–275**
McGovern, George, 1972 presi-
    dential campaign of, 19
mean regression, relative price
    strength and, 239–240
median return, 45
Meehl, Paul, 14
micro-cap stocks, 36–37, 58, 60,
    61, 329, 330, 356–357
Minnesota Multiphasic Personality
    Inventory (MMPI), 15
models for predicting and decision
    making, 15–17
Money Magazine, 379
Montier, James, 4
Morningstar, 2, 56, 325, 332
M–Squared, 320
multifactor models, 243–258, 383
  All Stocks universe
    growth models using, 253–254,
      254
    P/E, P/B, and PSR combined in,
      248, **249**
    price-to-book ratios and,
      245–246, **246**

multifactor models *(continued)*
    price-to-earnings (PE) ratios
      and, 243–244, **244**
    price-to-sales ratios (PSR) and,
      247–248, **247, 248**
    return on equity (ROE) and,
      255, 256, **255, 256, 257**
    value factors added to,
      243–244, **244, 245**
  base rates and, 245
  deviation from benchmark testing
    in, 249–250, 249
  growth factors and, 253
  growth models using, 253–254,
    254, 307
  implications for investing and,
    257–258, **258**
  Large Stocks universe and, 250,
    251
    price-to-sales ratios (PSR) and,
      252, **252–253**
    return on equity (ROE), 256,
      257
  Market Leaders universe and,
    264
  P/E, P/B, and PSR combined in,
    248, **249**
  price-to-sales ratios (PSR) and,
    247–248, **247, 248,** 252,
    252–253
  return on equity (ROE) and,
    255, 256, **255, 256, 257**
  value factors added to, 243–244,
    244, 245
  worst-case scenarios and, **258**
multiple or blended strategies in,
    367
mutual funds, active vs. passive
    managed, 2

NASDAQ crash of 2000, 17
Neff, John, 8
Netscape, 304
New Economy, 377–378
new research initiatives, 319–334
  correlation matrix analysis in,
    327–331, **328–330**
  Fama-French data series in, 328,
    328–330
  future projects in, 332–334
  holding period analysis in, 324,
    324
  intersection portfolios and,
    332–333, **333**
  randomization of in-sample data
    in, 325

new research initiatives (continued)
  regression-to-long-term mean within strategies and, 331–332
  seasonal analysis of stock performance in, 321, 322–323
  sector-specific analysis in, 326–327, 326
  statistical analysis of stock performance in, 320–321
  summation models in, 327
Newbould, Gerald, 46
Newton, Isaac, 33
NTT, 260
number of stocks in portfolio, 45–46

O'Shaughnessy Capital Management, 37, 24, 379
O'Shaughnessy Cornerstone Growth Fund, 298, 325, 385
objectiveness of investment strategy, 35
Ockham, William of, and Occam's Razor, 21, 378
Odean, Terrance, 20
OnDisc CD (Morningstar), 332
101 Years on Wall Street, 142
out-of-sample holdout periods, 38–39

panics, 27
parsimony principle, 21–23
passive management investing, 1
Pelli, Cesar, 197
performance analysis, past vs. future performance, 13–30
personal experience's influence on decision making, 19–20
personality testing, 15
Philadelphia Enquirer, 12
philosophy of investing, 377
pitfalls of investment strategies, 35–38
Polaroid, 34, 77, 304, 335
Poon, Percy, 46
Pope, Alexander, 32
portfolio management, 8, , 42–43, 45–46, 332–333, 333
  holding period analysis in, 324, 324
  intersection portfolios and, 332–333, 333
  number of stocks in, 45–46
predicting future performance, 13–14
  anecdotal evidence in, 34–35
  approaches to, 13–15

predicting future performance (continued)
  base rates and, 17–18
  collective intelligence theory, 221–222
  history as guide in, 22–23
  individual vs. group and, 18–19
  long-term data in, 24–30
  models vs. man in, 15–17
  parsimony principle in, 21–23
  personal experience's influence on, 19–20
  psychology of, 16–17
  simple versus complex theories in, 20–21
pretax profit margin, 390
price-to-book ratios, 91–107, 390
  All Stocks universe and, 245–246, 246
    high P/B stocks and, 96–100, 96–98, 99, 99–100
    low P/B stocks and, 92–96, 92, 94–95
    overall peformance using, 104–107, 105, 106
  base rates and, 93–94, 94, 159–160, 160
  best- and worst-case returns by, 102, 103, 104
  bubble markets and, 100
  decile analysis by, 103, 103, 104
  high P/B stocks and, 92, 96–102, 97, 98–99, 100, 101, 102, 104–107, 105, 106, 380
  implications for investing using, 104–107, 105, 106
  Large Stocks universe
    low P/B stocks and, 93–96, 93, 94, 95–96
    overall peformance using, 104–107, 105, 106
    low P/B stocks and, 92–96, 92, 93, 94–95, 95–96, 104–107, 105, 106
  Market Leaders universe and, 262, 263
  multifactor models and, 245–246, 246
  PE and PSR combined with, 248, 249
  risk assessment in, 156–159
  Small Stocks universe and, 271–272
  value investing and, 281
price-to-cashflow ratios, 109–125, 391

price-to-cashflow ratios (continued)
  All Stocks universe
    best and worst returns using, 113–115, 114, 115, 122–123
    high P/C stocks and, 109, 110, 110, 111, 116–120, 116, 117, 118
    low P/C stocks and, 109, 110, 110, 111, 113
  base rates and, 112–113, 113, 159–160, 160
  best and worst returns using, 113–115, 114, 115, 122–123
  decile analysis using, 123–125, 123, 124, 125
  high, 109, 110, 110–113, 116–120, 116–119, 122–123
  implications for investing using, 126
  low, 109, 110, 110–113
  Large Stocks universe
    best and worst returns using, 113–115, 114, 115, 122–123
    high P/C stocks and, 109, 110, 110, 111, 117, 118, 120–122, 120–121
    low P/C stocks and, 109, 110, 112–113, 110, 111, 112, 113
  Market Leaders universe and, 262, 263
  risk assessment in, 156–159
  Small Stocks universe and, 272
  value investing and, 281
  worst-case scenarios and, 113–115, 114, 115, 122–123
price-to-earnings (PE) ratio, 1, 71–89, 390
  All Stocks universe, 243–244, 244
    high-PE stocks vs. 78–83, 78–83
    low-PE stocks vs., 72–76, 72–75
    summary of performance using, 85–88, 85–88
  base rates and, 159–160, 160
  bubble markets and, 89
  deciles and, 84
  high-PE in, 81, 77–83, 78–83
  implications of, 84–88, 85
  Large Stocks universe
    high-PE stocks vs. 78–83, 78–83
    low-PE stocks vs., 72–77, 72–75
    summary of performance using, 85–88, 85–88

price-to-earnings (PE) ratio
    (continued)
  low-PE in, 72–77, **72–75**
  Market Leaders universe and,
    262, **263**
  multifactor models and,
    243–244, **244**
  P/B and PSR combined with,
    248, **249**
  real-time investing using, 88–89
  relative price strength and, 229
  risk assessment in, 156–159
  sector-specific analysis in,
    326–327, **326**
  Small Stocks universe and, 271–272
  summary of performance using,
    85–88, **85–88**
  value investing and, 281
price-to-sales ratios (PSR), 1,
    127–142, 128–131, **128–131**,
    155, 390
  All Stocks universe, 128–131,
    128–131, 247–248, **247, 248**
    best- and worst-case scenarios
      using, 132–134, **133–134**
    decile analysis and, 139–141,
      139–141
    high PSR stocks and, 134–139,
      135–139
    low PSR stocks and, 128–131,
      128–131, 132–134, **133–134**
  base rates and, 131, 159–160, **160**
  best- and worst-case scenarios
    using, 132–134, **133–134**
  decile analysis and, 139–141,
    139–141
  earnings gains and, 183–184
  high, 127, 134–139, **135–139**
  low, 128–131, **128–131**
  Large Stocks universe, 128–131,
    128–131, 252, **252–253**
    best- and worst-case scenarios
      using, 132–134, **133–134**
    decile analysis and, 139–141,
      139–141
    high PSR stocks and, 134–139,
      135–139
    low PSR stocks and, 128–132,
      128–131, 132, 132–134,
      133–134
  Market Leaders universe and,
    262, **263**
  multifactor models and, 247–248,
    247, 248, 252, **252–253**
  PE and P/B combined with, 248,
    249

price-to-sales ratios (PSR)
    (continued)
  risk assessment in, 156–159
  Small Stocks universe and, 271,
    273
  value investing and, 281
profit magins, 197–207, **198**
  All Stocks universe, 197–207,
    198, 199–202
    best- and worst-case returns
      using, 203, **203–205**
    decile analysis using, 205,
      205–207
    Sharpe ratio and, **202**
    worst-case scenarios in, **201,
      202**, 203, **203–205**
  best- and worst-case returns
    using, 203, **203–205**
  decile analysis using, 205, **205–207**
  implications for investing and, 205
  Large Stocks universe, 197–207,
    198, 197
    best- and worst-case returns
      using, 203, **203–205**
    decile analysis using, 205,
      205–207
    Sharpe ratio and, **202**
  Sharpe ratio and, **202**
  worst-case scenarios in, **201,
    202**, 203, **203–205**
psychology of investing, 16–17
*Psychology of the
    Non–Professional Investor,
    The*, 16
public nature of investment strategy,
    35

quantitative approach to decision
    making, 14–15

Radio Corporation, 34
random walk theory, 3–4, 5, 155,
    383
randomization of in-sample data,
    325
ranking the strategies, 335–376, 389
RBC O'Shaughnessy U.S. Growth
    Fund and, 298
Real Estate Investment Trusts
    (REITs), 144
rebalancing the portfolio. *See* port-
    folio management
regression, relative price strength
    and, mean, 239–240
regression-to-long-term mean
    within strategies, 331–332

relative price strength, 221–242
  All Stocks universe, 222–225,
    223, 224, 225–227
    base rates and, 225, **226**
    best and worst returns using,
      230–231, **231–234**, 234,
      234–235, 236–237
    decile analysis using, 235, **237**
    over longer term, 239–240,
      241–242
    over shorter term, 240, **241, 242**
    Sharpe ratios and, 224
    worst-case scenarios and,
      226–227, 230–232, **231–234**
  base rates and, 225, **226**
  best and worst returns using,
    230–231, **231–234**, 234,
    234–235, 236–237
  decile analysis using, 235, **237**
  earnings per share growth rates
    and, 229
  implications for investing and, 238
  over longer-term, 238–240,
    241–242
  Large Stocks universe, 222–225,
    223, 224, 225–227, 227,
    227–229
    base rates and, 225, **226**
    best and worst returns using,
      230–231, **231–234**, 234,
      234–235, 236–237
    decile analysis using, 235, 237,
      235
    over longer term, 239–240,
      241–242
    over shorter term, 240, **241,
      242**
    Sharpe ratios and, 224
    worst-case scenarios and,
      226–227, 230–232, **231–234**
  mean regression and, 239–240
  over shorter term, 240, **241, 242**
  price performance in, 229
  price-to-earnings (PE) ratio and,
    229
  Sharpe ratios and, 224
  volatility and, 224–225
  worst performing stocks in,
    230–231, **231–232**
  worst-case scenarios and,
    226–227, 230–232, **231–234**
reliability mathematics, 38
reliability of investment strategy, 35
research initiatives. *See* new
    research initiatives
Research Insight backtesting, 385

research methodology used in book, 31–32, 385–391
returns calculation, 44, **44**, 337–346, **338–345**, 387
return on equity (ROE), 209–220, 390
  All Stocks universe, 209–212, **210–213**, 255, 256, **255**, **256**, **257**
    base rates and, 210, 212, **212**, 210
    best and worst returns using, 215–216, **216**, 215
    decile analysis using, 216, **217**, **218**, **219**, **220**, 216
    Sharpe ratio and, **211**, 211
    worst-case scenarios using, **213**, **214–215**, 215–216, **216**
  base rates and, 210, 212, **212**
  best and worst returns using, 215–216, **216**
  decile analysis using, 216, **217**, **218**, **219**, **220**
  implications for investing and, 218–219, **219**, **220**
  Large Stocks universe, 209–212, **210**, **211**, **212**, **213**
    base rates and, 210, 212, **212**
    best and worst returns using, 215–216, **216**
    decile analysis using, 216, **217**, **218**, **219**, **220**
    Sharpe ratio and, **211**
    worst-case scenarios using, **214–215**, 215–216, **216**
  multifactor models and, 255, 256, **255**, **256**, **257**
  Sharpe ratio and, **211**
  worst-case scenarios using, **213**, **214–215**, 215–216, **216**
risk assessment, 156–159, **158**, **159**, 337, 382
  bubble markets and, 158–159, **158**, **159**
  Capital Asset Pricing Model (CAPM) and, 156
  downside risk in, 357–366, **358–365**, **366**
  price-to-book ratios and, 156–159
  price-to-cashflow ratios and, 156–159
  price-to-earnings (PE) ratio, 156–159
  price-to-sales ratios (PSR) and, 156–159

risk assessment *(continued)*
  risk-adjusted returns in, 347–357, **348–355**. *See also* Sharpe ratios
  Sharpe ratio in, 157
risk-adjusted performance, 44, **44**, 309–318, **312–318**, 347–357, **348–355**
Riverside Forest Products, 356
Royal Bank of Canada, 325
Runyon, Damon, 221
Russell 1000,, 66–67, **66**, **67**, 69
Russell 2000, **68–69**, 281–293
Russian default crisis, 347

S&P 500
  absolute returns in, 337–346, **338–345**
  active vs. passive managed funds and, 2, **3**
  All Stocks vs., 49–51, **50**, **51**
  annual performance of, 66–67, **66**
  average annual compound rates of return by decade for, 51, **52**, 65
  best and worst average annual compound returns for, 52–53, **52**, **53**, **64**, **64–65**
  correlatioin with, 45
  correlation matrix analysis in, **328**
  Dow Jones vs, 6–7
  downside risk in, 357–366, **358–365**, **366**, 357
  indexing to, 5
  Large Stocks vs., 49–51, **50**, **51**
  Market Leaders universe vs., annual data, 260, **260**
  Market Leaders universe vs., monthly data, 261–262, **261**
  risk-adjusted returns in, 347–357, **348–355**
  summary return and risk results for, 67, **67**
  total returns by universe in, 69–70, **70**
  value investing strategies for, 281–293
  worst-case scenarios for, 53–55, **53**, **54**, **55**
sales increases vs. earnings gains, 183–184
sales–to–price ratio, 390
sample bias, 36
Sawyer, Jack, 15
seasonal analysis of stock performance, 321, **322–323**

sector-specific analysis, 326–327, **326**
Security Analysis, 89
semi-standard deviation of return below zero, 45
share-weighted funds, 8–9
shareholder yield, value investing and, 286–288, **287**, **288**
Sharpe ratio, 44, 347–357, **348–355**. *See also* risk-adjusted returns
  dividend yields and, 149, **149**
  earnings per share percentage changes and, 187, **187**
  Large Stocks universe, 163, **163**
  market capitalization and, 58–59, **59**
  Market Leaders universe and, 259
  profit margins and, **202**
  relative price strength and, 224
  return on equity (ROE) and, **211**
  risk assessment and, 157
Shleifer, Andrei, 32
short-term data, 32–34, 36, 379–380
shorting strategies, 334
Siegel, Jeremy, 331
simple versus complex theories in decision making, 20–21
Sixties bubble market, 32–34, 335–336
small-cap stocks, 28–29, 55–57, **56**, **57**, 60
small sample bias, 36
Small Stocks universe, 59–69, 269–279
  10- vs. 25-stock version of, 278–279
  absolute returns in, 337–346, **338–345**
  annual data on, summary return and risk results for, **270**
  annual performance of, **68**
  average annual compound rates of return by decade, 65
  base rates and, **65**, 273–274, **276**
  benchmarks in, 70
  best and worst average annual compound returns in, **64**, **64–65**
  concentrated investing in, case study of, 277–279
  downside risk in, 346–347, 357–366, **358–365**, **366**, 357
  implications for investing in, 275–277, **276**

Small Stocks universe *(continued)*
    maximum declines in, 274–275,
        274–275
    Market Leaders universe vs.,
        annual data, 260, **260**
    Market Leaders universe vs.,
        monthly data, 261–262, **261**
    monthly data on, summary
        return and risk results for,
        270–273, **271, 272**
    price-to-book ratio and, 271–272
    price-to-cashflow ratio and, 272
    price-to-earnings (PE) ratio and,
        271–272
    price-to-sales ratios (PSR) and,
        271, 273
    risk-adjusted returns in,
        347–357, **348–355**
    selection criteria for, 269–270
    standard deviation of returns in,
        277–278
    stocks in, 269
    summary return and risk results
        for, **62–63, 68–69**
    total returns by universe in,
        69–70, **70**
    value investing strategies for,
        281–293
    volatility and, 278–279
    worst-case scenarios for, 61,
        63–64, 272–273, 274–275,
        274–275
Smart & Final, 356
Sortino ratio, 320
South Sea Trading Company, 33
speculation, 335
standard deviation of returns, 45,
    277–278
statistical analysis of stock perform-
    ance, 14, 18, 38, 320–321
Staunton, Mike, 32
Stocks for the Long Run, 331
structured portfolio, 8–9
summary return and risk results,
    62–63, 67, **67, 68–69**
summation models, 327
Super Stocks, 127
Surowiecki, James, 221–222
survivorship bias, 38
Systematic Equity Group, Bear
    Stearns, 37
Szent-Gyorgyi, Albert, 155

T-bills, 346
    absolute returns in, 337–346,
        338–345

T-bills, *(continued)*
    downside risk in, 357–366,
        358–365, 366, 357
    risk-adjusted returns in,
        347–357, **348–355**
T-statistics, 45
Taoism, 377, 378
taxes, 391
technology stocks, 34
Texas Instruments, 34
time horizons used in book, 386
Time Magazine, 11–12
*To Divine the Future, Study the
    Past,* 25–27
transaction costs, 46–47, 391
Treynor ratio, 320
Triumph of the Optimists, 32
Twain, Mark, 143

U.S. News & World Reports, 379
Union Carbide, 46
universe of stocks in presented
    investment strategies, 38–39,
    386

value factors, 155–166
value investing, 1, 281–293
    10-stock Cornerstone Value
        strategy in, 289–290,
        290–291
    All Stocks universe and,
        282–284, **283,** 292
    base rates and, **292**
    best and worst average annual
        returns in, **292–293**
    Cornerstone fund and, 284,
        285–286, 289–290, **290–291**
    dividend yield and, 286
    downside risk and return in, 282
    implications of, 291–292,
        292–293
    Market Leaders universe and,
        284–291, **285–286**
    price-to-book ratios and, 281
    price-to-cashflow ratios and,
        281
    price-to-earnings (PE) ratios and,
        281
    price-to-sales ratios (PSR) and,
        281
    real-time performance and, 289
    risk-adjusted performance and,
        309–318, **312–318**
    shareholder yield and, 286–288,
        287, 288
    worst-case scenarios and, **292**

Value Line Investment Survey, 17,
    325
Vermeulen, Menno, 32
Vishny, Robert W., 32
volatility, relative price strength
    and, 224–225

Ward, Artemus, 167
Warner Brothers Corporation, 34
Winchell, Walter, 185
Windsor fund, 8
Wisdom of Crowds, The, 221–222
Wittgenstein's maxim, 377
worst-case scenarios, 49–50,
    51–55, **53, 54, 55,** 381
    All Stocks universe, **161, 165**
    best and worst average annual
        compound returns for, 52–53,
        52, 53
    dividend yields and, 150–151,
        150–151
    earnings gains and, 171–173,
        172–173, 178–180, **179, 180**
    earnings per share percentage
        changes and, 191–192, **192**
    growth investing and, **304, 306**
    Market Leaders universe and, 63,
        265
    multifactor models and, **258**
    price-to-book ratios and, 102,
        103, 104
    price-to-cashflow ratios and,
        113–115, **114, 115,** 122–123
    price-to-earnings (PE) ratios and,
        high-PE, 84
    price-to-sales ratios (PSR) and,
        132–134, **133–134**
    profit margins and, **201, 202,**
        203, **203–205**
    relative price strength and,
        230–232, **231–234,** 226–227
    return on equity (ROE) and,
        213, 214–215, 215–216, **216**
    Small Stocks universe, 61,
        63–64, 272–275, **274–275**
    value investing and, **292**
wu wei, 377

Xcelera, 82
Xerox, 335

Yahoo, 77

Zweig, Jason, 379–380